The Ciano Diaries

1939-1943

The ciano diaries

1939 - 1943

*the complete, unabridged diaries of Count Galeazzo Ciano,
Italian minister for foreign affairs, 1936 - 1943*

Edited by Hugh Gibson

Introduction by Sumner Welles

Simon Publications

2001

Library of Congress Card Number: 47002678

ISBN: 1-931313-74-1

Distributed by Ingram Book Company

Printed by Lightning Source Inc. La Vergne, TN

Published by Simon Publications, P.O.Box 321,
Safety Harbor, FL 34695

Editor's Note

IN LATE AUGUST 1943 Count Ciano disappeared from Rome. On December 23 he wrote to King Victor Emmanuel that the Germans, on the pretext that his children were in grave danger and that they were taking him to Spain, trapped him and took him to Bavaria. Shortly afterward he was moved to Verona, where for three months he was held in custody by the Gestapo and treated with their customary brutality. In this letter Ciano stated that he could testify to the King's heroic struggle against the crime of waging war at the side of Germany; he insisted that neither the Italian people nor the government itself should be held responsible for the sufferings of all. One man, he said, and one man only—Mussolini—driven by sinister personal ambition and a thirst for military glory, had brought about the downfall of his country and his people.

Ciano told the King that he had arranged for the publication of his diaries as soon as possible after his death. Before his execution in January 1944 they were confided to his wife with instructions to have them published. Edda Ciano was faced with the difficult problem of smuggling the diaries out of Italy. She was herself under constant surveillance. The Nazis had offered a large reward for delivery of the manuscript, and the Fascists were also intent on preventing these revealing documents from leaving the country.

For her perilous journey from the neighborhood of Milan to the Swiss frontier Edda Ciano disguised herself as a peasant woman and concealed the diaries under her skirts fastened to a belt. She had an anxious time at the frontier, but, fortunately for her, was not recognized and was given special consideration because of what appeared to be her delicate condition.

The Swiss authorities, to whom she reported on arrival, consigned her to a convent near Berne, where for some months she was allowed no communication with the outside world except through Swiss official channels—a natural precaution in such troubled times.

Paul Ghali, of the Chicago *Daily News,* who had been reporting the war from his post in Switzerland, heard of Countess Ciano's escape and got in touch with her after she had been moved from the convent to a sanitarium. Ghali heard from her the story of how she had contrived to get the diaries out of Italy.

After some weeks of negotiations Ghali, acting for the Chicago *Daily News,* concluded a deal for world newspaper serial rights. Edda Ciano then consented to have the diaries photographed on microfilm. Each bit of film reproduced a full page of the diary in Ciano's handwriting. When received in this country, enlarged photographs were made from the microfilm, and it is from these enlarged facsimiles that the translation was made.

The text of the diaries is given unabridged. It will be observed that for several periods there are no entries—on account of illness, absence on military service, or other obvious reasons. In several places pages were removed from the diaries before they were turned over for photographing; this has been clearly indicated by notes in the text.

The task of translation was exacting, as Ciano employed a highly colloquial style, with free use of Fascist jargon. The translation made under some pressure for the Chicago *Daily News* has been painstakingly revised with the help of V. Umberto Coletti-Perucca, LL.D., former managing director of the Italian Labor Office and Allied Italo-American societies, and publisher of the *Rivista Illustrata d'Italia,* which was suppressed by the Fascist Government.

In view of the frequency with which many names are mentioned, an index in the usual form would be cumbersome and not particularly helpful. It is felt that the purposes of the reader are better served by a chronological list of important events as they appear in the diaries and a list of characters to facilitate the identification of persons who are referred to in the diaries. In this connection, every effort has been made to see that spellings and identifications are correct. This was made somewhat difficult because Ciano himself was often in doubt as to the spelling, and in general he seemed to regard the spelling of proper names as a matter of taste.

HUGH GIBSON

Chronology

(Events as they appear in the diaries)

1939

Dramatis Personae

ABETZ, OTTO, Nazi Ambassador to Vichy Government; High Commissioner for occupied France

ACERBO, GIACOMO, proposed successor to Ciano's father in the Italian Chamber of Deputies

ACQUARONE, COUNT, Minister of King Victor Emmanuel's household

AGNELLI, GIOVANNI, Italian senator; owner of Fiat Company

AGO, GENERAL, Italian Army officer

AGOSTINO, D', director of Italian Bank of Labor

AGOSTINUCCI, GENERAL CRISTINO, member of the Italian General Staff; called the "Stuffed Lion" by the Albanians

AIELLO, a provincial secretary of the Fascist party

AIETA, BLASCO LANZA D', diplomat; Ciano's secretary, 1933–43

ALBINI, UMBERTO, Prefect of Genoa; later Prefect of Naples

ALDROVANDI-MARESCOTTI, COUNT LUIGI, Italian Ambassador to Germany, 1939; senator; diplomat

ALEMAN, GENERAL, Italian Army officer

ALESSANDRI, ARTURO, former President of Chile

ALESSI, CHINO, Italian journalist; correspondent in Egypt for *Trieste Piccolo*, newspaper; seized by British

ALFIERI, DINO, member of the Fascist Grand Council; Minister to Poland; Ambassador to Germany

AMANTEA, GENERAL, Italian Army officer.

AMBROSIO, GENERAL VITTORIO, leading Fascist; Chief of the Italian General Staff succeeding Cavallero

AMÈ, COLONEL, Italian aviation specialist belonging to both staffs

AMÈ, GENERAL, head of Military Intelligence Service, 1942

ANDO, YOSHITAKA, Japanese diplomat; Counselor of Embassy at Rome

ANFUSO, FILIPPE, one of Ciano's secretaries; Minister to Hungary

ANOS, chief of a Spanish mission sent to Rome to negotiate a commercial treaty

ANSALDO, Italian senator; industrialist

ANSALDO, GIOVANNI, editor of Ciano's paper, *Il Telègrafo*, at Leghorn

ANTIC, COLAK, Yugoslav Minister of the royal household

ANTONESCU, MARSHAL JON, "Führer" of Rumania

ANTONESCU, MIHAI, Rumanian lawyer, delegate to anti-Comintern meeting in Berlin

AOSTA, DUKE OF, Commander in Chief of the Italian forces in the East African campaign, 1939–41; cousin of King Victor Emmanuel III

ARITA, HACHIRO, Japanese Minister for Foreign Affairs; Ambassador to Italy

ARMENISE, GIOVANNI, Italian banker

AROMA, D', journalist; provincial secretary of the Fascist party

ARPINATI, LEANDRO, former Italian Minister of Justice; lawyer in Venice

ASCENSIO, friend of Duke of Spoleto; owner of tavern in Rome

ASINARI DE BERNEZZO, GENERAL G. M., former head of the carabinièri

ATTOLICO, BERNARDO, Italian Ambassador to Germany; later to the Holy See

AURITI, GIACINTO, Italian diplomat; Ambassador to Japan

AXMANN, ARTHUR, Nazi director of European Youth Association

BADOGLIO, MARSHAL PIETRO (MARQUIS OF SABATTINO; DUKE OF ADDIS-ABABA), Italian Commander in Chief in Abyssinia; senator; Governor General of Libya; High Commissioner for East Africa

BAGNO, GALEAZZO DI, Italian diplomat

BAIOCCHI, Fascist informer

BALBINO, GIULIANO, leading Fascist; senator; Minister of Public Education

BALBO, MARSHAL ITALO, member of the Quadrumvirate in the March on Rome; Minister of Aviation; Governor of Libya

BALDONI (unidentified)

BARANAY, Hungarian politician

BÁRDOSSY, LADISLAS DE, Prime Minister of Hungary; Minister to Rumania

BARELLA, GIULIO, director of *Popolo d'Italia;* steward of Mussolini's personal fortune

BAROCCHI (unidentified)

BARTHA DE DÁLNOKFALVA, GENERAL KARL, Hungarian Minister of Defense

BARTOLI (pseudonym of Pietro Santi), Italian artist

BARZINI, LUIGI, JR., journalist; son of Italian-American publisher; at one time editor of Italian daily newspaper, *Corriere d'America,* in New York

BASTIANINI, GIUSEPPE, leading Fascist; Ambassador to Poland and Great Britain; Undersecretary for Foreign Affairs; Governor of Dalmatia

BASTICO, ETTORE, Italian general in Libya; also in Yugoslav and Greek campaigns; appointed Governor of the Aegean

BATISTA, FULGENCIO, President of Cuba

BATTAGLINI, COLONEL, Italian Chief of Staff of Third Celere Division in Russia

BAUDOUIN, PAUL, French banker and politician; Minister for Foreign Affairs in Pétain government; unofficial emissary of French Government to open discussion of colonial questions with Ciano in 1939

BEAUVAN, PRINCE DE, French brother-in-law of Prince Piero Colonna, Governor of Rome

BECHI, CAPTAIN, army officer and author; member of Fascist party intelligence service

BECK, JOSEPH, Polish Minister for Foreign Affairs

BELLINI, Hungarian Cabinet Minister

BELMONTE, NINON (unidentified)

BENEŠ, EDUARD, President of Czechoslovakia, 1935–38; President of Government in Exile, London, 1939

BENINI, GUSTAVO, Italian speculator; Lieutenant Governor of Albania

BENNI, ANTONIO S., Italian politician and industrialist; Minister of Communications; Minister of Public Works

BERGAMO, DUKE OF, son of the Duke of Genoa and cousin of King Victor Emmanuel III

BERGONZOLI, ANNIBALE, Italian general, served in North African campaign; called "Electric Whiskers"

BERNARDINI, MONSIGNOR FILIPPO, Papal Nuncio at Berne

BERTI, FRANCESCO, Italian general, known as the "Sly Murderer"

BESNARD, RENÉ, former French Ambassador to Italy; French lawyer and politician; commissioner for 1942 Fascist Exposition in Rome

BETHLEN, COUNT STEPHEN, former Hungarian Prime Minister

BIANCHI, MICHELE, one of the Quadrumvirate; died in 1926

BIGLIARDI, commander in the Italian Navy

BISEO, GENERAL ATTILIO, member of air corps, Italian Army

BISMARCK, PRINCE OTTO VON, Counselor of German Embassy in Rome; his wife, Princess Anna Maria von Bismarck

BLUM, LÉON, Prime Minister of France, 1936–37

BOCCHINI, ARTURO, senator; chief of police under Mussolini

BODINI, staff officer of Italian Army Intelligence Service

BOMBELLES, MARQUESS OF, Croatian; mediator between Ciano and the Croatian Agrarian leader, Matchek

BOMBIERI, ENRICO, Italian Consul General in Tunis; Minister to Guatemala

BONCOUR, PAUL, French Prime Minister and Minister for Foreign Affairs; delegate to the League of Nations

BONNET, PIERRE, French Minister for Foreign Affairs at the outbreak of World War II

BONO, MARSHAL EMILIO DE, one of the Quadrumvirate; senator; instigator of the murder of Matteotti; shot with Ciano

BOREA D'OLMO, DUKE GIOVANNI BATISTA, Italian statesman; senator; died in 1936 at the age of one hundred and five; former secretary to Cavour

BORGHESE, RODOLFO, Prince of Nettuno; member of Chamber of Deputies; served in Libya and was sent on military mission to Budapest

BORIS, King of Bulgaria, succeeded to the throne on the abdication of his father, King Ferdinand, 1918

BORRI, Prefect of Genoa

BOSCARELLI, RAFFAELE, Italian Ambassador to the Argentine Republic

BOSE, SUBHAS CHANDRA, Indian Nationalist

BOTTAI, GIUSEPPE, leading Fascist; member of Grand Council; Minister of Education; Civil Commissioner in Greece

BOTTONI (unidentified)

BOVA-SCOPPA, Italian representative at Geneva; Minister to Rumania

BRAUCHITSCH, MARSHAL WALTHER VON, German conqueror of Poland

BRINON, FERNAD DE, Vichy Ambassador to the Nazis in Paris

BRIVONESI, BRUTO, Italian admiral

BUFFARINI, GUIDO, Italian Minister of the Interior; leading Fascist politician

BUTI, GINO, Italian Ambassador to the Vichy Government; career diplomat; permanent secretary of Finance Committee, Ministry for Foreign Affairs

CALINESCU, ARMAND, leader of Rumanian Peasant party; pro-Nazi; murdered by insurrectionists

CAMPINELLI, popular leader in Corsica; anti-Italian

CANARIS, ADMIRAL WALTER WILHELM, head of German Naval Intelligence

CAPARMA, intimate of Admiral Ciano, father of Galeazzo

CAPODISTRIA, COUNT, mayor of Corfu

CARBONI, GENERAL, member of Italian General Staff

CARNELUTTI, special envoy from Croatian Agrarian leader Matchek; engineer of Italian origin

CAROL, King of Rumania

CARUSO, PIETRO, officer of the Fascist militia, in charge of civil police; Minister to Czechoslovakia

CASARDI, AUBREY, Secretary of Embassy in London, and later in Berlin

CASERO, COLONEL GIUSEPPE, head of Italian Air Bureau; served in North Africa

CASERTANO, ANTONIO, lawyer of Naples; a secretary of the Fascist party

CASINI, GHERARDO, Italian journalist; official of the Ministry of Popular Culture

CASTELLANI, ALDO (COUNT OF KISYMAIO), senator; authority on tropical medicine and diagnostician in Mussolini's illness

CAT, GENERAL AIMONE, Italian Army officer; aviation expert

CAVAGNARI, ADMIRAL DOMENICO, Undersecrétary of State for the Navy and Chief of Naval Staff

CAVALLERO, COUNT UGO, Italian Army officer and politician; Chief of Staff of Duke of Aosta in Ethiopia; Chief of Staff after resignation of Badoglio; senator

CAVOUR, COUNT CAMILLO BENSO DI, Italian statesman, 1810–61

CECCHI, EMILIO, attaché at Italian Embassy in Berlin

CERRICA, chief of carabinièri

CESABIANCHI, doctor called in to attend Mussolini

CESARE, DE, secretary to Mussolini

CHAMBERLAIN, NEVILLE, British Prime Minister at outbreak of World War II

CHARLES, SIR NOEL HUGHES HAVELOCK, British Chargé d'Affaires in Rome

CHIANG KAI-SHEK, Generalissimo of China

CHIANG TSO-LIN, GENERAL, Chinese war lord

CHIESA, EUGENIO, leader of the Republican party in the Parliament at the time of Giolitti

CHILANTI, FELICE, Italian journalist; involved in plot to assassinate Ciano and bring about a leftist revolution

CHIRICO, GIORGIO DE, Italian surrealist artist; painted portrait of Ciano

CHRISTIC, Yugoslav Minister to Italy

CHURCHILL, WINSTON SPENCER, British Prime Minister succeeding Neville Chamberlain

CHWALKOSKY, GENERAL, Sudeten German; supporter of the Nazis

CIANETTI, TULLIO, Italian industrialist; Italian Minister of Propaganda; member of Grand Council; Undersecretary for Popular Culture

CIANO, COSTANZO, Count of Buccari, father of Galeazzo Ciano

CIANO, GALEAZZO, Count of Cortellazzo e de Buccari; his wife, Countess Edda Mussolini Ciano, daughter of Mussolini; his eldest son, Marzio; his daughter Dindina

CICCO, DE (unidentified)

CINI, VITTORIO, Italian industrialist of Venice; leading Fascist

CLEMMA, [CLEMM] BARON and BARONESS VON, attaché at German Embassy, Rome

CLODIUS, KARL, head of Economic Section of German Foreign Ministry

CODREANU, CORNELIU ZELEA, head of Rumanian Iron Guard

COLIJN, HENDRIKUS, Dutch economist and politician; ex-Prime Minister of the Netherlands

COLONNA, PRINCE ASCANIO, Italian Ambassador to the United States

COLONNA, ISABELLA, wife of Prince Piero

COLONNA, PRINCE PIERO, Governor of Rome; ultra-Fascist

CONDE, PEDRO GARCIA, Spanish Ambassador to Italy

CONRAD, Prince of Bavaria

COOPER, ALFRED DUFF, leading figure in British politics and diplomacy; First Lord of the Admiralty and later Minister of Information

COPPOLA, FRANCESCO, senator; author; Fascist journalist

CORTESE, GUIGI, Italian Consul General in Geneva

COURTEN, ADMIRAL RAFFAELO DE, Italian naval officer

CRIPPS, SIR STAFFORD, British politician and member of Cabinet

CROIX, DEL, wounded veteran of World War I; ardent Fascist; orator

CRONETTI, Fascist party journalist

CZAKY, COUNT, Hungarian Minister for Foreign Affairs

DALADIER, EDOUARD, French Prime Minister, 1938–40

DALMASSO, GENERAL, commanded Italian Army in Albania

DANILO (PETROVICH), Prince of Montenegro

DARLAN, JEAN FRANÇOIS, admiral, Commander of the French Navy under the Vichy Government

DENTICE DE FRASSO, COUNT ALFREDO, Rear Admiral; Italian naval officer and shipowner; senator

DENTZ, French general and colonial administrator; High Commissioner and Commander in Chief, Syria

DINGLI, legal adviser to the Italian Embassy in London

DOLMANN, CAPTAIN, head of Gestapo in Rome

DOMBERG (unidentified)

DONADIO, go-between for Buffarini with the Petacci family

DONEGANI, Italian industrialist; head of Italian Chemical Trust

DORIOT, JACQUES, French politician; collaborator with the Nazis

DRAGO, PRINCE DEL, attaché of the Italian Embassy in Paris

DRUMMOND, SIR ERIC. See PERTH, EARL OF

DUCCI, ADMIRAL GINO, Italian naval officer

ELENA, Queen of Italy, consort of King Victor Emmanuel III, former Princess of Montenegro

ESSAD, PASHA, Albanian-born Turkish general and politician

ESSER, HERMANN, German politician; Nazi Gauleiter; head German Tourist Traffic Department; Secretary of State in Reich Ministry for People's Enlightenment and Propaganda

FACCINI, professor in Leghorn

FAGIOLA, active Fascist; secret service agent and intimate of Ciano

FALCHETTO, writer for *Osservatore Romano*

FARINACCI, ROBERTO, Italian politician and journalist; firebrand of the Fascist party; member of Grand Council; secretary general of the party; shot with Mussolini

FARINACCI JR., son of above, Italian Consul in Germany

FARNESI, MARIO, leading Fascist; a provincial secretary of the Fascist party; Chief of Cabinet under Vidussoni

FAROUK, King of Egypt

FAVAGROSSA, GENERAL UMBERTO, Italian Army officer

FEDERZONI, LUIGI, Italian politician and journalist; member of Grand Council and President of Senate; Minister of Colonies and Interior

FELICI, Italian senator and professor

FELLERS, COLONEL B. F. (now General), U.S. military attaché in Cairo

FERNANDEZ-CUESTA, Spanish Ambassador to Italy

FERRARIS, COLONEL MARIO DE, member of Italian Intelligence Service

FERRERI, ADMIRAL, Italian naval officer

FERRETTI, LANDO, official Italian propagandist; national councilor

FILIPPO, one of Ciano's secretaries

FIORAVANZO, ADMIRAL, an ace of the Italian Air Force

FLANDIN, PIERRE ETIENNE, French Minister for Foreign Affairs for the Vichy Government, 1940–41

FORBES, LORD, twenty-second baron; major, Grenadier Guards, retired

FORZANO, GIOVACCHINO, Italian playwright; wrote *Julius Caesar* in collaboration with Mussolini

FOUGIER, GENERAL RINO CORSO, in command of Italian aviation

FRANCISCI, SENATOR DE, Professor-Rector of the University of Naples

FRANCO, FRANCISCO, Spanish Chief of State, the "Caudillo"

FRANÇOIS-PONCET, ANDRÉ, French diplomat; Ambassador to Germany

FRANKLIN, MARTIN, Italian Ambassador in Paris

FRANZONI, Italian Minister to Portugal

FRITSCH, GENERAL BARON WERNER VON, German Chief of Staff; lost favor of Hitler and was relieved of command in 1938; killed in action before Warsaw; murder by Nazis suspected

FROELICH, CARL, German film manager and producer who gave Goebbels a thrashing in public

FRUGONI, PROFESSOR CESARE, leading Italian physician; treated Mussolini at times

FUNK, WALTHER, German journalist and economist; Minister of Economics; President of the Reichsbank

GABRIELLI, LUIGI, Italian military attaché in Albania

GAETANI, vice-secretary of the Fascist party; Prefect of Florence

GAFENCU, GRIGORE, Rumanian politician and diplomat; Minister for Foreign Affairs

GAILANI, EL, Prime Minister of Iraq

GALBIATI, GENERAL ENZO, leading Fascist; member of Grand Council; commander of University Student Volunteers; successor to Starace as secretary of the party

GAMBARA, GENERAL GASTONE, Italian Army officer and diplomat; commander of Italian expeditionary force in Spain; later in North Africa

GAMELIN, MARSHAL MAURICE GUSTAVE, Commander in Chief of French Army, relieved in 1940

GANGI, PRINCESS DI, Sicilian; friend of Mussolini

GARIBOLDI, GENERAL ITALO, commander of Italian forces in Russia

GASTALDI, federal secretary of Turin

GAVRILOVIC, one of heads of opposition to Christic in Yugoslavia

GAULLE, GENERAL CHARLES DE, leader of the Free French movement

GAYDA, VIRGINIO, Italian journalist; editor of *Giornale d'Italia,* mouthpiece of Mussolini

GAZZERA, GENERAL PIETRO, Italian Army officer and administrator; commander of troops and Governor of Galla and Sidama Gimma, Italian East Africa

GELOSO, GENERAL CARLO, commander of Italian Army in Greece

GERALDINE, Queen of Albania, wife of King Zog

GHIGI, PELLEGRINI, Italian diplomat; Minister to Rumania

GIACOMO, DE, Italian diplomat

GIANNINI, ALBERTO, Italian Minister of Foreign Commerce; diplomat; Director of Commercial Affairs

GIOLITTI, GIOVANNI, Italian statesman; five times Prime Minister; opposed entry of Italy into World War I

GIONI, MARKA, Albanian Catholic leader of Scutari

GIOVANNA, DELLA, Italian diplomat; attaché in Germany

GIRAUD, GENERAL HENRI HONORÉ, Commander of Allied defenses in northern France, 1940; succeeded Admiral Darlan as High Commissioner in Northwest Africa

GIROLDI, MARSHAL PECORI, served under Marshal Graziani

GIULIANO, BALBINO, former Italian Minister of Education; professor; senator

GIUMEDI, Corsican secret agent in service of Fascist party

GIUNTA, FRANCESCO, Italian lawyer and politician; Undersecretary of State to Prime Minister; deputy of party; secretary general of party

GOEBBELS, JOSEPH PAUL, Nazi Minister of Propaganda

GOERING, HERMANN, Reichsmarshal of Germany

GOLDONI, CARLO, Italian playwright, 1707–93

GOTZAMANIS, Greek expert in economics

GOVONI, CORRADO, modern Italian poet

GRANDI, COUNT DINO, leading Fascist; member of Grand Council; Minister of Justice; Minister for Foreign Affairs; Ambassador to Great Britain

GRAZIANI, MARSHAL RODOLFO (MARQUIS OF NIGHELLI), commander of the Italian Army in Libya; Viceroy of Ethiopia

GRAZIOLI, EMILIO, Italian Commissioner in Slovenia

GRAZZI, EMANUELE, Italian Minister to Greece; diplomat attached to Ministry for Foreign Affairs

GRIO, Inspector General of the Fascist party

GROBBA, FRITZ KONRAD FERDINAND, head of Arab service of the German Foreign Service

GUARIGLIA, RAFFAELO, Italian Ambassador to France; Ambassador to Germany; Ambassador to the Holy See

GUARNERI, FELICE, Italian Minister of Foreign Exchange

GUZZONI, GENERAL ALFREDO, Italian Undersecretary of War and Assistant Chief of the General Staff; commander of expeditionary force in Albania

HACHA, EMIL, President of Czechoslovakia; later President of the Nazi Protectorate of Bohemia and Moravia

HAILE SELASSIE, Emperor of Ethiopia (the Lion of Judah, the Negus)

HALDER, GENERAL FRANZ, Chief of Staff of the German Army

HALIFAX, VISCOUNT (now Earl), British Secretary of State for Foreign Affairs at outbreak of World War II

HASON, chief of the carabinièri

HELFAND, LEON, Soviet Chargé d'Affaires in Rome

HENDERSON, SIR NEVILE, British Ambassador to Germany, 1937–39

HESS, RUDOLF, Hitler's deputy and next in succession; flew to Great Britain in 1942

HESSE, PRINCE PHILIP OF, husband of Princess Mafalda, second daughter of King Victor Emmanuel

III; go-between for Mussolini, Hitler, and Himmler

HEWEL, WALTER, confidant of Hitler; Nazi official

HIMMLER, HEINRICH, Chief of the Gestapo

HITLER, ADOLF, Nazi Führer

HOARE, SIR SAMUEL (now Lord Templewood), British Ambassador to Spain

HOFER, FRANZ, Nazi Gauleiter at Bolzano

HORIA, SIMA, head of Rumanian Legion

HORICHIRI, Japanese Ambassador to Italy

HORTHY, ADMIRAL NICHOLAS, Regent of Hungary; his son, Stephen Horthy, Vice-Regent

HOST VENTURI, GIOVANNI, leading Fascist; Minister of Communications

HUMBERT, PRINCE OF PIEDMONT, son of King Victor Emmanuel III; heir to the throne

HUNTZIGER, GENERAL CHARLES L. C., member of French commission to sign the armistice with Italy

INDELLI, MARIO, Italian Ambassador to Japan; Minister to Yugoslavia

IRABO, an agent of the Slovaks

JACOMONI DI SAN LAVINO, GENERAL FRANCISCO, commander of Italian forces in Albania

JODL, GENERAL GUSTAV, member of German General Staff

JORDANA, GENERAL F. GOMEZ, Spanish Army officer and politician; Minister for Foreign Affairs and President, Council of State

KALLAY, NICHOLAS, Hungarian Cabinet Minister

KANYA, KALMAN DE, Hungarian diplomat and politician

KEITEL, MARSHAL WILHELM, supreme commander of German Army in World War II

KERILLIS, HENRI DE, French politician and journalist

KESSELRING, MARSHAL ALBERT, Chief of German Air Forces in Italy, 1942

KESTERER, German quack doctor; called by Hitler the "Magic Buddha"

KINDELAN, GENERAL ALFREDO, Spanish General of Aviation

KLEIST, GENERAL PAUL LUDWIG VON, commander of Nazi forces on southern front against Russia

KOCI, JAKE, Albanian chieftain

KOLIEGI, Albanian Cabinet Minister in pay of Ciano

KOO, WELLINGTON, Chinese diplomat

KRUIA, BEY, Albanian Prime Minister

KWATERNIK, MARSHAL, Yugoslav commander of Ustaci forces

LANZA, secretary at the Embassy in Berlin

LAPPUS, SIGRID VON, reputed mistress of Hitler

LAVAL, PIERRE, French politician; Prime Minister; Minister for Foreign Affairs, 1940; collaborator with the Nazis

LEGER, ALEXIS, French diplomat; Secretary General of the Ministry for Foreign Affairs, 1939–40

LEOPOLD III, King of the Belgians, brother of the Princess of Piedmont

LEPERA, Italian prefect involved in financial scandals in treatment of Jews

LEQUIO, FRANCESCO, Italian Ambassador to Spain

LETO, Inspector General of Police

LEY, ROBERT, Nazi Minister of Labor

LIBOHOVA, EKREM, Albanian Minister for Foreign Affairs

LINDBERGH, CHARLES A., American aviator

LIOTTA, GENERAL AURELIO, Italian Army officer

LIST, GENERAL SIEGMUND WILHELM WALTHER, commander of German Army in Greece; commanded German troops at Polish front and in Rumania

LITVINOV, MAXIM, Soviet Commissar for Foreign Affairs; Ambassador to the United States

LLOYD, LORD, British colonial administrator

LLOYD GEORGE, DAVID, British Prime Minister, World War I

LOMBRASSA, Italian official in charge of mobilization of civilians

LORAINE, SIR PERCY, British Ambassador to Italy, succeeding Lord Perth

LÖRZER, COLONEL GENERAL BRUNO, German Army officer

LUCCA, provincial secretary of the Fascist party

LUCCA, COLONEL, military attaché in Ankara

LUCIOLLI, Italian diplomat in Germany

LUTZE, GENERAL VIKTOR, German Army officer and politician; chief group leader of S.S.; Chief of Staff S.A. troops

LYAUTEY, MAJOR, son of Marshal Lyautey of French Army

MACKENSEN, HANS GEORG VON, German Ambassador to Italy

MAGISTRATI, MASSIMO, Ciano's brother-in-law; Italian diplomat stationed in Berlin, Berne, and Bucharest; his wife, Maria Ciano Magistrati

MAGLIONE, CARDINAL LUIGI, Secretary of State of Holy See under Pope Pius XII

MALBRAN, MANUEL E., Argentine Ambassador to Italy

MAN, HENRY DE, member of Belgian Cabinet; pro-Nazi

MANCINI, ADMIRAL, Italian naval officer

MANCINI, modern Italian artist

MANOÏLESCU, MIHAIL, former Prime Minister of Rumania; Minister to Austria; Rumanian politician and economist

MANORESI, member of Fascist Chamber of Deputies

MARAVIGNA, GENERAL, Italian Army officer

MARCHESI, GENERAL, Italian commander of air squadron in Libya

MARIASSY, Hungarian Minister to Italy; politician

MARKA, GIONI, Albanian politician

MARKOVIČ, T. JOVAN, Yugoslav Minister for Foreign Affairs

MARMI, GENERAL, Italian Army officer

MARRAS, GENERAL EFISIO, Italian military attaché in Berlin

MARTIRE, EGILBERTO, Fascist deputy; professor of economics

MARZIALI, Prefect of Milan

MASSIMO, Italian diplomat in Berlin

MASTROMATTEI, Prefect of Bolzano; member of commission for repatriation of Germans in Alto Adige

MATCHEK, JOSEPH, Croatian leader of

National Agrarian party opposed to the Serbs

MATERA, GENERAL, Italian Army officer

MATSUOKA, YOSUKE, Japanese Minister for Foreign Affairs

MATTEOTTI, GIACOMO, Italian Socialist deputy; murdered by Fascists in 1924

MATTEUCCI, clerk in Italian Consulate at Prague

MAZZASO (unidentified)

MAZZETTI, MARIO, former member Chamber of Deputies

MAZZOLINI, COUNT SERAFINO, Italian diplomat; Minister to Uruguay, Egypt, and Montenegro

MELCHIORI, ALESSANDRO, Italian journalist; an informer very close to Mussolini

MESOHEGEYS, Hungarian with whom Ciano hunted in 1942

MESSE, GENERAL GIOVANNI, Italian Chief of Staff at the last stage of the war; made prisoner of war in Tunis

MESSINA, Italian sculptor; protégé of Bottai

METAXAS, JOHN, Prime Minister and dictator of Greece

METAXAS, Greek Minister in Rome

MEZZASOMA, FERNANDO, a secretary of the Fascist party

MEZZI, Italian prefect stationed in Sicily

MICHAEL, Prince of Montenegro

MICHETTI, FRANCESCO PAOLO, artist, 1851–1929, of the modernistic school

MIHAEL, King Michael of Rumania, who succeeded his father, King Carol

MIHAILOFF, VASIL LACI, Macedonian-Greek who made an attempt on the life of King Victor Emmanuel III on his visit to Tirana

MILCH, FIELD MARSHAL ERHARD, Commander of the Nazi Air Force

MILONE, DR., secretary of the Fascist party in Naples

MISSIROLI, MARIO, Italian journalist in Fascist pay

MOELDERS, COLONEL WERNER, Nazi Number 1 ace; killed in plane crash; state funeral which Hitler attended

MOLLIER, press attaché of German Embassy in Rome

MOLOTOV, VYACHESLAV MIKHAILOVICH, Soviet Commissar for Foreign Affairs

MOLTKE, HANS ADOLF VON, German diplomat; Ambassador to Poland

MONTEZOMOLO, COLONEL GIUSEPPE, member of Italian General Staff; secretary to the four marshals, Goering, Kesselring, Rommel, and Cavallero

MONTGOMERY, MARSHAL SIR BERNARD L., British Commander in Chief in North Africa

MONTINI, MONSIGNOR GIOVANNI B., assistant to the Cardinal Secretary of State

MORGAGNI, MANLIO, Fascist journalist; administrative director *Popolo d'Italia*

MOSCHI, AUGUSTO, nephew of Donna Rachele Mussolini

MOURAD PASHA, Egyptian Minister to Germany

MUFTI, THE, head of Islamic community in Palestine

MUSSOLINI, ARNALDO, brother of Mussolini and his successor as editor of *Popolo d'Italia*

MUSSOLINI, BENITO (IL DUCE), his wife, Donna Rachele; children, Edda (wife of Ciano), Vittorio, Bruno, Vito; grandchild, Marina, daughter of Bruno; his sister, Donna Edvige Mussolini

MUTI, ETTORE, Italian politician; secretary of the Fascist party

NAVARRA, doorkeeper for Mussolini at the Palazzo Venezia

NECCHI, friend of Badoglio to whose villa in Milan the latter retired

NEUBACHER, HERMANN, German municipal administrator; commissioner for Greek economic and financial affairs

NISTRI, ardent Fascist; officer in the African campaign

NITTI, FRANCESCO SAVERIO, Italian politician and economist; Prime Minister of Italy, 1919–20

NOBLE, ADMIRAL SIR PERCY LOCKHART HARNAM, R.N., Commander in Chief of British forces in China

NOËL, LÉON, French diplomat; Ambassador to Poland; member of the commission to sign the armistice with Italy

OLIVA, COLONEL, referred to in Countess Ciano's letter to her husband; otherwise unidentified

ORANO, PAOLO, Fascist journalist

ORIANI, ALFREDO, philosopher; journalist; friend of Mussolini (Father, also named Alfredo, was called "the intellectual forerunner of Fascism")

ORLANDO, GENERAL, Italian Army officer

OSBORNE, SIR FRANCIS D'ARCY GODOLPHIN, British Minister to the Holy See

OSHIMA, HIROSHI, Japanese Ambassador to Italy

OSIO, president of Italian Bank of Labor

PACELLI, CARDINAL EUGENIO, later Pope Pius XII

PANSA, MARIO, Italian diplomat

PAPEN, FRANZ VON, German Ambassador to Turkey

PARENTI, GINO, Fascist leader

PARESCHI, GIUSEPPE, Italian Minister of Agriculture

PARIANI, GENERAL ALBERTO, Italian Chief of Staff; military adviser to Albanian Army before the Italian occupation; Undersecretary of State for War

PARINI, PIERO, leader in Fascist party; Italian diplomat

PARISOT, GENERAL, member of French delegation to sign the armistice with Italy

PASCOLATO, MICHELE, official of Italian Government

PATER, engineer and builder in high favor with Donna Rachele Mussolini

PAUL, PRINCE, Regent of Yugoslavia

PAVELIĆ, ANTE, Croatian dictator subservient to Fascists; protected by Mussolini

PAVOLINI, ALESSANDRO, Fascist enthusiast and holder of many offices; killed with Mussolini

PECORI, COMMANDER, naval attaché in Berlin

PEPPO, GIUSEPPE DE, Italian diplomat; Ambassador to Turkey and Spain

PERSANO DI PELLONI, COUNT CARLO (1806–83), Italian admiral in war of 1856 against Austria; dismissed from the Navy

PERTH, EARL OF, British Ambassador to Italy; formerly Sir Eric Drummond, Secretary General of the League of Nations

PERUGI, GENERAL, Italian Army officer

PETACCI, family to which Clara, mistress of Mussolini (slain with him), belonged; Dr. Marcello Petacci, father of Clara

PÉTAIN, MARSHAL HENRI PHILIPPE, head of Vichy Government; succeeded Reynaud as Prime Minister in 1940

PETRALIS, agent of secret Fascist information bureau

PETROGRANO, Italian Director of Public Health

PFITZNER, DR. JOSEPH, Sudeten German; vice-mayor of Prague

PHILLIPS, WILLIAM, U.S. Ambassador to Italy

PICCIO, GENERAL PIERO RUGGERO, Italian Chief of Staff for Aviation

PIETRI, Corsican secret agent in the service of the Fascists

PIETROMARCHI, LUCA, Italian diplomat

PIGNATTI MORANO DI CUSTOZZA, COUNT BONIFACIO, Italian Ambassador to the Holy See; career diplomat

PINNA, GENERAL PIETRO, member of the Italian General Staff

PINTOR, GENERAL PIETRO, Italian Army officer

PIRELLI, ALBERTO, Fascist industrialist; head of the rubber trust; newspaper owner

PISTOIA, DUKE OF, son of Duke of Genoa, cousin of King Victor Emmanuel III

PITASSI, MANNELLA, Italian general called "King of Artillerymen"

PITTALIS, Italian Ambassador to Argentine Republic

PIZZARDO, CARDINAL GIUSEPPE, Papal Nuncio, 1939

PLESSEN, BARON JOHANN VON, Minister attached to German Embassy in Rome

POHL, GENERAL RITTER VON, German Army officer in Libya

PONCET. See FRANCOIS-PONCET

PONTANO, DR., one of Mussolini's physicians

POTOCKA, COUNTESS, a member of the Radziwill family; wife of Count Joseph Potocki, a Polish diplomat

PRICOLO, GENERAL FRANCESCO, Italian Chief of Staff for Aviation

PRINI, Italian sculptor from Genoa

PRUNAS, GENERAL, Italian Army officer

QUEIPO DE LLANO, GENERAL GONZALO, chief of Spanish military mission to Italy

RAEDER, ADMIRAL ERICH, Commander in Chief of the German Navy

RANZA, GENERAL, Italian Army officer, member of General Staff

RAVASIO, CARLO, vice-secretary of the Fascist party

RENATO, Ciano's fisherman at Leghorn

RENZETTI, Italian military attaché in Berlin; Consul at Leipsic

REVEL. See THAON DE REVEL

REYNAUD, PAUL, Prime Minister of France preceding Pétain

RIBBENTROP, JOACHIM VON, Nazi Minister for Foreign Affairs

RICASOLI, BARON BETTINO, Italian Prime Minister during the War of Independence

RICCARDI, ADMIRAL ARTURO, Chief of Naval Staff and Undersecretary of the Navy

RICCARDI, RAFFAELO, Italian politician; Minister of Currency and Exchange

RICCI, RENATO, Italian politician; Minister of Corporations, nicknamed the "Earthquake"

RIDOMI, Fascist journalist; informer, secret agent

RINTELEN, GENERAL, German military attaché in Italy

RIOS, JUAN ANTONIO, President-elect of Chile, 1942

ROATTA, GENERAL MARIO, Chief of Italian General Staff; called the "Butcher of Yugoslavia"; military attaché in Berlin

ROCHIRA, UBALDO, Italian Consul General in Vienna

RODINIS, Italian diplomat; associate of Ansaldo as editor of Il Telègrafo, Ciano's newspaper in Leghorn

ROEHM, ERNST, Nazi leader, executed at Munich in the "blood bath," 1934

ROMAN (PETROVICH), Prince of Montenegro

ROMANO, Italian observer in Vienna

ROMMEL, MARSHAL ERWIN VON, German general in North African campaign; called the "Desert Fox"

ROOSEVELT, FRANKLIN DELANO, President of the United States

ROSENBERG, ALFRED, Nazi writer and politician; in charge of wartime youth education

ROSEO, intriguer at court for a separate peace

ROSSO, AUGUSTO, Italian diplomat; Ambassador to Soviet Russia and Turkey

RUEGGER, PAUL, Swiss Minister to Italy

RUSSO, DOMENICO, Fascist leader

SALAZAR, ANTONIO DE OLIVEIRA, Prime Minister of Portugal

SALZA, ADMIRAL, Italian representative on the Armistice Commission in North Africa

SANSONETTI, ADMIRAL LUIGI, Assistant Chief Italian Naval General Staff

SAPUPPO, GIUSEPPE, Italian Minister to Denmark; career diplomat

SARACOGLU, SHUKRI, Prime Minister of Turkey

SAUER, DR., cultural attaché of German Embassy in Rome

SCANDERBEG, Albanian national hero of the fifteenth century

SCANNAVACCA, Italian Army officer on General Staff

SCHIRACH, BALDUR VON, leader of Nazi Youth Movement

SCHMIDT, GENERAL ARTHUR, Nazi Army officer made prisoner at Bardia

SCHMIDT, GUIDO, German diplomat, formerly Austrian Cabinet Minister

SCHMIDT, GUSTAVE PAUL, Hitler's interpreter

SCHULENBURG, FREDERIC WERNER, GRAF VAN DER, German Ambassador to Soviet Russia

SCHUSCHNIGG, KURT VON, Austrian politician; Chancellor; Minister of Defense and Foreign Affairs

SCILTIAN, modern Italian painter

SCORZA, CARLO, early Fascist; last of general secretaries of the party

SEBASTIANI, OSWALDO, secretary of Mussolini; Italian Minister of Finance

SENISE, CARMINE, Italian chief of police; successor to Bocchini

SENNI, COUNT CARLO, Italian Army officer in African campaign; family socially prominent in Rome

SEREGGI, GENERAL ZEF, Albanian envoy from King Zog; Minister to Italy

SERENA, ADELCHI, secretary general of the Fascist party

SERRA DI CASSANO, Italian Consul

SERRANO SUÑER, RAMÓN, Spanish Minister for Foreign Affairs, 1940–42; brother-in-law of Franco

SEYSS-INQUART, ARTHUR, Nazi Governor of Austria; High Commissioner in the Netherlands

SHAW, GEORGE BERNARD, British playwright and author

SHIRATORI, TOSHIO, Japanese Ambassador to Italy

SIDOROVICI, GENERAL TEOFILE, head of Rumanian Youth Movement

SILIMBANI, Italian Consul General at Tunis

SMIGLY-RYDZ, MARSHAL EDWARD, Commander in Chief of Polish Army

SODDU, GENERAL UBALDO, member of Italian General Staff; resigned after failure to stop Greeks in Albania

SOMIGLI, ADMIRAL EDUARDO, Italian naval officer

SONNINO, BARON SIDNEY, Italian Minister for Foreign Affairs; Prime Minister; representative at Paris peace conference of 1919

SORICE, GENERAL ANTONIO, Italian Chief of Staff, 1940; fought in Greek campaign

SORRENTINO, Fascist journalist

SPISANI, spokesman for and agent of Clara Petacci; a "third-rate dancing teacher"

SPOLETO, DUKE OF (AIMONE), Vice-Admiral; brother of Duke of Aosta, received offer of the crown of Croatia

SQUERO, GENERAL, Italian Army commander

STACKIC, Yugoslav lawyer, sent on mission to Italy

STALIN, JOSEF, chairman of the Council of People's Commissars; Generalissimo of the Soviet Union

STARACE, ACHILLE, Italian officer and politician; Chief of Staff of Fascist militia; served longest term as secretary of the Fascist party; slain with Mussolini

STEFANI, ARMANDO, member of Fascist university group who disclosed plot against party to Ciano

STEPHENS, COLONEL, British Broadcasting Corporation military commentator

STHYKA, Albanian diplomat; Minister to Yugoslavia

STORER, BARONESS VON, wife of German Ambassador to Spain

STOYADINOVICH, MILAN, Prime Minister of Yugoslavia; Minister for Foreign Affairs

STUMM, GENERAL VON, officer killed in North Africa; his wife, Baroness von Stumm, daughter of Bismarck

STURDZA, PRINCE LUCA, Rumanian diplomat

SUARDO, GIACOMO, Italian senator; diplomat

TACCHI VENTURI, Jesuit priest who served as unofficial liaison officer between the Holy See and Fascist leaders

TALAMO STENOLFI, GIUSEPPE, MARCHESE DI CASTELNUOVO, Italian diplomat; Minister to Bulgaria

TALIANI, FRANCESCO, Italian Ambassador to China

TAMARO, ATTILIO, Italian diplomat; Minister to Switzerland

TAMBURINI, TULLIO, Fascist prefect; Minister of the Interior succeeding Buffarini

TASSINARI, GIUSEPPE, Italian senator and general director of food administration

TAYLOR, MYRON C., American representative at the Vatican

TELEKI, COUNT PAUL, Prime Minister of Hungary

TERUZZI, ATTILIO, leading Fascist; Minister of the Colonies

TESEI, young Italian diplomat in Berlin

TESTA, GENERAL, in command of Italian troops in Dalmatia

TEUCCI, COLONEL, Italian military attaché in Berlin

THAON DE REVEL, COUNT PAOLO, Italian Minister of Finance, called the "Red Count"; senator

THOMA, GENERAL RITTER WILHELM VON, Nazi commander of Afrika Korps; captured by British forces in Libya

TORINO, COUNT OF, cousin of King Victor Emmanuel III

TORRE, COUNT GIUSEPPE DELLA, director of *Osservatore Romano*, Vatican newspaper

TRIONFI, GENERAL, Italian Army officer

TSOLACOGLU, GENERAL GEORGE, Greek officer who offered to collaborate with the Axis to negotiate a surrender

TURABONI (unidentified)

TURATI, AUGUSTO, a secretary of the Fascist party

UDET, GENERAL ERNST, Chief of German General Staff

URACH, PRINCE ALBERTO VON, Nazi press official

VACCA MAGGIOLINI, leading Fascist

VACCARI, MARCELLO, Prefect of Venice

VALACI, Albanian bey

VALENTINO, BARON ARONE DI, Italian diplomat in Warsaw

VALERA, EAMON DE, President of Irish Free State

VALLE, GENERAL GIUSEPPE, Italian Minister of Aviation

VECCHI, DI VAL CISMON, COUNT CESARE MARIA DE, Fascist leader; holder of many offices

VERCELLINO, GENERAL MARIO, Italian Army officer

VERLACI SHEVKET, Albanian landowner and political leader; Albanian quisling

VEZZARO, business partner of Dr. Petacci

VICTOR EMMANUEL III, King of Italy

VIDUSSONI, ALDO, leader of the University militia; general secretary of the Fascist party

VIELI, Swiss banker

VILLANI, BARON FREDERICK, Hungarian Cabinet Minister and diplomat

VIOLA, GUIDO, COUNT DI CAMPALTO, Italian diplomat; Ambassador to Spain

VISCONTI PRASCA, GENERAL, Italian Army officer and official

VITETTI, COUNT LEONARDO, Italian diplomat; Director General, Ministry for Foreign Affairs

VOLPATO, Italian professor; economic consultant of Ministry for Foreign Affairs

VOLPI DI MISURATA, COUNT GIUSEPPE, Fascist leader; Minister of Finance; president of Italian-Croatian Economic Mission; senator

VRIONI, KENSAL, Albanian Minister for Foreign Affairs

WANG CHING-WEI, Japanese-controlled puppet Prime Minister of China

WEIZSÄCKER, ERNST VON, German Undersecretary of State; Ambassador to the Holy See

WELLES, SUMNER, Undersecretary of State of the United States

WEYGAND, MARSHAL MAXIME, French Commander in Chief French forces overseas, 1940

WIENIAWA, GENERAL BOLESLAW, Polish Ambassador to Italy

ZAMBONI, GIUSEPPE, Italian military attaché in Berlin

ZINGALES, GENERAL, in command of German expeditionary force on Rumanian-Russian border

ZOBUNE, Turkish Ambassador to the Soviet Union

ZOG, King of Albania

ZORLU, Turkish Ambassador to the Soviet Union

ZVETKOVIC, DRAGISHA, Prime Minister of Yugoslavia, 1939–41

Introduction

I FIRST met Count Ciano in Rome on February 25, 1940, and I saw him for the last time on March 19 of that year. During most of the intervening period I was away from the Italian capital. Gauged by time alone my knowledge of him both as a man and as a statesman must be regarded as exceedingly slight. Yet in the circumstances under which I knew him, and in the nature of the discussions which brought us together, I find a measure of justification for undertaking to write this introduction to Count Ciano's Diaries and to offer my own estimate of its author.

In the early winter of 1940 I was sent by President Roosevelt as his personal representative to visit the capitals of the Allied nations and of the two Axis powers in order to report to him upon the situation in Europe and upon the possibilities for the establishment of a just and lasting peace. As is now well known, no such possibilities existed. The Nazi Government was already fully prepared for an immediate all-out offensive, and the German onslaught was inevitable unless the French and British governments were willing to submit to a Hitler-dominated Europe. The Soviet Union was not to be invaded until more than a year later, and Japan's aggression upon the United States was still almost two years away.

The prospects for the Western democracies already seemed very dark indeed, although not yet so hopeless as they became a few months later.

The ability of the United States to arrest the catastrophe was tenuous. European public opinion generally believed that American sentiment was largely isolationist and that it would prevent President Roosevelt from undertaking any effective measures of assistance to England or to France when Germany's full war effort was finally exercised. The Axis governments were convinced that, should the United

States finally rouse itself from its lethargy, adequate military preparation, even for self-defense, would prove to be so long delayed as to be of no practical value. Only one thing could have prevented the German offensive in the west, and that was the knowledge on the part of the Nazi leaders and of the German General Staff that the United States was fully armed as well as determined to use force if necessary to prevent the outbreak of a new world war.

In such circumstances the maximum of what the United States could hope to accomplish was to prevent the entrance of Italy into the war at the side of Germany. Even though Italy's so-called non-belligerency was being notoriously utilized to render all assistance short of war to the Germans, an actual declaration of war by Italy would necessarily imply a far greater threat to France and to Yugoslavia, as well as a vital thrust at the British life line through the Mediterranean to the Suez Canal.

With the exception of a very small group of Fascist leaders, the Italian people as a whole, as well as every potent influence within Italy, were vehemently opposed to a declaration of war. While this opposition was primarily due to a general fear and hatred of Germany and of its Nazi Government, it also stemmed from the popular conviction that, however great the artificially engendered friction with Great Britain and with France might be, the future of Italy would be far more secure in a world in which the Western Powers remained to the fore than in a world in which Nazism had become the sole authority. Finally, there was a great mass of Italian public opinion which was hostile to the thought of war because of its realization that Italy would commit a fatal error by taking part in a war of which the outcome was problematical, and as a result of which, whoever the victors might be, the Italian people had nothing to gain and everything to lose.

Count Ciano shared the viewpoint of all of these groups. Of all the men possessing high authority within the Axis governments, he was the only one who made it clear to me, without subterfuge and without hesitation, that he had opposed the war, that he continued to oppose the war, that he foresaw nothing but utter devastation for the whole of Europe through the extension of the war, and that every effort which he personally could undertake would be exerted to prevent the entrance of Italy into the conflict.

His efforts, of course, were futile, as were the efforts of all other Italians. One man, and one man only, the Dictator Benito Mussolini, made the decision which plunged Italy into the holocaust and brought about the tragedy from which the Italian people have already so grievously suffered, and from which they will continue to suffer for many years to come.

Italy had prostrated itself before Mussolini. He was thus enabled to achieve an almost complete control over every form of activity in Italian life. From top to bottom the Italian social system had become wholly corrupt through the corroding influence of Fascism. The structure had already become so rotten by 1940 that no effective means existed whereby the will of the Italian people could combat the fatal determination of their dictator.

The members of what was politely termed the Italian Government were no more than Mussolini's lackeys. Count Ciano himself was wholly subservient to him. Count Ciano was a man who lacked neither personal dignity nor physical courage, and yet I have seen him quail at an interview with Mussolini when the Dictator showed irritation. The will of the Duce, however perverse, however ignorant, and however blindly mistaken the Fascist leaders knew him to be, was law. For no one in Italy from the King to his ministers, from the generals to the industrial magnates, dared to oppose him.

I first knew of the existence of this Diary, now for the first time published in full, from Count Ciano himself. He showed it to me and read me excerpts from it in my first conversation with him. There is no question of its authenticity, nor have I any reason to believe that in the last tragic days before his execution as a "traitor," at Mussolini's order, he had the opportunity or the desire to make any changes in what he had previously written. The record stands as he wrote it down day after day from the beginning of 1939 until he was removed by Mussolini from his position as Minister for Foreign Affairs in the early winter of 1943.

I believe it to be one of the most valuable historical documents of our times. To some who have read mutilated passages previously syndicated through the press, the Diary has proved a disappointment because of its lack of those sensational revelations which they had apparently anticipated. But those who will read the Diary in its complete text will obtain an opportunity to gain a clearer insight into the manner of being of Hitler's Germany and of Mussolini's Italy, and a far more accurate understanding of the degradation of the peoples subjected to Hitlerism and to Fascism during the years when almost the entire world trembled before the Axis partners.

They will find in the Diary a hitherto unrevealed picture of Germany's machinations during those fateful years. They will see perhaps more vividly than before how stereotyped was Hitler's course in utilizing his most solemn pledges to other governments, and by no means least to his ally, Italy, as a means of deluding them as to his real intentions.

Notwithstanding the recent assurances emanating from the Japanese war lords that the attack upon Pearl Harbor was carried out by a small group of militarists without the knowledge of Japan's responsible officials, the readers of this Diary will see how the Government of Japan actually notified the German and Italian governments that the United States was to be attacked four days before the date of the assault upon Pearl Harbor.

They can read the unvarnished account of the devious preparations made by the Fascist Government for its perfidious invasion of Albania and for its even more treacherous attempt to invade Greece.

There is scarcely an event in the dreary list of maneuvers and countermaneuvers in eastern Europe and in the Balkans which is not graphically portrayed in this Diary.

But what is perhaps most valuable of all is the picture which the Diary presents of Italy under the climactic stage of Fascism.

The partially unconscious analysis of Mussolini, undertaken by a man who was not only his son-in-law but who also obviously admired him, and who loyally served him until only a few months before his death, could hardly be more devastating.

As Count Ciano states in one entry, "action," no matter what kind of action it might be, was the only spring to which Mussolini's nature responded. The Dictator's obsession that Germany's armed might could overcome every other force in the world, his black rancor, his ruthless cruelty, his dense ignorance of the world at large, his gross failure to comprehend the power which men's passion for freedom represents, and, above all else, his utter contempt for the Italian people themselves, stand out unforgettably in the passages of this Diary.

To those Italians who actually believed in Mussolini and who sincerely regarded him, at least during the years prior to World War II, as Italy's savior, these appraisals of his fellow countrymen made by Mussolini in complete confidence to his son-in-law will come as a revelation:

"The Italian race is a race of sheep. Eighteen years is not enough to change them. . . . We must keep them disciplined and in uniform from morning until night. Beat them and beat them and beat them.

. . . To make a people great it is necessary to send them into battle even if you have to kick them in the pants. This is what I shall do."

But, as is natural, it is the author of the Diary himself who is most clearly depicted in these pages.

Galeazzo Ciano, Count di Cortelazzo, was born at Leghorn on March 18, 1903. He was the only son of Costanzo Ciano, who served with gallantry as a captain in the Italian Navy during World War I. The elder Ciano was one of those most responsible for the initial success of the Fascist movement. Promoted to the rank of admiral and ennobled immediately after Mussolini rose to power, he subsequently served for many years as Minister of Communications and as President of the so-called Fascist Chamber of Deputies. Today he is best remembered for the immense fortune which he accumulated through the opportunities offered him by his controlling influence within the Fascist party and, in particular, during the years when he held office as Minister of Communications.

Galeazzo Ciano graduated in law at the University of Rome in 1925, and during his university years, which coincided with the first period of Fascism, also worked as a dramatic and art critic on a Roman daily newspaper. Strangely enough, during these years he adopted a critical attitude toward the Fascist party, of which his father, whom he greatly revered, was already an outstanding leader.

Immediately after his graduation he entered the Italian Diplomatic Service. During his first five years in the service he was stationed at Rio de Janeiro, Buenos Aires, Peking, and the Vatican City. It was at the close of this period that he married Mussolini's daughter, Edda. Simultaneously he became an ardent Fascist.

From then on his rise was rapid. Serving briefly as Consul General at Shanghai, he was promoted in 1932 to be Minister to China. By 1933 he had again returned to Italy and, receiving an appointment as a member of the Italian Delegation to the London Economic Conference in June 1933, he was immediately thereafter made chief of Mussolini's press office. In 1935 he was promoted to be Undersecretary of State for Press and Propaganda. Shortly thereafter he was named a member of the Fascist Grand Council. The following year, at the age of thirty-three, he was appointed Minister for Foreign Affairs.

In his Diary Count Ciano shows himself to be precisely what he was in life—the amoral product of a wholly decadent period in Italian, and, for that matter, in European, history. To him morality in international relations did not exist. He was wholly seized of the concept that only might makes right. The question whether the Italian people should be consulted before the nation was plunged into war, since it would be their lives which would be lost, and since it would be they who would make the sacrifices involved, simply did not occur to him.

Yet where he showed himself far superior to the man who was his father-in-law, his political chief, and finally his executioner, was in his ability to see clearly where Italy's real security lay. He appears to have had no illusions from the time of the German occupation of Austria as to the danger inherent to Italy in German ambitions and in the extension of Hitler's sway. Time and again in his Diary he emphasizes his belief in the accuracy of the reports which come to him of the indications given by members of the Nazi hierarchy of Germany's ultimate intention to seize Trieste from the Italians and to occupy Italy's northern plains.

The Diary proves that, as a statesman, Ciano saw the major issue accurately. He was under no illusions as to what a German-dominated Europe would imply for Italy. He was convinced that only through the defeat of Germany could any world order be established in which a sovereign Italy could survive.

But what is equally apparent is Ciano's total inability to change the course upon which Mussolini had embarked. He relates the warnings against Germany which he gave to Mussolini and the occasional efforts which he made to establish some better relationship between Italy and the Western Powers. There is, however, never a sign that either his advice or his efforts were fruitful. During the earlier years in which he held high office he was wholly under Mussolini's sway. During the last two years of his life at times he made attempts to rally support among the members of the Fascist Grand Council in order to block Mussolini's growing subservience to the increasingly overbearing German taskmaster. Finally, at the crucial meeting of the Fascist Grand Council, on July 25, 1943, he took a leading part in the *coup d'état* against Mussolini, and the Dictator was at length overthrown. It was then far too late. The Armistice was consummated, but the Italian people were already prostrate.

Had Count Ciano possessed either moral courage, the true patriotism which in his Diary he not infrequently claims for himself, or the tough ability possessed by so many of the leaders in the *Risorgimento,* he would have resigned his office in August of 1939, when Mussolini ordered him to obey the German demand for the Axis alliance, and joined from outside Italy in the fight against the egregious policies of the dictatorship.

But such a course would have been wholly contrary to Count Ciano's manner of being. Family ties hemmed him in. The corrupting effect of Fascism upon his character, the decadent atmosphere in which he lived, all combined to render impossible any such hazardous exploit on his part. However much he opposed Mussolini's uninterrupted march toward disaster, however clearly he foresaw the inevitable results, he invariably acquiesced until the final tragedy was already at hand.

As an individual, Count Ciano, like most human beings, possessed his qualities and his defects. He was sincerely attached to his parents, and to all those who had been close to him in his early youth. He was a devoted father to his three children.

Of medium stature, well set up, with aquiline features, he possessed both dignity and personal charm. In intimate conversation or at informal gatherings there was not the faintest trace of the pompous and self-conscious Fascist dignitary who appeared in public and who so sedulously aped the absurd mannerisms of the Duce himself. As a companion he was frank, often surprisingly outspoken, and possessed of a keen wit and of a mordant sense of humor. He spoke well and fluently and with no inconsiderable knowledge of modern history. He was keen in his perception of the relative significance of men and of events.

Corrupt in a financial sense he undoubtedly was. Whether he was personally responsible for the assassination of several enemies of the regime in the earlier years of his tenure of the Foreign Office, as has often recently been alleged, I have no conclusive evidence. But I am inclined to the belief that Count Ciano possessed many of the qualities of the men of the Italian Renaissance, and that such crimes would have by no means been outside the bounds of his toleration.

The final passage in this Diary, that written by Count Ciano in his prison cell in Verona some two weeks before his execution, is the most revealing epitaph that can be written for him.

Galeazzo Ciano was the creature of his times, and the times in which he had his being are the least admirable mankind has known for many centuries.

SUMNER WELLES

Memoriale

di

Gabinetto

per l'anno

1939

XVII

January 1, 1939

The Duce returned to Rome last night, and we have had a long conversation. He is very much dissatisfied about the situation in East Africa, and has pronounced a severe judgment on the work of the Duke of Aosta. In fact, Asmara is still in a state of complete revolt, and the sixty-five battalions that are stationed there are compelled to live in *fortini* [literally, little forts, but actually temporary fortifications]. Mazzetti has acted wrongly. He attributes the responsibility for the appointment to Teruzzi, who acted on considerations of a personal character, while, when a political appointment is made, it is necessary to· be ready to accept the consequences, even though they may jeopardize one's life. The Duce spoke of the situation with the Holy See. He sees in the policy of the Catholic Action Movement an attempt to build up a real political party, which, foreseeing a difficult time for Fascism, aims at being ready to become its successor. He defended Starace; whatever he does, he does on the explicit orders of the Duce. He has rejected the suggestion of the Papal Nuncio that something be done about the celebration of the tenth anniversary of the Conciliation [Vatican Treaty].

In conclusion, he communicated to me his decision to accept the proposition of von Ribbentrop to transform the anti-Comintern pact into an alliance. He wants the pact signed during the last ten days of January. He considers more and more inevitable a clash with the occidental democracies, and therefore he wishes to effect a military alignment in advance. During this month he plans to prepare the acceptance of his views by public ·opinion, about which he doesn't give a damn. . . . I am going to write von Ribbentrop a letter in which I shall announce our acceptance of his proposal (which will be filed in the volume of official documents).

January 2, 1939

The letter to von Ribbentrop has been approved. Tomorrow I shall deliver it to Attolico together with some instructions as to what he

3

should say to the Germans, especially about the commercial relations between the two countries and concerning the Alto Adige. It would be well to put into execution Hitler's idea to evacuate those Germans who wish to leave this region. I have telephoned von Ribbentrop to communicate the decision briefly to him. We spoke with some difficulty because of poor connections and we were not able to say very much to each other, but he was satisfied, and he agreed that by the end of the month everything can be ready, even on the Japanese side.

A conversation with the Duce and Pignatti. The Duce told the Ambassador to tell the Vatican that he is dissatisfied with the policy of the Holy See, especially with reference to the Catholic Action Movement. He spoke also of the opposition of the clergy to the policy of the Axis, as well as to racial legislation. Let them not be under any illusion as to the possibility of keeping Italy under the tutelage of the Church. The power of the clergy is imposing, but more imposing is the power of the state, especially a Fascist state. We do not want a conflict, but we are ready to support the policy of the state, and in such a case we shall arouse all the dormant anti-clerical rancor; let the Pope remember that Italy is Ghibelline. Pignatti acted in a satisfactory manner. He said that the Vatican has made many mistakes, but that the Pope is a man of good faith, and that he is the one who, more than any other prelate, thinks in terms of Italianism. I have given him instructions to act tactfully. Notwithstanding Starace, I should like to avoid a clash with the Vatican, which I should consider very harmful.

January 3, 1939

I have given instructions to Attolico on his mission to von Ribbentrop. He will leave this evening. Whereas, in the past, I have found him rather hostile to the idea of an alliance with Germany, today he showed himself openly favorable to it. He said, during this particular stay in Italy, that he has been convinced that nothing would be more popular among us than a war against France. During the afternoon I also informed von Mackensen, who, having just returned from Berlin, came to pay me a visit. The Polish Ambassador announced to me the coming visit of Beck to Berlin, and of a later visit which von Ribbentrop is to make to Poland. This will make more feasible my visit to Warsaw, which will probably take place during the last week in February.

At the headquarters of the Duce, with the American Ambassador, bearer of a message from Roosevelt, and some suggestions regarding the settlement of the Jews, for whom President Roosevelt has thought of a part of Ethiopia and surrounding colonies. The Duce rejected this proposal, and said that only Russia, the United States, and Brazil have the material possibilities for solving the Jewish question, allotting to the Jews a part of their territories. He declared himself favorable to the creation of an independent Jewish state, and in general he promised to support it. In Spain the Corpo Truppe Volontarie has resumed its offensive and, it seems, with some success.

January 4, 1939

Conversation with Grandi. He is just back from a rather long vacation in Sicily, therefore he does not have much to tell me. I gave him a rather vague idea about our future alliance with Germany in order to get his reaction. He has declared himself to·be favorable and does not believe that there can be very serious repercussions in the British world. Great Britain is prepared to accept this. The memory of the Triple Alliance is still alive, which for a period of thirty years did not prevent the maintenance of cordial relations between Italy and Great Britain.

At Bagdad there have been demonstrations against our mass immigration to Libya; they think that this nucleus of Italians will break the Arabic preponderance in the Mediterranean. They are right; this is our objective; but the Duce desired me to reassure the Minister from Iraq. Since he was annoyed at the publicity that Balbo has acquired through this initiative, he ordered that future immigration should take place secretly. This pretext will help the situation.

I have informed von Mackensen about the American proposals of yesterday. He poked fun at them, and made some sharp comments on American lack of political sense.

In Spain we are going ahead at full speed. Gambara has executed a very brilliant maneuver. He has freed himself from the threat to his flanks and in turn has attacked the Reds on their flanks, producing a very serious crisis.

Attolico, after a preliminary conversation with von Ribbentrop, favors the twenty-eighth as the date for the signing of the alliance.

January 5, 1939

Good news from Spain. The only danger in sight is a possible mass intervention of the French, coming through the Pyrenees. There are already rumors on this subject. In order to avert such a threat, I have informed London and Berlin that, if the French move, this will be the end of the policy of non-intervention. We, too, will send our regular divisions. This means that we shall make war against France on Spanish territory. I have asked the Germans to publish a note on the diplomatic correspondence in support of our thesis.

The Duce tells me that he has informed the King about the forthcoming military alliance with Germany. He seemed satisfied with it. He does not like the Germans, but he detests the French and holds them in low esteem. However, he considers them capable of a sudden attack against us, and therefore looks with satisfaction upon an obligation on the part of Germany to come to the military aid of Italy.

Besides, times change. The anti-Italian manifestations in France and Tunis, the gesture of Daladier, who wanted to cut our throats with a Corsican dagger, the press which insults us create an atmosphere of hate toward France, especially among the common people. I have told Cianetti to give a social flavoring to anti-French propaganda among the workingmen. France is a bourgeois state, the defender of bourgeois privilege; this creates a tremendous effect. Today, even Alberto Pirelli [outstanding industrialist], sad-looking, skeptical, distrustful Pirelli, declared his fidelity to the policy of the Axis and his aversion to the Western democracies.

January 6, 1939

Calm in Spain. Gambara is counting upon mustering his forces in order to relaunch the attack tomorrow. I spoke this evening with the head of the Spanish economic mission [a Señor Anos], who has arrived in Rome for his commercial treaty. He is a very verbose individual, a little frivolous, very vain, but he is a Catalan and therefore knows at least the geography of his own country. He considers the victory of the past few days very important, perhaps decisive for the purpose of Catalonian liquidation, and therefore of the war itself.

The Duce is concerned with the Czech-Hungarian frontier incidents. This time it seems they have reached more serious proportions than usual. I have direct news which the Italian Legation has not yet received. The Duce wanted to have information from Grandi about the coming of Chamberlain, his state of mind and his intentions. But Grandi has been absent from London for twenty days. He has been having a good time in Sicily and in the mountains. When the Duce heard of this he was quite resentful. He said, "He is all petered out; after the visit I shall fire him." But I am certain that, as has happened frequently, he will save him at the last moment. After all, he may be right, because Grandi, in spite of his shortcomings, is a good ambassador; it would not be easy to find a better successor, since our diplomatic representatives at this moment are not brilliant.

January 7, 1939

Attolico has written about his conversation with Ribbentrop, who is very enthusiastic about our decision, but Attolico has gone too far in bringing out the economic question and that of the Alto Adige as conditions to the alliance. While, as a matter of fact, the first interests us a great deal more on account of the political repercussions on public opinion, the second must be solved calmly, without useless and excessive publicity. It is sufficient that the Germans, who at this moment need men badly, take those natives that do not desire to remain in Italian territory south of the Alpine range. I have telephoned about this to Magistrati.

Prepared a moderate toast for the coming of Chamberlain; I do not believe the situation calls for or will permit the expenditure of too many idle words. I have seen the Japanese Ambassador, who spoke to me about the alliance; he fears that Arita, the new Foreign Minister, is rather indifferent, while the Prime Minister is openly favorable. This will not have any influence upon the conclusion of the pact, but might delay the date of signing. Meanwhile, the Ambassador wishes to be received by the Duce in order to feel out the situation so that he may expedite a reply from his government. The Ambassador is very favorable to the alliance, which he considers an aggressive instrument to obtain from Great Britain "the many things which it owes to us all."

Von Ribbentrop has sent me the text of the pact, as well as that of the secret conventions on the subject of the military commissions.

Gambara has been wounded, but not seriously. This is fortunate, because his role has been magnificent.

January 8, 1939

Except for certain changes in the preamble, the Duce approves the texts sent by Ribbentrop. The change was useful. In one paragraph was mentioned "the threat of Bolshevist dissolution" as the aim of the pact. In reality, where is this threat? And even if such a threat existed, though not to our countries, why should we be concerned about it? We should not. Every possibility of dissolution and breakdown of other peoples should be encouraged and favored by us at the proper moment.

Señor Anos has brought the Duce a message from Franco, in which a résumé of the situation is given and in which also imminent victory is confirmed. The Duce was very appreciative of the message, and also praised it for the manner in which it was conveyed, defining it as "the report of a subordinate."

Then with the Duce we examined at length the action to be taken: closer relations with Yugoslavia, Hungary, Rumania, and possibly Poland, for the purpose of insuring raw materials. Alliance with Spain as soon as the war is won. Settling the account with France. No Nice, no Savoy, for they are outside the Alpine range. Corsica: autonomy, independence, annexation. Tunisia: minority settlement for the Italians, autonomy of the Bey, Italian protectorate. Jibuti: free port and railroad, administration in common with France, annexation. Suez Canal: strong participation in the administration, liquidation of Albania by agreement with Belgrade, eventually favoring Serbian settlement in Salonika.

January 9, 1939

I have secretly informed Starace about the treaty of alliance. He was enthusiastic about it, and said that for some time he had hoped for some such solution. It is true: even in the moments of crisis for the Axis, as, for instance, after the *Anschluss*, Starace was among the few who openly favored our understanding with Germany. I gave him these instructions: to stay calm until Chamberlain, to whom must be accorded a not too enthusiastic welcome, leaves Rome; then, afterward, steadily increasing propaganda against France, such that the alliance will take place when anti-French feeling is at its height; at the news of the signing of the pact there must be manifestations with a

sharp flavor of Francophobia. Starace says that not too much work is
needed for all this, since the change has already occurred, and thus it
is easy to create national feeling against France.

The Duce has answered quite cordially a letter from Franco, urging
him to proceed with caution up to the conclusion of the war, without
accepting compromises or mediations of any kind. Also as regards the
restoration of the monarchy, the Duce suggested that Franco go slow.
He prefers a united and pacified Spain under the guidance of the Caudillo, head of the country and of the party. It will be easy for Franco
to govern if he first achieves full military success. The prestige of a
leader victorious in war is never questioned.

January 10, 1939

From the information we now have, it is clear that not all responsibility for the frontier clashes between the Hungarians and the Czechs
is on the side of Prague. On the contrary. The Hungarian attitude is
not so good. From the beginning they tried to sabotage the Vienna arbitration. This is stupid politics, since it irritates both us and Germany
and certainly cannot modify the situation. I spoke clearly to Villani.
I told him to urge his government to stay in line and to abstain from
provoking incidents for which I would assume no responsibility either
for us or for the Germans. The Duce also is resentful, especially since the
French press might exploit the situation in order to discredit the influence and action of the Axis in Central Europe. He said, "These
Hungarians begin to fall in my esteem. They didn't have the courage
to act when they could have acted, and now they carry on like Jes-
uits. . . ."

Things are going well in Spain; the offensive is proceeding at a
rapid and regular pace.

January 11, 1939

Arrival of Chamberlain. In substance, the visit was kept on a minor
tone, since both the Duce and myself are scarcely convinced of its
utility. The welcome of the crowd was good, particularly in the middle-class section of the city, where the old man with the umbrella is
quite popular. The welcome was colder in the outskirts, where the
workers are less emotional. Chamberlain, however, is very happy over

the reception. Undoubtedly he still remembers the boos with which he was received some months ago in friendly France. . . .

6 P.M.: Conference at the Palazzo Venezia. The recorded conversations were in a tired tone. The matters which were discussed were not highly important, and both parties betrayed their mental reservations. Today's conversation has been rather one of exploration. Effective contact has not been made. How far apart we are from these people! It is another world. We were talking about it after dinner with the Duce, gathered together in a corner of the room. "These men are not made of the same stuff," he was saying, "as the Francis Drakes and the other magnificent adventurers who created the empire. These, after all, are the tired sons of a long line of rich men and they will lose their empire." Then, speaking of France, the Duce was quite offended by an article in *Europe Nouvelle* which made unpleasant remarks about his private life. He said, "These will be the first to fall. Certain offenses are punished with cannon and bombs."

January 12, 1939

Conference at the Palazzo Chigi with Lord Halifax. A tête-à-tête is preferable to discussion in public. He talks of politics with a certain impersonal interest. The conversation turned especially to Spain. I repeated to him our point of view and he gave his. But he does not seem to be very convinced, and at heart I think he would be happy if Franco's victory were to settle the question.

I shall let von Mackensen read yesterday's record. The recorded discussion of the afternoon was characterized by the profound sense of preoccupation which dominates the British with respect to Germany. German rearmament weighs on them like lead. They would be ready for any sacrifice if they could see the future clearly. This dark preoccupation of theirs has convinced me more and more of the necessity for the Triple Alliance. Having in our hands such an instrument we could get whatever we want. The British do not want to fight. They try to draw back as slowly as possible, but they do not want to fight. Mussolini defended Germany with strong loyalty, and he was also a bit secretive regarding his future projects and those of the Führer. Our conversations with the British have ended. Nothing was accomplished. I have telephoned von Ribbentrop that the visit was a "big lemonade" [a farce], absolutely harmless, and I thanked him for the attitude of the German press.

January 13, 1939

During the morning and the afternoon no contact with the British, who have gone to the Vatican. The atmosphere is now one of vague skepticism. English newspapers defined the meeting as a game ending in no score. The definition is good. I prepared a perfectly innocuous press release which I showed to the Duce at the Palazzo Venezia late this evening when he returned from the Terminillo Mountains where he had gone skiing. He approved it. Dinner at Lord Perth's. Afterward, a short conversation between the Duce, Chamberlain, and me. We spoke of the Jewish question, and it was interesting to note that Chamberlain did not know the number of Jews in Great Britain. He thought there were probably sixty thousand. The Duce said that they were in excess of two hundred thousand. Chamberlain is very much concerned with the problem and he said that any further Jewish immigration to England might increase the anti-Semitism which already exists in many parts of the country. During the meeting François-Poncet tried to get close to the Duce, who proudly turned his back on him. The French Ambassador cannot get anywhere; the Duce hates him. It has been learned from the Minister from Uruguay that Poncet has said that the Duce is in the period of intellectual decay. An intercepted letter from him had this to say: "In Germany I had to deal with real gentlemen; here, instead, I have to deal with servants who have become bosses." These are the rocks on which the Poncet mission was shipwrecked. He has been disoriented by the coolness of our reception, and so he now piles mistake on mistake.

I have sent Hitler true copies of the two reports of the meetings at the Palazzo Venezia.

January 14, 1939

I accompanied the Duce to the station on the departure of Chamberlain. He is furious about the British press in general, but especially with the *Daily Express* for an editorial by Lord Forbes, full of idiotic commonplaces, concerning the hostility of the Italian people toward Axis politics.

The leave-taking was brief but cordial. Chamberlain kept repeating his thanks for the treatment that was accorded him during his stay in Italy.

Chamberlain's eyes filled with tears when the train started moving and his countrymen began singing "For He's a Jolly Good Fellow." "What is this little song?" the Duce asked Grandi. Chamberlain is a pleasant fellow, and quite aside from any other consideration I can understand the cordial atmosphere which has grown up around him.

Mussolini indirectly inspired a violent editorial in the *Times* entitled "Spitting on France." Tomorrow I shall propose to him that wide publicity be given to a lengthy speech made by Campinelli in a hotel in Bastia, reported to me by two of our Corsican secret agents, Giumedi and Pietri. The speech threatens war against Italy in June and reveals exact plans of aggression by France. The report is absolutely authentic. I think that if properly used by the press, this report will go a long way toward creating a tremendous sensation, and, at any rate, will increase the wave of hatred against the French, which in Italy is already impressive.

January 15, 1939

News of the troop advances in Catalonia is more and more encouraging. General Gambara has luckily assumed the role of leader for all Spanish forces. Rumors are beginning to circulate about intervention of the French in large numbers. I do not believe them. For the French to intervene now, in the present state of the war, they would have to send great forces or else risk being defeated by the Catalans. They are in no position to do this; they would have to mobilize on a large scale. Moreover, a country which in the second half of the year just past has had forty thousand more deaths than births cannot permit itself the luxury of wasting the blood of its limited population. If the French intervene, so shall we. Mussolini said this morning, "If Paris sends forces we shall unload thirty battalions at Valencia, even if this should provoke a world war."

I discussed with the Duce what I must say and do in Yugoslavia. The Albanian question was the principal point of the discussion. We agreed that it would not pay to gamble with our precious friendship for Belgrade to win Albania. Therefore, as things stand, we shall take action only if we can arrive at an agreement on the following bases: increase of the Yugoslav frontiers, demilitarization of the Albanian frontiers, military alliance, and absolute support to the Serbs for their conquest of Salonika.

January 16, 1939

The forces are advancing in Catalonia at an accelerated pace. Reus and Tarragona fell yesterday; today, it appears, Cervera as well. At this pace the situation in Barcelona will also become untenable. The Duce is convinced of this: he says that an exhausted army becomes paralyzed when it is running. Victory now seems certain. For this reason we will not permit the French to intervene. This morning I called Lord Perth and spoke to him as follows: "I warn you that if the French intervene in force in favor of the Reds in Barcelona, we shall attack Valencia. Thirty battalions, fully equipped, are ready to be embarked at the first sign. We shall do this even if it should provoke a European war. Thus I ask you to urge the French to be moderate and to realize the sense of responsibility the situation demands."

I do not believe that France will act, even though with the taking of Barcelona a crisis will arise, the full import of which cannot be clearly appraised today.

Conference with Sereggi, bearer of a letter from King Zog, who asks for a kind of mediation with the Yugoslavs regarding the treatment of the Albanian minorities living in Kossovo; if everything goes well, and if Stoyadinovich is able to march ahead with determination, I shall certainly give Zog the mediation!

January 17, 1939

The advance continues well. Many rumors of French intervention and a great deal of agitation among the extreme political parties, but nothing serious; at least for the time being.

The German Ambassador, acting for von Ribbentrop, asked me to sound out Belgrade in order to ascertain whether Stoyadinovich intends to give his approval to the anti-Comintern pact. I shall try; but in my mind this is premature. There is no doubt about the intentions of Stoyadinovich with respect to the Axis and full solidarity. Personally, he would like to go even further. But I wonder if the present internal situation will allow him to make decisions of such a nature, and I am inclined to think not.

Dentice di Frasso has given us information about an astonishing American invention of a very powerful smokeless, colorless, and flashless gunpowder. Dentice vouches for this claim but I am skeptical about such inventions. However, I am inclined to have one of our specialists take a trip to the United States in order to meet the inventor and look into the matter. It is always worth trying. Who knows?

A long conversation with Lord Lloyd, to whom I repeated briefly and with some reserve what I had said to Halifax with respect to France.

January 18, 1939

Departure for Belgrade. Normal trip; cordial manifestations at Trieste and Postumia.

January 19, 1939

Arrival at Belje. Hare hunt. I returned by train, and Stoyadinovich and I had a conversation. I approached the Albanian question. At first Stoyadinovich seemed perturbed. Then he broke the ice, and spoke of the partition of Albania as the best way out.

January 20, 1939

Hunt in the forest. Good news from Spain. Stoyadinovich received it, shouting, "Corsica, Tunis, Nice!"

January 21, 1939

Last hunt at Belje. Departure for Belgrade during the evening. Stoyadinovich requested me to speak at length with the Regent and to inform him thoroughly of the international political situation. He is anxious about his relations with the monarchy, which do not seem good.

January 22, 1939

Belgrade. A hunt and a long conversation with the Regent. I am particularly moved by the spontaneity of the welcome accorded me, which was very different from my last visit here. I made a report on my treatment to be filed in Rome in my volume of notes.

January 23, 1939

Return trip to Rome. Many manifestations at the various stations.

January 24, 1939

This morning I went to Villa Torlonia, where I informed the Duce about my trip and its results. He was very well satisfied. He was particularly interested in hearing that in Yugoslavia I found such widespread anti-German feeling. He was also delighted so far as Albania is concerned. He informed me about what had happened during my absence. Nothing very important, except the news that the first woman was executed. There was a great deal of opposition to this punishment, in view of the popular reaction. The Duce, instead, approved of it because he was convinced of the approval of the masses. And in reality, while the execution of a man was accepted in silence, this one was greeted with applause. A woman killed her own child. The crime took place in Terni.

I met Lord Perth. I had previously communicated with him, before my departure, about French intervention in Spain. It caused alarm in London. They request that we do nothing before we consult the British Government. In principle I reassured Lord Perth.

Excellent news from Spain. The troops are taking up positions in the suburbs of Barcelona, so that they may occupy the city at any moment.

We ask that our Legionaries be among the first units to enter. They deserve it.

January 25, 1939

Conversation with Villani. I informed him as to what I had done at Belgrade, particularly regarding Hungary. I recommended moderation regarding Rumania. I do not understand how a country like Hungary, preoccupied with the German danger, does not seem to be able to see the danger of aggravating the crisis with Rumania, toward which the most dangerous ambitions of Berlin seem to point. What would be the Magyar position on the day when the Germans reach the frontiers of Transylvania?

The Duce is very anxious to have word about the occupation of

Barcelona. He calls often, because he fears a repetition of what took place in Madrid; I doubt it.

I informed von Mackensen of the outcome of my trip to Belgrade, and received Lord Perth, who came to ask us to warn Franco, so that he will not give way to vengeance against all his enemies after victory. I reassured him and told him that we have always tried to act as moderators. I recall that after the taking of Bilbao the Duce sent a letter which, when it is made known, will redound to the honor of its author.

Our volunteers are overcoming a final resistance of the Lister division. Barcelona is also within reach for them, who have had the hardest task, and they are anxious to reach it.

January 26, 1939

Long conversation with the King of Bulgaria. I had not met him before. My first impression was not good, in view of his physical appearance. My later impression was better. We spoke at length about the international situation, with particular reference to the Danubian basin and the Balkans. He asked for news about my trip to Yugoslavia, and he spoke about his agreement with this country with such feeling that I had the impression he was sincere. He was very bitter against Rumania, but his violence was such as would be expressed by a lymphatic person. He wants the province of Dobruja [a province taken from Bulgaria after World War I], and he wants it particularly because there is great Irredentist agitation. He spoke also of an outlet on the Aegean Sea, but added that this must be considered as the second step in the settlement of Bulgarian claims.

While I was at the golf club the news arrived that Barcelona had fallen. I notified the Duce at Terminillo [a winter resort near Rome] and came to an agreement with Starace about the celebration of the event all over Italy. All that was necessary was to fix the time, without any pressure, because the Italian population was very enthusiastic about the news and spontaneously so.

The Duce, too, was deeply moved, despite the fact that he would like to show himself to be imperturbably calm.

But he has good reason to be really satisfied, because victory in Spain bears only one name, that is the name of Mussolini, who conducted the campaign bravely, firmly, even at a time when many people who now applaud him were against him.

January 27, 1939

The Duce has called to his presence the Minister of Greece. From a report coming from Bucharest it appeared that the Greek military attaché had made insulting remarks about our Army in a conversation with a Hungarian colleague. The poor Minister from Greece trembled like a leaf when Mussolini, with a face metallic in its hardness, told him that if, within three days, full satisfaction was not given us, there would be serious complications. It is his intention to hand his passport to the Greek Minister, who, during this stormy scene, had nothing to say except to congratulate us on the capture of Barcelona.

Lord Perth has submitted for our approval the outline of the speech which Chamberlain will make before the House of Commons, in order that we might suggest changes, if necessary. The Duce approved it and commented, "I believe this is the first time that the head of the British Government submits to a foreign government the outline of one of his speeches. It's a bad sign for them."

At my suggestion Gambara has been promoted in the field to the post of divisional commander. He has deserved it, both because of his talent and because of the blood he has shed.

The Spaniards are preparing to make a political pact with Germany, of which the Germans have communicated the text to us. If it happens to be secret, like ours, there will be no opposition. But if it is to be made public I consider it imperative that we be the first to release the news. Otherwise people will say that Italy makes war in Spain and Germany profits from it.

January 28, 1939

Fagioli gave me an account of a conversation he had in France with Monsieur Baudouin, administrator of the salt mines in Somaliland, who stated that he had been secretly placed in charge by Daladier to start conversations with us about this matter. François-Poncet must not be informed about it, because in Paris he is no longer considered an authority on the Italian situation. It seems that Daladier is ready to make many concessions in these three fields: Jibuti, the Suez Canal, and statutes regarding the Italians in Tunisia. I informed the Duce, although he also is very skeptical about these clandestine ambassadors.

He suggested, however, that Monsieur Baudouin come to Rome for a possible conversation.

Long conference with Silimbani, Consul General in Tunis. The French authorities are exerting a great deal of pressure, with every means in their power, to nationalize the Italians. They are preparing a *coup d'état:* simultaneous publication of a great number of applications for naturalization, which will be the proof that the Italians do not care about their national aspirations. In order to ward off the blow and oppose the maneuver, we will organize a collective return to Italy of one thousand Italians who wish to escape the French pressure aimed at forcing them to become naturalized. We will create Tunisian refugees, just as there have been Austrian and Sudeten *émigrés* and refugees.

January 29, 1939

Nothing interesting except good news from Gambara about a further advance by the CTV [Corpo Truppe Volontarie—Corps of Volunteer Troops] toward the Pyrenees.

We have destroyed by bombs twenty-four batteries and an airplane which was about to take off. Gambara requests the sending of food, because the population is literally starving. They share the mess of the Legionaries, at the same time shouting, "Long live Franco! Long live Italy!"

January 30, 1939

The Minister from Greece brought the answer of his government; it is an act of abject submission made in terms which do not leave any doubt as to the Greeks' fear of us. A guilty conscience weighs upon them, and recent experiences have proved that small countries can count only on the friendship and the enmity of their geographical neighbors.

We sent provisions to Barcelona. The Duce had a terrible cold, but at the same time he is very much concerned about the preparation of the militia for the parade of February first. He is personally concerned about the most minute details. He spends many· a half-hour at the window of his office, concealed behind the blue curtains, looking at the movements of the various units. It was his order that the drums and trumpets be used at the same time. It was he who chose the bandleader's baton, and in person he teaches the movements to be made, and he changes the proportions and design of the baton. He is a strong believer that in the armed forces it is the form that determines the substance as well. He says that 1,400,000,000 men were required in order to defeat 60,000,000 Germans; the reason being that the rigid Prussian military training has made the soldiers invincible. Very often he accuses the King of having diminished the physical prestige of our Army in order to harmonize it with his own "unhappy physique."

January 31, 1939

The Führer's speech has produced the best impression everywhere. Even the Duce was very well satisfied with it, and he had me telephone von Ribbentrop so that he might tell Hitler that the words uttered last night have given a great deal of joy and satisfaction to all the Italian people. In fact today the Duce and I observed that the crowd applauded with much warmth in the Piazza Venezia some officers of the S.A. [Sturmabteilung]. The Axis is becoming popular. The Germans are working to this end as well as the French with their politics, based upon coarse insults and ill-concealed spite.

Conference with King Boris. Ostensibly it was to confer a decoration upon me, but in reality it was to protest politely against the exuberant activity of some members of the Italian Legation, Talamo included, who have created a difficult and uncomfortable situation. I shall intervene.

The Turkish Ambassador renewed the invitation of his government that I should come to Ankara. I replied that I had not gone previously because I had become aware that the Turks themselves preferred that the visit be postponed. I had read it in a decoded telegram. He became as red as a lantern [red as a beet], and said, "This delay was because of the health of Ataturk." However, I was noncommittal about the invitation.

Grandi telephoned late today that Chamberlain's speech in the House of Commons with reference to his trip to Italy has been very well received.

February 1, 1939

Review of the militia. Altogether it was very beautiful. The units are not truly ready. Masses both of men and steel. The defile, however, was monotonous. Nobody more than myself is in favor of the Roman step. [A step introduced by the Fascists in imitation of the German "goose step."] It imposes a form which gives life to the substance itself. But abolishing the bands during the march past creates a sense of heavy monotony, even if this hammering of steps on the pavement acts by itself to create a sense of strength. The Germans fuse together step, band, and drums with excellent effect. We ought to do the same; it is not bad to use their own experience in view of the undeniable fact that this particular step is a genuine imitation of the Prussians. Casini proposes to create a political daily in Rome, which nowadays does not exist. I agree that it must not be owned by industrialists. What need do they have for it? If a daily must be created, logically the Fascist party must be the owner. Afterward I was visited by Pignatti, and by the Nuncio. The atmosphere for the celebration of the tenth anniversary is becoming murky; the Duce has no intention of answering the Pope's letter, nor of granting the changes in the law concerning mixed marriages. [Mussolini's law on mixed marriages, between Catholic and non-Catholic, was directed particularly against Jews.] I have charged Pignatti to find out at the Vatican because we must be sure to avoid sharp statements by the Pope when he speaks to the bishops if we are to accept invitations to St. Peter's.

Muti came back. Things are going extremely well in Spain. He asked for reinforcements and arms for the final blow at Valencia and Madrid. We decided to give both.

February 2, 1939

A short meeting with von Mackensen. He says that the German Government has in no way dissuaded Budapest from coming to an accord with Bucharest. They agree with us that no opportunity should be missed to do everything in our power to bring Rumania in line with our system. I thanked von Mackensen for the Führer's speech and told him that we are preparing to have a solemn manifestation confirming our sentiments. In reality, by order of the Duce I prepared the agenda for the meeting of the Grand Council in honor of Hitler.

I received M. Baudouin. He strikes me as being a quiet and well-mannered person. He tells me that he had a conversation with Daladier and Bonnet on Sunday and he speaks for them. Naturally, he does not commit either Paris or Rome; his visit can be denied at any moment if we so choose. In conclusion, Daladier does not intend to make any open territorial concession; if we asked for territories there would be war. However, he is ready to make the following concessions: a large free zone in Jibuti; a share in the administration of the port; cession to Italy of the railroad in Ethiopian territory; support of our demands with regard to Suez; revision of the agreements of 1935 concerning Tunis, provided Tunisia is not made into an "Italian Sudetenland."

I made clear that with regard to Tunis we ask but one thing: the right of the Italians to remain Italians. I reserved the right to give him an answer only after having spoken to the Duce.

February 3, 1939

I reported to the Duce the conversation with M. Baudouin. He agreed that the proposals are interesting. As things stand, there are only two alternatives: either to deal on this basis, postponing the solution of the whole problem to a more favorable date, or face it now; the latter alternative would mean war. The Duce has prepared a report to the Grand Council, which he read to me. He is in favor of diplomatic negotiations; therefore, he authorized me to answer M. Baudouin that we consider the proposals worthy of consideration. He prefers that the negotiations be carried on through the Ambassador. "If we reach port through the mediation of a banker, suspicions of a moral character will be aroused against us." He ordered me, moreover, to keep von Mackensen secretly informed of everything.

Conversation with M. Baudouin. He was moved when I told him that it was through his action that the contact was made, and he understands that it is not his task to handle the negotiations to follow. We agreed that he will report to Paris and that the French Government will have François-Poncet officially repeat to me all that M. Baudouin told me yesterday, unless something new comes up. If there are unforeseen details to be discussed, he will write to me through Fagioli. I recommended also the most thorough discretion, for if the press gets hold of these plans for an understanding there will be an explosion.

February 4, 1939

While at golf I received Gambara's telegram announcing the occupation of Gerona by the Littorio division [division of Fascist militia]. Catalonia is now completely occupied, and there remains only the final blow at the center.

To that end we shall immediately begin to reorganize the CTV, which must again take on itself the task of carrying the Spanish along.

I informed von Mackensen of my conversation with Baudouin; so far as I could judge he received with pleasure the news of our possible diplomatic settlement of the dispute with France.

Lord Perth is concerned about our sending fresh troops to Libya. I avoided a definite answer, but I made it a point to reassure him on two items: that nothing is done in the direction of the eastern border, and the trips of Lutze and of General Udet to Libya have no military purpose. Stoyadinovich has offered his resignation. Is this a maneuver or a genuine fall? We shall see. In any case it disturbs me.

Meeting of the Grand Council. The Duce read his report (a copy of which will go in the volume of his writings), and said that it represents a password to future generations. For the first time he prepared a document for the Grand Council and he wishes that it be included in the record under the title, "The March to the Sea." I, too, made my report, and it was greeted with hearty applause.

February 5, 1939

The Duce explained in detail what has been done for Libya: there are thirty thousand men now, and thirty thousand more will be sent there. In order to understand why this must be done, one need only compare the extent of our forces with those of the French in Tunisia, Algeria, and Morocco.

For the celebration of the tenth anniversary of the Vatican Treaty in St. Peter's I have been delegated to represent the government. Prince Humbert will represent the royal house. The Duce had in mind to send less conspicuous personages, but Pignatti asked him not to do this, in order to avoid giving offense to the Pope, as he was already exasperated.

No definite news about the Yugoslav crisis. The Duce said that this is another proof that we can do business with one country alone, that is, with Germany, which, like ourselves, is not changeable in its directives and in the obligations it assumes. Stoyadinovich's position seemed to be secure; he himself asserted a fortnight ago that nothing and no one could get him out of power. Now, things are different. Now, the crisis interests me, not so much with regard to our relations with Belgrade, which will not change very much for a certain length of time, but rather with regard to Albania, with which we had almost reached an agreement. Anyway, we agreed with the Duce on the following formula: to go ahead just the same, with Stoyadinovich, partition of Albania between us and Yugoslavia; *without* Stoyadinovich, occupation of Albania by us without Yugoslavia, and, if necessary, even against Yugoslavia.

February 6, 1939

Ribbentrop telephoned to tell me that a Frenchman, de Brinon, has been to see him and made mention of the possibility of diplomatic agreements between Rome and Paris. He seems also to be informed about Baudouin's trip. I got the impression that Ribbentrop wanted us to proceed with the negotiations. I told him that we are taking no initiative, but in any case this shows that the secret mission of Baudouin is now known. It is becoming more and more difficult to work with these democracies. Ribbentrop also spoke with optimism of the Tripartite Alliance with Japan and of the Yugoslav crisis; he believes that the new Foreign Minister is oriented to the line of the Axis.

At the nunciature I saw Poncet. He made some mention of the futility of his stay in Rome, but I let the subject flag, and spoke instead of sports and art. The Japanese Ambassador is skeptical about the possibility of quickly realizing the Triple Alliance; he believes that the Japanese counterproposal is an expedient which he himself advises us not to accept.

I saw the Duce at the Palazzo Venezia. He believes that the liquidation of Stoyadinovich is a veritable *coup d'état* on the part of the Regent, who wanted to prevent the strengthening of the Fascist dictatorship in Yugoslavia. I gave the Duce my point of view in the Albanian matter: we must work faster. He agreed with me. We shall begin immediately to recall ground forces and to concentrate air forces. We shall intensify local revolutionary preparations. The date of the action: Easter week.

February 7, 1939

The Duce is right. Stoyadinovich informed Indelli that the Regent was aware of what was going on, and was, perhaps, himself at the center of the plot against him. However, Stoyadinovich has no intention of giving up. He has not yet decided how to proceed, but is determined to take revenge, and popular feeling is more and more openly with him. However, I wonder whether he will take action, and, if so, to what effect? His position was gaining in strength, but not yet strong enough to permit him to face a coalition which, with the encouragement of the Regent, was growing against him.

During the evening I saw the Duce, and we spoke at length about the situation. I repeated my views on the necessity of acting more quickly in the Albanian question for the following reasons: (1) the Yugoslavs now know that we are thinking of the matter, and the rumor may spread; (2) with the removal of Stoyadinovich the Yugoslav card has lost for us 90 per cent of its value; (3) since the enterprise will no longer be undertaken in conjunction with Yugoslavia, but without her, and perhaps even against her, we must not give her time to strengthen her contacts with France and with England on political, diplomatic, and military grounds. Barring unforeseen circumstances, we fixed with the Duce the date for the attack between the first and ninth of April. In the meantime, I will see Ribbentrop, and perhaps give him an account of the matter.

February 8, 1939

The Duce is not satisfied with the Japanese delays concerning the Tripartite Alliance, and he deplores the light way in which Ribbentrop assured us that the government at Tokyo agreed. He is of the opinion that an alliance between Germany and Italy should be concluded without Japan. He observes that such an alliance would alone be sufficient to meet the array of Anglo-French forces, and at the same time would not appear to be anti-English or anti-American.

We sent a telegram to Berlin, urging them to reach a conclusion quickly on the agreement with Spain, in order to counteract the *rapprochement* between Burgos and Paris. We shall then make it known that we have had an agreement with Spain since November 1936.

I received De Man, who had the mission to organize a four-power conference for the King of the Belgians. I told him that it seems to me that the necessary and sufficient conditions for the realization of such an initiative did not exist. De Man expressed his point of view in a trivial way; what interested me most about him was a slight tan which he got some place in the mountains. Jacomoni arrived, and confirmed the fact that this was the time to act quickly. The air is tense in

Albania; unquestionably all the chiefs are with us. But how long can the secret be kept? We studied at length the details of the operation.

February 9, 1939

The Royal Signature. [Periodical audience at which the members of the Cabinet submit documents for the King's signature.] Among other things the King told me that yesterday two persons had reported to him that in the last meeting of the Grand Council the Duce had deplored the meeting of November 30. I reported this to the Duce: still another proof that the Grand Council is not a completely reliable organ of the government. We must change its composition and reduce to a minimum the number of its members.

I proposed to the Duce, who approved, that we put to vote tomorrow evening in the Grand Council the agenda for the celebration of the tenth anniversary of the Vatican Treaty. Our relations with the Church have in these last few days greatly cleared. I did my best to bring this about. In the evening news arrived that the Pope's condition had become worse. His death would be rather upsetting at this time. Our attempts then to influence the conclave would have to be made in an atmosphere of prejudice quite hostile to our purposes. We might have to expect disagreeable surprises. During the meeting of the mission for the supreme defense of the country I showed the Duce the typewritten record of the telephone call by Pignatti concerning the heart attack suffered by the Pope, and he only shrugged his shoulders with open indifference. Strange. For some time now Mussolini exhibits an increasingly strong detachment from anything related to the Church. Once it was not so.

February 10, 1939

The Pope is dead. The news leaves the Duce completely indifferent. During my personal report to him he mentioned the death only in order to inform me that this evening he will postpone the meeting of the Grand Council out of respect to the memory of the Pope, and also because the public is too much concerned about the mourning to be preoccupied with scholastic reform. [The question was whether religious education should have a place in the schools, which would have been on the agenda of the meeting.]

Great resentment concerning the will of Germany to put its hands on the Albanian oil. The evidence comes from an official communication received by Attolico. I called Mackensen and informed him that we considered Albania just like another Italian province, and that any German intervention would create a strong resentment in Italian public opinion. This fact also proves that the Albanian boil will come to a head in a short time. The Serbians have spoken. King Zog is alarmed and very much agitated. Some move could be made in order to oppose our action.

I went to the Holy See to offer the respects of the government at the bier of the Pope, and was received by the dean of the cardinals and by Pacelli, today Camerlengo [cardinal in charge, pending the election of a new Pope] of the Holy Roman Church. I conveyed the sympathy of the Italian Government and of the Fascist people, and I said that the former Pope had bound his name for eternity to history through the Lateran Treaty. They liked my expressions very much. Pacelli directed me to the Sistine Chapel where the Pontiff rested on a high catafalque, and he spoke to me in a very agreeable and hopeful tone about relationships between State and Church. Of the Pope himself we could see nothing—only his enormous white sandals and the hem of his robe; but the atmosphere was one of infinity.

February 11, 1939

The Grand Council approved the agenda, and postponed the meeting as a manifestation of mourning. Starace and Farinacci were opposed to such a statement, but I insisted, and Federzoni and Balbo agreed with me. The Duce is always bitter about the Church. I called him in order to report what Pignatti had said; the Holy See was expecting a gesture of respect from him at the bier of the Pope, and he answered that it was too late: "That he is not interested at all in the conclave. If the Pope is an Italian, all right; if he is a foreigner, all right just the same."

I received Ambassador von Mackensen, who gave me the following explanations about the question of the Albanian oil. They had received a proposal, but nothing had been done, and nothing would be done. The haste with which the answer was given was a proof of the German eagerness to dispel any suspicion of the word of the Axis.

The Duce praised the activity in the field of public assistance, organized by the Princess of Piedmont in Alto Adige. He said that the

Princess had a holy fear of him and that very often she would ask him questions and seek his instructions. Once, he said, she took out a notebook and, following a line with her finger, asked the Duce what was the meaning of the statement that now the Grand Council must regulate the succession to the throne. The Duce answered that this would be the case only for lack of continuity in the direct line, or in exceptional circumstances. She seemed to be satisfied, but the question proved how much the members of the royal family are worried about the future.

February 12, 1939

The Duce agreed to take part in the funeral of the Pope, which has been fixed by the nunciature for the seventeenth. That decision pleases me, because it will create a good impression upon the Conclave. In some American circles it is rumored that the Camerlengo has a document written by the Pope. The Duce desires Pignatti to find out, and, if it is true, to try to get a copy of the document and that ". . . in order to avoid a repetition of the Filippelli incident." [Filippelli, a high Fascist official and journalist, who exposed the facts of the murder in 1924 of Matteotti, a Socialist leader in the Chamber of Deputies.]

Calm, for the time being, in other fields.

Gorgeous Sunday of a Roman winter, warm and sunny day. I spent a great part of it at golf.

February 13, 1939

General Piccio: pro-French. He reported some conversations of minor importance with Flandin and Laval, both of whom complain that they had been put in a difficult position through our requests, just when they had been able to obtain approval for the appointment of a new French ambassador. Paul Boncour was more inclined to be conciliatory. He said: "You have been too exigent; but we are too intransigent." Piccio says that the French armaments are going to be very imposing in a very short time.

Lord Perth spoke to me again about our forces to be sent to Libya. Nothing to be done. The proportion between the Arabic population of Libya and that of the French empire is 18 to 1; that of the armed forces is actually 1 to 8. We must put ourselves in a defensive state, and such a right cannot be denied us by any clause in any Italo-British agreement.

The Duce comments on the incident between Goebbels and Froelich and says: "Goebbels is wrong, not because he raped Froelich's wife, but rather because he permitted his face to be slapped." The commercial agreement between Italy and Germany has been signed. It embraces many points and, as the technicians say, is very satisfactory.

February 14, 1939

The Swiss Minister came to express his regrets for the misdoings of his country's press, and the Spanish Ambassador told me that General Jordana has rejected the French suggestion to send a secret agent, and also France's request for a declaration of Spanish neutrality. The Duce said that with regard to Albania we must await two events: the settling of the Spanish affair, and the alliance with Germany. In the meantime, we must spread the most varied rumors; like the octopus we must darken the waters. With regard to France, he repeated that it is desirable for the moment to await the development of Baudouin's undertaking. If such an undertaking should not develop, we shall put the question: Will you or will you not do business? If not, we shall prepare for war without delay. He also told me that we are in possession of a secret weapon which, "though not miraculous, could, nonetheless, affect the course of the war."

The Dutch Minister made a tentative but energetic representation with regard to the problem of the Dutch Jews, but he slowed up when I told him that we might have done something as a gracious gesture, but never under pressure. Imagine the Dutch trying to play the tough man!

February 15, 1939

A little personal episode: Starace caught the honorable Martire, former member of the Popular party, and a Fascist since 1932, in the corridors of the Chamber of Deputies in the act of trying to cast a slur on my name, saying that I had the "evil eye." As the candle of his petty malice was guttering out, he would have done well to tumble into bed in the dark; but he had other ideas, and preferred to try to "stab me in the back," as the Duce said later. Moral: Martire was properly handcuffed and sent to jail; Ferretti, who was present at the incident, and who failed to report it, was expelled from the party. In itself the incident was insignificant, but from it the following good and bad deductions can be made. Bad: the moral inadequacy of certain people whom we have admitted to our ranks, and who, in the shadows of the Littorio [coat of arms of Fascism], continue their shameful mudslinging. Good: it proved the Duce's psychological position with respect to me, since he reacted and acted with a violence such as, according to Starace, had never been shown before. Starace also acted in an admirable way: loyal, strong, a friend.

In the evening the Grand Council met. They approved the school reform. The Duce spoke to me of the Martire affair, and expressed his regrets for not having been able to beat him up. And he added that seventeen years of governing have denied him "the pleasure of fighting several dozen duels." [Dueling had been abolished by the Fascist Government.]

February 16, 1939

Albania is restless. We received a telegram from our military attaché to Tirana, which has somewhat disturbed the Duce; he said that the King [of Albania] wanted to order partial mobilization, and that Jacomoni had left by air for Rome. The situation is not so dramatic. I had a conference with Jacomoni, who, to tell the truth, appears quite calm. Yesterday he saw the King, who, after having listened to our complaints, said that he, too, had something to say. It appears that in Belgrade they discussed the partition of Albania, but he mentioned certain particulars which show that he was only partially and incorrectly informed. He also mentioned the preparation for an internal revolt, supported especially by refugees—a statement which was completely false. He cited the names of many people who were involved; except for Koci, these names were not exact. He concluded by reaffirming his desire to reach an understanding with us, and he sent Jacomoni as his representative with full powers to make the agreement. When I reported to the Duce by telephone he answered: "If we had already signed our pact with Berlin we could attack immediately. As things stand, we have to procrastinate." Then he confirmed the instructions which I had already sent to Jacomoni two days ago, which are as follows: to keep alive the popular agitation, but not fail to placate King Zog's doubts, giving him every reassurance he desires. To keep the waters troubled, so that our real intentions will not be known.

[*Entries February 17 and 18 missing.*]

February 19, 1939

The recall of Grandi from London is due to some information about him which has come to the Duce, but of which I know nothing either of the tenor or the source. The Duce said, "It is time that this gloomy, ambiguous, and unfaithful Grandi comes back to bathe in the atmosphere of the regime, and that he become de-Anglicized eventually. I will tell him personally that I have come to know things about him which have displeased me." The Duce read carefully a letter written by Nitti to Aldrovandi after the publication of his memoirs. The letter pitilessly attacks Sonnino, who is called "a bad Christian and bad Jew, and, above all, a bad minister." Mussolini himself admits that the letter is written with a good sense of humor.

The Duce is becoming more and more bitter against France, and he said that in these last months the French have reached the maximum of their perfidy and of their hate. He defined them as a "mean people." The Italians already hate France, but the Duce has intentions of increasing this hatred to an extreme in the course of the next few months. When he has waged war and beaten France he will show the Italians "how a peace in Europe should be made." He will not ask for indemnities, but will destroy all, and level many cities to the ground. He is, however, dissatisfied with the preparation of the two military departments of state: war and aviation. While naval preparation is perfect, he does not know what is going on in the other two departments. I warn him again about Valle, who, on too many occasions, has made assertions and promises which are either not true or not possible.

February 20, 1939

On his return from Belgrade, Christic repeated to me what we already more or less knew of the Yugoslav crisis. He conferred with the Regent, who is very much bent on justifying himself with us for having double-crossed Stoyadinovich. In any case, his assurances of continued good relations with the Axis are many, and such that we cannot ignore. Christic informed me also of a meeting he had had with one of the heads of the opposition, Gavrilovic, who asked him to tell me that if he comes to power he will strengthen his ties with us. The present situation of the Cabinet is weak; either Stoyadinovich will return to power by April, or the new government will be of the opposition.

The Duce has referred Nitti's letter to the King, and had a copy sent to me. The King generally shares Nitti's opinions on Sonnino, and, talking about Nitti, said that he was a man of clear vision and of great ability, but that these fundamental qualities were spoiled by "an unreasonable fear" which took possession of him at any rustling of the leaves.

Exchange of telephone calls with Ribbentrop, in order to settle a joint action of our ambassadors with Franco to talk him into adhering to our anti-Comintern pact. The step will be taken when the Japanese Ambassador has also received his instructions. If Franco joins, we shall have to put an end to the rumors which are spreading, even in Italy, about his too many intimate contacts with the Western democracies.

February 21, 1939

The joint action is no longer necessary, since Franco has decided to adhere to the anti-Comintern pact, communicating this decision to our ambassadors, even though it is to remain a secret until complete victory. Together with the Germans, we have accepted this solution, which is a good one because, in substance, it gives us the egg today and the chicken tomorrow.

Jacomoni referred to the Albanian situation: the King and his men have declared formally that they wish to re-establish the most cordial relations with us, but Jacomoni fears that this may be a maneuver to gain time to permit the success of the King's many attempts to draw up pacts and understandings with third powers. Jacomoni feels that the situation should be changed abruptly. The Duce and I do not agree with him. I instruct him by telegraph to steer cautiously for some time yet, while we are waiting for certain events in the international field, which will make it easier for us to deliver our blow. Grandi returned to Rome and received with much distress the news about his recall from London. He still hopes, however, to be able to change Mussolini's decision in a coming meeting with the Duce. However, he realizes that something has happened to his relations with Mussolini, who, for some years now, has treated him coldly and with detachment.

The Fascist legions have marched into Barcelona in great form and amid enthusiastic applause. Gambara will be in Rome tomorrow for a conference.

February 22, 1939

The Duce is very happy about Franco's decision to adhere to the anti-Comintern pact. The event is of great importance and will have influence in all future European happenings. After three centuries of inactivity Spain thus again becomes a living and dynamic factor, and, what is more important, an anti-French factor. Those silly people who tried so hard to criticize our intervention in Spain will one day perhaps understand that on the Ebro, at Barcelona, and at Malaga the foundations were laid for the Roman Mediterranean Empire.

Villani referred to a trip by Teleki to Italy for next April. I accepted with great pleasure, because I like Teleki, and I respect him as the best chief of government Hungary ever had.

Christic gives me hopes about Stoyadinovich. He said that the personal jealousy of the Regent played a great role in the crisis, but he believes and hopes that in a few months Stoyadinovich will be in power again.

Arrival of Gambara. He made a very good report about matters in Spain. Either Madrid will capitulate dramatically in a short time, or else at the end of March five columns will give the deathblow to Red Spain. The situation in Catalonia is good. Franco improved it with a very painstaking and drastic housecleaning. Many Italians also were taken prisoner: anarchist and communist. I informed the Duce about it, and he ordered that they all be shot, adding, "Dead men tell no tales."

February 23, 1939

Attolico has sent a very interesting account of his conversation with the Egyptian Minister to Berlin, Mourad Pasha. He speaks in the name of his king, who declares himself to be one who hates the British, and asks whether in the event that Egypt should proclaim its neutrality and Great Britain should attempt to intervene directly or indirectly, the Axis will be ready to support the position of King Farouk. This matter is so serious that it makes me want to make a number of reservations, even though the source of information is very reliable. In agreement with the Duce I authorize Attolico to continue his conversations and to make it clear that any effort to weaken the ties between Egypt and London finds approval here.

The Duce eulogizes Gambara in grand style. Gambara expounds his coming plan of action, which is not generally approved by the Duce, who would like to see the forces more concentrated. The Duce realizes, however, that in the present state of disintegration of Red Spain, Franco's plan to spread out the national armies all over the country might give excellent results. He offers Gambara still another division, but Gambara refuses, and asks instead for two battalions of Alpini and a group of Alpine artillery, and these are immediately granted.

Discussion between the Duce and Grandi in the afternoon. The Duce was more clever than hard on him. In any case, he told Grandi that his mission was finished, since it would lose its purpose after the signing of the Tripartite Alliance, and since he, Grandi, is becoming too English. He promised to give him another job when he leaves London.

February 24, 1939

On my way to Warsaw. Stopped at Vienna, where we had dinner at the Three Hussars. This city has a sleepy and tired appearance. Rochira made the statement that high life in the central section has considerably deteriorated, but that the great mass of the people are working, live better, and are more and more favorable to the regime.

February 25, 1939

I arrive at Warsaw. The welcome of the population was characterized by curiosity and perhaps by a certain amount of sympathy, but there was no great enthusiasm. The city is gray, flat, and very gloomy, even though a tired and unusual-looking sun lighted without warming the streets of this characterless capital. I was very much bored with the information I have received relative to small anti-German demonstrations that had broken out here and there in all the Polish cities. They had been provoked by some incidents which have been taking place at Danzig and which are peculiar to it. Poland, in spite of all the efforts and the politics of Beck, is fundamentally and constitutionally anti-German. Its tradition, its instincts, and its interest make it opposed to Germany. It is a Catholic country with large nuclei of Jews as well as strong German minorities. It inevitably contains all the elements of opposition toward imperialism. On the other hand, for us Italians it has the positive element of a general sympathy for us which has no practical results. The Poles are more interested in our art than in our way of living. They know our monuments better than our history. Basically, they do not consider us as we like to be considered. Too many painters, sculptors, and architects have represented Italy in Poland in the past, and continue to represent us with the inevitable servility of the artist who, in distant lands, finds a foreign Maecenas.

February 26, 1939 [continuation of February 25]

They love in us our artistic nature rather than the strength of our arms in which they still do not completely believe. We must work hard to correct the bad name the past three centuries have given us.

I discuss a little with everybody, but especially with Beck. There were no sensational elements in our discussion. Poland will continue in her policy of harmony, such as is called for by her geographical situation. With Russia, nothing more than strictly necessary contacts. With France, defensive alliance on which the Poles do not rely more than is necessary. With Germany, a good-neighbor policy, maintained with difficulty because of many spiritual and concrete elements of difference. It will be necessary to arrive at a solution regarding Danzig, but Beck wants this solution to emerge from free diplomatic negotiations, avoiding any useless and damaging pressure by public opinion. There is still a great deal of unrest on the Ruthenian problem. We and the Poles are unwilling to consider Czechoslovakia's frontiers as final, and they still hope for the realization of a common frontier with Hungary. Concern for the Ukrainian problem presses heavily on the Polish mind, though the Poles are not talking about it; however, Beck frequently emphasizes with satisfaction, though without conviction, the assurances given him by Hitler.

February 27, 1939

In speaking about the present situation of Czechoslovakia he defined it as "a temporary arrangement that may last for some time without, however, ceasing to be a temporary arrangement." I limited myself to a general discussion, in the course of which I stressed as much as possible the ties that link us to Germany.

I had conversations with the ambassadors from Germany and from Japan, with the Papal Nuncio, and with the ministers from Hungary and Yugoslavia. I visited military organizations, particularly those relating to aviation, which made a good impression on me. I am not able to say much about the internal structure of the country, because I have not been able to observe it to any extent. But it is far from being a totalitarian regime, in spite of the fact that the only voice which counts in Poland is that of a dead man, Pilsudski, and there are far too many who vie for the title of being the true depositories of his wisdom. Besides, the fact that he has remained as a posthumous dictator proves that no new force has as yet affirmed and manifested itself. Otherwise, even Marshal Pilsudski, like all dead people, would have quickly petered out.

Summarizing my impressions in terms of our own interests, it would be foolish to conclude that Poland has been won over to the Axis or to the triangle [Germany, Italy, Japan], but it would be too pessimistic to describe it as altogether hostile.

February 28, 1939

When the great crisis comes Poland will remain a long time on the alert, and only when the issue of the struggle becomes clear will it come in on the side of the victor. And this is right, because it is a country that has friends and enemies on both sides.

Hunting at Bialowieza, a magnificent forest, wild and primitive, and very well stocked with rare game.

March 1, 1939

Cracow: monuments and palaces, which to the Poles seem so many and so beautiful, but which in our eyes amount to very little.

March 2, 1939

Return trip. At Tarvisio I received the report of the election to the papacy of Cardinal Pacelli. It did not surprise me. I recall the conference I had had with him on the tenth of February. He was very conciliatory, and it seems also that in the meantime he has improved relations with Germany. In fact, Pignatti said only yesterday that he is the Cardinal preferred by the Germans. At the dinner table I had already said to Edda and to my collaborators, "The Pope will be elected today. It is going to be Pacelli, who will take the name of Pius XII." My prediction interested everybody.

March 3, 1939

The Duce is very dissatisfied with Guariglia, and intends to have him retired in a short time, together with Rosso and Valentino.

I have arrived in Rome. I found nothing particularly new in internal politics. At the Ministry I saw my collaborators and Alfieri, who gave me a résumé of the events of the last few days. The Duce has gone to Terminillo. He telephoned me, saying that he would like to see me, and in the afternoon I went to him.

He was interested in my none too optimistic report on Poland. I must admit that he, the Duce, had always seen, even from Rome, the Polish situation with greater clarity than those who had spent many long years on the spot. He called Poland "an empty nut." He is satisfied with Pacelli's election. He promised to send the Pope some advice on how he can usefully govern the Church. He does not, however, intend to use Tacchi-Venturi [Jesuit priest unofficially used by the Vatican to convey its views to the Fascist leaders], who, in his opinion, has outlived his usefulness. We discussed at length the Tripartite Alliance. New delays have been injected by Japanese procedure and formalism. The Duce is more and more favorable to a bilateral alliance with Berlin, leaving out Tokyo. As our ally Japan will definitely push the United States into the arms of the Western democracies. He wanted to accelerate the completion of the Italo-German alliance. He said that the delay has been the cause of certain unpleasant events recently, such as the fall of Stoyadinovich. He thinks that Stoyadinovich will return to power when we sign the pact with Berlin. With reference to Albania, he approves of letting matters slide but has it in the back of his mind to act as soon as the Spanish affair is settled and the alliance concluded —whether of two or three.

March 4, 1939

I communicated to the Minister from Switzerland that the measures taken in my absence against Swiss journalists have been suspended. These might have been revoked if the press had taken a more moderate attitude. I saw Lord Perth—a conference of little importance since he kept referring to the article in *Relazioni Internazionali* [a review dealing with international relations which had been founded by Ciano and Pirelli and was published in Milan], which threatened war against

France. I answered that the article reflected the personal opinion of its author and that, strange as it may seem, the review is directed by Pirelli, that is by a man notoriously tied to London and Paris by bonds of sympathy. On the other hand, I called his attention to the re-inforcement of the British contingents in Egypt.

During the afternoon I saw Lyautey; it was a useless conversation. He spoke a great deal but said little. However, he said enough to make it clear that his government was very much concerned about our attitude. I was personally cordial to him, but as far as politics was concerned completely uncommunicative.

I spoke briefly to von Mackensen of my trip to Poland and gave him my impressions, which coincide with those expressed by Ambassador Moltke.

The Duce had me decline a dinner invitation sent by François-Poncet to meet the special mission for the coronation of the Pope. Many of its members have written against Italy, and it is this which prompted the Duce's action.

Telephone conversation with von Ribbentrop; he is still certain of the participation of Japan in the Tripartite Pact but feels that weeks are necessary in order to reach a conclusion.

March 5, 1939

Gambara came to say good-by. We agreed on some details related to the despatch of further contingents to Spain. I brought him with me to see the Duce, who confirmed the instructions given in previous con-versations. He added that he means to keep the troops in Spain so long as there is fighting but does not intend to leave them there for police purposes. He instructed Gambara to tell Franco of his distinct aversion to the restoration of the monarchy. "The return of the monarchy would be equivalent to plunging Spain into a new civil war within three years. The King is an ultra-discredited man, and the best that can be said of his sons is that they are morons, completely at the service of England and France." I reported to the Duce on my conversation with Ribbentrop. The Duce is vexed by the delay in signing the alliance. This delay leaves the small countries at a loss. They see in the present situation only one stable element: the rearmament of France and Britain.

Jacomoni assured us that order has returned in Albania, and that the King, after having had the greatest fear of his life, goes to extremes in showing signs of friendship for us. He has sent me his "fraternal" greetings. The fact is that none of the plotters has talked, and that the play has only been postponed. Pignatti said that the Vatican is beginning to outline a maneuver in order to make it appear that Italy is opposed to the nomination of Cardinal Maglione to the Secretariat of State—a nomination which the Pope has at heart. I spoke to the Duce in order to get his authorization to retract. He answered, "Tell Pignatti that I don't give a damn about the Pope, the Cardinal Secretary of State, or anybody who occupies such positions." I carried out the retraction just the same, though in different language.

March 6, 1939

Last night at the Colonna residence [Prince Colonna was the Governor of Rome] I was informed through a telephone call from Pietromarchi of the insurrection at Cartagena and of the escape of the Red Spanish fleet as well as Franco's request for our co-operation in the air to trace the eleven vessels wandering in the Mediterranean and to prevent them from crossing the Sicilian passage, in case they should try to go to Odessa as has already been stated. I notified the Navy and the Air Force, and this morning at eight o'clock I informed the Duce, who approved what I had done. The fleet was pursued during the day; it wanted to enter Algiers but it was denied permission to do so. It now seems to be going in the direction of Bizerte.

Considerable rivalry among the aspirants to candidacy in the National Council of Corporations. Names may change but not the spirit, nor is it easy to eradicate from the hearts of Italians, even though they may be Fascists, their attachment for parliament. Information from Berlin indicates that the Japanese Government is raising objections to signing the Tripartite Pact.

Oshima plans to resign. He affirmed that it is necessary for the cabinet to fall. What will happen after this? I do not understand. But is it really possible to take into European political life a country like Japan which is so far away, which has become more and more convulsed and nervous and susceptible to modification from one hour to the next by means of a simple telephone call?

March 7, 1939

Nothing outstanding.

March 8, 1939

Meeting of the central corporative committee at the Palazzo Venezia for the adjustment of wages of private and governmental employees on the occasion of the twentieth anniversary of the Fascisti. The Duce was very well satisfied with the provision made, and he told me, "With this we really shorten the distance between social classes. Socialism used to say all equal and all rich. Experience has proved this to be impossible. We say, all equal and all sufficiently poor."

I saw the Japanese Ambassador. He confirmed what Attolico has written concerning the Japanese answer on the Tripartite Alliance. Many reservations are made, and there is the intention to give to the pact only an anti-Russian character. The answer was so unsatisfactory as to make one doubt the possibility of effectively concluding this alliance. Oshima and Shiratori refused to carry out the communication in an official way. They asked Tokyo to accept the pact of alliance without reservations, otherwise they will resign and will provoke the fall of the cabinet. We shall have a decision in the coming days. Shiratori maintains that if the decision is favorable the signature of the pact in Berlin can be realized in the month of March, otherwise everything will be postponed indefinitely. The delay and the procedure of the Japanese make me very skeptical about the possibility of an effective collaboration between the phlegmatic and slow Japanese and the dynamic Fascists and Nazis.

March 9, 1939

At Belgrade during a royal hunt organized by the Regent, Paul, I met a Croat, the Marquess of Bombelles, who was described to me as a country gentleman, friend of the Prince, and a great hunter. Today I received him at Rome, believing that he was making a courtesy call. Instead, he went directly into the political situation and revealed himself to be the secret agent of Ustasci [Fascist party of Croatia]. He spoke of the relations between Croatia and Serbia and pointed out that the chasm which separated these two countries is so wide as to make vain any idea of conciliation from now on. The Croats are kept in a state of moral, political, and economic servitude. If, someday, it should come about that through mobilization arms should be put in the hands of the Croats, their rifles would fire by themselves at the Serbs. His idea of Croatia is an autonomous kingdom with an Italian prince, particularly one connected with the royal Italian family. Bombelles did not ask anything. He merely wanted to inform us and to put us on guard against the politics of Belgrade, which have always been treacherous, but which particularly, since the fall of Stoyadinovich, are clearly favorable toward the democracies and therefore against the Axis.

For obvious reasons I was quite prudent. I confirmed our adherence to the Belgrade pacts so long as the Serbs behave well toward us. However, I told Bombelles that I am always ready to keep in contact with him and that whenever the situation changes we might listen to the Croat point of view in deciding our political attitude.

March 10, 1939

The Duce was impressed by a report from Attolico which substantially confirmed two things: (1) that the Führer is fully committed to solidarity with Italy and is ready to march with us; (2) that the German people, while firmly supporting their chief, would prefer to avoid any danger of war. The Duce commented, "The German people are a military people, not a warrior people. Give to the Germans a great deal of sausage, butter, beer, and a cheap car, and they will never want to have their stomachs pierced."

Von Ribbentrop has accepted our proposal immediately to begin contacts between the two staffs and has proposed, in turn, a conference between Keitel and Pariani. We have accepted, and have suggested Innsbruck as the place of meeting, which should be held as soon as possible and with considerable publicity. We must let the world know that the Axis is also preparing and it does not intend to leave the initiative to the French and British, as seems to have been the case for some time.

The American Ambassador has asked me whether it is true that a tripartite meeting is being planned in Berlin for the purpose of signing the alliance. I said that for the time being there is nothing in all this, but that it is possible it might take place in case developments should necessitate the three anti-Comintern countries making more binding the ties between them.

March 11, 1939

Gambara reported on his meeting with Franco. During the period between the sixteenth and eighteenth of this month final action will begin. We will operate on Toledo. Our meeting was militarily and politically well posted. Franco expressed himself in clearly anti-monarchical terms, and he insisted that even if it should be necessary to come to a restoration it would be a matter of waiting for many years.

The Polish agitation has aroused new hopes in the heart of the Hungarians on the Ruthenian problem. If the Germans go into Slovakia the Hungarians intend to achieve a common frontier—a dream which they will not give up. Villani came to tell me this. I asked him to be calm and to wait. In the meantime the news that arrived by telephone in the evening made the crisis appear less serious, and we are told in Berlin that the Slovaks will find the solution on their own. Christic and I confirmed the celebration of the second anniversary of the Belgrade pact. He reaffirmed his belief in the return of Stoyadinovich after the present government has failed with Matchek. He said, "The Croat problem goes back for generations. King Alexander, who put all his authority behind it, did not succeed in reaching a solution. Certainly a government with so little authority and so short-lived cannot find it either."

March 12, 1939

Coronation of the Holy Father. I attended the ceremony as head of the Italian delegation. It is quite cold and there was considerable disorder in the organization of the pontifical protocol. The Pope was as solemn as a statue; a month ago he was a cardinal and a mere man among men. Today he seemed truly touched by divine spirit, which spiritualized and elevated him.

March 13, 1939

Nothing of particular importance for us, inasmuch as the Duce does not intend to give any special significance to the Slovak crisis, which is developing and assuming disquieting proportions. Goering left San Remo in order to take part in a cabinet meeting. What can be Germany's intention? For the present nothing has been said except that there have been vague expressions of dissatisfaction against the Prague Government.

Naturally they are also beginning to be excited at Warsaw and Budapest.

Let us wait. Nevertheless, our role in this case can only be that of awaiting the development of events.

March 14, 1939

A long conversation with Wellington Koo about the Sino-Japanese situation. He, too, like all the Chinese, puts his trust in the time factor in order to exhaust Japan. I advised him to come to an agreement directly with Tokyo without depending on the not disinterested promises of help that have come from the so-called democracies.

The Duke of Aosta spoke with considerable optimism about the condition of the Ethiopian Empire. I must, however, add that among the many people who have come from there he is the only optimist. He urges us to avoid a conflict with France which would bring on to the high seas the task of pacifying our empire and would jeopardize the conquest itself. I do not quite understand whether he was speaking as the Viceroy of Ethiopia or as the son of a French princess.

News from Central Europe is becoming increasingly grave. For the first time von Ribbentrop has spoken with Attolico and has given him to understand that the German program has been completed; namely, to incorporate Bohemia, to make Slovakia a vassal state, and to yield Ruthenia to the Hungarians. It is not known as yet when all this will take place, but such an event is destined to produce the most sinister impression on the Italian people. The Axis functions only in favor of one of its parts, which tends to have preponderant proportions, and it acts entirely on its own initiative, with little regard for us. I expressed my point of view to the Duce. He was cautious in his reaction and did not seem to attach great importance to the event. He has sought a counterproposal with reference to the advantages which Hungary will have upon achieving a common frontier with the Poles and he had me tell Budapest to move boldly. But to me this seems very little.

March 15, 1939

Events are precipitated during the night. After a meeting between Hitler, Hacha, and Chwalkosky, German troops began their occupation of Bohemia. The thing is serious, especially since Hitler had assured everyone that he did not want to annex one single Czech. This German action does not destroy, at any rate, the Czechoslovakia of Versailles, but the one that was constructed at Munich and at Vienna. What weight can be given in the future to those declarations and promises which concern us more directly? It is useless to deny that all this concerns and humiliates the Italian people. It is necessary to give them a satisfaction and compensation: Albania. I spoke about it to the Duce, to whom I also expressed my conviction that at this time we shall find neither local obstacles nor serious international complications in the way of our advance. He authorized me to telegraph to Jacomoni, asking him to prepare local revolts, and he personally ordered the Navy to hold ready the second squadron at Taranto.

I conferred with Cavagnari, and after having given telegraphic instructions to Tirana, I was able to speak by telephone with Jacomoni, who was on his way to headquarters. He said that tomorrow he will telegraph us what he thinks can possibly be done, and foresees also the eventuality of handing this ultimatum to the King: either he accepts the arrival of the Italian troops and asks for a protectorate, or the troops will arrive anyway. I conferred again with the Duce, and he seemed to me to be less cool about the operation.

In the meantime Hesse [prince of German origin, married to Princess Mafalda, daughter of Victor Emmanuel III] arrived with the usual message. This time it is a verbal message, and not very satisfactory. The Führer sends word that he acted because the Czechs would not demobilize their military forces; because they were continuing to keep their contacts with Russia, and because they mistreated Germans. Such pretexts may be good for Goebbels' propaganda, but they should not use them when talking with us; we are guilty only of dealing with the Germans too loyally. In adding the Führer's thanks for unshakable Italian support, Hesse said that this operation frees twenty divisions for use in some other zone and for the support of Axis policy. But Hitler advises Mussolini that if he intends to undertake an action in grand style, it is better to wait a couple of years, when the available Prussian divisions will be one hundred. They could have spared themselves this addition. The Duce reacted, asserting that in case of war with France we shall fight alone, without asking Germany for a single man, happy only to receive from them arms and other equipment.

I returned to the Duce after Hesse left. I found him unhappy and depressed over the message. He did not wish to give Hesse's news to the press ("the Italians would laugh at me; every time Hitler occupies a country he sends me a message"). He continued to talk about Albania, but he has not as yet made a decision. Some doubt, which he has not yet revealed to me, disturbs his mind. He was calm, as always when the situation is grave, but he has not yet reacted in the way I expected. He wants me to return during the evening.

I received the Polish Ambassador and the Minister of Rumania, who accept with dignity the accomplished fact. [The Nazi occupation of Bohemia.]

I saw the Duce again in the late afternoon. He is fully aware of the hostile reaction of the Italian people, but he affirms that we must, after all, take the German trick with good grace and avoid being "hateful to God and to His enemies." [The *Divine Comedy,* by Dante.] He mentions again the possibility of a blow in Albania, but is still doubtful. Even the occupation of Albania could not, in his opinion, counterbalance in world public opinion the incorporation into the Reich of one of the richest territories of the world, such as Bohemia. Furthermore, to Admiral Cavagnari, whom the Duce received before me, he put only general questions regarding the possibility of making a landing, but did not give instructions of any kind. Too bad! I am convinced that our going into Albania would have raised the morale of the country, would have been an effective result of the Axis, after which we could have re-examined our policy with regard to Germany, whose hegemony begins to take on a disturbing form.

March 16, 1939

Mussolini called me to the Villa Torlonia at nine o'clock in the morning. He looked sullen. He said that he had thought a great deal during the night, and that he had come to the conclusion that the Albanian operation must be postponed because he fears that, shaking the unity of Yugoslavia, it might favor an independent Croatia under German rule, which would mean that the Ustasci would be in Sussak [Fiume]. It is not worth while to take this risk in order to get Albania, for we can have her at almost any other time. I can see that Mussolini has made up his mind; no use insisting. I ordered Jacomoni to let everything rest. I kept a note written by the Duce, in which he lists the reasons for the postponement of the Albanian action.

I had another meeting with the Duce. He now believes that Prussian hegemony in Europe is established. In his opinion a coalition of all other powers, including ourselves, could check German expansion, but could not undo it. He did not count too much on the military help which the small powers could give. I asked whether, as things stand, it would be more desirable for us to bind ourselves in an alliance rather than to maintain our full freedom of action to orient ourselves in the future according to our best interests. The Duce declared himself decidedly in favor of the alliance. I expressed my misgivings, because the alliance will not be so popular in Italy, and also because I fear that Germany might take advantage of it to push ahead its policy of political expansion in Central Europe.

Finally, I saw the Duce for a third time during the evening. He saw de Valera, with whom he had a short and insignificant conversation. Later he received Muti, who submitted to him the plan for operations in Spain to begin the twenty-fifth of this month. He approved it without discussion. Muti, who had not seen the Duce for two months, said that he found him tired and "aged many years." This is a temporary condition; but it is true that the latest events have profoundly shaken him. The Duce showed me the King's speech to the Chamber of the Corporations to which I contributed some modifications.

A great crowd of diplomats at the Palazzo Chigi [Ministry for Foreign Affairs]. The most worried of these was the Minister of Yugoslavia, who saw in Hitler's policy the marks of his Austrian origin. He said that the Germans will now aim at Budapest, and from there will launch their offensive toward the Balkans. They should not delude themselves, however, into thinking that they can subdue the Serbs without fighting, and fighting hard. He is concerned over the repercussions in Croatia, where the separatist movement will draw new life from what has happened. Stoyadinovich has emerged strengthened from the present situation, but the time for his return to power has not yet arrived. I received von Mackensen. In a matter-of-fact way I expressed our congratulations on the German success. He did not succeed very well in hiding a gesture of surprise. This time the Germans really feel that they are double-dealers.

I also saw the Japanese Ambassador, who spoke optimistically about the decisions of his government with respect to the Tripartite Alliance.

March 17, 1939

World opinion is very depressing. From all the capitals disturbing telegrams have arrived. Even in Hungary there is no celebration on account of the occupation of Ruthenia. Worse things are feared; I saw some diplomats: the ambassadors from Belgium and the United States. They expressed to me their concern about the future in their indignation against Berlin. I confess that it is not easy for me to find any justification for the German action. I allowed them to infer that we were in agreement or had at least been informed, but it is such a nuisance to lie!

The Duce was anxious and gloomy. It was the first time that I had seen him thus. Even at the time of the Anschluss he had shown greater indifference. He is preoccupied by the Croatian problem. He is afraid that Matchek may proclaim independence and put himself under German protection. He says, "In such a case these are the only alternatives: either to fire the first shot against Germany or to be swept away by a revolution which the Fascists themselves will bring about. No one would tolerate the sight of a swastika in the Adriatic." He is thinking also of the possibility of delaying the sending of troops to Libya, coming to an agreement with France through London, but later he abandons the idea. Upon my advice he decided to discuss the Croatian problem with the Germans. He said, frankly, that a change of the Yugoslav *status quo* in Croatia could not be accepted by us without a total and fundamental re-examination of our political policy.

I called von Mackensen and spoke to him calmly but with considerable firmness. I recalled that the Führer had said both to me and to the Duce that the Mediterranean does not interest the Germans; and it is upon this premise that we have formulated the policy of the Axis. If such a premise should not be adhered to the Axis would be broken and German intervention in questions relating to Croatia would automatically bring about its failure. Von Mackensen seemed to be impressed by my declaration. He insisted that the rumors which have reached us are without foundation and he assured me "that nothing has been changed from the point of view of the Führer." He hopes that the Duce has not taken tragically the information which has reached him. I assured him that the contrary was the case and that I was talking with him about this for purposes of clarification and so that we might act always in full harmony.

Christic asked to see me, and he denied rumors of Yugoslav military movements to the Hungarian frontier. On my part I denied rumors of an Italian military expedition in Albania and assured him that nothing would ever be done by Italy to weaken the territorial unity of Yugoslavia.

March 18, 1939

Audience with the Pope; I found him exactly as he was as Cardinal Pacelli, and, as before, he was benevolent, courteous, and human. We spoke of the situation. He did not conceal his concern over the aggressive German policy and added that as an Italian he was uneasy. He was very pleased when I told him that the Duce had already taken appropriate measures to hold back the German flood into zones of the most vital interest to us. On the religious problem he declared himself optimistic as to the Italian situation. He informed me that we can come to an agreement and that he will remove Cardinal Pizzardo and will entrust the direction of the Azione Cattolica to a committee of diocesan archbishops. He was most concerned about Germany and intends to follow a more conciliatory policy than Pius XI, but in order to do this co-operation from the other side is necessary; otherwise what he would do would be reduced to "a vain soliloquy." The audience lasted for a half-hour. I believe that we can get along well with this Pope. I spoke at length with Cardinal Maglione. He is a southerner, full of talent and spirit, and in spite of his ecclesiastical education he can scarcely hide the impulses of his exuberant temperament. Maglione, too, is concerned about the German advance, but he gave a discreet hint of the French desire to come to agreement with us, at the same time stressing the fact that he has not received any such commission nor does he intend to solicit any.

A long conference with the Duce during which he re-examined the King's speech and decided to bring it up to date. I expressed clearly to the Duce my concern about Berlin. It has increased greatly since I have had proof of German disloyalty, but he still seems to be quite favorable to the Axis. I did not succeed in convincing him even when I referred to an eventual German absorption of Hungary. He said that in this event he would not react. He personally outlined the editorial for the *Giornale d'Italia* in which he maintains that what Germany has done is logical and that we would have acted similarly under like circumstances.

Fagioli brought to me the record of a conversation with Baudouin. In it there are two interesting points: one, the French are ready to make further concessions; two, the person who revealed Baudouin's mission to the press was Ribbentrop himself on the basis of the information we had given him. Is it worth while to deal loyally with such people?

March 19, 1939

Long conversation with the Duce; during the last few days he has meditated a great deal about our discussion and agrees that it is now impossible to present to the Italian people the idea of an alliance with Germany. Even the stones would cry out against it. Our anxiety over what is going on in Croatia is becoming more serious since all our information confirms the fact that agitation is becoming more bitter. We decided upon sending a telegram to Belgrade in order to inform the Regent, Paul, that we have called a halt to German action and at the same time to advise him to hasten negotiations with Zagreb [the capital of Croatia, i.e., with Matchek, leader of the Croatians], because any loss of time might be fatal.

Meanwhile, the Duce has ordered a concentration of forces on the Venetian border. If the Germans think they can stop us, we shall fire on them. I am more than ever convinced that this may take place. The events of the last few days have reversed my opinion of the Führer and of Germany; he, too, is unfaithful and treacherous and we cannot carry on any policy with him. I have also worked today with the Duce for an understanding with the Western Powers. But will they have at least a minimum of good sense in Paris, or will the possibility of an understanding be compromised once more due to unwillingness to make any concession? The Duce thinks that British irritation runs very deep at this time. "We must not forget that the English are readers of the Bible and that they combine a mercantile fanaticism with a mystical one. Now the latter prevails, and they are capable of going into action."

Fagioli was sent to Paris to continue negotiations with Baudouin. The Duce proposes to make our demands clear in his speech of the twenty-sixth of March: Jibuti, Suez, Tunis.

March 20, 1939

I received the engineer Carnelutti, the special envoy of Matchek. He is of Italian origin. His brother was in the Italian consular service. He was very much excited at the beginning of the conversation and appealed to me to keep it secret because his life would be in danger. I have summarized what he said in a note. In brief, the Croats are anti-German but ready to fall into the arms of Berlin if they should be repulsed by us, if only to escape from Serbian tyranny. He repeated what had been said by Bombelles: negotiations to obtain concessions toward autonomy from Belgrade. If these should fail, an insurrection and an appeal for Italian military aid. The creation of a Croatian republic linked to us by a pact of alliance similar to the one which we have made with Albania but in addition including a customs and monetary union. Second phase: personal union with Italy. The Duce ordered me to accept the Croatian program. Tomorrow I shall confer with Carnelutti.

Von Mackensen brought in an answer to my remarks of last Friday: Germany is not interested in the fate of Croatia and recognizes the pre-eminence of Italian interest. He repeated that the Mediterranean is not, it cannot, nor should it become a German sea. I reported this to the Duce, who found the communication quite interesting "provided we can believe in it." Nevertheless, in spite of the fact that this morning he was very anti-German this evening he said, "We cannot change politics because after all we are not prostitutes." He had me reject the proposal which had been made for Laval to journey to Rome which "would be of no use except in so far as it would be a great piece of advertising for him."

The King is more than ever anti-German. He alluded to Germanic insolence and duplicity and at the same time praised the straightforwardness of the English, but in speaking with the Duce he went so far as to call the Germans rascals and beggars.

Fagioli, returning from Paris, has brought communications from Daladier through Baudouin. They are rather unsatisfactory. Now it will be necessary to wait for the speech of the Duce on the twenty-sixth of March for which both of us have added the portion which deals with foreign policy.

March 21, 1939

The Western Powers have today lost much ground, which was won by the Germans. News about the attempts to constitute a "democratic bloc" has hardened the Duce in favor of the Germans. The title itself identifies our destinies with those of Germany and makes skeptics of those countries such as Rumania, Yugoslavia, Poland, France, and Greece, who, while still concerned about the German progress, must preserve their internal regime built on authoritarian lines. And Germany has gained another point with us since Ribbentrop, in a letter addressed to me, renewed the solemn promise to recognize exclusive Italian rights in the Mediterranean, in the Adriatic, and in adjacent zones.

I had a conference with Carnelutti and told him: first, seek an agreement with Belgrade if for no other purpose than to gain time; second, if this should fail, and you revolt, we shall intervene at the call of the Croat Government; third, abstain from every contact with Berlin, and forewarn us of your actions.

The Grand Council met during the evening. The Duce talked about the necessity to adopt a policy of uncompromising loyalty to the Axis. He made a marvelous speech which was argumentative, logical, cold, and heroic. Balbo and de Bono were derisive. As a matter of fact, Balbo permitted himself to make an unfortunate remark, "You are shining Germany's boots." I reacted to this violently, and I proved to them that Mussolini's policies had always been those of a proud man. The Duce approved of what I had done, and told me that Balbo will always remain "the democratic swine who was once the orator of the Loggia Girolamo Savonarola of Ferrara." [The Masonic lodge in Ferrara, where Balbo was prominent.]

March 22, 1939

Christic assured me that Yugoslavia would not adhere to the bloc proposed by London, adding that it might do so only in the eventuality that Italy, if it changed policy, adhered to it. I went with Attolico to the Duce, who was again irritated against Germany, driven on under the lash of the French press, which never loses the opportunity to exploit his personal susceptibilities. Attolico talked at length about the situation and about his conferences with von Ribbentrop and Hitler. He did so wisely and courageously. He stressed the fact that Germany had not desired to be dragged into a war for the reasons that Hitler has outlined as follows: armaments are not ready and will not be ready for two years more; a navy is lacking; Japan is too engaged to be able to give any effective aid. He did say, however, that, should a crisis arrive, Germany will support us. Finally, he emphasized the necessity of dotting our *i*'s in our reciprocal relations, since the Germans are on the skids, perhaps without being aware of it, from the plane of overbearing power to that of arrogance, and might strike at our interests. The Duce analyzed the present-day situation with respect to Italian public spirit, and came to the conclusion that in order to continue the policy of the Axis it is necessary to fix the objectives of our respective policies, to establish zones of influence and of action for Italy and Germany, and to have Germany reabsorb the non-German residents of the Alto Adige. He also intends to send a personal letter to Hitler stating that certain events represent blows which his personal prestige cannot overlook.

March 23, 1939

Inauguration of the Camera dei Fasci e delle Corporazioni. [The new corporative parliament created by the Fascist Government.] The wording of the oath has been changed; we no longer swear allegiance to the "Royal Successors." (From later explanations I have learned that this has always been the formula. But there has been an alarm just the same. And how!) There is a great deal of talk about this matter, and those who are most outspoken are, as usual, Balbo and de Bono, who profit from it in order to further their petty anti-Fascist speculations. However, I do not know whether the innovation is appropriate at this time. I knew nothing about it. If I had been forewarned I should have been strongly against it.

The Duce has decided to move more rapidly on the Albanian question, and he himself has drawn up the project of agreement which is very brief, consisting of three dry clauses which give it more the appearance of a reprieve than of an international pact. I am also preparing one with Vitetti. It is an accord which, though couched in courteous terms, will permit us to effect the annexation of Albania. The Duce has approved it. Either Zog accepts the conditions which we lay before him or we shall undertake the military seizure of the country. To this end we are already mobilizing and concentrating in Puglia four regiments of Bersaglieri, an infantry division, air force detachments, and all of the first naval squadron.

Chamberlain has sent a letter to the Duce. He expresses his concern over the international situation and asks the help of the Duce to reestablish mutual trust and make certain the continuance of peace. Mussolini will answer after striking at Albania. This letter strengthens his decision to act because in it he finds another proof of the inertia of the democracies.

March 24, 1939

We discussed with the Duce and Pariani our plan for action in Albania. We agreed that it is not advisable to send an ultimatum im-

mediately, but rather to begin our negotiations with King Zog. If he
tries to resist, or to outsmart us, we will use force. The Duce was concerned about reactions in Belgrade, which must, for many reasons, be
kept at a minimum.

Acquarone came from the King to ask for advice on a certain
matter. It seems that His Majesty would like to show some apprecia-
tion of the Duce the day after tomorrow; but what? A title of nobility
would not be welcome. A nomination as Chancellor of the Empire?
Very well, but what difference would this make? In any case I cannot
assume the responsibility for an answer without having conferred with
the Duce, a matter which I will attend to tomorrow morning. I believe
that he will turn it down. But the King's gesture is significant just at
this moment, when certain people are speculating and attempting to
create the impression that there is dissension between the regime and
the dynasty.

March 25, 1939

As I had foreseen, the Duce refused every title and every honor. "I
do not know what they could ever give me," he said. "Make me a
prince? I would be the first to laugh at the idea; imagine people calling me Prince Mussolini! As for Chancellor of the Empire, all right,
but what does it mean? I suppose it would mean that I would continue
to be the head of the government as I am now. No, nothing doing.
Tell Acquarone to thank the King for me and tell him that the only
thing that I want from him is his continued co-operation."

De Ferraris left for Tirana taking with him the planned agreement
for the protectorate. It is not yet possible to foresee what the developments will be, but it seems probable that King Zog will give in. There
is, above all, a fact on which I am counting: the coming birth of
Zog's child. Zog loves his wife very much as well as his whole family.
I believe that he will prefer to insure to his dear ones a quiet future.
And frankly I cannot imagine Geraldine running around fighting
through the mountains of Unthi or of Mirdizu in her ninth month of
pregnancy.

I had a meeting with Prince Beauvan. I talked to him briefly about
our situation with respect to France, and although he is a good friend
of Italy he did not know very much about it. The speech which the

Duce will make tomorrow and which is awaited by everyone will be most useful and will present the picture clearly to the whole of Europe.

March 26, 1939

Meeting of the Fascist militia. The past twenty years have certainly left their mark on the body, but the spirit always remains vibrant and willing.

The Duce's speech made a great impression. Only the Quadrumviri [The original Quadrumviri were Mussolini, Bianchi, Balbo, and de Bono. Bianchi died of tuberculosis in 1926.] were obviously ill at ease, particularly de Bono. The Duce, who knew of this, said that de Bono "is an old idiot, with all respect for his age and for his mind if he ever had one; he was always an idiot, but now he is old on top of it."

After the news of the fall of Madrid, Franco began the attack. To-morrow the CTV will also go into action. There is every hope, even though the Reds give signs of wanting to resist from their positions.

March 27, 1939

Reactions to the Duce's speech are rather favorable. Even in France, where the fear of war dominated all minds, they prefer to accentuate the pacifist elements in the speech, rather than its hostile notes. The Duce was quite angry with the King this morning, when the King found ways of telling him three distasteful things: (1) he was not in agreement with the policy on Albania since he did not see the point of risking such a venture in order to "grab four rocks"; (2) that the offer made by Acquarone to give the Duce some honorary title on the twenti-eth anniversary of Fascism was decided upon in order to "forestall any repetition by the Fascists of the 'humiliation' inflicted upon the King when, without his knowledge, the Duce was given the title of Marshal of the Empire—a humiliation which the King still resents"; (3) that Conrad of Bavaria had told him that in certain quarters of Munich Mussolini is called "The Gauleiter of Italy." The Duce commented bitterly on these words of the King. He said, "If Hitler had had to deal with a nincompoop of a King he would never have been able to take Austria and Czechoslovakia," and he went on declaiming that the monarchy does not like Fascism because Fascism is a unified party, "and the monarchy desires that the country be divided into two or three factions, which could be played one against the other in such a way as to permit the monarchy to control everybody without compromising itself."

Our troops have attacked in Spain and are going ahead very well.

March 28, 1939

I informed the German Ambassador of Chamberlain's letter to the Duce as well as our plans for an answer which will reaffirm our desire to preserve peace and at the same time stress the effective and substantial recognition of Italian rights.

De Ferraris has returned from Albania with a memorandum from Jacomoni. It seems that the King is up to some sort of trickery. His answer is yes and then he has his ministers say no. Nevertheless, the machine is in motion and can no longer be brought to a stop. Either it will be carried out with Zog or else it will be carried out against him. For many reasons, primarily because we Italians do not want to be the ones to start a war in Europe, I should prefer the first alternative, but if Zog does not yield it will be necessary to have recourse to arms.

Madrid has fallen and with the capital all the other cities of Red Spain. The war is over. It is a new formidable victory for Fascism, perhaps the greatest one so far.

Conversations of minor interest with Hesse, and with the Minister of Rumania, who tried to affirm and to defend the necessity of the pact between Berlin and Bucharest.

Demonstrations in the Piazza Venezia because of the fall of Madrid. The Duce is overjoyed. On pointing to the atlas open at the page containing the map of Spain he said, "It has been open in this way for almost three years, and that is enough. But I know already that I must open it at another page." He has Albania in mind.

March 29, 1939

I had two meetings with the Duce for the purpose of making decisions regarding Albania. Since he is leaving for Calabria, and will return on Saturday, he insisted on bringing the matter up to date. (1) The Army, Navy, and aviation continue their preparations. They will be ready on Saturday. (2) Jacomoni must, in the meantime, exert his diplomatic pressure on the King, reporting its effects. (3) At a certain point, unless he gives up before this, we shall send our ships into the territorial waters of Albania and present an ultimatum. (4) If he persists in his refusal we shall raise the tribes in revolt, publish our declarations, and land. (5) Having occupied Tirana, we shall gather the Albanian chiefs into a constituent assembly, over which I should preside, and offer the crown of Albania to the King of Italy.

No one will react. Not even Yugoslavia, which is too preoccupied with recent Croat events. This evening I talked at length with Christic; I gave him the broadest assurances regarding Croatia, but held back on Albania. He offered no objections; he proposes, as a condition, that Albania shall not be used against Yugoslavia.

Badoglio went to the Duce to say that he was in agreement with him on the Albanian undertaking; his only suggestion was that a larger contingent of forces be mobilized. We shall mobilize an additional division, and also a battalion of tanks.

March 30, 1939

Jacomoni unexpectedly announced that he would arrive this afternoon. But because of engine trouble he has stopped at Brindisi and will arrive tomorrow.

Laval's speech is considered by everybody to be a stiffening of the French position. I told the Duce so by telephone. He answered, "So much the better; it was just what I desired."

I received Bombelles. He brought grave news from Croatia. The secession movement is spreading extremely fast. I do not as yet quite understand the real motives for his visit with the exception of two to which he has clearly alluded: to make personal contacts with Pavelić, who was one of the most aggressive men in the country and has the means of carrying on a strong campaign in favor of Italy among the Croatian masses. I made a new appointment for Sunday, after having conferred with the Duce.

The tension between Germany and Poland which had become so alarming during the last few days seems now to be lessening. I am glad of it because the German move would have disastrous repercussions here. Poland enjoys a good deal of favor, and besides the Germans must not overdo things. It is now difficult to find anyone that has faith in their word. They would be completely discredited should they fail to carry out their pact of collaboration with Poland which they have reaffirmed over and over again.

Conference with Shiratori and Oshima to announce that they will present the proposals for the alliance on the second of April.

March 31, 1939

After a long series of more or less useless discussions with, among others, Spoleto and Suardo, I had a meeting with Pariani, Jacomoni, and Guzzoni, who had been appointed as commander of the expeditionary corps in Albania. Jacomoni had no particular reasons for coming to Rome, except perhaps that by his absence he would introduce a little calm into the atmosphere of Tirana, which by this time was pretty much disturbed. It would appear that the King [Zog] has decided to refuse to sign a treaty which formally and substantially violates the integrity and sovereignty of Albania. Pariani said that he preferred such a determined attitude which permits a definitive liquidation of the Albanian question. We studied the military action and its close connection with the diplomatic moves. It appears that this connection is possible. But Jacomoni returned in the afternoon after his meeting with the military heads to give me his disquieting impressions regarding the organization of the expeditionary corps. It appears that they cannot, by all their efforts, put together a battalion of trained motorcycle troops, which could make a surprise arrival in Tirana. Unforeseen difficulties arise also with regard to the landing operations. In the meantime, news from Tirana confirms the fact that the King is preparing to resist—a matter which annoys me greatly, because I consider it rather dangerous to fire the first shot in this disturbed and inflammable Europe. Since the Duce will arrive tomorrow afternoon, his decisions cannot be altered, but while waiting I instructed Jacomoni to prepare a draft treaty which in his opinion might be accepted by King Zog.

Charles brought me the text of Chamberlain's declaration to the House of Commons on assistance to Poland. He also asks, as a personal matter, if he might take a step in London, to say that Italy is ready to discuss with France, if France will take the initiative. I reserve the right to answer after I talk it over with the Duce. If it had not been for Daladier's speech I should have said yes without hesitation.

Wieniawa talked about German-Polish relations. They hope for a peaceful solution, but if the Germans follow their usual unyielding procedure the Poles will fight. Wieniawa declared that he is sufficiently optimistic as to the resistance of the Polish armies.

April 1, 1939

The Duce returned and I had a preliminary conference with him, Jacomoni present. He approved the outline of the treaty with some slight modifications, which are more matters of detail than of substance, but which will have the effect of saving the King's face. For an Oriental, this means a lot. We planned this line of action: tomorrow Jacomoni will appear before the King with a new outline of the treaty and will make it clear that the situation is now serious. Either he will accept, and in that case I will go to Tirana to attend the solemn ceremony of signing the treaty, naturally accompanied by a strong squadron of planes, which will be a symbol of the fact that Albania is Italian. Should he refuse, disorders will break out in all of Albania on Thursday, making armed intervention on our part an immediate necessity. In this case, we shall land on Friday morning.

During the afternoon Sereggi, the new Minister from Albania, came to see me. He begins his mission at a stormy time. Passing by Bari, he saw the concentration of troops and realized that the music was about to begin. I spoke frankly to him; in a friendly tone but quite firmly. He said that he was in agreement with us. He urged me to save appearances in such a way as to make the solution acceptable to the King and to the people. I accompanied him to the Palazzo Venezia where the Duce repeated the warning to him in more precise terms. He added that if the King should refuse to sign the pact, a crisis will be unavoidable. Sereggi decided to leave for Tirana, together with Jacomoni, in order to persuade the King. Then, on the pretext that he was not able to exchange his Albanian money, he had Jacomoni loan him 15,000 lire, a first installment on a bribe!

April 2, 1939

Muti arrived in Rome, and I got ready to send him to Tirana with a small band of men as enterprising and boastful as himself, in order to create the incidents which are to take place next Thursday evening if the King, in the meantime, has not had the kindness to capitulate. I gave him freedom of action, but he is under definite orders: to respect the Queen and the child, if it is already born; to create terror during the night; at daybreak to hide in the woods and await the arrival of our troops, trying, in the meantime, to impede Zog's retreat toward

Mati [a mountain district west of Tirana], where he might attempt some resistance.

I authorized Bombelles to make contact with Pavelić in a very secret way. As regards propaganda, I am thinking things over and shall soon come to a decision, although the Duce has already approved a subsidy to be given to the Croats.

I received von Mackensen, bringing to his attention the Duce's letter in answer to Chamberlain. I also received Shiratori, bearer of the Japanese answer for the Tripartite Alliance. In general this answer is good. It makes, however, two reservations: (1) to make known to London, Paris, and Washington that in the mind of the Japanese the alliance is directed against Moscow; (2) and to add the declaration that, in case of a European war, Japanese aid would be limited. O.K. for the second. But with reference to the first, it seems to me that such a reservation might alter the value of the pact, and I want to set this down clearly.

The reactions in the various capitals, including Belgrade, are rather moderate. Christic, on the other hand, is more alarmed, but in answer to a question he declared himself convinced that the Albanian question cannot change the relations which happily exist between Rome and Belgrade. He recommended that no action be taken without first informing Belgrade, and that somehow the existence of the Albanian state be preserved as a matter of form.

Many contradictory news despatches during the morning. Jacomoni telegraphed an Albanian counterproposal presented before the Duce's ultimatum, but we did not take it into consideration. Sereggi telegraphed to offer his resignation. From Durazzo and Valona news arrived that the embarkation of Italian refugees is proceeding normally. Fortusi and the aviator Tesei, who arrived at noon from Tirana, said that the exodus of the Italians has filled the population with terror. They crowd the streets, weeping, and accusing King Zog of having brought this calamity upon them. The Duce telephoned the order for the embarkation, saying that the order for departure would come during the evening. At my suggestion he decided to carry out this afternoon a demonstration flight by a hundred planes over Durazzo, Tirana, and Valona.

4 P.M. A telegram arrived from Jacomoni. It appears that the King does not wish to take upon himself the responsibility for a complete capitulation, and intends to convoke the Council of Ministers to take the extreme decision of resisting or giving up. Quite justly, Jacomoni

observes that, in this way, the King puts himself outside the terms of the ultimatum, but he agreed to transmit the information, nonetheless.

The Duce, whom I have kept informed, gave the order to launch the expedition, reserving the right to make public news of its progress, if any.

From the telegraph offices we learn that long code messages are going from Tirana to the Foreign Office [the British Foreign Office]. We cannot stop them. I gave orders, however, that they be delayed, and that many errors in the code groups be repeated. It is well that we gain time, even though Chamberlain gave Commons an account of what has happened which was very favorable to us, and has also declared that Great Britain has no specific interests in Albania.

7 P.M. Jacomoni telegraphed saying that he was burning the secret code, that he had told the officials of the naval mission to leave, and that the entire legation might have to get on the submarine which is at Durazzo. The Duce repeats the order to attack, while specifying that the aviation must spare the cities and the populations.

Badoglio has written a letter to the Duce, criticizing the plan of operations. The Duce paid no attention to it. In a letter the King takes note of the communication made by the Duce yesterday, but expresses his doubts regarding the possibility of our installing ourselves solidly in Albania, basing his opinion on historical memories of Venetians and Aragonese. Evidently he does not remember that the Romans installed themselves there very well.

9 P.M. I communicated to Villani and to von Mackensen our decision to proceed with the military occupation. I received assurances from them both as to their solidarity and their absolute understanding of the motives which made us act. Subsequently, I saw Christic. I acquainted him with the maneuvers to create a crisis between us and Belgrade. I gave him the fullest assurance regarding the extent of our action and of our understandings. It seemed to me that he took it all with a remarkable dose of resignation. As he went out he said, "So Zog is coming to the same end Beneš came to."

At last Albanian proposals arrive. They would like to deal with Pariani. This is not possible, especially since Pariani is in Germany. We answered that eventually we shall send a plenipotentiary to Guzzoni.

I returned home at about 10:30 P.M. I am tired and don't feel well. I should like to rest, especially since tomorrow I must make a flight in order to observe the landing of our forces. Nothing to be done about it.

At dawn Zog's son was born. How long will he be the heir to the Albanian throne?

[*There are no entries for April 3 and 4 because Ciano had left Rome by plane for Albania.*]

April 5, 1939

Two ships will go to Valona and Durazzo to withdraw the Italians, who are now seriously threatened by the bandits to whom Zog has given orders to start a reign of terror. For the time being international public opinion is calm, so calm that I suspect it does not realize the tension between us and Zog and thinks Zog is going to appeal for help.

Germany, meanwhile, behaves well. Von Ribbentrop has communicated to Attolico that Berlin looks upon our action at Tirana with sympathy since any Italian victory represents a strengthening of the power of the Axis. Budapest has also reacted well. Villani informs me that six Hungarian divisions already mobilized are ready to go to the Yugoslav border if it should be necessary to exert pressure on the Serbs. The time required, forty-eight hours.

I also saw Bombelles, who has had a satisfactory conference with Pavelić. He is now going to return to Zagreb, where he will speak with Matchek, then he will come to Rome again in order to take up the question of our financial contribution to the propaganda movement.

I saw the Duce several times. He is calm, frightfully calm, and more than ever convinced that no one will want to interfere in our affair with Albania. However, he has decided to march, and he will march even though all the world may be pitted against him. He repeated this aloud to Muti, who has hurried to Tirana and confirmed our impression that Zog will resist with the small forces which he has at his disposal. Inasmuch as the King requests twenty-four hours so that he can think the matter over, the Duce, through a personal telegram, fixed the expiration of the ultimatum for twelve o'clock Thursday, the sixth of April.

April 6, 1939

Christic asked for another appointment. He seemed to want to say something urgent and serious to me. I was afraid that it was going to be a change in the line of conduct of Yugoslavia. Instead, it was a question of new requests for clarification and for details about our action and our future program. I tendered the olive branch. Christic himself, on telephoning to Belgrade, showed satisfaction over what I had said to him.

April 7, 1939

I got up at 4 A.M. Starace was waiting for me in the entrance hall with many communications, among which was a telegram from Zog to the Duce. It confirmed his decision to arrive at a military understanding and asked for negotiations. We answered that he should send his negotiators to Guzzoni. The Duce, having got up during the night, which is a very unusual thing, would like to have news and explanations that I am not in a position to give him because I have none.

The military attaché, Gabrielli, who in the last few days has behaved very strangely, telegraphs that Zog has at his disposal forty-five thousand men. It seems that he is exaggerating.

At 6 A.M. I left by plane. The weather is calm and warm. Buti, Vitetti, and Pavolini came with me. We were at Durazzo at seven forty-five. It was a beautiful spectacle. In the bay, motionless and solemn, were the warships, while motorboats, lighters, and tugs moved in the port, transporting the landing forces. The sea was like a mirror. The countryside is green and the mountains, which are high and massive, are crowned with snow. We saw only a few people in Durazzo. But there must have been some resistance because I saw detachments of Bersaglieri, crouched behind piles of coal, defending the port, and I saw others going up the hill in Indian file in order to surround the city.

From some of the windows there was occasional firing. I continued to Tirana. The streets were deserted and undefended. In the capital the crowd moved through the streets quite calmly. The legation was barricaded. On the roof was a large tricolored flag and in the courtyard many vehicles. I was convinced that in case of danger it would be easy to defend it from above and I gave orders to this effect.

I reported to the Duce, who was quite satisfied, particularly because international reaction was almost non-existent. The memorandum which Lord Perth left with me in the course of a cordial visit might have been composed in our offices.

During the afternoon everything changed. Guzzoni received Zog's negotiators, and instead of proceeding as the Duce had ordered, suspended everything for six hours. The Duce was furious, because this delay might have serious consequences. It is necessary for us to arrive in the capital in order to carry on our political maneuvering. Through Valle, the Duce ordered the march resumed, but meanwhile a day has been lost and this permits the usual mudslinging French press to say that the Italians have been beaten by the Albanians. News about the advance of the columns is lacking. The only one who telegraphs is Jacomoni, who is hiding with other Italians in the legation. The information he sends gives rise to more and more concern about its fate; the bandits are ransacking the royal palace and threaten the legation. The Duce, in a very nervous state of mind, telephones continually during the night, demanding information which I am unable to give. Only in the early hours of the morning does Jacomoni indicate that the city has quieted down, but we do not know anything about the advance of Guzzoni.

April 8, 1939

D'Aieta telephoned at eight o'clock in the morning, saying that Jacomoni gives every assurance that the aviation field at Tirana is usable. I decided to leave immediately, and I informed the Duce, who approved. I arrived in Tirana at ten-thirty, after having flown over the armored column, which is marching on the Albanian capital. The forward elements are already at the gates of the city. I found Valle, Guzzoni, and Jacomoni on the field, together with many units of airborne grenadiers. I must admit that a violent emotion has taken possession of me and of everybody else. I saw Guzzoni, who explained the reasons for the delay: landing difficulties, fuels not adaptable, and, finally, lack of communications, because the radio operators who were recalled are not up to the mark. The situation is now excellent. I received many Albanian commissions which paid me homage. In reply I said that Italy will respect Albanian independence, insuring her political development, as well as the social and civil growth of the people.

With the news of Zog's flight to Greece vanish all our fears about resistance in the mountains. In fact, the soldiers are already returning to their barracks, after having deposited their arms in the garden of the legation. I gave orders that the soldiers be treated well, and especially the officers. I took some steps in the direction of re-establishing order and the normal rhythm of civilian life. I gave orders that all of Zog's political prisoners be freed. These prisoners had been sentenced to one hundred years in jail. I distributed money to the poor. I conferred with the most important men of Tirana, in order to get a definite idea of the wishes of the Albanians and also to make decisions regarding the new form of government to be given to the country. Mixing with the troops and their officers, I found them all very proud of the undertaking.

April 9, 1939

I return to Rome to confer with and make a report to the Duce. Many Albanians greet me on the aviation field with considerable cordiality. They give me Albanian flags and ask for Italian flags in return. This morning Tirana is decorated with tricolored Italian flags.

The Duce is happy. He listens attentively to my report and decides to send a congratulatory telegram to General Guzzoni. He really deserves it.

Regarding the new constitutional setup of Albania, the Duce has prepared a regency project, which does not seem good to me. I tell him so, and explain my plan as follows: to create at once a government council, to announce a body of electors for the twelfth of April, to have it vote a decision which will sanction the personal union between the two countries, conferring on King Victor Emmanuel III the crown of Albania. In principle he approves. During the afternoon I draw up the document and discuss it with some jurists and other picayune professionals, such as Buti, Vitetti, et al. [In reality these men were not jurists but functionaries of the Ministry for Foreign Affairs.] All agree that while such a decision will give us possession of Albania it will not look like an aggression. This is useful, the more so because our tension with Great Britain appears to be decreasing after a conference I had this morning with Lord Perth, and the Yugoslavs behave in such a friendly way as can be explained only by their boundless fear. The same may be said of the Greeks.

April 10, 1939

We examine with the Duce the project drawn up yesterday which is approved, except for a few formal variations. Program: the electoral body at Tirana on the twelfth, the Grand Council at Rome on the thirteenth, my speech to the Chamber on the fifteenth, and Sunday, the sixteenth, a great national celebration of the event.

Reaction abroad begins to lessen. It is clear above all that the British protests are more for domestic consumption than anything else.

News from Albania is good; military occupation is carried out according to plan and without obstacles.

April 11, 1939

I got to work on the preparation of the speech for the Chamber. The reaction of foreign countries has toned down; with tomorrow's ceremonies we shall give the democracies a good pretext, since they ask for nothing better than to wash their hands of the whole affair.

I communicated to Pignatti the Duce's decision to erect a mosque in Rome in view of the fact that six million Italian subjects are now Mohammedans. After having spoken with Maglione, Pignatti reported to me that at the Vatican they are horror-stricken at the idea, which they take to be contrary to Article I of the Concordat [Vatican Treaty of February 11, 1929]. But the Duce has made up his mind, and he is supported in this by the King, who is always at the spearhead of any anti-Church policy. Personally, I do not see any need for such a thing, and, at any rate, I would be more inclined to have this mosque constructed in Naples, since that city constitutes a veritable bridge with our African domains. In so far as this proposal concerns the Albanians, we realize that they are an atheistic people who would prefer a raise in salary to a mosque.

April 12, 1939

I arrive at Tirana by plane at ten-thirty and am received at the airport by members of the new Albanian Government. I did not know Verlaçi and, had I known him, I should have opposed his nomination. He is a very surly-looking man and will give us a great deal of annoyance. The crowd receives me triumphantly; there is a certain amount of coolness, especially among the high school students. I see that they dislike raising their arms for the Roman salute, and there are some who openly refuse to do it even when their companions urge them.

However, things are not going so smoothly as it might appear. There is a great deal of opposition to a personal union. All are in agreement on having a prince of the House of Savoy or, better still, they would like to have me. But they understand that giving the crown to Victor

Emmanuel III means the end of Albanian independence. I have long discussions with many chiefs; the most stubborn are those from Scutari (who have been incited by the Catholic clergy) whom it will be easy to convince, however, as soon as I distribute bundles of Albanian francs, which I have brought with me. Nevertheless, things go well during the meeting of the electoral body; there is a unanimous vote which is also very enthusiastic. They come as a delegation to bring me their decision. I speak from the balcony of the legation and am especially successful when I give assurance that the decision will prejudice neither the form nor substance of Albanian independence. Let it be understood that this success refers to the masses, because I see the eyes of some patriots flaming with anger and tears running down their faces. Independent Albania is no more.

April 13, 1939

I return to Rome and go at once to the Palazzo Venezia. I find the Duce on the roof observing anti-aircraft experiments. I inform him as to what has happened. He would like to go further at once and abolish the Ministry for Foreign Affairs [evidently in Albania]. I do not share his views. We must proceed gradually unless we want to antagonize the rest of the world. So far matters have run as smoothly as oil because we have not had to have recourse to force, but if tomorrow we should begin firing on the crowd, public opinion would become excited again. On the other hand, the Ministry for Foreign Affairs is of use to us in order to have the new state of things legally acceptable without having to pass through an interminable polemic on recognitions. [That is recognition of the new Albanian Government by foreign governments.] Later on it can be quickly suppressed. I propose to the chief of the Albanian Government the creation of an undersecretary of Albanian affairs [that is, under the Italian Minister for Foreign Affairs] by naming Benini as undersecretary. I want a technical expert because it will be necessary quickly to carry out a program of public works. Only thus will we definitely link the people to us and destroy confidence in the authority of their chiefs, showing that only we are capable of doing what they have not been able or did not want to do.

During the evening a short session of the Grand Council for the approval of the decree.

April 14, 1939

Council of Ministers. Then I work on my speech which I send to the Duce in the late afternoon. He makes a few changes in it, then he defines it: "One of the best speeches that has ever been made in Parliament."

I receive the Yugoslav [evidently the Yugoslav Minister accredited to the King of Italy]. We reach an agreement on a meeting we are going to have in Venice with Marković on Saturday, the twenty-second.

Goering arrives. I receive him at the station and accompany him to Villa Madama [a famous Roman villa which the Italian Government used for the housing of official guests]. On our way he stresses the situation of the Axis which he defines as formidable. He harshly attacks Poland.

April 15, 1939

The Albanians have arrived. Some among them have a depressed air. The Duce received them at the Palazzo Venezia and addressed them. I noted that they listened anxiously for the word "independence," but this word did not come, and they were saddened. Jacomoni confirmed this later.

I made my speech at the Chamber. It went over in a big way. Later there was a meeting of the Senate which was hurried and not too imposing.

Finally, a meeting with Goering and the Duce at the Palazzo Venezia. The record was preserved. Roosevelt has sent a message proposing a ten years' truce. At first the Duce refused to read it, then he defined it: "A result of progressive paralysis."

April 16, 1939

The ceremony of offering the Albanian crown to the King of Italy takes place at the royal palace. The Albanians, who seem to be lost in the great halls of the Quirinal, have a depressed air. Verlaçi especially appears depressed as he pronounces, with a tired air and without conviction, the words he has to say in offering the crown. The King answers in an uncertain and trembling voice; decidedly he is not an orator who makes any impression on an audience, and these Albanians who are a warrior mountain people look with amazement and timidity on the little man who is seated on a great gilt chair beside which stands a gigantic bronze statue of Mussolini. They cannot understand what this is all about.

I talked to the Duce about the state of mind of the Albanians. He, too, was aware of it, and he assures me that he will talk to them today about their national independence and sovereignty in a way that will send them home reassured.

I have had two long conversations with Goering, one at the Ministry of the Armed Forces and the other at the Palazzo Venezia. The second of these was recorded. Although he speaks a great deal about war for which preparations are being made with great attention, yet it seems to me that he does not completely close the doors to peace, at least for a few years. The thing that disturbs me most in his conversations is the tone in which he described relations with Poland; it reminds me peculiarly of the same means used at other times for Austria and for Czechoslovakia. But the Germans are mistaken if they think they can act in the same way; Poland will undoubtedly be overrun, but the Poles will not lay down their arms without a hard fight.

April 17, 1939

I accompany Goering to the station. He is rather pleased with his stay in Rome, for it has given him contacts with me and with the Duce. Generally speaking, the impression is that even Germany intends to keep the peace. Only one danger: Poland. I was impressed not so much by what he said, but by the contemptuous tone he used in talking of Warsaw. The Germans should not think that in Poland they will make a triumphant entrance as they have done elsewhere; if attacked, the Poles will fight. The Duce also sees it in this way.

April 18, 1939

We received the Hungarians at the station. Teleki makes a good impression on the Duce; Czaky is what he appears to be: a small, presumptuous man and, most disturbing to note, apparently is a physical and spiritual weakling who wishes always to assume heroic airs.

The first meeting takes place in the afternoon. Nothing very extraordinary. Czaky expounds the situation in detail and tries to give his words an anti-German flavor. Above all, he keeps harping on Slovakia; he hopes—or, better, he deludes himself into thinking—that Germany might make a kind gift of it to Budapest.

It is useless to summarize the conversation since it is not important. In the Duce's words: "Only a bottle of wine was missing from the table."

We begin to draw our plans of action in Albania with Benini. I think much good will come of it since he is a man of action and is clear in his ideas and in his judgment. The Duce, too, had a good impression of him.

April 19, 1939

The more or less useless conversations with the Hungarians are continuing. Czaky becomes more and more prolix and futile in his arguments. He specializes in saying the obvious, and in saying it as if it were a matter of great importance. Mussolini says of him that "he takes a long running start to jump over a straw."

Conversation with Perth. The British raise some difficulties connected with the title: King of Albania. Some lively arguments with Perth, in which I maintained that the change in dynasty is a matter of internal affairs in which no one has a right to interfere.

April 20, 1939

After the Duce made his controversial speech with respect to Roosevelt's message, I accompanied him to the Palazzo Venezia and showed him a very serious report by Attolico, which announces imminent German action against Poland. This would mean war; hence, we have the right to be informed in time. We must be able to prepare ourselves and we must prepare public opinion so that it will not be taken by surprise. Hence, I have given orders to Attolico to hasten my meeting with von Ribbentrop.

During the afternoon the third, and fortunately the last, conference with the Hungarians. That is to say with Czaky, because Teleki has scarcely opened his mouth. My impression of Czaky is more and more negative. Today, in a very offhand way, he declared that it was his conviction that Hitler is crazy. He bases this observation on the look of the Führer's eyes, and he said such absurdities with a great deal of assurance. We hope that this presumptuous individual will not be the

Guido Schmidt of Hungary. The Duce has summarized the situation:
(1) Italy and Germany desire some years of peace and are doing all
they can to preserve it. (2) Hungary is carrying on and will carry on
the policy of the Axis. (3) No one wants the dismemberment of Yugoslavia, but everyone is working toward the maintenance of the *status
quo*. If, however, any dismemberment should come about, Italian interests in Croatia are paramount. (4) As to the Slovak problem, Hungary will adopt a watchful attitude and will do nothing contrary to
German wishes.

April 21, 1939

A day particularly devoted to Albania. I have a conference with
Sthyka, Albanian ex-Minister to Belgrade. He gives information above
all on the problem of the Cayovesi, that is, eight hundred and fifty
thousand physically strong Albanians, morally firm, and enthusiastic
at the idea of a union with their mother country. It seems that the
Serbs are in a panic over it. For the moment we must not even allow
it to be imagined that the problem is attracting our attention; rather
it is necessary to give the Yugoslavs a dose of chloroform. Later on it
will be necessary to adopt a policy of real interest in the Cayovo question; this will cause an "Irredentist" problem in the Balkans that will
absorb the attention of the Albanians themselves and will be a dagger
thrust into the back of Yugoslavia.

In the afternoon a meeting of the ministers to pass the budget of the
undersecretariat for Albania. It is set at 430,000,000 lire. Although I
protested very much against it, I am convinced that it is a sum that
will permit us to carry on a large-scale action.

A conference with Viola to discuss my trip to Spain, which is to
precede the trip that Goering will make there. It would make a bad
impression on the Italians if that fellow should get there before us.

At the Palazzo Venezia I greet Lord Perth. The Duce has treated
him very courteously and seems to like him now. It has been decided
that we will accept the credentials of his successor without the title
of King of Albania.

April 22, 1939

In Venice for the arrival of Marković. The population gives me a
cordial welcome. Evidently the Albanian question has had a particular

echo in this great Adriatic city. Marković makes a good impression on me. He is a kind, temperate, and modest man. He has all the characteristics of the career diplomat. The arrival in Venice was a great event for him. This was the first time he has traveled abroad as a minister. The applause, the flags, the bands, and an enchanted Venice full of sun and springtime had touched his spirit deeply.

Our first meeting went very well. I immediately discovered him to be reasonable and understanding, while, on the other hand, Indelli, who is an unreasonable alarmist, had made us believe in some excitement among the Yugoslavs which did not really exist; even if such feeling existed among some elements of their public opinion it had not reached responsible quarters. Our conversation touched on the following points:

Albania: has accepted the *fait accompli*, including our reasons for sending troops. It has appreciated our decision not to have the troops go in large numbers beyond Durazzo-Tirana to the north. On my part, assurances of our disinterest in Kossov.

Germany: there will be closer and closer co-operation among the members of the Axis, without, for the moment, adhering to the anti-Comintern pact for reasons of internal policy, but without at the same time destroying all possibility of such adherence.

April 23, 1939 [continuation of April 22]

Refusal of any kind of British guarantee. A political formula for Yugoslavia; a hint at conflict, disarmed neutrality with the economic support of Italy and Germany. Naturally, within the system of the Axis and gravitating principally on Rome.

Hungary: gradual bettering of relations in order not to compromise our existing obligations to Rumania, on which policy Marković has made open and sharp criticism.

League of Nations: progressive indifference.

In general the visit has brought excellent results. The communiqué issued at the end of the conversation has pleased our journalists and has very much displeased the Franco-British journalists, which is a proof of its goodness. Marković has made a good impression on all those who have come to know him; Stoyadinovich has been liked even more, perhaps because he is more modest and is more physically attractive. He [Marković] is very careful to hide the great expanse of his bald pate, and to this end he mobilizes all the hair of his temples and of the nape of his neck. He has said that his hairs are like the mobilized Yugoslavs in the Albanian crisis.

After my return to Rome I make a report to the Duce, who is quite satisfied. Jacomoni, following a request from me, has confirmed the agreement for the equality of civil and political rights of Italians and Albanians. The matter is very important, in fact as important as the annexation itself.

April 24, 1939

I received numerous diplomats and, particularly, the Polish Ambassador, who complains about certain strong reactions by our press against articles appearing in Warsaw opposition newspapers. He finds that such stuff is not worth bothering about; perhaps he is right.

The Minister from Holland, a good, vague gentleman, whom I see rarely, comes to spin me a strange yarn. He says that he is very much alarmed over what is happening in Europe and above all over what people are whispering is yet to happen. Certain officers have told him that we and the Germans have decided to divide Europe between us; Holland would belong to Germany. He asked me how much truth there was in all this. I answered him jokingly, and then I reported the conversation to the Duce, who was very much amused. They are the ideas of an official who is a little stupid and very timid, but they are none the less indicative of a state of mind spreading over the world.

Starace and Benini on their return from Tirana say they are enthusiastic over all they have seen, and admit that Albania is in reality far better than they had thought.

I go to the theater, where *Cesare*, by Forzano, is being given. The Duce also attends this show. He himself collaborated in the work, and some years ago, through me, he sent to Forzano the opera's scenario. Frankly, I think this opera is ugly, without originality and without technique. It affords neither pleasure nor interest. Besides, adulation is an art which one must practice with control. Forzano evidently goes too far in identifying the Duce with Caesar. On the other hand he has let everything get out of hand, and the results are anything but those he wanted to produce.

April 25, 1939

From Berlin comes the news that the Japanese still maintain their reserve with reference to the Tripartite Alliance; hence the signature is to be postponed *sine die*. Mussolini, whom I telephoned at Forlì, where he happens to be today, declares that he is satisfied. In reality, for some time past he has considered Japanese participation more harmful than useful. I shall see von Ribbentrop on the sixth in some city in northern Italy in order to discuss common policies.

François-Poncet uses the pretext of a commercial agreement to talk to me of Italo-French relations. He says he has been informed by Lord Perth as to what the Duce said about negotiations begun with Baudouin and later interrupted. He wants us to know that the French Government is always ready to continue discussions on this basis. I make sweeping reservations, but at his request I add that I do not consider anything changed in our political directives. In turn I ask him if I must consider this *démarche* as official. He tells me that he has made it on the authorization of his government.

April 26, 1939

I report to the Duce by telephone on my conversation with François-Poncet. He doesn't seem to give it much weight. He says: "Anyway, I have no intention of starting negotiations with France until after the signing of the treaty with Germany." I received many foreign diplomats; they are all appreciably flabbergasted about our foreign policy and all of them, including the more pessimistic, like Helfand, who is a professional Cassandra, admit that our successes have been greater than could have been thought possible.

We decide on certain important works in Albania, among them the construction of hotels in the larger centers, and for these the Duce gives a personal contribution of a million lire.

The English Chargé d'Affaires sends me a brief résumé of all that Mr. Chamberlain is planning to tell the House of Commons with regard to military conscription. The project seems to me of very modest proportions.

April 27, 1939

Nothing new, except a conference with the Japanese Ambassador, who says that the last word about the Nipponese decisions on the Tripartite Pact has not yet been said. However, I stress the point that we must know it before the sixth of May.

From Berlin they informed me that the Führer in his speech tomorrow will denounce the naval pact with Great Britain as well as the pact of friendship with Poland. This is very serious. The situation which during the past few days had an undeniable clarity may become very obscure from one hour to the next. The Duce, to whom I transmitted the information at Rocca delle Caminate [the castle-villa, reconstructed by the Fascist party and offered as a gift to Mussolini, is in the Apennines at an altitude of twelve hundred feet not far from Forlì and near Mussolini's birthplace], has telephoned for more particulars. He, too, does not hide his concern about the denunciation of the pact with Poland. However, on the other hand, as regards the pact with Great Britain, the situation is less alarming.

April 28, 1939

The Führer has delivered his speech. It lasted exactly two hours and twenty minutes; it cannot be said that brevity is the foremost quality of this man. Generally speaking, the speech is less warmongering than one might have supposed on the basis of information coming to us from Berlin. The first reactions to the speech in the different capitals are also rather mild. Every word which leaves any hope of peaceful intentions is received by the whole of humanity with immeasurable joy. No nation wants war today; the most that one can say is that they know it is inevitable. This is worth something to us and to the Germans. As for the others, I do not know. I ask myself seriously whether a German move against Poland, notwithstanding the many declarations and mutual guarantees, would not, in the end, lead to a new Munich. On the other hand, the British-French war against a Germany which is on the defensive on its western frontier is practically an impossible one.

I received news from Japan. It appears that they have now decided to sign the alliance. I tell Shiratori that it is necessary in any case to have a yes or no quickly. In a few days I shall meet Ribbentrop and we must make our decisions, especially since the diplomatic work of the democracies has been greatly intensified in the last few days, and that the Anglo-Soviet alliance seems now to be a concrete and accomplished fact.

The Duce returns to Rome.

April 29, 1939

Council of Ministers. Some decisions are approved to increase the power of the armed forces. The Duce is very much dissatisfied with it all, with the exception of the Navy. He has the feeling, and he is right, that beyond appearances, which are more or less carefully put on, there is little underneath. I think so too. I do not have any exact information as to the Army, but the many rumors which I hear are distinctly pessimistic. Also some impressions which I formed on the occasion of mobilization for the Albanian undertaking, a small mobilization after all. This has increased my doubts. The military make a big ado with a lot of names. They multiply the number of divisions, but in reality these are so small that they scarcely have more than the strength of regiments. The ammunition depots are lacking in ammunition. Artillery is outmoded. Our anti-aircraft and anti-tank weapons are altogether lacking. There has been a good deal of bluffing in the military sphere, and even the Duce himself has been deceived—a tragic bluff. We will not talk about the question of the air force. Valle made the statement that there were three thousand and six first-class planes, while the information service of the Navy say that they amount to only nine hundred and eighty-two. A gross exaggeration. I report the matter to the Duce. I believe that it is my duty to speak with absolute honesty about such a matter, even though it makes him bitter. This will serve to avoid greater sorrow in the future.

April 30, 1939

The Duce is furious on account of the photograph taken of the grenadiers of honor [a special unit of the infantry in the city of Rome] presenting arms on the arrival of General Brauchitsch. He is right, for it is difficult to find anything more badly done. The Duce sees in this an indication of the spiritual and physical lack of discipline in the Army. He explains it by saying that the Army was at one time the exclusive property of the Italian monarchy and had, above all, the simple function of a subsidiary police force for the preservation of public order; today, on the contrary, its main business is to wage war. This confuses many officers.

I discussed with Alfieri the advisability of accepting the title of Prince of Kruia which the Albanians would like to bestow on me. This would be the first and only thanks received so far for having given Albania to Italy. Nevertheless, my inclinations are to refuse it.

I had my first conversation with Gafencu. He is a likable man, a little timid, but quite sharp. We explore the situation. I do not conceal my disappointment over Rumania's acceptance of the British guarantee. What purpose would it serve if Hungary or Bulgaria attacked? He talks about relations with Budapest and stresses the intransigence of the Magyars. I agree with him on this point; the Hungarians are always absurdly insistent. I don't like their attitude toward us either. They condescend to accept favors which they first solicit. Gafencu talks also about our relations with France. He knows about my last conversation with François-Poncet. He says that Bonnet's tendency is for conciliation; that of Leger is to wait until we take the initiative. They certainly have a long time to wait.

May 1, 1939

The ceremony of submitting the reply to the King's speech [opening the session of the Fascist Chamber] at the royal palace. The Duce criticizes the eighteenth-century character of the ceremony, the use of gala carriages, et cetera, and says this is the last time it is going to happen.

Gafencu is received by the Duce. The conference starts off in a rather cool way. In general Mussolini is prejudiced against the Rumanians, whom he despises as soldiers. Then he allows himself to be carried away by his love for discussion and polemics. He criticizes openly the Rumanian acceptance of the British guarantee; as a result Rumania assumes the role of a protected country. Gafencu explains the reasons that have induced him to accept it; above all the pressure of public opinion which has been greatly concerned over German territorial demands for *Lebensraum*. We continue to explore the general political situation; nothing particularly interesting results.

In the afternoon I have a long conference with Christic. He is concerned about a possible German-Polish crisis during Prince Paul's stay in Rome. I reassure him, giving him some information as to my meeting with von Ribbentrop, which will take place during the week.

Von Mackensen at Rome and Attolico from Berlin make known to me Turkish anxiety about our intentions. They suggest our giving the Turks some reassurance sufficient to calm them down. Mussolini, to whom I refer the matter, approves this reassurance but says: "This is the fruit of a bad conscience. They deserve an act of aggression because of the mere fact that they fear one."

May 2, 1939

General Carboni, who has the reputation of being a deep student of military matters, today confirms the reports that our armament situation is disastrous. I have received this information from too many sources not to take it seriously. But what is the Duce doing? His attention seems to be spent mostly on matters of form; there is hell to pay if the "Present Arms" is not done right or if an officer doesn't know how to lift his legs in the Roman step [Fascist equivalent of the goose step], but he seems to concern himself only up to a certain point about the real weaknesses which he certainly knows very well. In spite of my formal charges in connection with the results of Cavagnari's investigation of the efficiency of our aviation he has done nothing, absolutely nothing; and today in his conversation with Cavagnari he didn't even mention the matter. Why? Does he fear the truth so much that he is unwilling to listen?

I received Bombelles. After what has happened with Yugoslavia we have no intention of doing anything that might weaken the unity of the state. On the other hand, it is not clear what the Croats are doing. It appears that agreement with the Serbs has been reached. Therefore, I fully confirmed all that I had said in previous conversations regarding our active interest in the destinies of Croatia, but I said that for the moment I intended to do nothing.

My last meeting with Gafencu. We became decidedly good friends. He invites me to Bucharest in October, which is all very well, but might it not be that by October many plans will have to be revised?

May 3, 1939

To calm Turkish apprehensions with regard to us and above all to please the Germans, who consider a countermaneuver on the part of Great Britain and France as possible, I have given the Turkish Ambassador reassurances to the effect that Italy has neither economic, political, nor territorial aims with respect to his country. The Ambassador was well satisfied with these statements. This was evident, notwithstanding his effort to hide his feelings.

Have made arrangements with Parenti so that the arrival of von Ribbentrop at Rome will be marked by particular solemnity. This is necessary in order to squelch the rumors appearing in foreign papers of the strong and clamorous opposition of the citizens of Milan to the policies of the Axis.

I receive Sir Percy Loraine, the new British Ambassador. Our conversation is purely conventional and hence is dull. However, Loraine made a good impression upon me. In my opinion he is a man who is naturally timid. He is very much concerned with the environment in which he is to carry on his mission. Rome, for a foreign diplomat, is a difficult post; but particularly is this true for an Englishman who finds himself in the ambiguous situation of an unpredictable friend, *amico incerto*. [An allusion to one of the characters in the comedies of Goldoni.] He must put on the appearance of formal friendship but in reality carry on political action which is hostile toward us. Lord Perth had adapted himself so as to fit in and interpret our point of view. Will Loraine do the same? That is possible.

May 4, 1939

I remained at home because I did not feel well. The Duce writes down some instructions for the conversation with Ribbentrop and sends me his notes. He emphasizes the necessity for a peaceful policy.

May 5, 1939

Many conversations, but none of any particular interest except one with the Japanese Ambassador. The final draft of the Tripartite Pact has been communicated to Arita in Tokyo. Ribbentrop is also dissatisfied with it. But the Ambassador tells me it is difficult to go any further, and that we are now near the breaking point.

A speech by Beck. It is hard to judge it on the basis of the short résumés of it in our possession. It does not seem aggressive or unyielding. But they are not satisfied in Berlin. The conversation with Ribbentrop will take place in Milan rather than Como. This is what the Duce wanted in order to refute the French rumor about a bloody anti-German demonstration in Milan. In the evening I leave for Milan.

May 6, 1939

Milan's welcome to von Ribbentrop dispels the legend which had been spread by the usual police informers that northern Italy was deeply anti-German. The Milanese population is very much flattered that the Lombard city had been chosen as the meeting place for an important event, and has shown considerable enthusiasm. I, myself, was surprised, not at the thing itself, but at the proportions of the demonstrations.

I have had stenographic notes taken of my conversations with von Ribbentrop.

Some comments: For the first time I have found my German colleague in a pleasantly calm state of mind. He did not, as usual, do a great deal of boasting. Rather, he has made himself the standard bearer of the policy of moderation and understanding. Naturally, he has said that within a few years we must go here, and take there, but the slowing down of the speed of German dynamism is a very significant symptom.

The alliance, or rather the immediate announcement of the alliance, was decided Saturday evening immediately after dinner at the Continental following a telephone call from the Duce. After the conversation I had reported to Mussolini the satisfactory consequences from our point of view.

May 7, 1939

Mussolini, when he has obtained something, has always asked for more; and he has asked me to make a public announcement of the bilateral pact which he has always preferred to the triangular alliance. Von Ribbentrop, who from the bottom of his heart has always preferred the inclusion of Japan in the pact, at first hesitated, but then yielded, pending Hitler's approval of the proposal.

The latter, when reached by telephone, gave his immediate approval, and has personally collaborated in drafting the agreement. When I informed the Duce on Sunday morning he expressed particular satisfaction.

Von Ribbentrop had a fair personal success, even in that useless and snobbish world of so-called society—indispensable when one must give a dinner. The men who accompanied von Ribbentrop are also liked by those with whom they come in contact. They are not the usual wooden and somewhat boring Germans; they are likable young men, who speak foreign languages well, and who, in a drawing room, are able to forget all their heel clicking when addressing a lady.

May 8, 1939

I returned to Rome. Starace is very happy over what I had to say to him on the state of mind of the Milanese. The Duce, too, is pleased by what has happened.

I received Christic, whom I told about the official meeting, and also Helfand, to whom I emphasized the fact that the pact as drafted has no anti-Russian character. I tried to facilitate the exchange of Russian prisoners held as hostages by Franco.

May 9, 1939

Review of troops in Via dell'Impero. The Albanians have for the first time paraded in Rome; I confess that this moved me. In the afternoon the sittings of the Roman Curia are resumed; the arrangements are entrusted to the Senate. My father protested against this, recalling that the Senate was the very body which opposed Caesar, and that Caesar was killed between those walls.

Conversation with von Brauchitsch. He, too, like all the Germans, is repeating the password of peace.

Conversation with Shiratori, who was very much impressed by our treaty of alliance with Berlin. I hope that Tokyo will wake up in time to join. I doubt it.

May 10, 1939

Paul of Yugoslavia arrives. The Duce, as always in such ceremonies when the subject of monarchy comes up, was critical, saying the monarchy was the sworn enemy of the regime. He is of the opinion that a manifesto would be enough to liquidate it. Someday he thinks he will do it.

At the Palazzo Venezia there is a meeting between the Duce, myself, and Marković. Nothing new in regard to the direct relations between Rome and Belgrade. The points settled at the meeting in Venice have all been confirmed. But a new factor is the definite position taken by Yugoslavia against Turkey and the proposal to form a Rumanian-Yugoslav-Bulgarian bloc for the purpose of opposing Turkey. In order to achieve this, an agreement between the Magyars and Rumanians is necessary. All this is quite interesting.

A conversation with Poncet at his request. He comes to tell me that the French Government is happy about the fact that we are still disposed to negotiate on the basis of Baudouin's proposals. But while exploring the matter he tried to save what he could in the usual French way, especially as regards Tunis. I immediately asked that he should not change the cards on us, as this would upset all prospects of success. And, very cleverly, he quickly drew in his oars. I cannot say if these deals will come to any conclusion, but I do know that François-Poncet has become a different person. His ideas on Italy and on the regime have become clearer, and perhaps he has also changed his ideas in general. He tells me that he now detests freedom of the press and that he is coming closer and closer to totalitarian ideas.

May 11, 1939

Naval review. During the sea trip I had a long conversation with the Regent, Paul. He is very much concerned about the threats of war, and I believe that only up to a certain point has he placed any faith in my assurances of peace. He tried to give me some explanations regarding Stoyadinovich. Quite apart from the weakening of the government, which had taken place during the time Stoyadinovich's group had had a parliamentary majority, the man had discredited himself by shady business speculations, carried on partly by him and partly by his satellites. It seems that he has been able to accumulate, especially in foreign countries, very considerable sums of money. Paul also hinted at the possibility of a lawsuit. I advised him against it, but would not swear that my words had any effect. The Duce, to whom I told these things, commented that this mania for wealth is a kind of disease. Otherwise it could not be explained, particularly because man's capacity to enjoy has a limit beyond which gold becomes an obstacle. Besides, as a kind of vengeance wreaked by fate, it is the richest men who can least enjoy their wealth; Rockefeller was obliged to live on milk and oranges during the last sixteen years of his life.

The King, on board ship, expressed his belief that Corsica must inevitably become Italian when the great crisis breaks out in Europe. The Duce, at the dinner at the Quirinal, spoke with some diplomats.

Nothing special except a warning to Greece because it had accepted the Franco-British guarantee. He used some harsh words even to Ruegger because of the attitude of the Swiss press.

May 12, 1939

This morning I found the Duce very nervous and concerned about the international situation. I believe that Daladier's speech, which was needlessly stubborn, has contributed to his state of mind. He told me that this speech renders worthless my conversations with Poncet and that therefore I should forget about them. On Yugoslavia he has also many reservations; as proof of the sincerity of their attitude he would like a definite gesture, such as their withdrawing from the League of Nations. I think this is premature, and also that we must take into account the difficulties which still exist in this country.

The Duce is also disturbed about Bulgaria; he instructed me to send a telegram to Talamo to sound out the real intentions of that government. The proper place of Bulgaria is in the Axis fold, but I believe that we must still make other efforts to convince that trembling king of this more than evident truth.

There was a bit of a storm in the intellectual spheres of Albania, which explains why twenty or so persons will immediately be sent to concentration camps. There must not be the least sign of weakness; justice and force must be the characteristics of the new regime. Public works are starting well. The roads are all planned in such a way as to lead to the Greek border. This plan was ordered by the Duce, who is thinking more and more of jumping on Greece at the first opportunity.

May 13, 1939

Departure for Florence with the Yugoslavs. While on the train the German scheme for the pact of alliance is handed to me. In general it is acceptable. We should, however, like to add a clause regarding frontiers, forever guaranteed, Lebensraum as concerns Italy, and the duration of the pact. I have never read such a pact; it contains some real dynamite.

Welcome in Florence was curtailed on account of a downpour which has lasted for hours and hours. I speak with Marković about the problem of Yugoslavia's remaining in Geneva. He still offers some resistance, but he realizes the advisability of deserting the mausoleum at Geneva. I believe he will end by accepting our advice.

May 14, 1939

Von Ribbentrop makes still another attempt to add to the signature of the alliance a tripartite pact with Japan. I offer no objections, although I am thoroughly skeptical of the possibility and also the usefulness of the matter.

The Duce makes a very fine speech at Turin. He is calm in his delivery but emphatic in the substance of his speech. He then calls me by telephone. We have our last discussion relative to the signing of the alliance. The Germans propose that I go to Berlin from the twenty-first to the twenty-fourth of May. I ask that the time be delayed or advanced. It does not seem to me that the twenty-fourth of May [the anniversary of Italy's entrance on the side of the Allies against the Central Powers in World War I] is the most appropriate date to sign such a formidable pact of military understanding with the Germans.

May 15, 1939

I return to Rome. The Yugoslav visit went well even though nothing new was decided. The Turkish threat is what particularly concerns Belgrade; we must take advantage of this psychological condition to pull the Yugoslavs more and more into the orbit of the Axis.

Useless conversation with the Belgian Ambassador.

Conversation with Wieniawa. He had asked to see me several days ago so that when he did meet me his request was no longer up to date. Beck had been informed by Valentino of our complete solidarity with the Germans in case of war. Wieniawa is pessimistic; he believes war is inevitable. Besides, he has no desire to remain in Rome under these conditions; he has asked to be recalled. After our official conversation was finished we spoke as friend to friend and I advised him to be very moderate. Whatever happens Poland will pay the price of the conflict. Because there are two alternatives: either the Axis wins and Germany will absorb Poland, or the Axis loses and Poland becomes a province of Bolshevist Russia. No Franco-British help is possible, at least in the beginning of the war; Poland would be soon reduced to a heap of rubble. Wieniawa admits that I am right on many points, but he has faith in the ultimate success which would give new power to

Poland. I fear that this illusion of his, unfortunately, is shared by too many of his countrymen.

I inform Villani about the conversations with the Yugoslavs. Especially of the idea of a four-party treaty against the Turks.

May 16, 1939

Nothing new.

May 17, 1939

The American Ambassador is very anxious to explain to me a conversation which the Duce had with him some days ago at the Quirinal. He is resentful, particularly because Mussolini said that America is in the hands of the Jews. He wanted to deny this, but used very weak arguments. He stressed one point, namely, that the American people, who originated in Europe, intend unanimously to concern themselves in European affairs, and it would be folly to think that they would remain aloof in the event of a conflict. I reported this to the Duce, who did not seem to be very much alarmed.

During the afternoon I received Alessandri, ex-President of Chile and a good friend of Italy. He has been defeated by a popular-front coalition, but he considers the Red regime to be ill-suited to his country, and foresees, he says with horror, that he will be recalled to power. Like all Americans he is anxious about the international situation, and is dreaming of a formula that may have the magic power to stifle all controversies.

Mussolini approves the definitive pact of alliance, and authorizes the bestowal of the Order of the Annunziata on von Ribbentrop. He says, too, that he is preparing an exchange of telegrams between the King and the Führer in order "to prevent the usual malicious interpretations that might be made by the French press."

May 18, 1939

Christic thanks me for the courtesies accorded to the Regent, Paul, and Marković, and asks for information regarding the Bulgarian attitude. I let him examine Talamo's telegram, which states that Bulgaria is ready to align itself with the Axis provided Yugoslavia does likewise and guarantees Bulgaria against Rumania. In Belgrade they are increasingly concerned over the enigmatic Turkish policy, and are trying to create a Slav bloc of an anti-Turkish character. This is what we also desire.

I see Irabo and he brings me an album of photographs of Ruthenia. Upon my asking him he affirms that Hungary is already in a position to beat Rumania. It only needs heavy artillery.

Guzzoni and Messe send excellent news about the situation in Albania. I come to the conclusion that we should effect the total absorption of the Albanian armed forces.

Carnelutti, sent by Matchek, wants information as to our conversations with and commitments to the Regent, Paul. Nothing is changed on our part, since Belgrade has made no formal commitment of adherence to the Axis. Then he informs me: (1) Matchek no longer intends to come to any agreement with Belgrade; (2) he will continue his separatist movement; (3) he asks for a loan of 20,000,000 dinars; (4) within six months, at our request, he will be ready to start an uprising. I make an appointment with him following my return from Germany, in order to continue our negotiations.

May 19, 1939

Nothing particularly important.

May 20, 1939

Departure for Berlin. During my trip I speak with Mastromattei, the prefect of Bolzano, to whom I show the text of the treaty. He states that the preamble with its definitive recognition of frontiers will strike a great blow at the Irredentism of the Alto Adige.

May 21, 1939

I arrive in Berlin. There are great demonstrations, clearly spontaneous in their warmth. My first discussion with Ribbentrop. Nothing has changed in regard to what was said and decided upon in Milan. He repeats Germany's interest in and intention to insure for itself a long period of peace—at least three years. He dwells on the desirability of binding Japan to our system. He maintains that Russia is too weak to give much help to the Western democracies even if she should take her stand with them. He speaks also of the Turkish situation. He has been influenced by the suggestions of the superficial von Papen and so he believes that the Turkish attitude has been determined by fear of Italy. I proved to him with original Turkish documents, intercepted by our secret service, that Turkish hostility is also directed against Germany. Finally, I talked to him about Yugoslavia. I tell him that our conversations in Rome have not been really satisfactory, even if they appear to be so. I declare that we shall not take the initiative in anti-Yugoslav movements, until Belgrade adopts a correct policy toward the Axis, but that we shall immediately revise our stand if Belgrade tends toward the democracies.

May 22, 1939 [continuation of May 21]

I go on to say that an internal revolt in Croatia would not leave us indifferent. Ribbentrop approves, but I can see that he really prefers to maintain the Yugoslav *status quo*. Himmler, on the other hand, tells me definitely that we must hurry and establish our protectorate over Croatia.

We repeat more or less the same discussion with the Führer. He states that he is very well satisfied with the pact and confirms the fact that Mediterranean policy will be directed by Italy. He takes an interest in Albania and is enthusiastic about our program for making of Albania a stronghold which will inexorably dominate the Balkans.

I found Hitler very well, quite serene, less aggressive. A little older. His eyes are more deeply wrinkled. He sleeps very little. Always less. And he spends a great part of the night surrounded by collaborators and friends. Frau Goebbels, who is a constant member of these gatherings and who feels quite honored by them, was describing them to me without being able to conceal a vague feeling of boredom on account of their monotony. It is always Hitler who talks! He can be Führer as much as he likes, but he always repeats himself and bores his guests. For the first time I hear hints, in the inner circles, of the Führer's tender feelings for a beautiful girl.

May 23, 1939 [continuation of May 22]

She is twenty years old with beautiful quiet eyes, regular features, and a magnificent body. Her name is Sigrid von Lappus. They see each other frequently and intimately.

The ceremony for the signature of the pact was very solemn and the Führer was sincerely moved.

Goering, whose standing is always very high, but no longer in the ascendency, had tears in his eyes when he saw the collar of the Annunziata around the neck of Ribbentrop.

Von Mackensen told me that Goering had made a scene, complaining that the collar really belonged to him, since he was the true and only promoter of the alliance. I promised Mackensen that I would try to get Goering a collar.

Himmler talked at length about relations with the Church. They like the new Pope and believe that a *modus vivendi* is possible. I encouraged him along these lines, saying that an agreement between the Reich and the Vatican would make the Axis more popular.

Ribbentrop is making a name for himself. In speaking to Signora Attolico, Hitler said: "Whatever has been said about him, it must be admitted that this man has a swelled head."

May 24, 1939

Return to Rome.

At the station all the high Fascist officials and a considerable crowd welcome me on my arrival with warm demonstrations. However, it is clear to me that the pact is better liked in Germany than in Italy. Here we are convinced of its usefulness and hence accept it as a matter of course. The Germans, on the other hand, put into it a warmth of feeling which we lack. We must recognize that hatred for France has not yet been successful in arousing love for Germany.

At the station Anfuso hands me a telegram from the King. I learn afterward from the Duce that he had thought of conferring upon me the title of marquis, but that he had been very wisely advised against it by the Duce himself. He considered that it would not be helpful to me because of the disapproval it would arouse in the great Fascist masses. The Duce had suggested the sending of the telegram to greet me.

I reported to Mussolini on the details and impressions of my trip to Germany. I find him quite satisfied, and, what is most unusual, he repeatedly expressed his satisfaction. Then he went on to speak of Yugoslavia. He was more than ever distrustful of it, and he authorized me to strengthen Matchek's movement by timely financial aid.

May 25, 1939

I thank the King for the telegram. He answers: "From 1900 to the present time I have never sent a telegram to a Minister. I believed that it would be worth while to break a tradition in order to express my own deep feelings." He then quickly made a jibe at the Germans: "The Germans as long as they have need of us will be courteous, and even servile, but at the first opportunity they will reveal themselves as the great rascals they really are." He recalls certain bitter contacts that he had with them on the occasion of one of his trips in 1893, and he does not think that things have changed since that time.

A long conference with the Duce. He harps increasingly on the anti-Yugoslav, anti-Greek note. We decide to close the Albanian Ministry for Foreign Affairs and to remove foreign diplomats from Tirana. He is thinking also of denouncing the London pact in consequence of the Anglo-Turkish accord. He will bring it up for the first time next Saturday in the presence of Percy Loraine on the occasion of his presentation. The King has made a strange prophecy with unusual confidence: "The day will come," he said, "in which Italy and Germany will come to an agreement with England. Then peace and progress will really be assured." There is no doubt that the King is anti-German, but it is likewise certain that he detests and scorns the French with profound conviction.

The Duce attacks the monarchy and says: "I envy Hitler, who need not drag along with him so many empty baggage cars."

May 26, 1939

A meeting with Carnelutti, who has just returned from Zagreb. He confirms Matchek's full decision to turn down every agreement with Belgrade and to refuse to prepare the rebellion. We agreed and embodied in a memorandum the following points: (1) Italy will finance Matchek's Croat revolt with twenty million dinars; (2) he undertakes to prepare the revolution within four to six months; (3) he will quickly call in the Italian troops to insure order and peace; (4) Croatia will proclaim itself an independent state in confederation with Rome. It will have its own government but its ministries for foreign affairs and of national defense will be in common with Italy; (5) Italy will be permitted to keep armed forces in Croatia and will also keep there a lieutenant general as in Albania; (6) after some time we shall decide on possibilities for union under a single head.

The Duce read the report and approved. He desires, however, that Matchek countersign it. In the meantime, I have sent it to Zagreb by safe means. In the coming week we shall begin our payments via Zurich [the twenty million dinars to finance the revolution].

Mussolini is taken up with the idea of breaking Yugoslavia to pieces and of annexing the kingdom of Croatia. He thinks the undertaking is sufficiently easy, and, as things stand, I agree with him. Meanwhile, I am thinking of better organizing the Albanians of Kossovo, who could be turned into a dagger pointed at the side of Belgrade.

May 27, 1939

This is a crucial day in our relations with Great Britain. The Duce received Percy Loraine for his formal presentation; but soon the visit assumed an entirely different character. The Duce, who ordinarily is courteous and engaging, was very stern; his face became absolutely impenetrable; it looked like the face of an Oriental god sculptured in stone. He began by asserting that in view of the manifest British policy of encirclement it was necessary to ask, as he now was asking, whether the agreement of April 16 had any tangible value left. Percy Loraine was not expecting this blow; he blushed and struggled for words, then he composed himself quite well. He asked if, while reserving the right to call for instructions from his own government, he could not at this time expound his own personal views. Then he began to argue with a certain professional ability. His strongest argument was the one which had to do with the attitude maintained by the British during the Albanian crisis. There is no question that the status quo of the Mediterranean had been changed by us; yet Chamberlain had assumed the responsibility of confirming the value of the pact. The Duce countered harshly in an argumentative tone. He declared that British politics were leading the whole of Europe into war. Through her guarantees to the small powers, Great Britain had brought about a very dangerous aggravation of the situation.

May 28, 1939 [continuation of May 27]

Agreement between the Germans and the Poles could have been reached if the British had not interfered. At this point Loraine reacted

more strongly; for a moment I had the impression that he was about
to get up and ask permission to leave. He controlled himself with difficulty, but emphasized his regret that Mussolini's point of view was so
far removed from that of the British. Mussolini answered that time
will prove who is right. The Duce made a brief and cutting comment
on the Anglo-Russian alliance, and then the conversation was brusquely
ended. During the course of the long walk between the table and the
door, Loraine sought for some human contact with the Duce. But it
was impossible. He walked slowly and gravely, with his eyes on the
floor and his mind elsewhere. His leave-taking was icy.

Mussolini then told me that he had meditated long and that he
thought the moment had arrived to make all positions clear. He handed
me a memorandum, which I am to give to Hitler on my meeting with
him, which he had written regarding the necessity for immediate Axis
occupation of Central Europe and the Balkans in case of war.

The Master of Ceremonies, who knows nothing of these conversations, and who accompanied the British Ambassador home, said:
"Loraine, on his return, was red and congested and he was bothered
by a nervous tic. He looked like a man who had received a slap in the
face. He talked to himself all the time."

Let us see what will happen now. In my opinion the British-Italian
agreement is dead and maybe Chamberlain will die with it.

May 29, 1939

A long conversation with the Minister from Bulgaria. Naturally the
attitude of his country was the principal subject of our talks. I maintained that the geographic and political situation of Bulgaria as well
as her best interests require that she come with the Axis. It may be
possible for Yugoslavia to remain neutral, but for Bulgaria, surrounded
by enemies, such a possibility is excluded. The Minister, who was in
morning dress, seemed to share my point of view. He said, however,
that from the military point of view Bulgaria is as yet unprepared. I
did not fail to reply that if Bulgaria adopts a well-defined policy, it
will be to the interest of Italy and Germany to make up for her deficiencies. I informed Talamo of the conversation and authorized him
to speak along these lines with the leaders in Sofia. I attributed the
greatest importance to the Bulgarian paper [sic].

Christic informed me that Yugoslavia has asked Turkey to declare that the Anglo-Turkish pact has no effect in the Balkans. The distrust between Belgrade and Ankara becomes more accentuated.

Cavallero has been nominated vice-president of the Italo-German mixed commission, as prescribed in the treaty. I shall leave Wednesday for Berlin as bearer of a note written by the Duce.

I made certain general provisions for Albania, among them the more important are the unifying of the armed forces and suppression of the Ministry for Foreign Affairs.

May 30, 1939

The Senate approves by acclamation the budget of the Ministry for Foreign Affairs. I received François-Poncet. He has nothing important to tell me and brings up only a few trifling routine matters, but he is trying to see the lay of the land and find out our reaction. He does not speak about continuing negotiations nor do I. We are in agreement in thinking that it is preferable to wait until the situation develops. I criticize the policy of encirclement; he answers that it is a simple, defensive action on the part of those who fear further aggressive ventures by the Axis. In his opinion, the fifteenth of March, the date on which Hitler tore up the Munich protocol, furnished the key to the new situation. He is quite pessimistic, but does not exclude the possibility of maintaining for a long time in Europe a peace based upon the balance of power. The first experiment lasted for some time— from 1871 to 1914. He alludes to the fact that Mussolini has refused to go on with the exchange of a fragment of the Ara Pacis now in Paris and deduces from this that his mind is extremely embittered against France.

I give to von Mackensen some documents furnished us by our secret service which prove that the Anglo-Turkish accord is a genuine offensive alliance against the Axis, and I give him information on the heated conference between Loraine and the Duce in the Palazzo Venezia.

May 31, 1939

Mussolini listens to my account of the meeting with Poncet with little interest. He says: "Had I accepted the fragment of the Ara Pacis the whole French press would have said that I would have to be satisfied with a few stones instead of Tunisia and Corsica." For the moment he has no intention of moderating relations with France. He would like, instead, to obtain from Switzerland three hundred millions in order to avoid revealing the decrease of our treasury reserves, which have come down to three billions. In the present political situation I am of the opinion that it would be difficult to get money from Berne.

The Duce sets down some directives in principle: (1) to get Hungary and Spain into the military alliance; (2) facilitate the entrance of Japan into the Pact of Steel; (3) make definite Bulgaria's position in favor of the Axis; (4) obtain a definite clarification of the Yugoslav attitude. In this connection it is necessary to note that Matchek has refused to sign the Carnelutti Report, saying that he has resumed negotiations with Belgrade and that he still wishes to clarify some points in the future relations between Rome and Croatia. This I have from Carnelutti. According to Bombelles, the refusal was much more categorical because Matchek has made other commitments and because he is a democrat and avoids any deep understandings with Fascism. The Duce, to whom I show Carnelutti's letter, is of the opinion that we must wait for the results of Prince Paul's visit to Berlin. He also believes that some concessions can be made on the future state of Croatia, contenting ourselves with having a common ministry for foreign affairs and the control of the Army.

June 1, 1939

Our Legionaries [the men who served in Spain] are displeased at the fact that the Duce will not review them. But he does not intend to change his decision: he will not come to Naples because the King is there; and he wants only a delegation to come to Rome. He will issue an order of the day. I am thinking of an assembly of the legions in September; it might be the occasion for a review.

The Ambassador [the Spanish Ambassador] comes to me for one of his pointless conversations. The conversation drifts to the monarchy [the Spanish monarchy]. I do not conceal our point of view from him, and am increasingly convinced that he is flirting with don Juan and is turning his smiles upon the English. I shall ask Serrano Suñer for his head.

I see Loraine for the first time since the conference at the Palazzo Venezia. He says that he will go to London soon and asks if there is anything to add to what the Duce said. Nothing so far as I am concerned. But we speak again of the situation, and he does not conceal the fact that the Anglo-Turkish pact is the direct result of our occupation of Albania. Hence it is that the confidence, which was the very basis for the pact of the sixteenth of April, has come to be questioned. We agree that for the moment there is nothing to be done; he repeats more or less what François-Poncet had said about the dangers of the present situation, which might crystallize into a situation of equilibrium between the two blocs.

June 2, 1939

I received at the station the Albanians, who come to receive the text of their constitution to be, that is to unify the armed forces and abolish their ministry for foreign affairs. As rewards, we shall give them certain compensations of a personal nature, such as nominations to the Senate, ambassadorial titles, et cetera. I must say that probably for the first time since the annexation they were visibly satisfied. Which goes to show that personal benefits will frequently silence even the most noble feelings. . . .

After the signature with Argentina, Guarneri relieved himself of some very pessimistic talk on the exchange situation. Our reserves are now reduced to three thousand two hundred millions [three billions two hundred millions]. Five hundred more will be necessary to carry through to the end of the year. Guarneri speaks openly of bankruptcy and says that it can be avoided only by bringing imperialistic policies to an end.

The Duce said today that Guarneri's talk is just one of the usual "exhalations" which expresses exactly the state of mind and the wishes of certain plutocratic circles. In any case, it made no great impression on him, since, after all, he has been listening to Guarneri's false prophecies for six whole years and they all fail to materialize with perfect punctuality, as democratic prophecies always do. I myself believe, however, that the truth is somewhere in between.

June 3, 1939

Ceremony at the court for the delivery of the constitution to the Albanians. The King asks who drafted the document and observes in a sarcastic tone that there is no heraldic symbol of the dynasty on the Albanian flag. I answer that this is not quite so, because it does have the blue Savoyard sash and the crown of Scanderbeg. This convinces him, but he remains in bad humor. I report this to the Duce, who seizes the occasion to lower his horns and charge the monarchy. Starace is also present. The Duce declares that he is sick and tired of dragging behind him "empty baggage cars, which, moreover, very often have their brakes on," that the King "is a small man, grumpy and untrustworthy, who at this time is concerned with embroidery on the flag and does not sense the pride which comes from seeing his national territory increased by thirty thousand square kilometers," and that, in conclusion, "it is the monarchy which, by its idiotic gassing, prevents the 'Fascistification' of the Army. The mediating agency for this 'gassing' is that disgusting Asinari de Bernezzo."

The Duce said, "I am like a cat, cautious and prudent, but when I jump I am sure of landing where I wish. I am now considering whether we ought to end it all with the House of Savoy. In order to liquidate it it is enough to mobilize two hundred and fifty thousand men in the two provinces, Forlì and Ravenna [the most revolutionary section of Italy]. Perhaps the posting of a manifesto will be enough." He spoke with such directness that Starace interpreted the words of Mussolini as marching orders for party action.

In the afternoon I settled the problem of the co-ordination of Albanian diplomatic services with the Italian services. A few decorations and a few jobs were enough to accomplish this.

The operation to emasculate Albania without making the patient scream—the annexation—is now practically realized. As I have already noted, for the first time the Albanians are not somber. Such is the advantage of cold-blooded and calculated decisions. The Duce and I have brought up the problem of the Irredentism of Kossovo and of Ciamuria. The Duce defines this Irredentism: "The little light in the tunnel." That is, the ideal spiritual motive that we must stimulate in the future to keep the Albanian national spirit high and united.

June 4, 1939

Nothing new.

June 5, 1939

Departure from Naples.

Serrano Suñer arrives with the Duke of Aosta. At the same time there arrives on the *Sardegna* the first contingent of the Arrow Division which had come to accompany their Fascist comrades who are being brought home. Considerable excitement; the Legionaries sing hymns of war; cannon and sirens fill the clear and sunny air. Serrano Suñer clasps my hands for a long time and repeats words of gratitude for what Italy has done and her way of doing it. I embrace Gambara; through him I clasp to my breast every one of those who return and every one of those who remain in Spain, the guardians of a friendship and performers of a task which will produce glorious results.

I have a long conference with Serrano Suñer while we are driving through the panoramic streets of Naples. He is a slender, sickly man— one of those creatures notable for study and reflection; a very conscientious man, honest and full of enthusiasm. Having been caught in the whirlpool of the revolution, he has become both actor and author, and brings to his task a passionate faith. Intelligent, but still somewhat inexperienced, he wavers in his judgment between the results of the practical knowledge he has acquired and the vague and metaphysical expressions of his reflections. But it is always feeling that dominates him: he hates and loves impetuously.

June 6, 1939 [continuation of June 5]

His *bête noire* is France. He said that he hates her in the first place because his two brothers were killed by French bullets, and also because he is Spanish, and for this reason considers France the eternal enemy of Greater Spain.

We touch on many points: *war*. Spain fears a war in the near future because she is today at the end of her resources. In certain regions there is famine. If she can have two or preferably three years' time, she can reconstitute herself and complete her military preparations. Spain will be at the side of the Axis because she will be guided by feeling and by reason. A neutral Spain would, in any event, be destined to a future of poverty and humiliation. Furthermore, Franco's Spain intends to solve the problem of Gibraltar; as long as the British flag flies on Gibraltar, Spain will not be a completely free and sovereign nation. The youth of Spain lives in the desire and hope of pushing the English into the sea, and is getting ready to do so. Spain also has accounts to square with France, that "dishonest and dishonorable France," and these accounts are called Morocco and political and economic independence.

Serrano Suñer was very happy to learn that we and the Germans also wish to postpone the conflict for some years.

June 7, 1939 [*continuation of June 6*]

Relations with Italy. The alliance is a fact in our minds; it would be premature, for the moment, to put it in a protocol. But it is the latter that he wishes. We spoke more pointedly with regard to Germany, especially, of the religious question. He is a believer, a convinced and fervent believer. The anti-Catholic excesses of the Germans offend his sensibilities.

Portugal. He considers it to be fundamental to Spanish policy and to the Axis to take Portugal out of the sphere of British influence. Difficult as this may be, he intends to exert his effort in this direction, and asks for our collaboration.

Monarchy. Perhaps "within twenty years Spain may have need of a king." Then if the Bourbons have behaved well, they can be put back on the throne, but not for the time being. The head of the state is Franco, and the necessity for a monarchy is felt in only a few quarters. Many who shout "long live the King" try to hide their opposition to the regime by this cry. Against these people Franco will act with the harshest energy.

These are more or less the statements which Serrano Suñer repeated to the Duce in the long conference which took place in the Palazzo Venezia. The Duce has reaffirmed his determined hostility to the restoration of the monarchy "which would become a center for opportunism and intrigue."

June 8, 1939

Percy Loraine communicates London's answer to the Duce's query. Chamberlain considers the pact of the sixteenth of April in full force and hopes that it might have further possibilities of development. I do not know whether such an answer will please the Duce, who is rarely satisfied with mere words and wants action, "extreme action," as he says, "for the time being the situation is negative; the Anglo-Turkish pact, the guarantees given to Greece and Rumania, the negotiations with Moscow, are elements of that policy of encirclement which London is directing against us."

I received from Hong Kong a document of the highest interest: it is a study made by Admiral Noble on British naval possibilities against the forces of the triangle. It is couched in pessimistic terms, especially as regards the Mediterranean dominated in his opinion by the aerial, naval, and undersea forces of Fascist Italy.

June 9, 1939

During the evening I have long conferences with Serrano Suñer. He is violent against Ambassador Conde, whom he calls an imbecile, and relates that Conde had even attempted to warn him against the Duce and myself. The fact is that Conde, who is really a big fool, is extraordinarily attached to the monarchy and traffics with the King and the princes for the restoration. He has served his time, and it is well that he should have a change of air. Suñer agrees, and will have him removed. Suñer also speaks to me disparagingly of General Jordana, as well as of all the Spanish diplomatic corps. He does not care to be made head of the government. He says that this is a French maneuver designed to disturb his good relations with Franco, but he would like to take the place of General Jordana. Evidently he is counting on our support and for this reason he would like to hasten the coming of Franco to Italy. He was somewhat prejudiced against the Axis. The words of Mussolini have dispelled his misgivings and he desires to establish contacts with the Nazis about whom he had been somewhat doubtful before. His Catholic faith and the propaganda of some hostile elements had succeeded in rousing in him the belief that Hitler's position had been shaky.

June 10, 1939

I report to the Duce on what Suñer had said to me. The Duce also would like to see him as head of the Foreign Ministry, even while holding on to the Ministry of Internal Affairs, for which, in the opinion of the Duce, his "fifteen years' experience constitute his best asset for leadership." I shall write a letter to Franco, which I will deliver personally on the occasion of my trip.

Naval review; very beautiful. It appears that the King of Italy has praised the Roman step, even recalling certain historical episodes which prove its high ethical value. The Duce's comment was: "I wanted to answer him: 'My dear, solemn idiot, it was precisely against you that I had to argue most in order to introduce it.' "

I handed to the Japanese Ambassador a copy of the Noble document. I translate a portion of it, and I can see that it is very impressive.

The Ambassador leaves tonight for Berlin, where new and it would seem better instructions have arrived for the conclusion of the Tripartite Pact.

I gave Mackensen the document and other telegrams which prove Yugoslav wavering. Mackensen was irritated by Serrano Suñer because he did not mention the Germans in his speech. In Suñer's defense I explained this by saying that he had little diplomatic experience, and I affirmed that Suñer represents in Spain the man who has the confidence of the Axis. I suggest the idea of a trip to Germany.

June 11, 1939

Nothing new.

June 12, 1939

The Duce speaks of De Vecchi and says that for eighteen years he has had to bear on his shoulders the embarrassing weight of this individual. "On the twenty-eighth of October 1922 [the date of the March on Rome] he was already willing to betray us to obtain a portfolio of some sort in the new cabinet to be formed by a coalition of different parties." After this statement he recalled, one after another, the blunders which De Vecchi had made in every one of the positions he had occupied. He aroused the wrath of God by threatening to take away the pensions of the war wounded, then made a speech that was a real shock to the regime. Then in Africa he did his best to occupy by force territories that already belonged to us and carried out a cruel and useless slaughter. In conclusion, he thinks that he is an "overbold clown," but he gives him everything he asks for. He has had two of his sons-in-law made barons. (Mussolini laughs about it, and will end by giving him the high military rank to which he aspires.)

A second conference at the Palazzo Venezia with Serrano Suñer. Nothing new. The Duce advises Franco to make the third of January a day memorable in the annals of Spain by freeing himself as soon as possible from all the elements that are not faithful to the revolution. Serrano Suñer says that he has spoken to the King and to the Prince of the Asturias. He had a good impression of the latter. Of the first he speaks ill; the King is an unreliable, domineering man. The Duce suggested bettering relations between France and Spain in the near future, which made Serrano Suñer indignant.

June 13, 1939

New tensions on account of the question of Danzig. As a matter of fact our military attaché in Paris should have given us warning of this two days ago. This leads one to suspect that the Poles planned some action in Danzig. The Duce receives von Mackensen, who brings a gift from Goebbels. He talks chiefly about the desirability of better relations between Germany and the Church for the purpose of strengthening ties with Spain. He reviews what he has done in Italy and arrives at the conclusion that when the interests of the state conflict with those of the Church the state should go ahead and take care of its own business. The Pope, he thinks, can go ahead and protest, if only "to save his own soul and maybe also mine."

We have decided on the construction of Pater Village in Tirana and also of five thousand buildings to house Italians returning from abroad. In this way we shall succeed in increasing the number of Italians living in Tirana. In Tirana the news is that everything is going well, both from the political and the military and economic points of view.

Serrano Suñer, on his farewell call, asks me to have the secret police keep an eye on the Spanish General of Aviation, Kindelan, during his visit in Rome. He accuses him of plotting for the monarchy and expects to have proof of this in his hands in order to denounce him to Franco.

The Duce calls me in to talk to me about Franco's visit. He is very much annoyed by the inevitable interference of the King [of Italy], since Franco is the head of the state. Says the Duce: "This time I don't want any meddling as there was with Hitler's visit. If the King doesn't have sense enough to withdraw, I will. It is necessary to put this paradoxical situation before the Italian people so that they may finally understand that there are certain incompatibilities, and may choose between me and the King as to who is going to be the head of the government."

June 14, 1939

Serrano Suñer leaves. He is visibly moved and repeats words of gratitude for me and for the Duce, as well as his love for Italy. He treats Conde coldly. Conde is scheduled to be torpedoed soon. Serrano Suñer told me that this idiotic individual had tried to influence him against the Duce and me, since he believes that we are opposed to the restoration of the monarchy. Relations between Serrano and Mackensen are now better, in fact, they are good. However, my intervention was necessary, because Suñer opposed the Germans, and von Mackensen was offended by his not too casual forgetfulness of the German contribution to the national cause of Spain.

The Duce desires that we begin to define with Spain the future program for the western Mediterranean: Morocco would go completely to Spain; Tunisia and Algeria would go to us. An agreement with Spain should insure our permanent outlet to the Atlantic Ocean through Morocco.

Dinner at the French Embassy, a useless, colorless, second-rate dinner, in the traditional diplomatic manner with the usual "dear colleagues" charged with uncertain and presumptuous undertakings and with old court dames whose only business is to gorge themselves with free food. We practically do not speak about politics. Still, the French press makes a big fuss over the event which, I repeat, represents nothing, absolutely nothing, and leaves our relations with France as before —even worse than before.

June 15, 1939

I go to Genoa. The fliers return from Spain.

Genoa, unexpectedly monarchical, gives the King such warm demonstrations as to lead me to reflect on many things.

I mention this to Starace.

June 16, 1939

I return to Rome. Nothing sensational.

June 17, 1939

During my absence a regrettable incident occurred in connection with an athletic parade of Nazis in Bolzano in which the secretary of the group was arrested. Von Mackensen speaks to me about it. I immediately take steps to get the secretary of the group out of jail, and the Duce gives his authorization to do so. They acted too impetuously. If I had been present things would have gone differently. What impression will be made abroad by the arrest in Italy of a Nazi official? And how about the impression in Germany itself? What would we say if they arrested our secretary of the Fascist party in Berlin or in Munich?

I receive Sthyka, ex-Minister of Albania to Belgrade. I intend to use him in connection with the Kossovo problem, concerning which he is very competent. I shall create at the undersecretariat for Albania an office for irredentisms.

Bottoni and Benini just arrived from Tirana, bringing excellent news on the Albanian situation.

The Duce has gone to Riccione for a short rest.

June 18, 1939

Nothing new.

June 19, 1939

Nothing new.

June 20, 1939

Hitler asks that the head of the Nazi group at Bolzano be sent to Germany because he intends to punish him in an exemplary way. It is an elegant gesture, for it is equivalent to proving publicly the importance which he attributes to Italian friendship.

Conference with Talamo. He says that Bulgaria continues in its uncertain attitude and that at least for the time being he does not have much hope of having it take a clear-cut position at the side of the Axis.

June 21, 1939

The functionaries of the commission for the repatriation of Germans residing in the Alto Adige leave for Berlin. There has been some uncertainty on the part of the Duce upon the advisability of sending Mastromattei; people might criticize the fact that a prefect is sent to Berlin on a diplomatic mission. But this is not quite the case; he is an expert who is going as a member of a commission. On the other hand, it seems that the Germans mean business. We must not, therefore, do anything that might put spokes in the wheel.

June 22, 1939

At Buffarini's office I lend support to the Slovenes' request for permission to publish some small non-political newspapers in their own language. If we really want to carry out a policy that will attract the Croats, Slovenes, and so forth, it is necessary to begin by giving them the feeling that we are showing them an intelligent liberality. We shall think later on of tightening the reins. As for the rest, there is nothing new.

June 23, 1939

I receive a letter from Serrano Suñer in which he invites me to go to Spain between the tenth and eighteenth of July. It is very courteously worded but appears to me to contain a certain amount of reserve. This may be due to the fact pointed out by Gambara; namely, that there is some rift between Serrano Suñer and Franco. We shall see. I should like to find out many things in Spain, and I should not like to have Serrano, even though it be in the best of faith, go too far in his predictions of total adherence to the Axis.

From Berlin they telephone that the first meeting on the Alto Adige has given concrete results and that the prospects are very encouraging.

June 24, 1939

Nothing new.

June 25, 1939

Nothing new.

June 26, 1939

Now that solitude has settled around me as well as within me, I wish, dear Father, to be in your company for a while in this great hall of Palazzo Chigi, where so often you came to support me with your trusting and farseeing optimism.

The cruel news of your death struck me suddenly like a treacherous

blow. We had seen each other only a few days before, on Wednesday
or Friday in your office. I found you in your office in what I thought
was good physical form. You spoke with your usual vivacity and you
were expounding to me plans and projects which you intended to carry
out in the space of a few years. You did not hesitate to plan ahead, for
you were now sure that your iron will had prevailed over the ailment
which, two years ago, had almost prevailed over you. And you gave
yourself sincerely, working without ever asking anything for yourself;
thus the ailment struck you down stealthily.

I returned home Monday evening, after having passed some hours
in the home of friends. I had no presentiment of the loss that would
befall me, but I was sad and a bit tired.

June 27, 1939 [*continuation of June 26*]

I went to bed at about one o'clock, or even before. I found that,
contrary to his usual habit, my servant was waiting for me to say that
they had telephoned from the Ministry for Foreign Affairs. This surprised me. A night telephone call, which at the time of Spain and
Albania was a common thing, appeared to me, in view of the present
conditions of European politics, somewhat unjustified. I learned quickly
that they were calling me from Ponte a Moriano because you were not
well. I had a foreboding of the truth, but I cast the thought away from
me with angry violence. I called Ponte a Moriano. A servant with a
sad voice answered me and gave the receiver to my mother, who,
between sobs, said at once that you, Father, our good, great, dear
father, were no more. It was a great blow. This is not a common, ordinary word which I now repeat: it was a great blow to me, physically
and mentally. I felt that something was torn away from my physical
being. Only at that moment, after thirty-six years of life, did I come to
realize how real and deep and indestructible are ties of blood. You,
Father, who have known from my infancy my admiring love for you,
you alone can thoroughly understand my sorrow.

June 28, 1939 [*continuation of June 27*]

Do you recall, when I was a child at Spezia, how I bade you good-by
every time you left the terrace of our house, which faced the sea? I was
unable to speak and my eyes filled with tears, but I restrained myself

as long as you were present, because I did not want to show my weakness to a grown-up. But my efforts were useless, and you knew very well that as soon as you had disappeared around the corner of Via dei Colli and del Torretto I would have collapsed to the ground, overcome by tears and solitude. Well, Father, the same thing has happened again. I have been overwhelmed by an unreasonable sorrow just as I was at that time, with the difference that I, no longer the child dressed as a sailor, proud of the ribbon which I wore with the name of your ship, but a man with many gray hairs, with a heavy burden of responsibility, of thoughts and worries, with my secret sadness, which I have hidden even from you—I am a man, in short, who is not cured of his wounds in one hour, but who carries them with him forever from now on.

I rushed to Ponte a Moriano in a car, all alone. Alone, not because some of my friends who had been informed by me had abandoned me, but because I wanted to remain with you and every other person would have been an obstacle to this, our first ultra-terrestrial communion.

June 29, 1939 [continuation of June 28]

My trip from Rome to Ponte a Moriano was long and terrible, but when dawn came, I do not know why, there arose in me a hope that perhaps I had misunderstood, and that your end had not come. I do not know, I cannot succeed in explaining the strange temptation that came to me which, however, lasted only a short time. Passing through Leghorn, in front of the telegraph office which you so carefully planned and which you loved so much, I saw the flag at half mast. For the first time, during the entire night, I wept.

Mother, overcome with a grief that only fifty years of a faithful and devoted love can explain, received me with despondent tenderness and led me to the room where you were lying calmly on the bed, wearing the gray suit in which death had overtaken you a few hours before. I should have said that you were sleeping were it not for a small crucifix that had been piously placed upon your great heroic breast. Mother had the strength to tell me, in all its details, your tragedy and her own. The illness that overcame you when you left Leghorn, your will power in attempting to dissimulate your ailment, the incessant alternation of slight improvements and more serious attacks, the useless search for help in the deserted and impassable countryside, all this Mother told me.

June 30, 1939 [*continuation of June 29*]

And she told me that, arriving home, your home in Ponte a Moriano, which you loved so well and where you played with my children for your joy and mine, and where even on that night little Marzio slept in blessed ignorance of what was happening, you insisted on getting out of the car without help, and, realizing that even an old fighter like you could not prevail in the matter, you put your arms around the doctor, saying calmly, "After all, the end has come," and breathed your last. You died as a soldier, as a Fascist, as a Christian.

Father mine, I do not speak to you about myself. You know, and you understand that any words of mine would be an offense to our great love as well as to my own sorrow. I shall tell you about the others instead. You were and you are very much beloved. More than anybody can believe. Your friends Rodinis, Baiocchi, Caparma, and many others were affected by your passing as animals wounded to death and seeking only to die in solitude. Starace arrived just a little after me and was terribly grieved. With his own hands he chose to place on your bed, to the right and to the left of your mortal remains, the party's insignia which you have honored so much by your work and by your faith.

Then, very shortly, the King arrived. He could not control his emotion. He spoke about you in generous terms. He greeted you with the Roman salute and his eyes filled with tears. Since he had arrived without any ceremony, in the company of only an aide in civilian dress, he laid aside all formality of his royal rank, and one could see in him only a poor old man burdened with sorrow, who wanted to weep over the coffin of a lost friend. On the stairs the King, who was going out, met the Duce, just arriving by air from Forlì. Your Chief, whom you loved so much and to whom you were always faithful, really loved you as you wanted him to love you and as on many an occasion you knew he loved you and wished that he would put it into words. But to put his love into words is not in his hard nature. He spoke it to you, however, after you were dead. He stayed long, looking at you with steady eyes and contracted face. Then he caressed you tenderly on head and shoulders, and twice he kissed you on the forehead. He repeated that with the death of Arnaldo [Mussolini's brother], your end was for him the hardest blow. He left after two hours, only to return the following day to pay you final homage in Leghorn.

What a strange and painful thing, Father, that I who have always obeyed you should now have the sad duty to carry out final preparations.

July 1, 1939 [continuation of June 30]

Still it was necessary to go through with it, and so I gave orders that they dress you in the uniform of an admiral with the decorations of the party and of the Fascist armed forces, and that the temporary burial take place at the cemetery of the Purificazione near your dear ones, and that the final burial be prepared at Montenero. The final burial must not take place in Famedio where the other great Livornese rest. You are the glory not only of a city, you belong to Imperial Italy. Your monument will rise from the top of the hill. It will be a monument that will recall your war [1915–18] and your heroism. On top of it will be a beacon which will be lit every night so that we may all be reminded from a distance of your immortal spirit. I say from a distance, because it will be seen even from that Corsica which encircles our savage Livornian Sea and in whose freedom you have always believed.

Late in the afternoon we carried you to Leghorn, and seeing you borne away forever from your home at the Ponte a Moriano was for me another blow. I followed you in the first car and beside me was Starace who, I repeat, has been like a brother. Almost the whole journey was made very slowly, often at a walking pace, for a great crowd of grieving peasants lined both sides of the street along the way. And all the flowers of Lucca were offered to you spontaneously.

July 2, 1939 [continuation of July 1]

We arrive in Leghorn at about seven o'clock in the evening. The weather is very fine: blue sky and warm air. All the church bells are ringing. The city seems to be stricken by an irreparable catastrophe, and it also seems that this is a drama that affects everyone. A silent and pensive people gathered on the sidewalks. Eyes are fixed and dry. Arms are raised in the Roman salute. Many women kneel and many are praying. This homage of love that your city pays you is such that only you could have imagined it. The love which you gave the people of

Leghorn during your lifetime is being repaid to you many times over if it were possible in the hour of your departure. In the hall of the Fascio, where you rest on the gun carriage fit for heroes, a great crowd passes silently and sadly. I remain near you for a long time. To look at you and to caress you lessens my sorrow, and I wish I could embrace one by one all who come to pay you homage. I recognize in their sorrow true sorrow—the sorrow which makes men brothers. The order to mount guard has been given to the best men of Italy, all those who have excelled in the last twenty years in arms, in politics, in the Faith. The war, and the determination, the new glory of Italy, are all there beside you personified in her best men.

Innumerable touching happenings, but I shall recall only one, because certainly it will be dearest to your heart. An old man, so old that he appeared to be ageless, dragged himself along to pay homage to your remains and said that he wanted to honor not only your memory but also that of your father, whose cabin boy he had been on board a sailing ship.

I have returned, Father, to see the house in which you were born. It is modest and somewhat ill-kept. This will no longer be the case in the future. I shall take an interest in it. And I shall see to it that it becomes, as it should be, a place sacred to all those people—and there are many of them—who have and will have the cult of your memory.

Yesterday, because of you, the King and the Duce met on the staircase of a modest country home. Today, again because of you, all of Italy has come to Leghorn. Never before in its history has the entire life of the nation been assembled within its walls.

The last solemn honors have been paid. The Duce came by plane from Romagna and followed on foot the caisson bearing your mortal remains. Next him was Mother, who has courageously kept her vow to remain near you to the last, and I, myself. Meanwhile, Maria [Ciano's sister], who is not altogether well but who will get better, had remained in Rome in her silent tears near the radio that transmitted the details of this occasion.

The religious ceremony took place in the cathedral. I had suggested St. Peter and Paul, the church of your childhood. But it was too small. The cathedral itself, which, when I was a child, seemed to have a boundless immensity, could not hold even a part of the high officials who were following you. As for the common people, they crowded the streets, and their attitude was so compassionate and humble that the entire city seemed to be transformed into an immense temple of sorrow.

After the blessing on the Piazza there took place the Fascist roll call. I am sure that among all the voices you recognized my own. "Present" is the only word, Father, that I can say with reference to you since you left me.

If in life you might at times be or seem to be far away, now that you are no more this is not possible. You are near me and with my spirit, endlessly and inseparably. The Duce and Mother had withdrawn. I followed your remains as far as the cemetery, and as you were crossing the fatal threshold of the Purificazione the naval squadron, having arrived during the night, let the cannon thunder in your honor. For some minutes you paused near the tombs of your forefathers, as you were wont to do every time you came to Leghorn. Then you were carried to a small chapel where you now rest in a niche until such time as a worthy monument is ready to receive you. I am grateful to those who have arranged for you to be put in a niche and not buried. It was nerve-racking to see the marble slab shut you off from the world of the living, but it would have been sadder still for me to see you buried in the earth.

The militiamen and my friends led me away as I was once again overcome by my grief. Then, with Mother, I started on my way back to Rome and, Father dear, life must again take on its usual rhythm within and without. This is inevitable and perhaps best. But today, as I write you, I am still upset. I feel a profound loneliness in my heart and a sweet and painful sadness. Someday, if I know that it would not be contrary to your wishes and to your nature, I will speak and write about you as I wish to do and as I must, so that so many beautiful things may be made public which you have stubbornly wanted to conceal. Today I would not know how, nor could I do it. But remember, Father, that among all those who honestly do you honor here, I do so now with my devotion, with my love, with my tenderness, which tragic fate has impressed on me profoundly, immutably, and completely.

July 3, 1939

Life goes on, and my work helps somewhat to draw me out of this great sorrow into which I have been plunged. The Duce was really paternal and uttered many expressions of great attachment and affection about my father. Then, this morning, he handed me the document that Father had in his possession since November 1926—a letter in which the Duce nominated him as his successor and gave him instructions on the measures to be taken in case of any sudden disappearance of the Chief. The Duce also spoke of his plans regarding the successor to my father in the chamber: Grandi and Farinacci. I inclined toward the candidacy of Farinacci, but this morning Starace, who has fought such a candidacy, and maybe with good reasons, came to see me. We agree on a colorless figure, such as Teruzzi or Acerbo, for the nomination.

The international situation has become obscure in these last few days because of the problem of Danzig. I remain calm, thinking that it is a false alarm. The fact is that the Germans haven't said a word on the subject, which cannot be reconciled with the commitments of the pact. The Duce has outlined a plan for a solution of the problem through a plebiscite. But this seems to me rather Utopian and I told him so.

Gathering at Palazzo Chigi to discuss the question of the return of the German population from Alto Adige to Germany. Things are going well, and I believe that in a short time we shall have satisfactory results.

July 4, 1939

The question of Danzig is slowly becoming more reassuring. From Berlin no communication, which confirms the fact that nothing dramatic is in the offing.

I have seen Christic, who has taken upon himself to tell me that his country does not intend to allow itself to be compromised by the pact which Turkey has made with the Western democracies. I have also seen the Japanese Ambassador, who states that his government is ready to sign the pact with some reservations, more pro-forma than anything else. I have likewise seen the British Ambassador, who spoke mournfully about the bitterness of our press with respect to his country. I answered that it is not the press but the facts which have created a new and very harsh state of mind between Italy and Great Britain.

The Duce received Cavallero in my presence. He said that the mixed Italian-German commission will have, in relation to the Axis, the same functions which the Supreme Commission for Defense has had for internal questions.

I have received Badoglio's report on Albania: *"Quam parva sapientia!"*

July 5, 1939

I see many diplomats, who are preparing to go on vacation, with their minds more at rest, now that the Danzig storm seems to have blown over.

François-Poncet tries to break a lance for a journalist who has been expelled. We discuss the matter of responsibility for the present situation and end in concluding that only time can better it.

The Greek, Metaxas, pays a courtesy visit, but he is stunned by my reception and by all the reservations which I raise on the matter of Greece's acceptance of a unilateral guarantee from Great Britain, which places his country in a somewhat unenviable position of a semi-protectorate.

July 6, 1939

Conferences with Villani, the Belgian Ambassador, and the Turkish and Yugoslav ambassadors. Nothing important. We urge Berlin to make a statement on the question of the exodus of the Germans from Alto Adige. It seems that the Führer is creating difficulties, and it is easy to see his reasons. However, the statement is necessary in order to re-establish the reality of the measure, since the foreign press is attempting to falsify its nature by every possible means.

July 7, 1939

Like a good ambassador who is new to his work with the Fascists, Percy Loraine makes a great to-do about communicating a personal message from Chamberlain, and succeeds in having himself conveyed to Palazzo Venezia. The message was of no special moment. It was a sort of charge in minor key against German claims to Danzig, as well as mentioning the dangers for the peace of the world that might come from such pretensions. The Duce debated the message immediately, point by point, and some of his arguments were truly brilliant, such as the one about Poland being the last country to speak about Czechoslovakia, since it was she, Poland, who struck the mortal blow when Czechoslovakia was down on her knees, and he concluded by saying twice, "Tell Chamberlain that if England is ready to fight in defense of Poland, Italy will take up arms with her ally Germany." Percy

Loraine practically never opened his mouth. The second interview at Palazzo Venezia had no more brilliant results than the first.

During the evening I acquainted von Mackensen with what had happened, and he seemed to be particularly satisfied with the attitude taken by the Duce on the British move.

July 8, 1939

Nothing new.

July 9, 1939

I leave for Spain.

[*Next entry is July 19, 1939*]

July 19, 1939

I have set down my impressions of Spain in a notebook. The Duce is quite satisfied with the report on my Spanish trip.

I summon Magistrati to Rome on the matter of the meeting between Hitler and Mussolini, which is set for the fourth of August. I fear that it is due to Attolico's endemic crisis of fear. Nevertheless, we must prepare the meeting well in order to prevent its being futile. Perhaps in view of the fact that for many reasons war plans must be delayed as long as possible he could talk to the Führer about launching a proposal for an international peace conference. This would offer the following advantages: either the democracies will agree to sit around a table and negotiate and then they will have to end by yielding considerably, or they will refuse, and in this case we shall have the advantage of having taken the initiative for peace, which will reveal the internal position of the others and strengthen our position in arguing for what we want. But what are the real intentions of Hitler? Attolico is very much concerned and warns of the imminence of a new and perhaps fatal crisis.

July 20, 1939

The information sent by Attolico continues to be alarming. From what he says, the Germans are preparing to strike at Danzig by the fourteenth of August. And for the first time Caruso from Prague announces movements of forces on a vast scale. But is it possible that all this should take place without our knowing it, indeed after so many protestations of peace made by our Axis comrades? We shall see.

By order of the Duce I have presented an ultimatum to the Nuncio for the *Osservatore Romano*. Either it will cease its subtle propaganda against the Axis or we shall prohibit its circulation in Italy. It has become the official organ of the anti-Fascists.

Villani speaks of the possibility of placing the Duke of Aosta on the throne of Hungary, but I have not succeeded in finding out whether he is acting on orders or on his personal initiative, in which case the matter is not of great importance.

July 21, 1939

Massimo is not so pessimistic about the situation and he confirms my suspicions: that Attolico permitted himself to be carried away in a fit of panic without very good reasons. Naturally Massimo expresses himself with a thousand reservations and ambiguities, as is his way. Such is his nature, which neither the years nor events will change. He is generally favorable to the proposal for a meeting. He agrees on the necessity of presenting it to the Germans very tactfully or in such a way as to avoid its being interpreted by them to mean that we would readily withdraw from our obligations to the alliance.

July 22, 1939

I take Magistrati to the Duce, who has worked out a plan of welcome for the meeting at Brenner Pass. It is based on the proposal of an international conference. The Duce outlines at some length the reasons for our proposal. I am skeptical of the possibilities of such a conference actually taking place, but I agree on the utility of our move which will, above all, throw confusion and dissension into the camp of the opposition, where many voices are already being heard against war.

I insist on two points: (1) that the condition must be included that our proposal be considered valid only if the Germans do not previously decide to wage war, since, in that case, it would be useless to discuss anything; (2) that Ribbentrop is interested in the question. I am doubtful, very doubtful, about Attolico's ability now. He has lost his head. I am sending a telegram to Magistrati ordering him to take part personally in all the negotiations.

I receive Koliegi, with whom I spoke about the problem of Kossovo and of Ciamuria. He will prepare a memorandum on the program. I give these instructions for the action which we must develop in three successive stages: (1) general broad propaganda laying stress on culture and religion; (2) same as to the management of public welfare; (3) clandestine military organization to be ready for the moment when the inevitable Yugoslav crisis comes to a head.

July 23, 1939

I tried to pay a visit to my children at Capri, but the rough sea prevented my landing. News from Spain minimizes the importance of the liquidation of Queipo de Llano. However, this liquidation was expected, and the speech was nothing but the pretext that Franco had been awaiting a long time. I remember that after having called General Queipo "crazy," Serrano Suñer said that it was his intention to kick him upstairs by sending him to the "golden exile" of the Buenos Aires Embassy. Events have permitted the realization of this idea sooner than expected.

July 24, 1939

Attolico will see von Ribbentrop. I am curious to know the German reaction to our proposal. I hope that it will be favorable but I do not believe that it will.

Villani brings the Duce two letters from Teleki. The first to confirm the absolute adherence of Hungary to the Axis; the second raises some reservations as regards a conflict with Poland. I vaguely suspect that the first letter was written in order to launch the second.

Villani also speaks of the dynastic question and frequently mentions the name of the Duke of Aosta. He says he speaks for himself, but he admits that such a possibility is being discussed even in government circles. He severely criticizes Czaky, whom he considers "lacking in balance, dominated by a boundless ambition, and without scruples."

The Minister of Yugoslavia repeats for the nth time his country's act of faith in collaboration with the Axis. They evidently feel our growing suspicions which have been accentuated by Prince Paul's trip to London.

July 25, 1939

Nothing new. The Hungarian move of yesterday made a bad impression on the Duce and on the Germans. That was to be expected. At Palazzo Chigi I had the first meeting regarding the reception to be given Franco.

In a long visit Guarneri sounded for the nth time the alarm on the monetary situation, which according to him is bad. He is preparing an alarming report for the Duce, who listens to him with "his imperturbable pessimism," and this is what most seriously troubles Guarneri.

July 26, 1939

I talked by telephone with Magistrati about the conversation with Ribbentrop. His reaction to the proposal of an international conference was unfavorable. He will talk about it to the Führer, but it is now easy to see that nothing will come of it. In which case, it would seem to be a good idea to postpone the meeting of the two chiefs. In any event, before suggesting a decision to the Duce, I prefer to await the arrival of Attolico's message that is to be sent by airplane.

I tell Villani confidentially of the impression caused in Rome and Berlin by the Hungarian note regarding non-intervention in case of war with Poland. He notes our disappointment and puts the responsibility on Count Czaky, a man whom I have always judged severely.

July 27, 1939

I go to Leghorn to attend the ceremony on the thirtieth day after Father's death. After a month sorrow grips my soul more deeply and more desperately than the first day. I can't get used to the idea of the loss of him whom I loved so much and who has done so much for me. May God watch over him.

I resume my work with the usual intensity. This relieves me. I receive Attolico's report, which I send to the Duce. The boner pulled by the Ambassador becomes more and more evident. Once again Ribbentrop has affirmed the German determination to avoid war for a long time. The idea of postponing the useless meeting at the Brenner Pass takes hold of me more and more. However, I ask the Duce to read the report before he makes any decision.

Franco submits the name of Queipo as head of the Spanish military mission in Italy, and, naturally, it is immediately accepted. This is a clever move in order to end all gossip of recent days, to get rid of Queipo de Llano and at the same time put him in his place.

Good news from Albania, where mining explorations are proceeding very well. The Ammi [a company for the mining of iron ore] has already yielded eight million tons of iron ore and many even greater deposits are being discovered.

July 28, 1939

After reading the report, the Duce decided to postpone his meeting with Hitler and I think he did well. I telephone Attolico, who is still trying to kid us. This time Attolico missed the boat. He was frightened by his own shadow and probably, with somebody in the German Foreign Ministry, was trying to save his country from a non-existent danger. It's too bad. This Ambassador has done good work, but now he permits himself to be taken in by the war panic. This may easily be explained by the fact that he is a rich man.

It appears that Ribbentrop has asked time to report to Hitler, who had expressed himself against the conference. Tomorrow we shall have a reply on the postponement.

The Bulgars are concerned about the alignment of Turkish forces. They are right. Ankara, with British help, again wants to try to play the game of supremacy in the Balkans. We must take advantage of this fact to put fear into the Greeks and Yugoslavs, both of whom still remember the stench of the Turks. Anyway, Marković has been greatly alarmed ever since news first arrived of the understanding between Turkey and Great Britain. I shall have Ansaldo write on this question. I don't expect too much, but it is always worth while trying to revive certain old hatreds which are not entirely dead.

July 29, 1939

Nothing new.

July 30, 1939

Nothing new. We have not yet been able to get a reply from Berlin regarding the Brenner Pass meeting.

Flying to Capri.

July 31, 1939

Nothing new except the postponement of the Brenner Pass meeting, decided personally by Hitler. I am happy that this meeting, which was meaningless and dangerous, has been avoided, at least for the time being.

August 1, 1939

Nothing new.

August 2, 1939

The Duce is irritated by the sending of Indian troops to Egypt. To-morrow I shall ask Percy Loraine for an explanation and particulars as to this British decision on the basis of the Italo-English accord.

I received the ministers of Yugoslavia and Hungary, as well as the Chargé d'Affaires of France. Conversations that had no importance.

Attolico continues to harp on his favorite theme of the meeting of Hitler and Mussolini, still insisting on the bugbear of a sudden decision that will be made by Hitler for the fifteenth of August. The insistence of Attolico keeps me wondering. Either this Ambassador has lost his head or he sees and knows something which has completely escaped us. Appearances are in favor of the first alternative, but it is necessary to observe events carefully.

August 3, 1939

Percy Loraine says that the information about Indian troops in Egypt was furnished to our military attaché in London. This is true, but the report has not yet reached us.

Massimo writes a private letter from which it appears that he is in disagreement with the Ambassador as to the danger of an approaching crisis. He advises us against asking the Germans for a clarification of their program. If Massimo, notwithstanding his considerable, his very great caution, has decided to take such a step, it means that he is sure of what he is doing. I have transmitted his letter to the Duce. Roatta, the new military attaché, on the other hand, informs us of the concentration of forces and movements on the Polish frontier. Who is right? I may be mistaken, but I continue to feel optimistic.

August 4, 1939

A brief conversation with Christic to call his attention to the danger presented by the excessive liberty of action allowed in Yugoslavia to certain emissaries of Zog. According to information in our possession, they are attempting to start frontier incidents. Christic promised he would intervene strongly, and I believe he will keep his word, because he is very much afraid of any possible complications.

Attolico's alarmist bombardment continues. *The situation seems obscure to me.* I am beginning to think of the possibility of a meeting with von Ribbentrop. The moment has come when we must really know how matters stand. The situation is too serious for us to view developments passively.

The Duce returns to Rome.

August 5, 1939

Nothing new.

August 6, 1939

I received from Christic ample assurances about the precautions that will be taken with reference to the Albanians. I confer with the Duce. The King has expressed his intention of giving me the collar of the Order of the Annunziata. The Duce was evasive at first, since "the collar may lead to compromises that it would be better not to make," but now he is persuaded as to the desirability of my having it, and tomorrow he is to write to the King about the matter.

We discussed the situation. We are in agreement in feeling that we must find some way out. By following the Germans we shall go to war and enter it under the most favorable conditions for the Axis, and especially for Italy. Our gold reserves are reduced to almost nothing, as well as our stocks of metals, and we are far from having completed our autarchic and military preparations. If the crisis comes we shall fight if only to save our "honor." But we must avoid war. I propose to the Duce the idea of my meeting with von Ribbentrop—a meeting which on the surface would have a private character, but during which I would attempt to continue discussion of Mussolini's project for a world peace conference. He is quite favorable. Tomorrow we shall discuss the matter further, but I am convinced that the Duce wants to move vigorously to avoid the crisis. And in so doing he is right.

August 7, 1939

The Duce has written a fine letter to the King to say that he approves my receiving the collar of the Order of the Annunziata. He writes among other things, "It is my duty to declare to Your Majesty that to Count Ciano is due the penetration of Albania from within which has permitted us to annex it almost without striking a blow. This in itself is worth the collar."

The Duce has approved my meeting with von Ribbentrop, and I have therefore telephoned Attolico instructions on this point. Attolico himself had thought of something of the sort and was very glad. I have added that the meeting between the Duce and Hitler can take place at some other time when the Anglo-French-Russian negotiations have been concluded.

We are favorably impressed by the measures taken by Franco to create a single party. The proof of this is the wild fury of the French press.

August 8, 1939

With Benini at the Duce's, to discuss the question of Albanian iron ore. The Duce is quite satisfied with the report. He decides that in the future I shall make a trip to Albania, during which the collar of the Order of the Annunziata will be conferred on me. Massimo writes in a rather soothing tone from Berlin. He does not foresee any immediate aggressive intentions on the part of Germany even though the Danzig situation is grave and dangerous.

August 9, 1939

Von Ribbentrop has approved the idea of our meeting. I decided to leave tomorrow night in order to meet him at Salzburg. The Duce is anxious that I prove to the Germans, by documentary evidence, that the outbreak of war at this time would be folly. Our preparation is not such as to allow us to believe that victory will be certain. The probabilities are 50 per cent; at least so the Duce thinks. On the other hand, within three years the probabilities will be 80 per cent. Mussolini has always in mind the idea of an international peace conference. I believe the move would be excellent.

The Japanese Ambassador informs me that adherence to the alliance has been decided by Tokyo. After so much uncertainty I wonder if this is true. And, if it is true, I wonder if it is for the best, since conversations with Moscow are as yet inconclusive. Besides, won't this fact make Germany more arrogant and encourage her to rush along a path of intransigence and thus bring the crisis to the boiling point as concerns the Danzig problem?

The King has very cordially confirmed to the Duce the matter of granting the collar.

August 10, 1939

The Duce is more than ever convinced of the necessity of delaying the conflict. He himself has worked out the outline of a report concerning the meeting at Salzburg which ends with an allusion to international negotiations to settle the problems that so dangerously disturb European life.

Before letting me go he recommends that I should frankly inform the Germans that we must avoid a conflict with Poland, since it will be impossible to localize it, and a general war would be disastrous for everybody. Never has the Duce spoken of the need for peace with so much warmth and without reserve. I agree with him 100 per cent, and this conviction will lead me to redouble my efforts. But I am doubtful as to the results.

August 11, 1939

In my book containing an account of my conferences I have a transcript of my conversations with von Ribbentrop and Hitler. Here I shall jot down only some impressions of a general character. Von Ribbentrop is evasive whenever I ask him for particulars about the German line of action. His conscience bothers him. He has lied too many times about German intentions toward Poland not to feel uneasy now about what he must tell me and what they are getting ready to do.

The decision to fight is implacable. He rejects any solution which might give satisfaction to Germany and avoid the struggle. I am certain that even if the Germans were given more than they ask for they would attack just the same, because they are possessed by the demon of destruction.

At times our conversation becomes very tense. I do not hesitate to express my thoughts with brutal frankness. But this does not move him. I am becoming aware of how little we are worth in the opinion of the Germans.

The atmosphere is cold. And the coldness between me and him is spread even among our secretaries. During the dinner hour not a word is exchanged. We are distrustful of each other. But I, at least, have a clear conscience. He has not.

August 12, 1939

Hitler is very cordial, but he, too, is impassive and implacable in his decision. He speaks in the large drawing room of his house, standing in front of a table on which some maps are spread out. He exhibits a truly profound military knowledge. He speaks with a great deal of calm and becomes excited only when he advises us to give Yugoslavia the *coup de grâce* as soon as possible.

I realize immediately that there is no longer anything that can be done. He has decided to strike, and strike he will. All our arguments will not in the least avail to stop him. He continues to repeat that he will localize the conflict with Poland, but his affirmation that the great war must be fought while he and the Duce are still young leads me to believe once more that he is acting in bad faith.

He utters words of high praise for the Duce, but he listens with a faraway and impersonal interest to what I tell him about the bad effects a war would have on the Italian people. Actually I feel that as far as the Germans are concerned an alliance with us means only that the enemy will be obliged to keep a certain number of divisions facing us, thus easing up the situation on the German war fronts.

They care for nothing more. The fate that might befall us does not interest them in the least. They know that the decision will be forced by them rather than by us. In conclusion, they are promising us only a beggarly pittance.

August 13, 1939

The second meeting with Hitler is briefer, and, I would say, more concise. Even in his gestures the man reveals more than yesterday his imminent will to action. Our welcome is cordial but well contained on both sides.

I report to the Duce at the Palazzo Venezia. And, in addition to reporting to him what happened, I make known also my own judgment of the situation as well as of the men involved and of events. I return to Rome completely disgusted with the Germans, with their leader, with their way of doing things. They have betrayed us and lied to us. Now they are dragging us into an adventure which we have not wanted and which might compromise the regime and the country as a whole. The Italian people will boil over with horror when they know about the aggression against Poland and most probably will wish to fight the Germans. I don't know whether to wish Italy a victory or Germany a defeat. In any case, given the German attitude, I think that our hands are free, and I propose that we act accordingly, declaring that we have no intention of participating in a war which we have neither wanted nor provoked.

The Duce's reactions are varied. At first he agrees with me. Then he says that honor compels him to march with Germany. Finally, he states that he wants his part of the booty in Croatia and Dalmatia.

August 14, 1939

I find Mussolini worried. I do not hesitate to arouse in him every possible anti-German reaction by every means in my power. I speak to him of his diminished prestige and his playing the none-too-brilliant role of second fiddle. And, finally, I turn over to him documents which prove the bad faith of the Germans on the Polish question. The alliance was based on premises which they now deny; they are traitors and we must not have any scruples in ditching them. But Mussolini still has many scruples. I am going to do my level best to convince him, because in so doing I am sure that I shall render a great service to him and to my country. Meanwhile, I tell Starace not to keep from the Duce the country's true state of mind, which is clearly anti-German. Tomorrow I shall also talk about this with the head of the police force. He should know that the Italian people do not want to fight alongside

Germany in order to give it that power with which one day it will threaten us. I no longer have doubts about the Germans. Tomorrow it will be Hungary's turn, and then ours. We must act now while there is time.

I go to the seashore with the Polish Ambassador. I speak with him in vague terms and advise moderation. Our counsellor at Warsaw says that Poland will fight to the last man. The churches are filled. The people pray and sing a hymn, "O God, help us to save our country." These people will be massacred by German steel tomorrow. They are innocent. My heart is with them.

August 15, 1939

The Duce, who at first had refused to act independently of the Germans, today, after examining the papers that I presented to him, and after our conversations, is convinced that we must not march blindly with Germany. However, he makes one reservation: he wants time to prepare the break with Germany, and he will do it in such a way as not to break relations brutally and suddenly. He is of the opinion that it may still be possible, though perhaps difficult, for the democracies to give in, in which case it would not be profitable for us to defend the Germans, since we, too, must have our part of the booty. It is, therefore, necessary to find a solution which will permit the following: (1) if the democracies attack, we should be able to free ourselves "honorably" from the Germans; (2) if the democracies simply swallow it, without fighting back, we should take advantage of it to settle accounts once and for all with Belgrade.

For this purpose it seems useful to put down in writing the conclusions of Salzburg. This is a document which we might either pull out in the open or leave buried in the archives, as the case may require. But the Duce is more and more convinced that the democracies will fight. "It is useless," he says, "to climb two thousand meters into the clouds. Perhaps we are closer to the Eternal Father up there, if He exists, but we are surely farther from men. This time it means war. And we cannot engage in war because our plight does not permit us to do so."

The conversations I had with him today lasted for six hours. And I talked to him with brutal frankness.

August 16, 1939

Today I have had two conferences at the Palazzo Venezia. I was alone in the morning and accompanied by Attolico in the afternoon. The Duce is more than ever convinced of the fact that France and England will enter the war if Germany attacks. "If they do not act," he says, "I shall send an ultimatum to the Bank of France, asking for the consignment of gold which is the thing that the French hold more dear than anything else." He is really beginning to react at German behavior toward him. I encourage him in this with every means in my power.

During the afternoon we examine at length the advisability of sending a note to the Germans, but then we conclude that it is better to make a verbal communication, since if it were written it might induce Germany to ask for clarification about our eventual position in case of war. This is the last thing that I desire.

Mussolini, impelled by his idea of honor, might be led to reaffirm his determination of going along with the Germans. He wanted to do it two days ago, and it was difficult to prevent him from doing so. It would be a mad venture, carried out against the unanimous will of the Italian people, who as yet do not know how things stand, but who, having had a sniff of the truth, have had a sudden fit of rage against the Germans.

Starace, who is in good faith in this matter, says that when Germany attacks Poland we must keep our eyes open to prevent public demonstrations against the Germans. A policy of neutrality will, on the other hand, be more popular, and, if it were necessary later, war with Germany would be every bit as popular.

August 17, 1939

I went with Attolico to the Duce. For a moment the fires of the old scruples of loyalty return to the Duce, and he wanted Attolico to confirm to Ribbentrop that, in spite of everything, Italy will march with Germany if the democracies throw themselves into the furnace of war. I fought like a lion against this idea and succeeded in making the Duce modify these instructions in the sense, at least, that we would say nothing until the Germans have renewed their request. The Duce, however, has still not settled on a precise line of action, and he is still capable of fastening our bonds with Germany more closely. Yet everyone tells him that our country no longer wants to have anything to do with the Germans, and he realizes this.

A brief discussion with von Mackensen, in which I tell him what Attolico must tell Ribbentrop tomorrow.

A brief conversation with Christic, who is, as always, fearful and uncertain. Finally I receive Percy Loraine. I do not conceal from him that I consider the situation very grave. And I tell him that Europe needs a great deal of common sense if it is to avoid the crisis. He answers that the common sense is there, but that Europe will still not tolerate the periodical *diktat* of Hitler. If the crisis comes, England will fight. Personally, he would like to participate in such a fight. He is sorry about only one thing: that for the first time in history our two countries may be at war with each other. I made no reply, but I think he knows that I, too, do not wish this to happen.

August 18, 1939

A conversation with the Duce in the morning; his usual shifting feelings. He still thinks it possible that the democracies will not march, and that Germany might do good business cheaply, from which business he does not want to be excluded. Then, too, he fears Hitler's rage. He believes that a denunciation of the pact or something like it might induce Hitler to abandon the Polish question in order to square accounts with Italy. All this makes him nervous and disturbed. My suggestions are given short shrift. He now suspects that I, too, am against the Axis, and that I have made up my mind, and he refuses to be influenced by me.

In the afternoon Count Czaky arrives suddenly. He is, as always, confused, muddled, and contradictory. He hurriedly submits the idea of making a pact of alliance with the Axis. He hopes in this way to save Hungary from a German invasion or from a "friendly occupation." I discourage him, above all because I see in this a new bond between us and Germany.

The Duce also is very reserved on the matter. Czaky has no definite ideas on the situation. He still thinks that the Germans may be bluffing. He says that 95 per cent of the Hungarian people hate the Germans. The Regent himself, speaking of them, called them "buffoons and brigands," and Madame Horthy said that even she would take up arms if they had to fight the Germans.

For the first time we have been approached in an official way about putting the Duke of Aosta on the throne of Hungary. The Regent would be favorable, but the obstacle is a German veto.

August 19, 1939

I arrive at Tirana, where the news of the conferring of the collar of the Order of the Annunziata reaches me. I inspect the public works of Tirana and Durazzo. In Albania much has been done along material and spiritual lines. Party organizations are excellent, especially work done with the younger people, who are now clearly oriented in favor of Italy.

There is no doubt that if we can work in peace we shall be in possession of the richest region of Italy within a few years.

I am quite satisfied with what I see, but today my spirit is absent. The vicissitudes of European politics are too serious and sad to permit me to concentrate my attention upon Albanian problems only.

August 20, 1939

On the steamer, the *Duke of Abruzzi,* I reach Valona. Here, too, the welcome given me was enthusiastic. What misery! Tirana and Durazzo are in contrast two metropolitan centers. And yet the locality is very beautiful, the bay spacious, and the sea rich in fish and fishing facilities. After a few years of work all will be transformed. We were to go to Korcia, but the weather was bad and we put it off. We return to Durazzo. There a telegram from Anfuso reached me to announce that my presence in Rome during the evening was "extremely desirable." I cancel my visit to Scutari and return to Rome.

This is what had happened: The Duce, in my absence, made an about-face. He wants to support Germany at any cost in the conflict which is now close at hand, and he wishes to send during the evening, through Attolico, a communication to the Germans stating this intention. In the meantime, the English have made an appeal to the Duce to settle the controversy peacefully.

Conference between Mussolini, myself, and Attolico. This is the substance: It is already too late to go back on the Germans. If this should take place the press of the whole world would say that Italy is cowardly, that it is not ready, and that it has drawn back in the face of the specter of war. I try to debate the matter, but that is useless now. Mussolini holds very stubbornly to his idea. I use the British communication as a pretext to obtain a delay in any decision until tomorrow morning. I still have hope that my point of view will prevail, but, on the other hand, Attolico leaves the Palazzo Venezia discouraged and overwhelmed with grief.

August 21, 1939

Today I have spoken clearly: I have cast aside every scruple. When I entered the room Mussolini confirmed his decision to go along with the Germans. "You, Duce, cannot and must not do it. The loyalty with which I have served you in carrying out the policy of the Axis warrants my speaking clearly to you now. I went to Salzburg in order to adopt a common line of action. I found myself face to face with a *diktat*. The Germans, not ourselves, have betrayed the alliance in which we were to have been partners, and not servants. Tear up the pact. Throw it in Hitler's face and Europe will recognize in you the natural leader of the anti-German crusade. Do you want me to go to Salzburg? Very well, I shall go and shall speak to the Germans as they should be spoken to. Hitler will not have me put out my cigarette as he did with Schuschnigg." I told him these and other things. He was much impressed, and approved my proposal; namely, to ask von Ribbentrop to come to the Brenner Pass, to speak frankly to him, and to reaffirm our rights as Axis partners. He does not want the Axis to collapse for the time being, but if it should I would not be the one to weep over it.

We telephoned von Ribbentrop, who was unavailable for some time. Finally, at 5:30 P.M., I speak to him and tell him that I want to see him at the Brenner Pass. He says that he cannot give me an answer at once because he "is waiting for an important message from Moscow (sic) and will telephone to me during the evening." I report this to the Duce, who asks me, as he frequently does these days, what the tone of the conversation had been and how the German humor was.

Another conference with the Duce. He approves the document that I have drawn up for my discussion with von Ribbentrop and we settle on four points relating to eventualities that might present themselves. In my opinion three do not count, but one is fundamental: the one which insists that we shall not intervene if the conflict is provoked by an attack on Poland.

August 22, 1939

Last evening at ten-thirty a new act opened. Von Ribbentrop telephoned that he would prefer to see me at Innsbruck rather than at the frontier, because he was to leave later for Moscow to sign a political pact with the Soviet Government. I suspended all decisions and reported to the Duce. He agreed with me in feeling that my trip to Germany would no longer be timely. I spoke again with von Ribbentrop to tell him that our projected meeting would be postponed until his return from Moscow.

A long telephone conversation with the Duce. There is no doubt the Germans have struck a master blow. The European situation is upset. Can France and Great Britain, who have based all other anti-Axis policy on an alliance with the Soviets, count upon the unconditional support of the extremist masses? And will the system of encirclement by means of small states continue to prevail now that the Moscow balance has collapsed? Nevertheless, we must make no hasty decisions. We must wait, and, if possible, be ready ourselves to gain something in Croatia and Dalmatia. The Duce has set up an *ad hoc* army commanded by Graziani. I have established contacts with our Croatian friends in Italy and in their own country.

In diplomatic circles there is a great deal of confusion about the Russian action. In general the representatives of democratic countries are inclined to underestimate the development. During the evening I see Percy Loraine, who would like an answer to the proposal he made on Sunday. My answer is vague, but not negative. In a general way I reaffirm our desire for peace and the disposition of the Duce to bring influence to bear on Hitler to continue negotiations.

August 23, 1939

The day is charged with electricity and full of threats. In the meantime anxiety about the German-Russian pact gives way to a more rational evaluation of this development, which to my way of thinking is not really fundamental. France and England trumpet to the four winds that they will intervene just the same in any eventual conflict. Japan protests. News from Tokyo signals their discontent, accentuated by the ignorance in which Japan has been kept up to this time.

The Duce followed my insistent suggestions. He authorized me to present to Percy Loraine a plan for a solution based on a preliminary return of Danzig to the Reich, after which there would be negotiations and a great peace conference. I do not know whether it was the emotion or the heat, but it is a fact that Percy Loraine fainted or almost fainted in my arms. He found a place to rest in the toilet.

A meeting with François-Poncet, who was rather discouraged and pessimistic. However, he, too, without underestimating the strength of Russian intervention, repeats that France will fight. Weizsäcker telephones me from Berghof to inform me of Hitler's harsh answer to the British Ambassador. Another hope is gone.

A new meeting with the Duce, with regard to my visit to the King. He does not wish me to show him the anti-German papers and he proposes that I limit myself to informing him of the four points which, however, have not yet been communicated to the Germans. Tonight the Duce is warlike. He talks of armies and of attacks. He received Pariani, who gave him good news on the condition of the Army. Pariani is a traitor and a liar.

Phillips, in the evening, brings me a long message from Roosevelt for the King. It doesn't seem to me to make much sense.

August 24, 1939

I went to Sant' Anna di Valdieri [a summer residence of the royal family in Piedmont] to confer with the King. This opportunity was created by my visit to thank him for the collar of the Annunziata, but we hardly spoke about the collar. He wants news on the situation. I quickly inform him of what has happened, and, with him, I do not have to attack the Germans, since his own mind is in a state of open hostility toward them. I show him the four points agreed on with the Duce regarding our attitude. He approves, especially the third: the one about neutrality. In his judgment we are absolutely in no condition to wage war. The Army is in a "pitiful" state. The military review and the maneuvers have fully revealed the unhappy state of unpreparedness of all our great units. Even the defense of our frontier is insufficient. He has made thirty-two inspections and is convinced that the French can go through it with great ease.

The officers of the Italian Army are not qualified for the job, and our equipment is old and obsolete. To this must be added the state of mind of the Italians, which is distinctly anti-German. The peasants go into the Army cursing those "damn Germans." We must, therefore, in his opinion, await events and do nothing.

Six months of neutrality will give us greater strength. In any case, if supreme decisions should have to be taken, he should like to be in Rome "not to be left out," and he hopes that the Duce, in case of conflict, would give to the Prince of Piedmont a command. "Those two imbeciles Bergamo and Pistoia have commands [two princes of the royal house, cousins of the King], my son should have one, too, for he has a head as good as that of the Duke of Aosta." He then added paternally that Prince Humbert likes me very much and that he speaks of me always with trust and hope.

August 25, 1939

During the night I had a telephone conversation with von Ribbentrop who, at the instigation of Hitler, makes it known that the situation is becoming "critical" on account of the usual "Polish provocations." His tone is less decisive and overbearing than it was before. I speak to him of the advisability of our seeing each other. The answer is evasive.

Bastianini informs me that during my absence the attitude of the Duce has become furiously warlike.

Indeed this is the state of mind I find this morning. I make use of the opinions of the King in order to dissuade him, and I succeed in having him approve a communication to Hitler announcing our nonintervention for the time being, pending a re-examination of our position, until such time as we have completed our preparations for war. I was very happy over this result, but the Duce calls me back to the Palazzo Venezia. He has changed his mind. He fears the bitter judgment of the Germans, and wants to intervene at once. It is useless to struggle. I submit and go back to the Palazzo Chigi, where consternation takes the place of the harmony that had reigned before.

Two P.M. I am told of a message of Hitler to the Duce. I go to the Palazzo Venezia with von Mackensen. The ambiguous message is couched in abstract language but gives one to understand that the action will begin in a short time and asks for "Italian understanding." I use this phrase as a pretext to persuade the Duce to write to Hitler. We are not ready to go to war. We shall do it if you will furnish us all the matériel and raw materials we need. It is not the kind of communication that I should have wanted to make, but it is something, anyway. The ice has been broken. I personally telephone it to Attolico, who will relay the information to Hitler. The German reaction is cold.

At 9:30 P.M. von Mackensen brings a brief note in which we are requested to make a precise list of what we need. During the drive von Mackensen, who is hostile to the military adventure, requests me to make out a complete list. He hopes that this will put the brakes on his government. In fact, there has been an initial suspension: Roatta has telephoned that the mobilization and marching orders for this evening have been postponed.

August 26, 1939

Berlin is showering us with requests for the list of our needs. We convene at the Palazzo Venezia at ten o'clock with the chiefs of staff of the three armies and with Benni. Before entering the Duce's room I remind these comrades of their responsibility. They must tell the whole truth on the extent of our stocks and not do what is usually done, be criminally optimistic. But they are all in precisely this state of mind, the most optimistic being Pariani.

Valle, on the other hand, is very much alive to his responsibility and is honest in his declarations.

We go over the list. It's enough to kill a bull—if a bull could read it. I remain alone with the Duce and we prepare a message to Hitler. We explain to him why it is that our needs are so vast, and we conclude by saying that Italy absolutely cannot enter the war without such provisions. The Duce makes some mention also of his political action to follow. In transmitting our request Attolico gets into trouble. (In a subsequent conference Attolico told me that this was not a mistake but that he had purposely done it in order to discourage the Germans from meeting our requests.) He asked for the immediate delivery of all the matériel, an impossible thing, since it involves seventeen million tons which require seventeen thousand cars for their transportation. I straightened things out. Soon Hitler's reply arrives. They can give us only iron, coal, and lumber. Only a few anti-aircraft batteries. He indicates that he understands our situation and urges us to be friendly. He proposes to annihilate Poland and beat France and England without help.

After Mackensen went away the Duce prepared the answer. He expressed regrets at not being able to intervene. He again proposed a political solution. The Duce is really out of his wits. His military instinct and his sense of honor were leading him to war. Reason has now stopped him. But this hurts him very much. In the military field he was badly served by his collaborators who, under the illusion of eternal peace, have lulled dangerous illusions in him. Now he has had to confront the hard truth. And this, for the Duce, is a great blow.

However, Italy is saved from a great tragedy, that very tragedy which is about to fall on the German people. Hitler is entering the war with an alarming scarcity of equipment and with a divided country.

The message is sent to the Führer at eight o'clock. He announces that he will reply.

August 27, 1939

Halifax has informed me, in a very courteous tone, that the precautionary measures taken in the Mediterranean must not be interpreted as a prelude to hostilities against us. I answer in an equally courteous tone: I am very much interested in keeping in contact with London.

Hitler's answer: He is still determined to go to war and asks us for three things: not to make known our decision to be neutral until it is absolutely necessary, to continue our military preparations in order to stop the French and British, to send agricultural and industrial workers to Germany. The Duce answers that he agrees to do all this and promises a reconsideration of our position after the first phase of the conflict. But when will this first phase end?

This morning he seemed satisfied with his decision "to stand looking out of the window." Meanwhile a singular incident takes place. The English communicate to us the text of the German proposals to London, about which there is a great ado but about which *we are 100 per cent in the dark*. Hitler proposes to the English an alliance or something like it. And this was naturally without our knowledge. I was indignant and so express myself. The Duce is indignant, too, but does not show it. He still wants to maintain an attitude of solidarity with the Germans, at least outwardly. Naturally, I do not reveal our ignorance of this document to Percy Loraine, whom I advise not to reject the German proposals and to begin to negotiate to gain time if for no other reason. We decide to make direct contact with Halifax and I telephone him.

This makes Percy Loraine and Halifax happy, the latter telling me that it is not the intention of the English to reject the offers but that at the same time they intend to safeguard existing commitments to Poland. The telephone call is characterized by extreme cordiality on both sides. The situation, therefore, is gradually improving. I have had to struggle hard to persuade the Duce to act as he has. And I must add that in this move I have been completely abandoned by the large group of men who are concerned with telling the Duce only those things that please him. To tell the truth is the least of their cares.

Starace, with his intellectual and moral shortsightedness, has the cheek to tell Mussolini that the Italian women are happy about the war because they are going to receive six lire a day and will not have the encumbrance of their husbands. How shameful! The Italian people do not deserve such a vulgar insult.

No matter. I am continuing my struggle alone because I am convinced that I am fighting for a good cause. War today, in view of our material situation and our morale, would be a great misfortune. I intend to avoid it at all costs.

In my conference this afternoon I tried to find out whether the Duce shares my opinion. In his judgment the question of a secret agreement with London has struck a strong blow at the Germans. He says that Hitler is acting in this fashion for fear that intervention on the part of the Duce will settle the crisis at the last moment, as was done last year at Munich. This would have the effect of raising his prestige, of which Hitler is jealous.

I am not sure that this explanation is correct. For me there is a simpler explanation; namely, that the Germans are treacherous and deceitful. Any kind of alliance with them becomes a bad alliance in a little while. From London we are informed that the Cabinet meeting has adjourned but will reconvene tomorrow at twelve o'clock for a definite answer to Hitler. Attolico has asked von Ribbentrop for information on the situation. He answered that there is little chance for peace and that Henderson has gone to London to express his own views only. Could there ever be a more revolting scoundrel than von Ribbentrop? But this is all very well, because it helps to dissipate the last scruples the Duce still entertains. Today he is relieved. He does not speak at all about what has been accomplished.

Halifax has informed me in courteous terms of the precautionary measures for intervention that will be taken later. He says that he will do only what is necessary after having awaited the development of the situation with a good deal of calm. It has been hard to draw him onto my side, but finally he is there, and has every intention of remaining there.

Hitler, at a secret meeting, has spoken to the Deputies of the Reichstag in strong terms. However, I do not know what he said nor has Attolico been able to tell me.

August 28, 1939

The day was quiet, so to speak. There was a pause which, according to Magistrati, was caused by the German need to send troops to the western frontier. We had no direct contact with Berlin, where, in fact, Weizsäcker said to Attolico that there was no communication in writing from the Führer to the English. Many cordial exchanges with the British, who have forewarned us of the tone of the answer that Henderson is preparing to take to Berlin in the evening. Once again they have appealed to the Duce to take pacifying action. But I do not believe that it is possible now to do more than has been done already. We might draw an unpleasant answer from the Germans. The Duce is now quite calm, as he always is after he has made a decision. He does not want to utter the word "neutrality," but it is this frame of mind that he has definitely reached. He even begins to hope that the struggle will be hard, long, and bloody for others, for he sees in this a possibility of great advantage for us.

During the night Percy Loraine sends me an outline of the British answer. It is not bad; in fact it leaves the door open to many possibilities. On the other hand, the British action has induced Poland to become more conciliatory. This is probably the key to the whole situation.

August 29, 1939

The Duce is restless. He would like to do something. Certain articles in the English press which speak of the necessity of Italian neutrality have had a bad effect on him. Meanwhile, he sets down a series of military and civilian measures of a warlike nature, which, in my opinion, need not be taken at this time. From Berlin, as well as from London, the news is better. Halifax telephones to tell me that the Führer has not rejected the English proposals and that there are still some possibilities of a peaceful solution. Attolico, who has conferred with Ribbentrop, says more or less the same thing. Under the circumstances, I induce the Duce to send a telegram to Hitler to advise him to pursue negotiations. I inform Sir Percy Loraine of this and he is very happy. I receive the German Ambassadress to Spain, Baroness von Storer. She is very pessimistic about the German internal situation. She believes that the outbreak of a total war might rapidly lead to Bolshevism. She says that the German people, which "is the most ungrateful people in the world," is at this moment agitated by very strong anti-Nazi currents.

Attolico has conferred with the Führer, who thanks him for the communication of the Duce. Hitler has told the British that he is "ready to receive a Polish plenipotentiary," but that in spite of this he is still skeptical about the possibility of a negotiated solution, since the two armies are now within rifle range and the slightest incident may cause a clash.

August 30, 1939

My first thought today is the memory of my father. He would have been sixty-three years old if unfair death had not stopped the beating of his great heart. May God welcome him and may his generous soul be always near me.

The situation has again become embittered. The British answer does not close the door to future negotiations, but it does not give, nor could it give, the Germans all they ask for. Our only hope is in making direct contacts, but time passes, and the Polish plenipotentiary does not arrive at Berlin. Instead, news reaches us of general mobilization at Warsaw, and it is not the kind of news that is calculated to calm our nerves. I continue and multiply my contacts with the English.

Percy Loraine came to my house tonight and all day he has been ringing me up, but we are not successful in changing the situation.

The Duce is convinced "that the invasion will take place tomorrow." Naturally, the idea of a neutrality imposed on us weighs more and more upon him. Not being able to wage war, he makes all the necessary preparations so that in case of a peaceful solution he may be able to say that he would have waged it. Calls to arms, blackouts, requisitions, closing of cafés and amusement places. . . . All this carries with it two grave dangers: one of an external character, since it would cause London and Paris to believe that we are preparing to attack, and hence induce them to take the initiative in moving against us; the other of an internal character, because it will alarm the population, which is more and more openly anti-German and opposed to war. Bocchini, whom I have urged to send to our Chief *true* reports on the situation, is very pessimistic. He went so far as to tell me that in case of uprisings in connection with the preservation of neutrality the carabinièri and police would make common cause with the people.

August 31, 1939

An ugly awakening. Attolico telegraphs at nine, saying that the situation is desperate and that unless something new comes up there will be war in a few hours. I go quickly to the Palazzo Venezia. We must find a new solution. In agreement with the Duce I call Halifax by telephone to tell him that the Duce can intervene with Hitler only if he brings a fat prize: Danzig. Empty-handed he can do nothing. On his part, Lord Halifax asks me to bring pressure on Berlin, so that certain procedural difficulties may be overcome and direct contacts established between Germany and Poland.

I telephone this to Attolico, who is more and more pessimistic. After a while Halifax sends word that our proposal regarding Danzig cannot be adopted. The sky is becoming darker and darker.

I receive François-Poncet. The conversation is without purpose and, therefore, vague and indefinite. The wish for peace is repeated on both sides. He seeks to learn what our attitude will be, but I make no reply. He is romantic, sad, and nostalgic. I must add also sincere.

I see the Duce again. As a last resort, let us propose to France and Great Britain a conference for September 5, for the purpose of reviewing those clauses of the Treaty of Versailles which disturb European life. I warmly support the proposal, if for no other reason than because it will widen the distance between us and Hitler, who wants no conferences and has said so many times. François-Poncet welcomes the proposal with satisfaction but with some skepticism. Percy Loraine welcomes it with enthusiasm. Halifax receives it favorably, reserving the right to submit it to Chamberlain. I insist on a quick answer, since time is pressing. But the day passes by without communications of any kind. Not until 8:20 P.M. does the telephone central office inform us that London has cut its communications with Italy.

Here, then, are the consequences of the measures taken in the last few days, or, in other words, the consequences of too much publicity on the meager results of the too many measures taken in the last few days. I go to inform the Duce. He is affected by it. "This is war," he says, "but tomorrow we shall declare in the Grand Council that we are not marching." Tomorrow will be too late. The English and French may have then committed acts that render very difficult any such declaration.

I propose that we call Percy Loraine and that I commit an indiscretion. If scandal come of it I am willing to be sacrificed, but the situation will be saved. The Duce approves. Percy Loraine comes to me. I acquaint him with what has happened and then, acting as if I can no longer contain my feelings, I say, "But why do you want to start the irreparable? Can't you understand that we shall never start a war against you and the French?" Percy Loraine is moved. He is on the verge of tears. He takes my two hands in his and says, "I have known this for fifteen days. And I communicated it by telegram to my government. The measures of the last few days had shaken my faith. But I am happy to have come to the Palazzo Chigi tonight." He shook my hand again and left happy. I inform the Duce of this by telephone. In the meantime he had given orders that the lights of the city be put on again, to lessen the alarm.

From Berlin there arrives the German communiqué summarizing all that has happened in the last few days, including the proposals to Poland. These are very moderate, but there is something obscure in the whole German attitude. The proposals are advanced, but at the same time it is stated that they are no longer open to discussion. In any case, all discussion is superfluous. Hitler's program announced to me at Berghof is being applied point by point. Tonight the attack will begin, since the thirty-first of August was given as the last possible date. The Duce, instead, thinks that negotiation is still possible. I do not, for I see in the communiqué a clarion call to war. At midnight Magistrati informs us that newspapers are being distributed free in Berlin with the headline, "Poland Refuses! Attack about to Begin!" In fact the attack begins at 5:25 A.M. I received news of this in the morning from Minister Alfieri and immediately afterward also from the Duce, who calls me to the Palazzo Venezia.

September 1, 1939

The Duce is calm. He has already decided not to intervene, and the struggle which has agitated his spirit during these last weeks has ceased. He telephones personally to Attolico urging him to entreat Hitler to send him a telegram releasing him from the obligations of the alliance. He does not want to pass as a welsher in the eyes of the German people, nor in the eyes of the Italian people, who, to tell the truth, do not show too many scruples, blinded as they are by anti-German hatred. Hitler sends the message through von Mackensen.

I receive François-Poncet and Sir Percy Loraine. It is now positive that France and England will do nothing against us. Nevertheless, I repeat to F. Poncet what I have said to Percy Loraine about our attitude. And this contact is useful to dissipate doubts. The French still insist that the Duce should take the initiative toward the conference which we talked about yesterday. The English are more skeptical. But more skeptical still are we Italians, who know how matters stand and know about the rabid determination of the Germans to fight.

At three o'clock Council of Ministers. The Duce speaks briefly. Then I speak, adopting a clear-cut anti-German tone. The agenda for non-intervention by Italy, already drawn up since morning by the Duce himself, is approved. They all reacted very well. Even ministers like Starace and Alfieri, who had been among the most vociferous warmongers, embrace me and say that I have rendered a service to my country.

During the evening information arrives as to measures taken in London and Paris, which preface a declaration of war.

There also arrive the first bits of news on the victories achieved by the Germans. The Poles are withdrawing everywhere. I do not believe their resistance can last long.

September 2, 1939

Yielding to French pressure we suggest to Berlin the possibilities of a conference. A mere hint for the information of Berlin. Contrary to what I expected, Hitler does not reject the proposal absolutely. I inform the Duce. I call in the ambassadors of France and England. I telephone personally to Lord Halifax and to Bonnet. (I note that my telephone call to Bonnet, to judge from the tone of his voice and from the words spoken, has produced lively satisfaction in Paris.) I find much good will among the French, and maybe as much among the English, but with greater firmness on the part of the latter. One condition is put forward: the evacuation of the Polish territories occupied by the Germans. This condition is confirmed by Lord Halifax, after the meeting of the Cabinet.

It seems to me that nothing else need be done. It isn't my business to give Hitler advice that he would reject decisively, and maybe with contempt. I tell this to Halifax, to the two ambassadors, and to the

Duce, and, finally, I telephone to Berlin that unless the Germans advise us to the contrary we shall let the conversations lapse. The last note of hope has died. Daladier talks to the French Chamber in a decisive tone and his English colleagues do the same in London.

Nothing new here. The Duce is convinced of the necessity of remaining neutral, but he is not at all happy. Whenever he can he reverts to the possibility of action. The Italian people, however, are happy about the decisions taken.

September 3, 1939

During the night I was awakened by the Ministry because Bonnet has asked Guariglia if we could not at least obtain a symbolic withdrawal of German forces from Poland. Nothing can be done. I throw the proposal in the wastebasket without informing the Duce. But this shows that France is moving toward the great test without enthusiasm and full of uncertainty. A people like the French, heroic in self-defense, do not care for foreign lands and for nations too far away.

At eleven o'clock the news arrives that Great Britain has declared war on Germany. France does the same at 5 P.M. But how can they fight this war? The German advance in Poland is overwhelming. It is not impossible for us to foresee a very rapid finish. In what way can France and England bring help to Poland? And when Poland is liquidated, will they want to continue a conflict for which there is no longer any reason? The Duce does not believe so. He believes, rather, after a short struggle, peace before the clash which he judges impossible from a military point of view. I agree. I am not a military man. I do not know how the war will develop, but I know one thing—it will develop and it will be long, uncertain, and relentless. The participation of Great Britain makes this certain. England has made this declaration to Hitler. The war can end only with Hitler's elimination or the defeat of Britain.

On his way to the front Hitler calls Attolico to the chancellery and entrusts him with greetings to the Duce. He was, I am told, calm and optimistic. He thinks that he will have Poland at his feet in four weeks, and in another four weeks will be able to concentrate his forces on the western front. He said nothing more. The Duce, who still prizes German friendship, was happy to know of Hitler's gesture.

September 4, 1939

I accompany Mackensen to the Duce. He handed him a message from Hitler, in which the conviction is reaffirmed that the two regimes, bound together by a common destiny, must follow the same path. Hitler shows much confidence in the success of his enterprise. The Duce expresses full solidarity with Germany, and this is what he really feels. He gives in to my suggestions momentarily, but later, as he is in the habit of doing, returns to his former ideas. He is convinced that France does not want and cannot fight this war, that the French people are tired even before they begin to fight, and he is still dreaming of heroic undertakings against Yugoslavia which would bring him to the Rumanian oil, forgetting completely the reality of our situation.

Favagrossa said tonight that he would be happy if our present stocks permitted us to fight for three months. At times the Duce seems attracted to the idea of neutrality which would permit us to gather economic and military strength, so that we could intervene effectively at the proper moment. But immediately afterward he abandons this idea. The idea of joining the Germans attracts him. The battle that I have to fight with him is hard, and at times I feel like giving it up, but I must fight to the end. Otherwise it will mean the ruin of the country, the ruin of Fascism, and the ruin of the Duce himself.

After a meeting with the American Ambassador I succeed in getting permission for our steamships to leave port. They will be full to capacity, especially since the sinking of the *Athenia*. In addition to the economic advantages we shall also be relieved of much worry.

Von Papen has been intriguing in Ankara. I propose to send a letter of protest to Ribbentrop. This will be another cause of friction—and I hope for many more.

September 5, 1939

I tell François-Poncet that the anti-Italian measures that are being taken at Tunis, Jibuti, Oran, etc., may lead to serious incidents. I shall telephone Bonnet. . . . I promptly received assurances that all these measures have been revoked. François-Poncet suggests that a meeting take place between one of their officials and Giannini in order to eliminate any possibility of friction between Italy and France. I speak to the Duce about it. After some hesitation he agreed. It is another step forward. François-Poncet believes that another attempt at mediation can be made by us after the occupation of Warsaw. To succeed, however, it would be necessary for Hitler to be endowed with the greatest wisdom—that sort of wisdom that does not desert one after victory. François-Poncet is doubtful because he knows the man and because, above all, he is afraid of the extremist influence of von Ribbentrop, whom he calls a dangerous imbecile.

Neutrality is beginning to bear fruit. The stock market quotations soar, the first orders to buy Italian industrial and financial stock come from France, boats resume their sailings at double the normal rates and are jam-packed. The Duce takes an interest in all this, but not a great deal as yet. He must be told that we need a long period of neutrality in order to enter the war later, as he desires, but not before the end of the year. General Carboni paints a very dark picture of the conditions of our military preparedness, our meager resources, disorganized command, demoralization among the masses. Perhaps he exaggerates, but there is some truth in it.

September 6, 1939

The Duce is in a more serene humor. He still believes that the opportunity of entering the game as a mediator will shortly present itself. Thus he is glad of the German successes in Poland, believing that they will shorten the conflict. Today Cracow fell, and the German generals paid their respects at the tomb of Pilsudski. The Duce feels that this fine gesture could never have been made by the Germany of the Kaiser. The Ambassador from Poland, whom I received this afternoon, was sad but not depressed. He says that the war will be continued until the last soldier is dead and that we shall yet have many surprises. What surprises, and when?

Conversation with Percy Loraine. I had asked him to let the Turks know that they keep up too much agitation against us and should keep quiet if they don't want all of the Balkans to catch fire. The English will do this, especially since Loraine has sent me a very honeyed note intimating that the English will take care to avoid incidents with our submarines.

Villani comes to speak to me in the name of Czaky about the danger of a German request for the passage of German troops through Hungary. He would oppose it, even by force of arms, although he would accept it if the Germans would agree to march against Rumania. This is one of Czaky's usual fantasies to which both I and the Duce give little credence. But we must keep an eye on him, since he is an irresponsible and vain man and also excitable—which means trouble.

Tacchi-Venturi brings a report of the Pope's desire for peace and his burning desire for Italian neutrality.

September 7, 1939

Nothing that is worth recording. Federzoni, Bottai, and other fellow Fascists come to assure me of their unconditional support of the position taken by me on the question of the alliance with Germany. They are in agreement in finding legal, ethical, and political reasons for our attitude.

The Duce still has intermittent belligerent flashes. Whenever he reads an article that compares his policy with that of 1914 he reacts violently in favor of Germany. He speaks of further consultations with Hitler in order to make decisions about intervention. But he will not do anything.

September 8, 1939

The Germans occupy Warsaw. The Duce is very much excited over the news. He sees in it some possibility of a rapid conclusion of the conflict through the proposals for agreement advanced by Hitler. But I do not believe that Hitler can have the wisdom to be moderate in victory, and I believe even less that the English, now that they have taken up the sword, are disposed to sheath it to their dishonor.

Indeed, this is repeated to me by Percy Loraine in a conference I had with him—a conversation marked by a sincere desire for understanding with us and a calm, inexorable intransigence with respect to Germany. On the other hand, Poncet, who is making ready to leave for France, seems more conciliatory. It is clear that there is some misunderstanding between London and Paris. The French recall too well the horrors of a war fought on their own territory to adopt without hesitation the British line of conduct.

September 9, 1939

Villani reports that the Germans have asked for the free use of the railroad at Kaya to attack Poland from the rear. The request, without threats at this time, was made today by Ribbentrop over the telephone. Czaky informs us at four o'clock that the first German troops will be despatched tomorrow at twelve. The Hungarians do not wish to yield to the demand. They are aware that this is a prelude to an actual occupation of the country. And they are right. On my return from Salzburg I indicated to the Duce that the Germans were using the same language to the Hungarians that they had used six months previously to Poland: *"querelles d'Allemands."* I accompanied Villani to the Duce. Villani is extremely anti-German. He talked clearly. He spoke of the menace that would weigh upon the world, including Italy, if Germany won the war. In Vienna they are already singing a song which says, "What we have we shall hold onto tightly, and tomorrow we shall go to Trieste." Hatred against Italy is always alive in the German mind, even though the Axis had for a time lulled this hatred to sleep. The Duce was shaken. He advised the Hungarians to turn down the German demand as courteously as they can.

Then, in talking with me, the Duce violently condemned German conduct. But he wishes to pursue a prudent policy, since a German victory cannot be completely discounted. I do not believe that he is wrong. I told him that I agreed with him, if the Germans would hurry. "If Germany wins before Christmas, well and good, otherwise she will lose the war."

September 10, 1939

Long conversation—the Duce, myself, and Attolico. The Duce is especially desirous of knowing the state of mind of the German people as regards us. Attolico reports that if the highest circles, where the truth is known, are calm and measured in their judgments, the masses, unaware of what has taken place, are already beginning to give indications of increasing hostility. The words treachery and perjury are often repeated. The Duce reacts with violence and wants Hitler to publish in Germany the telegram he sent the Duce which, since it is known to all the world, there is no reason to keep hidden from the Germans. Attolico also reports on the morale of Germany. It is quite depressed, even if military victories in Poland have galvanized it temporarily. During the conversation the Duce speaks with moderation and sometimes expresses himself against the Germans. Attolico, on leaving with me, shares my satisfaction in the change of Mussolini's psychology during these last weeks.

De Bono speaks of the situation of the Army and defines it as materially and morally disastrous. He, who has recently completed an inspection on the western front, is convinced that the present state of our defenses could not stand up against a French attack. He says that Pariani is a traitor and that Starace is a "sinister buffoon."

September 11, 1939

Villani reports that the Hungarians have denied the right of passage to German forces and that von Ribbentrop has not reacted. He had asked for the transit of some materials but I believe that this refusal will not be forgotten by the Germans and that at some time or other the Hungarians will have to pay for it. The English continue to use all sorts of blandishments on us. Percy Loraine came to make excuses for a hostile article written by Lloyd George and assured me that the British had pulled the Turks' ears for their hostile attitude toward us. As a matter of fact, the Turks have changed their tune in the last few days, especially in the press. Loraine also says that the Polish military position is not so bad as the Germans would make it appear. The Army is, for the most part, intact, and ready for the most severe tests. Can this be true? It is a fact that Warsaw has not yet been completely occupied, and recent experience has shown that fighting in cities is difficult.

Today, for the first time, the Duce alluded to the possibility of making a public declaration of Italian neutrality. Naturally, he says, this will be done in agreement with the Germans, but meanwhile we have taken one long step forward.

September 12, 1939

I received Villani early. He is very angry with the Germans. After the Germans accepted the refusal of transportation of their troops, they had the "Glorious Slovak Army" make the same request. The danger is still very great. According to Villani, the Slovaks are to the Germans what the jackals are to the hyenas—accomplices and pimps, with this added, that all the Slovakian minorities will raise their heads. Czaky refused in principle, and will confirm his refusal as soon as he gets orders from the Regent. The Duce, to whom I reported the matter, also found it ridiculous, and said that "against the glorious Slovakian Army it is necessary to oppose the not less glorious Hungarian Army."

Clodius, the German economic agent, gave Giannini to understand that in Berlin they would postpone the expatriation of the Germans from Alto Adige until the end of the war. The proposal is slippery. I remember that at Berchtesgaden Hitler twice said that the withdrawal of the minorities from Alto Adige had touched his prestige and that for this reason he would be more intransigent with Poland. I have a suspicion that the Germans are preparing to put one over on us. The Duce is indignant. He, who was ready to make great concessions to the Germans on economic grounds, remains unyielding on the question of minorities. I myself speak to Clodius, but succeed in getting only this concession: that the problem be again submitted to examination in Berlin. Orders come from on high.

I accompany Grazzi to the Duce, who gives instructions for an understanding with Greece, a country too poor for us to covet.

September 13, 1939

Important conversation with Percy Loraine, who hands me a very friendly letter from Lord Halifax thanking me for my part in the collaboration and hoping that it will be continued in the future. After this Loraine says, stating that he is speaking only for himself, "From various quarters I hear it said that England is getting ready to make threats against Italy. This is false. We are going to leave all this to the judgment of the Duce. I should like to ask one thing only, that if a change of policy should take place we be advised in time." I answered, "No change will take place. However, we will never take you by surprise. But I, too, want to tell you one thing—be careful not to dictate to us. Our position would stiffen immediately. If anyone should dictate to us from within or without we should naturally answer from within and naturally against the one who tried to force our hand." I reported the conference to the Duce and he completely approved it. He has also given me instructions to answer Halifax's letter in a very cordial manner.

Bocchini reports on the state of mind of the country, which is gradually getting better with the spreading of news of the certainty of our neutrality. Nevertheless, the country is and remains fundamentally anti-German. Germanophiles can be counted on the fingers of one hand. They are objects of scorn. The *Tevere,* an ultra-German paper, is called in Rome *The Rhinegold*. Farinacci is obstinately pro-German. Can the Rhine also have passed through Cremona? [The northern Italian city where Farinacci was born and where he rose to considerable power. He was the Fascist boss of the district.]

September 14, 1939

I have answered Halifax, ending my letter with an allusion to possible action by the Duce to re-establish peace.

Magistrati has had a very important conference with Goering, who seems to have been persuaded of the advisability of Italy's remaining neutral. Such a position will help Germany more than our eventual entrance into the conflict. One surprising thing—Goering gave a hint of the impending intervention of Russia, which is to absorb a part of Poland. In fact, Russia is showing signs of restlessness. It is mobilizing numerous classes and the *Tass* prints news of Polish boundary raids and provocations. How unimaginative people are when they intend to quarrel.

September 15, 1939

I have persuaded the Duce to appoint an ambassador to London. This move will have considerable repercussion in the world and will do a great deal to normalize our relations with Great Britain. I had chosen Bastianini, who, although he is not an eagle, is nevertheless a very trustworthy person and very much in accord with the policy of non-intervention. I am sure that he will render important services.

Today the Duce has come back to his idea of constituting a bloc of Danubian Balkan countries which we are to head. I have drafted a telegram of instructions for Attolico. But in the course of the evening Mussolini decided to put off the matter. He is thinking of postponing it until the end of German operations in Poland. He still believes it possible that the war can then be stopped, a European conference called, and a collective-security pact concluded among the six great European powers. I am sorry that I do not agree with him this time. In order to bring this about it would be necessary for Hitler to give evidence of a moderation of which I do not believe him capable. And then England will go ahead, will carry on the war implacably to the end, until her own defeat or that of Germany. I anticipate a bitter, hard, long, very long conflict, which will end in victory for Great Britain.

Graziani is pessimistic as to the condition of the Army. Pariani, on the other hand, is so optimistic and sure of himself as to make one wonder if perchance he is not right. However, as for myself, I do not believe him.

September 16, 1939

François-Poncet has returned from Paris less optimistic than when he left here. The war will last long. It will be continued to the end at any sacrifice. This is the spirit that predominates in France. I have had a transcript made of the conversation and have sent a copy to the King. In so far as it concerns us, unlimited smiles and polite words—a real serenade under the balcony. They are not sure of the situation and are afraid that one day they will have to settle with us. It now seems that Germany wants to attack Rumania. This disturbs the sleep of the French and British. But the fact that Russia is preparing to intervene should be even more disturbing. At this time an agreement has been reached with Japan, or is about to be reached. The Soviets can have a free hand in Europe. The Duce thinks that the Ukraine will have an internal uprising, will proclaim a Bolshevik republic, and be federated with Moscow. Russian intervention will thus find justification.

Other happenings have today darkened the horizon of the democracies. The Turkish Minister for Foreign Affairs is going to Moscow. Lindbergh makes a speech stating that whatever happens the United States must keep out of the fray. The Soviet military attaché to Berlin returns to Moscow to be received by the highest officials of the Soviet Union. The situation is developing in such a way as to make the position of the democracies precarious.

I have also seen Sir Percy Loraine. He is quite disturbed, and the information he gave confirmed the approaching German thrust into Rumania. This means that fire will be set to the Balkans and will probably make our neutrality untenable.

September 17, 1939

This evening the Russians entered Poland. On the pretext of avoiding disorders the Bolsheviks have crossed the frontiers. The Poles have put up some resistance, but what can they do at this hour? The Duce comments on the news to the effect that the situation of the democracies is becoming increasingly complicated. Although they are bound to action by the pact, he does not believe that France and England will declare war on Russia. Besides, the Duce does not believe that Germany wants to invade Rumania. It will be satisfied to impose economic servitude on it. I recall that during the Berghof conferences Hitler twice made the statement that King Carol will have to pay dearly for the murder of Codreano, who, on his mother's side, was of German blood. It would not surprise me if he should want to settle accounts today.

From the train of the Supreme Command in upper Silesia von Ribbentrop has talked to me over the telephone. He was calm and very cordial. He said that the Polish Army has already been liquidated and that within two or three days the last centers of resistance must give way. Russian intervention has taken place according to a prearranged plan. For the time being he was not able to say any more, but said that in a few days he would establish closer contacts with me. Although I didn't say so I have thought about eventual proposals for peace. I, too, was very cordial toward him and asked him to convey to Hitler our congratulations and greetings.

Wieniawa has informed me of the Russian invasion. For the first time he was very much discouraged, his eyes were filled with tears and showed that he had not slept for some time.

September 18, 1939

François-Poncet is gloomy. Although he does not want to admit it, he sees the situation in dark colors, but even today refuses to eliminate a priori the possibility of an understanding should Hitler be prepared to make reasonable offers. He says that during the first six months there have been many Franco-British failures, but that, as had happened in 1914, they would soon be corrected. He insisted that the course of the war is not quite similar to that of the other conflict and that it is not altogether certain, in view of the steady German progress, that six months more of war will be added to the first six months. The end may come quickly. Percy Loraine, whom I met at the Golf Club, was not happy. The sinking of the Courageous, about which he had just received news, did not help to keep him in good humor.

A long conference with the Duce in the evening. I reported what I had learned from General Graziani. At the present time our first-line forces amount to only ten divisions. The thirty-five others are patched up, incompletely manned, and ill-equipped. The Duce admitted that this was so and uttered bitter words as to the real condition of the Army, which at this time is so faulty. He boasts about our aviation. He has figures given him by Valle, which are absurdly optimistic. I advised him to start an investigation through the prefects: count the planes in the hangars and then add them up. This should not be an impossible undertaking. And yet until now we have not succeeded in finding out the truth.

September 19, 1939

The most important event of the day is Hitler's speech at Danzig, which may be called restrained and perhaps the precursor of a peace offensive. His references to us are friendly and cordial, which at this time has a special value. The Duce was flattered that the Führer had mentioned him twice.

From Rumania comes the information that the Polish military and political leaders have, for the most part, been interned at the request of the Germans. How can we put any trust in our allies? Wieniawa, who had come to protest because Italian newspapers had spoken of the flight of Smigly-Rydz to Rumania, wept when I furnished proof that the marshal, who had promised to sign a victorious peace in Berlin, had really crossed the frontier. I assured him that we intended to be humane and that Polish refugees would find a home and help in Italian territory.

As we had been led to expect, the conference between Grazzi and Metaxas has had good results. Tomorrow we shall issue our first report, which will give France and Great Britain another piece of bad news, of which they have had plenty the last few days.

September 20, 1939

No information worthy of mention. Our friends the Croats are waking up and I feel that we should not neglect them. The occasion may come for us to carry out our Croat action with the unwilling complicity of Germany and without incurring the hostility of France and England, which might welcome this new barrier to the German advance. I have spoken of it to the Duce and he has given me a hundred thousand Swiss francs to intensify our propaganda.

A long and somewhat useless conversation with Helfand, who made every effort, now that he is almost an ally of the Germans, not to speak ill of them as he has done for so many years.

September 21, 1939

Nothing new.

September 22, 1939

The Duce was somewhat shocked by the killing of Calinescu. He thinks there is some mysterious foreign plot at the bottom of it. The reaction to this has been so violent as to lead one to reflect. Only weak governments punish so severely.

I have spoken with Starace of the internal situation and told him that some of his methods are not of a kind to uproot anti-Fascism; they create it. In Via Veneto during the evening I saw a person beaten who was absolutely harmless (a patriot and a Fascist) by a small group of gangster elements protected by the fact that they belonged to the party and by the assurance that they would not be punished. They punished this Fascist, who has come from abroad, for having used "*lei*" [the polite form of address] rather than "*voi*." [The Fascist Government at this time was carrying out a plan to abolish the use of *lei* as a term of address because, according to them, it was an imported term and savored too much of the foreign rule to which Italy had been subjected in the past, and advocated the use of *tu* and *voi* as substitutes.] My presence was sufficient to end the incident quickly, but the look of the small crowd that had gathered was anything but reassuring and clearly hostile to the so-called Fascists. This unwarranted *squadrismo* action [a new word created by Fascism to indicate a group of men used for the purpose of attacking, arresting, and even killing opponents] is harmful, and I am going to speak to the Duce about it. I am far from deploring beatings when they are well deserved, but it disgusted me to see idiotic and cowardly acts of violence. Unfortunately this has become a habit with so many mercenaries employed by the higher-ups in the party.

September 23, 1939

After a long silence the Duce spoke today to the Hierarchy of Bologna. I saw him immediately after his speech. And, as often happens on these occasions, he was in a state of utter complacency. He read me what he had said, and together we changed some parts that concerned our foreign policy. As regards internal affairs, I gave him my point of view as follows: Never so much as today has the country been solidly behind the regime and the Duce. To speak of assassinations, plots, defeatism, et cetera, would be an attempt to give body to a shadow. The facts are quite otherwise. All the national resentment is directed against the person of Starace, who, in spite of having many good qualities, uses the wrong methods. "He is a vulgarian," the Duce said. "True," I answered. "Besides, we should not forget that he comes from Lecce, and that throughout all their history Milan, Turin, Rome, Florence, have never been governed by a southern man who was so typically southern. The sensibility of these cities rebels." The Duce agreed. It would not surprise me to see a change of guard, which, in view of the state of affairs, would be a very useful thing.

I received the Russian Chargé d'Affaires, who asked me for the *agrément* of the new Russian Ambassador, and I also received the British Chargé d'Affaires, who spoke to me about routine matters.

Nitti has addressed a letter to the Duce, for the first time in eighteen years, I believe. I do not know its contents as yet.

September 24, 1939

The development occasioned by the Russian occupation of Poland has led the Duce to revise the optimistic judgment that he had previously formed on the German situation. Indeed he now goes so far as to say that Hitler is bottled up and that by making able maneuvers the French and English may yet succeed in pitting Russia against Germany. The fact is that the Duce is in favor of peace only because the position of a neutral is not at all to his liking.

In the last few days he has repeated that a great nation cannot remain eternally in such a position without losing face, and that someday it should prepare to intervene. I cannot contradict him, because that would make matters worse. But he knows well by now the deplorable conditions due to an unprepared army, and this morning, for the first time, he admitted that Pariani has not been telling the truth [*ha molto piombo nell'ala*—his wing is overweighted with lead]. In his opinion the Army has two glaring defects: being excessively attached to the dynasty and being too much concerned about questions of supply. The second is perhaps true, but there are quite other reasons for the present state of utter confusion. Nevertheless, firing Pariani would be a good thing. I shall try to have Soddu succeed him because I hold him in high esteem. Sebastiani has said that the Chief wants to fire Valle, too, but he does not know how he is going to replace him. Why not with Ricci, who is a good pilot and who has given evidence of being a fine organizer?

We have asked Attolico to consider the idea of forming a bloc of neutrals and at least outwardly trying to give the matter an economic aspect. He agrees and has spoken to Weizsäcker about it.

September 25, 1939

"It is well to make use of a small person to kill a large one, but it is a mistake to make use of a large one to liquidate a small one." Such is the diagnosis that the Duce has made of the Russian intervention invoked by Germany. He is more than ever convinced that Hitler will rue the day he brought the Russians into the heart of Europe. They have two weapons that make them still more terrible: pan-Slavic nationalism, with which they can bring pressure on the Balkans, and Communism, which is spreading rapidly among the proletariat all over the world, beginning with Germany itself.

François-Poncet tries to find out whether the gentle hint for peace contained in the Duce's speech has any concrete basis in some German offer. No. Nothing new for the time being. Then he expresses himself pessimistically as to the possibilities of peace, and adds that for us Fascists it must be easy to understand how a country can struggle, and perhaps be defeated, to uphold a point of honor. It was difficult to contradict him.

Villani speaks of Hungary. In spite of the state of alarm there is a good deal of calm and as much decision to fight in case the Germans should want to invade the country. Teleki calls Hitler a gangster and Czaky has sent word to me that von Ribbentrop has not concealed his hatred for me. I feel very much honored.

Meeting to take up the matter of Alto Adige. Notwithstanding many objections made by the Germans, the exodus will begin again soon. Golden bridges. . . .

September 26, 1939

We already surmised during the last few days something was being hatched between Moscow and Berlin, and today we have had confirmation from Rosso. It seems that von Ribbentrop has returned to Moscow to sign a genuine military alliance to give Bessarabia and Estonia to the Russians and the remaining part of Rumania to the Germans. Absolute silence from Berlin. As usual we are told nothing. I telephoned to Attolico that he should obtain information, and after a few hours he reports that von Ribbentrop's trip to Moscow seems confirmed. Hitler and his associates have returned to Berlin and, after a statement which he is to make tomorrow, he intends to go to the western front for the first time.

During the evening Moscow confirms the visit of von Ribbentrop, who will arrive at 4 p.m. tomorrow. Berlin is still silent. All this is not clear. The Germans prepare to strike a blow without our knowledge— and from Vienna to Warsaw they have struck many. All this I tell the Duce, who telephones for news, and I give him to understand that it is very difficult to go on like this. The alliance between Moscow and Berlin is a monstrous union against the letter and spirit of our pact. It is anti-Rome and anti-Catholic. It is a return to barbarism, which it is our historic function to resist with every weapon and by every means. But will it be possible for us to do so? Or has not the outcome already been tragically decided?

September 27, 1939

Berlin gives us absolutely no information. It is from the press agencies that we find out that von Ribbentrop has left for Moscow. But the scope of his trip is entirely unknown to us. Alleging that he has very little time at his disposal, von Ribbentrop refused to receive Attolico. This is bad. . . .

In the morning the Duce received Commander Pecori, our naval attaché at Berlin, in order to discuss with him some requests made by the Germans for naval assistance. They would like submarine supply stations from us, help in the location of Franco-British naval convoys, and, in addition, the transfer of some of their submarines for opera-

tion in the Mediterranean. The Duce at first favored acceding to the
German requests, including the last point, which is the most dangerous. With Cavagnari, who agrees with me 100 per cent, we sabotaged
the plan. Pecori doesn't say anything very new except that the Germans will begin mass production of submarines in April. They think
they can produce about twenty every month, both of small and medium tonnage. Valentino, who has just come from Warsaw, tells his
personal experiences. From what he says German aviation has formidable power. It is absolutely pitiless and has constantly dropped bombs
on the civil population, but the German horror is surpassed a thousand
times by the unspeakable horrors of the Bolshevik advance.

September 28, 1939

Attolico reports that on Germany's part there is no opposition to our
grouping in a politico-economic system all the neutral Danubian-
Balkan states as well as Spain. The Duce still has many doubts. I, on
the other hand, firmly believe in the desirability of such a move, which
will give us a much broader political and economic base. Nevertheless,
I am of the opinion that we must wait and see what emerges from Ribbentrop's stay in Moscow before taking the initiative. We are still completely in the dark. Events in the Baltic states and in Bessarabia do not
lead me to expect anything good. That man Ribbentrop is a sinister
being and his influence on events is extremely dangerous.

I receive Villani. The Hungarians are restless. What can they do if
the Russians enter Rumania? In my opinion, make no move. They
are too weak and too exposed to get into the game until they are
obliged to do so.

September 29, 1939

We receive first through the press, and then from the ambassadors,
the texts of the Moscow agreements. They deal with an outright partition of Poland although they contain something which allows us to
foresee that on the German side at least there is some intention to do
something later on in the way of face-saving. The Duce, however, is
rather pessimistic and believes that in view of present conditions it is
almost impossible to attempt a peaceful solution. He is right. Besides,
it would not be admissible that the head of the Fascist party should

support a solution that will put into the hands of the Bolsheviks many millions of Polish Catholics.

I see François-Poncet, who is indignant at what has been done and how it was done. He expresses a hope that the Duce will not intervene and recommend a solution that will be inexorably rejected by France and England. François-Poncet, in addition, sees the day drawing nearer and nearer when Italy will stand beside these two powers to defend the liberty and dignity of Europe and its own national life as well. We speak of Franco-Italian relations. I voice severe criticism of the sordid French attitude toward us and he admits it. "What do you expect?" he adds. "The French are strange people who would like to win the lottery without buying a ticket." I am preparing the draft of a joint declaration to serve as the legal basis for constituting a group of neutrals which I should like to unite around Italy.

September 30, 1939

The Duce this morning was confirming his skepticism of the possibility of negotiation, when, during the meeting of the Council of Ministers, I received a telephone call from Ribbentrop. He was more careful and more courteous than during other recent telephone conversations. He advanced three proposals: (1) a Mussolini-Hitler meeting possibly at Munich; (2) a trip to Berlin by me, where Hitler would like to talk to me about the whole situation; (3) a meeting with him at the Brenner frontier. But the third solution was the least acceptable. I told the Duce that it was desirable to discard, for the time being, any idea of a trip by him. A meeting might place him in a difficult position, both with regard to the world in the event that Hitler advanced absurd proposals, as is likely, and, also, with regard to Hitler himself, if the latter asked him for immediate military collaboration. Therefore, my trip to Berlin would have to be made.

I personally called Ribbentrop, who emphasizes the need that I leave immediately today, at 6 P.M. I leave without any definite idea of what the Germans will propose to me, but I have the unshakeable and deeply rooted determination to safeguard our freedom of action. I do not believe that I can bring from Berlin any contribution to the re-establishment of peace in Europe, but it is certain that I will fight like a lion to preserve peace for the Italian people.

October 1, 1939

As usual I have summarized in a memorandum in my conference book the official account of my contacts with Hitler and other high officials of the Reich.

Here I record only some impressions. I found Hitler very serene. At Salzburg the inner struggle of this man, decided upon action but not yet sure of his means and of his calculations, was apparent. Now, on the other hand, he seems absolutely sure of himself. The test he has met has given him confidence for future tests. He was wearing a green-gray jacket with his usual black trousers. His face bore traces of recent fatigue, but this was not reflected in the alertness of his mind. Hitler spoke for almost two hours and cited figure after figure without referring to a single note. With respect to Italy, his attitude was the same as before. What is past is past. From now on he looks to the future and wants to have us with him. But I must say that all our suggestions as to military collaboration have been discussed quite openly. What most impressed me is his confidence in ultimate victory. Either he is under hallucinations, or he really is a genius. He outlines plans of action and cites dates with an assurance that does not admit of contradiction. Will he be proved right? In my opinion the game will not be so simple as he believes.

October 2, 1939

France and England still have a great deal to say. If it is to be war, it will be an implacable war. The eyes of Hitler flash in sinister fashion whenever he talks about his ways and means of fighting. I return from Germany with the strong conviction that the first months of the war will lead the Germans to believe in victory, but that the longer it lasts the harder will it be.

Ribbentrop says nothing new and nothing original. He is the exaggerated echo of Hitler. For the present he is all out for the Russians. And he expresses himself in favor of the Communists in such an imprudent and vulgar way as to perplex anyone who listens to him.

The German people are resigned but determined. They will wage war and will wage it well, but dream and hope for peace. The applause with which I was received clearly reveals this state of mind.

All the Italians in Germany heartily hate the Germans, but they are firmly convinced, without exception, that Hitler will win the war.

Goering did not show up. The tragicomedy of the decoration [the collar of the Order of the Annunziata] continues. At this juncture in the year of 1939 we are about to have a second *affaire du collier.*

October 3, 1939

I give the Duce my report and go into all of the details verbally. He does not share Hitler's confidence in victory. The French and English will hold firm. His conclusions are based on information given him by our military experts. And, besides, why hide it? He is somewhat bitter about Hitler's sudden rise to fame. He would be greatly pleased if Hitler were slowed down, and, hoping this, predicts that it will come about.

Nevertheless, for many months to come nothing can be changed as to our attitude, which is to remain neutral and go on preparing.

October 4, 1939

For the first time in six years Mussolini speaks to me about sacking Starace. I encourage him, and Muti's name is mentioned as the one to fill Starace's place. Muti is valiant and faithful, still without sufficient political experience, it is true. But he is full of natural genius and has a strong will. If he is appointed he will do well, if for no other reason than that he will be the successor of Starace, who is hated and detested.

A meeting with two ambassadors: those of France and Britain. I give them some information on the results of my interviews in Berlin. In accord with Mussolini, I gave them to understand that the German conditions are hard, possibly acceptable, but in any case hard. At heart the Duce wishes that the European giants fight bitterly against one another, and, in spite of all that is said about our will to peace, he prefers that with some measure of restraint I throw kerosene on the flames.

October 5, 1939

Hitler announces that tomorrow morning he will let us have the text of the speech he is to deliver at twelve o'clock. According to Attolico, appearances have been saved with respect to Poland. It is certain that tomorrow will be the fatal day; either peace or real war. I should not be surprised if Hitler became a little more yielding. Determined as he is to meet events with force, a bit of the old socialist yet remains in him, making him hesitate at the prospect of a European conflagration. Not so Ribbentrop. He is an aristocrat, or, rather, a *parvenu,* and shedding the blood of the people does not worry him. The case of Hitler is different. He was a worker, and he still has some indefinite repugnance to bloodshed. He would prefer victories without bloodshed. For these reasons I think that a faint though very feeble hope still exists.

October 6, 1939

I accompany von Mackensen to the Duce to deliver the text of Hitler's speech. The Duce speaks in a very cordial tone, and tells him that Italian military preparations are proceeding at a sure and rapid pace. If the war should continue, in the spring he will be able to give help rather than receive it.

When we were alone, the Duce read Hitler's speech and commented on it very favorably. He judges it to be so useful and effective in arousing emotion as to bring about a change in the international situation. He indulges himself in such a strain of wishful thinking that in the evening he telephones me to say that to his way of thinking the war is now ended.

I do not share this optimism. There is no doubt that the speech will create some emotion in the enemy camp which is divided by currents of pacifism. But what does Hitler offer except fair words? And how much are his fair words worth? I still have too much respect for France and England to believe that they will fall into Hitler's trap. The war did not end today; it will really start soon.

October 7, 1939

The first reactions to Hitler's speech are coming in. Though they are negative, I cannot find in them that violence which would seem to be called for by the real essence of the speech. The Polish Ambassador himself, while lightly reaffirming his old uncompromising attitude, this morning did not seem to reject *a priori* the discussion of German proposals.

Mussolini would like to do something that would get us into the game. He feels left out, and this pains him. The moment will arrive, but for the time being it is necessary to avoid taking any steps which would have little chance of success.

I gave the Duce a *curriculum vitae* of Muti. He was impressed by it. Muti is something of a warrior of the early Middle Ages.

October 8, 1939

Nothing new, except for an accentuation of the French-British reaction.

Only two voices were heard in England in favor of the conference proposed by Hitler: those of Lloyd George and Bernard Shaw. Which proves conclusively that the English consider Hitler's proposals absolutely unacceptable.

October 9, 1939

I have never seen the Duce so depressed as he was this morning. He now realizes that the prosecution of the war is inevitable, and he feels all the discomfort of having to stay out of it. He did what is for him an exceptional thing: unburdened his feelings to me. "The Italians," he said, "after having heard my warlike propaganda for eighteen years, cannot understand how I can become the herald of peace, now that Europe is in flames. There is no other explanation except the military unpreparedness of the country, but even for this I am made responsible—me, mind you—who have always proclaimed the power of our armed forces." He vented his feeling on Hitler, who, he said, placed him in a situation where he had to "throw overboard so many men and had cast a bad light even on a man like the Duce himself." He is right. Nothing to object to in this. In the country rumors are being spread against everything and everybody, himself included. But he has always acted in good faith. He was betrayed by four or five individuals whom he inadvisedly put into high positions and whom he still has not punished severely.

I am saddened. Maria is ill in bed. She seemed thin and bloodless, as if made of ivory. May God help her. I love her very much. She is the only connection with my passing youth.

October 10, 1939

I listen to Daladier's speech on the radio. It seems to me as if it were clearly uncompromising, even though it is measured and correct in form. Mussolini is not of this opinion. In fact, he telephones me with a rather satisfied air that "the French are beginning to weaken." Frankly, I don't believe this. We shall see.

October 11, 1939

Reactions to Daladier's speech confirm my first impression of its uncompromising character. In fact, Mussolini does not talk about it any longer. François-Poncet also is of the opinion that war cannot now be controlled and that operations will soon have a much broader scope. He does not deny the difficulties of the undertaking, but has faith in the victory of France—true confidence. I distinctly sense an accent of conviction in his words.

The German Government continues to put a thousand difficulties in the way of the evacuation of the Germans from Alto Adige. Requests and pretensions pile up every day. They ask quite seriously to take with them even the doorknobs and the locks. In the meantime the local situation becomes more disturbed. The people who know that they must leave are beginning to consider themselves somewhat outside the law. Some incidents have already occurred. I call Mackensen and ask him to deal with the question on a political plane. We must act quickly. The Italians are following this question with great interest and they cannot justify the delays, especially since, under Russian pressure, the Germans got eighty thousand men out of the Baltic states in a few hours.

October 12, 1939

Bombelles sends an interesting report on the situation in Croatia. Agitation is strong, and the money given by us has intensified it to the point of causing serious incidents between the mobilized Croatian troops and their Serbian officers. He considers the situation nearly ripe for intervention. I speak of it to the Duce. I, too, feel that we must strike a blow in Croatia but with the consent of, or at least without the opposition of, France and England. We must make these people under-

stand that it is to their interest if we barricade the path against the
Germans and if we save Hungary from the double pressure of Germany and Russia. Nevertheless, we must not be in a hurry. It is an
operation which will succeed, but it must be conducted like the one in
Albania.

Chamberlain speaks. It does not seem to me that his speech contains
any new elements when compared to those expressed by Daladier. As a
matter of fact, the first impression I received was rather of a more
determined intransigence.

October 13, 1939

Chamberlain's speech makes the hopes of even the most obstinate
pacifists sink. One recognizes the traditional British decision in the
voice of the old statesman. The Duce, after having read the original
text, concludes that every possibility for an understanding has now
disappeared. He was preparing to make a statement but is putting it
off for the time being. Well done. This is the real moment to keep
one's mouth shut.

In Germany the speech was received with indignation and fury.
Attolico telegraphs that it has turned out to be a call to war, and von
Mackensen expresses himself in similar terms. The latter comes in the
name of von Ribbentrop to request the support of our press on some
specific points of the polemic. Von Mackensen is rather depressed and,
notwithstanding all his efforts, he does not entirely succeed in hiding
his profound antipathy toward von Ribbentrop, whom he considers the
person most responsible for the war.

October 14, 1939

Nothing new.

October 15, 1939

Nothing new.

October 16, 1939

In the afternoon the Duce holds forth at length on the state of the
armed forces. He has to face the facts, and the situation known to

everybody can no longer be ignored even by him. Finally, he said that
he wishes to fire Pariani and Valle. This would be wise. He also said
there will be no possibility of entering the war before the first of June
or July, and even then we shall have at most three months' supplies.
Under such conditions it would be folly to enter the conflict. We must
wait, and I am sure that the Duce, who suffers to the death because of
his present position, will know how to wait until the best interests of
Italy can be served by such a move.

All over the world a deadly silence seems to presage bad news. When
the Germans shut themselves up in their silent resentment they prepare
a blow. I believe that the cannon will be heard soon. The Duce was
very much affected by certain documents and information on Russia
which have come into our possession, and wants to begin a press campaign to explain to the Italians that Bolshevism is dead and that in its
place is a kind of Slavic Fascism. I try to dissuade him. Russian friendship is a potion that the Italians would not drink too willingly, especially if served in a German beaker, as it would now have to be served.

October 17, 1939

The condition of Maria has become worse and the doctors have
lost hope of saving her. May the Madonna accomplish the miracle.
There is nothing sadder than to witness the gradual extinction of a
youthful life which has been filled with purity and goodness. This year
fate is trying me harshly.

October 18, 1939

Tonight passed tragically. The death of Maria seemed imminent
and unavoidable. Later she rallied and is now somewhat better. There
is a slender thread of hope, but I still cling to it. The mercy of the
Virgin may have descended upon a creature who richly deserves it.

Hitler sent his Ambassador to express his good wishes for the health
of Maria, and von Ribbentrop telegraphed.

Together with Clodius I have worked out the final clauses for the
agreement on the Alto Adige, which will be signed tomorrow. I have
also tried to satisfy some of Hitler's requests of an economic nature for
the purpose of facilitating the transfer. I believe we must do everything
possible for the Germans short of giving them our complete military
support.

The Duce confirms his intention of proceeding to a change of guard within the party by substituting the excellent Muti for Starace. Better late than never.

October 19, 1939

Maria continues to improve, and this leads me to entertain high hopes.

Today France and Great Britain signed an agreement with Turkey. This does not displease me, because it means Germany is losing a point. Poncet telephones to tell me, under instructions from Paris, that the agreement has no anti-Italian character, but is aimed only at the preservation of the *status quo* in the eastern Mediterranean. I don't know what this assurance is worth, but it is well that it has been given. A change of guard is about to take place in the government. The Duce is getting ready to make ministers out of my friends Muti, Pavolini, Riccardi, and Ricci. He sends Alfieri away, and this displeases me, because he has been a good comrade. I shall try to keep him afloat politically, and if I do not succeed in having him appointed President of the Chamber, I should like to appoint him Ambassador to the Holy See. Starace will perhaps pass into my jurisdiction as Governor of the Aegean, but I like this less. Pariani and Valle, too, are finally leaving.

October 20, 1939

Maria is worse. I now feel that misfortune is inevitable and close at hand. Anguish wrings my heart, because of my own sorrow and the deep, silent sorrow that has overwhelmed the heart of my mother.

October 21, 1939

The gravity of Maria's illness continues unabated. Slight and transitory improvements render the sad fact more evident, just as the lightning shows more clearly for a moment the horror of the tempest. Nothing is sadder than to have to watch this slow agony and to look on smilingly, because Maria, who is in complete possession of her intellectual powers, must not suspect the fate that awaits her. Up to this point she has not realized that death is ready to strike her, and this proves again that divine Providence is truly infinite.

October 22, 1939

At six minutes past midnight, the same hour at which my father passed into the shadows, Maria passed away. After a long and painful agony she breathed her last serenely, receiving the consolations of religion. But she had been unconscious for over half an hour.

This is a great blow which numbs me. Maria was a good sister. Always near me spiritually, but always discreet and thoughtful, she was for me a link with my past. Our early youth was spent in absolute intimacy, as was proper in the modest family of an officer. For a long time we slept in the same room, ate our meals together with the spontaneity of two colts who feed out of the same manger. Later on, even though life did separate us physically for a long time, it could never really separate us. Maria was proud, loyal, honest, and straight as a sword. The ailment which consumed her perhaps at times influenced her personality, but it could not in the least change the profound characteristics of her soul. Everybody who knew her never failed to be impressed by them. Universal and deep sorrow is felt for her. Melancholy dominates my spirit, and the void which has come into my heart with her disappearance can be filled neither by time nor events. A kiss to you, Maria. May God receive you in His great arms as you deserve. Adieu.

October 23, 1939

At Leghorn for the funeral of Maria. Once again, overwhelmed by sorrow, I have passed through the city of my childhood between rows of people who appeared to be suffering with me. Maria has been placed in the Purificazione Cemetery in a niche under that in which Father rests. When, a little later in the day, I returned alone to the cemetery to say an affectionate farewell to my dear ones, it seemed less hard for me to abandon my sister in that sad place, since our great, unforgettable father had received her there. And he will watch over her as he watched over us when we were children.

October 24, 1939

Life goes on its way. At the Ministry an audience with the Duce, who was paternal in his attitude. Visits, conversations, the press, telegrams. . . . But when, after a fall, we begin to walk again, the slope seems harder to climb, and one feels that the burden weighing on the shoulders has increased in weight.

October 25, 1939

The Duce plans to write a letter to Hitler to tell him that as things stand Italy represents for Germany an economic and moral reserve, but that later on it may also play a military role. I do not see the need of this document, but the Duce is a little restless and wants to do something. He also speaks of a meeting of the Grand Council to be held soon with the idea of informing it exactly as to what has happened. He also alludes to the timeliness of a very important speech by me to inform the country of what is taking place. If I tell the truth it will be difficult to reach the conclusion which the Duce intends and which he impresses upon me—that is, that the Axis and the alliance with Germany still exist and are fully operative.

October 26, 1939

The speech that Ribbentrop delivered at Danzig has had damaging repercussions. It was a mediocre repetition of Hitler's speech. Loraine said that Ribbentrop is a second-rate man with secondhand ideas. I agree with him.

Mussolini speaks again of the speech that I am to make on December 16, and, in listing the arguments that I must employ to establish the reasons for our attitude, the Duce, while still wishing to maintain a pro-German line, makes the sternest charges against the Germans. It will be a difficult task, but taking advantage of his state of mind I shall try to make a speech that will carry, save appearances as far as possible, but tell the truth and so widen the breach between ourselves and the Germans.

This morning the Duce said that Hitler is creating grave risks for himself, since, forced by circumstances, he is putting all power in the hands of the military leaders. Arms in the hands of the people and power in the hands of the officers are distinctly unfavorable for any dictatorship. The Duce discovered this in September, when anti-Fascism found in our barracks the best environment in which to grow and prosper. In time of war the influence of the party becomes more and more ephemeral, and the black shirts themselves are not held in

check by regular army officers. Recently we have had many proofs of
this.

October 27, 1939

Changes are about to take place in high positions, both in the party
and in the various ministries. The Duce has decided in favor of Muti,
but he is still somewhat doubtful as to Valle's successor. He is thinking
of General Pinna. I advised him against this, because this man is too
intimately linked with the work of his predecessor. We must choose a
new man. I suggest Pricolo. For the Navy, too, the Duce asked me for
a nomination, and he advances the name of Admiral Riccardi. My
father did not hold him in high esteem because he tried to shirk his
duty during the war [World War I]. I think the best thing to do is to
keep Cavagnari, who has served very well. The Duce agrees. The
changes will take place on Monday.

In the international field nothing new. Increasingly strong rumors
reach us about an imminent German offensive in the west. Mussolini
does not believe that this will take place. On the contrary, I believe it
will.

October 28, 1939

Nothing new. This year's celebration of the anniversary of the
March on Rome is somewhat lifeless and lacking in enthusiasm. The
Duce is the most dissatisfied and restless person among us all. He feels
that events have betrayed both hopes and promises. What does the
future hold in store? That depends upon us here. I am steadfast in my
ideas: that if we can be calm and if we wait and overcome our im-
patience, we can yet turn this disadvantageous situation to our profit.
But calm and caution are indispensable conditions for the attainment
of these ends.

October 29, 1939

Nothing new.

October 30, 1939

The Duce tells me that yesterday, returning from an excursion
to Pomezia, he informed Starace that he had been sacked. On re-

ceiving the news Starace objected to being replaced by Muti, and he proposed the nomination of certain *federali* [federal secretaries of the Fascist party in the large cities of Italy], friends whom he favored. But the Duce did not bite and insisted on the name of Muti. "After all," he said, "he was not able to make any substantiated accusation worthy of consideration. Only provincial gossip. I think Starace is jealous of Muti because Muti has more decorations than he."

I spoke at length with Muti, outlining directives to him. Muti will follow me like a child. In spite of my growing skepticism about men in general, Muti is one of the rare ones that I believe to be sincere.

Starace is sent to command the militia. Even there he will make trouble, but certainly less.

October 31, 1939

A bombshell bursts with the change in the ministries. There is general enthusiasm because of the departure of Starace and expressions of good wishes for the new ministers. Starace and Muti meet in my office and the meeting is almost cordial.

November 1, 1939

Nothing new in foreign affairs.

November 2, 1939

At Leghorn to visit my two dear ones. At Florence that evening, where the Fascist militia received me with considerable warmth.

November 3, 1939

The new ministry is called, *sotto voce,* the "Ciano cabinet." Job hunters begin to crowd me. I am also asked for opinions on foreign policy. How absurd!

November 4, 1939

Nothing new.

November 5, 1939

Nothing worth while is happening either in Italy or outside. In Berlin, Attolico has had a conference with von Ribbentrop, who has shown himself, as usual, an out-and-out warmonger. He said that just now there is no way to have peace but to make war. All this, beautified by many phrases about the certainty of a quick victory, about which events make us more and more skeptical every day.

November 6, 1939

Nothing new.

November 7, 1939

Lively reaction of the Duce to the Comintern manifesto attacking the middle classes of the warring countries, including Germany and Italy. At my suggestion his reaction takes shape in a strong article in the *Giornale d'Italia*. The friction with Russia certainly does not help to improve relations with Berlin. But other elements play their part in this. In the first place, the fact that Ribbentrop continues to say that England entered the war because she learned in time that Italy would remain neutral. This is a lie. If Ribbentrop is trying to find a justification for his errors, he makes a new and dangerous mistake. I wrote Attolico to clear up this point immediately. If Ribbentrop insists, we may move toward some real unpleasantness. This morning the Duce was indignant.

News from Germany, Austria, and Prague all confirm a definite worsening in their internal situation.

Conversation with Soddu. He is very well informed. He says that the present condition of our Army is much worse than had been thought. He excludes any possibility of being ready in April; maybe in October at the very earliest. Soddu, too, agrees with me in believing that Germany will inevitably be beaten. He will speak about this to the Duce.

November 8, 1939

The Duce is very much impressed by what General Liotta told him about the German tendency toward alcoholism. The General went so

far as to say that the "German peril can be held back only by means
of the alcoholization of Germany," and "that the world of tomorrow
will belong to the people who drink water." However, I have wondered whether it is worth while taking seriously that Sicilian clod-
hopper, Liotta, who, because he offered some bottles of bad wine to the
Germans, believes that he has won their confidence.

The initiatives for peace by the rulers of Belgium and Holland have
not had any success, at least for the time being.

Conference with Badoglio, who comes to put himself at my disposal.
He is pessimistic as to the condition of our armed forces and affirms
that if we work very hard for two years we may be in a position to
intervene if, in the meantime, the others wear out. Badoglio is deeply
neutral but on the whole would prefer to fight against the Germans
rather than with them.

November 9, 1939

The attempt on Hitler's life at Munich leaves everybody quite skeptical, and Mussolini is more skeptical than anyone else. In reality many
aspects of the affair do not altogether convince us of the accuracy of
the account given in the papers. Either it is a master plot on the part
of the police, with the overdone purpose of creating anti-British sentiment in the German people who are quite indifferent, or, if the
attempted murder is real, it is a family brawl of people belonging to
the inner circle of the Nazi party; perhaps a carry-over of what took
place on the thirtieth of June which cannot have been forgotten in
Munich. The Duce has tried hard to compose a telegram expressing his
delight that peril has been avoided. He wanted it to be warm, but not
too warm, because in his judgment no Italian feels any great joy over
the fact that Hitler had escaped death—least of all the Duce.

Information from several sources leads us to believe that a German
attack in Belgium and Holland is close at hand. Attolico acts as the
mouthpiece for these reports, but without guaranteeing them. The
Belgian Ambassador in Rome is very much concerned and feels that
the alarm finds considerable justification in the intensified preparation
of the Germans. On the other hand, François-Poncet is skeptical.

I have spoken clearly to von Mackensen and have given instructions
to Attolico on the situation which is developing in the Alto Adige,
where the action of the German propagandists is carried on contrary
to our agreements for the emigration of the people of non-Italian

origin. People speak guardedly of the return of the Alto Adige to the Reich and hopes are aroused that may unduly embitter a situation which is growing increasingly tense. If the Franco-British were clever, this would be a fine moment to create a major incident between us and the Germans.

November 10, 1939

Nothing new. Speculation continues on both sides regarding the attempt on Hitler's life in Munich, many aspects of which are undeniably mysterious.

November 11, 1939

Rumors about an imminent German invasion of Belgium and Holland become more intensified. News of this sort has now been coming from too many quarters not to be given serious consideration. However, I must say two things: that nothing on this matter has been communicated to me from Berlin, and that, as a matter of fact, Hitler and Ribbentrop have always specifically excluded an attack on the neutrals for moral and technical reasons. But this, considering what happened before, would lead one to think that anything is possible. . . .

Mussolini does not believe that such an attack will be made, but he admits that, if it did take place, Germany's actions would be totally discredited and that in Italy there would be such a wave of hatred for Germany as to make anybody think twice. The Duce in these last few days, probably because of the situation in Alto Adige, lines up and expresses himself more and more definitely as an anti-German.

November 12, 1939

Nothing new.

November 13, 1939

Nothing new.

November 14, 1939

I receive the Prince of Hesse. I find him rather depressed, in spite of his effort to appear in his usual good humor. He confirms reports that the German offensive will take place soon on the French front and not through Holland and Belgium.

As regards the frontier incident with Holland, he secretly informs me that it was the result of a raid that the Gestapo made in Holland in order to capture, as it did, the head of the English Intelligence Service.

He tells me little or nothing about the attempt on Hitler's life at Munich. He maintains that those responsible must be sought in the circle of Roehm's old friends.

November 15, 1939

Nothing new.

November 16, 1939

Nothing new.

November 17, 1939

Nothing new.

November 18, 1939

The Prince of Piedmont hands me a small personal gift—the evening dress button for the collar of the Annunziata. He takes advantage of the occasion to talk to me on certain matters: (1) he is happy over the change of guard. He does not conceal his dislike for Starace and for his followers and their ways; (2) the troops are always fraternizing with the French on the line of the French frontier, while dislike of the Germans is becoming more and more acute. The Germans also contribute to this. Their military attaché, Rintelen, arrived unexpectedly among the Italian troops and began to ask indiscreet questions with the air of one who is making an inspection of the front. This was resented by our soldiers, especially by the officers; (3) Hesse showed himself to be rather concerned about the situation. I also mentioned the possibility of changing Ambassador Attolico, but the Prince, naturally, let the conversation die out.

November 19, 1939

To Turin hunting on the Medici estate.

November 20, 1939

News from Prague leads us to believe that the situation is more difficult than is admitted in official reports. The Duce is satisfied especially because he thinks that a Bohemian crisis will retard or, perhaps, torpedo the projected offensive on the western front. For Mussolini, the idea of Hitler's waging war, and, worse still, winning it, is altogether unbearable. He gives instructions to our Consul at Prague to advise the Bohemians to side with the Communists. This will make German repression harder and will accentuate the causes for disagreement between Moscow and Berlin.

November 21, 1939

Matters go badly in the Alto Adige. The Germans, in attempting to carry out the agreement, are preparing to hold nothing short of a plebiscite. Up to this point no harm is done, provided the German population leave immediately after having expressed their choice. Instead, nothing happens. They have the privilege of remaining as long as three years, and nothing leads us to hope that on the German side there is any intention of shortening the time. Mussolini says that he does not quite understand. Today he affirmed that on this question we might get into a conflict with the Reich. Meanwhile, he strengthens the police and the carabinièri and also increases the forces on the frontier.

All this is very well, because the chasm which separates us from Germany becomes wider from day to day, even in the mind of the Duce. This is a good moment for Franco-British propaganda to get to work. If an incident were to break out in the Alto Adige our relations with Berlin would become extremely precarious.

November 22, 1939

Nothing new.

November 23, 1939

Nothing new.

November 24, 1939

I take steps at the French Embassy and at the office of the English Chargé d'Affaires to protest against the new blockade maneuvers. This protest is couched in mild terms. The Englishman takes this into account, but Poncet, who is always very brilliant, argues, saying that it is not to him but to the German Ambassador that we ought to protest, since the floating mines are the cause for the tightening of the blockade. Then, since with the French, as with heaven, reconciliation is always possible, he says that he will intervene so that the transport of German coal, which in reality is what interests us, be allowed to go on without too many difficulties.

November 25, 1939

Nothing new.

November 26, 1939

At Dresden the *Statthalter* said, after a banquet which was attended by our Consul, that Germany must fear friends that betray her even more than her enemies. I called von Mackensen and told him that this time if there is anyone who has been betrayed it is not Germany. He sought to excuse the Statthalter, saying that after the banquet he probably was not in a lucid state of mind.

The Duce is indignant because of this phrase uttered in Dresden. The German star is beginning to pale, even in his mind, and this is what counts most.

November 27, 1939

Attolico reports that a German Government official has protested because, according to him, our Navy serves the interests of the French and British, and he went so far as to say that some submarine might open fire on us also. A genuine diplomatic blunder, typical of a German mind, which I use effectively to exasperate the Duce.

I have finished writing the speech that I am to deliver on the sixteenth of December—a very insidious speech—which, if accepted in its present form by the Duce, will definitely liquidate or at least undermine our relations with Germany, which are materially worsening.

November 28, 1939

The Duce completely approves of the speech which, unless something new comes up, will be delivered on the sixteenth of December. He speaks to me about the new President of the Chamber. He had already chosen de Francisci. I dissuade him. It does not seem to me right that my father's place should be filled by a mediocre individual who has been rescued by Fascism. I talk in favor of the appointment of Grandi, and the Duce decides it this way.

In the international field, nothing new except the increasing tension between Russia and Finland, which forecasts a coming attack. What is the attitude of the Germans? One thing is sure, and that is that for many years Germany has been supplying arms to the Finns. I did not neglect to find ways of informing the Russians of this.

November 29, 1939

No important news.

November 30, 1939

Russia has attacked Finland.

A long conference with Sir Percy Loraine, who has returned from London. I vigorously attack the question of the blockade and tell him that it is utterly idiotic to compromise Anglo-Italian relations for questions of secondary importance. I have the impression that he has done his best, but that he has encountered difficulties of practical application. He speaks with serene confidence about the general situation. Germany, which had announced many offensive plans on sea, on land, and in the air, has not seriously carried out any of them. England is stronger every day, and more resolved to carry the war on to its logical conclusion: the end of that regime which has transformed Germany into a permanent peril for European peace.

Toward us a great deal of cordiality. He was also the bearer of a letter addressed to me by Halifax, which was very courteous but not of particular importance.

December 1, 1939

At the Golf Club I saw Lord Lloyd, who has just arrived from a trip to the Balkans. He had nothing special to tell me except to confirm what the Ambassador had told me yesterday: that England was determined to carry the war to full victory.

The German Ambassador asks me again what we intend to do on the question of the blockade. Ribbentrop showers us with telegrams, and wants to create a crisis between us and London at any cost. What annoys me most is that he gave orders to Mackensen to see the Duce. I have to take him there tomorrow. Such meetings always have a dangerous side to them.

General Carboni, new head of the SIM [Military Intelligence Service], is to meet with Canaris in Munich. My recommendation to him is that he make no serious commitment. He must say yes to the Germans in small matters so that we can say no in big ones.

December 2, 1939

This morning I called together Ricci, Riccardi, and Host Venturi to form an office of co-ordination for economic warfare. All three are 100 per cent anti-German, but I thought it advisable to bring them up to date by telling them briefly what happened at Salzburg and later. They were indignant, and I am certain that they will put forth their best efforts to straighten out matters with France and England and accentuate the differences with Germany.

The Duce received von Mackensen. When the Duce speaks with Germans he can't refrain from a warlike attitude. And this morning he did it again, though not too openly. It is clear that Ribbentrop, who is beginning to flounder in the bog, is making every effort to drag us into the war. It would be idiotic not to see through his game, as it would be criminal to play with him. In any event, the Duce has made no specific commitments and, what is more important, he clearly re-affirmed the anti-Bolshevist orientation of our policy.

In reality, the whole of Italy is indignant about Russian aggression against Finland, and it is only a sense of discipline that checks public demonstrations. I have prepared a letter for Lord Halifax on the question of the blockade. It is a fact that the blockade is hampering our navigation, and, given the Duce's still uncertain state of mind, it is advisable to avoid any incident that might provoke a crisis between us and London.

December 3, 1939

The Duce and I have drawn up the agenda to be voted on at the next meeting of the Grand Council. The Duce is very insistent on the insertion of a clause to reaffirm that relations between Rome and Berlin are unchanged—*palabras y plumas el viento las lleva*. I do not object, provided there is another clause which reaffirms quite as categorically that we are going to continue our policy of watchful but armed waiting.

Mussolini is more and more restless. He feels that he is out of this great struggle and in one way or another he would like to find a way to fit into it. He intends, after the Council meeting, to send a letter to Hitler asking him to find a diplomatic solution. The Duce is ready to support it. If, on the other hand, Hitler is planning to continue the war, we will intervene in 1942, as our obligations demand. All this seems useless and dangerous to me, but it is not yet the moment to contradict him. I shall do so if he wants to carry out his project. At this moment there is nothing better than to remain inactive, absolutely inactive. This gives us all sorts of advantages, even along moral lines. Besides, we should not delude ourselves in any way. The Italian people are growing ever more anti-German. Even their violent anti-Bolshevik demonstrations can be interpreted as anti-German manifestations. The fate of the Finns would be of much less concern to the Italians if the Russians were not from all practical points of view the allies of Germany.

December 4, 1939

In all Italian cities there are sporadic demonstrations by students in favor of Finland and against Russia. But we must not forget that the people say "Death to Russia" and really mean "Death to Germany."

I showed the Duce the report of an Italian, the Grande Ufficiale Volpato, the only foreigner permitted to live in Posen. [Ciano refers to the fact that the Germans did not permit foreigners to live in the restricted industrial area of Posen.] With a simplicity which accentuates the horror of the facts, he describes all that the Germans are doing: unmentionable atrocities without reason. The Duce himself was indignant; he advised me to see to it that by indirect channels the American and French newspapers get the contents of the report. The world must know.

Starace brings for our perusal a report from his information service in which it is said that the German Embassy is preparing news of a serious break between me and the Duce. The thing is over now. This is the tail end of an old maneuver which began after Salzburg. Starace, who wanted to give proof of his loyalty, told me that he had absolutely no intention of showing it to the Duce. I know that bird and fear his gifts. I told him that the report left me perfectly indifferent and that, as a matter of fact, I advised him to give the paper to the Duce. He persisted in saying he would not. But it was he who persisted, which leaves me absolutely out of it.

December 5, 1939

Conference with Dr. Ley. His visit to Rome bears a perfect German imprint. No one had asked him to bother us. He had insisted on seeing Cronetti at Venice, and as soon as he received our official permission he hurried to Rome to confer with the Duce and with me and to give his trip a distinctly political flavor.

Ley is a heavy person who in the past was a well-known drunkard living in a brothel in Cologne. He is not the best choice to carry on diplomatic missions. He repeats like a phonograph record whatever his master has charged him to say, and shies with noticeable fright when asked an unexpected question. I have had a stenographic note made of the conference. There is nothing sensational in what he said, but he hinted at several very important things: (1) that an attack on Holland is being prepared on the pretext that Holland is not abiding by her declaration of neutrality; (2) that Russia has been given more or less of a free hand in Sweden and Bessarabia; (3) that Germany foresees conflict with the Soviet within a few years; (4) that Hitler's only thought is to continue the war.

Percy Loraine is going to Malta to try to influence the Admiralty to make its blockade less irksome.

December 6, 1939

François-Poncet informs me that the Allies have decided not to interfere with the coal we are importing from Germany. We have a long conversation, in which the only important point is that the French admit the possibility of the Germans breaking through the Maginot Line, though they believe they can beat them subsequently in the open country. Paris, too, holds that the German offensive is imminent. I saw Attolico, who came from Berlin. He can tell me very little, since the Germans now say very little to us. To him they say less than to the others. He confirms what everybody is saying, and that is that the German people are more and more unfavorable to Italy, even though in some quarters our intervention in the spring is considered certain— a certainty presumably based on a conversation Mussolini had with Mackensen a month ago.

December 7, 1939

Nothing new. During the evening I made a long report to the Grand Council. I asked the Duce for permission to read all the documents and he consented. What I revealed made a great impression; and since I believe that the Grand Council might keep a secret . . . I am sure that all I said yesterday evening will slowly trickle down to the country and will have the effect it should.

December 8, 1939

The Duce was quite satisfied with my report. On the other hand, he was furious at Balbo, who continues to carry on a press campaign in the *Corriere Padano* [a Ferrara daily], which is so openly anti-

Communist that it implies an indirect crack at Germany. "He thinks," said the Duce in my presence and in the presence of Pavolini, "that he can fish in troubled waters at home but he should remember that I am in a position to put everyone, without exception, to the wall."

I receive the Minister of Finland, who thanks me for the moral assistance given to his country, and who asks for arms and possibly specialists. No objection on our part to the sending of arms; some planes have already been sent. This, however, is possible only so long as Germany will permit the traffic. But how much longer will Germany consent? The Minister replies that that side of the question is settled, and confides to me that Germany herself has supplied arms to Finland, turning over to her certain stocks especially from the Polish war booty. This proves that the German-Bolshevist understanding is not so complete as they would have us believe in Berlin and in Moscow. In reality, distrust, contempt, and hatred dominate.

December 9, 1939

Today I was somewhat troubled because the Duce wanted me to insert in my speech a statement on the relations between Italy and Russia which, if not couched in cordial terms, should at least be civil. This did not seem very timely to me and was in sharp contrast to all the rest of the speech. To settle the question, a note arrived during the evening from the new Soviet Ambassador notifying us that as he had been recalled to Moscow he would be unable to present his credentials on the twelfth, as had been arranged. I informed the Duce, stressing the extraordinary discourtesy of such a gesture. His reaction was immediate, and if my speech is going to be changed it will be to make the pill more bitter still.

However, the Duce's attitude has always been vacillating and fundamentally he is still in favor of Germany. He said today that the time will soon come when we shall demand Corsica and Tunisia from France. I answered that in that event we must be ready, because this would inevitably mean war. He was quite pleased with an English article which said that the Italian people might fight at the side of Germany for reasons of honor. This is also his point of view, and even when there are a thousand voices to the contrary, a single anonymous voice saying that he is right is sufficient, and he will cling to it and overlook, indeed deny, the others. I cannot conceal the fact that this state of mind troubles me.

December 10, 1939

Mussolini is becoming more and more exasperated by the British blockade. He threatens countermeasures and revenge. I believe, on the contrary, that we can do very little about it. Either we have the power to oppose, which means war, or else we keep our mouths shut and try to solve difficulties in a friendly way. The Duce is more and more nervous, but he proudly declares that he is calm. The position of playing a neutral part in a Europe that is fighting or getting ready to fight humiliates him. But I can't see a way out. Our absolute military unpreparedness, our lack of sufficient means, and our economic dependence will force us to remain in our present position for a long time, which doesn't displease me in the least. The day will come when everybody will see the great advantages that non-belligerency has given Italy.

December 11, 1939

Nothing new.

December 12, 1939

When the Germans discovered that we were working the Lokris mine, our only source of nickel, they asked us for it. I thought I would find a strong reaction from the Duce. Instead there was nothing of the sort. If he is not ready to grant the request, he is at least disposed to yield a part of the product. It is all very well, but it is enlightening to see how these gentlemen act—that is, as bullies and robbers. How long are we going to stand this?

December 13, 1939

A long conference with the King in relation to the Albanian decoration. We then have a general discussion. He tells me nothing new, but makes it clear that he is a neutral and an out-and-out anti-German. Neither does he like the French, and he rates their military efficiency lightly. He considers it likely, although contrary to his hopes, that the German military offensive will have positive results. The Duce has me introduce into my speech, in addition to a confirmation of our alliance with Germany, a reference to his speech to the Fascist militia. It is necessary to make clear to the press that this reference is important because of what was said in regard to international obligations, and not because of what was said against France, otherwise we are going to engulf ourselves in an argument that might become dangerous.

Von Mackensen comes back on the matter of the nickel mine. I answer with abundant proof that we can give up only a part, which will involve a small amount of mineral. He is not satisfied, and I am less satisfied than he.

December 14, 1939

In the Chamber they commemorate my father's death. Grandi [now President of the new Italian Parliament] delivers a very noble oration, and the Duce utters words which, for him, are rare. I had never seen the hall without my father. Today a great laurel wreath had been placed on his chair, but never was he so near to me as he was today.

December 15, 1939

Nothing new.

December 16, 1939

I spoke to the Chamber. My speech had great success, even if everybody did not discern the subtle anti-German poison which permeated it. The first impression seemed merely anti-Bolshevik, but in substance it was anti-German. They tell me that the German Ambassador listened to it in silence, and at times was not able to conceal his disappointment. Good.

During the evening I saw Sir Percy Loraine, who is highly satisfied and pays me his compliments.

December 17, 1939

The speech continues to be talked about. It has had much success in Italy as well as abroad. Politically, it went a long way. If it was difficult formerly to persuade the Italians to march side by side with the Germans, it is impossible now that they should snap into action despite their given word, since they know the whole truth and what is happening behind the scenes.

Everybody knows and understands that Germany has betrayed us twice.

December 18, 1939

Nothing new. There are still many comments and all of them good, including those from Berlin, where, nevertheless, they are swallowing a bitter pill.

I have finished making arrangements for the visit of the King to the Pope and for a return of the visit—an event without precedent. It will cause a lot of talk, and it will not help to draw Germany closer to us. The fight against Catholicism in Germany is being carried on pitilessly and idiotically.

December 19, 1939

I had thought that François-Poncet would have received my speech more sympathetically. Instead, during the visit that he paid me yesterday he did not complain about what I had said but emphasized the point that my reference to solidarity with Germany was too strongly expressed. To tell the truth, I do not know in what part of my speech this occurred. The English were more intuitive and have given my speech a welcome which caution alone has restrained. As to the Italians, they were the most intelligent of all, and have completely understood my lingo. They consider my speech to be the real funeral of the Axis.

A Finnish representative asks to purchase arms. There is no objection to this within the limits of our possibilities and on condition that they themselves take care of the transportation.

Wieniawa accuses me of being "the worst assassin in the world." According to him I had suppressed in my speech seven million Poles, who, according to him, are twenty-five millions.

A long conference with Albanian senators. They present their objections and their wishes. Insignificant things of a personal and local character, about which we can give them satisfaction. I am convinced, especially from what they themselves have said, that matters in Albania are moving in a satisfactory manner.

December 20, 1939

The Albanians take their oath in the Senate. The Duce was beside himself because the *Osservatore Romano* announced the visit of the Italian royal family with only a brief news article. "This is how the Vatican always acts. It's hard to make them understand." The Duce inveighs against the Pope. "I'm becoming more and more of a Ghibelline. In the crest of Forlì there is a white eagle." Another thing that enrages the Duce is that the British have stopped our ships. I don't know what to do about this. On the other hand, as long as we advertise our solidarity with Berlin, it is difficult for the British not to apply the rules of blockade against us. Tomorrow I shall accompany Percy Loraine to the Duce. It is well that he should see Mussolini's state of mind for himself.

December 21, 1939

Visit of the King and Queen to the Holy See. The King is in good humor and congratulates me on my speech. He is glad that I have given some annoyance to the Germans, who, in his opinion, and as he hopes, are destined to lose the war, above all if they cannot count on the full support of Russia. The visit takes place without complications, but there is some commotion when the Pope starts making an address. The King is always very much embarrassed and does not know what to do. He was afraid that he had to answer it, and as he does not excel in oratory he turned to me in despair. I made him a sign not to move and he calmed down. The Pope, in the conversation he had with the King, criticized Germany violently for its persecution of the Church.

I see Himmler and have quite an unimportant conversation with him. I tried to obtain information on the offensive, but the Germans now distrust me and the information was not given. The Duce was closeted with Himmler for two hours yesterday, and the latter left the Mappamondo hall well satisfied. What can Mussolini have promised him? In talking to me about the conference, the Duce said that Himmler was anti-Russian and somewhat discouraged and that he told Mussolini "that he would never allow a German defeat to take place." This is a great deal, but I fear that the conversation has gone much beyond this.

December 22, 1939

I confer at length with Percy Loraine on the question of the blockade. We must find a solution before some incident occurs which compromises the situation and shifts the problem from the commercial field to that of prestige, in which event conciliation is more difficult.

December 23, 1939

A long conversation with Antonescu, who was sent here by the King of Rumania to explore the ground and learn our intentions if the Russians attack the Rumanian frontier. I answered, reaffirming our anti-Bolshevist point of view, but avoided any commitments which might bind us to Rumania at a moment when we must have the maximum freedom of action. The Rumanians would like to have us work on the Hungarians, because any Hungarian threat on the Rumanian rear would oblige the Rumanians to come to an agreement with the Russians. This may be possible, although the stubbornness of Czaky does not give us much hope.

I gave von Mackensen a document of exceptional gravity which comes to us from Prague. It is a résumé of a lecture given by the vice-mayor of Prague, Dr. Pfitzner, a German, in which German imperialistic objectives are bluntly revealed. It refers not only to the Germans' intention of taking possession of Alto Adige and Trieste, but to their ambition of conquering the whole plain of Lombardy.

Mussolini was highly indignant and, since the document contained many threats against Russia, he ordered me to send the statement with an unsigned note to the Soviet Ambassador in Paris. I told Mackensen that if a thing like this were known by the Italian people there would arise an utterly uncontrollable movement of hostility to Germany. Mackensen was greatly impressed. Every time he is invited to confer with me now he trembles, because he well understands my line of action.

December 24, 1939

François-Poncet tells me that the French Government is worried over the situation in the Balkans, but this is only his personal opinion.

Weygand's army, which is ready in Syria, will intervene to repel any threat, be it German or Russian, but there is no intention in Paris of doing anything without previous agreement with Italy, whose paramount interests in the zone are recognized. I cannot for the moment assume any obligations, but it is important to note that France has taken the initiative.

December 25, 1939

Nothing new.

The holiday makes me feel more sadly the absence of those who are no more.

December 26, 1939

With Mussolini we talk about Rumania. He is in favor of having me transmit the Rumanian demand to Hungary, and he is even ready, in case of a Russian aggression, to give the Rumanians military support of the kind we gave to Franco in Spain. The report on the utterance of the vice-mayor of Prague has made him more and more distrustful of the Germans. Now, for the first time, he desires German defeat, and since Marras, military attaché to Berlin, indicated that from good sources he has had news of the imminent invasion of Holland and Belgium, the Duce invites me secretly to inform the two diplomatic representatives [of Holland and Belgium]. Mussolini always has in mind the occupation of Croatia, which seems to me possible, and I told him that it should be undertaken only in agreement with the French and the British.

I inform Antonescu of our program in connection with eventual Russo-Balkan complications. He is very happy about it. He tells me that he learned from the French Ambassador at Bucharest that Great Britain has recently sent a note to Paris couched in the following terms: (1) Italy must again be won over to the British side; (2) Italy wants to go into the Balkans; (3) if this is the condition for the realization of the first point, England is ready to let her go ahead. This is very probable, as it is just like the narrow and nearsighted Parisian policy. But it is a good sign that the British are in this frame of mind.

December 27, 1939

The Germans are greatly alarmed over the Prague speech, so much so that they have called von Mackensen to Berlin for a conference. Naturally they deny the speech, but it has its logical foundation in a whole mass of German literature which has for a long time spread propaganda along the same lines expressed by Dr. Pfitzner, the vice-mayor of Prague.

The Pope has conferred on me the Order of the Golden Spur. More than the decoration itself, I was pleased with the telegram sent by Cardinal Maglione, in which he praises my work in favor of the "most noble cause of peace," and of the *rapprochement* between Church and State. On the whole, Mussolini tends to underrate the importance of the Pope's visit to the King, and never so much as in the last few days he delights in calling himself "an unbeliever." On the other hand, the event is very pleasing to the Italian people, who attribute to the visit an anti-German and anti-Bolshevik flavor.

A long conference with Bocchini. He complained especially about the restlessness of the Duce, which has already been noticed by all the collaborators, and he even went so far as to say that the Duce should take an intensive anti-syphilitic cure, because Bocchini claims that the psychic condition of Mussolini is due to a recurrence of this old illness. It surprised and annoyed me very much that Bocchini should have said this, although I myself recognize the fact that Mussolini's present contradictory behavior is truly upsetting to anyone who works with him.

Verlaçi asks for my approval to ". . . take the initiative against King Zog, who, when he is dead, will be less embarrassing than he is today." The matter does not interest us, and I answer that only the Albanians can be the judges of the life of another Albanian.

December 28, 1939

The Pope visited the King. Everything went off according to plan. The King was pleased by the visit, and after the meeting he told me that the Pope repeated many times that he would like to improve relations with Germany but that this is rendered impossible by the increasingly uncompromising German attitude. Immediately after the visit I went to the Duce. Today, also, he was making ironical comments on the visit of the Pope, and depreciated its importance.

Czaky lets us know that he will be in Venice during the first week of January. I shall try to get him to understand that it is, above all, to the interest of Hungary to go along with Rumania, now that the Russian danger is coming closer and becoming more evident. If Hungary wants to live and even prosper moderately she must avoid becoming, more than she is today, a mosaic state. Past experience proves this to be very dangerous.

We have recalled Rosso from Moscow. As long as the Soviets do not send an ambassador to Rome our Embassy will also be headed by a chargé d'affaires. Our decision does not improve relations with Russia or with Germany. The ridiculous and lying telegram of Stalin to Ribbentrop, in which Stalin speaks of Russian and German blood shed in common (but where?) proves that the collusion between Bolshevism and Nazism is becoming more and more intimate and deep. So much the worse for them, because Russia and Germany will suffer the same fate.

December 29, 1939

I see Besnard, the French representative at the next Fascist Exposition in 1942. We speak somewhat of politics, but he does not say anything interesting. Ex-ambassadors generally flatter themselves in believing that they are in a position to accomplish what the ambassadors in charge of the affairs of their countries at the moment cannot do, and which they did not do themselves when they might have done it.

Sir Percy Loraine informs me that the English Government intends to act more generously toward Italy as regards the blockade. This is all to the good and will serve to calm the Duce's nervous tension.

I am somewhat alarmed over Muti's behavior. He is a fine fellow, attached and devoted, but one who has more guts than brains. And besides, he cannot resist the temptation of basing all his actions on personal considerations. For him to favor Dick and to deceive Tom is everything. The rest does not count. He does not see the essence of a problem. Unintentionally he acts on his own and heeds less and less what I say. He thinks that he has won over Mussolini, but he does not understand that the latter is the coldest judge of men; not contradicting his interlocutor, not arguing, never opposing, he destroys individuals by the most pitiless methods. Muti thinks that he is playing cat with

Mussolini, but he is really the mouse. It may be that I am giving substance to a shadow, but I am afraid that the Duce is in a quandary as
to the situation of the party, and I should not like Muti to have the
ephemeral and fleeting life of a political meteor.

December 30, 1939

I bring Verlaçi to the Duce. He makes a very optimistic report on
the situation in Albania and asks for a greater concentration of powers
in the Italian lieutenancy. Public power must be divided as follows:
the government of Tirana is answerable to the lieutenancy and the
lieutenancy is answerable to Rome. In order to carry out this concentration I have thought of calling Parini to the position of inspector
general of the party in the place of Grio, who has done well during the
preparation but who has compromised himself with too many people.

A long conference with Maria of Piedmont. She is especially disturbed by the threat of the German invasion of Belgium. I have told
her that in the light of our latest information it now seems very probable. She will immediately inform King Leopold. We have agreed
that whenever I obtain further information I will inform her through
a trusted person. She wanted to know the details of what I did at Salzburg and later addressed me in a very friendly and kindly manner.
She hates the Germans with all her heart and calls them liars and
swine.

Mussolini wants the Albanian plans against King Zog suspended.
He gives orders to this effect, and he is right, because we would not
derive any advantage from it but only blame.

December 31, 1939

Mussolini is still suffering from the usual recurrent waves of pro-
Germanism. Now he would like to send some advice to Hitler (his
previous advice made no impression), informing him that Italy is continuing to arm. But what are we preparing for? The war at the side of
Germany must not be undertaken and never will be undertaken. It
would be a crime and the height of folly! As for war against Germany, I do not for the moment see any reason for it. In any case, if
necessary I acquiesce in war against Germany but not in her company.
This is my point of view. Mussolini's point of view is exactly the opposite. He would never have war against Germany, and, when we are

ready, he would fight on the side of Germany against the democracies, who, to my way of looking at it, are the only countries with which one can deal seriously and honestly.

For the moment we must not talk of war. The state of unpreparedness of the country is complete. We are worse off now than in September. General Favagrossa said yesterday that if he could have all the material already asked for, which would permit our factories to work double shift, a sufficiently complete preparation could be reached by October of 1942. Generals Badoglio and Soddu agree that we cannot do otherwise.

Thus closes a year which, for me, has been so cruel in my personal life and so generous in my political life. In my opinion the coming year holds many surprises. Maybe we shall witness a rapid conclusion to a tragic upheaval which humanity did not want and is unable to understand. In the very fact that this absurd and inexplicable war is understood by no one, we can, perhaps, find the key to its end.

CROCE ROSSA ITALIANA
COMITATO CENTRALE · ROMA

AGENDA 1940
ANNO XVIII-XIX · E. F.

EDIZIONE DELLA CROCE ROSSA ITALIANA

January 1, 1940

Mussolini reproaches the democracies for talking too much of peace. This depresses public opinion and creates currents hostile to the conflict. Hence, a keen pro-German feeling is reawakening in the Duce. For this reason he sent a telegram today to Hitler, a telegram for which someday we are going to be reproached.

January 2, 1940

I persuade the Duce to allow volunteers to leave for Finland, where pursuit-plane pilots and artillerymen are needed. Tomorrow I will come to an understanding with the Finnish Minister.

Graziani, in a conference with me, reveals himself as an interventionist and a pro-German and denounces Badoglio because of the contacts he maintains with Gamelin. I have been at odds with Badoglio many times, but this time I am in agreement with him. Graziani, on the other hand, favors war at the side of Germany and tries to persuade the Duce to hasten it. We must neutralize his influence. I inform the Belgian Ambassador of the possibility of a German attack on the neutral countries. Two months ago I told him that I did not consider this probable. Today I told him that new sources of information have led me to change my opinion. He was impressed.

The Duce has expressed his regret that von Ribbentrop has not sent his usual New Year's telegram of greetings. Evidently my speech irks Ribbentrop. His anger leaves me indifferent. As a matter of fact it honors me.

January 3, 1940

The Duce has prepared a letter for Hitler. After a first reading it does not seem very compromising, but tomorrow I am going to analyze it thoroughly.

Von Mackensen brings along a large portfolio containing the German Government's inquiry on Pfitzner's speech, which, very naturally, appears negligible. The Germans would now like us to reveal the source of our information. This is not possible. We are not informers. Attolico has written us that he was under the impression that the investigation had produced results which, at least in part, support our contention.

I have arranged a considerable transfer of diplomats. I have personally appointed the son of Badoglio. He is not an ace, but his father adores him, and at this moment I mean to keep his good will at all costs. He is a valuable ally in the cause of non-intervention.

January 4, 1940

Nothing new.

January 5, 1940

Von Mackensen returns to see me to find out the name of the person responsible for the Pfitzner case. I give him to understand that it is an Italian already returned to Italy, who will be punished by us. He seems to accept this explanation. In reality, the document was furnished to Muti by a Czech lawyer, for whom Muti himself accepts personal responsibility. The translation was made by an employee of the consulate, a certain Matteucci.

After having made a few changes in it, the Duce gives orders that the letter he had been pondering over be sent to Hitler. It's a fine document, full of wisdom and restraint, but it leaves matters as they are. Mussolini's advice is accepted by Hitler only when it coincides with his own ideas.

This evening I am leaving for Venice, to meet that clever and cautious Count Czaky.

Mussolini gives these indications of the state of mind of the country: "Italy has no liking for Germany, is indifferent toward France, hates Great Britain and Russia." Here is a diagnosis with which I concur only with many reservations.

January 6 and 7, 1940

At Venice with Czaky. I have had a detailed report made of the results of the conference, which, in general, I consider satisfactory.

Czaky has assured me that Hungary will not take the initiative in the Balkans and thus spread the fire. As a matter of fact, I already knew about the Hungarian attitude. It recalls that of certain individuals who shout and gesticulate and threaten so that they be prevented from coming to blows. The Hungarians (they proved it at the time of the Czechoslovak crisis) are violent in their use of words but moderate in their actions. At times, too much so.

January 8, 1940

I report to the Duce, who is annoyed that Czaky should busy himself about Croatia, toward which country Mussolini's ambitions are increasingly directed.

Conversation with François-Poncet. Nothing new from him. I inform him with some caution of the results of the Venice conference. He complains about Mussolini's kicks. "It is too bad," he affirms, "because in France they are beginning to believe that the Duce himself is the only obstacle to an understanding between the two countries."

I receive the Prince of Hesse. For the nth time he announces that the conclusion of a *modus vivendi* between the Pope and the Reich is close at hand. He alludes to the possibility of a trip to Rome by von Ribbentrop. I do my best to discourage it.

January 9, 1940

Colijn, the ex-Premier of Holland, has come to Rome to ascertain our opinion on the situation and, if possible, to establish more direct relations. He informs me as to what his country has done to impede a possible German invasion. He is certain that the Dutch will fight with the energy that comes from desperation. The Prussians' break-through will not be easy. I tell Colijn that, for the moment, there is nothing to do but wait and see and, at most, to arm. Colijn said that he doesn't believe a German victory is possible. I gave him to understand that I feel the same way.

I inform Percy Loraine about the Venice results. He is satisfied with them. What we are doing for Rumania has the great advantage of placing us more and more in the anti-German camp.

January 10, 1940

Badoglio, who is now politically well set, no longer considers it possible that we can prepare our defenses in the coming year. We lack raw materials. It will take the whole of 1941, and not even in 1942 shall we be able to pass to the offensive. In agreement with Badoglio, we will put a brake on General Graziani's ambitions. Graziani has more ambition than brains, yet he is influencing the Duce in the dangerous idea of intervention.

The Duce's letter was received by Hitler yesterday. It appears that Hitler will reply in writing. Attolico sent word to me by one of his trusted clerks that he does not believe that the Duce's suggestions will find any welcome in Germany, and that the conviction that we will soon enter the war at the side of Germany is gaining strength. We now see the results of Mussolini's conversations with Mackensen and Himmler. The less Germans Mussolini sees the better.

Ambassador Rosso has returned from Moscow. He does not bring much news because diplomats are forced to lead a secluded life these days. He believes that the understanding between Russia and Germany is solid, but that the Russians are not inclined to render any appreciable aid on the field of battle. He emphasizes that this is his personal opinion, because he knows nothing definite.

January 11, 1940

Attolico reports a long conference with von Ribbentrop. Nothing but comment on the Duce's letter. The Germans are wondering whether Mussolini, in laying out a proposal for the reconstruction of the Polish state as a sufficient condition for the re-establishment of peace, does not anticipate what the Allies intend to do. Nothing of the kind. It is a personal conviction of the Duce, who continues to believe, and he is wrong, that the French and English do not want war. In the Goering circles they talk again of a German offensive within a short time, and anticipate victory. The Duce's letter has not, on the whole, been well received.

Mussolini talked to me today of "intervention at the side of Germany during the second half of 1941." He, too, is becoming convinced that the unpreparedness of the armed forces makes impossible any kind of warlike attempt by us before that time. I told von Mackensen that von Ribbentrop, in speaking with Attolico, denied that he had asserted that France and England would not enter the war. Von Mackensen, after I had reminded him of the Salzburg bet, beat his head and said, "I can't say anything, because von Ribbentrop is my Minister, but I am sorry that I should be the man who has such a short memory."

January 12, 1940

Nothing new.

January 13, 1940

The Duce talks to me about Muti. He says that in the management of the Fascist party the command has gone soft and a too violent contrast exists as compared with the rigid formalism of Starace, "whom he adored." I had to agree. Muti has found bad company, is presumptuous, and I don't think he will last long.

Our negotiations with the British to solve the problem of the blockade have run aground, in spite of a very courteous personal letter from Halifax, which reached me today.

We again discuss the crown of Hungary with Villani: union under one head, or else coronation of the Duke of Aosta. Doesn't matter which, so long as we proceed more rapidly, because the question of Croatia is quickly coming to a head.

January 14, 1940

The Germans make a violent kick against the sale of Italian airplane motors to France. The Duce wants to forbid the exportation of war matériel to the Allies. But after a long discussion, in the presence of Riccardi, he is convinced that we will quite soon be left without foreign exchange, and hence without raw materials that are indispensable to military preparedness—those raw materials that can be obtained only with foreign money owing to the devaluation of the Italian lira. Therefore, I can speak clearly to the Germans. I draw up a note, giving our point of view. I do not delude myself. The Germans will be furious, but this will make it possible for us to assure ourselves a greater freedom in international commerce which at this moment is quite favorable to us.

I tell Percy Loraine that it is not possible for us to accede to the British proposals in the matter of the blockade. The Italians will not allow their most elementary necessities to be rationed. British persistence would be equivalent to transferring the problem of blockade to the political sphere, and this is very dangerous. Sir Percy Loraine, who is every day becoming more understanding, has grasped the point.

January 15, 1940

Mussolini approves the memorandum, which, during the evening, I deliver to von Mackensen, who receives it with a few words and with great disappointment, and I do nothing to modify his impression.

The Duce is sad because of the state of our armed forces, which at last he has grown well acquainted with. The number of divisions that are ready are ten; by the end of January there will be eleven. The others lack more or less everything. Some are lacking 92 per cent of their equipment. Under these conditions it is folly to speak of war. Mussolini, according to what he says, is discouraged to the point of feeling the symptoms of a new stomach ulcer.

I set up a special office for Finland at the Italian Ministry for Foreign Affairs. The office is to co-ordinate all of our political, military, and economic efforts in favor of this Baltic nation. I entrust it to Captain Bechi.

Conference with Sir Percy. We try to settle our navicert [naval certificate which permits the passage of goods through a blockade] difficulties. He informs me that before long the embargo will also strike at German coal, which arrives by sea. Although the Duce does not seem to give much weight to such a decision, I am really anxious because of the consequences it will have on the entire economic life of our country.

January 16, 1940

The carabinièri give the Duce an alarming report on Albania. He takes it very seriously. The command of the carabinièri is a reliable source of information but they talk too much, and at times they limit themselves to passing on the observations made by non-commissioned officers. Jacomoni vehemently denies all that the carabinièri report and prepares, together with Benini, a counterreport. In Albania we are working methodically and without bluffing, which, in the opinion of a few persons, is perhaps a mistake. But I do not intend to change.

I prepare with Muti the agenda for the meeting of the federal secretaries of the Fascist party. We must give the impression that the machinery of the Fascist party is, as ever, in good working order. The Duce wants to add certain phrases with an anti-Allied flavor, but this is a mistake, because it will harden the Franco-British position against us and afford us no practical advantage.

A letter from the Princess of Piedmont thanking me in the name of her brother [the King of the Belgians] for what I have done for him. I believe that the warning was in time. And today Ambassador Attolico telegraphs that the attack on Belgium is not only probable, but may even be imminent. Attolico is very conscientious in his gathering of news.

January 17, 1940

Mussolini, in his present seesawing of feelings, is today somewhat hostile to the Germans. He says, "They should allow themselves to be guided by me if they do not want to pull unpardonable boners. In politics it is undeniable that I am more intelligent than Hitler." I must say that the Chancellor of the Reich has not given proofs of sharing this opinion.

Christic, on his return from Belgrade, renews his assurances of friendship for Italy, and insists on emphasizing that the understanding reached between Serbs and Croats is this time deep and active. However, the news that comes to us from another source is exactly to the contrary.

I received De Man, the Belgian Minister, on his way to Rome, as well as the Polish Ambassador, who tells me of the daily martyrdom that his country is undergoing under the terrible yoke of German bestiality.

Accompanied by Jacomoni, I discussed the Albanian situation with the Duce. Let the carabinièri think and write as they please. However, one thing is certain: for the time being Albania has not caused us the least trouble.

January 18, 1940

I went with Jacomoni to see the Duce. I think the Duce, too, realizes that the alarm created by General Agostinucci, who is called the

"stuffed lion" by the Albanians, is in large measure, at least, unjustified. The meeting was useful, at any rate, to agree on certain plans for
public works, especially in Tirana.

I confer with Ricci on the coal problem. The Duce told him: "I
have the pleasure, and let me emphasize *the pleasure,* to inform you
that English coal can no longer arrive in Italy." This he considers to
be a good lash of the whip for the Italians, so that they will learn to
depend only on their own resources. He counts on substituting our
own lignite for the coal which is now imported from Great Britain.
But will our own lignite be sufficient? And is the machinery to extract
it complete? Ricci does not conceal his skepticism.

Percy Loraine talks to me about the blockade and about commercial
problems; then he becomes thoughtful and intent. He seems to want to
say something but cannot decide. I encourage him to speak. He reveals
to me his concern over the attitude of the Duce, whom he feels and
knows to be fundamentally hostile. "The Duce must know," he concludes, "that the Britain of today is no longer the Britain of a year ago.
She is now strong and prepared for anything." It is hard for me to
argue with him because I am of the same opinion and he knows it.

January 19, 1940

Today, François-Poncet could not conceal his concern over the attitude the Duce is assuming. The declarations made by the secretary of
the party, of which, however, the origin is evident, had an unfavorable
echo in France and England, as they sound like threats. Nevertheless,
we must convince ourselves that the Allies will win the war and we
must not present ourselves at the peace table in the guise of accomplices, albeit non-combatant accomplices, of Germany. I tried to convince François-Poncet that he was wrong, but the facts, alas, count
more than words, including my own words. Even Balbo, who came to
see me and who thinks along all lines as I do, was very hostile to the
declarations made by Muti on foreign policy, as well as on domestic
policy.

January 20, 1940

Meeting of the Council of Ministers characterized by a phantasma-
goric display of billions which we do not have—provisional budgets

that would take anybody's breath away—anybody but the Duce, who maintains an imperturbable calm. He said that states are never shaken by financial questions; they fall either because of internal political instability or by military defeats, never because of economic causes. Revel weakly objected, saying that the French Revolution failed precisely because of the assignat, but the Duce did not encourage the discussion and cut him short, adding something about a possible advantage of inflation on a Cyclopean scale, but, fortunately, he spoke of it only academically.

January 21, 1940

Countess Potocka, with whom I hunted wild boar last year at Białowieza and whom I was instrumental in freeing from a Russian prison some weeks ago, came to see me. She described with dignity her life in Russia during her imprisonment, her return trip, her encounter with the German Gestapo. She wished neither to alarm me nor to seek my pity. She is too aristocratic for that. She despises the Russians. She hates the Germans. She said that Beck is not disliked in Poland, where his policies find comprehension and support, but that Marshal Smigly-Rydz can never again return to Poland.

Bombelles describes the visit of the Regent, Paul, to Zagreb as "a funeral during which no one took off his hat." He says that the situation goes from bad to worse, that the Serbian is hated more and more and is less efficient, and that shortly everything will be ready for the rebellion. He proposes my meeting Pavelić, which I neither accept nor decline. Our eventual line of action should be the following: insurrection, occupation of Zagreb, arrival of Pavelić, appeal to Italy for her intervention, formation of a kingdom of Croatia, and offer of the crown to the King of Italy. Bombelles is in agreement and says that our military effort will be minimum because the popular insurrection will be complete and the Serbs will be struck everywhere and implacably disposed of by the Croats.

January 22, 1940

Mussolini agrees on the need for my having a talk with Pavelić. This will take place tomorrow at home. In principle the Croat question seems to be on its way toward a solution. It is, however, necessary to prepare the ground with London and Paris. This is a fundamental condition. Otherwise it is better to do nothing about it. They will pay dearly for it, and soon. Mussolini, however, turns a deaf ear to all this. Yesterday, when I asked him for assurances regarding the future which I wanted to communicate to Loraine and Poncet, he said, "One thing is certain: we shall never join with them [France and England]." I took great care not to say this to the two ambassadors as Mussolini would have wished me to.

I appealed to the Minister from Rumania for the release of certain Hungarians who have been accused of plotting against the safety of the state. It will be a useful gesture, since a trial would make more acute the tension between those two countries.

January 23, 1940

Council of Ministers. Military budget. The Duce takes advantage of this occasion to speak of the international situation. All of his shafts are aimed against France and England, who "can now no longer win the war." He repeats that we cannot indefinitely remain neutral. To preserve neutrality until the end of the war would make us play second fiddle among the European powers. He foresees that our military possibilities will enable us to make a move during the second half of 1940, or perhaps during the early part of 1941. Every allusion to action is pointed toward the Allies. He speaks of terror bombings over France, of the control of the Mediterranean. His declaration greatly impressed the ministers, some of whom approved heartily, especially Ricci and Revel. Riccardi, on the other hand, speaking later in the antechamber, said that it is absurd to plan to arm seventy divisions when the raw materials at our disposal are hardly enough to arm ten of them.

I received Pavelić. Anfuso has made a stenographic memorandum of the conference. Pavelić is an aggressive, calm man, who knows where he wants to go, and does not fear the responsibility for attaining his ends. We have fixed upon the principal points of preparation and action.

I assure Sir Percy Loraine that I am doing "something and even more than something" in favor of Finland. He was satisfied.

January 24, 1940

Nothing new.

January 25, 1940

Nothing new.

January 26, 1940

Nothing new.

January 27, 1940

The Finnish Minister asks for additional supplies of arms, especially heavy artillery; and he asks for them in a tone of desperation. If things go on in Finland as they are now, the overwhelming superiority of Russian resources will break down Finnish morale and resistance will come to an end. Perhaps the Minister has painted too dark a picture, but it is certain that to hope for an unlimited resistance is a vain illusion.

Gamelin has said to General Visconti Prasca, who in turn has told me, that he would be ready to give a billion to the Germans, provided they would do him the favor of taking the initiative in the attack. Visconti Prasca thinks the French Army the best in the world. He is convinced that from this day Germany has lost the war.

January 28, 1940

The Duce has returned from Terminillo. He is not exactly nervous, but he appeared more than usually irritable. He takes it out, as usual, on France and England, because, owing to their policies, "they have lost the victory." And he takes it out on Germany for having hastened the war which, within three years, "would have been won because of the disunity among the democracies."

Even as to the internal situation, he is dissatisfied because of Muti. The latter has taken some disciplinary measures that have had a strong echo and have met with the approval of anti-Fascist circles, which makes Mussolini indignant. "We must act like the Church," he said, "which never strikes its members publicly. Once I denounced to Tacchi Venturi the Bishop of Jesi for moral turpitude. Notwithstanding overwhelming proof, no satisfaction was given me then and there, but some years afterward I learned that the guilty man had died in obscurity at Frascati."

I see Poncet. He is disturbed about the Italian attitude. He thinks that he can recognize the earmarks of warmongering and pro-German activities. He is convinced that Mussolini is blinded by his hatred for democracy, and that one day he will end by bringing about an unavoidable crisis.

January 29, 1940

After a long period I saw the King again. As usual he was very courteous to me, praising my work. He is anti-German, for such are his convictions and his nature, but no longer sure about a German defeat. He is doubtful about the power of internal resistance of the British Empire. He is disturbed about Italy. "With the present policy we risk becoming *'a Dio spiacente ed a' nemici suoi'*" [a quotation from Dante: "Hateful to God and to His enemies"]. He was sufficiently informed on Mussolini's plans for Croatia, but did not conceal his mistrust regarding the success of the undertaking if it is not preceded by a timely understanding with France and Britain.

The Duce is irritated by the internal situation. The people grumble. Food restrictions are a matter to be taken into account. War again casts its shadow on the country. He was annoyed with the Count of Turin, who was hoarding soap, he says, "to help wash his thirty-five thousand whores, with whom one cannot understand what he can do, considering the state of his health." He ranted about the possibility of an uprising, "When the instincts in a people are stationary and without ideas, only the use of force can save them. Those whom we strike will be grateful because the blow will save them from falling into the abyss toward which their own fear was pushing them. Have you ever seen a lamb become a wolf? The Italian race is a race of sheep. Eighteen years are not enough to change them. It takes a hundred and eighty, and maybe a hundred and eighty centuries."

January 30, 1940

Piero Parini points out that the professors and students of Corcia [Albania] who created disorders lately have been identified, and he believes that some harsh punishment is necessary. The Duce approves. I telegraph, ordering that they be arrested and deported to some island on the Tyrrhenian Sea. The Albanian intellectuals, as is logical, are those who most oppose the new situation, and it is necessary to absorb them wherever it is possible, or to deal severely with those who are unwilling to be convinced. It is not a very serious problem: a matter involving two or three hundred persons. The Albanian people do not give trouble. They work, earn, and enjoy a comfortable living, which they have not known until now, and most of them are satisfied.

January 31, 1940

The English Ambassador informs me that while his government is increasing the shipment of supplies to Finland, it has decided not to send military units. He is pleased when I tell him that we, too, are shipping supplies and a nucleus of specialists. At the end of the conversation he hints at the apprehension aroused by the personal attitude of the Duce. England feels in the Duce's hostility something that will prevent a deep and sincere *rapprochement*. I try to deny this, but he does not listen to me, nor can I proceed on this line with an intelligent and frank man like Percy Loraine, nor go very much beyond what is generally referred to as a conventional diplomatic white lie.

Hitler has made a speech for which I see no reason, except that of celebrating the date of his assumption of power.

February 1, 1940

Anniversary of the founding of the militia. Mussolini made a speech which I did not hear, but which is reported to me to be alarmingly radical. Brief, uncompromising, ending with the affirmation that the Italians are yearning to fight "that fight which is bound to come." Unfortunately, nothing can be done about it. His mind is set and decided on war. The only good thing in it is that he has given orders to Pavolini not to reproduce it in the press. At least there will not be a new crisis with France and England. That's something, when one lives from day to day.

Mussolini leaves for Romagna.

February 2, 1940

Nothing new.

February 3, 1940

The English Ambassador delivers a memorandum relative to our commercial negotiations. The terms are not bad, but one of the clauses must be considered *sine qua non,* and that is the sale to Great Britain of arms and ammunition. I am certain that the Duce will not like it, but Riccardi says that we must make a virtue of necessity, and reach an agreement with the English, otherwise the economic situation will become too burdensome.

February 4, 1940

Nothing new.

February 5, 1940

Nothing new.

February 6, 1940

Conference with General Carboni, just returned from Germany. He makes a frank and pessimistic report on the state of the country. Lack of food, and, above all, lack of enthusiasm. A great land offensive is being prepared, but it will not be possible to start it before the end of April, after the thaws.

I see the Prince of Hesse. He wants to confer with the Duce on behalf of Hitler, but has nothing special to say. He informs me that Goering is more than ever incensed against Italy, and apparently against me personally. That won't keep me awake. The real reason must be sought in the collar of the Order of the Annunziata given to von Ribbentrop when he expected it for himself. He blames me for it. He will calm down when he gets his.

Mussolini telephones from Forlì. He continues to object to the sale of arms to the English. He thinks that the British position is every day becoming more and more difficult. Why?

February 7, 1940

Return of the Duce, with whom I have a long conversation. Meanwhile, he refuses to sell arms to Great Britain. He says that he does not want to reduce the means of making war that are at our disposal, and that he intends to keep the obligations recently confirmed with Germany. "Governments, like individuals, must follow a line of morality and honor." He is not concerned about the English reactions, which I prophesy will be inevitable and harsh. Neither does the lack of coal weigh on his mind. He repeats that it is good for the Italian people to be put to tests that cause them to shake off their century-old mental laziness. He is bitter toward the people. "We must keep them disciplined and in uniform from morning till night. Beat them and beat them and beat them." He does not discriminate between the classes, and calls "the people" all those who wish to vegetate.

I inform Riccardi of the Duce's decision in the matter of commercial exchanges with England. He is very gloomy. He had counted upon the 20,000,000 pounds sterling that were a part of the agreement, and he is afraid that we shall no longer receive the raw materials, most of which come from the British market. Von Mackensen comes to plead for the usual illicit favors that Germany demands as a part of our participation. As usual, I am inclined to answer these secondary demands affirmatively, in order to be able to answer the larger demand negatively whenever it comes, as, unfortunately, come it will.

February 8, 1940

I inform Percy Loraine that the Duce has decided to turn down every request for war matériel [by England]. The communication had a strong effect. Loraine replied that this destroyed the basis of all negotiations and that shortly the transport of coal from Germany would be stopped. He emphasized also the political significance of our refusal. Italo-British relations are moving into a period of sharper tension. When I stated that the Duce is disposed to re-examine his decision in six months, he answered that by that time Europe will be reshaped for ten generations to come.

I take Prince Hesse to the Duce. Hitler proposes a meeting of the two chiefs at the frontier. Mussolini immediately declared himself favorable. I fear this meeting. When the Duce is with the Germans he becomes excited. Today, with Hesse, he used entirely warlike language. He said that he means to take his place at the side of Germany as soon as his armament preparations permit us to be a help rather than a hindrance to the Germans. Even with Hesse he maintained an attitude of complete indifference with regard to the coal crisis about which everyone is worried. Bocchini, the Minister of Police, confirms reports that the state of mind of the country is becoming more and more unsettled, and he fears regrettable incidents and disorders in the near future.

February 9, 1940

Clodius, who has been in Rome for some days on commercial matters, received with joy the news of the Duce's refusal to England. He declared that if Italian arms were sold to the Allies a violent reaction would develop, particularly in German military quarters. Clodius was unhappy over the progress of his negotiations. He asks for many things, perhaps for too many things, receiving from our officials many refusals. I limited myself to giving him assurances and good words. They cost so little.

The Duce is very proud of his "no" to the English. He repeats that states, like individuals, must have a moral standard on which no compromise can be made; the course of honor cannot be disregarded. Selling arms to the British would have dishonored us. Naturally, I replied, it remains to be seen for how long a time we can continue to be unyielding on practical grounds. The sources of raw materials are in the hands of others. How will these others react now?

The Duce has confirmed his statement that he is favorable to the meeting with Hitler. He also looks with favor on a trip by Ribbentrop to Rome, especially because this would permit him to visit the Pope.

February 10, 1940

Nothing new. I go to Leghorn for the celebration of the anniversary of Buccari [the famous Buccari raid by the Italian Navy against the Austrian Navy during World War I, led by Ciano's father].

February 11, 1940

The ceremony at my father's tomb arouses in me pride and sadness. While formerly it used to be a joy for me to go to the city of my childhood, now, it reopens old wounds. My father's death has changed my life, or, rather, my conception of life. My youth, too, was buried in his grave.

Benini reports that Riccardi made a very courageous speech before the Supreme Commission for the Defense of the Italian State on our present monetary situation, our stocks, and on the real condition of our armament. In the speech he reached totally pessimistic conclusions and spoke in a tone never heard before. Badoglio objected not so much to the substance as to the form, agreeing fully with the former.

February 12, 1940

I found the Duce irritated by Riccardi's speech. According to him, what Riccardi said pleased the critics of Fascist policy so much that as soon as the Duce had left the room Balbo went to shake hands with Riccardi, until then his implacable enemy. The Duce repeats that he does not believe in the cry baby of the Department for Foreign Trade and Exchange. Even Guarneri has for the last six years been announcing that we are on the brink of bankruptcy, but we have carried on quite well, thinks the Duce. But the Duce does not add that during that time we consumed twelve billions in foreign securities and five billions in gold. Now our reserves have been reduced to one thousand four hundred miserable millions, and when these are gone we shall have only our eyes to weep with. Riccardi erred in form, but he acted courageously, sounding the alarm.

February 13, 1940

Nothing new.

February 14, 1940

I communicate to Sir Percy Loraine the Duce's final decision to refuse the British all military matériel, including the training planes already contracted for. Sir Percy does not conceal his disappointment and says that the relations between our two countries are really moving toward a period of growing difficulties.

General Graziani, replying to Riccardi's speech at a meeting of the Supreme Council for the defense of the country, claims that the Army should be thanked for not having asked financial sacrifices of the country that might have been too heavy. The Duce takes on himself all responsibility and defends the armament program. He says that ever since 1935 the Italian economists have been threatening bankruptcy, and that, in spite of this, we have continued to carry on. In reply, Riccardi made up pretty well for his previous error, expressed regrets for the form of his speech, but in substance repeated what he had said on Saturday. The laws of economics cannot be changed.

Balbo accompanies me to the Palazzo Chigi. He can hardly control himself. He fully approves of my action. "Just whistle," he says, "and I'll come to your aid."

February 15, 1940

Bocchini's report on the internal situation was very pessimistic. The poverty of the nation is growing and all kinds of difficulties increase. The prestige of the regime is not what it used to be. But is Bocchini telling these things to Mussolini? He swears to me that he is.

February 16, 1940

François-Poncet, whom I had not seen for a long time, complains about our press attacks, and especially of those appearing in the *Popolo d'Italia*. The French newspapers, for the time being, are not reacting, but the relations between the two countries are suffering from it none the less, and the atmosphere of better understanding which we had established in months past is again disturbed. I used some kind words, but nothing more, since the press campaign is personally desired and directed by the Duce, my influence being very limited.

Donegani is overwrought about the coal question. If our supplies diminish or cease entirely in the coming week, industry will suffer a sudden stoppage with dire consequences in the field of production and labor.

I receive Sidorovici, head of the Rumanian Youth Movement. He is a dumbbell—a preposterous creature devoid of interest.

February 17, 1940

News from Finland confirms the fact that the position of its defenders is becoming more serious. The Russians are exerting more and more pressure with immense masses of men and arms. Resistance under such conditions cannot last very long. For obvious reasons we can do no more than has already been done. Nor is it advisable for us to commit ourselves too much in a military undertaking which is beyond our control.

Sir Percy comes to show me certain papers of minor importance which tend to prove collusion between Nazism and Communism. I needed no such proof. I conferred with the Duce on the necessity for stopping our petty newspaper campaign against France. He promised me that he would do it—but for how long?

February 18, 1940

Last night at the Colonnas' Percy Loraine told me that the first of March had been chosen as the date when England would stop all shipments of coal coming to Italy from Germany by sea. I talked about this to the Duce, who flaunts his indifference on the subject. He talks a great deal about national fuels and is counting on an increase of production in our lignite mines. He fools himself and others fool him. Technical experts, on the other hand (and I mean those who are really capable and honest), agree that the lack of coal will paralyze our national life to a large degree. The last few months should have taught Mussolini a great deal about the dangers of autosuggestion.

Sebastiani informs me that Mussolini intends to fire Revel because of the scandalous failure of the *tassa sugli scambi* [a special tax on all sales and exchange of goods]. This was an idiotic decree because there is nothing more hateful than a tax which keeps nagging millions of taxpayers at every turn.

I talked to Casertano about Muti. He affirms that Muti is acting in good faith, but that power has gone to his head, and he is under the influence of a group of friends, minor leaders in the Army and elsewhere, who push him into heaping error on error in their own personal interests. I don't think that Muti will last long as secretary of the Fascist party.

February 19, 1940

Nothing new in politics. The British attack on the German steamer *Altmark,* which was sailing in Norwegian territorial waters with English prisoners, has made a deep impression. I speak of it with Percy Loraine, and to his surprise I declare that the English action is justified and reminiscent of the boldest traditions of the Navy at the time of Francis Drake.

I advise the Hungarian Villani to be calm, very calm. If a conflict should break out within a short time, provoked by Hungary, we would not be in a position to give any help. Besides, even the Magyars do not approve the verbal but dangerous violence of Count Czaky. At the Golf Club on the same day Countess Betlem suggested that I should pull the coattails of her much too intemperate Minister for Foreign Affairs [Czaky].

February 20, 1940

Goering, in talking with Teucci, spoke clearly about the Italian position, pronouncing judgments which reveal that he is disappointed and very angry. We must keep this in mind. He is the most human of the German chiefs, but he is emotional and violent and might become dangerous. In the meantime, Clodius and Mackensen have come to protest about the difficulties they are encountering in the commercial negotiations. What do they want from us? I told them openly, as long as we maintain a hostile policy toward France and England we shall have increasing difficulties in providing ourselves with raw materials. They cannot demand, as they do, that we also renounce our Balkan markets.

Percy Loraine informs me in writing that today his government will declare in Commons that German coal en route to Italy is merchandise subject to confiscation. The crisis is approaching, and all the Stefani [Italian news agency] communications which today filled the newspapers with articles on our production and use of lignite will not suffice to divert it.

Ansaldo reports on a conversation with the Duce. Nothing essentially new. The Duce reiterates his firm hostility toward the democracies and his idea of waging war on the side of Germany, an idea in which I believe less and less.

February 21, 1940

The Duce intends to satisfy the Germans, and at the Palazzo Venezia there is a meeting with Riccardi and Giannini. Both of them are insistent on the need to refuse goods which we ourselves lack, such as hemp, copper, and other raw materials. But the Duce decides to give thirty-five hundred tons of copper anyway, from the amount which he is preparing to extort from the Italians. He thinks that this

requisition will amount to twenty thousand tons, but perhaps this estimate is too high. Nevertheless, the requisition will not be well received, and worse still if it becomes known that a part of the copper
will have to be ceded to the hated Germans. I insist to the Duce that
he should not requisition sacred objects in the churches. He refused.
"The churches do not need copper but faith, and there is very little
faith left now. Catholicism is wrong in demanding too much credulity
from modern man."

February 22, 1940

Our commercial agreement with the Germans was reached easily
after the intervention of the Duce.

I see the Prince of Piedmont. I apprise him of the situation which
he, moreover, knows very well and sizes up with prudence. But it was
clear that he liked to hear from me what he himself did not dare to
say. He is very anti-German and convinced that Italy must remain
neutral. He is skeptical, very skeptical, about the potentialities of the
Army in the present condition of armament—a condition which he
considers to be altogether pitiful.

February 23, 1940

Nothing new.

February 24, 1940

Nothing new.

February 25, 1940

Hitler has spoken. Contrary to the English comments which pass his
speech off as quite ordinary, the Duce considers that this time the
Führer wants to make known his peace conditions: recognition of the
principle of *Lebensraum* for Germany and restoration of the colonies.
These conditions seem to me such that it would be unworthy of London to discuss them, but the Duce considers them acceptable. The
Duce has once more confirmed his certainty that the Allies will lose
the war, and his whole policy is based on this conviction. In fact, he

has again spoken of claims against France, and has outlined his thesis on the necessity of free access to the open seas, without which Italy will never be an empire.

February 26, 1940

I received Roosevelt's representative, Sumner Welles. He is an American distinguished in appearance and in manner, who carries easily the weight of a mission that has put him in the limelight of American and world publicity. The conference was very cordial. I did not hesitate to inform him on events concerning which he was not informed and about my own plans. I give a normal, simple tone to the conversation and this impresses him, because he was not expecting it. He is anti-German, but makes an effort to be correctly impartial. He was glad, however, when I let him know my feelings and sympathies. Unfortunately, the conference with the Duce (detailed elsewhere) took place in a rather icy atmosphere. Mussolini stresses the note of aloofness that he is now showing openly in his relations with the Anglo-Saxons. Sumner Welles left the Mappamondo room more depressed than when he entered it. The Duce later commented sarcastically on the interview: "Between us and the Americans any kind of understanding is impossible because they judge problems on the surface while we go deeply into them." The Duce was not impressed by Welles's personality, but I do not agree with him. I have had too much to do with that pack of presumptuous vulgarians, for such the high German officials are, not to appreciate the fact that Sumner Welles is a gentleman.

February 27, 1940

I go to Naples to act as crown notary on the occasion of the birth of Princess Maria Gabriella, daughter of Prince Humbert and Princess Maria José. I also visit the work in progress for the Triennial Overseas Exposition and of the Ciano Shipbuilding Institute, an institution worthy of the name it bears. During my absence the Duce has an editorial published in italics in the *Giornale d'Italia* answering the *Daily Herald,* in which he says that in addition to being willing to join the Germans we are also ready to join the Russians if there is any intention on the Allied side of threatening our existence as a totalitarian regime. This caused considerable comment, none of it favorable.

February 28, 1940

The Duce said yesterday to Anfuso, "There are still some criminals and imbeciles in Italy who believe that Germany will be beaten. I tell you Germany will win." I accept "imbecile" if it is for me, but I think "criminal" is unjust. In any case, it is this deep, honest conviction of his that inspires his actions. The Duce ordered that the report of the conversation with Sumner Welles be given to Mackensen and Mackensen was very pleased. I can understand it. Mussolini defended the German thesis with absolute determination.

News comes from Paris that political censorship has been lifted. Here's an event that cannot fail to complicate matters.

February 29, 1940

Pavolini received orders to launch a polemic against some French newspapers, on account of an article by Kerillis [Henri de Kerillis, French journalist] on Italian neutrality. A very touchy subject. All we have to do is to start and the rest will follow. I am worried.

This morning the Duce let off steam against the people of Genoa, who, like the Milanese, "show themselves to be incurably pro-English and at the same time somewhat caddish." The reason is that in Genoa they are complaining more than elsewhere, despite the fact that Albini denies it.

Again Bocchini is concerned more and more about the internal situation. Economic difficulties, political uncertainty, scarcity of food: these are the fundamental reasons for the complaint.

From various sources it is confirmed that Germany is getting ready for an offensive on the western front. It cannot be immediate, however; in Goering's circle they mention the end of March, a month dear to Hitler's superstition.

March 1, 1940

The English press announces that as of today German coal will be treated as an article of contraband, and, hence, seized. We shall have moments of serious difficulty before provisioning from British sources can be straightened out, aside from the difficulties of making payment. The Duce has set aside for this use a billion in gold of the bank of

Italy. On the *Rex,* which is soon to leave, we shall send ingots valued at two million dollars. After this billion is withdrawn, our gold reserve will be about 1,300,000 millions against the deficit in the balance of payments estimated at four billions for the current year. Despite these difficulties the Duce repeats that never has a government fallen on account of financial and economic difficulties. Today he praised the broad vision manifest in the policies of Hitler, who has in mind "a real plan to regulate European life," based upon an exchange of populations so as to make political frontiers coincide with ethnical frontiers.

Revel is not at all pessimistic about the financial situation, and I am surprised. Today at the Golf Club he explained to me a fantastic theory of his according to which gold will no longer be worth anything, and we shall become rich through the sale of works of art. Revel is a fool, who has begun to play the part of an extreme interventionist in order to please his master. Nevertheless, this is dangerous, because the Minister of Finance, if honest and capable, ought to act as a sort of brake.

March 2, 1940

The coal blockade is causing a great deal of comment in the international press, and also a certain amount of excitement in Italy. The Duce thinks it necessary to address a note of protest in strong terms to the British Government. He himself dictates the concluding phrases of the note, which is harsh and threatening.

I receive Sir Noel Charles, who is replacing the ambassador who is ill. He seeks to clarify the measures taken by his government concerning the blockade, but the explanation is of slight significance. I take advantage of the occasion to tell him—as a good friend of the English —that the measures taken on the coal question are the sort that will serve to push Italy into the arms of Germany. It would be absurd not to admit that British stock is down in our estimation.

Charles informs me, too, of the impending despatch of new forces to the Near East, which should not be interpreted as having any connection with the Balkan situation.

March 3, 1940

The Duce approves the note I have prepared on the basis of his conclusions, a note, I believe, which is firm and to the point, and yet not such as to burn our bridges. Von Mackensen comes to see me. I give him a copy of the note. His government instructs him to say that the German press is at our disposal for an attack on Great Britain on the coal question. The game of Berlin is clear. The Germans are trying at any cost to embitter relations between us and London. I have not the least intention of encouraging this. I thank von Mackensen, and tell him that it is not necessary to take any further steps. We are able to take care of the matter with the means at our disposal.

Guariglia sends an interesting and adroit report on Italo-French relations. He goes so far as to propose negotiations and the conclusion of an agreement. Although the report contains phrases and arguments which will certainly be unwelcome to the Duce, I decide to submit it to him anyway, because it may have a wholesome influence on his line of thought.

I speak with the Duce about the eventual exportation of works of art. He is favorable, but I am not. He does not like works of art, and above all detests that period of history during which the greatest masterpieces were produced. I recall—he recalls it too—that he felt a sense of annoyance and physical fatigue unusual in him on the day he was obliged to accompany Hitler on a detailed visit of inspection to the Pitti Palace and to the Uffizi.

March 4, 1940

I go with General Marras to the Duce; the latter is very pessimistic about the German attitude toward us. He is convinced that the Germans, notwithstanding a certain respect for us, maintain their hatred and scorn unchanged, now aggravated by what they call a second treachery. No war move would be so popular in Germany, both for the older and younger generations, as an armed invasion pushed in the direction of our blue skies and warm seas. This and other things Marras frankly told the Duce, who is shocked by the report. The Duce repeated his theory of a parallel war and again insisted that Italy will never enter the war at the side of the Western Powers. Of this he is certain.

Bodini likewise presents a report on his trip to Germany, but it is very superficial. Two points emerge from it: the certainty of an approaching offensive, and the German conviction that they won the war last September. What a bitter delusion this will be if they find themselves in the trenches during the coming winter.

March 5, 1940

The American Consul at Naples, in order to find out the state of mind of the Italian people, questioned a beggar, who answered that he does not fear war, but rather revolution. The report, which has fallen into the hands of the Duce, has put him in a good humor. He observes: "Even the beggars are so well content with their condition under the Fascist regime as to fear a revolution." This was his final comment, but as Minister for Foreign Affairs I shudder at the sources of information used by consuls, naturally including our own consuls.

Another conversation with the King. I find him disappointed at the English attitude which, however, has not changed his stubborn anti-German view. "I know that I am in the German black book," he said. "Yes, Your Majesty. At the top. And if you will allow me to be bold enough to say it, I figure in it immediately after you." "I think so too. This honors both of us so far as Italy is concerned." Such is the tone of our conversation. I did not hesitate to tell him that I would consider a German victory the greatest disaster for our country. He asked what we might be able to obtain from the Allies. "The preservation of the liberty of Italy, which German hegemony would compromise for centuries to come," I said. He agreed.

I try in vain to assuage the worries of François-Poncet, who is very much disturbed over the resumption of the pro-German tendencies of the press, of the party, and above all of the Duce.

March 6, 1940

The Duce is more than ever irritated about the coal question. The first ships were held up yesterday, precisely as stated in Percy Loraine's report, although some information in the press and the optimism of the Minister of Communications had caused us to hope for a postponement. Mussolini is angered at this display of force more than by the practical consequences that might come. "Within a short time the guns will loose off by themselves. It is not possible that of all people I should become the laughingstock of Europe. I have to stand for one humiliation after another. As soon as I am ready I shall make the English repent. My intervention in the war will bring about their defeat." The Duce, alas, is still under illusions as to our chances of quick rearmament. The situation is still very difficult and lack of coal will only make it worse. Perhaps we shall go into war, but we shall be unprepared and unarmed.

For the first time I found a person who wants to declare war with the Germans against France and England. This person is no less than the intrepid Cesare Maria de Vecchi di Val Cismon! The Americans say that a sucker is born every minute; one has only to look for him. This time I have found one. Cesare Maria is, above all, a man of pomposity and vain illusions, who dreams of obtaining a marshal's baton and decorations and hopes to gain them through the blood of others.

March 7, 1940

The situation created by the confiscation of our coal is not at all changed, although Bastianini indicates from London a possible easing of the British attitude. Mussolini is brooding over his exasperation. Today he uttered between his teeth new and vague threats against the English. He said, "England will be beaten. Inexorably beaten. This is the pure truth, that you should get into your head." During our seven years of daily contacts this is the *first* time that he picks on me personally. If I considered my job more important than my conscience, I should be greatly worried tonight. Instead, I am perfectly serene. I know that I am honestly serving my country and him whom I love and to whom I owe so much.

The Yugoslav Minister is concerned about events in Croatia and asks us to increase our vigilance over Pavelić. On this matter I give him at once the most ample assurances.

March 8, 1940

A theatrical gesture, dear to the common tastes of the Germans: von Mackensen informs me that Ribbentrop will be in Rome on Sunday, bringing with him Hitler's reply to the Duce. He adds pompously that he [Ribbentrop] will pay a visit to the Pope. I telephone Mussolini, emphasizing the inadvisability of such a move, just at a time when the coal business has made our relations with London so delicate. But the Duce is perfectly satisfied, and nothing remains for me but to let the Germans know that we welcome the visit.

Frankly, I dislike all this. It will produce a far-reaching effect on the whole world, just when we ought not add fuel to the fire. Further-more, I dread the Duce's contact with the Germans. In these last few days his hostile attitude toward the Allies has become more pro-nounced. The thought of war dominates him, and it will dominate him even more if the offensive on the western front begins. Inaction will then go against the grain of his aggressive temperament. Under the circumstances, Ribbentrop will need no great power of oratory to urge on the Duce a course which he, the Duce, desires with all his soul. With respect to Ribbentrop's visit to the Pope, I judge it to be a ges-ture as phony as it is futile.

March 9, 1940

We were finally able to reach an agreement with the British on the matter of the ships held up by them. The ships were released with their cargoes on condition that none of our ships are to be sent to northern ports for the purpose of loading German coal for Italy. I tell Charles this evening that the agreement pleased me in a very special way, and he, being quicker than he would have me believe, replied that my remark made it unnecessary for him to ask any questions re-garding Ribbentrop's visit—one which will be very unpopular in Italy.

I tell Pavolini to feature in the best way possible the news about the agreement with London. Ribbentrop will not like this, but it will help to counteract, within and without our boundaries, the unfavorable impression of his visit.

March 10, 1940

The meeting at the station is rather cool. The crowd, that had with some difficulty been gathered by the Federale, showed a good deal of reserve. As we drove away von Ribbentrop at once stated that the fine weather we were having brought nearer the moment for action and arrogantly uttered this phrase, "Within a few months the French Army will be destroyed and the English on the Continent will be pris-oners of war." The same phrase is repeated also to the Duce during the conference.

Von Ribbentrop is the bearer of Hitler's letter: a long document in which there are many unimportant things, but in which two fundamental points are emphasized—that he intends to settle the conflict with arms and that the place of Italy will inevitably be at the side of Germany. Von Ribbentrop dilutes these ideas into many words. Mussolini listens and promises to answer tomorrow, after having meditated over the letter as well as over the interview. And he immediately joins Hitler in affirming that the place of Fascism is at the side of Nazism on the firing line. The conference was quite cordial and without outbursts on either side.

After the interview, when we were left alone, Mussolini says that he does not believe in the German offensive nor in a complete German success. He has not yet come to a firm conclusion. He wants to think it over further. As for today, von Ribbentrop has not scored any decisive advantage.

March 11, 1940

Today it has been Mussolini's turn to talk. The stenographic report of today's conference [with von Ribbentrop] has been made and will be kept elsewhere. The Duce expressed himself calmly, avoiding grandiloquent phrases, but could not restrain himself from alluding repeatedly to two obligations (implicit in the present state of things) which he intends to maintain, and which are above all his deepest convictions. He declared that, reserving his freedom to choose the date, he intends to intervene in the conflict and to fight a war parallel to that of Germany; in a word, to join the latter country. The principal reason for this is that he considers Italy imprisoned in the Mediterranean. Von Ribbentrop tried to dot his *i*'s as much as possible, asking permission to reinforce our troops on the French frontier in order to cause a concentration of forces on the other side. He then proposed that within a short time a meeting between Hitler and Mussolini should take place at the Brenner Pass. The Duce quickly accepted the proposal, which I find to be quite dangerous because of the immediate consequences it may have, and also because of its influence on the future. I shall try to talk it over with the Duce.

Thus von Ribbentrop's visit ended. If he wanted to reinforce the Axis, he has succeeded. If, on the other hand, he wanted to accelerate our intervention, he has not achieved his aim, although he may have secured from Mussolini some new but not very useful compromises.

March 12, 1940

This morning Mussolini insistently asked for the reports of yesterday's conversations, not yet back from Berlin. He says he fears that there might be some error, but in reality he believes he has gone too far in his commitment to fight against the Allies. He would now like to dissuade Hitler from his land offensive, an idea to which he returns over and over again. Italian inaction, which already weighs heavily on the Duce, would be unbearable if the German forces really entered the struggle. Thus he hopes to prevail on Hitler, and this is the result that he expects to achieve at the meeting at the Brenner Pass. I express my opposition to this.

The Germans know by now that the Duce is opposed to the land offensive, but they have let us know that they will go ahead just the same. It is therefore useless for us to insist. But if the German offensive is preceded by a meeting at the Brenner Pass I shall always consider Mussolini in a certain measure responsible for the great massacre. Neither can it be denied that the Duce is fascinated by Hitler, a fascination which involves something deeply rooted in his make-up. The Führer will get more out of the Duce than Ribbentrop was able to get. With the necessary tact, I told this to the Duce, who partly agreed with me, but he insisted that he cannot now decline the offer of a meeting with Hitler. He is probably right in this. I can therefore only redouble my recommendations for prudence.

March 13, 1940

Von Ribbentrop telephones and asks to set the date of the meeting at the Brenner Pass for Monday, the eighteenth of March. At first Mussolini exploded: "These Germans are unbearable; they don't give one time to breathe nor to think matters over." But then he concluded that in view of the state of affairs, since the meeting must take place, it had better take place at once. So I confirm to von Ribbentrop the date chosen by him. Nevertheless, the Duce was nervous. Until now he has lived under the illusion that a real war would not be waged. The prospect of an imminent clash in which he might remain an outsider disturbs him and, to use his words, humiliates him. He still hopes, but less than before, that he can influence Hitler and persuade him to desist from his intention to attack.

Poncet would like some information. I am quite reserved with him, but I do not conceal the fact that I consider the clash now imminent. As regards us, I tell him that we shall maintain the political line that we have followed up to this moment.

Casertano [new secretary of the party] makes a report of the condition of the party: terrible. Muti, on whose behalf I am not going to make any effort, has shown himself presumptuous and distrustful, and, as often happens, is less devoted to me than I thought he was. It only remains for me to abandon him to his fate.

March 14, 1940

While playing golf, Count Acquarone, Minister of the Royal House, approached me. He talked openly of his concern about the situation and assured me that the King is also aware of the impoverishment of the country. In his opinion the King feels that it may become necessary for him to intervene at any moment to give a different direction to things; he is prepared to do this and to do it with despatch. Acquarone repeats that the King has for me "more than benevolence—a real affection and much trust." Acquarone, I cannot say whether by his own initiative or by order of the King, wanted to go deeper into the subject, but I kept the conversation on general lines.

Mussolini is more and more preoccupied about the meeting at the Brenner Pass. He would like to get from Hitler a signed document in the shape of a communiqué which would give him a certain latitude or freedom of action to stay out, even if hostilities should begin on the western front. This seems difficult to me, because Hitler, too, has his public opinion to consider, and he would not be forgiven if he played his cards badly and lost his Italian trump. It would be better if we made the Germans understand that they are repeating the old Salzburg tune. They do things and undo them without consulting us, frequently acting against our point of view. Their present dealings, as those of former times, offer a suitable pretext to insist on our freedom of action.

March 15, 1940

Nothing new.

March 16, 1940

Two conferences with Sumner Welles—at the Palazzo Chigi and the Palazzo Venezia. Stenographic reports are to be found elsewhere. The most important result is this: in London and in Paris there does not exist any of the uncompromising attitude which their speeches and the papers indicate. If they had certain guarantees of security they would be ready to give in more or less and to recognize the *fait accompli*. I think that if they really go along this path, they are moving toward defeat. If Hitler is still doubtful about when to deliver the attack, his doubts will be dispelled at once when he learns from Mussolini of these shilly-shallyings of the democracies. But I do not believe he has any doubts. From the haste with which Hitler wanted to set the meeting, from the fact that he did not want to remain at the Brenner Pass more than an hour and a half, Mussolini deduces that within a short time he will set off the powder keg. Today the Duce is calmer. He intends to keep his solidarity with Germany, but he does not intend to enter the war—at least for the time being. He said, "I shall do as Bertoldo did. He accepted the death sentence on condition that he choose the tree on which he was to be hanged. Needless to say, he never found that tree. [Bertoldo is the Wise Fool in Giulio Cesare Croce's famous work, *Bertoldo, Bertoldino, and Cacaseno*.] I shall agree to enter the war, but reserve for myself the choice of the moment. I alone intend to be the judge, and a great deal will depend upon how the war goes." These intentions encourage me, but only up to a certain point. To push Mussolini on is an easy undertaking, but to pull him back is difficult.

March 17, 1940

Welles has telephoned Roosevelt, asking for permission to undertake a certain vague initiative for peace, but the answer is in the negative. The whole tone of the telephone call gives one the impression that Roosevelt does not wish to commit himself beyond a certain point, and certainly not before he has carefully examined the results of his collaborator's European mission.

At 1:30 P.M. we start for the Brenner Pass. Mackensen, rather embarrassed, tells me that the Führer has expressed a wish that the conversation begin between the Duce and himself alone. (Alfieri says that

he learned from Frau Mackensen that Hitler wishes to keep Ribbentrop at a distance, but this seems to me one of Alfieri's flights of imagination.) During the trip I talked at length with Mussolini. He is
calm and, at heart, happy that Hitler has called for him. He believes
that hostilities will start at any moment, and he repeats to me his latest
theory on our position if this should happen. The Italian forces, he
says, will constitute the left wing which will tie up an equal number
of enemy troops without fighting, but ready, nonetheless, to go into
action at a convenient moment.

During our trip the first telegrams begin to arrive from the capitals,
where news of the trip has been announced. They express surprise and
amazement, and, in general, the tendency to connect the event with
Sumner Welles's presence in Rome.

March 18, 1940

It is snowing at the Brenner Pass. Mussolini is waiting for his guest
with anxious elation. Recently he has felt more and more the fascination of the Führer. His military successes—the only successes that
Mussolini really values and desires—are the cause of this. While we
are waiting, he tells me that he had a dream during the night "which
tore away the veil from the future." But he does not say what the
dream is. On the other hand, he says that this has happened at other
times, when, for example, he had dreamed of fording a stream, and
learned that the Fiume question was about to be solved.

The Hitler meeting is very cordial on both sides. The conference,
of which a stenographic report is to be found elsewhere, is more a
monologue than anything else. Hitler talks all the time, but is less agitated than usual. He makes few gestures and speaks in a quiet tone.
He looks physically fit. Mussolini listens to him with interest and with
deference. He speaks little and confirms his intention to move with
Germany. He reserves to himself only the choice of the right moment
(it reminds me of the tree of Bertoldo). The conference ends with a
short meal.

Later Mussolini gives me his impressions. He did not find in Hitler
that uncompromising attitude which von Ribbentrop has led him to
suspect. Yesterday, too, von Ribbentrop only opened his mouth to
harp on Hitler's intransigency. Mussolini believes that Hitler will think
twice before he jumps into an offensive.

The meeting has not substantially altered our position.

March 19, 1940

The crisscrossing of speculations regarding the reasons for and the results of the Brenner meeting continue, and, as always happens, those reasons that are most natural and therefore truthful are disregarded. In Rome yesterday the meeting was interpreted as a step toward peace, and the city celebrated, which made me think how difficult it would be to cause it to celebrate in the same way an announcement of war.

I saw Sumner Welles and briefly posted him on the situation: nothing else but an event in the house of the Axis which leaves things exactly as they were before. He is happy that there is no threat of an immediate military clash. Roosevelt will in this way have time to study Welles's reports, and perhaps to take some peace steps. Welles also talks about a possible meeting between Mussolini and Roosevelt in the Azores—a rather complicated project for results so uncertain.

Percy Loraine is desirous of news. I put him at ease. The Brenner meeting is no prelude to surprises in our policy. This is what he wanted to hear.

In thinking over his meeting with Hitler, and while waiting to read Schmidt's reports, the Duce is convinced that Hitler is not preparing to launch the land offensive. As a matter of fact, Mussolini resented the fact that Hitler did all the talking; he had in mind to tell him many things, and instead he had to keep quiet most of the time, a thing which, as dictator, or rather the dean of dictators, he's not in the habit of doing.

March 20, 1940

Chamberlain's outburst yesterday in the House of Commons, in speaking of the "two gentlemen who have met at the Brenner Pass," is very significant, but Mussolini has not attached any importance to it nor has he alluded to it. Poncet, too, has expressed himself regretfully about the meeting, and my words did little to convince him that there is nothing new. "You are mistaken," he said. "You have bet, and in fact the Duce himself has put his money on the losing horse, and now he is doubling his bet. But the Franco-British horse, even if at the beginning of the race it may lag behind, will win in the last lap." He spoke of the French Cabinet crisis and very skeptically about Daladier, who will not form an important cabinet because he does not care to surround himself with strong men. He considers that Reynaud is the right man.

Sumner Welles before leaving spoke clearly to Blasco d'Aieta, who is a relative of his. Even without undertaking any offensive, Germany will be exhausted within a year. He considers the war already won by the French and English. The United States is there with all the weight of her power, to guarantee this victory. He deplored the fact that Italy, for which he has a great deal of sympathy, should continue to get more and more deeply involved with one who is destined to suffer a harrowing defeat.

March 21, 1940

Nothing new.

March 22, 1940

Nothing new.

March 23, 1940

I receive Count Teleki at the station, and later am present at the unveiling of the tablets with the new names of the streets near Montecitorio [the hill where the Chamber of Deputies is built], which are dedicated to the memory of my father's military deeds. Mussolini, who is in good humor these days and quite talkative, is growing every day more definitely pro-German. He now speaks openly of entering the war at the side of Germany and even defines our course of action: defensive in the Alps, defensive in Libya, offensive in Ethiopia against Jibuti and Kenya, aero-naval offensive in the Mediterranean. The Duce's attitude is beginning to influence many Fascist chiefs, who, either because they follow him, or out of personal conviction, are lining up in the ranks of the interventionists: Muti, Ricci, and, to a greater extent, Revel and Riccardi, who is no longer telling unpleasant truths as he used to do. Against the adventure are Grandi and Bottai. The latter naturally are among those who hold positions that they don't want to lose; the people of all social levels want nothing to do with war. Starace tells me that the Duce made some very warlike speeches to him, and that this morning he said to General Galbiati, commander of the University Student Volunteers, "Hold yourself ready. Shortly we will march in the west." Starace himself mixes much water with his wine. He affirms that the internal conditions of the country are precarious and "almost dangerous."

March 24, 1940

I play golf with Teleki. He repeats that 95 per cent of the Hungarians detest Germany. He desires only to keep his country out of the conflict and hopes that Italy may do likewise. Villani again alludes to the question of the crown. He confirms the Magyar intention to offer it to some member of the House of Savoy.

Mussolini again has one of his anti-clerical outbursts. He attacks the clergy on the grounds of faith, honesty, and morals. He says that in numerous towns in southern Italy the population almost forces the curate to take a concubine, since only in this way will their wives be left undisturbed.

March 25, 1940

A long conference with Count Teleki. I find him objective and reasonable as regards Magyar claims. He realizes what a danger it would be to Hungary to incorporate within itself a disproportionate number of foreign minorities. The very life of the country would be affected by it. Besides, he will not do anything against Rumania, because he does not want to make himself responsible, even indirectly, for having opened the doors of Europe to Russia. No one would pardon him for this, not even Germany. Teleki has avoided taking any open position one way or the other, but has not hidden his sympathy for the Western Powers and fears an integral German victory like the plague.

In the afternoon I talked with the Duce and General Soddu. The Germans offer us the immediate delivery of some anti-aircraft batteries. Mussolini plans on sending for them at once. Soddu agrees, but he does not want any German personnel. This supplying of weapons, which the Germans will hasten to reveal publicly, will make London and Paris still more acutely suspicious.

March 26, 1940

With the Duce during the morning. I do not talk of politics. He praises Friedrich Wilhelm who, by kicking the women who were out walking and cudgeling the clergymen who were looking at the soldiers, created the Prussia of today. During the conversation the Duce was scintillating and pungent; but he is wrong in admiring the Prussians as "a philosophical breed."

In the afternoon I bring Teleki to him, and there is more or less a repetition of yesterday's conference. The Duce makes it clear that he does not intend to remain neutral to the end, and that at a certain moment he will intervene at the side of Germany. Teleki receives this declaration with very limited enthusiasm.

March 27, 1940

A visit from Poncet, who is getting ready to confer with Reynaud. He was deeply impressed by the turn matters have taken, and he wanted to know if at the present state of affairs he must consider that the die has been cast. I tried to calm him, but did not succeed, because he is a keen man, and, besides, recent events have been too clear and eloquent. Poncet tried again to put before us the possibility of negotiations for conditions more favorable to Italy, and he has gone so far as to talk about the cession of French Somaliland. I did not accept these offers, which, for that matter, were vague, and have told him that Mussolini's state of mind is not much inclined to negotiation. In fact, when I told Mussolini about the conference with the French Ambassador, he quickly answered that French offers are always made in bad faith and with the sole practical aim of "compromising and defaming us."

Caruso presents a report on the conditions of the Bohemian protectorate. Apparently things are going better, and the ferocity of German pressure has abated. But there is a storm lurking. If one day the wind changes not one German will get out alive.

At luncheon Teleki asks me abruptly, "Do you know how to play bridge?" "Why?" "For the day when we are together in the Dachau Concentration Camp." This is the real state of mind of this man.

March 28, 1940

A long conversation last evening with the Prince of Piedmont. Though he is usually cautious and reserved, he revealed, without exposing himself too much, his concern about the growing pro-German direction of our policy—a concern which was aggravated, he said, by his knowledge of our present military condition. He denies that since September there has been any real improvement in our armament; supplies are scarce and morale is low. He talks apprehensively about the Fascist militia, which he thinks does not represent the volunteer spirit of the Army, but constitutes rather a group of dissatisfied and undisciplined men.

I talk about the party with the Duce. I agree with him that if we are really moving toward war Muti is not the right man to develop the Fascist organizations to the full, and to charge them with power. Mussolini is concerned about it, but then, as is usual for him now, concluded optimistically, "I myself will galvanize the party at the right time, and I will do it in the way of Frederick the Great."

Another conversation with Teleki. Nothing new, but he opens his anti-German heart to me. He hopes for the defeat of Germany, not a complete defeat—that might provoke violent shocks—but a kind of defeat that would blunt her teeth and claws for a long time.

March 29, 1940

A report presented by Melchiori, who has spent a month in Germany, has had a definite influence on the mind of the Duce. I do not know the value of this individual's observations. He is a shining example of amorality, of greedy ambition, ineptitude, and ignorance, who does not know a single word of German and spends his time in the anterooms of the consulates and the embassy begging for second-hand information, which he then cooks up in a rather vulgar style. The trouble is that Mussolini takes him seriously. Few documents have struck him lately as much as the Melchiori report, in which even though he reaches the conventional conclusion of "an unavoidable German victory" he also brings out the difficult living conditions of the German people. This report has not substantially modified the decisions of the Duce, but for the first time he has admitted that Germany is not resting on a bed of roses, and that the failure of the offensive or a long-drawn-out war would mean defeat, and hence the collapse of the German regime. "I do not understand," he said, "why Hitler does not realize this. I feel that Fascism is wearing out—a wear and tear which is not deep, but is nevertheless noticeable, and he does not feel it in Germany, where the crisis has already assumed rather alarming proportions."

March 30, 1940

The Germans raise objections to our recognition of the government of Wang Ching-Wei. It is now too late after the telegram which I sent him with the intention of digging deeper the gulf which separates our politics from the Russians. I speak of it to the Duce and point out the danger of doing something that is not welcome to Japan. He agrees, and inveighs against von Ribbentrop, "a truly sinister man, because he is an imbecile and presumptuous."

Molotov's speech cannot have pleased Germany, because it is quite different from the tone of that used by von Ribbentrop toward Moscow.

Mussolini is irritated for the nth time at Catholicism, which is to blame for "having made Italy universal, hence preventing it from becoming national. When a country is universal it belongs to everybody but itself."

March 31, 1940

Word reaches me from many quarters that the Duce has in mind to fire me from the Ministry for Foreign Affairs. I do not believe it. In any case, if this should happen, I would be delighted to leave this job in which I have served for almost four years—and what years!—carrying my head high. Everything that I have done was done for the sole purpose of serving my country and the Duce, and whenever I took a stand which seemed to conflict with that of the Duce I did so to defend the Duce's position against offense from abroad. This has been the true and inmost cause of my incurable resentment, a resentment which I have nourished and reaffirmed against the Germans since the days of Salzburg. But all this is of no account. The Duce will do whatever he wishes to do. *Dominus dedit, Dominus abstulit* [The Lord giveth and the Lord taketh away].

I read the whole text of Molotov's speech. On two points he is harsh with us, and this is of some help in avoiding the understanding which Berlin wishes us to have with the Russians.

Mussolini is indignant with Sumner Welles because he told Chamberlain that, while not actually having suffered a stroke, the Duce looks, nevertheless, very tired and perturbed. We learned this from one of the usual telegrams shown to us by the English Embassy.

April 1, 1940

Von Mackensen, on his return from Berlin, hands me a stenographic report of the Brenner Pass meeting. It is not in the stenographic style of other reports made by Schmidt. It is a much abridged summary. It appears that Hitler had made some objection about furnishing the copy. The Ambassador, on the orders of von Ribbentrop, speaks once more of Italo-Russian relations and he asks, with some hesitation, because he does not personally agree with his master, that our press publish articles "more or less praising the Soviet." I refuse flatly. We cannot do such an undignified somersault and Molotov's speech is certainly not a document that justifies such a gesture on our part. The Duce approves, and concludes that "the best we can do for Russia is to be silent, and that is a great deal."

After reading the report, Mussolini repeats that it is his intention to write to Hitler to dissuade him from attempting his land offensive, which is equivalent to putting all his money on a single card. I encourage this move by the Duce because either Hitler will attack just the same and Mussolini will be affected by it and, God willing, will have another pretext to break away, or Hitler will not attack and the war will end in the course of a few months, *en queue de poisson*. It will go well for us one way or the other. But von Mackensen and our embassy in Berlin agree in asserting that the offensive will take place, and perhaps in a short time.

April 2, 1940

Violent turn of the wheel in the direction of war. Today Mussolini wants full steam ahead to open conflict if France and England really intend, as they announce, to tighten the blockade. As Goering, in a conference with Colonel Teucci, had said that he wanted to be informed about the Italian position, Mussolini telegraphed that Goering be told that he is hastening preparations. And yet no one asked him to do so. The Duce tells me that he has drawn up a memorandum concerning our plan of political and strategic action. He will give me a copy and on Saturday he will get together with seven responsible men who will be informed about the document.

In the Council of Ministers, too, he expresses his belligerency. He foresees that the war may begin at any moment, and excluding the fact that he does not want to show himself servile to the democracies (which would bring us into conflict with the Germans), and excluding the fact that if we remain neutral Italy would lose prestige among the nations of the world for a century as a great power and for eternity as a Fascist regime, he concludes that we shall move with the Germans to promote our own purpose. He speaks of a Mediterranean empire and of access to the ocean. He believes blindly in German victory and in the word of Hitler as concerns our share of the booty. But even accepting German victory as an accomplished fact (and I strongly reject the hypothesis of victory), is it so certain that Hitler, who has never kept his word to anyone, will keep it to us?

April 3, 1940

Nothing new.

April 4, 1940

Nothing new.

April 5, 1940

Last night I saw the German film of the conquest of Poland. I had previously refused to attend, but if I had been absent last night also, my absence would have stood out in too equivocal a light. It is a good film if the Germans wish merely to portray brute force, but it is bestial for purposes of propaganda. The audience, composed partly of pro-German functionaries and partly of self-appointed pro-German pimps, did not go beyond the limits of mere courtesy in its applause.

I received an impression of weakness on the part of the Allies this morning in my conversation with Dingli, legal adviser of the embassy in London and friend of Chamberlain. Grandi had a great deal of respect for this man, who impresses me as being of rather secondary importance. He brought a useless and very general message from the Prime Minister, one of those messages of good will destined from the start to remain unanswered. But more important than this was the man's [Chamberlain's] lack of faith in victory. If this were really representative of British morale, the fate of Europe would be tragically sealed. But I do not believe that it is.

Sumner Welles sent his Ambassador to tell me that the whole story about the map has no foundation, and that Reynaud never spoke to him about the new territorial setup in Europe.

April 6, 1940

I received from the Duce one of the eight copies of the secret report prepared by him summarizing the situation and outlining the military political program for the future. It is a measured document in which he arrives at the double conclusion that Italy cannot make an about face nor remain neutral to the end of the conflict without losing standing among the great powers. Therefore, we must fight on the side of Germany for our interests and when conditions are favorable. The plan of military action is this: defensive action on all fronts and offensive action toward Jibuti; aero-naval offensive in grand style. But the Duke of Aosta, whom I saw this morning, said that it is not only extremely problematical that we can maintain present positions, because the French and English are already equipped and ready for action, but the population, among whom rebellion is still alive, would revolt as soon as they got any inkling of our difficulties. I talked about this to the Duce and, for whatever it was worth, repeated that Italy unanimously detests the Germans.

I informed Mussolini briefly of my conversation with Dingli and he wanted me to suggest to Dingli in his name that he attempt to bring about a compromise peace.

April 7, 1940

A year has passed since we landed in Albania. This is a day that I remember with emotion. And, talking about Albania, General Favagrossa today refused the minimum amount needed to solve the housing problem in Albania. With the best will in the world he can't give any money because he hasn't got it. With him I made a rapid survey of the situation with regard to our metal reserves. The results were very sad. Italy is losing all her foreign markets, and even the small amount of gold that we have to spend cannot be converted into the metals that we need. Internal resources are scarce, and we have already gone the limit in gathering copper pans and iron grates. Everything is gone. The truth is that we are worse off today with regard to reserves than we were in September. We have enough stocks for only a few months of war. This is what Favagrossa states. Under such conditions, how can we dare enter the war?

I talked to Dingli and told him that in the event Chamberlain is ready to offer possible conditions, we could become intermediaries for his proposals and facilitate a compromise. Otherwise, they must entertain no illusions. Italy will be at the side of Germany. Dingli is satisfied with his mission and is getting ready to return to London to report. I have the vague impression that I shall not hear of him again. A man of little account.

April 8, 1940

There is alarm in Budapest. Teleki has sent to Rome one of his messengers, Mr. Baranay, to inform us of an approach made by the German General Staff to the Hungarian General Staff. On the pretext that Russia will soon move into Bessarabia, Germany intends to occupy the Rumanian oil fields and asks for free passage through Hungary. The price for this permission would be Transylvania. For the Hungarians there arises the problem either of letting the Germans pass, or opposing them with force. In either case Hungarian liberty would come to an end. Acceptance would spare them devastation and ruin, while fighting, though more painful for the moment, would prepare for a future rebirth. Villani and Baranay advocated resistance and hoped for Italian aid. I accompanied them to the Duce, who reserved his answer, though in principle he advised acceptance. He repeated to them, also, that he stands firmly with Germany, that he is getting ready to fight against the French and English. We have sent a telegram to Berlin to learn how much truth there is in what the Hungarians say. Nobody has told us anything; in fact, the Germans have so far assured us of exactly the opposite. But experience proves that this doesn't mean very much.

April 9, 1940

They did not march in the direction of Rumania.

A secretary of the German Embassy, who came to my house at two o'clock in the morning, bearing a letter from Mackensen, asked to be received at seven o'clock in the morning. Nothing else. He arrived at six-thirty, pale and tired, and communicated Hitler's decision to occupy Denmark and Norway, adding that this decision had already been acted upon. He made no comments, but agreed with me wholeheartedly when I told him that the reaction of the neutrals, and especially of the Americans, would be violent. Then we went to the Duce to give him a written message from Hitler—the usual letter, in the usual style, announcing what he had already done. Mussolini said, "I approve Hitler's action wholeheartedly. It is a gesture that can have incalculable results, and this is the way to win wars. The democracies have lost the race. I shall give orders to the press and to the Italian people to applaud this German action without reservation." Mackensen went out of the Palazzo Venezia glowing.

Later, I returned with the Hungarians to Mussolini. Attolico has denied the rumor of an attack on Rumania. The Duce advised, therefore, that the Hungarians keep calm and moderate, and that they accede to the German requests. This was not the answer the Hungarians expected and hoped for. They went so far as to ask whether, in the case of military resistance, they could count on Italian help. Mussolini smiled. "How could this ever be," he said, "since I am Hitler's ally and intend to remain so?"

When we were alone, the Duce talked about Croatia. His hands fairly itch.

He intends to quicken the tempo, taking advantage of the disorder that reigns in Europe. But he didn't specify, except to say that he is convinced that an attack against Yugoslavia will not lead France and England to strike at us. But what if this should not happen? Are we ready to fight? Balbo and the Duke of Aosta have talked to me about their respective sectors of operation in the last few days in such terms as to leave very little room for illusions.

The first indefinite news of fighting and resistance in Norway is coming in. I hope that the news is true; in the first place, because of the reactions that such an unequal struggle will have on world opinion; second, to show that there are still people who know how to fight in defense of human dignity.

April 10, 1940

News of the German action in the north has had a favorable echo among the Italian people, who, as Mussolini says, "is a whore who prefers the winning mate." More surprising than the speed of the

German action is the Franco-British reaction. The Allies reply to Hitler's military success with a barrage of speeches and articles that is absolutely futile for purposes of war.

Returning from Paris, François-Poncet was very downcast today— a mood that sharply contrasts with his lively and provocative temperament. He spoke of "giving time to time," of "lost battles and wars that were won," of "the United States that will not permit a victory of Hitler." I agree. But I should like to see more decisive action. In France, everybody, or almost everybody, is now convinced that Italy is preparing to go against them, but nothing will be done that might provoke or accelerate such an Italian decision. They would like to leave the whole responsibility up to us. Poncet personally pointed out the dangers in precipitating things.

Mackensen came to see me on a pretext. He wanted to know what were our further reactions to what had happened. I showered him with felicitations and eulogies, since there is now nothing else to do, even though I am absolutely of the opinion that the last word has not yet been spoken, and that we may witness a complete change in the situation—perhaps soon.

April 11, 1940

An urgent message from Hitler to the Duce. I went with von Mackensen to Villa Torlonia at 11 P.M., where Mussolini, contrary to his usual custom, was standing waiting for us. He had a bad cold and was feverish and tired, but glad to receive Hitler's message. Today he has prepared an enthusiastic answer. In it he says that, beginning tomorrow, the Italian fleet will be ready, that our preparation in the air and on land is proceeding at an accelerated pace, and, finally, he calls Hitler's attention to the ambiguous Rumanian attitude, at the same time expressing a desire to safeguard peace in that sector of Europe for the time being. Hitler has received Attolico and mentioned with satisfaction the message from the Duce. He has given optimistic reports on the course of the present aero-naval battle. I wonder. Only time will prove whether the Führer has acted as a strategist or has run into a dangerous trap.

This morning Mussolini was gloomy. He had returned from a conference with the King that had not satisfied him. He said, "The King would like us to enter only to gather up the broken dishes. I hope that they will not break them over our heads before that. And then it is humiliating to remain with our hands folded while others write history. It matters little who wins. To make a people great it is necessary to send them to battle even if you have to kick them in the pants. This is what I shall do. I do not forget that in 1918 there were five hundred and forty thousand deserters in Italy. And if we do not take advantage of this occasion to pit our Navy against the French and British forces, what is the use of building six hundred thousand tons of warships? Some coast guards and some yachts would be enough to take the young ladies on a joy ride."

April 12, 1940

I go to bed with a very bad cold and remain there until the twentieth.

April 20, 1940

My illness gave rise to much gossip. They talked about "diplomatic illness," and Rome is filled with rumors about my resignation. Naturally, the German successes have caused many desertions in the ranks of my so-called friends. On the contrary, it was an old anti-Fascist, Alberto Giannini, who took a courageous stand by writing to the Duce, imploring him not to fire me, as this would increase the country's confusion. Mussolini reacted sympathetically and said that he wished, first of all, to do something that will cut short all these rumors; then he told Buffarini and Muti that I am the man who enjoys his full confidence.

No news from the interior of the country during my days of absence. A letter from Hitler to bring the situation up to date. The letter was naturally in an optimistic tone. To the Duce, Hitler uses words that go straight to his heart and produce the desired effect. In the evening Prince Hesse talked to me about the imminent offensive, and told me that Hitler blames the bad weather for his not having been able to celebrate his birthday in Paris.

After ten days I found Mussolini more warlike and more pro-German than ever, but he says that he will do nothing before the end of August, that is after improving preparations and after the harvest. Thus only three months remain to give us a ray of hope.

April 21, 1940

The Duce's speech from the balcony of the Palazzo Venezia was sober and controlled, while the one that he made to the representatives of the labor confederations inside the palace was radical and 100 per cent Nazi. Immediately afterward, however, he told me to try to lessen the eventual echoes of his speech in the diplomatic corps, because "up to the second half of August there is no sense in talking of war."

April 22, 1940

This morning the date for Italy's entrance into this war was changed to the spring of 1941 because, according to the Duce, Norway has further removed a solution of the conflict, as well as the center of the European field of operations. Naturally this does not mean that he has in the least changed his attitude. It seems that he had a rather excited meeting with the King, during which Mussolini asserted that "Italy today is in fact a British colony, and certain Italians would be disposed to make this a legal fact, that is, they would make of her a Malta multiplied by a million," and he added, "I saw that old man turn pale." But alas, the King, who is so much against the war, can do no more to guard against it.

I saw François-Poncet. He was excited and depressed and talked about Italian war enterprises so near, in fact, it seemed that they could begin any day now. I tried to put him right a bit, and he left my room better informed on our policy, and, above all, more serene. I did the same thing with the American Ambassador, who more and more reveals himself to be a friend and a gentleman. I did the same also with certain other foreign diplomats of minor rank.

April 23, 1940

I exercise a soothing influence on the English Chargé d'Affaires [Noel Charles] who, although he is of a reserved temperament, has not remained indifferent to the offensive of alarmist rumors during the last week, which had their start with my illness. I repeat: Italy stands solidly behind Germany, but does not intend, until further notice, to make its solidarity more concrete, which does not mean that it intends to make the few guns of Badoglio thunder in the place of the paper guns of Virginio Gayda. It seems to me that the French and English should be satisfied, and I believe that as long as it lasts they will certainly be satisfied.

Renzetti has spoken to me again about what might be called Goering's tragicomedy of the collar of the Annunziata. It seems that the heart of the big marshal is still as filled with desperate sadness as when he saw the picturesque, glittering scenes of the Annunciation hanging from von Ribbentrop's neck. I speak of it to the Duce. We must not let the voluminous quasi-dictator of the Reich suffer any longer. And Mussolini, who has a sincere scorn for these honors, authorizes me to write the King a letter of appeal to describe the pitiful situation of the tender Hermann and to propose that a suitable pendant be given him on the twenty-second of May, the sad anniversary of the Alliance. Let's hope the King will accede to the proposal, because in the matter of the collar of the Annunziata he is cautious and reserved.

April 24, 1940

François-Poncet has brought a sealed letter from Paul Reynaud to the Duce. He was somewhat resentful that he, the Ambassador of France, should be the bearer of a message as to the contents of which he is kept in complete ignorance, and he fired a few darts at his government while at the same time speaking well of Reynaud: "He is a man who has always had the courage to tell the bitter truth, but he has all the faults of men under five feet three. He elbows his way ahead for fear that he won't be taken seriously." Mussolini read the letter with pleasure and scorn. In truth, it is a strange message, a little melancholy and a little bragging, which, I believe, very well reflects the temperament of its author. It ends with a sort of invitation to a meeting before the two nations cross swords. Mussolini intends to answer with a refusal, adding some words to take the dramatics out of Reynaud's vision of things. Naturally, the first thought of the Duce was to send Hitler a complete copy of the letter.

Von Mackensen, on his return from Berlin, comes to see me, and I go with him to the Duce. He speaks of the Hungarian proposal for a three-nation conference, and is against it. This is a far-fetched idea of the restless Count Czaky. On his return from the Palazzo Venezia, in his car, he mentions the position of Attolico. I invite him to talk, and then he says that in Berlin they would now welcome his recall. That is natural. He is an Italian and a gentleman. As his successor, Hitler is thinking of Farinacci and Alfieri. I eliminate the first and dwell upon the second. I am sure that Mussolini will meet the German desire.

April 25, 1940

I speak with the Duce on the question of the Ambassador to Germany. Mussolini accepts the nomination of Alfieri without objection, and I accompany the latter to the Palazzo Venezia. The Duce at once gives him some instructions as to his approaching mission to Germany. He repeats his faithfulness to the pacts, but as regards war he says that "he will enter it only when he has a quasi-mathematical certainty of winning it." Alfieri leaves the Mappamondo hall with the conviction that he will have to go slowly and cautiously in Germany.

Giunta in the Chamber has made an inconclusive and ill-bred speech of a distinctly pro-German character, and with such absurd implications that it stunned the Chamber. Mussolini, who had approved the first part of it, was struck by the cold atmosphere which the vulgar Germanic adoration of Giunta created in the hall. On the other hand, Pavolini, who has made his debut as a minister, attained a great success.

April 26, 1940

Barzini, Jr., was arrested. From one of the usual documents shown to us at the British Embassy it appears that he had informed the British that we have a secret service operating effectively inside the embassy itself, and that he had said that "Mussolini is insane," and that the Italian newspapermen hated every line they were compelled to write by the Fascist party. Mussolini is furious and speaks even of the Special Tribunal [special court against the enemies of the Fascist state].

The answer to Reynaud is ready. A cold, cutting, and contemptuous letter. Tomorrow I shall hand it to François-Poncet. Tonight I shall send a copy to von Mackensen. I try to make the letter less harsh, at least in form, but my efforts had meager results. It is clear that the Duce's letter can be used by Reynaud against the remaining pro-Italian Frenchmen as proof of our provocative radicalism. The Duce also sent a brief telephone message to Hitler to advise him to hold on to Narvik at all costs.

I obtained from the Duce the nomination of Attolico to the Holy See. I do not wish to give the Germans the impression that they can so easily liquidate a man of ours who has done his duty very well. Otherwise, God only knows where it will end and who will be the next victim to be sacrificed on the Nazi altar.

April 27, 1940

After all, François-Poncet was neither surprised nor disturbed at Mussolini's answer to Reynaud. He did not know the text of the French letter, and I showed it to him. While he talked well of the spirit and the form of the paper, he said that it was evidently written by a man who, not knowing Mussolini, thinks that he can win him over on the sentimental side. This is a gravely mistaken idea which Poncet has tried for a long time and in vain to correct. His government, in turn, was prevented from correcting it by those pro-Italian Frenchmen of Laval's type, who are encouraged frequently by our own Ambassador Guariglia. Mussolini's letter, described by him as "dry," will go a long way to set things straight.

I communicate to Attolico Hitler's stab in the back. He takes it with a great deal of dignity and comes to the conclusion that it is an honor for him to end his mission in this manner. He is glad to go to the Vatican—from the Devil to Holy Water. He confirms briefly his judgment on the German situation: "A short war, a victory for the Reich; a long war, a victory for the Allies." He tells me that Ribbentrop does not conceal his dislike for me, and that he considers me responsible for Italian non-intervention. I am proud of it.

In Berlin, Ribbentrop makes some declarations, advertised as sensational, on the Norwegian question. On the basis of a first reading it seems to me to be a case of the mountain giving birth to a mouse.

April 28, 1940

Another letter from Hitler to the Duce to bring him up to date on his military successes in Norway. These letters are, in general, of meager importance, but Hitler is a good psychologist and he knows that these messages go straight to Mussolini's heart.

The Pope addressed a letter to the Duce, in which he eulogizes his efforts to keep the peace, and prays that for the future also Italy will stay out of the conflict. Mussolini's reaction to the letter was skeptical, cold, and sarcastic.

April 29, 1940

Mussolini relates that the King was against granting the collar of the Annunziata to Goering, but that, willy-nilly, he will do it in the end. On the other hand, he approved very much of the reply to Reynaud. From the Duce's account it is clear that the conversations between him and the King are anything but cordial. In fact, they are a continuous quarrel, in which the Duce reaffirms with all the impetuous violence of his nature the need for the policy he is advocating, and the King, with the prudence that his position and character demand, strives to put in evidence all the dangers implicit in such a policy. But, on the whole, Mussolini takes little account of the judgment of the King, and thinks that the actual strength of the monarchy is negligible. He is convinced that the Italian people follow him [the Duce] and him alone. This morning he praised Blum, who, in an article in *Populaire*, said more or less the same thing.

A long conversation with Helfand, who now is playing the part of an official pro-German badly and weakly. I gave him information of a general character, and avoided every mention of policy which might alter the present situation between the two countries. After all, many Germans remain cool toward Moscow. Bismarck himself was saying yesterday that the Russians must not be trusted for two reasons: because they are Bolshevik, and because they are Russians, and more for the second reason than for the first.

April 30, 1940

Nothing new.

May 1, 1940

Phillips has a message from Roosevelt for the Duce. It is a warning not to enter the war, dressed in polite phrases, but nonetheless clear. If the conflict spreads, some states that intend to remain neutral will be obliged to revise their positions at once. Naturally, Mussolini ac-

cepted this with ill grace, considering the fact that Roosevelt is openly
in favor of the Franco-British. At the time he said little or nothing to
the American Ambassador, except to reaffirm the Italian right to a
window on the open sea. Then he personally wrote an answer to
Roosevelt, cutting and hostile, in which he arrives at the conclusion
that if the Monroe Doctrine has force for Americans, it must also
have force for Europeans.

The English have decided to have their ships avoid crossing the
Mediterranean. I speak about it to Charles, and do not conceal my surprise at a measure that must be the prelude to war. (Fortunately, we
have not gone that far yet. It is important that London avoid measures
that increase the existing nervous tension.) Charles agreed, but he was
concerned about the speech of the Duce to the Fascist organizations on
the twenty-first of April. [The anniversary of the foundation of Rome.]
At a meeting of the ministers Mussolini reaffirmed his certainty in a
German victory in the formula he has adopted. "In the struggle between the forces of conservatism and those of revolution it is always
the latter that win."

Mussolini speaks to me again about a *rapprochement* with Russia.

May 2, 1940

The Duce sends a message to Hitler to inform him of the situation
as it has developed in the last few days. He starts from this premise:
"The feeling of the Italian people is unanimously against the Allies."
Where does he get this information? Is he really sure of what he writes,
or is it not true that, conscious of his personal influence, he is thinking
of the opportune moment for modifying the national mood at his
whim? Dino Grandi is dissatisfied with the hostile reaction his speech
in the Chamber has provoked in London and Paris. He recalls the
pro-Axis talk which he gave in London last year, and calls it a blot
on his character and on his life as well. He received only three telegrams: one from Starace, one from Morgagni, and one from an inmate
of the insane asylum in Catania, who offered to put the speech into
verse for a hundred lire.

The first accurate news on the German victory in Norway makes
a deep impression. Chamberlain's speech makes an even deeper impression. It is so resignedly pessimistic as to admit the possibility of a
German landing in England. Mussolini is exultant. He has nothing but
scorn for the sending of a Franco-English fleet to the Mediterranean,

convinced as he is that the Allies will never take the initiative against us.

May 3, 1940

The news from Norway literally exalts the Duce who, with ever-increasing emphasis, affirms his certainty in German victory. From Berlin come telegrams that are filled with positive optimism. Von Ribbentrop tells Zamboni that the offensive on the Maginot Line will be as rapid as it is sure. Goering, for the first time, urges Renzetti to hasten our intervention because the war, to which he admits he had reasons at the start to be opposed, is now on its way toward speedy victory. I don't believe it. And even though we want to intervene, can we do so?

General Soddu says that now even Graziani, concerned over his responsibilities, expresses himself as clearly hostile to any war action on our part, including that in Croatia.

Our greatest deficiency is in artillery. The Italian Navy knows the dangerous task that awaits it. The Duce complains of Admiral Cavagnari's lack of energy. Cavagnari is a gentleman and tells the truth.

Our aviation is being built up laboriously. General Aimone Cat, one of the best technicians, has expressed himself very pessimistically, at the same time recognizing that what Pricolo has done has brought about some notable progress. He speaks even worse about our anti-aircraft. Very bad weapons, and bad functioning of our services.

Franco sends a colorless message to the Duce, in which he confirms the absolute and unavoidable neutrality of a Spain preparing to bind up her wounds.

May 4, 1940

A new letter to the Duce from Hitler, which consists of disconnected paragraphs. It contains particulars on the development of the war in Norway. Hitler complains about the excessive rapidity of the victory, which has not permitted his involving the English forces more effectively to destroy them completely. For the first time the tone of the letter is ironical as to the military capacities of the Allies. He concludes by saying that he intends to obtain a victory in the west as soon as possible, and that he is impelled to do this by hidden threats of American intervention.

May 5, 1940

I spend the day at Leghorn. I wanted to kneel down before Father and Maria. Beautiful weather; from the windows of my home we could see Capo Corso [Corsica] almost within reach of our hands. And yet at Leghorn, too, and even on the part of those who are most enthusiastic, the Mediterranean question is not very deeply felt. Anyway, deeply enough to justify a war.

May 6, 1940

Audience with the King in order to obtain his signature to the laws that have been passed. His Majesty speaks today about his opposition to Germany, not very strongly, but with a good deal of moderation, and says that in his opinion the Italian military machine is still very weak. He advises going slow. For this reason the King recommends our remaining as long as possible in our present position of watchful waiting and preparation. He has decided to give the collar of the Annunziata to Goering, but rather unwillingly. Mussolini, who conferred with him about the matter, said: "Your Majesty, it's perhaps a lemon that you must gulp down, but everything advises us to make such a gesture at this moment."

Conference with Christic. His government receives the declarations I made the other day with a sigh of relief. I believe that our situation will oblige us to keep to them for a long period of time.

May 7, 1940

Nothing new.

May 8, 1940

Percy Loraine has returned from London. From what he says, his instructions are to do everything he possibly can to safeguard relations between Italy and Great Britain "honorably and in good faith." He mentions the fact that our press campaigns have already strengthened the conviction in large sections of English public opinion that Fascist Italy is to be numbered among the enemies. This is serious, especially when the time comes to settle accounts at the end of the war, which he is sure will end victoriously for his country. I have spoken frankly to him about our policy. The Duce intends to be true to the pacts that bind him to Berlin, but this does not mean that in the near future we are going to abandon our non-belligerency. These statements, ordered by Mussolini, disturbed Sir Percy, who, unfortunately, did not leave reassured. However, he remained very calm and altogether certain about the English future.

I give von Mackensen a record of the meeting of the British ministers in the Balkans, which was furnished me by the English Embassy. I also speak of the ceremony for conferring the collar of the Annunziata on Goering. We can have it take place on the twenty-second at the Brenner Pass, which will save me a speech and the making of a solemn reaffirmation of the Alliance—a task difficult and displeasing to me.

May 9, 1940

During the ceremony at the Tomb of the Unknown Soldier I spoke with Badoglio, who now is less anti-German than before, since the Norwegian victory has had its effect on him even while he still defends non-belligerency fanatically. In his opinion, an attack on the Maginot Line would not be successful; he knows the Maginot Line personally, and believes that a break-through would require six months' action and the sacrifice of a million men. In talking to me about Badoglio, Mussolini said that he has convinced the marshal of his thesis, as he had done before. I do not think this is so. In the face of the German successes, Badoglio is more prudent; but I do not admit that he is convinced.

Anfuso reports that Princess Bismarck, with whom he is on very friendly terms, told him with tears in her eyes that Germany is lost, that Hitler has ruined the country and its people. She spoke so convincingly that Anfuso suspected her of being an *agent provocateur*, but then many things in her speech changed his mind. Even more fiery words were pronounced by her against Ribbentrop and his policy.

May 10, 1940

This is for history: yesterday I dined poorly at the German Embassy. A long and boring after-dinner conversation, as varied as one can have it with Germans. Not a word on the situation. When we got out at twelve twenty-five von Mackensen said that *"perhaps* he would have to disturb me during the night about a communication that he expected from Berlin," and took my private telephone number. At 4 A.M. he called me to say that within three quarters of an hour he would come to see me and together we would go to the Duce, as he had had orders to confer with him at exactly 5 A.M. He would say nothing over the telephone about the reasons for the meeting. When he arrived at my house he had with him a large package of papers which certainly could not have arrived by telephone. He muttered with embarrassment an excuse about a diplomatic courier who had remained at the hotel until he got the "go" sign from Berlin.

Together we went to the Duce, who, forewarned by me, had already got up. We found the Duce calm and smiling. He read Hitler's note, which listed the reasons for the action [the invasion of Belgium and Holland], and concluded with a kind invitation to Mussolini to make the decisions he considers necessary for the future of his country. Then the Duce examined the accompanying papers for a long time. Finally, after almost two hours, he told Mackensen that he was convinced that France and England were preparing to attack Germany through Belgium and Holland. He approved wholeheartedly of Hitler's action.

After Mackensen left, the Duce repeated to me his certainty about rapid success of the Nazi armies, and also his decision to intervene. I did not fail to repeat that, for the time being, we should wait and see. This is a long-drawn-out affair, longer than we can possibly foresee now. He didn't deign to answer me. My remarks served only to annoy him. During the morning I saw him many times and, alas, found that his idea of going to war was growing stronger and stronger. Edda, too, has been at the Palazzo Venezia and, ardent as she is, told her father that the country wants war, and that to continue our attitude of neutrality would be dishonorable for Italy. Such are the speeches that Mussolini wants to hear, the only ones that he takes seriously.

I confer with Poncet, Loraine, and Phillips. They want news on the Italian attitude. They are rather skeptical and pessimistic. From certain intercepted telephone messages it appears that they are expecting our intervention at any moment. I try to calm them down and partially succeed. On the other hand, they know very well my own ideas and with what sincerity I am trying to postpone the intervention.

Poncet is rather downcast. He has a tired air, red eyes, is unusually unkempt in his attire. Loraine is cold and determined. With an emphasis that is startling in such a phlegmatic and courteous gentleman he asserts that Germany will be destroyed. For a moment all the determination of his race came into his eyes and words. Phillips said that what has happened is bound to stir America profoundly. He made no prophecies, but I should not be surprised if the United States immediately broke relations with Germany as a prelude to intervention. And the United States is a very important factor to consider, although erroneous judgments are generally made about her.

Mussolini is preparing a message in answer to Hitler which is warm but not such as to commit us. I ask him to delete a phrase in which he associates himself with an accusation against the Allies to the effect that they were threatening Belgian neutrality. He listens to me and makes the change.

In leaving for Florence, Edda comes to see me and talks about immediate intervention, about the need to fight, about honor and dishonor. I listen with impersonal courtesy. It's a shame that she, so intelligent, also refuses to reason. I think she does well to go to the Florentine musical festival, where she can more profitably busy herself with music.

I saw the Belgian Ambassador and the Minister from Holland. They are sad but dignified, and both express themselves with a great deal of faith in the ability of their countries to resist. General Soddu, on the contrary, maintains that the struggle on the Belgian-Dutch line will amount to nothing, while French defense will be absolutely unbreakable. He is, in any event, of the opinion that we should not take any initiative for at least a month after the beginning of the offensive.

I saw Pavelić. The Croatian situation is getting ripe and if we delay too long the Croats will line up with Germany. Now I shall prepare a map to indicate the precise positions of the forces and their most urgent needs. Then we shall pass to the phase of execution. I have not fixed any particular moment; in fact, I have recommended that we avoid any premature explosion. We have received proof of the fact that Bombelles is a traitor on the pay roll of Belgrade and he will suffer the merciless law of the Ustasci.

I report the conversation to the Duce. He says that we must act quickly. He makes notes on his calendar, somewhere near the first part of June, and decides to call Gambara back from Spain to take command of the forces that will carry out the break-through.

No direct news from the battle front, but from all that we hear it seems that things are going well for the Germans. What is especially surprising is the lack of Allied action in the air, while the others are bombing a hundred places.

The substitution of Churchill for Chamberlain is received here with absolute indifference; by the Duce with irony.

May 11, 1940

During the night some Fascists beat an English official who had torn down an anti-British manifesto, and Sir Percy Loraine came to me this morning to speak of the incident. Since he assumed a rather haughty tone, very much in contrast to our excellent personal relations, I answered in the same tone, refusing to give any explanation; on the other hand, emphasizing the fact that, while the British Army is fighting hard, English officials might better go to bed, rather than wander around bars until four o'clock in the morning. We parted so frostily that I thought it necessary to inform the Duce, because of possible future developments. But this evening Loraine telephoned me with his usual cordiality, and the incident has been closed.

Nothing new here. Today Mussolini is less bellicose than he was yesterday, and more disposed to wait. It seems that the Italian General Staff has thrown most timely cold water on our present military prospects. Even Balbo has told me that we cannot go into the field before two months, and before having received a definite quantity of arms and matériel.

May 12, 1940

The telegrams sent by the Pope to the rulers of the three invaded states have incensed Mussolini, who would like to curb the Vatican, and is inclined to go to extremes. In these last few days he often repeats that the papacy is a cancer which gnaws at our national life, and that he intends, if necessary, to liquidate this problem once and for all. He added: "The Pope need not think that he can seek an alliance with the monarchy because I am ready to blow both of them up to the skies at the same time. The seven cities of Romagna will be sufficient to knock out King and Pope at the same time." [The seven cities referred to here are Bologna, Modena, Reggio, Parma, Forlì, Ferrara, and Ravenna, that is the most revolutionarily inclined part of Italy.]

I do not share this policy of the Duce, because, if he intends to wage war, he must not provoke a crisis with the Church. The Italian people

are Catholic but not bigoted. Superficially, maybe, they scorn the
Church, but they are religious at heart, and especially in times of peril
do they draw near the altars. I believe that it is indispensable for us
to avoid any clash, and for this reason I give Alfieri instructions to
take a step that will not have any of the controversial character the
Duce wanted to give it.

The King sends word that he will give the collar of the Annunziata
to Goering, but, nevertheless, wants to avoid sending him a telegram
of congratulations and the notification. I shall try to find a way out.
His Majesty desires that his wish be kept secret from Mussolini.

May 13, 1940

Mussolini began to talk as follows: "Some months ago I said that
the Allies had lost the victory. Today I tell you that they have lost
the war. We Italians are already sufficiently dishonored. Any delay
is inconceivable. We have no time to lose. Within a month I shall
declare war. I shall attack France and England in the air and on the
sea. I am no longer thinking of taking up arms against Yugoslavia
because it would be a humiliating expedient." Today, for the first time,
I did not answer. Unfortunately, I can do nothing now to hold the
Duce back. He has decided to act, and act he will. He believes in
German success and in the rapidity of this success. Only a new turn
in military events can induce him to revise his decision, but for the
time being things are going so badly for the Allies that there is no hope.

Alfieri has spoken to the Pope. He will make a written report, but
meanwhile stresses the fact that he found a clear-cut intransigency in
the attitude of the Church. The Pope has said that "he is even ready
to be deported to a concentration camp, but will do nothing against
his conscience."

I see Poncet and Loraine. No discussion of any importance. More
than anything else tentative soundings. I try not to increase their
apprehensions, but I honestly do not wish to hide the fact that the
situation is growing more serious.

May 14, 1940

Letter from Hitler to the Duce. A long and calm account of
military events. It is an assured note: victories on land, and, above

all, victories in the air, over which at this time the Germans have an
uncontested dominion. Naturally, all this cannot but influence the
mind of the Duce to intervene. He has also announced to von
Mackensen his decision to enter the struggle soon. "It is now no
longer a question of months, it is a question of weeks and perhaps
days." I, at least, hope that it is more a matter of weeks than of days,
for although the vicissitudes of war are turning in favor of the Germans, it is too soon to count our eggs and before making a supreme
decision we must recall that Italy is not ready for war, or at least
is ready for a very short war. A mistake in timing would be fatal
to us.

The Duce informs me that General Soddu has spoken to the
King about the question of the Italian supreme command, which
Mussolini wants to assume personally. It seems that His Majesty has
resisted strongly, basing on the constitution his own right to decide.
However, he finally consented to a compromise, that is a delegation
of powers. Mussolini showed irritation. He said clearly that after the
war was won he intended to get rid of a monarchy that he does not
like and whose weight he can no longer tolerate.

May 15, 1940

Roosevelt sends a message to the Duce. The tone is changed. It is
no longer as it was the first time, in a covertly threatening style. It
is rather a discouraged and conciliatory message. He speaks of the
Gospel of Christ, but these are arguments that have little effect upon
the mind of Mussolini, especially today, when he is convinced that
he has victory in his grasp. It takes more than this to move him.

Great excitement over the news of the piercing of the Maginot
Line at Sedan. It is a piece of news that doesn't convince me completely, and I believe that it is dangerous to exaggerate information
of secondary importance. Public opinion has now improved because
of German victories, but the real feelings of the people have not
changed.

Naturally, in our political circle, one witnesses a headlong rush
to enlist in the Fascist party pre-dating the admission to emphasize
sympathy for the warmongers and for pro-Germans, and so forth. It
would be laughable if the optimistic bits of news we receive were followed by others less good.

May 16, 1940

The news was, in truth, very much exaggerated. The breaching of the Maginot Line has become a break-through! The proof is that during the evening Sir Percy sent a British report on the operations of a rather optimistic flavor. I show it to the Duce, who is impressed, although his nature compels him to believe only news favorable to his own longings. Nevertheless, during the day he has shown himself to be less anxious to set fire to the powder keg.

The conference that he had with the King has also irritated him. His Majesty still maintains an obstructionist attitude with reference to intervention, saying that public opinion is overwhelmingly against it. He raised numerous objections on the question of a military command, although he ended by yielding.

Loraine brings a message from Churchill to the Duce. It is a message of good will, couched in vague terms, but nonetheless dignified and noble. Even Mussolini appreciates the tone of it, and he means to answer that, like England, he, too, intends to remain true to his word. An increasing uneasiness in the Vatican on account of the daily incidents caused, above all, by interference with the sale of the *Osservatore Romano*. The Nuncio calls attention to these matters in a conversation with me, during which I was able to give him only kind and vague words.

May 17, 1940

News from the French front speaks of an overwhelming German advance. Saint Quentin has been taken, and Paris is directly threatened from there. We still lack confirmation from French sources, just as we lack details on the depth of the penetration of the lines. However, all this leads one to believe that it is a very serious situation. Italian public opinion (I mean honest opinion, not the clownish politicians, who have become exaggeratedly pro-German) reacts in a strange way to this news: admiration for the Germans, a wishful belief in the rapid conclusion of the war, and, above all, a great concern about the future. Mussolini is calm and at least until now has shown no desire to hasten intervention.

Von Mackensen proposes an exchange of telegrams between me and von Ribbentrop on the occasion of the anniversary of the pacts, and speaks of the bestowal of the collar of the Annunziata on Goering; this can be presented by Alfieri. But Marshal Goering insists on a telegram from the King. I fear that the present situation will not allow any alternative. The King must do it.

May 18, 1940

News of the conflict is increasingly favorable to the Germans: Brussels fallen, Antwerp demolished, columns of tanks running through France up to Soissons, followed, it seems, by German infantry. However, our military staff is withholding its opinion. General Soddu does not think it is a decisive battle and asks for two weeks more before pronouncing judgment.

I give Sir Percy Loraine the Duce's answer to Churchill. It is brief and needlessly harsh in tone. Loraine receives it without comment. In turn, he gives me his usual information on the military situation, which the English continue to describe in incredibly rosy colors.

François-Poncet is more concerned. He believes that during the last few hours the situation has become better, but he knows that the fate of France is at stake. He is concerned about our attitude and says that he does not "consider that it is to the interest of Italy to see France crushed." He refuses likewise to believe that Mussolini will want to rob Stalin of the glory of striking at a fallen man.

Without saying anything I hand Phillips the brief and dry answer to Roosevelt's message. He receives it without comment. Tomorrow I am going to Cremona and Milan. Mussolini orders me to give a definite intimation of our approaching intervention, as well as to indicate clearly that he will also be "the only head" of the nation while at war—the civil as well as military head.

May 19, 1940

Cremona. Milan. Very warm welcome in both cities. But in Milan the mention of intervention made in my brief speech, while received with enthusiasm by the Fascist militiamen, is greeted with limited enthusiasm by the great masses of the people. I gain the impression that Milan, which hates the Germans tenaciously, considers entry into the war, even under present conditions, as an unwelcome necessity.

May 20, 1940

I report to the Duce on my Milan visit, and he agrees with my opinion on the situation. Today he does not speak of intervention. He fully approves the text of the speeches delivered by me yesterday along the line of his suggestions.

Mackensen mentions the possibility of a rapprochement between us and Russia, through the medium of Ribbentrop. I answer that there is no objection on our part, provided the Russians take the initiative by sending back their Ambassador. They started the break and they will have to make the first gesture.

War news continues favorable to the Germans. They captured General Giraud, together with his general staff. François-Poncet talked of him a few days ago as the great hope of France, and predicted that he would be Gamelin's successor.

All this makes a great impression on many Italians, even those who are not capable of seeing what is coming. Even Dino Grandi came to see me, and said with a very dramatic air, "We should admit that we were wrong in everything and prepare ourselves for the new times ahead." I did not share his change of heart; not because I am stubborn, but because, in spite of everything, my opinions have not changed. The worth of a horse is tested in a long race, and nobody can imagine how long this race will be.

May 21, 1940

The King is nervous. This morning I went to the royal palace to accompany the Albanian mission, which has come to bring the Address in Reply to the Speech of the Crown. [A formality according to which every time a Speech of the Crown is made in Parliament, heads of the provinces offer what is called the Address in Reply.] The King almost attacked me on the question of the collar of the Annunziata for Goering. He said, "This thing has gone all wrong. To give Goering the collar is a gesture that displeases me, and to send him a telegram is distasteful for a hundred thousand reasons." On the military situation His Majesty expressed himself unfavorable to the Germans.

I talked to the Duce of the necessity of setting our aspirations clearly before the Germans. If we really have to leap headlong into war, we must make a definite deal. Even today the war remains for me an adventure with many fearful, unknown factors. I know these fellows too well, and I trust their written agreements very little and their word not at all. After the first of June I might see Ribbentrop and draw up a report on what should be our share at the end of the war.

May 22, 1940

I leave for Albania. I arrive at Durazzo and Tirana. A very warm welcome. The Albanians are far on the path of intervention. They want Kossovo and Ciamuria. It is easy for us to increase our popularity by becoming champions of Albanian nationalism.

May 23, 1940

I visit Scutari and Rubico. A very promising copper mine. The public works that I visited this morning are also satisfactory. Everywhere a warm welcome.

There is no question that the mass of the people is now won over by Italy. The Albanian people are grateful to us for having taught them to eat twice a day, for this rarely happened before. Even in the physical appearance of the people greater well-being can be noted.

May 24, 1940

I mingled with the workers at Ragosina. Italian laborers mix well with the Albanians. We find the greatest difficulties in the Italian middle classes, who treat the natives badly and who have a colonial mentality. Unfortunately, this is also true of military officers, and, according to Jacomoni, especially of their wives.

May 25, 1940

Stopped at Butrinto. Very beautiful. The Canal of Corfu. Port Edda. I returned to Italy.

In Brindisi, at Bari, and later at every station, I receive a hearty welcome. The people want to know what will be done, and I hear many voices calling for war. This never happened up to a few days ago.

May 26, 1940

I report to the Duce on my trip which, on the whole, has been satisfactory. Mussolini speaks to me of his disagreement with the King on the question of the military command during the war. It seems that before yielding to the Duce the King put up considerable resistance.

Hitler has sent another letter to the Duce and to Alfieri a report on his conference with Goering. The latter raised the question of the date of our intervention and suggested our attacking when, after the liquidation of the Anglo-French-Belgian strongholds, the Germans can throw the whole weight of their power on Paris. The Duce agrees in principle. He plans to write a letter to Hitler announcing our intervention for the latter part of June.

May 27, 1940

Long conferences with François-Poncet and with Phillips. The latter was the bearer of a message from Roosevelt for the Duce, but was not received and speaks with me instead. I have made a stenographic report of our interview. In short, Roosevelt offers to become the mediator between us and the Allies, becoming personally responsible for the execution, after the war, of any eventual agreements. I answer Phillips that Roosevelt is off the track. It takes more than that to dissuade Mussolini. In fact, it is not that he wants to obtain this or that; what he wants is war, and, even if he were to obtain by peaceful means double what he claims, he would refuse.

My conference with Poncet is also important, not because of its results, but as a psychological indication. He made some very precise overtures. Exclusive of Corsica, which is "an integral part of France," he said that we can make a deal about Tunisia and perhaps even about Algeria. I answered that he, too, like Phillips, is too late, and reminded him of the time when France, in 1938, objected to our having even those four reefs which England had ceded to us in the Red Sea. Once more the French have been, as Machiavelli says, "more niggardly than prudent."

Poncet recognizes the faults of the French, attacks the governments of the past, and throws a great part of the responsibility upon Leger, whom he calls a "sinister man." The conversation, naturally, was kept on an academic note.

May 28, 1940

My conference with Poncet, who is the picture of distress, and the events of the night (the Belgian capitulation) led Mussolini to speed up his planning, as he is convinced that things are now coming to a head, and he wants to create enough claims to be entitled to his share of the spoils. This is all very well as regards France. But England is still standing. And America? The Duce talks of the tenth of June.

I see Christic; he is terrified and would like to know if we shall attack his country. I can but partially reassure him. A painful conference with Sir Percy Loraine. He had come to discuss the question of blockade and complained about the interruption of the negotiations. I answered that all this was useless because we are on the brink of war. Although prepared for it, he did not expect such a brutal blow and grew pale. Then he recovered his bearings. "If you choose the sword, it will be the sword that will decide the future. It is well to establish this in connection with responsibilities for the war." Then he continued, changing tone, "We shall answer war with war, but, notwithstanding this, my heart is filled with sadness to think that blood must flow between our countries." I answered that this was very sad for me, too, but that I could not see any other way out.

On the situation in Flanders he expressed himself thus: "If the Allies win, the war will end in a year. If the Germans win, it will last more than three years. But this will not change the end, which will be our victory." He spoke with firmness, but his face was very sad and his eyes at times were dim.

May 29, 1940

Today at eleven at the Palazzo Venezia the High Command was born! Rarely have I seen Mussolini so happy. He has realized his dream: that of becoming the military Condottiero [leader] of the country at war. Under him will be Badoglio, Graziani, Pricolo, and Cavagnari. The decision is about to be taken; after the fifth of June any day may be good. I reported to the Duce on my conferences of yesterday, and advised him to give solemn assurances to Yugoslavia as to our neutrality, and especially evidence that we have no interest in setting the match to the Balkan powder keg. After the war is won we can obtain what we want anyway. He authorizes me to act in this way, and therefore I talked to Christic, who, having been called suddenly, came to my room as pale as a ghost, but he left comforted.

Badoglio now seems to accept a bad game with good grace, and prepares for war. He tries still to gain some days in order to look into the French situation more clearly, because he thinks that there may be some surprises. He is concerned about Libya, where a French move might have a chance of success. However, the war must be brief. Not more than two or three months, so, at least, according to Favagrossa, who is a pessimist, because our supplies are fearfully modest. We are literally without some metals. On the eve of the war—and what a war!—we have only one hundred tons of nickel.

May 30, 1940

The decision has been taken. The die is cast. Today Mussolini gave me his communication sent to Hitler about our entry into the war. The date chosen is the fifth of June, unless Hitler himself considers it convenient to postpone it for some days. The message is communicated in cipher to Ambassador Alfieri at Berlin with orders to deliver it to Hitler personally. At the same time I inform von Mackensen; although he was already prepared, the Ambassador received the news with great joy. He had words of admiration for the Duce and praised my decision to take part in the war as a pilot. "In Germany," he said, "the higher-ups in the party have not set a good example. Baldur von Schirach, at least until now, has been safely tucked away at the rear."

Mussolini plans to make a speech to the people on the afternoon of the fourth of June. One hour before this I am to announce a state of war to Poncet and Loraine. The Duce wanted to omit "this formality." I insisted on it in order at least to observe the forms.

The Minister from Egypt speaks on his own responsibility of an eventual proclamation of neutrality by his government. I encourage him. I do not believe that Egyptian neutrality would make a great deal of difference in the game, but, nevertheless, it might have a certain advantage.

May 31, 1940

Another move by Roosevelt, this time more energetic. After having reminded us of the traditional interest of his country in the Mediterra-

nean, he affirms that Italy's intervention in the war would bring about
an increase in armaments by the United States and a multiplying of
help in resources and matériel to the Allies. I reserve my answer until
I have conferred with Mussolini, but tell Phillips offhand that Roosevelt's new attempt will suffer the fate of his preceding attempts and
will not move the Duce.

Alfieri telephones that he has transmitted the message to Hitler, who
was "glad, in fact enthusiastic," and has reserved to himself the right
of letting us know, after having conferred with his generals, whether
the date chosen is satisfactory. I submit to the Duce the draft of a
communiqué for the declaration of war. He approves it but advises my
talking to the King about it, since the latter is sensitive and, besides,
according to the constitution, it is up to him to declare war. Daladier
delivers a note to Guariglia, the Italian Ambassador in Paris. No definite proposal, but many openings. It states clearly that every attempt
will be made to avoid war, but Mussolini refuses to take it into consideration; in fact, he decides that he will not even answer it.

June 1, 1940

An audience with the King. He approves the formula that I submit
to him. He is now resigned, no, more than resigned, to the idea of war.
He believes that in reality France and England have taken tremen-
dously hard blows, but, with good reason, he attributes great importance to the eventual intervention of the United States. He feels that
the country is going to war without enthusiasm. There is interventionist propaganda, but there is not in the least that enthusiasm we had in
1915. "Those who talk of a short and easy war are fools. There are
still many unknown factors, and the horizon is very different from that
of May 1915." Thus concludes the King.

Christic reports Belgrade's satisfaction at the communication of the
other day, and gives the fullest assurances of complete and almost benevolent neutrality.

I gave Phillips the Duce's answer. Briefly, it is as follows: America
has no more interest in the Mediterranean than Italy has in the Carib-
bean Sea. Therefore, it is beside the point for Roosevelt to insist; in
fact, he should remember that his pressures can only stiffen Mussolini's stand.

Mackensen brings Hitler's written reply to the Duce. The news of
our intervention is received by the Chancellor with enthusiasm. He

asks, however, that the date be changed by a few days, for he proposes to make a decisive attack on French airfields. He fears that the beginning of Italian action might cause a reshuffling of the French Air Forces, interfering with his plán of destruction. In principle the Duce agrees, because the postponement is useful to round out our preparations in Libya. He prefers the eleventh to the eighth, as the former is "a date of good omen for him."

Poncet speaks to me about Daladier's note. From my answers he understands that there is no longer ground for nurturing hopes and illusions. Mussolini's choice will be imposed by the sword. Poncet does not insist on a reply. In fact, if the reply is to be in any way quarrelsome, better to have none at all, because, in any event, "there will always be a future, and we must not think that contacts between France and Italy will no longer be necessary after the war." He says nothing about the situation. He believes that the game is not ended, and that the two great battles that Hitler must fight—the battle of Paris and above. all the battle of London—may still bring many surprises.

Bottai, who is one of the few who has not lost his head, proposed to me on the golf course today that in the face of so much official interventionism we form a new party: the "Party of the Interventionists in Bad Faith."

June 2, 1940

The Duce writes his answer to Hitler. While the postponement is advisable, especially to complete military preparations in Libya, Mussolini, who had already set June 5 as the day, is annoyed at having to change it. He selects the eleventh of June.

During the evening Mackensen urgently asks for an interview and, in the name of Hitler, withdraws the reservations made in the previous communication; in fact, it seems that now an earlier intervention would be most welcome. This is not possible. We have moved several divisions, and a declaration of war before the eleventh of June would catch us during the movement. The eleventh of June is confirmed as the definite date; it is sufficient that Hitler answer "go ahead." Having taken this decision, Mussolini becomes, as always after a decision, calm and sure.

In the evening I saw Balbo for a long talk. He is preparing to return to Libya. He has made up his mind to do the best he can, but he does not believe that the war will be quick and easy. The armaments at his disposal are sufficient for only a short conflict. What if the war should be long? At any rate, he is a soldier, and he will fight with energy and determination. Naturally, he doesn't withdraw even one of his objections to the policy of the Axis. Balbo does not discuss the Germans. He hates them. And it is this incurable hatred which guides his reasoning.

June 3, 1940

Alfieri telegraphs the "O.K." of Hitler. In reality the bombardment of Paris and of other French airfields proves that Hitler has already started to move.

Mussolini says that the King, too, finds the date of the eleventh satisfactory, perhaps because of the slight delay that will be granted to us, because it is his birthday, and because as a raw recruit he was given the number 1,111. Now that the sword is about to be unsheathed, the King, like all members of the House of Savoy, is preparing to be a soldier, and only a soldier.

Percy Loraine comes to see me on the pretext of small current affairs. We already talk as representatives of two countries in conflict, even though our own personal relations are excellent. He is sad but calm. He realizes that the next two or three months will be extremely critical for the Allies. But if they can hold out, Germany is lost. He would like to participate personally in the war. I answer that I have no desire to discuss the matter. Now that my country is in the war, or will be soon, I do not want to discuss his conjectures, nor can I tolerate such a discussion.

June 4, 1940

A meeting of the Council of Ministers. While all were expecting great political sensations, the Duce coquettishly gave today's meeting "a strictly administrative character, such as it has never had in eighteen years." No declaration. Only at the beginning of the meeting Mussolini said, "This is the last Council of Ministers during peacetime," and took up the agenda.

I have chosen my military position in the war. I assume command of a squadron of bombing planes at Pisa. I have chosen this field because it is closest to Corsica, and because it is dear to me to fight where

I was born and where my father sleeps his last sleep. The Duce approved my decision to join up as well as that of leaving Rome for Pisa, because he prefers that I become "a soldier-minister" rather than a "minister-soldier."

June 5, 1940

The Germans have attacked on the line of the Somme. For the present, information is lacking, but it is everybody's conviction that they will cross it rapidly. French morale has not yet improved, and the defensive organization is necessarily incomplete. Have we come to the decisive battle?

So far as we are concerned, nothing has changed in the program. Only this, that the Duce, though he had previously been thinking of launching an air attack against France as a beginning, has now decided to bombard British ports in the Mediterranean and to remain as an observer toward France, unless, he concluded, "before Monday they [the French] have been subjected to a new attack by the Germans and our action against them will serve to finish the work."

June 6, 1940

I find the Duce angry at the King over the question of the supreme command. He had hoped that the King would yield it without difficulty. Instead, His Majesty has written a letter in which he repeats that he assumes the command, at the same time entrusting to Mussolini the political and military conduct of the war. Mussolini finds this "an ambiguous formula through which he is given what he has virtually had for eighteen years." A great disappointment for the Duce, who plans to write the King that it is better to leave things where they are, and he adds, "After the war is over I shall tell Hitler to do away with all of these absurd anachronisms in the form of monarchies."

Little news about the battle of the Somme. The Germans are gaining ground, but a real break-through does not seem to have occurred. The French, now that they are on their own soil, fight with their traditional bravery, even if their hopes have in large part vanished. The reshuffling of the Reynaud cabinet has been interpreted as a sign of political collapse.

June 7, 1940

Nothing new in Italy. On the French front the struggle continues to be very hard. Although the French have had to retreat in a number of places, there are yet no signs of an actual break-through. The public is following the events of this battle with unprecedented anxiety. It knows that on the Somme decisive cards are being played for the history of the world.

An almost good-by visit from Percy Loraine. He is sad and feels fully the gravity of the hour for his country, but talks with imperturbable firmness about a fight to the last, confirming his faith in victory "because the British are not in the habit of being beaten." He is personally worried about his voyage home, but I have taken every precaution to insure him and his associates perfect treatment. He is also worried about a colt he has to leave in Italy.

June 8, 1940

The battle continues. New German successes, but still one cannot speak of a break-through at the front. French resistance is becoming tenacious, stubborn, heroic. Mussolini reads me the speech he will make on Monday, at 6 P.M., when the nation is to be called to listen. It is an appeal to the people in Mussolini's best classical style, in which he briefly outlines the reasons for our intervention.

The Duce is following with anxiety the battle in progress, and is happy over the resistance of the French because "the Germans are finally being weakened and will not reach the end of the war too fresh and too strong." The agreement is concluded for the return of Ambassador Rosso to Moscow and of the Ambassador of the Soviets to Rome. Ribbentrop will be happy over this, since it was one of the great objectives of his policy. Still, there is something not entirely clear in the conduct of the Kremlin toward Germany.

June 9, 1940

A rapid German advance seems to be deciding the fate of the battle irrevocably. In Badoglio's judgment, the battle will still be long and hard, because of the terrain.

The Duce was angry this morning at the Germans, because, having intercepted a telephone call, he learned that Ribbentrop had the cheek to ask for the text of Mussolini's speech. "He is the same presumptuous boor," said the Duce. "I am not his servant, and I do not intend to be."

Poncet comes to say good-by. He is sad and depressed, and at this stage admits that his country is beaten. He personally would accept a separate peace, but he does not know his government's intentions. A separate peace would probably be the lesser of two evils. The continuation of the war will be a frightful destruction of civilization, of riches, of life. Poncet wept, but he affirmed that France wishes to save at least its military honor in a hopeless struggle, three against one, five against one. We said good-by with emotion that neither of us was able to conceal. Poncet is a man like us: he is a Latin.

Mackensen brings the Duce a message received from Hitler by air. His best wishes for our coming entry into the war. He accepts the offer of the Bersaglieri [Italian light infantry], and will send, in exchange, some regiments of his Alpine troops. He describes with sober optimism the various phases of the battle of France.

June 10, 1940

Declaration of war. First I received Poncet, who tried not to betray his emotion. I told him, "You probably understood the reason for your being called." He answered, with a fleeting smile, "Although I am not very intelligent, I have understood this time." After having listened to the declaration of war, he replied, "It is a dagger blow to a man who has already fallen. I thank you nonetheless for using the velvet glove," he continued, saying that he had foreseen all this for two years, and that he had no longer hoped that he could avoid it after the signing of the Pact of Steel. He was not able to resign himself to considering me an enemy, nor could he so consider any Italian. However, as for the future it was necessary to find some formula for European life, he hoped that an unbridgeable chasm would not be created between Italy and France. "The Germans are hard masters. You, too, will learn this." I did not answer. This did not seem to me the time for discussion. "Don't get yourself killed," he concluded, pointing to my aviator's uniform, and he clasped my hand.

Sir Percy Loraine was more laconic and inscrutable. He received my communication without batting an eye or changing color. He confined himself to writing down the exact formula used by me and asked me if he was to consider it as advance information or as a general declaration of war. Learning that it was the latter, he withdrew with dignity and courtesy. At the door we exchanged a long and cordial handshake.

Mussolini speaks from the balcony of the Palazzo Venezia. The news of the war does not surprise anyone and does not arouse very much enthusiasm. I am sad, very sad. The adventure begins. May God help Italy!

June 11, 1940

A meeting of the Council of Ministers. Some war measures relating to finance and justice are rapidly adopted. The Duce wants our legislation to conform to that of the Germans.

I leave by plane for Pisa, where I assume command of a group of bombers assigned to me. The first day of war passes very peacefully on this happy yet rugged coast of Antiguano.

June 12, 1940

Nothing new.

June 13, 1940

Nothing new.

June 14, 1940

Nothing new.

June 15, 1940

I fly as far as Nice in order to look for the French ships which have bombarded Genoa. Very bad weather; dangerous flying. I return after two hours without having sighted the enemy.

June 16, 1940

Bombing Calvi [Corsica].

June 17, 1940

Bombing of Borgo, airport of Bastia [Corsica]. Accurate aiming.
French reaction is also active and accurate. On my return to the landing field it is reported to me that Reynaud has fallen and that Pétain
has taken his place. This means peace. In fact, Anfuso telephones me
to return at once to Rome in order to leave for Munich that evening.
The French have asked for an armistice, and Hitler, before dictating
his terms, wants to confer with the Duce.

I find Mussolini dissatisfied. This sudden peace disquiets him. During the trip we speak at length in order to clarify conditions under
which the armistice is to be granted to the French. The Duce is an
extremist. He would like to go so far as the total occupation of French
territory and demands the surrender of the French fleet. But he is
aware that his opinion has only a consultative value. The war has been
won by Hitler without any active military participation on the part of
Italy, and it is Hitler who will have the last word. This, naturally, disturbs and saddens him. His reflections on the Italian people, and,
above all, on our armed forces, are extremely bitter this evening.

June 18 and 19, 1940

During the trip by rail German welcome is very warm. At Munich
a meeting with Hitler and von Ribbentrop. The Duce and the Führer
are locked in conference. Von Ribbentrop, exceptionally moderate and
calm, and in favor of peace. He says at once that we must offer lenient
armistice terms to France, especially concerning the fleet; this is to
avoid the French fleet joining with the English fleet. From the words
of von Ribbentrop I feel that the mood has changed also as regards
England. If London wants war it will be a total war, complete, pitiless.
But Hitler makes many reservations on the desirability of demolishing
the British Empire, which he considers, even today, to be an important
factor in world equilibrium. I ask von Ribbentrop a clear-cut question,
"Do you prefer the continuation of the war, or peace?" He does not
hesitate a moment. "Peace." He also alludes to vague contacts between London and Berlin by means of Sweden. I speak of our desiderata with respect to France. In general I find him understanding,
but von Ribbentrop does not want to push the conversation further
because he does not know as yet the precise ideas of Hitler. He says

only that there is a German project to round up and send the Jews to Madagascar.

The conference then continued with Hitler, Mussolini, and the military authorities. In principle the terms of the armistice with France are fixed. Mussolini shows himself to be quite intransigent on the matter of the fleet.

Hitler, on the other hand, wants to avoid an uprising of the French Navy in favor of the English. From all that he says it is clear that he wants to act quickly to end it all. Hitler is now the gambler who has made a big scoop and would like to get up from the table, risking nothing more. Today he speaks with a reserve and a perspicacity which, after such a victory, are really astonishing. I cannot be accused of excessive tenderness toward him, but today I truly admire him.

Mussolini is very much embarrassed. He feels that his role is secondary. He reports on his conference with Hitler, not without a tone of bitterness and irony, and he concludes by saying that the German people have, in themselves, the germs of a collapse because a formidable internal clash will come that will smash everything. In truth, the Duce fears that the hour of peace is growing near and sees fading once again that unattainable dream of his life: glory on the field of battle.

June 20, 1940

The French have appointed the same delegates to deal with us who were appointed to deal with Germany, and they ask whether negotiations can take place contemporaneously at the same place. This was also our idea at Munich. But Hitler was opposed to it and specifically asked for "two commissions." The Duce thinks that he sees in this a psychological reason, mainly, that he did not want the French to face Italians and Germans in a position of parity.

Mussolini decided yesterday to attack the French in the Alps. Badoglio was energetically opposed, but the Duce insisted. Then I spoke to him. I consider it rather inglorious to fall upon a defeated army and I find it morally dangerous also. Armistice is at the door, and if our Army should not overcome resistance during the first assault, we would end our campaign with a howling failure. Mussolini listened to me, and it seems that he will limit the attack to a small sector near the Swiss frontier. He was persuaded to do this also by a telephonic interception of a conversation between Generals Roatta and Pintor, in which the latter declared that he is absolutely unprepared to carry on an attack tomorrow. This happens after nine months of wait-ing, and with the French reduced as they are! Had we entered the war in September what would have happened? Mussolini is very indignant with Balbo, who in Cyrenaica has met with a series of failures already, notwithstanding a great quantity of men and matériel at his disposal.

June 21, 1940

Alfieri transmits the German armistice terms. I examine them with the Duce and Badoglio. They are moderate terms which prove Hitler's desire to arrive quickly at an understanding. Under these conditions Mussolini does not feel inclined to advance claims to territorial occu-pation. This might provoke a rupture in the negotiations and bring about a real rift in our relations with Berlin. Hence, he will confine himself to asking for the militarization of a fifty-kilometer strip of the frontier and plans to advance our claims at the moment of peace. Mussolini is quite humiliated, because our troops have not made a step forward. Even today they have not succeeded in advancing and have halted in front of the first French fortification which put up some opposition.

In Libya an Italian general has allowed himself to be taken pris-oner. Mussolini is taking it out on the Italian people, "It is the mate-rial that I lack. Even Michelangelo had need of marble to make statues. If he had had only clay he would have been nothing more than a potter. A people who for sixteen centuries have been an anvil cannot become a hammer within a few years."

Hitler's ceremonial for the signing of the armistice has also dis-turbed the Duce very much. It explains why the Germans did not want a single commission.

June 22, 1940

We are waiting for the French delegates. There is a little delay be-cause of some discussions, but Alfieri telephoned that the signing will surely take place. The delegates, it seems, will come tomorrow. Musso-lini would like to delay as much as possible, in the hope that General Gambara, who in the meantime has attacked, will arrive at Nice. It would be a good thing, but will we have time? I received the Soviet Ambassador. The conversation was cordial but general. I say that the Italo-Russian relations are, above all, a psychological fact, because there are no conflicts of direct interest that separate the two countries. The Ambassador addresses some questions to me about the Balkans. I say that, in principle, our policy in that sector is to preserve the *status quo*.

Preparations are made for the ceremony of the armistice. The Duce desires that since there has been no struggle there should not be the least theatrical scenery. The meeting will take place almost secretly and hush-hush will be asked of the press.

June 23, 1940

The French plenipotentiaries have arrived in German planes. They are received by us at 7:30 P.M. at Villa Incisa on the Cassia Road. Badoglio does not hide his emotion. He wants to treat them with great courtesy. Among the French delegates is Parisot, who is a personal friend of his. Who knows how many times they have spoken ill together of the Germans? In the dining room, on the ground floor, there is a long table, and we sit down at one end. I have Badoglio at my right and Admiral Cavagnari at my left. We wait for the French standing, and we greet them with the Roman salute. They answer with a nod of the head. They are dignified. They do not show any pride nor, on the other hand, do they show any humiliation. Only Ambassador Noël is as white as a sheet. They sit down. I stand up and say that Badoglio has charge of communicating the armistice terms. Roatta reads the French translation of them. Huntziger answers that although he is a plenipotentiary, nevertheless, in as much as they are dealing with questions that involve the future of his country, he must report to Bordeaux, therefore he asks that the meeting be postponed until tomorrow. I approve, and fix the meeting for 10 A.M. Before leaving I shake hands with Huntziger, who was not expecting it. Then I say good-by to all the French delegates, followed by Badoglio and the others. The ceremony lasted twenty-five minutes in all.

From the Palazzo Chigi I report to the Duce by telephone; he is bitter because he had wanted to reach the armistice after a victory by our own armed forces.

June 24, 1940

Badoglio has asked to be left alone to continue negotiations. My presence would have had the appearance of a control which Keitel, at

Compiègne, did not have. No opposition on my part, particularly because from telephone interceptions I saw that they were in agreement at Bordeaux. The armistice was signed at 7:15 P.M. and at 7:35 P.M. I sent word to von Mackensen. Within six hours there will be no more fighting in France unless . . . I do not want to make any predictions, but I am not altogether certain that the Pétain government can succeed in imposing its will, especially on the empire and on the Navy.

Today, at Constantinople, all the French merchant ships raised the English flag. The war is not yet over, rather it is beginning now. We are going to have so many surprises that we shall not wish for more.

Russia is preparing to attack Rumania. This is what Molotov has told Schulenburg. Germany can do no more than acquiesce, but it is clear that Russian policy is increasingly anti-German. The capital in which there is the greatest amount of conspiracy against German victory is Moscow. The situation had appeared quite otherwise when, in August and September, the Bolsheviks signed pacts with the Nazis. At that time they didn't believe in a German triumph. They wanted to push Germany into a conflict and Europe into a crisis because they were thinking of a long and exhausting struggle between the democracies and Hitler. Things have moved fast, and now Moscow is trying to trouble the waters.

June 25, 1940

They do not know the armistice terms in Italy as yet, but already rumors are circulating which create a noticeable uneasiness. They were expecting immediate and gratuitous occupation. They thought that all the territory not conquered by the use of arms would pass over to us anyway, in view of the agreement. When the document is made public, delusions will increase all the more.

Starace, returning from the front, says that the attack on the Alps has proved the total lack of preparation of our Army, an absolute lack of offensive means, and complete lack of capacity in the higher officers. Men were sent to a useless death two days before the armistice, employing the same technique that was employed more than twenty years ago. If the war in Libya and Ethiopia is conducted in the same way, the future is going to hold many bitter disappointments for us.

I have solicited and obtained German intervention to save the life of Stoyadinovich, who, according to indications from our representative, is in the hands of his enemies and running grave risks.

June 26, 1940

After a communication from von Mackensen I have taken steps at the office of the Soviet Ambassador to discuss the question of Bessarabia. In short, Italy has no objection to the liquidation of this problem, but would prefer, in view of the present state of affairs, to see the controversy settled peacefully and without creating a new conflagration in the Balkans.

June 27, 1940

It is the anniversary of Father's death. I go to Leghorn for the occasion. My sorrow is not so bitter as it was at the time of his death, but even now the wound caused by his disappearance is painfully open in my heart. My dear, great, and good father, you who have given me not only my life, but also whatever I have found beautiful in it, know that I am always near you and that your spirit is my light and guide at all times.

June 28, 1940

Russian ultimatum to Rumania. From Bucharest they ask us directly what they must do. Yield, is our answer. We must at any cost avoid a conflict in the Balkans which would deprive us of their economic resources. For our part, we shall keep Hungary and Bulgaria from joining the conflict.

In fact, Rumania yields, rather sadly, but also with a rapidity worthy of Rumanian traditions as a belligerent people. I see many diplomatic representatives and give them all the Italian point of view.

The Pope intends to take the initiative for peace. I talk of it over the telephone with the Duce, who is immediately and decisively hostile.

Admiral Cavagnari complains of the High Command. There is disorder, and no one assumes responsibility. The submarines we have lost number eight.

June 29, 1940

Balbo is dead. A tragic mistake has brought his end. The antiaircraft battery at Tobruk fired on his plane, mistaking it for an Eng-

lish plane, and brought it to the ground. The news saddened me very
much. Balbo did not deserve this end. He was exuberant, restless, he
loved life in all its manifestations. He had more dash than talent, more
vivacity than acumen. He was a decent fellow, and even in political
clashes, in which his partisan temperament delighted, he never descended to dishonorable and questionable expedients. He did not desire war, and opposed it to the last. But once it had been decided, he
spoke with me in the language of a faithful soldier, and, if fate had
not been against him, he was preparing to act with decision and
daring.

Balbo's memory will linger long among Italians because he was,
above all, a true Italian, with the great faults and great virtues of our
race.

June 30, 1940

Ambassador Alfieri telephones that Hitler is going through one of
his periods of isolation, which, with him, precede the making of great
decisions. Therefore, he has not yet answered the Duce's message, in
which he [the Duce] offered the participation of our land and air
forces in the attack on Great Britain. But does he really want our
aid? From information sent by Teucci, it seems that the German
offensive will come only from the air, in grand style, and will take
place between the tenth and fifteenth of July.

The Duce continues his visit to the western front. This trip of his,
at the same time Hitler visits Paris, is arousing unfavorable comment.
Had I been able, I should have advised him against it.

July 1, 1940

Ambassador Alfieri has gone to confer with Hitler and will also
bring up my approaching trip to Germany.

Nothing more that is new.

July 2, 1940

Mussolini has returned from his trip to the western front, and, as I
foresaw, returned enthusiastic over what he had seen. He finds that
Italian armaments are in good shape. He speaks with fervor of the

break-through of the Alpine Maginot Line. As a matter of fact, there has been no break-through. Our storm troops have carried on infiltrations inside the French system of fortification and have occupied towns in the valleys, while the French forts cut off the path behind them. On all this the curtain of the armistice has providentially fallen. Otherwise, there might have been many not altogether joyful happenings. Now Mussolini considers the march on Alexandria as practically completed. He says that Badoglio also considers the undertaking easy and safe.

Ambassador Alfieri has reported on his conference with Hitler. I am convinced that there is something brewing in that fellow's mind, and that certainly no new decision has been taken. There is no longer that impressive tone of assurance that was apparent when Hitler spoke of breaking through the Maginot Line. Now he is considering many alternatives, and is raising doubts which account for his restlessness. Meanwhile, he does not answer Mussolini's offer to send men and planes to participate in an attack on England. On the other hand, he offers us aerial assistance to bomb the Suez Canal. Evidently he does not place much trust in us.

July 3, 1940

I ask Phillips the meaning of the Republican candidacy and if the United States is ready to enter the war. He replies, "In the field of foreign policy, Democrats and Republicans are almost entirely in agreement. For the moment we don't intend to enter the conflict. We are arming on a very large scale, and are helping the British in every way. However, some new fact might decide our intervention, such as a bombardment of London with many victims among the civilian population." This is why Hitler is careful and thoughtful before launching the final adventure. So much the more so, because, as we gather from many quarters, the Russians are preparing to assume a more and more hostile attitude toward the Axis.

I spoke clearly to the Greek Minister. De Vecchi telegraphs that English ships and maybe also English planes find refuge, supplies, and protection in Greece. Mussolini is furious. If this music should continue he is decided to take action against Greece. The Greek Minister tried weakly to deny it, but he left with his tail between his legs.

Limited firing between the French and English fleets at Oran. We still have no particulars, but it is a matter of no small moment.

This Sunday I shall be in Berlin and perhaps Hitler will speak. Will it be a speech of peace or one of total war against Great Britain?

July 4, 1940

News of the Anglo-French naval engagement is still indefinite. In any case, a good part of the French fleet has been destroyed, and perhaps another part has been seized. This disturbs Admiral Cavagnari, who this morning confirmed the fact that we had lost ten submarines. It is too early to judge the consequences of the British action. For the moment it proves that the fighting spirit of His British Majesty's fleet is quite alive, and still has the aggressive ruthlessness of the captains and pirates of the seventeenth century.

Ambassador Bastianini, who is back from London, says that the morale of the British is very high and that they have no doubts about victory, even though it may come only after a long time. Everybody—aristocracy, middle class, and the common people—is embittered, tenacious, and proud. Air and anti-aircraft preparation is undertaken on a large scale, such as to repulse and greatly reduce the offensive of the enemy. Hitler's indecision is thus explained.

Mussolini is worried over the possibility that the Germans may have got hold of certain documents among those that they captured from the French which might compromise us. So far as the Duce is concerned this isn't possible; they must be forgeries. For myself . . . I could not say the same! But the Germans know very well what I think, and have no need of any confirmation of my views by any French papers.

The Ambassador confirms my trip to Berlin for next Sunday.

July 5, 1940

The Duce gives me instructions for my trip to Germany. He wants definitely to participate in the attack on Great Britain, if it occurs, and he is concerned over the fact that France is trying to slip gradually into the anti-British camp. He fears that this may cause us to be defrauded of our booty. He charges me also to tell Hitler that he intends to land on the Ionian Islands and to tell him about the necessity of splitting up Yugoslavia, a typical Versailles creation, functioning against us. Through her Minister, Greece gives assurances of total neutrality, which the Duce receives incredulously, especially since De Vecchi maintains his accusations against Greece.

July 6, 1940

On my way to Berlin.

July 7, 1940

I arrive in Berlin. Warm reception. Conference with Hitler, of which there is a stenographic report elsewhere. I can add, personally, that he was very kind, extremely so. He is rather inclined to continue the struggle and to unleash a storm of wrath and of steel upon the English. But the final decision has not been reached, and it is for this reason that he is delaying his speech, of which, as he himself puts it, he wants to weigh every word. As to his health—he is well. He is calm and reserved, very reserved for a German who has won.

Von Ribbentrop, too, has changed, in contrast to his attitude at Munich. Then he reflected the warlike spirit of his master. Today he is again buoyantly belligerent.

July 8, 1940

A visit to the front: the Maginot Line, Metz, Verdun. The struggle has been less hard than I had believed it to be from a distance; except for a row of villages between the frontier and the Maginot Line, the other villages do not show any traces of war.

July 9, 1940

Still at the front: Lille, Dunkerque, Ostend, Bruges, Flanders. Here, too, many signs of flight and very few of fighting.

July 10, 1940

Munich. Meeting with the Hungarians at Hitler's residence. The latter clearly analyzes the situation in regard to the restless Magyars. If they are certain that they can do it alone, and if they are sure they must not expect any aid from Italy and Germany, who are involved elsewhere, let them attack. The Magyars left dissatisfied.

Salzburg. Great popular demonstration.

July 11, 1940

Report to the Duce on my trip. He is satisfied with the results. Von Ribbentrop spoke in clear terms about the Italian desiderata. Mussolini is good-humored, satisfied with the results of the aero-naval engagement, and optimistic about the approaching action in Egypt.

Von Ribbentrop telephones in a gruff and rude manner concerning some articles in our newspapers which have unmasked the Axis batteries as regards German intentions in the Balkans. He exaggerates. I know how to answer him, but for the time being mum's the word.

July 12, 1940

Nothing worth recording.

July 13, 1940

The real controversy in the matter of naval conflicts is not between us and the British, but between our aviation and our Navy. Admiral Cavagnari maintains that our air action was completely lacking during the first phase of the encounter, but that when it finally came it was directed against our own ships, which for six hours withstood the bombardment of our airplanes. Other information also gives the lie to the glowing reports of our air force. I confess that I am incredulous too. Mussolini, on the other hand, is not. Today he said that within three days the Italian Navy has annihilated 50 per cent of the British naval potential in the Mediterranean. Perhaps this is somewhat exaggerated.

We are awaiting a speech from Hitler. We shall learn the decisions from him.

July 14, 1940

Helfand, who directed the Soviet Embassy at Rome for many months, has to return to Moscow, but he sniffs the odor of the firing squad. That is why he has asked for help to escape to America, where he will leave his family, and, I believe, stay himself. He is a keen and intelligent man, whose long contact with bourgeois civilization has made a complete bourgeois of him. Under the stress of imminent misfortune all his Jewish blood has come to the surface. He has become extremely obliging and does nothing but bow and scrape. But he wishes to save his family and his daughter, whom he adores. He fears their deportation more than death for himself. This is very human and very beautiful.

July 15, 1940

Alfieri telephones that the date of Hitler's speech is not yet decided.

The outline of the letter that the Führer intends to send to King Carol on the Transylvanian question arrives. The Duce approves it.

July 16, 1940

Hitler has sent a long letter to the Duce. It announces the attack against England as something decided upon, but declines in a definite and courteous way to offer to send an Italian expeditionary force. He explains his refusal by saying that logistic difficulties would arise in supplying two armies. Goering, too, in a conversation with Alfieri, said that Italian aviation has too important a task in the Mediterranean to scatter its forces in other sectors. The Duce was very much annoyed by the refusal, but he finds solace in instructing the press to play up the naval battle of a week ago. But we have received information, even from German sources, that the damage inflicted on the British Navy is about nil. The Italian Navy is also of this opinion, while the Italian air force tends to exaggerate. I only hope that the version given by the air force is true, otherwise it will cost us dignity and prestige even with the Germans.

I took measures to give full help to the Italians in France. It is really humiliating to learn that they are forced to beg the defeated French for alms.

July 17, 1940

Nothing new.

July 18, 1940

The Germans inform us at the last moment that Hitler's speech will be made tomorrow at 7 P.M. I must leave at once.

July 19, 1940

I arrive in Berlin. Conference with von Ribbentrop. Hitler's speech will be a last appeal to Great Britain. I understand that, without their saying so, however, they are hoping and praying that this appeal will not be rejected.

Ceremony at the Reichstag. It is solemn and stagy. Hitler speaks simply, and, I should say also, in an unusually humane tone. I believe that his desire for peace is sincere. In fact, late in the evening, when the first cold English reactions to the speech arrive, a sense of ill-concealed disappointment spreads among the Germans.

July 20, 1940

Conference with the Führer, a stenographic report of which is to be found elsewhere. He confirms my impressions of yesterday. He would like an understanding with Great Britain. He knows that war with the English will be hard and bloody, and knows also that people everywhere today are averse to bloodshed.

In the afternoon a visit to Goering. He looked feverish, but as he dangled the collar of the Annunziata from his neck he was somewhat rude and haughty toward me. I was more interested in the luxurious decoration of his house than in him and his variable humors. It is an ever-increasing show of luxury, and it is truly incomprehensible how, in a country which is socialized, or almost so, people can tolerate the extraordinary pomp displayed by this Western satrap.

July 21, 1940

Return trip.

July 22, 1940

I report my impressions to the Duce. He, who had been against Hitler's speaking, defines it "a much too cunning speech." He fears that the English may find in it a pretext to begin negotiations. That would be sad for Mussolini, because now more than ever he wants war. And yet today he was depressed on account of the loss of the *Colleoni,* not so much because of the sinking itself as because he feels the Italians did not fight very brilliantly.

Halifax makes an inconsequential speech about Germany, in which Hitler's vague proposals for peace are not taken into account.

July 23, 1940

The Rumanian ministers go to confer with the Germans at Salzburg, then they will come to us.

July 24, 1940

Nothing new.

July 25, 1940

At Florence, to visit Marzio [Ciano's eldest son], who has been ill for some days. I am glad to find him lively and gay, as he always has been.

July 26, 1940

Our air losses during the first month of the war amount to two hundred and fifty planes; we are producing the same amount. The question of pilots is more difficult. Their losses cannot be too easily replaced.

I saw von Mackensen. The usual quarrel between Ribbentrop and Goebbels brings him to me. I do my best to eliminate every pretext for dragging us into this quarrel.

The Hungarians are nervous about the Rumanians' trip to Rome and to Berlin. They fear that Rumania, after so many years of boasting the Little Intente and "Genevaism," might ask and obtain admission to the Axis.

July 27, 1940

After a long period the Duce talks with the King. He saw him yesterday, and His Majesty's first question was "whether we shouldn't fear that Prussia might soon play a bad trick on Italy also." This question irritated the Duce because "it revealed that nothing has changed in the attitude of the King, who at heart still hopes for a British victory—a victory, that is, of the country where he has always kept his immense fortune."

I received the Rumanians. They are simply disgusting. They open their mouths only to exude honeyed compliments. They have become anti-French, anti-English, and anti-League of Nations. They talk with contempt of the *diktat* of Versailles—too honeyed. I have a first meeting with them at the Palazzo Chigi and I recall to their memory, with a certain brutality, their anti-Italian past. In the afternoon another meeting at the Palazzo Venezia. Mussolini, who had received in time the report of the German conversations with the Rumanians, repeated what Hitler said at Salzburg.

July 28, 1940

Sunday, I went to Leghorn with the children.

July 29, 1940

Mussolini calls many times by telephone from Riccione [a beach resort below Rimini on the Adriatic Sea] to have me modify the minutes of Saturday's conversation. He desires that I delete certain anti-Russian phrases of his and substitute for them some rather pro-Soviet remarks. The reports are to go to Berlin!

General Favagrossa brings me up to date on the problem of our supplies. It isn't so bad as we had thought. Our greatest need is for copper and steel alloys.

July 30, 1940

From Berlin comes news of absolute calm. Is it the calm before the storm? So affirms Alfieri.

I inform the Hungarians about the conference of last Saturday. Villani is rather satisfied with them.

July 31, 1940

Nothing new.

August 1, 1940

Nothing new.

August 2, 1940

Nothing new.

August 3, 1940

I ask the Greek Minister to withdraw his consul at Trieste, who is incurably anti-Italian. He attempts to defend him, but I have very clear proof as to his guilt and he must yield.

Soddu says that Graziani, after having emptied Italy in order to supply Libya, does not feel that he is prepared to attack Egypt, principally because of the heat. He intends to postpone the operation until spring. I do not yet know the reactions of the Duce, but I predict that they will be violent. From Germany, too, come rumors of a postponement of the attack. Can they be true?

Four agents of our Military Information Service (S.I.M.) were surprised this evening in the Yugoslav legation. We must encourage the rumor that they were only common burglars.

August 4, 1940

Mussolini has returned to Rome. He is in quite good humor, notwithstanding the postponement of the offensive in Libya and the reopening of an old leg wound which he suffered during the last war. He does not refer to the military situation. On the other hand, Badoglio informs me that Graziani has been ordered to Rome. Meanwhile, the Duke of Aosta has begun his offensive against British Somaliland, with excellent prospects.

Mussolini speaks of our relations with Russia, and believes that the moment has come to take further steps to better them. I agree.

From Berlin Alfieri reports that the sudden return of Hitler and of the highest Nazi officials leads him to suspect imminent operations about which we, as usual, have been told nothing.

August 5, 1940

Invectives by the Duce against "the Italians," which take place whenever he meets opposition to his projects. The principal points he made were: decrease in the birth rate, the tendency toward alcoholism, and complacency. He says that one day he will make a sweeping speech entitled "The Secret Wounds of Italy." He will do this in order to confront the nation with its own weaknesses. He said that the principal reason for the reforestation of the Apennine regions is to make the climate of Italy more rigorous. This will bring about an elimination of the weaker stock and an improvement of the Italian race.

Moral: the Duce is dissatisfied because Graziani, who has laid so much blame on Balbo, now refuses to face difficulties, and does not want to attack in Egypt. Today he has called him for an accounting, but I don't yet know with what results. Mussolini's uneasiness will increase if, as seems probable, Hitler soon launches his offensive against the British Isles.

August 6, 1940

Alfieri now says that German activity is slowed down and this time fails to explain the reason. Could there be anything in the rumors about a separate peace through the King of Sweden?

Mussolini talks very much about an Italian attack on Yugoslavia during the second half of September. Therefore, he wishes me to put aside the Croatian problem and arrive quickly at an agreement with Russia, which should have a "spectacular" character. He also raises the question of my going to Moscow. Litvinov's visit was never returned. All this seems premature. In any case, I shall talk to Mackensen about it. As regards the attack on Yugoslavia, I do not believe that, unless something new comes up, Hitler will permit the status quo of the Balkans to be disturbed.

The Duce telephones during the evening, exultant because our troops have entered Zeila. I do not know the real importance of this.

August 7, 1940

Nothing new.

August 8, 1940

Graziani has come to see me. He talks about the attack on Egypt as a very serious undertaking, and says that our present preparations are far from perfect. He attacks Badoglio, who does not check the Duce's aggressive spirit—a fact which "for a man who knows Africa means that he must suffer from softening of the brain, or, what is worse, from bad faith." "The water supply is entirely insufficient. We move toward a defeat which, in the desert, must inevitably develop into a rapid and total disaster."

I reported this to the Duce, who was very unhappy about it because in his last conversation with Graziani he had received the impression that the offensive would start in a few days. Graziani did not set any date with me. He would rather not attack at all, or, at any rate, not for two or three months. Mussolini concluded that "one should not give jobs to people who aren't looking for at least one promotion. Graziani has too many to lose." [Graziani, after the Ethiopian war, had been made a marshal. He could not run the risk of being demoted or put on the inactive list.]

Mackensen brings a plan for an identic protest to be made to Berne because of an insolent speech by a Swiss general. We agree on its general lines.

According to Alfieri, the offensive on the English Channel has been delayed because of bad weather. But, according to General Marras, the delay is caused by secret conversations supposedly going on now. The Alfieri version is the more probable.

August 9, 1940

Nothing new.

August 10, 1940

Meeting of the Council of Ministers. A long Mussolini monologue, which covered everything from the events of the war and alcoholism to his inevitable attack on the Italian middle class. "A bourgeois," he said, "is one who is neither a worker nor a farmer, and who is concerned only with his own interests." As for me, I still prefer Flaubert's definition: "Bourgeois is anything that is vulgar." The bourgeois concept has more of a psychological than an economic value. But on this problem of the so-called struggle against the bourgeois there are many things to be said, and someday it would be well to say them.

I talked to the Duce about the difficulties that have arisen on the Greek-Albanian frontier. I don't wish to dramatize the situation, but the Greek attitude is very tricky. The Duce is considering an "act of force, because since 1923 he has some accounts to settle, and the Greeks deceive themselves if they think that he has forgotten."

News of further delay in the offensive comes from Berlin. Will it take place? When? And in what form? We know nothing. The fact is that the Germans keep us in the dark about everything, just as they did when we were neutral, even though we are now fighting beside them.

August 11, 1940

Mussolini still speaks of the Greek question and wants particulars on Ciamuria. He has prepared a Stefani despatch, which will start agitation on the question. He has had Jacomoni and Visconti Prasca come to Rome and intends to confer with them. He speaks of a surprise attack against Greece toward the end of September. If he has decided this, I feel that he must work fast. It is dangerous to give the Greeks time to prepare.

The German air force has asked that our planes be sent to collaborate in the action against Great Britain. When we offered them a month ago they were promptly refused. Now Germany asks for them. Why? I am not very favorable to this for technical and also for political reasons.

Favagrossa compares the Italian situation to a bathtub with the stopper removed and with the taps turned off. Only from the shower, which is France, is it possible to expect a little water to run. But up to now this has not happened. We are very much concerned about tin, copper, and nickel. By the end of September we shall have exactly nothing so far as tin is concerned.

August 12, 1940

I accompany Jacomoni and Visconti Prasca to the Duce, who sets down the political and military lines for action against Greece. If

Ciamuria and Corfu are yielded without striking a blow, we shall not ask for anything more. If, on the other hand, any resistance is attempted, we shall go the limit. Jacomoni and Visconti Prasca consider the action possible, and even easy, provided, however, that it be undertaken at once. On the other hand, the Duce is still of the opinion, for general military reasons, that the action should be postponed until toward the end of September.

From Germany news about air attacks, but nothing more. I have spoken over the telephone with Alfieri, who was more than usually vague. A new and violent outburst by Mussolini against the middle class. "After the war is over, I shall begin my attack on the middle class, which is cowardly and despicable. We must destroy it physically, and save perhaps 20 per cent, if that much." And he added, "I shall strike at it, and I shall say, like St. Dominic, 'God will choose his own!' "

In Somaliland we fight and advance.

August 13, 1940

Mussolini is very resentful toward the Duke of Aosta because of the delay of operations in Somaliland. He repeats this formula: "Princes ought to be enlisted as civilians."

August 14, 1940

At Leghorn to see the children.

August 15, 1940

A Greek vessel has been sunk by a submarine of unidentified nationality. The incident threatens to become serious. As for me, I consider the intemperance of De Vecchi at the bottom of it. I confer with the Duce, who desires to settle this incident peacefully. It was not necessary. I suggest sending a note to Greece. This will place the question on a diplomatic plane.

August 16, 1940

Nothing new.

August 17, 1940

Alfieri has had an interesting conference with von Ribbentrop. It can be summarized as follows: (1) that the German Government does not desire that we make too close a *rapprochement* with Russia; (2) that it is necessary to abandon any plan to attack Yugoslavia; (3) that an eventual action against Greece is not at all welcome at Berlin. It is a complete order to halt all along the line. According to von Ribbentrop, every effort must be concentrated against Great Britain, because there, and there alone, is "the question of life and death." This leads me to think that even in German opinion the war is going to be hard. The Duce himself has dictated our counterproposal. Naturally, we accept the Berlin point of view, even as regards Greece. In fact, we put back in the drawer the note that we had already prepared.

At the seashore I saw Mollier, the press attaché of the German Embassy, who talks more than the Ambassador. He says that the landing is now imminent, and to this end thousands of landing craft are ready in the Channel ports; that the operation, which is a very bold one, will be hard and bloody, but certain as to its results. Mollier spoke of peace by the end of September.

August 18, 1940

Nothing very important. Only from Berlin a series of significant hints which lead us to consider as very imminent the decisive attack against Great Britain. Mussolini believes them to be true, and is convinced that we shall have victory and peace by the end of next month. For this reason he wants to move fast in Egypt.

Badoglio and De Vecchi insult each other by letter, so the Duce has told me. He was satisfied, and attributed to De Vecchi statements of which he could not be proud.

August 19, 1940

The Duce reads me a telegram he has sent to Graziani. He orders him to march on Egypt as soon as a German patrol lands in England. Mussolini himself assumes responsibility for the order, knowing full well the objections that Graziani will make.

August 20, 1940

Graziani sends in a copy of a report from which it appears that all his generals declare themselves against the offensive in Egypt. I shall refer it to the Duce.

A speech by Churchill. For the first time in a year I read an English speech which is definite and forward-looking. One can feel that behind the façade of beautiful words and strong affirmations there is a will and a faith.

August 21, 1940

Nothing new.

August 22, 1940

Mussolini gives me a copy of certain military directives he has formulated, in which the actions against Yugoslavia and Greece are indefinitely postponed. It appears that the Germans have renewed their pressure, even on our headquarters, for this very thing. The Duce wanted at first to give a copy of his directives to the German Embassy, then he telephoned to countermand his instructions. It appears that he prefers to send them in writing to Hitler.

Riccardi is now optimistic about our stocks. At the present rate of collection and acquisition there should not be any noticeable shortages until the end of 1941.

An important speech by Halifax. The British tone has changed, and the possibility of an understanding with Germany is not excluded. Is it possible that this explains the delay in the attack?

August 23, 1940

The Duce has prepared a letter—an outline of which goes to Hitler—and received an interesting one from Franco. The Caudillo talks about Spain coming into the war soon. He says that he has already approached the Germans to get what he needs. To us he has not specified what he had asked for.

August 24, 1940

Nothing new.

August 25, 1940

Nothing new. I am spending the day at Leghorn.

August 26, 1940

Von Ribbentrop telephoned several times. He is concerned about the turn taken by the controversy between the Hungarians and Rumanians. Germany wants, at all costs, to avoid a crisis in the Balkans. Hence, although he does not speak of arbitration, von Ribbentrop is thinking of calling the two ministers for foreign affairs to Vienna to give them the friendly advice of the Axis to seek a solution. All this is naturally to be accompanied by a threat: whoever does not accept the advice will take upon himself all responsibility for future consequences. I agree, and the Duce approves. I have Ghigi and Talamo come to Rome in order to obtain more information. We shall go to Vienna within two or three days.

Von Ribbentrop informs me that he has dealt harshly with the Greek Minister, who had tried to knock at the doors of Berlin. He did not receive him, and has told him it would be more useful to speak with Italy, since Germany is in perfect accord with us about everything.

August 27, 1940

The meeting at Vienna is decided for tomorrow. The Hungarians and Rumanians will come on Thursday. Von Ribbentrop telephones that the Führer is of the opinion that the Rumanians should give up forty thousand square kilometers to Hungary, which has asked for sixty thousand. Mussolini has no precise ideas on the subject, and gives me full liberty of action. He is entirely occupied with the plan of the attack on Egypt, and says that Keitel also thinks that the taking of Cairo is more important than the taking of London. Keitel has not said this to me. The attack is to take place on the sixth of September. What does Graziani think of it?

August 28, 1940

Hitler desires to speak to me before I go to Vienna. Hence we go by way of Salzburg. The weather is beautiful south of the Alps and cloudy in the north. The usual reception at Berchtesgaden. Hitler is cordial and serene as usual, but more tired than on other occasions. After lunch we speak first of the general situation. I have summarized the conference in a telegram to the Duce. Hitler explains the failure of the attack on Great Britain as due to the bad weather. He says that he will need at least two weeks of clear weather to neutralize British naval superiority, but from all that he said it seems to me probable that there is now a definite postponement of the assault. Until when? Nevertheless, Hitler seems resolved to go the limit, because, he tells me, he has rejected an attempt at mediation made by the King of Sweden.

We speak little of the Magyar-Rumanian question. He leaves the solution to von Ribbentrop and me. The only thing he has at heart is that peace be preserved there, and that Rumanian oil continue to flow into his reservoirs.

Air trip to Vienna. The city, compared to what it was a year ago, seems to be in a more miserable condition: little traffic, stores that are ill-supplied, and a heavy atmosphere. The people on the streets are badly dressed and listless.

August 29, 1940

With Ribbentrop we decide to solve the problem by arbitration. If we once started a discussion we should never be able to get out of it. We first talk to the Hungarians. Czaky is reasonable; Teleki is hostile. Then Ribbentrop assails the Hungarians. Courtesy is not his forte. He accuses Hungary of having engaged in anti-German policy on more than one occasion. His words are rather threatening. The conversation with the Rumanian is less violent. Manoïlescu doesn't know what to do or what to say and seems terrified for his country and for himself. We try to make him pay dear for our guarantee of his frontiers. He, too, is convinced that this is an excellent thing, but thinks the price is high.

The Hungarians accepted this afternoon. The Rumanians will make us wait for their answer until four o'clock in the morning. In the meantime Ribbentrop and I trace the new frontier and dictate the terms of the arbitration. It is a difficult problem to solve; in fact, impossible to solve with any absolute justice. We shall try to be as fair as we can.

In Vienna they are eating less and badly. Hotels are short of provisions and disorganized to the point where they don't seem to be the same. The war weighs more heavily on this city than elsewhere. Austrian morale is not good either.

August 30, 1940

Ceremony of the signature at the Belvedere. The Hungarians can't contain their joy when they see the map. Then we hear a loud thud. It was Manoïlescu, who fainted on the table. Doctors, massage, camphorated oil. Finally he comes to, but shows the shock very much.

In the evening there is a demonstration in front of the hotel. Since they went to the trouble of organizing one, it should have been bigger and warmer. Vienna is truly gray.

August 31, 1940

I went hunting with Ribbentrop.

September 1, 1940

I return to Rome. A conversation with the Duce. He is pleased by what has happened. He declares he is glad that the war will last beyond this month and, maybe, beyond the winter, because this will give Italy time to make greater sacrifices and thus enable him better to assert our rights. Will he prove right this time? And isn't there the danger that if the war doesn't end soon it may last beyond the time favorable for us? This is a question that is worth asking and which many Germans, among those who have their heads screwed on, are now asking.

September 2, 1940

Nothing new.

September 3, 1940

Nothing new.

September 4, 1940

The Americans lend fifty destroyers to Great Britain. In Berlin a great deal of excitement and indignation. The Duce, on the other hand, says that he is indifferent. At the request of the Germans we stop our radio transmissions at 10 P.M. It seems that this step was taken because of the advantage which English aviation derived from the prolongation of the transmission.

September 5, 1940

Mussolini returned to Rome. He is alarmed by the situation in Rumania as it is described by the military attaché. Ghigi is more calm. They are also calm in Berlin. Hitler has spoken, and has uttered harsh threats against England. But he makes no allusion to the blitzkrieg, and some expressions used by him, such, for example, as his clownish ridiculing of Duff Cooper, leave me greatly perplexed. He must be nervous.

September 6, 1940

The Duce is rather excited. I don't know why. He is taking it out on his generals, whom he removes, as well as on the Germans, who prevent our *rapprochement* with Moscow.

King Carol of Rumania has abdicated. He is paying, but only in part, for his silly buffoonery, his betrayals, and his crimes.

September 7, 1940

Council of Ministers. At the end of the meeting the Duce makes some political statements. He begins by affirming that, in his opinion, the war is now bound to last part of the winter, although he considers the landing of the Germans in England as a certainty. As to what concerns us more directly, he has again taken up the matter of our attack on Egypt. It was to take place today, but Graziani has asked that it be postponed for one month. Badoglio was in favor of the delay. Mussolini vetoes this, taking upon himself responsibility for the decision. If Graziani does not attack on Monday he will be replaced. He has also given orders to the Navy to make a move to meet the British fleet and to give battle. As to the more distant future, he said that he is now certain that between 1945 and 1950 war will break out between the Axis and Russia. By that time he will have ready his program of armament on the basis of one hundred divisions.

September 8, 1940

Graziani has answered that he will obey. The attack will begin tomorrow. Many military technicians are skeptical. Among them the Prince of Piedmont, who has expressed to me his doubts on the prospects and wisdom of the enterprise.

The naval encounter has not as yet taken place, because our aerial reconnaisance has not yet located the route of the British squadron from Gibraltar.

September 9, 1940

The drive against Egypt has suffered a new delay. Graziani is doing his best to approach his objective, and is preparing to begin action on the twelfth. Never has a military operation been undertaken so much against the will of the commanders.

What is happening in London under German bombing? From here it is difficult to judge. The blow must be hard. Decisive? I don't believe it.

September 10, 1940

Nothing new.

September 11, 1940

The beginning of the attack on Egypt is confirmed for tomorrow. Even General Carboni, who has never been unduly optimistic, says that our advance as far as Marsa Matruk is easy, and that it is possible to reach Alexandria.

German air action continues against London. We do not know exactly what the results are. It seems incredible, but we do not have a single informant in Great Britain. On the other hand, the Germans have many. In London itself there is a German agent who makes radio transmissions up to twenty-nine times in one day. At least it is so stated by Admiral Canaris.

September 12, 1940

Nothing new.

September 13, 1940

Von Ribbentrop telephones from Berlin. He wants to come to Rome next week in order to confer on two subjects: Russia and America. The trip may prove useful. I agree to it.

Graziani must have launched his attack, but up to now we have no precise information.

September 14, 1940

The attack on Egypt has begun. At the moment the British are withdrawing without fighting. They wish to draw us away from our base and lengthen our lines of communication. The Duce, whose good humor has returned, considers the arrival at Marsa Matruk as a great victory, especially since it permits our aviation to attack Alexandria by day, with fighter escort.

No definite news from the north. The Duce is still convinced that the landing will take place, while General Marras, who thought it certain until today, is beginning to doubt it. Maybe we shall learn the truth from Ribbentrop.

The Russian attitude is becoming alarmingly equivocal.

September 15, 1940

I go to Leghorn, later to Spezia, to preside at ceremonies in honor of my father. The statue by Messina is a work worthy of the Renaissance. When it was unveiled the image of my father seemed so powerfully alive that I was thrilled.

September 16, 1940

Mussolini is nervous because of the slow progress in Egypt. But he is angry at Berti who, because of his slowness, may lose us our booty.

The fact is that no fighting has yet begun. Only some rear-guard action.

Ribbentrop's visit has been confirmed for Tuesday.

September 17, 1940

It seems that things in Egypt are going better and better. The English are withdrawing with unforeseen rapidity. According to military experts there will be resistance at Marsa Matruk. Others believe, on the other hand, that it will come at Alexandria. Mussolini is radiant with joy. He has taken the entire responsibility of the offensive on his shoulders, and he is proud that he was right.

September 18, 1940

Nothing new.

September 19, 1940

Arrival of von Ribbentrop. He is in good humor and pleased by the welcome that is given him by "the applauding squad," which was very well mobilized by the police commissioner. In the car Ribbentrop speaks at once of the surprise in his bag: a military alliance with Japan, to be signed within the next few days at Berlin. The Russian dream vanished forever in the rooms of the Belvedere at Vienna, after the guarantee to Rumania. He thinks that such a move will have a double advantage: against Russia and against America, which, under the threat of the Japanese fleet, will not dare to move. I express a contrary opinion. The anti-Russian guarantee is very good, but the anti-American statement is less appropriate, because Washington will increasingly favor the English. As for England, von Ribbentrop says that the weather has been very bad and that the clouds even more than the R.A.F. have prevented final success. However, the invasion will take place anyway as soon as there are a few days of fine weather. The landing is ready and possible. English territorial defense is non-existent. A single German division will suffice to bring about a complete collapse.

In the afternoon a conference at the Palazzo Venezia, the stenographic report of which is filed elsewhere. In general I find von Ribbentrop in better spirits than at Vienna, and the principal reason for his elation is the pact with Japan, which he considers of fundamental importance, and which, in addition, is one of his own personal successes.

September 20, 1940

A second conversation with Ribbentrop. It has to deal principally with Spanish intervention, which now seems to be assured and imminent. Ribbentrop reads a message sent by Hitler to Franco. It is a paper partly political and partly military, written with the convincing logic which the Führer's writings frequently contain.

D'Aieta reports to me that Ribbentrop's optimistic forecasts are not shared by the functionaries with him here, who think that this may be a long war. Some of them think it will be a hard war.

September 21, 1940

I went with Ribbentrop to Villa d'Este and to Villa Adriana [two villas near Tivoli]. In the last few days Ribbentrop has wanted to meet many people both inside and outside political circles. Everybody disliked him.

September 22, 1940

Final conference with von Ribbentrop. It is panoramic in its scope. Von Ribbentrop alludes to the possibility of the Axis taking the initiative in breaking diplomatic relations with the United States. Mussolini is inclined to agree. I do not, first of all because I believe we must avoid a conflict with America at all costs, and then because I believe that we would be rendering a signal service to Roosevelt, for whom it would be advantageous to present himself at the elections in the guise of one who has been attacked. Anyway, the decision is not imminent, and I hope that I shall be.able to put in my oar.

The weather in the north continues bad, and along with the summer the prophecies made by von Ribbentrop disappear in the distance. The Hungarians are laying too heavy a hand on Transylvania. In agreement with von Ribbentrop, we take steps at Budapest to advise that moderation which, in the hour of success, represents the greatest wisdom. However, the Hungarians are beginning to circulate propaganda leaflets in which are printed the words: "The Trianon is dead. Vienna, too, will die."

September 23, 1940

No news.

September 24, 1940

The final text of the Tripartite Pact is agreed upon. The signature can now take place in a few days.

During the night Mackensen telephoned about de Gaulle. He appeared at Dakar with some English vessels and called on the French to give up. The governor resisted, and Pétain asked the Armistice Commission for authorization to send certain French vessels, among them the *Strasbourg,* into the Atlantic. The Germans objected. I, too, object. We cannot see clearly de Gaulle's attitude. In fact, I am convinced that as time works against the possibility of a British collapse, solidarity between Free France and the French Colonial Empire appears more evident.

I spoke about it to the Duce, who is also thinking of the occupation of Corsica. He is right. If we don't get there the British will, and from Ghisonaccia the Royal Air Force will attack Italy.

Cavagnari absolutely denies that a cruiser of the *London* type has been sunk. According to him, it is one of the usual bragging claims of the air force to spite the Navy, at which they poke fun.

September 25, 1940

I went to Florence on account of Marzio's operation; thank God everything goes well. At the station a telephone call reached me from Ribbentrop announcing that the signature of the alliance will take place on Friday. I must leave immediately.

September 26, 1940

I am on my way to Berlin. On Hitler's order the train is stopped at Munich. Attacks by the Royal Air Force endanger the zone, and the Führer does not wish to expose me to the risk of a long stop in the open country. I sleep in Munich and will continue by air.

September 27, 1940

The pact is signed. The signature takes place more or less like that of the Pact of Steel. But the atmosphere is cooler. Even the Berlin street crowd, a comparatively small one, composed mostly of school children, cheers with regularity but without conviction. Japan is far away. Its help is doubtful. One thing alone is certain: that the war will be long. This does not please the Germans, who had come to believe that with the end of summer the end of the war would also come. A winter of war is hard to take. More so since food is scarce in Berlin, and it is easy to see that the window displays of the stores promise much more than is actually inside.

Another thing that contributes to the depressed spirit of Berlin life is the constant recurrence of air raids. Every night the citizens spend from four to five hours in the cellar. They lack sleep, there is promiscuity between men and women, cold, and these things do not make for good humor. The number of people with colds is incredible. Bomb damage is slight; nervousness is very great. At ten o'clock in the evening everyone looks at his watch. People want to return home to their dear ones. All this does not yet justify the pessimism in certain quarters where the memory of the first war is being evoked and they are beginning to think of the worst.

September 28, 1940 [continuation of September 27]

But it is a fact that the tone of Germany today is not that of last June or even of last August.

I had two conversations with Hitler, one formal after the signing, the other the next day. He did not speak of the current situation. He spoke rather of Spanish intervention, to which he is opposed because it would cost more than it is worth. He proposed a meeting with the Duce at the Brenner Pass, and I immediately accepted. No more invasion of England. No more blitz destruction of England. From Hitler's speech there now emerges worry about a long war. He wishes to conserve his armed power. He speaks with his usual decision, with less impetuousness but with as much determination as ever. Ribbentrop is more nervous. Perhaps it is his bad health, and perhaps he has other reasons for complaint. He had relied too much on a lightning end of the conflict not to be disappointed. Toward us Italians the

Germans are impeccably courteous. Ansaldo judges that the courtesy is in proportion to the need the Germans have of us. With the Spaniards, on the other hand, the Germans are less courteous. Generally speaking, Serrano Suñer's mission was not successful, and the man himself did not and could not please the Germans.

September 29, 1940

On my way home.

September 30, 1940

I confer with the Duce. I find him in good humor and very happy that Italy could score in Egypt a success which affords her the glory she has sought in vain for three centuries.

He is rather irritated by Badoglio, who now seems to have assumed the role of delaying Graziani's march.

October 1, 1940

Serrano Suñer arrives in Rome. General Queipo de Llano is also at the station, but they do not greet each other and Queipo declines an invitation to lunch. In speaking of Queipo, Serrano Suñer called him "a bandit and a beast." All this has symbolical meaning: it represents the situation in Spanish public life today.

I have a long conversation with the Duce which is recorded elsewhere. There is one point in the record of the conversation which I had to take out of the copy given to the Germans: Serrano's colorful invectives against the Germans, for their absolute lack of tact in dealing with Spain. Serrano is right. The Germans are not models of courtesy, and Ribbentrop less so than the others, even though this time there is something to be said for him. For years the Spaniards have been asking for a lot and giving nothing in return. However, there are other ways in which Serrano could have expressed himself.

October 2, 1940

The Duce is very anxious about an attack to take place soon on Marsa Matruk, and is irritated by Badoglio because the latter does not think the action can be carried out in October. I speak of it with

Graziani because the Duce wants to know what he thinks of it. Graziani feels that we must still wait for some time, at least all of November, to complete our logistic preparation, which is the only real definitive guarantee of success.

He is afraid that the English may resist for a long time at Marsa Matruk. If our supply lines should not function well we would have to retreat. And in the desert a retreat is equivalent to a rout.

A conference with Serrano. He says nothing new but he is postponing his departure until after my return from the Brenner Pass in order to be duly informed.

October 3, 1940

Biseo, a man who really understands aviation, has painted a black picture of our air force in North Africa. Our logistic organization is bad, and we are short of pursuit planes. Although the English are numerically inferior, they cause us plenty of trouble. Biseo thinks it will be difficult to carry our attack on Egypt to its logical conclusion.

A partial crisis in London with the removal of Chamberlain from the government. Information is scarce and uncertain, nor does it enable us to make any kind of diagnosis of the significance of this development. A long conference with the King, who is vaguely pessimistic and fundamentally hostile to Germany. He repeats his favorite refrain on the scant feeling of security which German promises give. He is also skeptical as to the condition of our armed forces.

October 4, 1940

Rarely have I seen the Duce in such good humor and good shape as at the Brenner Pass today. The meeting was cordial and the conversations were certainly the most interesting of all that have taken place so far. Hitler put at least some of his cards on the table, and talked to us about his plans for the future. I have recorded the conversation elsewhere. These are my general impressions: (1) there is no longer any talk about a landing in the British Isles and preparations already made remain where they are; (2) it is hoped to attract France into the orbit of the anti-British coalition, since it is now realized that the Anglo-Saxon world is still a hard nut to crack; (3) greater importance is given to the Mediterranean sector, which is good for us. Hitler was energetic and again extremely anti-Bolshevist. "Bolshevism," he said, "is the doctrine of people who are lowest in the scale of civilization." Ribbentrop, on the other hand, was very silent and in noticeably bad health.

Anfuso, who remained long with the Germans of the entourage and who is the most pro-German of my collaborators, is not too well satisfied, and says that a spirit of adventure seems still to drive the Germans.

I had a long conversation with the Duce on the train. He said that he will soon fire Muti because he is incapable and an opportunist; he also said that he will spur Graziani on to start the offensive sooner, and that he detests the King "because the King is the only defeatist in the country."

October 5, 1940

I inform Serrano of the results of the meeting in so far as they concern Spain, and he is only half satisfied. Why hadn't he yet seen that for a long time the Germans have had an eye on Morocco?

The Duce approved the report on the Brenner meeting, and asks that a copy be sent to the King, as well as a résumé to Badoglio. He pronounced unfavorable judgments on Badoglio, and declared that in the spring he will think about finding a substitute for him.

October 6, 1940

I go to Leghorn.

October 7, 1940

Nothing new.

October 8, 1940

A telephone call from the Duce, requesting that we take action in Rumania to elicit a request for Italian troops. He is very angry because only German forces are present in the Rumanian oil regions. The step is delicate and difficult, but I imagine that Ghigi will carry it through all right.

October 9, 1940

Nothing new.

October 10, 1940

Ribbentrop telephoned, informing me that the Hungarian Government has again asked permission to adhere to the Tripartite Alliance. While formerly he was against it, Ribbentrop is now entirely favorable, because no one who wants to join in the anti-British fight must be turned down. Mussolini gives his approval, though a bit unwillingly, since he does not wish to enlarge the Tripartite Alliance. Once the Hungarians are admitted he believes we should have to open the door to the Rumanians also. I inform Ribbentrop of this, and he receives the idea with very measured enthusiasm.

October 11, 1940

Nothing new.

October 12, 1940

The return of the Duce. He is very much vexed at Graziani because the latter has once more answered in dilatory form his order to start the offensive. The Duce speaks of replacing him, and mentions the names of Generals Messe and Vercellino.

But above all he is indignant at the German occupation of Rumania. He says that this has impressed Italian public opinion very deeply and badly, because, in view of the decisions taken at Vienna, nobody had expected this to happen. "Hitler always faces me with a *fait accompli*. This time I am going to pay him back in his own coin. He will find out from the papers that I have occupied Greece. In this way the equilibrium will be re-established." I ask if he has come to an agreement with Badoglio. "Not yet," he answers, "but I shall send in my resignation as an Italian if anyone objects to our fighting the Greeks." The Duce seems determined to act now. In fact, I believe that the military operation will be useful and easy.

October 13, 1940

Nothing new.

October 14, 1940

Mussolini speaks to me again about our action in Greece, and fixes the date for October 26. Jacomoni gives very satisfactory information, especially on the state of mind of the population of Ciamuria, which is favorable to us.

October 15, 1940

A meeting with the Duce at the Palazzo Venezia, to discuss the Greek enterprise. Badoglio, Roatta, Soddu, Jacomoni, Visconti Prasca, and myself take part in it. The discussion is available in a stenographic report.

Afterward, at the Palazzo Chigi, I speak with Ranza and Visconti Prasca, who explain their military plans. I speak also with Jacomoni, who gives an account of the political situation. He says that in Albania the attack on Greece is awaited keenly and enthusiastically. Albanian youth, which has always been reserved in its attitude toward us, now makes open manifestations of approval.

October 16, 1940

I receive a copy of a report from Graziani. He declares that to resume his march in Egypt he will need at least two months' time. I immediately send the document to the Duce. I can imagine his indignation.

October 17, 1940

The Duce is at Terni [near Rome and center of the metallurgic industries]. Marshal Badoglio comes to see me, and speaks very seriously about our action in Greece. The three heads of the General Staff have unanimously pronounced themselves against it. The present forces are insufficient, and the Navy does not feel that it can carry out a landing at Prevesa because the water is too shallow. All of Badoglio's talk has a pessimistic tinge. He foresees the prolongation of the war, and with it the exhaustion of our already-meager resources. I listen, and do not argue. I insist that, from a political point of view, the moment is good. Greece is isolated. Turkey will not move. Neither will Yugoslavia. If the Bulgarians enter the war it will be on our side. From the military point of view I express no opinion. Badoglio must, without any hesitation, repeat to Mussolini what he has told me.

I go to Naples. I meet Edda, who is returning with a hospital ship. I speak with the wounded. They are magnificent.

October 18, 1940

I go early to see the Duce. I find Soddu in the anteroom. He has spoken with Badoglio, who declared that if we move against Greece he will resign. I report to the Duce, who is already in a very bad humor on account of Graziani. He has a violent outburst of rage, and says that he will go personally to Greece "to witness the incredible shame of Italians who are afraid of Greeks." He is planning to move at any cost, and if Badoglio presents his resignation it will be accepted immediately. But Badoglio not only does not present it, he doesn't even repeat to Mussolini what he told me yesterday. In fact, the Duce states that Badoglio only brought this up in order to obtain a postponement of a few days, at least two.

I go with Manoïlescu to the Duce. A long and gloomy lamentation over the insolence of the Hungarians, which is undoubtedly a fact but which we can hardly stop. On the other hand, after twenty years of Rumanian oppression a reaction was to be expected, especially as the Magyars are at heart of a savage and harsh temperament.

From an intercepted cable it seems that Turkey is preparing to move if Greece is attacked. I do not believe it, and the Duce considers it out of the question.

October 19, 1940

Council of Ministers. The Duce speaks of the situation, and gives us to understand that action is imminent, but he does not mention the date, nor does he give precise details about the direction it will take.

Anfuso returns from Sofia, where he delivered a letter from the

Duce to King Boris. It was not an invitation to action, but rather information on the decision taken. It was left up to him to decide his course as dictated by his conscience as King and as a Bulgarian. He answered with a written and sealed message, but in the long conference he had with Anfuso his attitude was rather evasive, in accordance with his habits and his character. Above all, he fears the Turks.

October 20, 1940

I see Bismarck, who informs me of two matters, both of them very important; namely, that during the next week Hitler will meet Franco somewhere in France, and that, during the course of his trip, he will speak with French Government officials to see if he can put into practice the projects discussed at the Brenner Pass. These are not very satisfactory to me. In the long run, a *rapprochement* between Berlin and Paris could not but work against us. But is this possible?

October 21, 1940

Nothing new.

October 22, 1940

This is a sad day, more than ever because it is the anniversary of the death of my good sister, Maria.

Mussolini returns. He has prepared a letter for Hitler on the general situation. He alludes to our impending action in Greece, but does not make clear either the form or the date, because he fears that once again an order might come to halt us. Many indications lead us to believe that in Berlin they are not very enthusiastic about our going to Athens. The date fixed is now the twenty-eighth of October. General Pricolo reports that Badoglio has given orders for a limited air action. The Duce does not agree. He wants us to attack very vigorously, because he would like everything to go to pieces at the first clash. If we leave the Greeks too much time to reflect and to breathe, the English will come, and perhaps the Turks, and the situation will become long drawn out and difficult. The Duce can now hardly stand Badoglio, whom he considers a barrier between himself and the troops.

I begin to draw up the ultimatum which Grazzi will hand to Metaxas at two o'clock in the morning of the twenty-eighth of October. Naturally it is a document that allows no way out for Greece. Either she accepts occupation or she will be attacked.

October 23, 1940

Nothing new.

October 24, 1940

With General Pricolo I examine the plan of the air attack on Greece. It is good, because it is energetic and bold. By a hard blow at the start it will be possible to bring about a complete collapse within a few hours.

During the evening von Ribbentrop telephones from a little railway station in France. He reports on a conference with Franco and with Pétain, and is, on the whole, satisfied with the results achieved. He says that the program of collaboration is heading toward concrete results. I do not conceal my doubt and suspicion. Nevertheless, it is essential that the inclusion of France in the Axis shall not be to our detriment. Von Ribbentrop also speaks of an impending trip of Hitler to a city in northern Italy, to confer with the Duce.

October 25, 1940

With the Duce I settle upon our diplomatic lines of action for our move in Greece. He also approves of having a meeting with the Soviet Ambassador immediately after the attack. It is a gesture that may calm the troubled waters, perhaps prepare the ground for the future. In the meantime, von Mackensen conveys some more particulars on Hitler's conferences with the French and Spaniards, and announces the terms of a secret tripartite protocol with Spain.

The Duce sends a letter to General Visconti Prasca, spurring him on to action.

Von Ribbentrop telephones. He proposes a conference and the proposal is accepted. It is to take place on Monday, the twenty-eighth, in Florence, between Hitler and Mussolini. This rush of the Führer to Italy so soon after his conference with Pétain is not at all pleasing to me. I hope he will not offer us a cup of hemlock because of our claims against France. This will be a bitter pill for the Italian people, even more so than the Versailles delusion.

October 26, 1940

Nothing new.

October 27, 1940

Numerous incidents in Albania. Action is expected at any moment. And yet the four diplomats, German, Japanese, Spanish, and Hungarian, to whom I handed the text of the ultimatum to Greece, were rather surprised.

I have prepared the agenda for the meeting at Florence tomorrow. Hitler will remain there for only a few hours, and then will leave for the Brenner Pass.

October 28, 1940

We attack in Albania and carry on a conference at Florence. In both places things have gone well. Notwithstanding the bad weather, the troops are moving fast, even if air support is lacking.

At Florence the conference, of which there is a stenographic report elsewhere, is of the greatest interest and proves that German solidarity has not failed us.

The Duce is in very good humor. He speaks at length about the situation of the party. He lays aside Ricci's candidacy [as secretary general], and accepts the name of Serena. He would also like to consider Marziali, the Prefect of Milan, but I dissuade him. It would be a disaster—worse than that caused by Muti.

October 29, 1940

The weather is bad, but the advance continues. Diplomatic reactions in the Balkans are quite limited for the time being. No one makes a move to defend the Greeks. It is now a question of speed, and we must act quickly.

I leave for Tirana during the evening.

October 30, 1940

At Tirana. Bad weather. I do not fly. I inspect the public works, the roads, the port. Things are going a little slowly. It's because of the rain.

October 31, 1940

Continued bad weather. I write a long letter to the Duce. Here they complain of the ill will of the General Staff, which has not done what it should have done to prepare for the action. Badoglio was convinced that the Greek question could have been settled at the peace table, and his attitude was affected by this prejudice. This has resulted in a much weaker preparation than we were led to expect.

November 1, 1940

The sun has finally come out. I take advantage of it to carry out a spectacular bombardment of Salonika. On my return I am attacked by Greek planes. All goes well. Two of theirs fell, but I must confess that it is the first time that I had them on my tail. It is an ugly sensation.

I went from Tirana to Taranto to confer with the Duce, and then from Taranto to Rome, whence I will leave for Germany.

November 2, 1940

On my way to Sudetenland.

November 3, 1940

I made a report of my conversations with Ribbentrop. I have nothing to add. I saw no one except the people on the official committee, and the foresters—not enough to get any impressions.

Last night, while Ribbentrop talked to his guests, repeating his favorite motto that the war was already won, a German Army major turned to me and said in his labored French: "This phrase was given to us in 1914, in 1915, in 1916, and in 1917. I believed it. In 1918 I

wished I were dead." His calm sincerity and sadness impressed me.
Let's hope that too many of them don't get to thinking this way.

November 4, 1940

I leave for Italy.

November 5, 1940

On my way home.

November 6, 1940

Mussolini is dissatisfied over the way things are going in Greece. The
attack on Corcia did take place, even though the results were not those
bragged about by the English radio. The enemy has made some progress and it is a fact that on the eighth day of operations the initiative is
in their hands. Soddu has left for Albania and will assume command.
Visconti will remain in command of the Army of the Epirus.

I don't think that we have come to the point where we must bandage
our heads, although many are beginning to do so. As a matter of fact,
in the evening Mussolini is calmer. The forces now gathered in the
Corcia sector indicate that the Greek push may be definitely slowed up.
Afterward the counterattack and success will come. Perhaps even much
sooner than is expected.

November 7, 1940

I confer with Benini, who has just returned from Tirana, and accompany him to the Duce, to whom he makes a long report. On the
Corcia sector our collapse began when a frightened battalion of
Albanians ran away. It seems there was no treachery. Our soldiers did
miracles. Entire Greek divisions were stopped by the resistance put up
by platoons of custom guards, and the Greeks did not pass until the
defenders died to the last man. We withdrew to a defensive line. Soddu
maintains that the arrival of a few regiments of Alpine troops would
definitely eliminate all dangers. On the Epirus sector Visconti is still
relatively optimistic and thinks that we can place ourselves in a position
to bring about the fall of Jianina. Soddu is not of this opinion and

thinks we ought to cease our maneuver, augment our forces, and repeat our attack.

The civilian organization is excellent. The port of Durazzo is operating at full capacity, but not too crowded with ships. So also are the roads, which insure an intense and safe traffic between the front and the rear.

In the afternoon I go to the reception given by the Soviets. This creates a profound sensation in the diplomatic corps. It is the first time that I have crossed the portals of this embassy as Minister for Foreign Affairs.

November 8, 1940

The news given by Jacomoni does not coincide with that of headquarters, which is more pessimistic. The Duce has a long conversation with Badoglio and Roatta and makes plans for the sending of troops. It appears that Badoglio is lugubrious and this irritates the Duce. He is especially irritated because Badoglio asks for four months more. Too long. We must act immediately and energetically. The attack of the Greeks is slowing down and they have no reserves. Grazzi, returning from Athens, confirms that the internal conditions of the country are very bad, and that their resistance is made of soap bubbles. According to him, Metaxas, receiving our ultimatum in his night shirt and dressing gown, was ready to yield. He became unyielding only after having talked with the King, and after the intervention of the English Minister.

In the evening news is better. The Greek attack is weakening on all sectors.

November 9, 1940

The situation is stationary on the Albanian front. The Greek attack has lost its impetus and is dying out. But we, too, unfortunately, have not the strength to resume our advance. We shall do so in a few weeks. The Duce is now very angry with Jacomoni and Visconti, who had represented the operation as too easy and sure of success.

Hitler has made a speech. I didn't like it. Too many personal arguments to be convincing. The purpose of the speech is to raise the morale of the German people, who are disappointed at the results of the American elections. But did the Führer succeed? Mussolini plans to speak on the eighteenth of November. He is aware of the fact that

the internal situation has become difficult and that a word from him
is needed.

November 10, 1940

An offensive thrust by our cavalry carried far in the vicinity of
Prevesa, meeting no resistance, which proves that the Greeks have only
a thin military line and that having broken this we shall go on with
ease. If we had two divisions in Albania today we could launch them
with certainty of success.

Neville Chamberlain is dead. Of the two occasions I saw him, in
Munich and in Rome, I have pleasant memories. He was a simple
man, spontaneous and human. Mussolini does not attach any weight
to the event, and commented: "This time he definitely missed the
bus," and he was so pleased with his own remark that he asked me to
include it in my diary.

November 11, 1940

I received today Stackic, a lawyer from Belgrade, who was introduced to me by Galeazzo di Bagno. He is on a mission from the royal
house of Serbia and, more precisely, for Antic, Minister of the Royal
House. It appears that Antic would like to meet me for the purpose
of strengthening ties between Italy and Yugoslavia. He even talks of an
alliance with far-reaching guarantees, among which is included the
demilitarization of the Adriatic. I referred the matter to Mussolini,
who encouraged the project. I am extremely favorable to it. I always
considered an attack on Yugoslavia a difficult undertaking and not
useful for the future equilibrium of Europe. Instead of bringing home
to us a mass of nervous and untrustworthy Croats, I believe it is better
to create a solid basis of understanding between Italy and Yugoslavia.
This would be useful if the morrow brings us an anti-Russian or an
anti-German policy.

From Albania we receive news that the situation is re-established.
Had we had more adequate forces we could have gone far. Now we
can only wait. Unfortunately, success, when it does come, will no longer
be of the first magnitude.

From many sources, and especially from Moscow, comes news of a
certain anti-Italian attitude, and even actual anti-Italian propaganda
that the Germans are spreading in Greece.

November 12, 1940

A black day. The British, without warning, have attacked the Italian fleet at anchor in Taranto, and have sunk the dreadnought *Cavour* and seriously damaged the battleships *Littorio* and *Duilio*. These ships will remain out of the fight for many months. I thought I would find the Duce downhearted. Instead, he took the blow quite well and does not, at the moment, seem to have fully realized its gravity. When Badoglio last came to see me at the Palazzo Chigi, he said that when we attacked Greece we should immediately have to move the fleet, which would no longer be safe in the port of Taranto; why was this not done a fortnight after the beginning of operations and with a full moon?

The British bombardment also did serious damage to Durazzo. The Agijo [oil refinery] is burning. Fortunately the port is intact. It is very important to keep it from being damaged, since it is our only access to Albania. It has worked well and is still working splendidly. No slowing down or bottleneck in this port. I remember what happened at Massawa at the beginning of the Ethiopian campaign, and the comparison is gratifying, but anti-aircraft defense is scarce and the British attacks will most certainly be intensified.

November 13, 1940

The Duce is beginning seriously to lose faith in Badoglio. He has given me orders to keep my eye on him carefully and constantly to find out what he really says to the Germans in his coming meeting with Keitel at Innsbruck.

Mussolini read me the speech which he will deliver to the chiefs of the party on the eighteenth of November. It is good, but contains nothing new or different. I shall be absent, because on that day I shall be at a meeting with Hitler; Serrano Suñer will also be present.

November 14, 1940

Antonescu and Sturdza arrive. My impressions of the first man are fair. As to the second, he isn't even worth talking about. Mussolini has called him "one of those who performs Russian dances."

The interview at the Palazzo Venezia is rather dull. Antonescu makes a very strong attack on the decision at Vienna, and says that the verdict was given on the basis of a colored sheet of paper printed by the Hungarians. If the colors had been reversed the verdict would have been favorable to the Rumanians. I did not want to go on arguing, but I must confess that he was not very courteous in speaking with one of the two arbiters.

Farinacci tells me that Mussolini, in speaking of the Greek affair, told him that "even Count Ciano has given him inexact information," and then, speaking of the Fascist party, that "Count Ciano had made a present of Muti to the party." Farinacci said that he protested vigorously. I shall only answer that I had the same information as Mussolini about Albania, and as regards Muti it is timely to recall that from the first of January on I constantly denounced his incapacity and advised that he be replaced at once.

November 15, 1940

It seems that the Greeks have resumed their attack all along the front, and with considerable forces. Up to now we have resisted very well. This is also confirmed by a letter from Starace, which, with all its realism, is not pessimistic. Above all, he blames Visconti Prasca, who had too lightly asserted that everything was ready to the last detail, while, as a matter of fact, the organization of our forces was altogether defective.

The King does not like colored shirts very much, whatever their shade. Yesterday, at the court, he told me, "These Rumanians in their green shirts are really ridiculous. They remind me of the hotel porters in old Russia."

In the evening the news from Albania is more serious. Pressure continues, and resistance is more difficult. And then we lack guns, while the Greek artillery is modern and well handled.

Under the circumstances, Comrade De Vecchi is thinking seriously of offering his resignation as Governor of the Aegean, and yet he was one of the most active, in fact the most active, inciter of Mussolini in the war against Greece. But now that he realizes the time has arrived for the rats to scuttle he wants to be the first to land.

November 16, 1940

We are putting up a strong resistance in Albania.

Departure of the Rumanians, who, on the whole, have not made a deep impression.

November 17, 1940

I leave for Salzburg. News from Albania is uncertain; an eventual withdrawal is not to be excluded.

November 18, 1940

A rather enigmatic Ribbentrop meets me in Salzburg. Before lunch, in his house at Fuschl, he decides to talk, that is to announce that Hitler will speak on the situation created by the Greek crisis. The Germans are gloomy, and it is not difficult to understand why. I had lunch with Serrano and Ribbentrop. Serrano is outspoken. He chats away with a freedom the Germans don't like, criticizing especially the German effort to get together with the French. He thinks this understanding is difficult and he doesn't believe that Laval is the right man to bring it about.

In the afternoon I saw Hitler at Berghof. A long tea with Serrano and the others, and then a personal conversation with Hitler, Ribbentrop, and an interpreter. I outlined the conversation in a letter to the Duce. There was a heavy atmosphere. Hitler is pessimistic and considers the situation much compromised by what has happened in the Balkans. His criticism is open, definite, and final. I try to talk to him, but he does not allow me to proceed. Only in the second part of the conversation, that is, after Hitler gave his consent to eventual negotiations with Yugoslavia, does he become warm and cordial, at times almost friendly. The idea of an alliance with Yugoslavia excites him to the point that while his pessimism at first appeared too black now his optimism seems too rosy.

November 19, 1940 [continuation of November 18]

He tells me some secrets: even that Horthy urged him at the time of his trip to Italy to raise the question of Trieste, that is, he wanted to launch Hungarian nationalistic pretensions to Fiume. (Can I believe all this?) "For the moment," Hitler added, "it is necessary to dissemble with the Hungarians, as we need their railroads. But the moment will come when we shall speak clearly." (However much he dissembles, the Hungarians know his ideas very well.) From the hotel I write a long letter to the Duce. I lay emphasis on the Yugoslav affair, because I am convinced that it will be very much to the liking of the Germans at this moment. I believe that Mussolini will raise strong objections, at least he will refuse all military help in the matter before he has taken his revenge on the Greeks.

Alternative news of defeats and victories on the Albanian front. I fear that we shall have to withdraw to a pre-established line. The loss of Corcia is certainly not the loss of Paris, but it will serve to give a name to the battle and help the enemy to beat the drums of propaganda against Italy. This is why I hope that we may hold on to Corcia.

On my way to Vienna by train.

November 20, 1940

Signature of Hungary's adherence. Rumanian and Slovakian adherences will follow. I do not attach much importance to the adherence of these states, which are vassals of Germany, or almost so. In fact, they weaken the tripartite agreement itself, and seem to be the useless bits of ersatz diplomacy of our victory. In Germany they talked too much about everything being finished by October, and in fact the Viennese people, who always have their witticisms ready, said, "They were right: oil, butter, and meat are finished." Austrian morale is low.

A few not very interesting words with the Hungarians.

Again a conference with Hitler. He speaks exclusively of Yugoslavia and is satisfied that the Duce has, in principle, given his consent. He plans to call the Regent, Paul, to Berlin, and to propose the big deal to him. He is disposed to favor the accession of Paul himself to the throne. His wife is ambitious. This seems difficult to me. Paul is not enough of a Serb in spirit and ways to be loved by his people. In the end, Hitler has one of his characteristic fits of emotion. "From this city of Vienna, on the day of the Anschluss, I sent Mussolini a telegram to assure him that I would never forget his help. I confirm it today, and I am at his side with all my strength." He had two big tears in his eyes. What a strange man! He hands me a sealed letter.

November 21, 1940

Hitler's letter to the Duce is in the same tone as the first part of the conference—critical and full of concern. I expected a violent reaction from Mussolini. Instead, there is nothing. He does not seem to attribute any importance to a document which, indeed, has a great deal. I find the Duce calm, decided, not concerned. What is happening in Albania saddens but does not disturb him. He is critical of our military men, of Badoglio, and announces an imminent change of guard in the military sector.

During the evening Soddu announces that he intends to abandon Corcia and withdraw on the entire front. And yet the Greek pressure seems to be less. Mussolini intervenes to get him to reconsider, but the machine is in motion and it cannot be stopped now.

November 22, 1940

Mussolini is preparing his answer to Hitler's letter—on rereading it he had realized its full import. "He really smacked my fingers." Thus he concludes. The answer is brief and calm. He accepts Hitler's political and military proposals.

Pavolini recounts confidentially that Badoglio said to him: "There is no doubt that Jacomoni and Visconti Prasca have a large share of the responsibility in the Albanian affair, but the real blame must be sought elsewhere. It lies entirely in the Duce's command. This is a command that he, the Duce, cannot hold. Let him leave everything to us, and when things go wrong let him punish those responsible." Pavolini dutifully informed the Duce about it. The Duce's reaction was like a flash. He called Badoglio names like "enemy of the regime" and "traitor," which are strong epithets for him to use about his own Chief of Staff in wartime.

November 23, 1940

Sebastiani revealed to me this morning that the Duce is studying the military *Annuario* [an official state publication listing the officers of the armed forces in order of their age and seniority], in order to find substitutes for Badoglio and Soddu. His eye seems to have rested on the names of Pintor and Orlando, the latter being an unknown. Mussolini himself said nothing to me about it. In any case, even if he asks me, I intend to keep out of it, since I know little about military affairs. Personally, I like Messe, and I recall that my father thought well of Gazzera.

In the *Regime Fascista* [Fascist daily in Cremona, published by Farinacci] Farinacci makes an open attack on Badoglio, thereby precipitating a crisis.

I had a brief telephone conversation with Ribbentrop. Hitler has not yet examined the Duce's letter, and therefore can make no reply. I shall talk to him again tomorrow. News from Albania is of an orderly retreat without pressure from the enemy.

November 24, 1940

Nothing new.

November 25, 1940

Soddu confirms our information on better news from Albania. He considers that the forces under him are sufficient to guarantee a stabilization of the line. The Badoglio crisis is out in the open. Badoglio calls for a denial from Farinacci, couched in such terms that I am certain the latter will dynamite the rotary press of his paper rather than accept. Badoglio insists that if a denial is not published he is going to leave. Mussolini now desires to liquidate him. He goes slowly, because this is his nature in such matters, and because he wants to let time take its course. He speaks about Pintor and Gazzera.

November 26, 1940

Badoglio, after a conference with the Duce, has handed in his letter of resignation. Farinacci persists in his refusal to publish a retraction. We cannot go on in this way. When we add to this that Badoglio was confronted with Pavolini's written statement, we begin to see the outlines of the situation. Today the ushers at the doors of the Palazzo Venezia were given instructions to accompany the most important Italian big shots into different rooms, in order to prevent a general brawl.

November 27, 1940

The General Staff crisis continues. Mussolini has accepted in principle the resignation of Badoglio, but he must yet overcome some last-minute uncertainties. He wants to draw up a despatch in which it is said that "Badoglio has submitted his resignation for reasons of health and age." This formula does not suit Badoglio, but Mussolini insists, for in this way he intends to nip in the bud the candidacy of "that roguish old madman, General de Bono." Meanwhile, Badoglio has retired, not to his tent, but to the villa of his friend Necchi in the vicinity of Milan. Nevertheless, this is a situation that cannot go on.

From Albania the news from Soddu indicates progressive improvement. News from Starace, on the other hand, is not very optimistic, since he still feels that our situation is hanging by a thread.

I see De Vecchi. He speaks with less logic than usual, and cannot explain his resignation.

He would really like to leave, but knows he will cut a bad figure. Notwithstanding his incomparable conceit, he is ashamed, but not to the point of refraining from applying for another post at the same time.

November 28, 1940

Conference between De Vecchi and Mussolini, which ends in no decision. De Vecchi said that "he is ready to serve elsewhere, but that he expects lots of chevrons on his sleeve." The Duce did not react.

Bad news from Albania. Greek pressure continues, but above all our resistance is growing weak. If the Greeks had strength enough to penetrate our lines we might yet have a great deal of trouble.

November 29, 1940

The Duce has appointed Guzzoni Undersecretary of War and Assistant Chief of the General Staff. In general, this appointment is well received.

Starace, who has just come from Albania, sees things in pretty dark colors, and passes severe judgment on the behavior of our troops. Our soldiers have fought but little, and badly. This is the real, fundamental cause of all that has happened.

November 30, 1940

Meeting of the Council of Ministers. The Duce talks at length about the situation. He reads the principal documents and, while personally assuming responsibility for the political decisions, he directs some hard blows at Badoglio as regards military action. The Duce's thesis is this: Badoglio was not only in agreement, but even over-enthusiastic. The political side of the question was handled perfectly; military action was entirely inadequate. He did not conceal the gravity of the situation, that is the imminent retreat to the south and the enemy's attack now going on in the Pogradec zone. "The situation is serious," said the Duce. "It might even become tragic." In the Council of Ministers there was a genuine rebellion against De Vecchi when the Chief mentioned his name and read the telegrams in which he had spurred him on to the attack of Greece.

The Duce called in General Cavallero, and this reveals his intentions. Cavallero is an optimist who does not believe in the possibility of a defeat in Albania, having full faith in our ability to take the offensive once more. I record everything but guarantee nothing. I am becoming more and more cautious in military matters. The Duce does not mention any appointments or jobs to General Cavallero. He listens to him at length, and invites him to another meeting tomorrow. In the meantime, Badoglio continues to shoot pheasants.

December 1, 1940

News from Albania has improved. We are holding and even counterattacking in the north, while in the south the withdrawal continues without enemy pressure. In his conversation with Cavallero the Duce tells him about his impending appointment as Chief of the General Staff. It is still impending, being delayed until Badoglio returns to Rome.

We have indirect news of German-Yugoslav negotiations. Nothing has been communicated to us, although they are discussing matters which concern us.

I can't say that the Germans are very tactful with us.

December 2, 1940

Nothing worth mentioning. A discussion with the Nuncio about the abolition of holidays on New Year, Epiphany, and St. Joseph's. This is a bright idea of the Duce, who is very proud of it. At my insistence he relented as to the celebration of St. Joseph's day, but he holds firm on the other two holidays, and especially on New Year's, "since it is no other than the day of the circumcision of Christ, that is, the celebration of a Hebrew rite, which the Church itself has abolished." I wonder whether, in times like these, it is worth while irritating the people with whims of this sort.

December 3, 1940

Greek pressure has started again on the Albanian front, and it seems that the 11th Army must now make that withdrawal from Argirocastro and Port Edda which we had hoped to avoid.

December 4, 1940

Sorice telephones at an early hour that we have lost Pogradec and that the Greeks have broken through our lines. Then he informs us that Soddu now thinks that "any military action has become impossible and the situation must be settled through political intervention." Mussolini calls me to the Palazzo Venezia. I find him discouraged as never before. He says: "There is nothing else to do. This is grotesque and absurd, but it is a fact. We have to ask for a truce through Hitler." This is impossible. The Greeks will, as a first condition, ask the Führer's personal guarantee that nothing will ever be done against them again.

I would rather put a bullet through my head than telephone Ribbentrop. Is it possible that we are defeated? May it not be that the commander has laid down his arms before his men? I am in no position to give military suggestions, but rigorous logic tells me that if a rout has not already started it is still possible to form a bridgehead at Valona and, with fresh forces, a safety line on the river Skumbini. What counts now is to resist, and to stick to Albania. Time will bring victory, but if we give up it is the end. Mussolini listens to me and decides to make a fresh attempt. He sends Cavallero to the front. Later, he has a new attack of discouragement and says, "Every man must make one fatal error in his life. And I made mine when I believed General Visconti Prasca. But how could I have avoided it when this man seemed so sure of himself and when every indication had given us full assurance? The human material I have to work with is useless, worthless."

The idea strikes me that I can perhaps verify the situation through Jacomoni, and I call him on the telephone. I immediately get the impression that in Tirana they are more at ease than in Rome. I fear that some misunderstanding lurks in the air. In fact, Jacomoni says that "as a political solution, Soddu had intended a military diversion on the Greek flank, such as a German or Yugoslav intervention." News from the High Command also improved during the day, and Soddu and Cavallero leave for Elbasau, to study the situation on the spot.

During the evening I see the Duce again. He was more relieved. He has had a talk with Badoglio, who meant to withdraw his resignation. Too late. Mussolini asserts that the King himself encouraged him to accept it, saying that, "in his opinion, Badoglio is now too tired."

December 5, 1940

News from Albania indicates that the situation is unchanged. The time gained is entirely in our favor, the more so since the Germans have given us fifty transport planes. In this way traffic is facilitated.

De Vecchi's resignation has also been accepted, and he will be replaced by Bastico. The Duce intends to replace Admiral Cavagnari by Admiral Riccardi. My father's opinion of the latter was not very high.

I succeed in having the Duce restore the New Year and Epiphany holidays. I inform the Nuncio of it. It was not worth while to create a crisis with the Vatican in times like these.

December 6, 1940

News from Albania unchanged.

Conference with Marshal Milch, who has come to Rome to settle the question of the Stukas in the Mediterranean. He was calm and optimistic on the situation in general, as well as on the Greek question. Hitler's letter, of which he was the bearer, also differs substantially in content and in form from the one sent from Vienna. The Albanian affair is minimized, considered certain of solution, an episode in the great picture in which the prospects are good. All this has greatly relieved Mussolini, who passes on to a counterattack, even about internal matters. "If, when I was a Socialist," he said, "I had had a knowledge of the work of the Italian middle class, not purely theoretical as learned by the reading of Karl Marx, but practical, based on experience such as I have now, I would have launched a revolution so pitiless that, by comparison, the revolution of Comrade Lenin would have been child's play."

Cavallero has been appointed [Chief of the General Staff]. Repercussions are not good, especially in military circles. The man is much discussed. Opinions vary, but no one says that he is stupid.

December 7, 1940

A speech by Zvetkovic marks the beginning of a maneuver for the conversion of Yugoslavia. Stackic also announces that he will soon make a trip to Italy and will be followed shortly by Antic, Minister of the Court. In a conference with Christic I underlined our good disposition toward his country, and alluded to the Slavism of the Vardar Valley. Mussolini is calm, and as firm as a rock. Now that he has removed De Vecchi he is glad he has done it. He put in the despatch the words "at his request," in order to make it clear to all concerned that "at the time when these men should have made a request to reenter the ranks of the Fascists, they have asked to leave them."

Cavallero returns from Albania. He still considers the situation critical but on the way to a solution. Within a week our lines, which still suffer from slight oscillations, will be definitely stabilized. Within a short time he is thinking of making a local counterattack that would again assure us of the possession of Corcia, which, from the point of view of prestige, would be a great thing. News from Greece confirms reports that the situation is serious.

December 8, 1940

Nothing new.

December 9, 1940

The Fascist party has launched a counterattack against Badoglio which is probably exaggerated; as it even speaks of treason. Serena [new chief secretary of the Fascist party] has told me what he was doing and explained his tactics. I do not entirely agree. Every exaggeration hits back because it touches on the honor of the Army itself. In fact, Badoglio went to protest to the Duce and obtained a rather friendly reply.

December 10, 1940

News of the attack on Sidi Barrani comes like a thunderbolt. At first it doesn't seem serious, but subsequent telegrams from Graziani confirm that we have had a licking. Mussolini, whom I see twice, is very calm. He comments on the event with impersonal objectivity. It almost seems that what has happened doesn't concern him in the least, he being more preoccupied with Graziani's prestige, and disposed not to recognize the seriousness of what has happened. But it is serious, at home and abroad. It is serious outside of Italy because from the tone of Graziani's telegrams it does not appear that he has sufficiently recovered from the blow to prepare a counterattack. Inside of Italy, because it makes matters worse. Public opinion had already been shaken and too much divided to receive this new and heavy blow.

Hitler's speech did not make a good impression. It is more defensive than offensive, and one feels that Italy plays a very secondary role.

December 11, 1940

Things are really going badly in Libya. Four divisions can be considered destroyed, and Graziani, who reports on the spirit and decision of the enemy, says nothing about what he can do to parry the blow. Mussolini becomes more and more calm. He maintains that the many painful days through which we are living must be considered inevitable in the changing fortunes of every war. He still hopes that Graziani can and will stop the English advance. If it can be stopped at the old boundary, the situation will not be serious, he thinks; if the English should reach Tobruk, then he thinks the situation would verge on the tragic.

During the evening news arrives that the Catanzaro division did not hold against the English push but was itself torn to pieces. Something is the matter with our Army if five divisions allow themselves to be pulverized in two days.

December 12, 1940

We are easing up in Albania. Doing poorly in Libya. Graziani telegraphs little news and gives no details. He has not yet recovered from
the blow he has suffered, and besides, it seems that his nerves are quite
shaken since the time of the attempt on his life in Addis Ababa. They
tell me that even in Italy he was so much afraid of attempts on his life
that he had his villa at Arciruzzo guarded by at least eighteen carabinièri. In Libya he had a refuge built in a Roman tomb at Cyrene,
sixty or seventy feet deep. Now he is upset and cannot make decisions.
He pins his hopes on the possible exhaustion of the adversary, and not
on his own strength, which is a bad sign. The Duce now feels the
gravity of events. "In Libya we have suffered a real defeat. This time
it will not be said that politics is to blame. I have left the military
authorities the most ample freedom of action. Today the King is very
gloomy."

I have seen von Mackensen. He came on a pretext. Naturally we
spoke of the situation, and I did not conceal how matters stand. He
has shown solidarity and comprehension. Ansaldo reports that von
Ribbentrop has done the same in a conference he had with him in
Berlin. During the evening Sebastiani suggests that I should go to the
Palazzo Venezia. A catastrophic telegram has arrived from Graziani, a
mixture of excitement, rhetoric, and concern. He is thinking of withdrawing to Tripoli, "in order to keep the flag flying on that fortress at
least," but he is inclined to make accusations against Rommel, that
is, Mussolini, for having obliged him to wage a war "of the flea against
the elephant."

I visit Mussolini and find him very much shaken. I have nothing to
tell him, but desire only by my presence to give him to understand
that I am more than ever with him. He realizes how the country will
feel the blow. He listens to my suggestion about doing something to
raise the morale of the people. We must speak to the hearts of the
Italians. We must make them understand that what is at stake in
the game is not Fascism—it is our country, our eternal country, the
country of all of us, which is above men and times and factions.

December 13, 1940

The morning news seems better, and the Duce is relieved. For my part I am skeptical, since the force of the attack and the feeble resistance of the troops do not give us grounds to hope for anything good. I do not at all believe, as the Duce does, that the English will be content to eject us from Egypt and stop at the frontier. They have more far-reaching objectives.

December 14, 1940

News from Libya seems to improve. Graziani sends less telegrams and is not so gloomy as before. Soddu continues to send disturbing reports from Albania, while Cavallero's telephone calls are quite serene. Mussolini says, "Five generals are prisoners and one is dead. This is the percentage of Italians who have military characteristics and those who have none. In the future we shall create an army of professionals, selecting them out of twelve or thirteen million Italians— those in the valley of the Po and in part of central Italy. All the others will be put to work making arms for the warrior aristocracy."

During the evening bad news again. While I am dining at the German Embassy the Duce telephones to inquire about a crisis in the French Government. The Germans don't seem too concerned about it. Their attitude toward us is grim. In German eyes one does not yet read the verdict of guilty but surely finds in them many questions.

December 15, 1940

I find the Duce calm but indignant toward Graziani because of a long telegram of recrimination in which he talks "man to man" and scolds the Duce for having permitted himself to be betrayed by his Roman military collaborators, for never having listened to him, and for having pushed him into an adventure which leads us beyond human possibilities into the realms of destiny. Mussolini reads it to me and says, "Here is another man with whom I cannot get angry, because I despise him." The Duce still believes that the British advance can be stopped at the approaches to Derna.

In Albania also there was a retreat, which Cavallero considers not to be serious and of purely strategic value to the enemy. He believes that his reserves are sufficient to stop the gap.

I receive Marchesa Graziani. She is beside herself. She has received a letter from her husband containing his will, and in it he says that "one cannot break steel armor with fingernails alone." He asks for a mass intervention of German aviation in Libya, which might still change the present rout into a victory. Even if this idea were taken into account, would the Germans risk sending their planes on such short notice without time to prepare for replacements and transports? I don't think so. The only thing that is certain is that Marshal Graziani has lost his self-control.

December 16, 1940

A lull in Albania and in Libya, where, however, the enemy is massing for an attack on Bardia. A meeting with the Duce concerning the request to Germany for raw materials. The sad story begins. We are not asking for too much, but it is always hard to ask for anything, especially at this moment.

December 17, 1940

Again a bad withdrawal in Albania toward Clisura and Tepeleni. The Duce has prepared a letter, a harsh letter, to Cavallero, with an order to the troops to die at their posts. "More than an order from me," he wrote, "it is an order from our country." Let us hope that this lash will have its effect.

In the city the rumor has spread of a great Italian victory with tens of thousands of prisoners and hundreds of tanks destroyed. In a flash the rumor has swept the peninsula. There is no truth in it. It is a maneuver, cunning and base, to break down our morale. They tell me that after Caporetto, too, the same thing happened, and that the country was inflamed by the hopes aroused by false news and was then plunged into an even gloomier desolation. Anticipation of the war of nerves.

December 18, 1940

I confer at length with Cavallero, who has returned from Albania. He is distinctly optimistic. He not only thinks that a notable surprise is possible, but he also believes that the critical phase is almost over, and he is planning to strike the first offensive blow at Clisura day after tomorrow. This is to be followed by another in the Tomorrizza Valley. He thinks that by the first of February he will have completed preparations for an offensive that should bring us to Corcia; from there on he will press the offensive as rapidly as possible. Being in this spirit, he attaches little importance to the vicissitudes that our lines have suffered in the last few days.

Little news from Libya, where English forces continue to press us around Bardia. Nevertheless, its means of defense are such that if Bergonzoli holds firm the English will not have an easy task.

I received the National Council of the Veterans' Association and speak to it. It does not take many words to kindle the faith that is in the hearts of all Italians, and which only awaits an occasion to express itself.

December 19, 1940

I cannot say that what has happened has proved Cavallero right. The Siena division, which was operating on the shore line, was broken to pieces by a Greek attack. The position is dangerous. Once they enter the valley of Sciuscizza the march on Valona is easy and natural, and it is not difficult to see how heavy a loss the fall of Valona would be. Mussolini is irritated because he feels that our forces are not fighting back and their officers are low in morale. To this must be added the fact that when Soddu talks to the Duce he says one thing, and when he talks to Sorice he says another. For him, the important strategy is not the one directed at the Greeks, but the one directed at the Palazzo Venezia.

December 20, 1940

Jealousies among generals are worse than among women. One should hear Soddu's telephone calls to Sorice. He demolishes all the generals. Geloso has softening of the brain, Perugi is a disaster, Trionfi is bankrupt. Today, for some unknown reason, he speaks well of Vercellino, saying, "Poor Vercellino. He is such a dear. He came to see me and he wept."

The Duce has prepared a message for Hitler. He presents things as they are and asks for German intervention in Thrace through Bulgaria. I don't think that Hitler can do this before March. In any case, the message will not be sent immediately. The Duce awaits Cavallero's report and probably also the results of our counterattack at Tepeleni, where two fresh divisions have arrived, the Cuneo and the Acqui.

Churchill has made another speech. It is, naturally, hard on us, for he says cruel things as to the value of our forces in Libya, where the situation continues to be serious. It is an able speech, in which many hints can be read between the lines.

December 21, 1940

Nothing new or noteworthy on the two fronts.

Mussolini, who feels a little better, has a long conversation with the military attaché, Marras, in my presence. It deals with eventual German military help. Marras comes to these conclusions: (1) before March Hitler can engage in no actions in Thrace; (2) it is useless to ask for German troops in Valona because they could not arrive within a month; (3) they might consider sending two armored divisions to Libya. The Duce is in agreement on these points.

December 22, 1940

Cavallero, who is the fellow who always sounds the optimistic note, says that the counterattack on the coast line will be ready tomorrow or the day after. We do not expect great results, but hope to lessen pressure on Valona. This would be a success, because Valona represents a strategic objective of the first order for the Greeks and the English, and also because we shall recover the initiative.

December 23, 1940

Nothing new, but I find the Duce rather irritated over Saturday's withdrawal, contrary to the expectations of Cavallero. Instead of lessening, the pressure on Valona is now increasing. The Duce no longer believes what Cavallero says. "These generals have become," affirms Mussolini, "like those country innkeepers who paint a rooster on the wall and under it write 'When this rooster begins to crow, to you credit I'll bestow.' I, too, will grant the military men credit when they prove by some action that the situation has changed." Then, speaking of the rather indifferent behavior of our troops, he added, "I must nevertheless recognize that the Italians of 1914 were better than these. It is not flattering for the regime, but that's the way it is."

December 24, 1940

It is snowing. The Duce looks out of the window and is glad that it is snowing. "This snow and cold are very good," he says. "In this way our good-for-nothing men and this mediocre race will be improved. One of the principal reasons I have desired the reforestation of the Apennines has been to make Italy colder and more snowy."

A long conference with Melchiori, who has come from Cyrenaica. He is Graziani's liaison officer, hence, pretty much in the heart of things. In his opinion the situation has clearly grown better, and we shall no longer have any sudden surprises. Graziani openly accuses Badoglio of treachery, and says that even in his gloomiest hours the only thing that prevented him from committing suicide was his strong desire to drag Badoglio one day to the dock.

December 25, 1940

Christmas. The Duce is somber, and speaks again about the situation in Albania. He appears more tired than usual, and this saddens me very much. The energy of the Duce at this time is our greatest resource. He no longer believes in Cavallero. He says that his optimism is like that of one whistling in the dark. In fact, Cavallero reports from Tirana that "the height of the crisis has been passed, and now there is a complete change of spirit in the troops."

December 26, 1940

Nothing new.

December 27, 1940

The usual story in Albania, and this displeases the Duce. He is right. Notwithstanding Cavallero's bright words one cannot read the situation clearly. He promises this offensive of the valley of Sciuscizza, but it does not take place, and we would not be surprised if once again the Greeks should launch theirs first.

December 28, 1940

Nothing new.

December 29, 1940

I went to Cortellazzo for the inauguration of the village dedicated to my father. A simple and brief ceremony.

In Venice I saw little and can say little about how the people feel. Some degrees below freezing, and the lagoons are covered with ice; such being the case, the Venetians are unwilling to interest themselves in politics.

December 30, 1940

During my absence the Duce conferred the command of the armed forces on Cavallero, and took it away from Soddu. For some time he had been dissatisfied with Soddu's temperamental changes of humor. One day all rosy, and another all black. The final blow came when the Duce learned that Soddu, even in Albania, was devoting his evening hours to composing music for the films.

December 31, 1940

Cavallero transmits a copy of a letter addressed to the Duce, in which he asks his permission for an offensive action in grand style along the coast. It is like inviting the hare to run. No one more than the Duce gnaws his lips on account of this interminable defensive that day after day forces him to swallow bitter pills.

Parini at the Palazzo Venezia. He speaks of what the party is doing for the troops. His opinion of the future is rather bright, but he is very severe about the past.

AGENDA

1941

Anno XIX - E. F.

Agenda tipo 524 marca A.G.B

January 1, 1941

The year has begun with a violent emotion about Mother's health. A heart attack put her dear life in danger. Then she improved, but all this has left me in great anxiety.

The Duce has received a long letter from Hitler; it contains a full survey of the situation. The Führer is serene about the future prospects of the war, but he thinks that many decisions are still necessary and he enumerates them with his usual precision.

I write to Alfieri to acquaint him with our negotiations with Russia, and to inform Ribbentrop also. These are no longer in the stage of broad and superficial conversations; the Russians wish to go to the bottom of many fundamental and important questions, on which I would consider it imprudent for us to commit ourselves without first having agreed with the Germans.

Cavallero announces as imminent his attack along the coast.

January 2, 1941

News from Hungary leads us to believe that internal conditions in Greece are serious. The Greek military attaché to Budapest is himself supposed to have said that there is very little his country can do now. On the other hand, Bulgaria seems to have decided to align itself with the Axis. Filof will soon go to confer with the Germans.

January 3, 1941

Prince Hesse asks, on behalf of Hitler, the Duce's feelings toward the Führer, since certain attitudes on the part of the military have created the impression in Germany that the Duce is showing some coolness. I replied that never before has the Duce been more grateful to Hitler for his solidarity and for his friendship—a reply that corresponds to the truth 100 per cent.

During the conversation with Hesse, Guzzoni telephones, saying that a British attack on Bardia makes the situation there extremely precarious. This is painful, but it should not surprise us. To think that, after its initial success, the British attack could be exhausted was, in my opinion, comforting but very erroneous.

I inform Mackensen, who is going to Berlin about our negotiations with Moscow.

January 4, 1941

A meeting of the Council of Ministers. The Duce makes a long exposition of the military situation in Libya as well as in Albania; the first rather somber, the second somewhat optimistic. In reality, the attack on Bardia seems to have fully succeeded, for only two hours after the fighting began Bergonzoli considered the situation of the stronghold very critical. The Duce read all documents, including Graziani's telegrams written "during the time that this man had lost his senses, or at least his mind." He is very hard on all the marshals, except Pecori Giraldi, for whom he has great respect. He confines himself to naming de Bono, adding quickly afterward, "I want you to note that I have said nothing about him." On the whole he seems to be unmoved and hopeful of a solution, after which "a third wave will come, the most formidable of all, one which will upset institutions and men who have revealed their real nature in this hour, and of whom I am now quietly preparing the lists."

Grandi is displeased and terrified because of a letter sent him by Farinacci, who invites him to come out in the open and drop his self-imposed equivocal reserve.

January 5, 1941

Ever since 4 P.M. yesterday the Bardia radio has been silent. We know what transpires only from the British communiqués. The resistance of our troops was brief—a matter of hours. And yet there was no lack of arms. The guns alone numbered four hundred and thirty. Why didn't the fight continue longer? Is this still a case of the flea against the elephant? "A peculiar flea," says Mussolini, "one that between Sidi el Barrani, Bardia, and Tobruk, had at its disposal more than a thousand guns. One day I shall decide to open the dikes and tell the whole truth to the Italians who have been befuddled by too many lies. After my speech of January 3 I shall speak again on the third of February—one of those speeches that draw blood. I am waiting only until Cavallero succeeds in striking a first blow at the Greeks, then I shall speak."

During the evening news arrives that Bardia, though cut in two, is still resisting. For how long? It would be important if we could wear out the British and prevent their carrying out more ambitious programs, such as the recent successes might very well have inspired.

I telegraphed Alfieri for a Hitler-Mussolini meeting somewhere between the twelfth and the nineteenth. Up to this point Mussolini has procrastinated. He does not like to meet Hitler, burdened by these numerous failures, until they have been at least in part redressed.

January 6, 1941

After a long time I again saw the King, who was preoccupied and shaken by the situation in Libya. He does not believe that the forces arrayed at Tobruk and on the approaches of Derna are sufficient to stop the British advance. He is incredulous with regard to Germany. And even when I talk to him about Hitler's perfectly loyal attitude toward us he is skeptical. "He has treated you courteously only because he had to and could not do otherwise," he said. "But he is a German like the others, and will deal with Italy only on the basis of a brutal utilitarianism. Nor do I believe that Hitler has the power to do anything he wishes. The military element is strong in Germany, and even Bismarck, who has a really good head on him, had to submit to it." Then he went on to criticize our military organization. "For too long a time a chair has been called a palace in Italy," he said; "but this does not change the fact that a chair remains a chair. Thus it happens that our divisions, small and unarmed, are divisions in name only." Then he mentioned an eventual British landing in Italy, which explains why he is against any excessive weakening of the home front. In spite of all this he maintains that the war will end in a German victory, because Hitler has unified the European continent against England.

January 7, 1941

The fall of Bardia has again shaken public morale. The internal situation becomes grim. "This is a washing," says Mussolini, "for the drying of which at least a week is necessary." [It will take a week for the nation to get over it.] In the meeting of the Council of Ministers the Duce surveyed the situation without comment, soberly, fearlessly, with a calm which in these days seems really superhuman. He read the list of the generals and colonels who have been replaced in the course of recent weeks because of their lack of human or professional value, deducing from this many bitter judgments on the Army and on its personnel. Finally, he proposed an order of the day which was approved by unanimous vote. The last phrase is significant: an appeal to the Italian masses, "proletarian and Fascist." The hostile and complaining middle class is playing a dangerous game. It does not know Mussolini and is not aware that he can take an awful amount of punishment, and is capable, at the same time, of harboring deep resentment. If he wins, in fact *when* he wins, the obstructionist bourgeoisie will have to deal with the old Socialist from Romagna it has succeeded in awakening.

Cavallero confirms his decision to attack soon, maybe tomorrow. It will be a limited attack, but one which in these times would have great moral worth.

[*January 8 and 9, 1941. No entries.*]

January 10, 1941

In my presence the Duce received the German Ambassador, who has just come from Hitler in regard to the date of a meeting between the two chiefs. It is decided for Sunday, the nineteenth, at Berchtesgaden. Mussolini is in excellent humor because the air and naval battle, now in progress in the Sicilian channel, is going very well. A British aircraft carrier and two destroyers are in flames. And this is not the end of it. The Duce says: "At last the moon has changed; a good one is out." He speaks of the necessity of always telling the people the truth, in the first place in order to raise morale, and, second, to win its confidence. "The people must know that life is a serious thing and that war is the most serious thing in life."

January 11, 1941

Yesterday evening's news on the air and sea battle was perhaps exaggerated. We cannot as yet establish whether the English carrier has been sunk or not. On the other hand, from Cavallero we are not getting very good news on the course of affairs in Albania. Clisura is lost.

In itself this means nothing. It is a mass of huts in a more or less dilapidated condition, but it is a name, and Anglo-Greek propaganda is already sounding all the trumpets of the press and radio. It also proves that the wall of resistance, that famous wall which we have been waiting for for seventy days, has not yet been formed. Our troops, even the fresh ones, hold out until Greek pressure starts, but they yield ground rapidly under attack. Why? Mussolini finds that the entire situation is an inexplicable drama, so much the more serious because it is inexplicable. Cavallero, with whom I have spoken by telephone, does not hide the gravity of what has happened, but he does not feel that the situation at Berat, and hence at Valona, has been compromised. He continues to speak of the famous attack along the coast, but of this, however, we see no concrete evidence.

January 12, 1941

Nothing new.

January 13, 1941

Tomorrow morning Mussolini is going to Foggia to meet the generals from Albania. He considers the moment has come to make some decision, especially because Guzzoni is very insistent that the offensive take place along the coast. He thinks that this will have the effect of exploding the Greek offensive plans and even of bringing us back to the old frontier.

The movement begins in Bulgaria. The nearness of the German troops already gives the impression that the tempo of events is about to quicken. Magistrati feels that Bulgaria will not openly array itself with the Axis but will allow itself to be invaded without too much opposition, even of a perfunctory character.

January 14, 1941

Nothing new. I conferred with von Mackensen to organize the Duce's trip to Berchtesgaden.

Alfieri, in a very secret letter, informs me that the campaign against me of the last few weeks has had a certain echo, though now it is all over, he says, even in Germany. This does not surprise me. The Germans have an old resentment for my non-belligerency and, even when they try to save appearances, cannot entirely conceal this resentment. This is so especially of Ribbentrop. Ever since Salzburg, 1939, our relations have changed, and my bet with Joachim on Anglo-French intervention is completely forgotten. I made the mistake of being right. Useless for them to split hairs about whether or not I was for the war with Greece; one thing is certain—I wanted no war at all.

January 15, 1941

No important news.

January 16, 1941

During the morning I had a meeting with the King; in the afternoon, another with the Duce. The King, who maintains an attitude which is more than cordial toward me, said that, with the German descent into Thrace, he considers the end of the Greek affair imminent. On the other hand, he considers the situation in Libya grave and thinks that the defense of Tobruk is a very serious mistake. It will have no practical results, and will only further weaken our already limited forces, while a courageous retreat on the coast line of Derna might have permitted us to resist, perhaps even victoriously. The Duce has returned from Puglie [a southern Italian province], where he conferred with Cavallero. He is somber and pessimistic. The front is not yet stabilized, notwithstanding the fact that we have sent many men and much matériel. The military sector is completely bankrupt. "Greece," he says, "was a political masterpiece; we succeeded in isolating that country and in having it fight against us all alone. Only the Italian Army failed us completely." He is concerned about his trip to Germany. He feels that he will meet Hitler under conditions of obvious inferiority.

On the Clisura front another Greek attack takes place. Let's hope that our troops will hold.

January 17, 1941

The topic of the day is the Duce's decision to mobilize by the first of February all the high Fascist officials—government, Grand Council,

Chamber, and party. When Serena made some objections about the practical possibility of the project, he answered that what he, the Duce, intends to do by working directly with the bureaucracy is an interesting experiment in government. We shall see. Nevertheless, in all the higher government circles there is a good deal of dissatisfaction over the decision and the manner in which it has been brought about.

In the anteroom of the Duce this morning I heard phrases and comments that surprised me. There is something in all of this government machinery that does not function well and it would be wise not to ignore it. Some people, such as Bottai, go so far as to speak of a real "*coup d'état* on the part of the Duce in order to get rid of Fascism and to place his reliance on other political currents." I do not believe all this. The more time passes the more I am inclined to discard anything too complicated. But the decision is certainly ominous, and perhaps this is not the time to undertake experiments "on the domestic front."

Cavallero is not going to Germany because a Greek attack is taking place. Guzzoni replaces him on the trip. I don't like this very much. I don't like him. He is a man who stirs up trouble, untrustworthy, and, besides, it is humiliating to present to the Germans such a small man with such a big paunch and with dyed hair.

January 18, 1941

Departure for Salzburg. Mussolini arrives at the train frowning and nervous. He is shaken by the news from Albania. Nothing too dramatic, but once again we have had a kick in the pants, leaving many prisoners in the hands of the enemy. The serious thing is that it involves the "Lupi di Toscana" [wolves of Tuscany], a division which has an excellent reputation and a grand tradition, landed only a short while ago in Albania, and on which we had put many hopes. The Duce talks at length about all this. He repeats his pessimism concerning the Army and the Italian people. He can't explain it all. He keeps repeating, "If anybody had predicted on October 15 what later actually happened, I would have had him shot." Then he changes the subject. He is very much amused by reading a comedy which has had great success in Germany, entitled *Cherry Trees in Rome*. The subject matter has to do with Lucullus and tries to prove that even a great strategist can have refined tastes and love comfortable living. Mussolini attributes the success of this comedy to a hidden vein of political satire, which escaped Nazi censorship.

January 19, 1941 [*continuation of January 18*]

He repeats one of his slogans to the effect that the German people more than any other love their food, their drink, and their entertainment, and says that, when he has time for it, he, too, will give himself over to self-indulgence.

We arrive at a small station. I think it is Puch. Hitler and his chiefs of staff are waiting for us on the platform in the snow. The weather is fair and the cold not too intense. The meeting is cordial, and, what surprises me most, spontaneously cordial. There are no hidden condolences in the air—condolences that Mussolini feared. There is, without delay, a meeting between Hitler and the Duce, and also one between me and Ribbentrop. A written report of the latter was presented. I am briefly informed about the other by Mussolini himself, who says that he found a very anti-Russian Hitler, loyal to us, and not too definite on what he intends to do in the future against Great Britain. In any case, it is no longer a question of landing in England. Hitler said that the undertaking would be extremely difficult and that if it failed the first time it could not be attempted again. Added to this there is the fact that, while England now fears the loaded pistol of invasion, after a failure she would know that Germany holds only an empty pistol.

January 20, 1941 [*continuation of January 19*]

Mussolini said that he brought Hitler up to date on Italian matters, including the undecided attitude of the King, which, however, does not influence others, and finally, also, about the Badoglio case, which Hitler compared to the Fritsch case. On the whole, the Duce is satisfied about the conversation. I am less so, especially because Ribbentrop, who in the past had always had an attitude of bravado, now, in answer to a definite question of mine on the length of the war, said that he sees no possibility of ending it before 1942. And how about us?

Subsequently, many conversations take place, the most important on Monday in the presence of military experts. Hitler talked for about two hours on his coming intervention in Greece; he dealt with the question primarily from a technical point of view, placing it in the general political panorama. I must admit that he does this with unusual mastery. Our military men are impressed.

January 21, 1941 [continuation of January 20]

Guzzoni, with his tightly stretched paunch and his little dyed wig, according to Alfieri, made a mediocre impression on the Germans. He expressed surprise about Hitler's deep understanding of military matters.

Result of the visit, generally good. There is absolute solidarity between the countries of the Axis, and we shall march together in the Balkans. To us is assigned the hard task of bringing back home the Spanish Prodigal Son. I wish to add that, in my opinion, if Spain falls away the fault rests in great part with the Germans and their uncouth manners in dealing with Latins, including the Spanish, who, probably because of their very qualities, are the most difficult to deal with.

On his return, Mussolini is elated as he always is after a meeting with Hitler.

I wrote a letter to Serrano, proposing a meeting in Genoa between the Duce and the Caudillo. We shall soon see the Spanish reaction.

January 22, 1941

The news from Rumania worries Berlin. The conflict between Antonescu and the Legionaries had been foreseen by Hitler on account of the equivocal situation that was created. Here the Führer has had no hesitation about his choice. His sympathies go to Antonescu, who has shown himself to be "a man of good faith, who is resolved to hold firm the baton of command, and a very thorough nationalist." In fact, von Ribbentrop telephoned late in the day that instructions have been given to the German Minister to support Antonescu in every way. He requests that the same thing be done with respect to Ghigi. Naturally I carry out the request, but I have the vague suspicion that the influence of our Minister is not so decisive as that of his German colleague.

Tobruk has fallen. There has been a little more fighting but only a little. The Duce is allowing himself to be lulled by his illusions. I thought it necessary to speak to him with brusque frankness. "At Sidi Barrani," I said, "they spoke of surprise. Then, you counted upon Bardia, where Bergonzoli was, the heroic Bergonzoli. Bardia yielded after two hours. Then you placed your hopes in Tobruk because Pitassi Mannella, the king of artillerymen, was there. Tobruk has also been easily wrested from us. Now you speak with great faith of the escarp-

ment of Derna. I beg to differ with your dangerous illusions. The
trouble is grave, mysterious, and deep." This is what I said, but in
reality there is very little mystery in it. The reasons for this frightful
collapse of the Italians of today in contrast to the Italians of 1918 appear very clearly to any modest observer. I was not wrong in not wanting war.

In Albania, Cavallero is preparing an offensive action. I am waiting
without excessive illusions but with faith. The Greek sector is probably
the only one that holds out hopes of a few hours of sunlight.

Conversation with Gambara. I had him received by the Duce. Notwithstanding my efforts, I have not succeeded in having him given a
command in Albania, although he lived there for four years. The
Italian General Staff does not like him; he is not one of them, and he
has committed the unpardonable sin of advancing by leaps and bounds
in his career, a career to which are linked the names of our victories
in Spain.

I have given the Duce a serious and harsh letter from Professor
Faccini of Leghorn, whose eighteen-year-old son, mobilized on the
seventeenth of January, was sent to Albania on the same day, without
knowing what a firearm was. This explains so many things.

January 24, 1941

The Duce conferred for a long time with Gambara and is becoming
more and more favorable to the idea of putting him at the head of the
army now under Vercellino. It seems to me that Gambara is not in the
King's good graces, and probably for this reason the Duce suggests
that Gambara ask to be received by the King. I tell this to Gambara,
who admits that he has never been to see the King once in his whole
career. He will go tomorrow.

Grandi got his orders to report for service. He wasn't expecting it
and didn't welcome it at all. In addition to the convenience of staying
at home, he attached a political significance to his not being called. So
like his complicated nature. All his hopes now have fallen at one blow.
What remains is the stark fact of having to return at the age of forty-
five to pound the snow with his Alpine mountain boots, so worn out
that he had considered them done for.

As I foresaw the day before yesterday, Mussolini is concentrating
his hopes on the escarpment of Derna. What has happened up to now
has taught very little—at least to him.

January 25, 1941

I say good-by to the Duce. Tomorrow evening I will join my air group in Bari. He wasn't so cordial as he should have been. But Mussolini in these last few days has begun to feel that the order to send the ministers away from Rome has not met with public favor, and, as always happens in such cases, he becomes more stubborn in his decision and more brusque in speech. In saying farewell he made certain observations which he might very well have omitted.

In the afternoon I saw Donna Rachele [Mussolini's wife]. She is very much alarmed at the way things are going. As is her simple nature, she follows gossip and small talk, especially in the matter of money, and has no definite sense of proportion. In any case, she thinks that the barometer indicates stormy weather, and she affirms that everything and everybody take it out on the Duce. She is canny in her own way. She complained that the starlings that she loved to shoot had deserted the pines of Villa Torlonia. "With the wind that blows even the starlings have changed direction; they are flying to the trees of Villa Savoia [the King's villa]," she said.

Cavallero has attacked in the direction of Clisura, and it seems that everything is proceeding well.

January 26, 1941

Departure. This time, as I have a certain amount of experience in such departures, I find it hard to leave. I have no apprehensions, only a small amount of conviction, and consequently less enthusiasm. All of my comrades who have become volunteers by force feel this way, and many do not hide their feelings.

[*No entries January 27 to April 23 inclusive*]

Ciano joined his air group in Bari on January 26, 1941.

April 24, 1941

I resume my notes. I have made an appointment with Pavelić for tomorrow at Lubiana. It is a matter of finding out what the Croatians think more than to reach any definite conclusions. It will not be easy.

In Italy, too, there is a strong propaganda in favor of the acquisition of Dalmatia, which is carried on by the usual agitators. To be pro-Dalmatian is a profession for many. Nevertheless, we have prepared two solutions: one that involves a continuous stretch of territory from Fiume to Cattaro, and one limited to historic Dalmatia. This last-named portion should be integrated by a political contract which would practically put the whole of Croatia under our control. The attitude of the Germans in all this is ambiguous. When we met at Vienna they gave us a free hand. But up to what point are they sincere?

With Acquarone we settle on a visit that the King wants to make to Albania. He also talks about the restoration of the Petrovichs in Montenegro. "Danilo, that perpetual libertine Danilo," as Mussolini calls him, has a son. We must go easy in this, especially so as not to arouse hope in Albania for a dynasty of their own. But the Queen [Elena] is using her influence to push the issue. Meanwhile, I have sent Minister Mazzolini as our representative to Cettigne.

April 25, 1941

In Lubiana. A hell of a day. It is raining and there is a freezing wind. The people have a distraught air but are not hostile. I see Pavelić, surrounded by his band of cutthroats. He declares that the solutions proposed by us would have him thrown out of his job. He makes a counterproposal: the Dalmatia of the London pact, with Trau added, goes to us. Spalato and Ragusa, in addition to some islands, would remain Croatian. His followers are more radical than he. They invoke statistics to prove that in Dalmatia only the stones are Italian. On the contrary, Pavelić is favorable to the political pact. He doesn't even exclude the eventuality of a union under one head, or a monarchy under an Italian prince. He asks for time to think about it for a few days, then we shall meet again.

I see the ex-Ban [governor] of Slovenia. I have known him since the times of Stoyadinovich. He is unhappy over the fate of that part of Slovenia which has remained under the Germans. Commissioner Grazioli tells me that German treatment of the population is actually worse than cruel. Robberies, armed thievery, and killings occur every day. Churches and convents are looted and closed.

April 26, 1941

Except for Spalato, Mussolini is in agreement with Pavelić and justly maintains that it is better to attract Croatia into our political orbit than to gain a little more territory populated by hostile Croats. With the Duce we prepare the decree for the annexation of Lubiana. It will be an Italian province with broad administrative autonomy, both cultural and fiscal. Our humane treatment of them, as compared with inhuman treatment by the Germans, should attract to us the sympathy of the Croats. The Duce is also resentful of the German attitude in Greece. The Germans have practically assumed the air of protectors of the Greeks, and there was nearly an incident between the soldiers of the Casale division and S.S. troops of Hitler's regiment at Ponte di Piernacti.

Even Farinacci telephones me to deplore the attitude of the Germans. When he does that it means a lot.

Grandi wrote a letter to Cavallero refusing the nomination as Civil Commissioner in Greece. It appears that Bottai, on the other hand, would go willingly.

April 27, 1941

Von Mackensen comes to my house at one o'clock in the morning, and together we go to Villa Torlonia, where we find Mussolini half asleep but quite courteous. Hitler says that the Greek general, Tsolacoglu, or some such name, is ready to establish a Greek government in Athens with which we might be able to negotiate the surrender of Greece. He is favorable to this. In fact, he considers all this as a "heaven-sent favor." We must send a delegation to Larissa early tomorrow morning. I suggest Anfuso, and the Duce approves. We are naturally less enthusiastic than the Germans, and it seems to us that we can discern in all this the explanation of much of the German attitude in Greece, including what has occurred within the last few days. However, Anfuso, having arrived early in the morning at Larissa, informs us that he finds there neither the German nor the Greek delegation, and that, besides, Marshal List had not in any way been informed of his arrival. This puts the Duce in good humor, because it proves "that even in Germany things don't run smoothly," and gives us another singularly important instance to add to the many that have formed a constellation during these six months of German-Greek relations. Later, List informs us that the two delegations will arrive tomorrow morning.

I request the Duce to give the Stefani agency his telegram of praise for Cavallero, and he agrees.

April 28, 1941

This affair about Tsolacoglu pleases me less and less. Anfuso informs me that it is a matter of recognizing a government which enjoys sound and legal backing; although the territorial occupation of the country is a fact, it is clear that this general proposes to save the national and ethnic unity of Greece, and German connivance is equally clear. It seems to me that the least we can do is to ask the Germans to leave to us the civil government of the territories that we claim. Otherwise, I fear that what we get out of it will be very small.

Casertano telephones that much progress has been made with the Croatians in regard to the frontiers of Dalmatia and also as to the possibility of instituting a monarchy under a prince of the House of Savoy. I called him to Rome.

The King insists upon a restoration of the monarchy in Montenegro. I fear that this will create tension with Albania, which will exact a national dynasty. But the Duce has already agreed, and I don't want to play the spoilsport. The King of Montenegro will be a nephew of the Queen, a young man whom the Duce calls "a son of many and poor parents." He lives in Germany, in obscurity and almost in poverty.

April 29, 1941

With Buffarini I prepare a political map for the creation of the Province of Lubiana. It is inspired by very liberal concepts. It will have the effect of attracting sympathies for us in Germanized Slovenia, in which the worst abuses are being reported.

Casertano at the Duce's. The Croatian affair has taken many steps forward. The crown is offered to a prince of the House of Savoy, but no compromise in respect to Spalato. Pavelić declares that if he were to relent on Spalato he would have to resign, and with him would collapse all his pro-Italian policy. The Duce is aware of our real interest, but is stubborn about yielding on the question of Spalato. In him there come to the surface once more the same words that he used during the Fiume-Dalmatia conflict [in 1919–20]. I am more and more convinced of the necessity of advancing the problem toward a political solution, which also seems to me to be the most convenient from the military point of view. Is it really worth the trouble of saving a city in which the only thing Italian is its monuments, and so lose control over a large and rich kingdom? The rights of the stones are undeniable, but even stronger are the rights of the living.

Conference with Roatta. The General Staff warmly advocates a political solution with respect to Croatia, and considers as dangerous any extremist step as regards Dalmatia.

April 30, 1941

A meeting with the King on the Croatian question. On his part there are no objections to concessions about Spalato. On the contrary, he is pleased. The King is of the opinion that the less of Dalmatia we take the less trouble we will have. "If it were not for a certain understandable sentimentality," he said, "I would be in favor of relinquishing even Zara." He is very happy, on the other hand, about the bestowal of a crown on a prince of his house. If the Duke of Aosta had been in Italy the King would have designated him without hesitation; as things stand, the only choice is between the Duke of Spoleto and the Duke of Pistoia. The King favors the first, because of his physical appearance and also, up to a certain point, because of his intellectual capacities. I found the King in good health, sunburned from his tour of the Alps, and, generally speaking, in good humor. As usual, he is anti-German.

The Duce replies to Pavelić's letter, accepting the crown, and he gives last instructions to Casertano: to insist on Spalato but not to the point of creating a break. Today our paratroops occupied Cefalu. They are only a few, about one hundred and fifty, and we hope that they will not be thrown into the sea by the local garrison. The Duce is anxious to make the announcement "because since we now have a good number of paratroops we can, even if it be only one regiment, say that it is a division." This upsets me. We are at it again, and the lessons of the past have taught us little.

May 1, 1941

All the grumblers who most criticized the Greek affair are now extremists in the matter of Dalmatia. This is particularly true in the Senate, which distinguished itself during the debates on Albania by its blattering. Senator Felici speaks to me of a sort of petition to the Duce to ask that not even a centimeter of coast line should go to Croatia. I have told Acquarone that it would be timely for him to make clear that it is useless to undertake such an absurd campaign. In the Senate the word of the royal household is very much heeded.

May 2, 1941

The second son of Badoglio has died in Libya as a result of a motor accident. I am sorry. In spite of the fact that Badoglio has given me good cause to dislike him, I am really sorry for the loss of his son.

Casertano telephones that all hope for Spalato is not lost.

May 3, 1941

Mussolini has me read an order of the day which Rommel addressed to our divisional commanders in Libya. He goes so far as to threaten to denounce them before the military tribunals. It seems that, owing to this, some trouble has arisen and I would be surprised if it were otherwise. In Albania, too, where at a certain point our Army has had to face considerable obstruction from the Germans, the feeling of resentment toward our Allies is marked. The Duce realizes this and gives Farinacci the responsibility of drafting a letter to Hitler to call attention to what has happened. He has chosen Farinacci because he has no official position and because there are no possible doubts as to his pro-German feelings.

May 4, 1941

Casertano reports that Spalato might also be given to us with some reservations on the administration of the city. The Duce is satisfied. It now seems that Pavelić wants to have some preliminary talks with the Duce. I should prefer that we arrive at a quick conclusion, especially because the German attitude toward us with reference to Croatia is anything but clear. Alfieri, for what he is worth, continually sounds the alarm from Berlin, and considers that a meeting between Hitler and Mussolini is necessary to settle on the principal points of our claims.

A long speech by Hitler. I am not acquainted with it yet, but Mussolini, who listened to it, judges it with considerable detachment and says that it is a useless speech that might much better not have been made.

May 5, 1941

Farinacci's letter to Hitler is not sent. The Duce is satisfied with the Führer's explanation, and, on the other hand, does not like the introduction of Farinacci's letter, which vaunted his own exploits in Albania.

For the day after tomorrow we have set a conference between Mussolini and Pavelić. It will take place on the frontier, as near Zagreb as possible, because it will not be very prudent for Pavelić to be absent too long from his capital. The Duce has put a stop to the Dalmatian agitation by the usual overzealous people, many of them acting in bad faith, with the aim of creating expectations that might bring delusions later on.

As always, Hitler's speech was excellent. I like the oratory of this man more and more. It is strong and persuasive. It was an informative speech, but at the same time one in which no assurances were given. All those who, on the basis of previous declarations, believed that the end of the war would come in 1941, have been bitterly disappointed. For my part I have entertained but few hopes of this kind.

On the advice of the Duce I have written a letter to Serrano Suñer. I congratulate him on his speech and give him advice about Axis intransigence. *Palabras y plumas el viento las lleva* [The wind carries away both words and feathers].

May 6, 1941

Departure for Monfalcone. On the train Mussolini is wrapped in thought. We speak at length of the future prospects of the war. I cannot say that now that he has laid aside his optimistic view of a rapid end he has any clear idea of the future. I give him my ideas, the tenor of which is that a compromise peace should be welcomed by us, especially now that we have acquired our share of booty. He appears to agree, now that recent vicissitudes, and above all tension with the German troops in Greece, have opened his eyes to many things.

May 7, 1941

We arrive at Monfalcone. It is an overcast and cool day. Pavelić is escorted by some carloads of Ustasci, which give his trip a strange cowboy character. We receive him in a little waiting room of the station. Nothing sensational happened. There is confirmation of the results that have been reached in previous conferences. On some points Pavelić appeals to the generosity of the Duce, and the latter naturally agrees—a matter of customs union and of some bits of territory. On my part, I hold firm on Curzola and Buccari [the Beffa di Buccari is famous in the annals of World War I on account of a brilliant maneuver by the Italian Navy against the Austrian Navy, directed by Admiral Ciano, the father of the writer of the diaries. It was because of this that the Admiral was made Conte di Cortellazzo]. I want to see a monument erected to my father at Buccari. The ceremony of the offer of the crown will take place on Sunday the eighteenth.

On the train Mussolini is in good humor and loquacious. He evinces satisfaction with the results obtained and criticizes those who would like a totalitarian solution of the Dalmatian problem, neglecting that of Croatia. He is particularly amusing when he describes at length the old Italian socialistic world. All the men of those days are brought to life in his colorful description. "They were bourgeois," he concludes, "who were terrified of the proletariat and were afraid of only one thing: revolution."

He will take care of the question of the army commands and will liquidate Guzzoni.

May 8, 1941

Through Acquarone I inform the King of the results achieved, and he decides to leave for Albania the day after tomorrow. Acquarone says the Duke of Spoleto is proud of the task which awaits him, but concerned about losing his liberty. "When we looked for him, to give him the news, we managed to find him, only after twenty-four hours, in a Milan hotel, where he was hiding in the company of a young girl."

Mussolini informs the Council of Ministers of what has been done and what will be done. The Council's approval appears to be complete and enthusiastic. I leave for Tirana, where I will receive the King.

May 9, 1941

At Tirana. The general feeling is good; the soldiers feel more and more that Italian effort has worn out the Greeks, and they are proud of it.

May 10, 1941

The King arrives. The weather is bad—cold and rainy—which does not prevent the streets being crowded with enthusiastic people—sincerely enthusiastic. The King is in very good humor and is moved. He didn't think that he would find Albania so developed and fertile. In his mind was the memory of that heap of arid, hard rocks which is Montenegro, for which he holds, nonetheless, a great deal of affection, even to the point of wanting to re-establish it with the boundaries of 1914. I do not think this is possible. The Albanians would rebel violently against any such decision. We have enough to do to restrain their ambitions, which now go so far as Antivari and beyond.

The King is very courteous to me. He repeatedly said that it was I who "built up" Albania, and he tried in every way to show his friendliness to me. He was rather distant with Cavallero, who noticed it and did not conceal his resentment. I had to work hard to get him an invitation to lunch with the King, and I did it because Cavallero's exclusion from such an intimate repast would have given rise to many rumors.

May 11, 1941

All the ceremonies were carried out well. During the evening reception the royal palace was used by us for the first time. Afterward there were missing eight cigar lighters, a silver case, and sixty knives and forks. As a debut on the part of Tirana high society, that's not bad.

Acquarone has spoken to me of the personal financial situation of the King. I, like everyone else, thought he was very rich. On the contrary, he is not. He probably has something between twenty-five and thirty millions. As for the jewels, they are the property of the Crown, and they are linked to the entail established by Charles Albert in order to safeguard the family from the prodigality of Victor Emmanuel II, who died loaded with debts. The King gives a monthly allowance of 20,000 lire to each of his daughters and keeps 100,000 lire for himself. He is concerned about the expenditures of his son, for he foresees "that, like his grandfather, he will always have money troubles."

I return to Bari by air and proceed to Rome by train.

May 12, 1941

Mussolini was annoyed because the King, in Tirana, had presided over the Council of Ministers. He was reassured only when I explained that it was more a meeting for the Royal Signature than anything else. The Germans have taken a step in Tokyo, with which we have associated ourselves, inviting the Japanese to adopt a definite anti-American stand. I don't know whether the note will have any great effect. Matsuoka does not conceal his great friendliness and respect for the United States. Phillips, with whom I spoke today, no longer excludes the possibility of intervention by his country, and, as usual, he talks of a very long war. Even the Duce, who had always talked about a blitz war, now believes in a long one, mentioning the year 1948. He bases all this on information given him by Forzano, that buffoon Forzano, who, in Athens, is supposed to have talked with Marshal List, which I doubt very much.

A strange German communiqué announces the death of Hess in a plane accident. I cannot conceal my skepticism of the truth of this version. I even doubt whether he is dead at all. There is something mysterious about it, even though Alfieri confirms the report that it was an accident.

May 13, 1941

The Hess affair has a tinge of tabloid news. Hitler's substitute, his second-in-command, the man who for fifteen years has had in his grasp the most powerful German organization, has made an airplane landing in Scotland. He fled, leaving a letter for Hitler. In my opinion, it is a very serious matter: the first real victory for the English. In the beginning, the Duce believed that Hess had been forced to make a landing while he was on his way to Ireland in order to start a revolt, but he very soon abandoned this thesis, and he now shares my impression of the exceptional importance of this event.

Von Ribbentrop unexpectedly arrives in Rome. He is discouraged and nervous. He wants to confer with the Duce and me for various reasons, but there is only one real reason: he wants to inform us about the Hess affair, which is now in the hands of the press all over the world. The official version is that Hess, sick in body and mind, was a victim of his pacifist hallucination, and went to England in the hope of facilitating the beginning of peace negotiations. Hence, he is not a traitor; hence, he will not talk; hence, whatever else is said or printed in his name is false. His conversation is a beautiful job of patching things up. The Germans want to cover themselves before Hess speaks and reveals things that might make a great impression in Italy. Mussolini comforted von Ribbentrop, but afterward told me that he considers the Hess affair a tremendous blow to the Nazi regime. He added that he was glad of it because this will have the effect of bringing down German stock, even with the Italians.

Dinner at home with von Ribbentrop and his associates.

The tone of the Germans is one of depression. Von Ribbentrop repeats his slogans against England with that monotony that made Goering dub him "Germany's No. 1 parrot."

It seems that Bismarck, who hates von Ribbentrop, emphasized every phrase of his Minister with heavy kicks under the table at Anfuso, to whom he finally said: "He is such an imbecile that he is a freak of nature."

May 14, 1941

Ribbentrop left after having said good-by to Mussolini in a brief meeting at the Palazzo Venezia. The Hess affair has had no developments so far. The British radio says that he spends his time writing, which disturbs Ribbentrop. When Ribbentrop's four-engined plane was taking off, Bismarck said to Anfuso, "Let's hope that they will all fall and break their necks; but not here, or we'll have some unpleasant work to do." That's German national solidarity for you!

In the meantime, in Japan, things are not going as they should, and still worse in Russia. Ribbentrop himself, when questioned by the Duce, avoided giving a definite answer, and said that if Stalin is not careful "Russia will be despatched in the space of three months." The chief of the Military Service of Information, on the basis of information gathered in Budapest, says that the attack is already decided upon, and will begin on the fifteenth of June; Hungarians and Rumanians are meant to collaborate. This may be. But it is a dangerous game and it seems to me without a definite purpose. The story of Napoleon repeats itself.

A long conversation with Spoleto. He is proud of having been chosen as King of Croatia, but has no exact idea of what he is supposed to do and is vaguely uneasy about it. I emphasize that he will be a lieutenant general with a crown at the service of the Fascist Empire. In any case, it will be necessary to keep the reins tightly in our grasp.

May 15, 1941

Contrary to expectations, the speculation of Anglo-American propaganda on the Hess case is quite moderate. The only documents that are really harmful are the German despatches, confused and reticent. Alfieri writes that the confusion in Berlin is at its height in all circles. He stresses the fact that the Germans, despite their efficiency and determination, are poor sports when fortune turns against them.

A long conversation with the Prince of Piedmont. Although he has been personally courteous to me, yet I have felt that there is considerable bitterness in his heart. For a man so prudent he has frankly criticized the Fascist system in general and the Fascist press in particular. He now lives among the military, and, during the last few months, has absorbed a good dose of poison which has had some effect on him. He does not yet know how to analyze or synthesize very well. He has neither the experience nor the acumen of his father, though I consider him a very much better man than his reputation has made him out to be. He recalled what I predicted about two years ago on the development of the Croatian question.

May 16, 1941

A lull of expectancy in the Hess case. Even the British press mentions a mysterious peace mission, going so far as to imply a prearranged agreement between Hitler and Hess. This is in contrast to Ribbentrop's declarations, and also to German agitation, which isn't decreasing.

Augusto Moschi came to see me; he is the nephew of Donna Rachele, who for a long time has held the keys to the heart of his pow-

erful aunt. And now he has been dethroned, his place being taken by
Pater, a no-good engineer, who builds houses of sawdust and card-
board. Moschi violently attacks Pater, accusing him of having disturbed the peace of Villa Torlonia with intrigues and evil doings of
every kind. He is a sort of puny Rasputin in disguise, who takes advantage of his influence to secure all kinds of personal benefits. Maybe
Moschi is exaggerating, but there must be something to it. Edda, who
is intelligent and outspoken, pointed out to me some months ago the
strange role that Pater was playing with her mother, and concluded
by attributing the situation to "the effects of the menopause."

For some months, in fact, Donna Rachele is disturbed, diffident,
and busies herself like a detective with a thousand things that don't
concern her. It even seems that she goes snooping around dressed as a
bricklayer, a woman of the people, and God knows what else. All this
will end in a formidable turmoil, and it is well to keep out of it. Pater's
influence may be behind Starace's imminent and unjust liquidation,
since Pater is Starace's bitter enemy. One of the ways in which the
Duce explained it to me was to say that he had learned from his wife
that Starace sends a militiaman to walk his four dogs. "Italy," said
Mussolini, "is still too fed up with D'Annunzio's dogs to tolerate those
of Starace." [D'Annunzio became the laughingstock of the Italians
when he had his many dogs paraded on leash by liveried flunkies.]

May 17, 1941

An incident on the departure of the King from Tirana was the only
sour note of an otherwise very successful trip. A nineteen-year-old boy,
a certain Mihailoff [a Macedonian-Greek], fired a few pistol shots at
the royal carriage; the boy, who seems to be half unbalanced, wanted,
in this way, to voice his indignation for not having been recognized as
a poet by the local authorities. Needless to say that his poems are
worth a great deal less than the few lire of subsidy which he had repeatedly received. The King attached no importance to the incident
and remained very cool. It appears that he even said to Verlaçi, who
was seated at his side, "That boy is a poor shot, isn't he?"

Starace has been ousted, and I must say that nothing was done to
make the blow less painful. When he came to see me he was sad and
apparently hardened by his sorrow. Unless there are reasons that have
escaped me, Starace's liquidation and especially the manner in which
it was done were unjust.

May 18, 1941

The Croatians arrive with Pavelić at their head. They are in good humor and well disposed toward us. I should say that they are better disposed than the Albanians when they offer the crown. The ceremony is more or less the same as that with the Albanians. In the streets, few and undemonstrative people. Not many realize the importance of the event. When His Majesty designated the Duke of Spoleto and the delegates saw him, there was a murmur of approval among them. Let us hope that it will be the same when they hear him speak. Everything went on in due form; also the signing of the Acts, the content of which seemed to those who had knowledge of them to bear a better political meaning than was expected. It now remains to be seen if what we have built will be lasting. Maybe I am mistaken in my personal impression, but there is a feeling in the air that Italian domination in Croatia is to be temporary. And this is why the public is indifferent. Only one piece of news would really send the country wild with enthusiasm: the news that peace had been declared.

Pavelić is rather sure of himself, and today he is calm and modest, as he was in Rome when living like an expatriate. He asks for some privileges, which are of secondary importance, and advisable for us to grant in order to consolidate his position. During the evening, after one of the usual dinners at Court, formal and boring, the Croatian delegation leaves.

May 19, 1941

I present to the Duce two nominations: Volpi as president of the Italian Croatian Economic Commission, and Bastianini as Governor of Dalmatia. Both are accepted, and I believe that the public will receive these names with favor. Yesterday's announcements, which were printed in the press only today, are meeting with considerable favor, but there is no manifestation of that enthusiasm which one might have expected at other times.

I see Bottai. He is cordial and, I believe, sincere. He would like very much to free himself from the office of Minister of National Education, which for too long a time has overwhelmed him with work without giving him any satisfaction. I believe that deeply within himself he nourishes the ambition of being sent as Ambassador to Berlin. He would certainly do well, but at least for the time being it is out of the question. I should not want to cause Alfieri grief, even though he didn't know yesterday, after six months of war with Greece, what Florina was. [A Greek village, the scene of critical fighting.]

The Duce, when speaking to me of Bismarck [old Prince Bismarck], went on at some length to say that as great and as big as he was he had an intense sentimental life and wrote "schoolboy letters." From what the Duce related it was not difficult to perceive what I should call a personal interest in this side of the Iron Chancellor's private life. . . .

May 20, 1941

Pavelić has found at Zagreb a fairly good situation. One could not ask more.

Bastianini is going to Dalmatia as Governor. He is prudent, honest, and faithful.

Cavallero informs me of his intentions in his undertaking. Good. Meanwhile he will liquidate Guzzoni, the dyed-haired general—and that is perfect!

May 21, 1941

I accompany Mazzolini to the Duce's in order to settle the Montenegrin question, which is especially complicated on account of the sentimental interest attached to it by the royal family. It seems that the idea of Prince Michael for the position is not popular in Montenegro. They do not know him; he has married a French woman and until now has lived on the pay of Belgrade. On the other hand, the consensus of opinion is unanimous in favor of the Queen. She is the one who ought to wear the crown of the Petrovichs. Such a solution would also be very pleasing to me, because it would tend to place the country solidly in our hands. For the time being the King is recalcitrant. Now we have sent Mazzolini to explain to him how matters stand we hope that he will give his consent. As for the frontiers, the King would like to restore Montenegro to its 1914 borders. This is impossible. Albania would start an uprising, and we know from experience how invincible is the bitterness provoked by deceit on the part of allies. Versailles teaches us this lesson.

Pavelić made his first speech at Zagreb, which, to judge from the first press reports, seems good. They say that he is an impressive orator.

Grandi has returned to the fold with solemn affirmations of Franciscan devotion and humility. That was to be expected.

May 22, 1941

The King continues to object to the Queen's taking the crown of Montenegro, and suggests the son of Prince Roman, who is the son of a Petrovich [Montenegro's royal house]. Let us hope that the son is better than the father, who is a prototype of fat head. Moreover, he has a raucous voice. Mazzolini will try to speak about the matter to Cettigne, but maintains that it is very improbable that the idea will be received with favor, for the simple reason that everybody is unaware of the existence of this dear little boy.

May 23, 1941

I went to the country to see my mother. I find her rather well and this gives me great joy.

Then I went to Leghorn. Although the city has always stayed in line, Rodinis tells me that even recent events have caused no enthusiasm. He, who bases all his judgments on how many copies of our paper are sold, repeats that circulation has not increased either for the success of Dalmatia or for Croatia.

May 24, 1941

No news of any importance.

May 25, 1941

The Duce, yielding to Riccardi's insistence, had decided to remove Giannini as Director of Commercial Affairs. Clodius intervened in his favor, courteously but firmly, saying among other things that Giannini's dismissal would render more complex the commitments of both countries on the question of fuel oil. Riccardi is indignant and calls this blackmail. Anyway, the Duce has revoked his order and Giannini stays in.

Bismarck gave Filippo to understand that the Germans are in possession of our secret codes and read our telegrams. This is good to know; in the future, they will also read what I *want* them to read.

May 26, 1941

The King has informed us, through Acquarone, that Prince Roman does not wish to hear about the throne of Montenegro; therefore, we must come back to Prince Michael, who is living on Lake Constance. If he, too, refuses, we shall think of a regency. Frankly, I never dreamed we should waste so much brain power on a country like Montenegro.

No political news. In Crete, military operations are going well and there is great talk in the world on account of the naval victory of the *Bismarck*. In the meantime Otto [Bismarck] does not like it a bit that his grandfather's name should be involved in this anti-English struggle, and he foresees that the *Bismarck* itself, pursued by the *King George,* is about to pay dearly for its adventure.

I see Bottai. He, like all those who return from Slovenia, is very anti-German. He speaks pessimistically of our internal situation, which, in his opinion, is characterized by the formation of two groups, extra-legal, so to speak, asserting a strong and dangerous influence on the Duce. On one side are Donna Rachele and Pater (and people in all quarters are talking a great deal about this affair), and on the other are the Petaccis and their satellites. Like all outsiders, such people intrigue against those who hold some legal and constitutional power, and it is in this way that Bottai explains the cold and almost hostile attitude which Mussolini has assumed against the highest Fascist officials.

The Starace affair has made a deep impression on older Fascists, including the enemies of Starace, because everyone sees in this summary but unmotivated sentence a direct personal threat. Perhaps Bottai draws too dark a picture, but it is undeniable that among our Fascists one can perceive a marked uneasiness.

May 27, 1941

The *Bismarck* has been sunk. This is important especially on account of the repercussion it will have in the United States, where it will prove that the sea is dominated by the Anglo-Saxons. Alfieri has arrived. I can't say that he is a pessimist, but he doesn't show his old optimism. He says, "The war is won. All we have to do is find a way to stop it." This formula is dangerous. Mussolini is always in bad humor and resentful toward the Army. This morning he was tempted to "get out of his car and whip the officers who were going to the Ministry of War—they were so unworthy of the uniform."

In the afternoon the Duce telephoned me asking me to speed up the negotiation with Russia, so that we can get a bit of fuel oil. "Otherwise," said the Duce, "a little while longer and we will be compelled to sit with folded hands."

May 28, 1941

Cavallero has now resolutely assumed control of military affairs. From what he tells me I understand that the military undersecretaries will be reduced to the position of managers with respect to men and materials in their own bureaus, and this is right. I have also received Squero, the new Undersecretary for War. He is an upright soldier, timid, modest, and very much surprised at the burden of responsibility that has landed on his shoulders. After the nomination he wept on Cavallero's breast because it seems that he has a horror of speaking in public. And he considers as a public three or more persons.

Speech by Roosevelt. It is a very strong document, even though it is not clear as to plans of action. Mussolini inveighs against Roosevelt, saying that "never in the course of history has a nation been guided by a paralytic. There have been bald kings, fat kings, handsome and even stupid kings, but never kings who, in order to go to the bathroom and the dinner table, had to be supported by other men." I don't know whether this is historically exact, but it is certain that Roosevelt is the individual against whom the Duce's greatest hostility is directed.

May 29, 1941

I accompany Alfieri to the Duce, who asked him for news on the Hess affair. I must say, to judge from Alfieri's replies, that he knew little about it. Alfieri was the first who, taking seriously the first communiqué, practically broke his neck to telegraph Hitler his condolences for the "loss of his favorite collaborator." The Duce later said that, in his opinion, the tone of German-Italian relations was lowered a bit, and from this observation went on to say that Italy is indispensable to Germany, exalting our co-operation and even our military contribution to the war.

The Duke of Spoleto comes on a visit. He wishes to take Guariglia with him to Zagreb, and this seems to me an excellent choice. He said nothing of any particular importance, but the tone of his conversation was distinctly anti-German.

I had lunch with Acquarone, who, with great reserve, put me on my guard against Cavallero, "who, according to the King, has a tendency to boast and who cherishes exaggerated ambitions." But he also said that the King is thinking of nominating the Duce Chancellor of the Empire, and me President of the Council, thinking thereby to insure succession in office. But Mussolini, I am sure, will have none of this.

May 30, 1941

Information from Iraq is bad and, what is worse, our planes, a month after the conflict, have not yet gone into action. If there were any need of it, here you have new proof of the lack of preparation of our air force. Things are going better in Crete, on the other hand, where the liquidation of the English seems imminent. Mussolini speaks of a hop on to Cyprus, but I know they are quite skeptical about this at the German Embassy. Mussolini has had a violent anti-German outburst, apropos of German meddling at Zagreb. "They should leave us alone," he said, "and they should remember that through them we have lost an empire. I have a thorn in my heart because the vanquished French still have their empire, while we have lost ours." The ill temper of the Duce is due to this. He was very much attached to Ethiopia, which he called "the Pearl of the Regime," and the years 1935 and 1936 the "Romantic Years of Fascism." Now he is trying to console himself by preparing for the reconquest of the empire, but he is the first to grasp the risks and difficulties this will involve.

Bottai was saying today that Roosevelt is a real dictator, and that our system of government, like those which have always flourished on the shores of the Mediterranean, ought to be interpreted as a tyranny. He is more and more skeptical on the progress of public affairs in Italy.

May 31, 1941

Hitler has sent word that he wishes to confer with the Duce at the earliest possible moment: tomorrow or the day after. Neither the invitation nor the form of invitation pleased the Duce. "I am sick and tired of being rung for." And he decided on the day after tomorrow for the meeting at Brenner Pass. We have no idea of the purpose of the meeting, but at first sight I think that it must deal with either one of two subjects: France or Russia.

Sebastiani was liquidated by Mussolini, who explained it by saying that his family doesn't like him, and also reproached him for having built a villa at Rocca di Papa. Whoever has seen this villa says that it is a very modest place. The fact is that Sebastiani, too, is a victim of the campaign started against him by Donna Rachele—an exaggerated campaign, even if not altogether unfounded. I myself know the names of persons from whom Sebastiani took money to facilitate the establishment of industries in Apuania [a new town created by Fascism].

Galbiati, who is taking the place of Starace, comes to pay me his formal visit. He interprets the function of the Fascist Voluntary Militia as a watchdog for the revolution, rather than as an armed force at the service of the country, and says it will operate along that line.

I learn from Bottai that the Duce is exasperated by the publication in the *Minerva Review* of Turin of a motto by some Greek philosopher or other. The motto reads: "No greater misfortune can befall a country than to be governed by an *old* tyrant."

June 1, 1941

Departure for the Brenner Pass. On the train I had a long conversation with Bismarck on men and things of the Nazi regime. According to him, Goering has lost a good deal of his influence on Hitler because he "admonishes him too much," and dictators do not like it. Von Ribbentrop is very much listened to and Himmler very powerful also. Lutze's star is in the ascendency. Since Hitler proved to be right on the offensive against the Maginot Line, the military men no longer dare open their mouths. The best of them are with the troops, not those who surround the Führer.

The Duce is quite good-humored, but he cannot understand the reason for this hastily arranged conversation. He is afraid that the Germans will want to expedite their agreement with France, and that this will take place at our expense. Repercussions in Italy resulting from an eventual renunciation of our Western aspirations would be very serious and damaging to the prestige of the regime.

June 2, 1941

I have summarized our conversations elsewhere. The general impression is that for the moment Hitler has no precise plan of action. Russia, Turkey, Spain, are all subsidiary elements: complements or dispersion of forces, but it is not there that one can find the solution of a problem. The greatest German hope is now in the action of its submarine fleet, but one does not know what the summer will bring, with its starlit nights and calm sea. A slaughter of ships, some people say. A slaughter of submarines, others think. The Duce, too, is convinced that a compromise peace would be received by the Germans with the greatest enthusiasm. "They are now sick of victories. They now want the victory—a victory which will bring peace." The atmosphere of the meeting was good. Mussolini states that during the conversation he had privately with Hitler the latter spoke about Hess and wept. The Duce was satisfied with the meeting, especially because he was able to note that for us there was no lowering of tone on the matter of Italo-German relations.

An opinion of the Duce on monarchies: "They are like those thick and strong trees, very flourishing on the surface, but hollowed by insects from within. All of a sudden they are struck down by lightning and there is no human power that can set them up again."

June 3, 1941

On the instructions of the Duce I have drafted a letter to Serrano Suñer, emphasizing the advisability of Spain's adhering to the Tripartite Pact. Mussolini added a personal note to it.

On the whole, the Duce has a favorable opinion of yesterday's conference, at the same time commenting upon the excessive verbosity of Hitler. He thinks that personal ties should be strengthened "by means of pairs." It is my duty, therefore, to establish closer ties with von Ribbentrop. About Keitel the Duce expresses this opinion: "Keitel is a man who is happy that he is Keitel." The opinion expressed by Bismarck is more to the point: "Keitel is an imbecile."

During my absence Anfuso had to put up with a telephone assault from Donna Rachele about certain offenses of the Duce, which, parenthetically, are not our concern but the concern of the Ministry of Popular Culture. She didn't express herself in very refined language and said that she will come to the Palazzo Chigi and start "shooting up the place." I don't know who puts certain things into her head, but I am not going to speak to the Duce because of the high and noble feeling he has of maintaining his prestige in public affairs. But this increasing interference is a serious matter, and perhaps one day I shall be obliged to overcome all my reticence and speak to the Duce.

June 4, 1941

Bárdossy arrives—a man whose career has been rapid and ominous, at least for his superiors. I remember him in Vienna a year ago at the meeting on arbitration for Transylvania. He was a modest plenipotentiary at Bucharest. Later, Czaky's death brought him to the government, and Teleki's suicide brought him to the presidency. What will become of the Regent? Bárdossy is a person of distinction and restraint, a career man. He offers a balanced judgment on the situation and reveals no attitude beyond that inspired by the orthodoxy of the moment. Villani, however, says "that Bárdossy in reality has the same ideas that he has," which would mean that he hates the Germans. The conversation with the Duce had nothing particularly important about it, until Bárdossy went into ecstasy with regard to Hungary's love for Rome. Then Mussolini, with the air of a sharp old wolf, or some diabolical and over-intelligent animal, said that the Hungarians were for Fiume what the Swiss were for Genoa. Bárdossy was floored by these few words better than by any long conversation.

I saw Donna Rachele. She is in a continuous state of over-excitement for no reason at all. Her arguments are of no particular account. She could live quietly and undisturbed, but instead embitters her days by futile controversies.

June 5, 1941

After one has been with Bárdossy for a little while one recognizes in him the classical career diplomat, devourer of cakes at ladies' teas, frequenter of South American legations and salons of unknown countesses. Even the language he speaks is that of the traditional chief of mission. He forgets that he is the man responsible for the policy of his country, and assails you with the traditional *"qu'est ce que vous pensez, monsieur le Ministre,"* et cetera, which distinguishes those who belong to the diplomatic career from other mortals. Nevertheless, Bár-

dossy is a good fellow, and he, too, will pass, like the others, hurriedly
and pompously, through the kaleidoscope of Hungarian politics. At
any rate, he has left, and his visit to Rome was one of the most clas-
sically useless.

June 6, 1941

Commercial negotiations in Berlin do not at present give very much
satisfaction. Reductions in the coal quota, difficulties in the transportation of oil. Even scrap iron, which we were to receive from France,
has been delivered to us only in very small quantities. Mussolini is resentful and this gives an anti-German tinge to his words. "This means
that in the future we shall wage 'an ersatz war.' I would not be at all
sorry if Germany in her conflict with Russia lost many feathers, and
this is possible because the Russians are not lacking in armaments, and
the only problem is whether twenty years of Soviet propaganda have
been enough to create in the masses a heroic mysticism."

I receive Bose, head of the Indian insurgent movement. He would
like the Axis to make a declaration on the independence of India, but
in Berlin his proposals have been received with a great deal of reserve.
Nor must we be compromised, especially because the value of this
youngster is not clear. Past experience has given rather modest results.

June 7, 1941

Information from Berlin is still less favorable, which accentuates the
anti-German tinge in the mind and words of the Duce. In fact, he was
even thinking of postponing the speech which he was going to make
at the Chamber on the tenth—the anniversary of our entrance into the
war. "I would be expected to exalt our collaboration with Germany,
and now this is repugnant to me."

Tassinari informs me about the food situation. It is not brilliant but
not very bad, and we may foresee an improvement as to fats. Prince
Michael, who has refused the crown of Montenegro, opened his heart
to Consul Serra di Cassano. He does not want to compromise himself
because he is convinced that in the end Germany and Italy will be
beaten, and for this reason he considers that any present solution is
transitory and ephemeral. I do not believe that the Queen is very
proud of the ideas of this sprig of the Petrovichs.

June 8, 1941

Starace mopes about his personal misfortunes, but not like a cry-baby; he weeps from anger, and without saying so, out of hatred. I talk about him to the Duce. The most serious complaint that the Duce makes about him is that Starace wears a distinguished service medal without authorization. The criticism regarding financial doings finds less echo in Mussolini's mind. I was not very successful in defending Starace to the Duce, but it is my impression that the Duce's anger doesn't go deep. If Starace will swallow the Duce's scolding without kicking, in a short time we shall see him raised to power again.

De Gaulle has entered Syria. What will be the reaction of the French? Mussolini takes it out on the Germans: "They are not intelligent, that is all. They should have occupied the whole of France at the armistice."

June 9, 1941

No particular news. News from Syria is still quite uncertain, but it seems that a considerable contingent of Dentz's army has joined forces with the Gaullists. Which doesn't displease me at all; a Vichy French alliance with the Axis would have been at the expense of Italy.

The Hungarian Minister of Defense, General Bartha, who is visiting Rome, maintains that a Russo-German clash is more than inevitable —it is actually imminent. He is optimistic as to what is to be expected. He believes that the Russian Army cannot resist for more than six or eight weeks, because the human element is weak. It remains to be seen, however, how twenty years of Communist revolution have influenced them.

June 10, 1941

What a strange anniversary of our entry into the war! Using as a pretext the increased German meddling in Croatia, Mussolini uttered against Germany the harshest charges that I have ever heard from him. He was the aggressive Mussolini, and hence Mussolini at his best. "It is of no importance," he said, "that the Germans recognize our rights in Croatia on paper, when in practice they take everything and leave us only a little heap of bones. They are dirty dogs, and I tell you that this cannot go on for long. I do not even know if German intrigue will permit Aimone [Duke of Spoleto] to ascend the Croatian throne. Besides, I have been thoroughly disgusted with the Germans since the time List made an armistice with Greece without our knowledge and the soldiers of the Casale division, who are natives of Forlì and hate Germany, found at Ponte di Perati a German soldier barring the road and robbing us of the fruits of victory. Personally, I've had my fill of Hitler and the way he acts. These conferences called by the ringing of a bell are not to my liking; the bell is rung when people call their servant. And besides, what kind of conferences are these? For five hours I am forced to listen to a monologue which is quite fruitless and boring. He spoke for hours and hours of Hess, of the *Bismarck,* of things more or less related to the war, but he did not propose an agenda, he did not go to the bottom of any problem, or make any decisions. Meanwhile, I continue building fortifications in the Vallo Alpino. Someday they will be useful. For the moment there is nothing to be done. We must howl with the wolves. Today at the Chamber I will cajole the Germans, but my heart is filled with bitterness."

The Duce has shown me his speech. I suggested that he use the soft pedal about the Turks, who are still allied to the English and who may have some surprises in store for us, especially since French resistance in Syria seems to be petering out.

The reception the Chamber gave to the speech was nothing to talk about, and the first comments to reach us are not altogether enthusiastic. But, I ask, could the Duce have acted any differently or better in the present situation?

June 11, 1941

I tried here and there to sound out the reaction to the Duce's speech. But even among the die-hard Fascists the reactions are not good. Reactions are quite unenthusiastic at the German Embassy. Bismarck told Anfuso that some employee or other expressed himself as follows: "I have listened to seventeen speeches by Mussolini. This one is, without doubt, the worst." At lunch Farinacci, Cini, Volpi, and Bottai subjected the speech to an intense fire of criticism. The uneasiness which lurks in the minds of all the party heads has a lot to do with these acid comments. I cannot agree with them. Perhaps the Duce should have said nothing, but since he did speak, I don't see what other line he could have taken.

The newspapers of the GUF [Fascist University Group] have abused a certain freedom of discussion which is granted them, and are inveighing against the party heads. They exaggerate—so much so that their arguments are influenced by the absurd and irresponsible grumblings of the mob. Although these youngsters were in the wrong, it must be admitted that the regime has also made a mistake; for twenty years it has neglected these young men, and has had them in mind only to deck them out in uniforms, hats, and capes, and herd them against their will into the squares to make a lot of noise.

June 12, 1941

Nothing new.

June 13, 1941

Negotiations with Berlin are dragging. Giannini does not blame the difficulties on the ill will of the Germans, but on an authentic scarcity of recourses. Mussolini is in a black humor. He says that he is glad that the people of Europe should see what German domination means. "We may be willing to give up our shirts, but the Germans remove even pieces of hide."

With Jacomoni, the Duce settles upon some new directives concerning Albanian policy. A greater autonomy without eliminating the beys, who still count in the country, as recent events have proved, and also to receive into the government some new elements which are closer to the intellectual classes and to the people.

June 14, 1941

In Venice for the adherence of Croatia to the Tripartite Pact. When Ribbentrop arrives he is exceptionally gay and jovial. At dinner in a Venetian inn he is even amused by the vulgar repartee of a waitress. I myself, and all those who are with me, are astonished. We drop politics.

June 15, 1941

As usual, I have had a stenographic report made of the conferences. The ceremony at the Ducal Palace was impressive, but more important than the frame is the canvas, since the participation of Croatia has the domestic flavor of homemade spaghetti. The political value of the event is about zero.

Von Ribbentrop hastens his departure and gives us to understand clearly that this is due to an imminent crisis with Russia. Naturally, he raises no objections to this, approving all his master's exploits. But he is less ebullient than usual, and had the nerve to recall his enthusiastic praise of the Moscow agreement and of the Communist leaders, whom he compared with those of the old Nazi party.

Pavelić is satisfied with the course of events, and the others also confirm that the situation is becoming consolidated. He has already assumed the tone and gestures of a dictator, at least toward his satellites. He is very much of an extremist in the social sphere. In his discussion with Vittorio Cini he maintained that the land must go to the peasants, and that as to industry, we must lead the way to the formation of state ownership of property. All this in ten years. Ansaldo, who is put into a rage by such ideas, said, "We must not take the man seriously. Within ten months he will be liquidated."

June 16, 1941

First I go to Ponte a Moriano, and then to Rome. There isn't much news except the talk by Churchill to the representatives of the invaded powers. He was intransigent and arrogant. He called Mussolini a "tattered lackey." I am unable to find out what the reactions are because the Duce went to Riccione today for a short vacation.

June 17, 1941

Nothing important.

June 18, 1941

Long telephone call from Ribbentrop. Two pieces of news: one good and the other not so good. The first is that an agreement has been reached between Turkey and Germany, consisting of neutrality, reciprocal respect, and peaceful solution of all controversies, and no secret protocols. The second news is the expulsion of all United States consuls from Axis territory, and vice versa. Which means that we are moving headlong toward an open state of war.

The Prefect of Bolzano has been in Germany to deal with the question of the evacuation of non-Italians from Alto Adige. The movement is slowing up under the specious pretext that Hitler has not yet chosen the territory where they are to go. The Prefect is convinced that the Germans want to mark time, in order to bring the question on the carpet again after the end of the war.

Things are better in Libya. The British attack was broken, and we have had a notable success. Bismarck didn't hesitate a minute to make the following comment: "It won't be this sort of thing that will end the war."

June 19, 1941

I conferred with the Turkish Ambassador on the possibility of a pact similar to the one concluded with Germany. If anything, we could go even further, since our two countries have near and mutual interests. The Ambassador did not answer, but seemed to be pleased. He is an odd type, with whom I have had little to do so far. In five years I have seen him no more than ten times, and the principal topic of our conversations has been the cure of his rheumatism.

June 20, 1941

Nothing new.

June 21, 1941

Many signs give the impression that operations against Russia are about to begin. Bismarck secretly tells Filippo that he is expecting a message from Hitler during the night. The idea of a war against Russia is in itself popular, inasmuch as the date of the fall of Bolshevism should be counted among the most important in civilization. Considered as a symptom, such a war is not liked. An obvious and convincing reason is lacking for such a war. The current explanation is that this new war is a *pis aller*, that is an attempt to find a way out of a situation that had developed unfavorably and not as had been foreseen. What will be the further course of the war? The Germans believe that it will all be over in eight weeks, and this is possible, since military calculations in Berlin have always been better than political calculations. But what if this should not be the case? If the Soviet armies should show the world a power of resistance superior to that the bourgeois countries have shown, what results would this have on the proletarian masses of the world?

June 22, 1941

At three o'clock this morning Bismarck brings me a long missive from Hitler for the Duce, which seeks to explain the reasons for his move [the invasion of Russia], and although the letter begins with the ritualistic assertion that Great Britain has lost the war, its tone is far from being puffed up as usual. By telephone I inform the Duce, who is still at Riccione. Then, still early in the morning, I try to get in contact with the Soviet Ambassador in order to notify him of the declaration of war. I do not succeed in seeing him until twelve-thirty, since he and all the employees of the Embassy have, quite calmly, gone bathing at Fregene. He receives the communication with a rather lackadaisical indifference, but that is his nature. I submit the communication to him without idle words. The conversation lasted two minutes and was quite undramatic.

Tomorrow Mussolini will send his answer to Hitler. The thing that is closest to the Duce's heart is the participation of one of our contingents, but from what Hitler writes it is clear that he would gladly do without it.

Riccardi makes a great outburst about the trends of our economic situation, and ends with this phrase: "At this stage of affairs of the regime the only thing that might yet surprise me would be finding a pregnant man; aside from this we have seen everything."

June 23, 1941

From Russia the first news of German successes begin to arrive. They talk about seventeen hundred Russian planes destroyed in one night. Cavallero, who conferred with the Duce at Riccione, is of the opinion that the Germans can easily gain a great victory, and he believes that the Bolshevist armed masses will be dispersed, causing a collapse. According to Bismarck, in German military circles they expect to take five million prisoners, "five million slaves," as Otto says. We are sending an expeditionary corps under the command of General Zingales, which will operate on the borders between Rumania and sub-Carpathian Russia.

Since the Hess affair, all fortunetellers and astrologers in Germany have been arrested.

I see Phillips. He thinks that American intervention is inevitable and coming soon. He desires this intervention against Germany, which he hates, but a war between his country and Italy saddens him a great deal.

Churchill has made a speech which, it must be objectively recognized, carries the mark of the great orator. I talked about it to Grandi, who, having lost his self-control for a moment, expressed an extreme admiration for Churchill. "In England," he said, "I had few friends, but Churchill was really a friend."

June 24, 1941

No definite news on the Russian front. Marras telegraphs that the German forward elements have met first-line Bolshevist resistance, and are preparing an artillery attack. Our first contingents will leave in three days. The Duce is very much excited at the idea of this participation of ours in the conflict, and telephones me that tomorrow he will review the troops. I despatch to Berlin Mussolini's reply to Hitler.

June 25, 1941

The Turkish Foreign Minister has told De Peppo that the proposal of a pact with us has had a favorable reception. Conversations may take place shortly.

Falangist contingents leave Spain for the Russian front. Mussolini does not like this and would like to prevent it, but I do not know what to do since the German-Spanish agreement was made completely without our knowledge.

June 26, 1941

At Verona, Mussolini reviewed the first division on its way to Russia. By telephone he defined it as perfect. Be that as it may, I am concerned about a direct comparison between our forces and the Germans. Not on account of the men, who are, or who may be, excellent, but on account of their equipment. I should not like to see us play once more the role of a poor relation.

The Japanese desire the recognition of the government of Wang Ching-Wei, and they agree to it in Berlin. Von Ribbentrop telephones me about it, and adds that he is quite satisfied with the course of operations on the Russian front. In fact, the Germans have made considerable progress, while the Rumanians, as was to be foreseen, have allowed themselves to be thrust back.

June 27, 1941

I go to Leghorn to pray at the tomb of my father. As time passes, his personality becomes greater, not only in my heart, but also in the memory of all those who loved him. Today, as when I was a child, and as always, I feel strongly the need for his protection and his help. I know that he watches over me.

June 28, 1941

Nothing new.

June 29, 1941

German bulletins describe victories in Russia in simple and exultant terms. Also Ribbentrop telephoned Alfieri that the progress of operations has surpassed the most favorable predictions. Notwithstanding this, it seems that Ribbentrop is in very bad humor; Alfieri explains it on the basis of internal German conflict.

Mussolini has returned. He looks well but is in an extremely sour humor. In the Gimma [a kingdom in Ethiopia] there was the usual surrender in great numbers, with generals at their head, despite a large amount of arms and equipment at their disposal. But even the most modern weapon, as Moltke says, is of no use when it is thrown in the ditch. The Duce is also concerned about the situation in the Alto Adige. For some time now the repatriation of the non-Italians is almost totally stopped. The letters which arrive from those who have left are filled with threats and insults against us. Mussolini fears "that the Italians will have to learn the hard way that every agreement with the Germans is nothing but a *chiffon de papier* [scrap of paper]." This, too, he blames on the military, who have ruined our prestige, Graziani in particular.

June 30, 1941

We must define the question of the Albanian and Montenegrin frontiers, otherwise there will be a multiplication of incidents, above all with Croatia, which, like all new countries, is beginning to toy with imperialism. Pavelić now would like to have the sanjak of Novi Bazar [a district of Bosnia], an absurd and unjust pretension. I am preparing a letter signed by the Duce to refuse this request. At the Palazzo Venezia there is a meeting between Mussolini and Pietromarchi; the main points are put down and it is decided that if the Croatians and Bulgarians should play tricks, the frontiers will be decided upon by decree, without their advice.

Mussolini gives vent to another anti-German outburst. He fears that the Germans are getting ready to ask for the Alto Adige; he says that he would resist this with armed force, but I do not see that he has the means to carry out such a threat. He was offended, especially by the way the Germans treated him with regard to the Russian question. There was absolute silence on their part and only a "night alarm" to inform him of the accomplished fact. "Not even I disturb my servants at night," said the Duce, "but the Germans make me jump out of bed at any hour without the least consideration." The Duce realizes that Hitler did not welcome the participation of our troops on the Russian front, but he insists on sending them just the same. I tried my best to change his mind, but he is immovable and convinced that they are "divisions superior to the German, both in men and equipment." I know that Rintelen's judgment was very different. Now the Duce hopes for two things: either that the war will end in a compromise which will save the balance of Europe, or that it will last a long time, permitting us by force of arms to regain our lost prestige. Oh, his eternal illusions! . . .

July 1, 1941

It seems that at Minsk the Germans are now meeting with stronger Russian resistance, which is very much to the liking of the Duce. He says, "I hope for only one thing, that in this war in the East the Germans will lose a lot of feathers. It is false to speak of an anti-Bolshevik struggle. Hitler knows that Bolshevism has been non-existent for some time. No code protects private property like the Russian Civil Code.

Let him say rather that he wants to vanquish a great continental power with tanks of fifty-two tons which was getting ready to settle accounts."

July 2, 1941

A long letter to the Duce from Hitler. It is a résumé of the operations, all of which are favorable even though harder than had been foreseen. The Russian array of forces was such that one is led to believe that they were prepared to attack. Hitler also proposes a meeting of the two chiefs at his headquarters while operations are still going on. Mussolini liked the idea so much that he accepted immediately.

July 3, 1941

I hope that I am wrong, but the star of our Alfieri in Berlin seems to be paling. Von Ribbentrop, who was indignant at the visit of Pavolini to Goebbels, has started a serious and laborious investigation on the origins of this trip, and Dino Alfieri will come out of it with his feathers plucked. The affair has amused the Duce, who considers the incident quite serious but who is obliged to laugh at it as he laughs at everything, even those dramatic things that happen to Alfieri. [Allusion to the fact that Alfieri was thrashed by a German officer.]

July 4, 1941

Nothing important.

July 5, 1941

Meeting of the Council of Ministers. Financial measures were considered, and then the Duce gave a long dissertation on the politico-military situation: The United States will intervene, but its intervention is already discounted. Russia will be beaten in short order, and this may persuade Great Britain to yield. The Duce was very unhappy over the almost total loss of the empire, "for which loss I [Mussolini] have sworn hatred against the British for all time, bequeathing this hatred to all Italians." The reconquest of the empire will be undertaken at any cost, even if it should impose on us the most extreme sacrifices.

Pavelić has replied on the Montenegrin question: he agrees on the establishment of the 1914 boundaries. I will send to Mazzolini the text of the proclamation on the establishment of the frontiers, after which the constituent assembly will meet to create the new kingdom of which Mazzolini himself will be the regent. Silimbani gives an interesting exposition of the situation in Tunisia: even the stones are Gaullists, and 80 per cent of the middle classes believe in a British victory. They hate the Germans but admire them; they simply despise us.

July 6, 1941

A report from our Consul at Innsbruck informs me of the resumption of German activities to keep the Alto Adige in their hands, under the leadership of Gauleiter Hofer himself. The Duce has been flabbergasted and irritated by it. "Note it down in your diary," he says, "that I foresee an unavoidable conflict arising between Italy and Germany. It is now evident that they are preparing to ask us to bring our frontiers to Salerno and perhaps even to Verona, which will produce a terrible crisis in Italy even for the regime. I shall overcome it, but it will be the hardest of all. I feel this by instinct, and I now seriously ask whether an English victory would not be more desirable for our future than a German victory. Meanwhile, the English are flying over Germany by day. Bruno [Mussolini's son] has told me so, and this pleases me very much. For this reason, since we shall have to fight the Germans, we must not uphold the myth of their invincibility. Anyway, I have little faith in our race; at the first bombing that might destroy a famous campanile or a painting by Giotto, the Italians would go into a fit of artistic sentimentality and would raise their hands in surrender. We must thank Graziani; it is to him we owe it if our prestige is going by the board, as a matter of fact already half gone. The war over, he will no longer be Marshal of Italy."

July 7, 1941

Anti-German resentment by the Duce is still keen. "The Germans insist upon the loyalty of others, but they are themselves incapable of being loyal."

I see Della Giovanna, who returns from Germany. His impressions on the situation are mediocre; little enthusiasm, much uneasiness on account of living conditions that are becoming more and more difficult.

The Duce leaves for Puglia.

July 8, 1941

I met Admiral Fioravanzo, who is a young ace of the Navy; he is lively and interesting, though a bit too conceited. He does not conceal his anti-German feelings and is concerned about German hegemony in Europe. He considers our Navy still very efficient in dreadnoughts and cruisers, but believes that the Italian undersea craft have received a hard blow from which it will be difficult to recover because of our lack of raw materials. He criticizes our program for naval armaments in which we sacrificed armor for speed.

July 9, 1941

Acquarone comes to make two complaints in the name of the King: first, that in the proclamation to the Montenegrins we spoke about the Duce and not about the King—and this I remedy immediately, since the proclamation has not yet been published. Second, that the Duce reviewed the divisions returning from the front. This, in the past, was always done by the King. I shall talk about this to Cavallero, whom the royal house continues to distrust because, according to Acquarone, "he has ambitions which are more of a political than of a military order."

The German advance in Russia proceeds at a somewhat slower pace. Resistance is serious; I saw a set of documents sent by Goebbels in which this is clearly evident.

Buffarini paints a very, very dark picture of our internal situation: anti-Fascism is taking root everywhere threateningly, implacably, and silently. He is preparing a documented report, but does not dare show it to the Duce.

July 10, 1941

The Duce has returned to Rome. The Hungarians have annexed the Mura territory, which produced great resentment in Zagreb. I did not conceal my disappointment from Villani and told him that Hungary will end badly if she follows this line. A country of fifteen million inhabitants and five million minorities is inconceivable. The Hungarians will have the same fate as all mosaic states.

Naples is bombed, and Cologne very badly also. From the Russian front news is quite serious; the Russians are fighting well, and, for the first time in the course of the war, the Germans admit withdrawing at two points.

The Bulgarian Minister for Foreign Affairs is ill and his visit to Rome will be postponed. I gain the impression that the Bulgarians have little desire to talk to us, preferring that the frontiers be established unilaterally, so that they can always contest the justice of the decision, which they could not do if a regularly signed pact were made.

July 11, 1941

I saw the Duce after a few days' absence. He is well and happy about his inspection of the troops in Puglia. "The Tridentina division," he said, "is superb. I affirm without hesitation that there are no more perfect soldiers in Europe."

An aerial attack on Naples—a very bad one. Not so much on account of the number of victims as because of the damage, of which the most serious was the fire of the Italo-American refineries. We lost six thousand tons of oil, and God only knows how much we needed it. The Duce said, "I am happy that Naples is having such severe nights. The breed will harden, the war will make of the Neapolitans a Nordic race." On this I am very skeptical.

A meeting with Domberg. He is calm but not joyful. Losses in Russia are heavy, and the war may bring us big surprises. His wife is more sprightly than he, and she does not conceal her judgment of the situation. "This is a war," she said, "that we cannot get away with."

News from the Russian front is so-so. The abridged bulletin on the battles of Bialystok and Minsk evidently deal with things that should have happened but did not.

July 12, 1941

Nothing new.

July 13, 1941

Mussolini is more and more alarmed about the situation in the Alto Adige. He had a meeting with Signora de Paoli. She preferred Italian citizenship, though she is of German origin and mother of a fallen soldier with an Italian gold medal. With concrete and irrefutable arguments she completely disillusioned the Duce, stating Germany's real decision to annex the Alto Adige no later than after the war. The Duce repeated his usual anti-German arguments and concluded by saying that he will bring clearly to Hitler's attention the fact that an event of this kind would constitute "the collapse of the regime."

Notable German progress on the Russian front; the Stalin line has been broken through at various points, and they are moving toward Leningrad, Moscow, and Kiev.

Frau Domberg is anti-Nazi but she is German, and therefore I must speak with prudence. Last night she asked me point-blank, "Is it true that you love Mussolini more than Hitler?" To which I replied, "I fear that I do not feel as you do. I love your chief very much." She was left out on a limb!

July 14, 1941

Disorders in Montenegro. Shooting by armed bands, an assault on the royal villa of Budua. It appears that this has no connection with the constituent assembly, but the coincidence of events is at least strange. In the meantime we have postponed the arrival of the Montenegrins in Rome, and on the King's initiative the regency will be assumed by three Montenegrins instead of by Mazzolini.

The Duce is furious with the military who "mislead him." They had assured him that the Galileo Factory of Florence would produce eight anti-aircraft searchlights a month, and instead he learned that the first thirteen of them, in two types, would be ready only at the end of December. All this is particularly serious for organizing our anti-aircraft defenses. We have had to stop sending Italian workers to Germany because it was becoming more and more difficult for them to live with the Germans, and fist fights were a daily occurrence.

July 15, 1941

We receive particulars on the surrender of Debra Tabor [Ethiopia]. In eight weeks our losses amounted to two killed and four wounded out of four thousand men. Notwithstanding that, the surrender took place with full honors. Mussolini affirms that this is one of the "classical Italian *combinazioni*." They have discovered this form of sur-render that saves their hides, and which it is easy to obtain from the mercenary English, who thus save themselves sacrifices and losses.

In Montenegro things are going rather badly. The capital is isolated and all the roads leading to it are blocked by the rebels. We have sent forces there from Albania.

A strange thing from Mussolini: he has reproached Pavolini be-cause in an article by Ansaldo the latter referred to "the war in Rus-sia, under the direction of Hitler, et cetera . . ." "In this way," the Duce said, "the Italian people is getting accustomed to thinking that it is only Hitler who directs the war." I wonder. Are we playing tiddlywinks, or are we serious?

July 16, 1941

The Duce is not convinced as to the course of affairs in Russia. The tone of his conversation today was distinctly pessimistic, particularly as the Anglo-Russian alliance makes Stalin the head of Nationalist Russia. He is afraid that Germany is facing a task that is too much for her, and will not reach a complete solution of the whole problem be-fore winter, which reveals a lot of unknown factors.

July 17, 1941

The Montenegrin insurrection continues; in fact, it is assuming greater proportions. If it did not have a deep and bitter significance, it would be grotesque that war exists between Italy and Montenegro. We hope that our military men will settle it without having to call for German intervention.

Mussolini, as usual, speaks in a bitter tone of the military men, and says that he likes only one general, I forget his name, who, in Al-bania, said to his soldiers, "I have heard that you are good family men. That's very well at home, but not here. Here, you will never go too far in being thieves, murderers, and rapers."

July 18, 1941

Anfuso has had an intimate and very interesting conversation with Frau Mollier, the wife of the German press attaché. She revealed

that the Russian campaign has caused a deep crisis in the German rul-
ing classes. Hitler went to war believing that the struggle against Bolshevism might lead the Anglo-Saxon countries to end the conflict. Von
Ribbentrop did not agree; in fact, he was convinced that Churchill is
ready to make an alliance even with the devil himself if he can only
destroy Nazism. And this time he was right. Now the struggle is hard
and bloody, and the German people, who are already tired, wonder
why. Frau Mollier used harsh terms. She said that Hitler is a Dumm-
kopf [blockhead]. In fact, the war is harder than the Germans had
foreseen. The advance continues, but it is slow, and harassed by the
very vigorous Soviet counterattacks. Colonel Amè and General Squero,
who made a report on the military situation today, believe that the
Russians will succeed in maintaining a front even during the winter.
If this is true, Germany has started a hemorrhage that will have incalculable consequences.

July 19, 1941

Some battalions have reached Cettigne, and hence the situation in
Montenegro, though it has not been solved, is noticeably improved.

I accompany Villani on his farewell visit to the Duce. The man continues with his anti-German ideas that amuse the Duce at this time
and do not cause any reaction from him. The end of the conversation
is less happy. "I am going home because I have reached the age
limit," he says. "I'm an old man. I am your age, as a matter of fact
one year older." Mussolini did not like this comparison, especially because Villani is the real physical image of old age.

We have fixed the Bulgarian-Albanian frontier by a unilateral decree. Stormy weather at Sofia, where the Cabinet talks of resigning.
The approaching and futile visit of the Bulgarian ministers to Rome
begins under bad auspices.

July 20, 1941

The Duce continues his anti-German outbursts. Today he said,
"Meditating over the words of Villani, I wonder if at this time we do
not belong among the vassal nations. And even if this is not so today, it
will be so on the day of total victory for Germany. They are treacherous, and without a sense of restraint. I have proofs that the in-

trigues in Croatia have all been hatched by the Germans. I foresee an unavoidable crisis between the two countries. We must place thousands of guns along the rivers of the Venetian region, because it is from there that the Germans will launch their invasion of Italy, and not across the narrow valleys of the Alto Adige, where they would be easily cut to pieces. For the time being there is nothing that can be done. We are on this track, and we must stay on it. But we must hope for two things: that the war will be long and exhausting for Germany, and that it may end by a compromise that will save our independence."

The news from the Russian front tells of a costly and hard-contested advance. From some reports from Moscow, intercepted from American-Turkish sources, we learn that disorder is beginning to be noticed among the Soviet troops, and that a collapse might now be near. That may be. However, a heavy price has been paid for it, and even if Russia is beaten, what will become of the rest of the world? Is this a decisive victory? I do not believe it.

July 21, 1941

The arrival of the Bulgarians: two traditional democratic-parliamentary ministers, whom the raging tempest over Europe obliges to deal with dictators, uniforms, and parades. They have come to beg for some frontier concessions, particularly in the zone of the Ochrida and Prespa lakes, indispensable for the strengthening of their personal situation in their own country. I have held firm, more for reasons of form than from conviction. Some small concessions may be made at the meeting of the mixed commission. I have seen the King and the Prince of Piedmont, the former more calm and cordial, the latter dissatisfied and critical. Hitler addresses a long letter to the Duce. It is a summary of military operations in Russia, the course of which he thinks is favorable. It is a broad politico-military survey, and finally —this is the real reason for the letter—asks to take over our air and navy commands. I don't know what they can do more or better than we can. Our Navy, especially, is giving excellent results in proportion to its opportunities and equipment. I do not believe that this request will increase fondness toward Germany in many circles.

July 22, 1941

False air alarms continue at Rome. It was the Duce who, personally, ordered an alarm in the capital every time there is an alarm at Naples. He does this because he wants to give the country the impression that a war is on. He has also ordered that at the first opportunity the anti-aircraft should fire in order to make it more exciting. Is all this worth while? If we listen to comments on the street, I should say not at all. News is more insistent about the approaching English offensive in Libya. Squero considers that there is something true in the report but doubts that we can resist a mass shock attack.

Matters in Montenegro are going pretty badly. The rebel forces are being increased by Croats and Serbs, and our divisions cannot keep contact with them. All this is grotesque, but it makes one think a great deal.

[*No entries July 23 to September 21 inclusive—Ciano was suffering from a throat infection.*]

September 22, 1941

I return to the Ministry after a long absence, due to a throat infection which compelled me to undergo an operation. Practically two months of inactivity without contacts with the Duce, except for the very sad day of the death of Bruno [Mussolini's son, who died in an airplane accident while experimenting with a new type of plane]. I found the Chief well, physically and spiritually. He has recovered from the blow. As always, the main note of his conversation is the military progress of the war. He says that the uneasiness of the Italian people is due to the fact that they are not participating in the war on the Russian front on a larger scale. I cannot agree with him. The people are not interested in this Russian war, and the real misery of our people is due to lack of food, fats, eggs, et cetera. But this aspect of the situation is not the one that disturbs the Duce.

It does, however, disturb Serena, who, after all, is now responsible— or at least passes as the one who is responsible—for the food situation. It was a big mistake on the part of the party to take this problem on its own shoulders—one which will be the foundation of all complaints, because, if today the situation is disturbing, it is not difficult to foresee that it will become more acute later on when the lack of fodder and the scarcity of fertilizers further reduce the harvests and production drops to still lower levels.

September 23, 1941

The event of the day is the matter of private ownership of the industrial and state bonds [making them non-negotiable]. Revel plays the victim, says that he knows nothing about it, and that he is against it. The Duce would favor it, but more out of spite than from conviction. According to Revel the one who inspired this measure is an informer of the police, ex-employee of the Bank of Italy, who has written to Mussolini to the effect that he, Mussolini, doesn't have the courage to do what Giolitti did. Volpi is furious and tries with every means at his disposal to block the measure.

I saw Phillips, who has been called to Washington for consultation. He was, as always, cordial. We entered into no particular discussion. He merely emphasized that the American press is no longer attacking Italy. He made mention of the Battle of the Atlantic, which he considers already won by the democracies. Von Mackensen also came to pay me a courtesy visit. We did not speak of politics. Generally speaking, he was calm and spoke in cordial terms about Italian affairs.

September 24, 1941

The Duce told me that Alfieri put him on guard against rumors that are circulating about the Duce himself. The rumor is that the Duce returned from Germany with a rather pessimistic impression of the progress of operations, and that he expressed himself in harsh terms about the Germans. (In reality he has done this even with me sometimes, but more often in my absence.) Alfieri, when pressed for the source of such information, kept his conversation on a vague and general level, and this made the Duce indignant. "Alfieri lost much ground." Alfieri had talked to me along these same lines with respect to what was being said about me. I sent him to blazes, where I frequently send this petty braggart. Nevertheless, the Duce was disturbed by it all, and on the first of October he will speak to the Italo-German Association to deny all rumors of this kind.

I saw a report by Cecchi on the treatment of our laborers in Germany. In certain camps, in addition to beatings, large watchdogs are used which are trained to bite at the legs of those workers who are guilty of only slight misdemeanors. If a report of this kind were known to the Italians they would revolt with a violence that few could imagine.

September 25, 1941

I showed Cecchi's report to the Duce. He was shaken by it and requested me to take this up with Mackensen to acquaint him with the gravity of what has happened. The Duce added "that I should take the step as on my own personal initiative, unknown to the Duce, who is supposed to have no knowledge of it." I did, in fact, talk with Mackensen, who took his cue from my words to embark on an attack on the presence of our workers in Germany "destined to sharpen the deep state of irritation which already exists between our two countries."

I saw Cavallero, who, as the good hot-air artist that he is, admits all the difficulties and concludes with the inevitable *"tout va très bien, Madame la Marquise."* In reality, the Mediterranean situation is dark, and will become even more so on account of the continued loss of merchant ships. Commander Bigliardi, who is in the know and is a reliable person, says that in responsible naval quarters they are seriously beginning to wonder whether we shouldn't give up Libya willingly, rather than wait until we are forced to do so by the total lack of freighters. From a report by the Duce, of which I have a copy, it appears that German armed units are installing themselves in the principal Italian cities. What for? We must keep our eyes on them.

September 26, 1941

From other sources, too, the news about the dogs being sicked on our workers in Germany has reached the Duce, and he was shaken and disturbed by it. "These things are bound to produce a lasting hatred in my heart. I can even wait many years, but in the end I shall square this account. I will not permit the sons of a race which has given to humanity Caesar, Dante, and Michelangelo to be devoured by the bloodhounds of the Huns." He suggested that I meet Ribbentrop for discussions and bring this up. I have written a letter advancing the proposal to Comrade Joachim!

A short conversation with Acquarone without any particular interest except the fact that the Court atmosphere is becoming more and more somber, down in the mouth, and anti-German.

The new Minister from Hungary, Mariassy, is the typical example of the classic career busybody, ceremonious and empty. He wanted to address some political questions to me, and began by asking me if I thought that the Axis would win the war! I wonder what kind of an answer he expected in wartime from the Italian Foreign Minister whom he had met for the first time in his life. A fine specimen of an imbecile.

September 27, 1941

Meeting of the Council of Ministers. One must take more notice of the Duce's state of mind than of the measures taken at the meeting. He talked for three hours almost without interruption. His arguments were directed against the bourgeoisie, "against the well to do, who are the worst type of Italians." He made a few references to the war and its development, only to say that he now believes that the war will last many years. Bread is rationed at two hundred grams, with an increase up to three hundred or four hundred for heavy laborers. "Let no one think," he said, "that rationing will end after the war. It will stay as long as I want it to. Only in this way will the Agnellis and the Doneganis eat the same as the least of their employees. If two hundred grams are little, then I tell you that around springtime the ration will be even less, and this delights me because we will finally see signs of suffering on the faces of the Italian people, which will be valuable to us at the peace table."

The Duce took delight in the fact that bonds now bear the names of their owners, but his arguments were hardly convincing and technically meaningless. The Council of Ministers remained silent. Only Revel—who loves to call himself the "Red Count"—was satisfied. Grandi, who accompanied me to the Ministry, was horrified by what he called the "white Bolshevism of Mussolini" in which he found the editor of *Lotta di Classe* [the Class Struggle, a Socialist newspaper of which Mussolini was once the editor], which he had read in school, utterly foreign to his way of thinking.

September 28, 1941

A long conversation with Gambara. Both the Duce and Cavallero had depicted him to me as an optimist, confident of the future of the I.N.R.A. [an industrial company which owned the mining rights in Albania and electric interests in Italy]. He is nothing of the kind. He talked to me with a profound sense of responsibility and sees the future full of clouds and dangers. He thinks that, compared to last year, the situation has greatly improved, but it is only a relative improvement, and replacements of raw materials are becoming scarce and more difficult to get. Now they are talking about attacking Tobruk. He thinks this is a serious error, an action in which we may exhaust our best forces, leaving the door open to the inevitable English offensive. It is Cavallero who supports this plan to please the Germans and the Duce. Therefore, Gambara attacks Cavallero violently, saying that "he was not able to win for himself the esteem of the Army, and wastes his time in vain political activities instead of proceeding with a real organization of the armed forces. If we continue at this pace, we will lose the war. This is also the opinion of Roatta and Squero." Gambara is right. Cavallero is revealing himself a perfect peddler who has found the secret way to Mussolini's heart, and who is ready to follow this path of lies, intrigue, and imbroglio. He must be watched; he is a man who can bring us great trouble.

September 29, 1941

Nothing new.

September 30, 1941

Mussolini is elated at the successes of the expeditionary force to Russia. Our naval victory, 90 per cent of which is discounted by London, and the prisoners captured on the eastern front, have cheered the heart of the Duce, who now sees a rosy future, even from the military point of view. But this represents the continual highs and lows of his nature.

Phillips is about to leave, and he comes to say good-by. He talks at length about the discouraged state of mind of the Italians, and ends by repeating the sympathy of America for our country—a sympathy which will be of indispensable help to us on the day of our reconstruction. I did not make any report [of the conversation], especially as the military intelligence service has come into possession of the American secret code; everything that Phillips telegraphs is read by our decoding offices, and my report might therefore be given the wrong interpretation. This, naturally, paralyzes any possibility of a rapprochement with the Americans.

Today, for the first time, there is a report signed by Alfieri (the real author of the political reports is always Ridomi) in which it is said that the German people are moving farther and farther away from the idea of a total victory and toward the idea of a compromise peace.

October 1, 1941

From Munich comes a report from Petralis, which, if it does not paint the situation in dark colors, certainly is not rosy. Of great significance is the clash which is shaping up between the Prussians and the Bavarians. It is certain that the religious factor is of considerable importance, but also we must not neglect the fact that many foodstuffs have disappeared from the Bavarian market because of the well-to-do Prussians who have taken refuge in Bavaria. And then there are those who are surprised at the Italians becoming irritated with the Germans when they ransack our warehouses!

A conference with Admiral Ferreri. He is concerned about the fate of Libya, especially if the sinkings of our merchant ships continue to be as numerous as in September. While in the past the percentage of ships lost had reached a maximum of 5 per cent, in September it jumped to 18 per cent. Like all our naval officers, he is outright anti-German.

Inauguration of the academic year of the Italo-German Institute. That simple-minded man, Balbino Giuliano, made a very unconvincing speech on the common traditions of the Italian *Risorgimento* and the corresponding movement in Germany. The presence of the Duce at this unimportant ceremony is intended as a denial of the rumors spread by Alfieri of a cooling of feelings on the part of Mussolini toward his Axis associate.

October 2, 1941

Nothing new.

October 3, 1941

Speech by Hitler in Berlin, which was unexpected, or almost so. First impressions are that he has tried to explain to the German people his reasons for the attack on Russia and to justify his delay in ending the war, about which he had made very definite commitments. There is no doubt that he has lost some of his vigor. This time there are no fulminating anti-English threats. As for us, we were given no particular attention; he lumped us with the others, and this will not produce a good impression in Italy, where the wave of anti-German feeling is growing stronger and stronger. Plessen has sent to our Ministry a note, which is rather strong, to point out "that in Greece the people are starving, and that we are responsible for whatever may take place there." The least I can say is that we are dealing with a puzzling document.

De Chirico is painting my portrait. He is a strange man, this artist, opinionated and very timid, at times absent-minded and at times deep and sharp. He has a surprising culture, which runs through his conversation almost without his being aware of it.

October 4, 1941

Mussolini, who was at Riccione, telephones concerning Hitler's speech. He does not like it a bit, "although he is satisfied as far as he himself is concerned." He is provoked by the step taken by Plessen as to Greece. He says, "The Germans have taken from the Greeks even their shoelaces, and now they pretend to place the blame for the economic situation on our shoulders. We can take the responsibility, but only on condition that they clear out of Athens and the entire country."

The internal situation, which is bad in many sectors, is becoming serious in Sicily. This region, which has suffered all the woes of war and enjoyed none of its benefits, has been particularly annoyed by a personal decision of the Duce to remove Sicilian civil-service employees from the island. To the misery of the Sicilians has been added what they consider an outrage. Why this was done I do not know. I have seen Gaetani, who wishes to resign his position as vice-secretary of the Fascist party, and who weeps when he speaks of conditions in Sicily. I have seen Mezzi, who is to be transferred to northern Italy, and who refuses to accept. He said, "My father is Genoese and my mother is Sicilian. If she were a Jewess I would be Aryanized. In this case, however, there is no indulgence for me. Is it, then, worse to be a Sicilian than to be a Jew?"

October 5, 1941

Nothing of importance.

October 6, 1941

Mussolini, to judge from what he told me over the telephone, from Riccione, is irritated by Hitler's speech. In the fact that he has spoken impromptu he finds the explanation "of that which otherwise would be unpardonable."

Squero has had a long conference with me on the situation of the Army. He is not a man with a great breadth of view, but he is honest, and he does not bluff. While Cavallero speaks of dozens of divisions that can be made ready by winter, Squero is of the opinion that we cannot have more than four or five new ones that are really well equipped. Supplies for Libya are becoming more and more difficult. Only 20 per cent of the materials set aside for September has been shipped and delivered. On the other hand, the percentage of men is higher: 50 per cent.

A good deal of dissatisfaction on account of the food situation. And in some provinces there have been small demonstrations by women, which are difficult to suppress. In Rome they grumble a great deal and are sarcastic. They now call the Campidoglio Campidaria. [*Campidaria*, as a pun, "live on air," and *campi d'olio*, "live on oil."]

October 7, 1941

Nothing new.

October 8, 1941

Some people can be hard-boiled! When I was in Albania, Verlaçi, in the presence of Jacomoni, talked to me about the Albanian Government's intention to offer Cavallero a parcel of Albanian soil. At the moment I thought that it had to do with the usual urn filled with earth, as with the earth of the Grappa or water from the Piave, as the custom is, and I made no objection. But when I learned that the offer was not so symbolical, since it had to do with a grant of almost twenty-five hundred acres of land in Fieri, I definitely opposed it. Which did not please the interested parties, who are now trying to twist things around with a letter from Verlaçi announcing the accomplished fact. I spoke to Cavallero about the matter and I will stop it. But Cavallero is not grateful to me. Just the contrary. Yet he cannot realize that for a man like himself, on whose fame as a strategist people disagree, but on whose reputation as a grafter all agree, the acceptance of such a gift would spell his doom. When bread is being rationed and the people are hungry is not the time to announce that Cavallero is celebrating a very dubious Greek victory by accepting a present of a few millions.

October 9, 1941

The conditions in Greece, according to Ghigi, are getting so desperate that there is fear the population will get out of hand. The bread ration is already reduced to ninety grams a day. They have nothing else. If a load of grain does not arrive at Pireus tomorrow, the ovens will be cold. What is the remedy? Ghigi makes no definite proposals, but he declares that, in the first place, it is necessary to straighten out the misunderstandings arising from the division of command between ourselves and the Germans, which paralyzes many undertakings and which burdens the food situation in Athens with too many heavy-eating officer gangsters. Tomorrow I will see Ghigi again. Today he did not conceal his profound unhappiness but did not explain himself, saying only that he would like to be transferred.

News from the German front in Russia is more and more favorable to the progress of operations: as paeans of victory. Will this prove to be true, or will we, after so many losses in men and matériel, be reading simply that a new front was saved a hundred or two kilometers farther back? This is what is really important for the whole course of the war.

October 10, 1941

Mussolini has returned and is in good humor, especially because of his trip to Bologna and Parma, which "received him very enthusiastically, once more giving proof of the fact that they are ultra-political cities." On the course of operations in Russia he is reserved. There have been successes, and that is undeniable, but he considers that the communiqués also bear evidence of propaganda for internal consumption, in view of the approach of a winter which will be hard. This opinion is corroborated by some telegrams from Alfieri, who pours not a little water in our wine and says that there is a difference of opinion between the most conservative military men and the politicians, who are sounding the trumpets of victory. The whim of the Duce is to send forces to Russia. He wants to send another twenty divisions there in the spring, because "in this way our war effort will compare favorably with Germany, and to prevent Germany, in the moment of final victory, from dictating to us as it will to the conquered peoples." I also brought the Duce up to date on the Cavallero question—of his property in Albania—and the Duce was deeply and unfavorably impressed.

October 11, 1941

Ghigi talks honestly with the Duce on the Greek situation, which is, in a word, hunger. Anything is possible, from epidemics to ferocious revolts on the part of people who know that they now have nothing to lose. Something will be done. Mussolini has given orders that seventy-five hundred tons of wheat be sent immediately. A very small amount compared to the needs for November. But we can do no more. The Italians, too, are pulling in their belts to the last hole: the one that the Italians call the "*foro* Mussolini"—"the Mussolini hole." [The Italian word *foro* means both forum and notch, or hole. Hence the pun on the Foro Mussolini.]

The Undersecretary to the Food Administration said that rations must be further decreased because there is no choice but to limit further the consumption of food, unless we want to be without food for a month. Frankly, this would be too much. Meanwhile, what most concerns the Duce is our absence, or practical absence, from the eastern front. He wants to send twenty divisions there in October, and Cavallero encourages him to do so. But aside from the fact that in the spring we could never, never have twenty divisions ready, would it be wise for us to send the little matériel that we still have at home and which is our only protection? The King, who is in San Rossore, definitely objects to such a proposal.

October 12, 1941

Nothing new.

October 13, 1941

Through Mackensen, Ribbentrop has asked me to join him at Schönhof to go pheasant shooting toward the end of the month.

The Duce received news that during his trip to the Russian front a German is supposed to have said about him, "There goes our Gauleiter for Italy." An employee of the Embassy is supposed to have heard this remark. The Duce wrote to Alfieri to ascertain the truth. Mussolini said, "I believe it. In Germany there exist certain phonograph records. Hitler makes them; the others play them. The first record was the one about Italy being the loyal ally, on an equal footing with Germany, mistress of the Mediterranean as Germany was of the Baltic. Then came the second record, that of the victories, that Europe would be dominated by Germany. The conquered states will be colonies. The associated states will be confederated provinces of Germany. Among these the most important is Italy. We have to accept these conditions because any attempt to rebel would result in our being reduced from the position of a confederated province to the worse one of a colony. Even if they should ask for Trieste tomorrow, as part of the German Lebensraum, we would have to bow our heads. As a matter of fact, there is the possibility of a third phonograph record, the one which will be made if Anglo-American resistance makes our collaboration more useful to the Germans. But that is yet to come."

I confined myself to saying that with such a prospect one can easily understand why Italian enthusiasm in this war is so slight.

Serena is worried about the food situation, and he took it out on the Chief, who, agitated as he is, would—if told—make impulsive decisions on the basis of intercepted telephone conversations and anonymous messages which in a short time cause a dangerous state of disorder. Perhaps the Duce might act differently with me, but I cannot agree with Serena's judgment. Mussolini at times is a little in the clouds, but he is always calm, attentive, and in possession of himself. He also has completely recovered from the sorrow of Bruno's death.

October 14, 1941

Nothing new.

October 15, 1941

The King sent for me. He had no particular question to ask, and the pretext that he used with the Duce for his talk with me was the Croatian situation. As usual, he gave a cautious but definite opinion on the situation. He is against sending any more Italian troops to Russia, and he deplores Cavallero's talk about the possibility of forming ninety-six divisions by spring. He doesn't believe that we have well-supplied army stores "including the three million rifles, which he would like to count for himself, because many of these rifles were given to the Fascist militia, and to the GIL [Fascist youth organization], who stole even the bolts of the rifles." He criticizes the militia; the Mantua Legion was abandoned by its consul [corresponding to the rank of colonel in the Army], who returned to his unit only when the engagement was over and was booed by his men, "who, in reality, are nothing but civilians in uniform." The internal situation also disturbs him. Above all, he thinks we must avoid any act of force and all incidents that might exasperate the Italian population, which is already exasperated to the danger point by present restrictions. He fears a German-French agreement at our expense, and he even fears an agreement between London and Berlin. He has no trust in the Germans, and every time he talks of them he calls them "those ugly Germans."

Today the Duce was under the influence of a talk with General Marras, who confirmed to him the imperialistic plans of certain German social groups, according to whom, after the war, Germany alone will be an armed and industrial power, while the other nations will have to play a more or less agricultural role and become political vassals of Berlin. Mussolini said, "I believe it. The German people are dangerous because they dream collectively. But history teaches that all attempts to unify Europe under a single rule have failed."

Tassinari is very much alarmed and disturbed about the food situation. He fears the worst and would like to pass the buck to a successor, on the excuse of being tired and ill. Naturally, I dissuaded him.

October 16, 1941

I didn't know Arpinati except through my father, who spoke very
well of him. I met him today and we had a long conversation at the
Palazzo Chigi. Before receiving him I informed the Duce, who is very
suspicious about those I receive. Among the men of the regime Arpinati
is important. I don't know if this is owing to his intelligence, but it is
certainly because of his character—a somewhat rare gift among Italians. He talked about the past and his misadventures calmly, and, I
would say, with pride. He didn't ask to be reinstated or to be forgiven;
in fact, without any backbiting he reaffirmed his loyalty to his beliefs
which irritated Mussolini at the time. He is opposed to the system of
the Corporations, is an anti-Communist, an anti-German, but he realizes that no other policy was possible, since, had we followed a different line of conduct, "we would have been swallowed up like an egg by
Germany." He was cautious in his judgments on men: only of Grandi
he said that he is a traitor and that he, Arpinati, "can knock him off
his pedestal whenever he wants to."

Marras had a second conversation with the Duce and said that in
German quarters they are quick at making plans: 1942, liquidation of
Russia and attack on Egypt; 1943, occupation of the island [Britain].
I have heard about such programs many times before, yet . . .

October 17, 1941

The taking of Odessa has saddened Mussolini, who now sees himself taking second place to the Rumanians. Every day he vents his
anger upon the Italian generals, and particularly upon Graziani, whom
he wants to court-martial. The Riom trial [the trial of various French
statesmen by the Vichy Government with a view to establishing responsibility for the war] has had an influence on him.

Von Ribbentrop invites me to Germany for the twenty-fifth at
General Headquarters, where Hitler wants to confer with me, and after
this to Schönhof for the usual shooting party.

At the Attolicos' [Attolico is now Italian Ambassador to the Vatican]
a luncheon in honor of Frau Goebbels, who is passing through, accompanied by a sister-in-law. This is how Bismarck addressed Anfuso on
the subject: "Frau Goebbels is the typical wife of a high Nazi official.
She was first married to a crook, and earned money through prostitu-

tion. Later she became the friend of Goebbels, but this did not prevent
her from going to bed with many of the frequenters of the party meetings at the Sports Palace. Goebbels married her one night when he was
drunk. They have had several children together, and maybe not together, because Frau Goebbels has continued her former ways. Now
she goes around looking for men, and when she does not suffice, there
is also her sister-in-law, who is another prostitute. I am ashamed to
think that my wife has anything to do with such people." This is how a
Bismarck has expressed himself about the wife of one of the most outstanding men of the Nazi regime.

October 18, 1941

According to some sources of information the Germans are beginning
to slow down before Moscow. Isn't this a case of their having sung their
hymn of victory too soon?

I leave for Ponte Ciano [Ponte a Moriano has now changed its name
in honor of Ciano's father].

October 19, 1941

My day was divided between the farms and the sea. Nothing interesting at Leghorn, but the spirit of the citizens is low. The approach
of winter is viewed with great concern by all. Too many illusions have
been built up, purposely or involuntarily, on the shortness of the conflict and on a victory which was supposed to be easy.

October 20, 1941

Alfieri reports about a long conference with von Ribbentrop, who
has sung his usual song: victory is achieved, the Russian Army crushed,
England has reached the end of her days. And yet at Moscow the
armored divisions are at a standstill before a very strong resistance,
and many German soldiers are bound to die with their mother's name
on their lips before the flag of the Reich flies over the Kremlin. Meanwhile, winter is drawing near, and military operations will soon become
very limited.

October 21, 1941

Funk and Clodius are in Rome. With the first I had a conversation that was more general than substantial. With Clodius we talked especially about the Balkan situation. He has returned from Turkey and believes that in Ankara they are desirous of keeping to the middle of the road, hoping for a compromise peace. This would be ideal for the Turks: an exhausted Russia, and a Europe in which a balance of power remains between Britain and Germany.

To Anfuso he said some hard things about our financial status: "Italy is running toward inflation and there is no way to stop its course."

Bottai is increasingly pessimistic. His judgment of the Chief is now violently bearish. He said, "My friendship for Balbo was always an argumentative friendship, since our ideas were frequently different. As time goes on I must confess that he was right. I remember that he called Mussolini 'a product of syphilis,' and that I used to object to his words. I wonder now if this judgment on Mussolini wasn't correct, or at least very close to the truth. The Duce has decayed intellectually and physically. He doesn't attract me any more. He is not a man of action; he is presumptuous and ambitious and expects only to be admired, flattered, and betrayed."

This is the anniversary of Maria's death, the dear, unforgettable soul.

October 22, 1941

Among the many individuals with no earnestness of purpose that life puts into circulation every day, General Cavallero easily carries off the palm. Inasmuch as he feels that an ill wind is blowing from my direction, he is now attempting to get around me and at the same time to seek favor. Today, with his artificial, hypocritical, and servile optimism, he was unbearable. He says that he has solved the problem of motorization not by giving the troops trucks but by increasing the rate of march of the infantry from eighteen to forty kilometers a day. Tomfoolery. To this I reacted violently, and he was forced to back down. He then goes on to assure me that by spring he shall have ninety-two divisions ready for use. This is a shameless lie. He knows very well that we shall not have even one third of this number. But in this way he spurs the Duce's imagination.

The Duce insists more and more upon sending forces to Russia, indicating a contingent of fifteen divisions. He has given me instructions to speak to Hitler to this effect during the meeting that we are to have on Saturday, insisting at the same time that the number of our workingmen in Germany be replaced by soldiers to be sent to the front. Mussolini holds that in this way we shall acquire a greater merit with our ally, who continues to mark time before Moscow.

Del Croix gives vent to his hatred of Germans, and he speaks very freely of the Duce as follows: "For some years now he misses his mark. He [the Duce] speaks of collaboration with Russia, and the war against Russia breaks out. He says that the march on Rome paved the way for the march on Moscow, but we have not reached Moscow yet. He announces the blitzkrieg, and there is no question but that the war will last many years."

October 23, 1941

Cavallero realizes that he has boasted too much, and came to me to pour some water in his wine, and so slip out of his previous statements. "It's true," et cetera, et cetera, he said, "we can't send to Russia more than six new divisions, and only on condition that the motorized equipment be furnished by Germany." He states that he has explained the reasons for his change of mind to Mussolini, but, even if this is true, he got little result, since the Duce confirmed yesterday's instructions, which he expressed in the formula, "more soldiers and less workers" [to Germany]. Even with regard to the food situation, the Duce assured Hitler that Italy will get along on its own. "In 1926, when we had to pay our first installment on our debt to America, one appeal from me was sufficient to bring in the hundred millions necessary for the purpose. I am certain that even today, if I made another appeal, many millions of Italians would sacrifice their bread and meat rations."

Aside from the fact that to contribute a few lire is something very different from giving up one's own already meager food ration, is Mussolini sure that things haven't changed profoundly in the mind of the Italian people since 1926?

At 8 P.M. I leave for General Headquarters, where I shall meet Hitler on Saturday.

October 24, 1941

On my way to headquarters.

October 25, 1941

I arrive at headquarters. Welcomed at the station by von Ribbentrop and by Hitler at the entrance of his fortified cabin. They had told me that he was looking tired and old. This is not true. I found him in top form, physically and mentally. He is very courteous, or perhaps I should say chummy. He quickly has me come into his studio, together with von Ribbentrop and Schmidt. I have made a report of the conference to the Duce, and it is filed elsewhere. I have also frankly added my own observations, but now I shall limit myself to jotting down a few episodes and impressions.

Von Ribbentrop speaks in a strangely confidential tone. Usually he is very reserved and dignified, so all this surprises me. He goes so far as to busy himself about my personal comfort, and has sent to my room warm, sweetened milk to help my cough. They say in Tuscany that when you are being made more of than usual people are getting ready to cheat you, or you have already been cheated.

He is distrustful of the monarchy. While we were hunting in the woods, von Ribbentrop asked me point-blank, "What is your King doing?" "He is hunting," I answered.

October 26, 1941 [continuation of October 25]

"No, I mean in politics."

"Nothing that is particularly interesting. The King is informed about politics, but does not meddle."

"Yet in court circles they intrigue."

"I deny it most decidedly. Perhaps, at times, they gossip, and even this to a limited extent. If you know the people at Court you would soon realize that but for one or two exceptions they are not even worth suspecting."

"I am pleased to hear this. But you will not say the same about the Prince of Piedmont. That fellow is hostile."

"Not at all. I can give the most ample assurance regarding the

Prince of Piedmont. He is young. He has neither the prestige nor the experience of his father, but he is very respectful of the regime, and devoted to the Duce. I beg you, my dear Ribbentrop, don't listen to gossips. They flourish in every country, but are of no account. One must not fish up information from the gutter of public gossip."

The shoot was very beautiful. Everything was perfectly organized. The game was driven by four hundred soldiers commanded by their officers, and they all took their task seriously, as if it were a question of ejecting the Russians from the forests of Wiesma or Briansck.

October 27, 1941 [continuation of October 26]

If in Italy a party leader dared to assign soldiers for a similar purpose, there would be a tremendous scandal.

At the final dinner Ribbentrop took the floor and spoke very tactfully to the guests and to the organizers of the shoot. He concluded thus: "Next year, my dear Ciano, our game will be better, not only because we shall kill double the number of animals, but also because England will have finally realized that she can no longer win the war. The bag of 1943 will, in the end, be that of peace." For a man like Ribbentrop, who has always, from 1939 on, been announcing victory in fifteen days, this was a big jump to take.

Roosevelt's speech made a great impression. The Germans have firmly decided to do nothing which will accelerate or cause America's entry into the war. Ribbentrop, during a big lunch, attacked Roosevelt.

October 28, 1941 [continuation of October 27]

"I have given orders to the press to always write 'Roosevelt, the Jew'; I wish to make one prophecy: that man will be stoned in the Capitol by his own people." I believe personally that Roosevelt will die of old age, because experience teaches me not to give much credit to Ribbentrop's prophecies.

On our way to the station Ribbentrop repeated a phrase that I have heard many times: "Hitler's New Order in Europe will insure the peace for a thousand years." I remarked that a thousand years is a long time. It is not easy to hang a couple of dozen generations on the achievements of one man, even if he is a genius. Ribbentrop ended by making a concession: "Let's make it a century," he said. For my peace of mind I was satisfied with the reduction, which was certainly considerable.

Domberg, in his cups, said to my collaborators: "Our next colony in Europe will be Hungary. I have hopes of becoming its governor." In spite of the wine, I think that, unfortunately, he was talking seriously.

October 29, 1941 [continuation of October 28]

My general impression of Germany is good; the country is in fine shape. The people are calm, well-fed, well-dressed, well-shod. When the Americans speak of an internal collapse they are mistaken, or, to say the least, they are premature in their judgment. Germany can hold out for a long time yet, especially since there is the spirit of victory; under such conditions revolt will not break out.

I have come across a train filled with our workingmen—long beards, open shirt collars, bottles of wine, some guitars. They are similar to the immigrants I used to see sixteen years ago in South America. Nothing is changed. Sympathy and esteem for us in Germany are in inverse ratio to the number of our men working in any particular district.

The sight of prisoners of war is a sad spectacle. They can be found everywhere in the open country, and serve in farming families where men are lacking. Domberg says, "Every German has his Frenchman," which is equivalent to saying that he has his cow or his horse. They are bound to the soil—slaves. If they touch a woman they are shot. And yet they have the blood of Voltaire and of Pasteur.

October 30, 1941

I reported to the Duce. He wished me to send the King a copy of the report I sent from Germany.

Mussolini asserted this morning that now he believes less than ever in the intervention of the United States. "It is quite clear that Roosevelt is barking because he cannot bite." Could he be right?

October 31, 1941

Nothing new.

Just now, late in the evening, I read that the American destroyer, *Reuben James,* was sunk last night west of Iceland. It appears that there were many victims. I fear that the incident this time is of such a nature as to provoke, or at least accelerate, the crisis.

November 1, 1941

A letter has arrived from Hitler, but I have not discussed it at length with the Duce, because the translation had not yet been made this morning, and I did not know its contents. What struck Mussolini more than anything else was that the Führer, throughout the long text, referred but very little to our army divisions. Little politics and a great examination of the military situation. It was a fragmentary and casual examination that does not foretell future undertakings by the Axis, but rather tends to point out the blows which England may strike at us. He is evidently concerned about us. During the past winter we have had too much trouble to be able to face another lightly. He fears English landings in Corsica, Sicily, and Sardinia, and offers, beginning today, all his support in the language of one who does not know what a successful blow by the English may do to us. Fundamentally, the Germans distrust us, and in my opinion this letter is proof of it. Nevertheless, it is the document of a man who is aware of what might happen and who is not free from great worry. He knows that he is playing a difficult game with a strong and dangerous adversary. The letters that arrived after the French campaign had quite a different flavor.

A long conversation with the chief of police, Senise. This is the first time I have spoken with him at length. Until now our meetings have been fleeting and a wary attitude maintained by us both. After all, he is a sleuth. But today I was amused. He is a Neapolitan, both intelligent and ignorant, a queer mixture; he follows natural instincts and is a blackmailer; fundamentally he is easy going, a chatterbox, superficial, and a gesticulator. It is enough to think that a man like him is the chief of police in the twentieth year of Fascism, to be con-

vinced that in this country, *plus ça change et plus c'est le même chose.*
He might better have been a Bourbon minister. In brief, he tells me
that the internal situation is restless, but not dangerous, that Mussolini
likes to be deceived by crooks, who are always successful with him,
that Buffarini is a hypocrite and a thief because he demands money
for the aryanization of the Jews, and receives money from Bocchini,
a bigger thief than he, if possible, and that the new secretary of the
Duce, De Cesare, has the evil eye as well as being an imbecile. The
information is not really very important, but I shall see him more often
because it is amusing.

November 2, 1941

Nothing new.

November 3, 1941

The Duce is indignant with Pavelić, because he claims that the
Croats are descendants of the Goths. This will have the effect of bringing them into the orbit of the German world. Even at the present time
we have clear signs of this maneuver.

A ceremony of the Garibaldi legion on the Janiculum to honor the
soldiers who fell in 1849. Mussolini delivered a short talk, filled with
dark threats against the French. This will not please the French, and
will perhaps please the Germans even less.

November 4, 1941

Nothing new.

November 5, 1941

Cavallero speaks to me of the coming of Marshal Kesselring to Italy.
He will assume command of the joint forces operating in southern
Italy and on the islands, which means all the combat forces. Cavallero
also brings out that this will have an ugly repercussion in the country.
But personally he would like, at least, to draw one advantage from it,
and gives me to understand that if he is granted the rank of marshal

the trouble might in part be remedied. Mussolini has swallowed the toad. He realizes the meaning of this fact in the general picture of the war and within the country, but, like a good player, he takes the blow, and pretends that he doesn't feel it.

I accompany Ghigi to the Duce's, and he draws a very dark, realistic picture of the Greek situation. He confirms the fact that within a short time there might be free-for-all shooting in the streets. We must clarify our position with the Germans: it is either they or us. This double-harness situation complicates everything, and prevents a solution of any problem. Mussolini has given Ghigi some good words, and nothing more. Perhaps he couldn't offer anything else.

November 6, 1941

Anna Maria Bismarck said to Anfuso that when General Rintelen went to see the Führer on the eastern front he was approached by the German marshals and generals, and that a sort of meeting took place. During the meeting they entreated him to find some way of making Hitler understand that the way the war in Russia is conducted is pure folly, that the German Army is gradually wearing out, that it cannot hold on, and that, finally, he is leading Germany to the brink of ruin. It seems that this is the unanimous opinion of all the military leaders, but that no one dares tell it to Hitler. Naturally, Rintelen, too, was careful not to do so. But if this is true—and it is probable that it is true —it is serious, because in Germany the generals still count a great deal.

Today Mussolini said, during one of his usual anti-German out-bursts: "We can do nothing against Germany for the time being. We must bide our time. It is a country that no one can vanquish militarily, but it will collapse through lack of internal equilibrium. For us, it is a problem of 'holding out' and waiting until this takes place."

November 7, 1941

I had not seen Prince Humbert for a long time and today he was very cordial. He wanted to know about Germany, and listened with a great deal of interest and with an effort to appear impartial, while his prejudice against our allies was clear: he considers them insufferably crude. Then the Prince spoke about the Armed Forces. He is, or believes himself to be, competent; therefore, his appraisal of the past is severe. He blames Badoglio, but repeats that it was an error to have him liquidated by the argument of "any old Farinacci." Badoglio has by now disappeared from the memory and the hearts of the Army, but the moral crisis which his leaving engendered still exists, and it will take time and care to heal it. The Prince's judgment on Cavallero was almost favorable.

I again called Mackensen's attention to what is happening in Mitrovica, in the Kossovo region, where, with the complicity of German propaganda, there has arisen a small local government composed of refugee elements from Albania. This creates confusion and disorder, serving to attract all those who wish to disturb relations between ourselves and the Germans. Mackensen agrees. But what can he do about it?

Stalin has made a speech which lags and is full of absurdities, such as the one "that the Russian forces proved themselves to be strong and the German forces weak." But, quite aside from this, it is clear that he intends to fight and resist.

November 8, 1941

The figures sent by our Embassy in Washington on American war production have impressed Mussolini, who has asked that a chart be prepared comparing present production with preceding months. In reality, the increase is impressive.

It seems that von Plessen, during a dinner in the home of Clemma, asked a lady point-blank, "When will the revolution start in Italy?" To which the lady replied calmly, "As you know, we follow you in everything. Therefore, it will take place after it happens in your country." What a charming atmosphere! After all, Baroness von Clemma herself told Anfuso that the Germans have a right to a warm-water outlet, and so one day they will demand Trieste. Anfuso gave her the twofold advice, not to talk politics, and to dedicate her energies to another occupation in which the Baroness is notoriously something of an expert.

November 9, 1941

Since September 19 we had given up trying to get convoys through to Libya; every attempt had been paid for at a high price, and the losses suffered by our merchant marine had reached such proportions as to discourage any further experiments. Tonight we tried it again; Libya needs materials, arms, fuel, more and more every day. And a convoy of seven ships left, accompanied by two ten-thousand-ton cruisers and ten destroyers, because it was known that at Malta the British had two battleships destined to act as wolves among the sheep. An engagement occurred, the results of which are inexplicable. All, I mean *all* our ships were sunk, and one or maybe two or three destroyers. The British returned to their ports after having slaughtered us. Naturally, today our various headquarters are pulling out their usual inevitable and imaginary sinking of a British cruiser by a torpedo plane; nobody believes it. This morning Mussolini was depressed and indignant. This will undoubtedly have profound repercussions in Italy, Germany, and, above all, in Libya. Under the circumstances we have no right to complain if Hitler sends Kesselring as commander in the south.

November 10, 1941

The photographs taken by our reconnaissance planes show four English ships moored in the port of Malta. Notwithstanding, it is reported in the bulletin that one of the cruisers has been struck. Pricolo insists upon it, and uses the argument that this ship had gone to moor near the dry dock. This is equivalent to declaring that a man is probably slightly dead because he has gone to live near the cemetery. Clowns, tragic clowns, who have brought our country to the present-day necessity of accepting, in fact, of invoking, outside intervention to be protected and defended!

From now on, until the Germans come, English aviation will dominate our skies almost like their own. I have asked Cavallero what will be done to the responsible admiral. Until last night Cavallero did not even know his name. I reminded him that the democratic Italy of Ricasoli had the courage to court-martial Persano when, after the battle of Lissa, he telegraphed that he dominated the seas. I also told this to Mussolini, who was still discouraged, and is right in considering yesterday the most humiliating day since the beginning of the war. "I have been waiting for a piece of good news for eighteen months now, and it never comes. I, too, should be proud to send a telegram like the one Churchill has sent his admiral, but for too long a time I have been vainly trying to find the opportunity."

November 11, 1941

Irritation and misery for what has happened persist in the country and in the Duce. Mussolini is exasperated and takes it out on the Croatians from Spalato who throw bombs at our soldiers. "I, too, will adopt the method of hostages," he said. "I have given orders that for every one of our men who is wounded, two of theirs must be shot, and for every one of our dead, twenty of theirs." But he knows that he won't do it.

Galbiati, returning from Greece, said that Greece is not yet at the point of starvation, but will be shortly. The rebellion will begin when the first children starve to death.

Jacomoni proposes that we change the Albanian Government. Kruia in the place of Verlaçi. Which means a further concession to the extremists of Albanian Nationalism. Up to now the results of this policy have not been good; things went better when Benini concentrated authority in Rome. In any case, Mussolini has agreed, and we shall see what will happen.

I read *Parlo con Bruno* by the Duce. [A book Mussolini wrote to commemorate the death of his son Bruno.] It is a collection of articles and various writings held together by Mussolini's style. But this style is very different from that of the book on Arnaldo. [Another book that Mussolini wrote on the death of his brother.]

November 12, 1941

At navy headquarters they were scandalized by what has taken place in the Mediterranean, but with the present command it is impossible to expect anything better. Bigliardi has described to me the different phases of the encounter. All of this would be inexplicable if it were not known that Admiral Brivonesi is said by Cavagnari to be unfit for command. After the battle Bigliardi was reached by telephone by Riccardi, who told him that in order to neutralize the bad impression in our country it was imperative to send out a bulletin about successes in the Atlantic. But where were these successes? Relying upon some very uncertain information, a bulletin was drawn up which attributed to the submarine *Malaspina* the sinking of two steamers aggregating ten thousand tons. The only real sinking was that of the Italian submarine which has been missing from its base for ten days. The assistant head of the General Staff, Admiral Sansonetti, picked up his pencil and increased the ten thousand to thirty thousand, because "this would create a greater effect." Comment is superfluous. The Navy has had the reputation of being serious and honorable and cannot tolerate certain actions without going through a profound crisis. Besides, all the Navy knows and repeats that Admiral Riccardi owes his position to the protection of Signora Petacci [the mother of Mussolini's mistress], and this is certainly not a rumor designed to increase his prestige.

November 13, 1941

Tassinari is more pessimistic than ever in his forecasts. If Germany does not, or does not want to, give us five hundred thousand tons of cereals, it will be necessary to reduce by one half the bread and pasta rations beginning the first of March to the end of June. Now Mussolini is absolutely against asking the Germans for wheat; he feels humiliation at military developments, including the coming of Kesselring, and he does not wish to add any more reasons for being grateful, and therefore more humiliated.

We have had to change the system of pay for our foreign diplomatic agents, because we have no more foreign exchange and the end of the conflict is still so far away.

Anfuso leaves. He will go as Minister to Budapest. He desired this very much, and now he has been satisfied. I am sorry he is leaving, not so much on account of his collaboration as because of his companionship.

November 14, 1941

Alfieri transmits a communication from von Ribbentrop on the behavior of our workingmen in Germany. We must recognize that among them is a noticeable percentage of hoodlums, idlers, and intemperate men. Even the Germans make a clear distinction between the northern and southern workingmen, and they state that the first do between 80 and 90 per cent of what a German workingman can do and the second not more than 40 per cent. Hatred against Germany must be at white heat, in view of the fact that they have gone so far as to repeat aloud, "We shall all march together against the Germans." Von Ribbentrop's communication is harsh but frank, and hence praiseworthy, but not to the point of my thanking von Ribbentrop as Alfieri would like me to do.

November 15, 1941

Change of guard in the Air Force Command. It is about time. Pricolo had greatly disillusioned us, and had shown himself increasingly shortsighted, envious, and mean. Fougier is replacing him. At least he is likable and a real pilot, not a dirigible officer. He will have as head of his bureau Casero, my old faithful Casero, who is certainly an officer who takes his duties seriously. With him things should be better.

November 16, 1941

In Genoa for the dedication of the monument to my father. It was a simple ceremony, an intimate one, for it was thus that I desired it because I do not feel that this is a moment to assemble people in large gatherings. The statue is huge but not very well done; it is by Prini, a Genoese sculptor who yesterday moved us to pity because he had recently lost a son who was a submarine commander. I recalled when my father lived in Via Corsica in 1919 he made Genoa the center of his activities. To see his likeness perpetuated in marble is to me today a sad but pleasing sensation.

November 17, 1941

No news during my absence. Mussolini tells me that he has persuaded Rommel to hasten the attack at Tobruk and that it is to begin some time this month. I recall that Gambara has expressed himself as distinctly opposed to this because he fears that when we attack Tobruk this will be followed by an English attack on our flank at Sollum, which he feels we cannot resist.

Cavallero informs me that the Duce has ordered an enquiry into the conduct of Graziani. The head of the commission is old Thaon de Revel, and General Ago, General Marmi, and the National Counselor Manaresi formed part of it. This idea had been fixed in his head for some time. But is this really the time to stir up a hornets' nest?

The King wants the Duke of Spoleto to leave Rome, and Mussolini will inform him through Russo. In fact, the behavior of this young man is quite absurd. He is living with a well-known society girl and brings her to his private car. He frequents restaurants and taverns and gets tight. A few nights ago, in a restaurant near Piazza Colonna, he put a twisted towel around his head in imitation of a crown, amid the applause of the waiters and of the owner, a certain Ascensio, who spends part of the time in his kitchen and part of the time in jail. Ascensio happens to be the Duke's best friend. He is a fine man to be a king!

November 18, 1941

A serious matter: Bismarck has told Anfuso that there is some alarm at the German Embassy because it is learned that Pricolo has been removed by the government on account of his opposition to the coming of Kesselring to Italy. This is entirely false. Bismarck, when pressed, declared under the seal of absolute secrecy that the information had been given to Rintelen by Cavallero, who boasted of the service that he had thus rendered Germany. There is no need of comment. This fact is enough to prove what Cavallero is. The real truth is that he had quarreled with Pricolo for entirely different reasons, and that in this way he has tried to besmirch him.

Mussolini tells me that he has learned from His Majesty that the King of the Belgians has married the daughter of the Governor of Liége [really Governor of Western Flanders], upon whom the King had brought public scorn on account of his having gone to meet the Germans. [When they invaded Belgium.] The King now lives at Laecken in his castle, and he is disinterested in his government. "Another sovereign who has been liquidated," says Mussolini, who is more and more anti-monarchical. "This proves that dynasties are a useless inheritance of the past which nations can no longer tolerate."

Meeting at the Palazzo Venezia to carry on negotiations with France. Although the situation is not of the best, I have expressed the opinion that we must do something, especially since the Germans are carrying on a conciliatory policy and are grabbing everything.

November 19, 1941

Casertano gives the Duce and me a rather discouraging account of the situation in Croatia. The instability of Pavelić's power, domestic intrigues, and growing German meddling are the elements that make the life of the new state uncertain and our influence precarious. There is no longer an Italo-Croatian problem but an Italo-German problem as regards Croatia. It is a controversial problem, but we do not wish nor can we afford to make it such.

Bartoli is painting my picture. He is a truly great artist. He is human. His feet are on the ground, and he refuses to follow styles and trends in which he does not believe, even if they would bring him fame and easy money. Besides, he has a rare wit and vivacity. He does not dare touch on certain subjects, but rumor has it that his witticisms are very keen. I know that he recently drew a cartoon in which one sees the Lion of Judah leaving the station of Rome, while Mussolini says politely to him, "Let us hope the next time you will remain longer." He is pitiless, but those who know him assure me that Bartoli is a good patriot and a sincere Fascist, even if he indulges in biting satire.

November 20, 1941

English attack in Libya. At some points resistance is effective, at others, the offensive penetration has been rapid and deep. Cavallero is optimistic and considers the situation "normal." This is reflected in Mussolini's attitude. I am especially fearful of the lack of supplies and the insufficiency of our aviation, which, during this initial attack, has suffered serious losses.

Riccardi takes advantage of the occasion of the selection of a commercial attaché to Spain for a violent attack on Dr. Petacci—the brother of that notorious woman—who, in his opinion, is a crooked speculator. In support of his assertions he repeats this phrase of Leto, the Inspector General of Police: "Dr. Petacci is doing the Duce more harm than fifteen battles."

The Germans at Frascati have eyed the Collegio di Mondragone [famous Jesuit school], and they want to ·requisition it as a barracks. This is an extremely unpopular measure, calculated to hit five hundred families. The Nuncio has protested, adding that the presence of the Germans at Frascati will prevent the Vatican from carrying out its plan to keep Rome safe from bombing.

November 21, 1941

The battle of Libya is in full swing and our responsible military leaders are optimistic. Churchill in one of his speeches has been outspoken about the objectives of the action but very prudent as to the course of the operations. Nevertheless, we must admit that it is a disturbing speech. The Duce is not of this opinion.

Serrano has sent me a long letter which ends with the proposal of a meeting at Genoa in December. I shall speak of it with the Germans in Berlin. I shall leave tomorrow night, and if they do not raise objections the meeting with Serrano might take place.

November 22, 1941

No positive news about the Libyan battle. Cavallero is undisturbed; Mussolini is definitely satisfied as to how things are going. On the other hand, von Rintelen appears to be worried. The convoy which was to cross last night direct to Tripoli by following the route east of Malta has not succeeded in passing. The boats under the attack of torpedo planes turned back toward Taranto, and at the same time two cruisers, the *Trieste* and the *Duke of Abruzzi*, were struck by torpedoes. Fortunately they were not sunk. There is no doubt that the task of moving supplies is most difficult, and it is that which keeps our hearts in our throats.

I leave this evening for Berlin. There are few instructions from the Duce: I must insist on the question of the troops to be sent to Russia. I must clarify Germany's intentions as to Croatia and Greece. I must not speak of the food problem, and I must reach agreement as to an eventual meeting between myself and Darlan.

November 23, 1941

On my way to Berlin.

November 24, 1941

I have made notes on my conferences and on my impressions of Berlin. I add here something more indiscreet.

The atmosphere of the anti-Comintern meeting was truly singular. The state of mind of the delegates differed very much. Serrano Suñer was aggressive and sharp but quite pro-Axis. The accusation that the Germans make against him of having prevented Spanish intervention is unjust. He really hates the English, the Americans, and the Russians.

But he cannot behave properly with the Germans and is ironical with them. Bárdossy had a resigned air and as often as he could he launched a modest and cautious dart against Germany. Mihai Antonescu is a novice in foreign politics. Until a short time ago he was an unknown lawyer in Bucharest; now he represents his country, and he does a pretty good job. But he remains a Rumanian and has an equivocal air. The Danish representative was like a fish out of water—a little old man in a morning coat who wondered why he was there but who, on the whole, was glad that he was there because things might have gone worse.

November 25, 1941 [continuation of November 24]

The Germans were the masters of the house, and they made us all feel it even though they were especially polite to us. There is no way out of it. Their European hegemony has now been established. Whether this is good or bad is neither here nor there, but it does exist. Consequently, it is best to sit at the right hand of the master of the house. And we are at the right hand.

Goering was very much offended because of some secondhand gossip concerning our Embassy. After venting his feelings to me the air was cleared. He was impressive when he spoke of the Russians, who are eating each other and have also eaten a German sentry in a prison camp. He recounted the incidents with the most absolute indifference. And yet he is kindhearted, and when he spoke of Udet and Moelders, who have lately disappeared, tears came to his eyes.

A dramatic episode: Goering told me that hunger among the Russian prisoners had reached such an extreme that in order to start them toward the interior it is no longer necessary to send them under armed guard; it is enough to put at the head of the column of prisoners a camp kitchen, which emits the fragrant odor of food; thousands and thousands of prisoners trail along like a herd of famished animals. And we are in the year of grace 1941.

November 26, 1941 [continuation of November 25]

An amusing episode: The Spanish Blue Legion is sturdy but undisciplined and restless. The soldiers suffer from the cold and they want women. Anti-erotic pills so efficacious with the Germans do not have the least effect on them. After many protests the German command authorized them to go to a brothel and had contraceptives distributed among them. Then came a counterorder: no contact with Polish women. The Spaniards in protest inflated the contraceptives and tied them on the ends of their guns. Thus one day in the suburbs of Warsaw one saw a parade of fifteen thousand contraceptives carried by Spanish legionaries.

The battle of Marmarica has raised us in the esteem of the Germans. For the first time they speak of Italian bravery and of our military contribution. The optimistic outlook on the development of operations was more pronounced in Berlin than in Rome, where we maintain a prudent reserve. Two days ago the Führer considered the battle won.

[*No entry for November 27.*]

November 28, 1941

Return by train.

November 29, 1941

I hand the Duce my report. He is satisfied but is in a hurry, and we shall speak of it tomorrow. I accompany him in his car to Villa Torlonia.

The battle of Marmarica has aroused in the Italians more interest than any other episode of this war. This is as it should be. If we win this battle, the English situation may become very insecure, perhaps untenable. Within a short time we may also have favorable and unforeseen developments. England would have to face four crises and all of them of the first importance: public opinion at home, American delusion, a more clear-cut separation from the French, and, finally, a loss of face in the East, with repercussions in Turkey and even in India.

November 30, 1941

Cavallero sums up the Libyan situation. He is aware of its gravity but is neither pessimistic nor optimistic. The hardest problem is that of supplies. This evening we are going to try to send through a convoy of five boats by breaking the blockade. How many will get through?

December 1, 1941

Out of the whole convoy two ships arrived, one was forced to beach at Suda Bay, and two were sunk. The result is not brilliant. But it might have been worse. The Libyan situation has crystallized somewhat, but the English are receiving reinforcements. Cavallero defines it as difficult but logical. God only knows what he means. Experience tells me that when generals entrench themselves behind unintelligible jargon it means that there is a nigger in the woodpile. . . .

I have protested to the Nuncio about the publication in the *Osservatore Romano* of some photographs showing that our prisoners in Egypt are having a great time—football games, concerts, gaiety. Mussolini is concerned about it. "It is a known fact," he says, "that they are inclined to let themselves be taken prisoners. If they see that their comrades are having such a good time over there, who can hold them back?"

On the advice of the police, who do not guarantee that they can keep order, I postpone my trip to Zagreb until a better time. This time it will be Pavelić who will come back to Italy—I believe to Venice.

December 2, 1941

Another of our ships has been sunk, almost at the entrance to the port of Tripoli. It was the *Mantovani* loaded with seven thousand tons of gasoline. It cannot be denied that the blow is a hard one. The battle—for the moment—has no new developments, but it is clear that time is working against us. My meeting with Darlan has been arranged with Vacca Maggiolini. It will take place in Turin on Thursday. This will be the first political contact with the French since the beginning of the war. I do not believe, however, that very much will come of it, and Cavallero's hope to have free transit to Bizerte seems to me doomed to failure.

The Duce is concerned about the food problem. He is now convinced that we lack five hundred thousand tons of grain for our needs. We must borrow it from Germany. We might be able to pay it back in July, since our harvest, on account of climatic conditions, comes two months before theirs. But Mussolini cannot make up his mind to write to the Führer making the request, and I can understand this. If we could do without this help it would be very fortunate, but it seems to me absolutely necessary. The fact is that even those responsible for domestic order—Serena, Buffarini, et al., believe that any more food restrictions would surely cause disorders.

December 3, 1941

A stunning move by the Japanese. The Ambassador asks to be received by the Duce, to whom he reads a long declaration on the progress of their negotiations with America, concluding that they have arrived at a dead end. Then, invoking the pertinent clause of the Tripartite Pact, he asks that Italy declare war on the United States as soon as the conflict begins, and proposes also that we sign a pact with Japan on making no separate peace. The interpreter who was taking down these requests was trembling like a leaf. The Duce gave general assurances, reserving the right to get together on the matter with Berlin. The Duce was pleased by the communication, and said, "Thus we arrive at the war between continents, which I have foreseen since September 1939." What does this new event mean? Now that Roosevelt has succeeded in his maneuver, not being able to enter the war directly, he has succeeded by an indirect route—forcing the Japanese to attack him. Now that every possibility of peace is receding farther and farther into the distance, to speak of a long war is an easy, very easy prophecy to make. Who will have the longest wind? This is the way the question should be put.

The reply from Berlin will be delayed because Hitler has gone to the southern front to see General Kleist, whose armies continue to fall back under the pressure of an unexpected Soviet offensive.

December 4, 1941

Berlin reaction to the Japanese step is extremely cautious. Maybe they will go ahead, because they can't do otherwise, but the idea of provoking American intervention is less and less liked by the Germans. Mussolini, on the other hand, is happy about it.

I receive a message from Gambara. Naturally, he is offended because Rommel was given command, but aside from this he sees the situation as delicate and filled with unknown factors. Nistri, who is a convinced Fascist and an intelligent officer, is very pessimistic, and adds by word of mouth the things Gambara did not wish to write, that is that the exhaustion of our forces is noticeable, that enemy infiltrations reach every point of Cyrenaica, and that, finally, we are in no condition to resist another offensive by the British. "Our men die gloriously," he concludes, "which does not change the fact that they die."

December 5, 1941

A night interrupted by Ribbentrop's restiveness. After having delayed two days he now hasn't a minute to lose in answering the Japanese, and at three o'clock in the morning he sends Mackensen to my house to submit a plan for a Tripartite Pact of Japanese intervention and the promise not to make a separate peace. They wanted me to wake up the Duce, but I did not do it, and the Duce was very pleased.

I gave Mussolini a copy of Gambara's letter, in which, however, I omitted the anti-Rommel phrases. The Duce is now so proud of having given the command to the Germans that he would have been very angry with Gambara—and Cavallero is urging him on. He dislikes Gambara. They have entirely different natures. One is a soldier, the other plays politics.

December 6, 1941

A few words in reply to Gambara, words of friendship and good wishes. But things in Libya are not going well, and I fear that sad days are near at hand.

December 7, 1941

Dark news from Libya. Our forces are no longer such as to attempt a long resistance; they must break contact with the enemy, and break it decisively, in order to try to defend the Gebel. Mussolini is calm; in fact, he talks about the possibility of a counterattack. Cavallero, on the other hand, is obscure, and thinks that it all depends on cession of the port of Bizerte by the French. I am supposed to speak about it to Darlan on Thursday, but during the evening Mackensen comes to tell me in the name of Ribbentrop that I must start no such negotiations with the French. This is the will of Hitler, communicated to Mussolini through Rintelen.

Hitler is right: Tunisia is de Gaullist 101 per cent; any unwelcome pressure would in itself accentuate the separation which is developing between the French Empire and the government of Vichy. But without Bizerte Libya is lost; so says Cavallero.

This morning the Duce was very much irritated by the paucity of losses in eastern Africa. Those who fell at Gondar in November number sixty-seven; the prisoners ten thousand. One doesn't have to think very long to see what these figures mean.

December 8, 1941

A night telephone call from Ribbentrop; he is joyful over the Japanese attack on the United States. He is so happy, in fact, that I can't but congratulate him, even though I am not so sure about the advantage. One thing is now certain: America will enter the conflict, and the conflict itself will be long enough to permit her to put into action all her potential strength. This is what I said to the King this morning, when he, too, expressed his satisfaction. He ended by admitting that in "the long run" I might be right. Mussolini was happy. For a long time now he has been in favor of clarifying the position between America and the Axis.

It seems that in Libya things are going a little better. In the Duce's judgment the gloom of the last forty-eight hours has passed. Cavallero, as well as Admiral Riccardi, announce to me a great naval operation against the blockade for the twelfth, thirteenth, and fourteenth of this month. All the ships and all the admirals at sea. May God help us!

Mackensen sends me the résumé of the meeting between Goering, Pétain, and Darlan. It accomplished nothing, only words, suggestions, advice. I don't think my meeting will have any better results.

December 9, 1941

I go to Turin to await the arrival of Admiral Darlan.

December 10, 1941

I took notes on my meeting with Darlan. My impression of the man was good. He is a small man, energetic, willful, and rather boastful, who talks without reticence, and calls a spade a spade. He is a military man, who is beginning to develop a taste for politics, and because he is French, he does it with a certain finesse. Is he sincere? I can't say, except for one thing: he hates the British. Some ways of speaking and some expressions cannot be simulated. On the other hand, there is no choice for him, and he declares it: if the British should win the war, his fate would not be a happy one.

Results of yesterday's meeting: none, except a clearing of the atmosphere which, with the French, it is not difficult to achieve. It is enough that we meet. In order to have bad relations with them, all we have to do is not to meet. And this has always been the recipe used by Mussolini for a break. He himself, when he spoke to them, could not prevent a rapprochement. Even the population of Turin was cordial to the guests; applause was not wanting, though it was scattered.

News of the amazing Japanese naval victories continues to arrive. Against this the land fighting in Libya and in Russia is not going well. Such are the incredible surprises of this war.

December 11, 1941

Mussolini is very little interested in my discussions with Darlan. It is the American war that occupies him. At 2:30 P.M. I receive the Chargé d'Affaires, a good man, somewhat timid, with whom I have had little to do. He thinks that I have called him to discuss the arrival of certain newspapermen, but I disillusion him immediately. He listens to the declaration of war, and turns pale. He says, "It is very tragic." Then he hands me a personal message from Phillips. Feeling that zero hour was approaching, he had telegraphed to express his gratitude and his good wishes. Phillips is an honest man, and he loves Italy. I know that for him this is a day of mourning.

Mussolini made a speech from the balcony—a brief and cutting speech, which fell on a great crowd. A very pro-Japanese setting. News of the naval victories has excited the Italian imagination. The demonstration, however, was not very enthusiastic. We must not forget that it was three o'clock in the afternoon, the people were hungry, and the day was quite cold. These are all elements which do not make for enthusiasm.

In the evening Ribbentrop asks that we join a German proposal that the countries of the Tripartite Alliance declare war on the United States. How about Spain?

December 12, 1941

The Vichy press spoke with cordiality about the welcome of the French in Turin, and this rasped the Duce's nerves. I gave Mackensen the report of my conversations with Darlan, underlining the need to send a political representative to Vichy for the purpose of taking away from the Armistice Commission the political functions which do not belong to it, and which generals do not always know how to exercise.

December 13, 1941

The usual naval woes. Tonight we have lost two five-thousand-ton cruisers: the *Barbiano* and the *Giussano,* and also two large ships, the *Del Greco* and the *Filzi,* loaded with tanks for Libya. This happened even before the great convoy (accompanied by battleships) ever had put out to sea. What is happening in the Navy is baffling, unless what Somigli says is true, and that is, that our General Staffs are possessed by an inferiority complex that paralyzes all their activities. The fact is that our naval losses become more serious every day, and I wonder whether the war won't outlast our Navy.

The Minister from Cuba came to declare war. He was very emotional, and was disappointed that I did not share his emotion. But, after having had the good fortune, or is it the misfortune, to declare war on France, on Great Britain, on Russia, and on the United States, could the good man really think that I would turn pale on learning that Sergeant Batista was mobilizing against us the forces of Cuba on land and sea and in the air? Ecuador, too, has declared war, but I had my secretary receive the Minister.

December 14, 1941

Cavallero justifies our naval defeats with an impudence that can't be equaled. He has become the defender of the office of Admiral Riccardi, and this morning I had an earful which I shall never forget. It is strange that this Piedmontese general should have the mentality of a Neapolitan deputy.

Mussolini is calm. This morning he jested a long time with me in a tone of impersonal argument. He took it out on Christmas, Christmas gifts, and the gifts of all holidays in general. He says that the offering of gifts is the alibi of the rich to justify their good fortune in the eyes of the poor. The fact is that in these days the people feel more than ever the lack of food, and complain, but Mussolini, as is his custom, takes it out even on the Almighty when things go wrong.

I leave for Venice, where I will meet Pavelić. He will ask for many things, but I know already that I shall have to refuse them all. I shall use good manners, and sugar-coat what I have to say, but its substance will have to be negative.

December 15, 1941

I have had the usual stenographic transcriptions made of the conferences.

Impressions: Pavelić is growing more and more confident as he continues to rule. He is more resolute, casual, and calm. He has complete domination over his ministers and even treats them harshly. In my presence he reproached his Minister of the Treasury, who blushed to the roots of his hair and hung his head.

It all depends on the Germans. If they keep their obligations under which Croatia has become a zone of Italian influence, a great deal can be accomplished by us yet. If, on the contrary, they should again try to force our hand and press their penetration, there is nothing for us to do but to haul down our flag and return home. The Croatians are very sympathetic toward us. Pavelić also likes us, but all of them are terrorized by the Germans, and it does not even occur to them to offer resistance to any pressure from Berlin.

The monarchical question has for the moment been laid aside. That does not displease me, especially because I still think that it is possible to have a real union under our King. Naturally, all this is premature, and we should always have to give the most ample guarantees with reference to local independence.

December 16, 1941 [continuation of December 15]

Army, diplomatic corps, police, courts, all of this geared to an imperial system which in the beginning would be easier to realize in practice than to fix in terms of constitutional formulae.

In summary, it seems to me that the boat continues to float with some difficulty, and that it begins to unfurl some timid sails. We are far from the end, but something has been done, and as for the future, everything will depend upon us and upon the men who work for us in Croatia.

Venice was sad, empty, tired. Never have I seen it so squalid. Empty hotels, deserted streets. Fog. Misery. Darkness. I have only vague memories of the Venice of the other war, but it was not at all like this. If nothing else, there was the sentimental attraction of a first-line city.

December 17, 1941

I confer with Mussolini, who was very skeptical on the progress of things in Croatia. He is happy about it, especially since the Germans have asked us to assume territorial military control over the whole country. This is certainly due to the fact that the Germans have to withdraw their divisions, because in Russia the winter threatens to be hard, and Serbia gives them too much trouble, although it also proves that Croatia is really considered in Berlin as our Lebensraum. Mussolini wants to accept the proposal immediately. Roatta, who two days ago took Cavallero's place in Libya, is favorable, but asks if he may not study the proposal because he fears that the available military forces may not be sufficient, and he does not want to start something he cannot finish.

Things are not going well in Libya. Even Mussolini is beginning to admit it, and he blames Rommel, who, he believes, spoiled the situation with his recklessness. Today the whole fleet is at sea, and Riccardi believes that a clash with the British is inevitable. He says that we are definitely superior in quantity and quality, and he promises success— the success we have been waiting for for so long in vain. Can it be that our luck will change?

December 18, 1941

The convoy has gone through without battle and without trouble. On the other hand, the situation is reaching a crisis in Cyrenaica. The headquarters and motorized forces are withdrawing to Agedabia, while the infantry is turning toward Bengasi, where the General Staff is thinking of forming an entrenched camp and resisting as the English did at Tobruk. Can this be possible in view of the fact that we do not have control of the sea as they had? I am somewhat skeptical about it.

A meeting at the Palazzo Venezia to extend our occupation to all Croatia. On the military plane it is a question of troops. We must send strong forces because a revolution may break out in the spring when the woods afford cover and concealment. If we undertake to garrison the country we must do it 100 per cent. However, this does not concern me and I am not interfering with it. Politically I have expressed my opinion that we must do things simply: communicate to the Croatians that on account of a special decision of the Axis command the Germans are leaving and we are arriving. We should avoid at all costs presenting the decision as a success gained by us. That would mean putting all Croatians against us.

December 19, 1941

News is still bad in Libya, in spite of the official optimism of our General Headquarters. God confound servile optimists! They are the ones who have cooked our goose. They have ruined us. In the meantime, Rommel announces that he, with his slender armored resources, will break into Tunisia, because he does not wish to be made prisoner by the British. All this while Cavallero continues to swear that nobody can make him fall back from the wastes of the Sirte, and Mussolini believes him.

I saw Verlaçi, who spat venom when talking about Jacomoni, and this is natural, because he was shown the door. It is the way in which it was done that most offends him. He would have desired longer notice, but this, too, would have been a double-edged sword. He says that now matters are troubled in Albania, and that the people are dissatisfied. He might be exaggerating, but there must be something to it. However, when I asked him what remedy he could offer, he had none to suggest. Jacomoni, with whom I conferred at length, is not pessimistic, and believes that, with good steering, we can set our ship on its course again. So far he has never been mistaken.

December 20, 1941

Mussolini is satisfied with the way the war is going in Russia. He talks about it openly. The failure of the German troops cheers him. "As long as this doesn't go too far," I suggested. He even called

Alfieri to Rome to learn more about it. Nothing new in Libya on what had been forecast yesterday. The official slogan is that if the Littorio division is brought to the African shore we shall be in Sollum in a few days. Let's hope so.

Mackensen informs us that the Germans not only approve our sending a representative to Vichy, but are favorable to our sending an ambassador to Paris, in a position indentical to that of Abetz. I asked Buti if he was willing to go, but up to now he has raised many objections. Truly, I can't make it out.

December 21, 1941

The Duce approves the sending of an ambassador to Paris and the choice of Buti. The latter has now overcome his instinctive timidity and has accepted. I have informed von Mackensen of all this and intend to draw up an official communiqué with him.

I am informed by Cavallero of the development of operations in Cyrenaica. As usual, he finds everything "logical." He says that it is due to him that all our infantry has not fallen into the hands of the English. He repeats that we shall hold firm at Agedabia and he denies any danger for Tripolitania. Let us hope that he is right. On the other hand, he considers the situation of the Germans on the Russian front quite difficult. Bismarck has communicated to d'Aieta that Brauchitsch has been liquidated. It's a sign of a serious crisis. It must be added that in Germany the General Staff is of real importance and has an enormous following in the country.

Goebbels' and Hitler's messages have not made a good impression. The humble but pressing request for warm clothing for the soldiers on the eastern front is in direct contrast to the arrogant tone that up to now has characterized their speeches. It also proves the Germans are unprepared for a winter struggle.

December 22, 1941

The liquidation of Brauchitsch is on the agenda. English and American radios talk of nothing else. The German Embassy is staggered by the news. Mackensen expressed no opinions, but didn't conceal his concern. Bismarck didn't conceal his joy, and turning to Anfuso he said: "We have come to the fifth act of the great tragedy. This goes to show that Hitler is a blundering ass." The young man is exaggerating, but he isn't the only one in Germany who plays at opposition. The crisis is in the regime itself; it isn't only between men, and I must add that the General Staff supports its chiefs. Cavallero also told me that General Rintelen is very reserved on the subject.

Mussolini does not attach very great importance to the matter. He believes, in fact, that in the last analysis it will be advantageous. because "this war has proven that only political armies have something to say, and now Hitler is making his army more political." I wonder if this is the proper moment to do it—between frostbites and Russian beatings. Mussolini has again attacked Christmas. He is surprised that the Germans have not yet abolished this holiday, which "reminds one only of the birth of a Jew who gave to the world debilitating and devitalizing theories, and who especially contrived to trick Italy through the disintegrating power of the Popes." He has prohibited newspapers from mentioning Christmas, yet all you have to do is to look out of the window to see that the people remember it and love it just the same.

December 23, 1941

I accompanied Verlaçi to the Duce's. He did not behave well. He strongly attacked Jacomoni, and also requested that he be replaced by Guzzoni, who, in a few months, would be capable not only of eating up Albania, but all the Balkans as well. He naturally detests Kruia, but he does not have any solid arguments against him. He confines himself to saying that a country cannot be governed by a man who is the son of a servant by whom Verlaçi himself had been served a cup of coffee in the home of Essad Pasha. Verlaçi is a feudal lord, and those things that to us may appear to be prejudices are sacred principles to him.

Serena and Tassinari have insulted each other in the presence of the Duce, and almost came to blows in the anteroom. It seems that the Duce is about ready to put thumbs down on Serena, pushed on by Buffarini, who, as always, works in the dark. He is a snake. I have seen a letter he has sent with the *curriculum vitae* of Serena's eventual successor. The Duce opened it in my presence. Buffarini has denied to me having sent such a letter, but I believe more in my eyes than in his word.

Von Mackensen comes, on the advice of von Ribbentrop, to ask my personal opinion on the approaching three-man meeting with Darlan. He says that we must talk politics. I answer that such a conference, if it has an exploratory character, should not turn out harmful or useless.

December 24, 1941

Nothing new on foreign politics or on the war fronts.

At home, attention is beginning to concentrate on the case of Serena, who for two days has not been received by the Duce. Candidates are cropping up. Riccardi has his name proposed by Osio, but the Chief has not spoken to me of the dismissal and I am not taking any initiative on the question. I should indeed consider a Riccardi secretariat a real disaster.

Serena, whom I saw in the afternoon, continues to say that it was a plot by Buffarini, who now has the Duce in his hands and maneuvers through indirect and disloyal channels. He intimates that on the pretext of compensation he would give more than one hundred thousand lire a month to the Petacci woman, upon whom, meanwhile, he exerts influence by means of a certain Donadio, whose role is not clear. Indeed, Serena says that a racket of the Petaccis has been formed around the Duce, manipulated in the background by Buffarini and served by De Cesare, who is acquiring more influence every day and acts in a sinister fashion. He is unperturbed as regards himself. He wants a decision as soon as possible because he does not consider it good for the dignity of the party that the secretary be allowed to stew for so long a time.

December 25, 1941

Alfieri writes that the disasters on the Russian front have gone farther than is desirable for us. I glean this from the Germans of the Embassy. They are very much discouraged. The Duce, who in the beginning underestimated the problem, now affirms that it is serious and that perhaps it will have further consequences.

The Pope has delivered a Christmas address and naturally it did not please Mussolini because he found that out of the five points it contains at least four are directed against the dictatorships. This is unavoidable, in view of the anti-Catholic policy of the Germans. Isabella Colonna told me last evening that she had recently spoken with Cardinal Maglione, who told her that at the Vatican the Russians are preferred to the Nazis.

Anyway, the Duce increasingly reveals his anti-religious attitude. The Christmas holidays afford him a pretext. "For me," he has declared, "Christmas is nothing more than the twenty-fifth of December. I am the man who in all this world feels least these religious anniversaries." To prove it he has made a list of appointments which is longer than usual. This year, however, the crowds in the churches are overflowing.

December 26, 1941

Serena and Tassinari have been replaced. The first is going to the front, and the second is returning to his university teaching. Pareschi, who is a technician, and who seems good to me, even though he talks too much and is ambitious, is going to the Ministry of Agriculture; a certain Vidussoni, who has a gold medal [military decoration], is twenty-six years old, and a candidate for a law degree, will become General Secretary of the Fascist party. I know nothing else about him. Evidently this is an audacious experiment, and we hope that fortune will this time be a faithful companion to audacity. I know nothing about him, and haven't even seen him.

Vacca Maggiolini has come to tell me that he has received instructions from the Duce to begin conversations with the French with a view to obtaining Tunisian ports, such conversations to be carried out on a political plane. This surprised me for two reasons: in the first place, because our understanding with the Germans is different, or at any rate nothing has been settled with them; and, in the second place, because just a few days ago Mussolini told me that Vacca Maggiolini is an imbecile who should not concern himself with politics. To Vacca Maggiolini, who asked me what to do, I naturally gave the advice that he should follow the instructions of the Duce to the letter.

December 27, 1941

Council of Ministers. The Duce summarizes the military and political situation. He says nothing that is new to me. He foresees a very long war, lasting at least four or five years, and that humanity is moving toward complete "proletarianization." He distinctly undervalues America and her real weight in the conflict.

I received Vidussoni, whose appointment has aroused a unanimous feeling of astonishment. From the golf caddies to Count Volpi, everybody is commenting on it sarcastically. Until now very few knew him. Bottai, Russo, Host Venturi, all have taken the trouble to say that he is a nincompoop. I cannot yet judge. I have talked with him for about a half-hour, and the conversation remained more or less vague. He seems enthusiastic and loyal, but is a novice. He will sweat blood in that environment of old whores which is the Fascist party. I have spread the denial that he is a creature of mine, as was beginning to be rumored. Not at all. Let it be clear that he has come out of the mind of Mussolini as Minerva sprang from the brow of Jupiter.

Gambara, in a letter addressed to me, assures me that if "supplies" arrive Tripolitania can be saved, and he takes it out on Rommel, who, "as leader, is a flop."

December 28, 1941

Indelli reports from Tokyo that the Prime Minister of Japan has made some discreet allusions to the possibility of a separate peace between the Axis and U.S.S.R. Mussolini has dashed headlong into an examination of the problem and is very favorable. The vicissitudes of the war, particularly the recent ones, have convinced him that Russia, that ocean of land, may have innumerable surprises in store. He is right. I do not believe a separate peace is possible. The manner of the German attack, the German declaration as to the objectives of the anti-Bolshevik war, the development of events, all seem to preclude this possibility.

We learn from Berlin of an English landing in Norway and of a Russian landing in Crimea. There is no alarm, the German Embassy reports, but the two incidents are not at all underestimated.

The Germans have changed their minds on the Croatian question. They will no longer withdraw their troops, but offer only a military collaboration with us. Perhaps this is not bad, because in the spring Bosnia, Serbia, and Montenegro will give us plenty of headaches.

December 29, 1941

Mussolini says that he will write to Hitler on the question of the Tunisian ports; either France comes to an agreement with us and grants them, or it will be necessary to take them by force. I hope that he doesn't write the letter, because it would bring no good results.

Bismarck talked to d'Aieta about the nomination of Vidussoni. It has made a very bad impression in German quarters, and particularly at the Embassy, where they have had an opportunity to know the youth and to see that he is poor stuff.

December 30, 1941

The letter to Hitler on the question of Tunisian ports was written and sent through Rintelen. I am certain that Hitler's reaction will not be good, especially since news from the Russian front has been anything but favorable. Even Mussolini is concerned about it. He believes, and with good reason, that the physical factor is predominant, and that the Germans will succeed in creating a wall of resistance against Russian pressure only if they are in good physical condition. This is his chief conclusion, but it is certain that the German situation is not at this moment very rosy.

Mussolini asks me to go to Bologna to speak there on the third of January. He realizes that Vidussoni's nomination has shaken the old Fascism and now he wants to do something that will temper the reaction.

December 31, 1941

At the Russian front things continue to be not so good.

I see Kesselring, with whom I have a more or less formal conversation.

Memoriale

di

Gabinetto

per l'anno

1942

(XX)

January 1, 1942

Cavallero comes to see me on a number of pretexts, but actually because he wants the Germans to know through me that he is not responsible for the idea advanced by the Duce of attacking Tunisia. As a matter of fact, it was he who put it in the Duce's head.

A letter arrives from Hitler. It crossed the Duce's letter. It is a long résumé of how things have gone in Russia; mostly excuses, not explanations. The tone is courteous and vaguely subdued in regard to Italy. Very different from the tone used last year about this time when we had our war in Albania.

Alfieri came to the Palazzo Venezia. He paints a vague and disjointed picture of the situation in Germany. He knows nothing and says nothing, and does it with a lot of words.

January 2, 1942

Nothing new here. From our Embassy in Berlin news from the Russian front is steadily worse, but Mussolini doubts its accuracy.

Talking with Alfieri he said, "Tell the Germans that three years from now Italy will still be in the war under exactly the same conditions as today."

It does one good to find a dissenter. Today Barella said that the appointment of Vidussoni has been well received in the country.

January 3, 1942

I was in Bologna for the celebration of the third of January and made a rather long speech at the Medica theater. I curbed the publicity on my speech for the following reasons: I had nothing new to say; I think the less one says at the moment the better; all my government comrades were talking in other cities and it wasn't advisable to arouse or accentuate jealousies by disparity in treatment. The audience listened with attention and applauded warmly, but wanted to be shown. Even a Fascist audience reasons, doesn't get excited, wants to understand things. The warmest acclamations were for Hitler and for the King. The Duce, in Bologna, is one of the family.

On my return I met von Mackensen on the train returning from Germany. He didn't say much but was somewhat low; the retreat in Russia weighs heavily on every German, almost as if it were a personal misfortune.

January 4, 1942

The Duce gives unusual praise to my speech at Bologna. There is no news except the sailing of a convoy to which are entrusted our arms and hopes for the resistance in Libya.

January 5, 1942

Mussolini today repeats his praise of my speech, but shows me a clipping from the *Resto del Carlino* [daily newspaper of Bologna], and criticizes my Fascist salute, which was not according to regulations. Is there nothing really better to think about? Vidussoni comes to see me. After having spoken about a few casual things, he makes some political allusions and announces savage plans against the Slovenes. He wants to kill them all. I take the liberty of observing that there are a million of them. "That does not matter," he answers firmly; "we must imitate the Ascari [Negro soldiers from Italian colonies] and exterminate them!" I hope that he will calm down. Now they say that the motto of the party is no longer "Book and Musket," but "Book and Youngster." [Pun—*Libro e Moschetto—Libro e Maschietto.*]

The convoy has reached Libya without being attacked by air or sea. This will stimulate resistance.

The police advise against my trip to Zagreb. The situation is not good, and there has been shooting in the vicinity. On the other hand, I should not like to disappoint Pavelić, who is expecting me. I have telegraphed Casertano to get his opinion.

January 6, 1942

Mussolini is indignant with the Germans for two reasons—because General Schmidt, who was made prisoner at Bardia, declared to the correspondent of the *Daily Herald* that he could not hold out because he was commanding Italian soldiers. But it seems that it was Schmidt himself who took the initiative in giving up. And because the Germans in Rumania, according to Antonescu's communication, took for themselves the oil which was meant for us. This is why Mussolini called them "highway robbers."

Our public-relations officer with the second army in Croatia sends bad news on the situation and on the morale of the troops. Some units permitted themselves to be captured without firing a shot.

Ravasio comes to pay me a visit. He was appointed vice-secretary of the party by the Duce, with instructions to function as "supervisor of orthodox morality and policy of the party"—an assignment which is obscure, difficult, and indefinite. Ravasio, whom I know very slightly, has the reputation of being a Savonarola, who, in the Cova Café and in the columns of the *Popolo d'Italia*, has uttered thunderous threats against the lukewarm members of the Fascist party. But who are the lukewarm, so-called impure? It is so easy to engage in paper demagogy, but, in reality, whom are we supposed to be accusing? Let them first name names and prove guilt; then, and only then, let them bring out the rope and the soap. I put the question up to Ravasio, and he himself was able to give me no more disturbing example than a butcher who dug up and sold a hog, declared to be infected by the veterinary. A bad thing, to be sure, but not a matter to justify an accusation against the whole class of Fascist leaders.

January 7, 1942

Nothing new.

January 8, 1942

Nothing new.

January 9, 1942

Anti-Italian demonstrations at Zagreb. Everything tends to discourage the trip. It must be for another time.

Mussolini is concerned about the fate of the four transatlantic liners, which are supposed to go to Ethiopia to bring home a first group of Italians who had been sent there after the Ethiopian occupation for colonizing and public works. He fears that the British will stop the ships at Lisbon [the ships circumnavigated Africa] on their return and seize them. I do not think so. I exclude the possibility that the British Government will want to be guilty of breaking promises. In any case, since the Duce feels as he does, I cannot take upon myself the responsibility, and I leave the decision to him.

Acquarone talks to me about the Duke of Spoleto. The Duke doesn't give a damn about Croatia, and wants only money, money, and more money. On the whole, it is to our interest to hand him at least a little. I shall propose to the Duce that we give him a hundred thousand lire a month.

January 10, 1942

Mussolini holds firmly to his point of view regarding the ships we are sending to Ethiopia. However, he does not want to take on his shoulders the weight of a refusal and he gives these instructions: we should postpone decision in this case without breaking off negotiations.

My article on Albania has received favorable comments and, strangely enough, even the German press has laid stress on it as an expression of the policy of the Axis. Nevertheless, it does not seem that that is really their line of conduct in the occupied countries.

January 11, 1942

Germany is in a state of nerves. The denial made to the foreign press about disorders at home is the proof of it. The Duce deplores it. He says, "Had I ever denied that I fought a duel with the heir to the throne, the people would have really begun to believe it." Alfieri sends bad military news and telegraphs that the divisions withdrawn from the Russian front are stationed in occupied territories, but not brought back to the Reich for fear they will spread propaganda. From Vienna Romano also informs me that the state of mind is very bad and that many soldiers have committed suicide rather than return to the Russian front.

January 12, 1942

The Duce protests against the conduct of the German soldiers in Italy, especially the non-commissioned officers, who are presumptuous, quarrelsome, and drunken. Last night in Foggia two of them forced their way into the house of a man who was about to go to bed and said to him, "We have taken possession of France, Belgium, Holland, and Poland. Tonight we are going to take possession of your wife." To which the man replied, "You can take possession of the whole world, but not of my wife. I haven't any. I'm a bachelor." In their disappointment they broke all the furniture before they withdrew. If they go on in this way even Mussolini, who protested to Rintelen, foresees some *"vespro."* [Mussolini refers to the famous Sicilian vespers, where the population rebelled against tyrants.]

Generally speaking, nothing new. The Japanese are doing well, the Germans not at all well in Russia, and we, in Libya, so-so.

January 13, 1942

Politically these are rather empty days. From the military point of view attention has turned toward the Russian front, where difficulties continue for the Germans. Alfieri, too, who as a rule paints everything in rosy colors, begins to admit openly that in Russia they are swallowing a bitter pill. The retreat continues under the growing pressure of the enemy. The Duce does not seem to be excessively worried, but considers the situation very serious. He criticizes Hitler for the entire Russian campaign and says that he has falsified his communiqués. "He has used big figures to impress people like that jackass of a Roosevelt," he said, "and the results have been sinister. In fact, they are both big jackasses and belong to kindred races."

Buti is received by Mussolini before his departure for Paris and listens to these instructions: he is to take no political initiative. He should try to stimulate economic and commercial exchanges; not do very much in the cultural field except to send to France some of our products, such as books, plays, films, and not to take anything from the French.

I have seen von Mackensen. I had not seen him for ten days, as he has been ill. As always happens to the Germans when times are bad, he appeared dejected. I tried to inject some energy into him.

January 14, 1942

On my way to Budapest. Brief stop at Vienna. The city is sad and tired-looking. Romano confirms that the people are not in a good mood.

January 15, 1942

Elsewhere I have put down my impressions of and my conversations with the Hungarians, but since my notes were going into many different hands I was very cautious. The truth is that the Hungarians are exasperated with the Germans. You can't remain long with any Magyar before he speaks ill of Germany. All of them are like this, from the Regent to the last beggar on the street.

Admiral Horthy said, "The Germans are a courageous people, and I admire them for this, but they are also an unbearable, tactless, and boorish people." Kanya was even more cutting. Bethlen weighed his words, but in talking about German interference he was so violent, even though restrained, that I can't describe it.

January 16, 1942

In Budapest. Military ceremonies, and a free afternoon.

January 17, 1942

I was hunting with Mesohegeys. It was a good hunt, but not so rich as the one of 1938. Ribbentrop had already killed most of the wild game, and the Regent [Horthy] was too tired to engage in a long hunt.

January 18, 1942

With the Italians in Budapest, a patriotic ceremony at Fascist headquarters. In the evening I leave.

January 19, 1942

On the train for Rome. I stopped in Venice for supper.

January 20, 1942

I report to Mussolini on my trip. He seems to be interested in what I said in my report and what I say personally to him. He, in turn, gives me the latest news.

France. The Führer does not care to accept the terms which Vichy lays down for placing Tunisian ports at our disposal. He is right. They are excessive. Besides, I have never doubted the intentions of Hitler in this respect.

Rio de Janeiro. America is insisting that all South American countries break relations with us. If this happens, the Duce believes that it would be to our interest to declare war without loss of time. In this way we shall impose upon the United States the burden of a military defense on a vast front. "They want a white war," says Mussolini, "but they will get a red one."

Libya. The situation is precarious. Our supplies are scarce, while the English forces are extremely well supplied. The Duce fears that it will not be possible to hold the present line. I have talked this over with Cavallero, proposing a withdrawal to the Sirte-Homs line. Cavallero has written a memorandum opposing this. Nevertheless, Mussolini has not yet abandoned his project and will come back to it again.

Today the Duce was in good humor but tired-looking.

The King has added to the noble title of Buccari that of Cortellazzo. I am proud of this because of the memory of Father. [That is, Ciano would now be called Cavaliere Galeazzo Ciano, Conte di Cortellazzo e di Buccari. Both Cortellazzo and Buccari are places where Admiral Ciano had distinguished himself.]

January 21, 1942

Cavallero, on his way to Libya, explores the situation with me. Naturally he persists in his official optimism. He uses propagandist slogans, such as "We will resist," "They shall not pass," and "The difficulties will strengthen our will," which displease me when mouthed by a general. Anyway, he says, (1) that the Russian push on the eastern front is almost exhausted; (2) that in Libya we shall be able to resist an eventual British attack; (3) that the preparation of the Italian Army continues at a favorable pace. We shall see to what extent Cavallero is right.

January 22, 1942

I went to see the King. He talked little. As always he is anti-German. He criticized the organization of the Italian Army.

I received General Roatta on his farewell visit. He was embittered but dignified. He said he realized that his association with Cavallero could not continue because "Cavallero is a man who loves to create and believe in illusions, while Roatta wishes always to keep his feet on the ground." He maintains that the war is now in its critical phase; even for Libya he isn't at all confident, and fears that we shall soon have more British pressure which we shall not be able to resist. He is happy over his new command in Croatia. In the spring he will get plenty of fighting. Roatta may not be a very pleasant person, but he is the most intelligent general I know.

Osio, founder of the Labor Bank, was kicked out of his job. He came to tell me, and, although he is a strong man, he had tears in his eyes. The reason for his dismissal is not clear, but it appears that Osio made some comment not entirely orthodox, and some say he had a quarrel with Petacci's brother over business matters. In fact, Osio talked about it a little too freely, calling him [Petacci] "Lorenzino de Medici." [nephew of Lorenzo the Magnificent, who murdered his brother.]

Today Grandi could no longer contain himself and said, "I don't know how I was able to disguise myself as a Fascist for twenty years." Arpinati tells me that Grandi plays the liberal reactionary and royalist in Bologna. He told me that the King frequently invites him to lunch. I asked Acquarone if this were true, and he denied it in the most categorical fashion.

January 23, 1942

News from Rio de Janeiro is contradictory regarding the decision of Argentina and Chile. I fear that notwithstanding controversies these countries will also line up against us in the end. Mussolini is almost happy about it. I confess that I am most distressed. Not only because every hope of peace is vanishing, but also because I think with sadness of the collapse of so much good will created by our industrious immigrants during a hundred and twenty years of work. In certain places undoubtedly the memory of the mother country is pretty much forgotten, but in many others they still love Italy with a deep nostalgic attachment. If war comes, many Italian tears will be shed.

News from Russia is bad. The Russian advance continues at an accelerated pace, with growing strength. Alfieri, in one of his reports which betrays the style of Ridomi, describes the internal German situation in dark colors, though he does not come to pessimistic conclusions. It is still too early to say, but, as Grandi said yesterday, a Beresina [where Napoleon was defeated on his retreat from Moscow in 1812] wind is blowing. In contrast to this we are getting along better in Libya, according to our military people.

January 24, 1942

The Duce was quite disturbed by Alfieri's report, which "really is not encouraging." On the other hand, he is happy about the progress of operations in Libya, and about our naval traffic, even though the *Victoria,* which was the pearl of our merchant fleet, was sunk today.

Mezzasoma wants to leave the party and hopes to become director of the *Nazione* of Florence [daily newspaper]. He isn't wrong. He cannot get along with Vidussoni. Somebody wrote an anonymous letter in which all the secretaries of the party are given titles: Turati is called an epileptic and a dope fiend; Farinacci, one who inflicts wounds upon himself to escape military duty, and also a thief, and so on down the line to Vidussoni, who is called the perfect champion of Fascist youth, depraved, ignorant, and moronic. Naturally they exaggerate, and a great many unjust rumors about Vidussoni are going the rounds. However, I cannot say that he has yet given any evidence of qualities which would justify his appointment. I believe the Duce himself will soon see that he has to do with a pupil unworthy of his teacher.

Pareschi would like to get grain from Hungary. They will not give it to us, particularly since they fear that the Germans, whom they hate, intend to impoverish them further. Yet in Hungary there is an abundance of everything. The only thing lacking is the desire to make war.

January 25, 1942

Again Mussolini complains of the behavior of the Germans in Italy. He has before him the transcript of a telephone call by one of Kesselring's aides, who, speaking with Berlin, called us "macaroni" and hoped that Italy, too, would become an occupied country. The Duce is keeping a dossier of all this, which "is to be used when the moment comes." In the meantime, he reacts strongly against the request of Clodius to have still more Italian workingmen sent to Germany. They would like to raise the number from two hundred thousand to three hundred and twenty-five thousand. It is too much. Moreover, it is impossible because, aside from other considerations, our own labor supply is running short and we shall soon have to call new classes to the colors.

The breaking of diplomatic relations with South American countries begins. Today it is Peru, tomorrow it seems it will be Uruguay and Brazil. I have seen the Argentine Ambassador, who has just returned from Buenos Aires. His country has held firm and will still hold firm, but will not be able to resist isolation for an indefinite period. We must, therefore, expect the breaking off of relations with all of South America. He indicated the possibility of discriminating between us and Germany. I unhesitatingly dispelled all his illusions on this point. The Duce would never accept it, nor would it be to our interest.

January 26, 1942

Hunger grows in Greece. We can give very little, but even less are our means of transportation to get it there. The Italian merchant fleet has not a single ship to put at our disposal. We shall have to turn to the Italian Red Cross and have them try to get some ships. The Duce has agreed to this solution.

We are getting on well in Libya. The Germans are intensifying their propaganda about it to raise morale at home, which is quite low over the way things are going on the Russian front, where the Germans continue to be beaten.

January 27, 1942

Nothing new.

January 28, 1942

Goering has arrived in Rome but I have not seen him. In the first place this is because the visit is of a military character and our military men have insisted on monopolizing his reception. In the second place, it is because this paunchy individual has for some time—that is from the time of the granting of the collar to von Ribbentrop—adopted a haughty attitude toward me that I do not like very much. When I was in Berlin the last time he received me with an almost regal ceremony, to which he did not try to add any personal cordiality. He knows my address is the Palazzo Chigi. If he wants me, he knows where to find me.

The Duce has told me that Goering said on getting off the train, "We are having hard times." Cavallero later telephoned to inform me that Goering is optimistic about the possibilities of an understanding with France. How much truth is there in it?

I have read Churchill's long address attentively. It is clear that times are hard for them, too, and that many disappointments are in store for the future. But it does not seem that he has faltered in his decision to carry on the struggle to the end.

January 29, 1942

The Duce talked to Goering for almost three hours yesterday. Schmidt took the conversation down as usual. I shall try to get it, but it is not so easy to get it from them. Goering is bitter about things in Russia and takes it out on the German generals, who have little or no sympathy for the Nazis. He thinks that difficulties will last throughout the winter, but is just as convinced that Russia will be defeated in 1942 and that Great Britain will lay down her arms in 1943. I took all this with a grain of salt. Goering is skeptical about the possibilities of an understanding with France, which is taking every opportunity to boycott the armistice, remaining at heart irreconcilably hostile. Goering has taken all measures for the attack on Malta. In a few days the intensive air bombardments will begin, then it will be decided whether we can or cannot land. The Duce summarizes his impressions as follows: state of mind toward us, very good; general morale, pretty good.

Brazil has broken diplomatic relations. Mussolini wanted me to say to the Chargé d'Affaires who made the declaration that he, Mussolini, has the memory of an elephant, and someday he would make them pay dearly for it. But how? And when?

January 30, 1942

Nothing new.

January 31, 1942

Nothing new.

February 1, 1942

Nothing new.

February 2, 1942

Mussolini is very happy about operations in Libya. He wants us to push them because, from some intercepted American messages, it appears that the English forces are somewhat disorganized.

For the first time since his presentation visit two years ago I have seen the Ambassador of Chile. He does not believe that his government will ever go so far as to break diplomatic relations with the Axis. The new President-elect, Rios, notwithstanding the fact that he belongs to the popular front, will follow the same line. Nevertheless, the Ambassador is doing his best to influence him in this respect, especially since he is profoundly convinced of Anglo-American defeat.

Luncheon with Goering at Cavallero's. As usual he is bloated and overbearing. He said nothing that is especially worthy of mention. The only thing, and indeed it is very sad, is the servility of our leading military men toward him. Following the example of that perfect clown, Cavallero, who would even go so far as to bow to the public lavatories if this would be helpful to him, the three heads of our military staff acted today in the presence of that German as if he were their master. And he strutted blissfully. I know that it is futile, but I swallowed a great deal of bile—more bile than food.

February 3, 1942

The Duce has me read two letters which Melchiori sent from Libya. They are typical of this unpleasant figure, two reports against our command and in praise of Rommel. I do not know whether he is right or wrong, but I distrust the individual and everything he does. Nevertheless, there is nothing more humiliating than the manner of Melchiori, who has placed himself at the service of the Germans and is cheating the Italians. Mussolini, who had taken the letters seriously, inveighed strongly against Gambara and Bastico especially because Gambara is reported to have said at a dinner—but I do not believe it —"Mussolini has sold out Italy to Germany. I hope to live twenty years longer in order to command an army to fight the Germans at that time."

In addition, I have received a long report by Gambara on the situation in Libya. It is an interesting document that is worth keeping. Gambara was against Rommel's withdrawal as he is now against his rapid advance. We shall see if and to what degree he is right.

February 4, 1942

Goering leaves Rome. We had dinner at the Excelsior Hotel, and during the dinner Goering talked of little else but the jewels he owned. In fact, he had some beautiful rings on his fingers. He explained that he bought them for a relatively small sum in Holland after all jewels were confiscated in Germany. I am told that he plays with his gems like a little boy with his marbles. During the trip he was nervous, so his aides brought him a small vase filled with diamonds. He placed them on the table and counted them, lined them up, mixed them together, and became happy again. One of his high officers said last evening: "He has two loves—beautiful objects and making war." Both are expensive hobbies. To the station he wore a great sable coat, something between what automobile drivers wore in 1906 and what a high-grade prostitute wears to the opera. If any of us tried a thing like that we would be stoned in the streets. He, on the contrary, is not only accepted in Germany but perhaps even loved for it. That is because he has a dash of humanity.

February 5, 1942

No news of any particular importance. Now that the pendulum swings in our favor and against the British in Libya, the Vichy Government is anxious to smile at us. We must take it for what it is worth.

On his arrival from Germany I accompanied De Cicco to the Duce. He painted the situation with notable optimism. Hitler is nervous, and the people are strong and determined to fight to the end. In substance I think he is right, even though Lanza, secretary of Legation, who has been in Berlin a few years, paints a darker picture. According to him, hopes for a total victory went up in smoke on the Russian steppes, and the Germans now aim at a negotiated peace.

I have learned that the Prince of Piedmont will be chosen to command an Italian army in Russia. Is this a good thing? Is it wise to send him? I would think long about it before answering.

I see Ravasio. He found some pretext to come to see me, but in reality he wanted to expound his own situation and that of the party. His disagreement with Vidussoni, or rather with the people around him, was inevitable, and it can clearly be seen in outline. Ravasio will explode before long because he feels that he is being attacked from above and wants to react, but Vidussoni has put him in a modest corner of the Department of Propaganda. Ravasio knows that Vidussoni is a dumbbell, and is convinced that it will go from bad to worse. He wants no responsibility, not having been at fault. All this makes more precarious the situation of the party, which is already very shaky and weak.

February 6, 1942

Nothing new.

February 7, 1942

Meeting of the Council of Ministers. Mussolini makes a rather brief statement on the progress of the war in Libya and concludes with his usual attack on our generals. On the other hand, he extolls Rommel, who is always in his tank at the head of the attacking columns. The Bersaglieri are enthusiastic about him and give him their feathers, bearing him in triumph on their shoulders, shouting that with him they are sure they can reach Alexandria. The measures taken today are of no particular importance, but Revel announced a new loan in order to reduce circulation of money, declaring that after the end of the war interest on state bonds will be greatly lowered.

Grandi, accompanying me to the Ministry, made his usual attack on the social policy of the regime and also took it out on the King, who, he said, has become "nutty." I had to raise my voice to stop him because, aside from everything else, this is not true.

Complaints from von Mackensen about an article by Admiral Ducci in which it is shown that it would be to the advantage of the British to make a landing in northern Norway. According to Mackensen it seems that his arguments are excellent. But for this very reason could he say anything more idiotic?

February 8, 1942

The German objection has resulted in the suppression of the newspaper *Oggi*. When the Duce mentioned it to me I encouraged him to suppress it. It was the organ of very questionable individuals, who accepted the regime but with considerable and ill-concealed reservations. The second-rate and discontented intellectuals are headed by Bottai, who boasts that he has accredited an ambassador, whose name he conceals, to the house of the Petaccis.

Admiral Courten, who commanded a convoy for Italy, told me of the struggle he had against the torpedo planes. It is due to a whim of fate that all of his division was not lost. De Courten gives a very optimistic view of the development of the naval war. There is only one dark spot—the lack of oil. Just now we have barely a hundred thousand tons, and only a negligible quantity comes to us from abroad. This immobilizes the Navy, particularly the large ships, which, as matters stand, enjoy a total supremacy in the Mediterranean.

February 9, 1942

Attolico died suddenly, and this grieves me very much. Not only for personal reasons (since he was bound by strong friendship to poor Maria), but also because I greatly valued his collaboration. Of all the ambassadors who have worked with me through the years he was among the most intelligent and certainly the most courageously honest. In Berlin he foresaw the power of the new Reich and favored the understanding and friendship between the two regimes. He didn't believe in the supposed miracles of blitz warfare, and fought tenaciously, first of all against the outbreak of the conflict; second, against our entry into it. We owe it to him in large measure if in September we did not immediately join the Germans, and thereby incur the consequences which would have followed. With Attolico, we lose a man who in other times would have been called *"un grand commis de l'état."* Bottai wants to succeed him at the Holy See. The Duce was against it. He said, "I refuse to believe that at forty-six years of age Bottai would want to end as a sacristan. Besides, he still has to carry through the educational reform which he invented and which he would now like to sidestep. We shall appoint Guariglia, whom I esteem both for his intellect and for his character."

Baldur von Schirach is in Rome. He is convinced we shall have a long war. He is an optimist who doesn't exaggerate. He sees in our food situation the main cause for alarm.

February 10, 1942

I have received El Gailani, the Prime Minister of Iraq, who started the anti-English movement and now circulates between Rome and Berlin to lay the foundation of the future Arab nations. The Germans are prudent and do not wish to sign any pact with him for the present. He is a vivacious and resolute man, who enjoys a great influence among his people, both through his rank and personality. He has faith in the victory of the Axis and says that when our forces arrive at Tiflis the English will not be able to prevent an insurrection of the peoples subject to them. He is skeptical about the Turkish attitude. Except for some military leaders the Turkish people heartily favor the English and hope they will win. I must add that Bismarck, while speaking with Vitetti this morning, gave him to understand that Germany is preparing to attack Turkey, which is necessary if the Germans want to reach the oil wells. But is this calculation right? It seems that Bismarck sees things from the dark side. He always has been so, and the development of affairs in Russia cannot but have discouraged him. At this point he will little by little reveal something more.

News from the eastern front is again alarming. The Russians are attacking everywhere, and a new and clear withdrawal of the line is to be expected.

Vidussoni has appeared for the first time at dinner at the German Embassy. He had rigged himself out in a shirt with blue stripes and a red tie and handkerchief. He was not very much at ease.

February 11, 1942

Attolico's funeral gave evidence of the esteem and affection in which he was held.

In the afternoon there was a ceremony for the inauguration of the headquarters of the Association of the Friends of Japan. Much to everybody's surprise, the Duke of Pistoia asked to be heard, as he had prepared a clever little speech. The speech was, I am tempted to say, violent. Anyway, it was a tone unexpected and unusual for a Royal Highness.

February 12, 1942

The British have torpedoed one of our tankers, the *Lucania,* en route from Taranto to Genoa to join the convoy of ships destined for the evacuation of our compatriots from East Africa. The ship was traveling according to plan and under the agreement with Great Britain. They really broke their word, and there is no justification for it. The Duce and the Navy, which were always against the idea, now take advantage of what has happened to drop the whole undertaking. Frankly, I can no longer oppose them. I should have rendered myself personally a guarantor of British good faith, but after what happened yesterday this becomes very difficult.

I handed Mackensen the text of a telegram from the American military attaché at Moscow, addressed to Washington. It complains about failure to deliver arms promised by the United States, and says that if the U.S.S.R. is not aided immediately and properly she will have to consider capitulating. Still, up to the present, Soviet attacks have continued at an accelerated pace, and it is now a question of the Germans either holding or abandoning the whole sector of Vitebsk-Smolensk. Alfieri telegraphs that the German position is not serious because it responds to modern criteria of elastic defense, but I must confess that his arguments do not convince me.

February 13, 1942

The submarine which torpedoed the *Lucania* has been rammed and many of those picked up from the latter have been saved. We must, therefore, eliminate the hypothesis that it was sunk by a drifting mine.

The Duce, as usual, is irritated at the military. In order to send two divisions to Russia in March, we must ask the Germans for anti-tank guns, anti-aircraft batteries, and motorcars. Notwithstanding this, Cavallero has presented Mussolini a list which indicates that we are producing two hundred and eighty anti-tank guns a month. When this figure was questioned he confessed that it was not correct but represented our theoretical possibilities, and, in pencil, before the Duce himself, he corrected the two hundred and eighty to one hundred and sixty. This was a sensational reduction. Like the Jews in Campo dei Fiori [peddlers' market in Rome]. Mussolini was indignant and explained that the only reason he did not throw him out was because after so many changes he realizes that they are all equally deceitful. He said, "Only Squero is sincere. He is a fool, but an honest man."

I received Marshal Kwaternik, who handed me a letter from Pavelić. He wants to meet the Duce. I believe this can be done in Rome, but not very soon.

February 14, 1942

Nothing new.

During the evening, in the Clemma home, Ninon Belmonte tells me a story that I still can't believe. Two things are clear: that Revel has lost his head over Ninon, and that Revel hates the banker Armenise. His hatred is unreasonable, without explanation, but nonetheless unyielding and like that of Cataline. Armenise, who was beginning to feel the weight of this persecution, turned to Ninon, to whom he was introduced by Rudolfo Borghese. Ninon took up Armenise's cause. Well, Revel not only swore that he will do nothing against him, but also that within a week he will see him to re-establish cordial relations. "He was blushing and sorry," said Ninon, of this fifty-year-old Minister [Revel], "like a child caught in a naughty prank. But now that he promised me, I am certain that he will behave." Here is an episode which illustrates certain negative aspects of present-day Italy more than any number of volumes could do.

February 15, 1942

Mussolini has not yet made up his mind to break off negotiations with England for the evacuation of Italians from East Africa. He prefers to consider it further. He is opposed in principle to sending our ships, but realizes it would be too serious a responsibility to refuse.

I write to Bárdossy with the idea of acquiring some wheat. Pareschi and Pascolato have come to speak to me of the cereal-production situation. They consider it bad. By March it will be necessary to reduce rations by fifty grams, but this will not be enough to carry us through.

The Duce is much more optimistic. He believes that enough wheat will yet come out, and that in any case his appeal to the people will make them patient and understanding.

February 16, 1942

Kruia has come to Rome for the first time since the installation of his cabinet at Tirana. When he was appointed there was considerable criticism: among the Italians because he is considered too nationalistic, among the Albanians because he is of humble origin and the Albanian tradition is still feudal. Verlaçi said of him, "I shall never be able to respect a man whose father waited on me in the house of Essad Pasha." It is too early to pass judgment on the Kruia experiment. So far things have gone well, and even the indignation that had been aroused in many Albanian circles has calmed down. It was feared that he would be an extremist, but instead he has shown himself moderate. Now that he is in power he, too, realizes that *"la critique est aisée, mais l'art est difficile."* He has not asked me for anything unexpected, except some small rectifications on the Montenegro frontier and some changes in the flag. They do not want the eagle imprisoned between the lictors' fasces and the knots of the House of Savoy. The question is a delicate one and not to be too quickly rejected.

Churchill made an address today which I should call firm but grave. The fall of Singapore has been a great blow to the British Empire. "I should like to know," Mussolini said today, "the effect four English officers, presenting themselves with a white flag to surrender, has had upon those whimsical Orientals. If it had been us, no one would have attached any importance to it, but they are English."

February 17, 1942

A conversation between Mussolini and Kruia. The Albanian President talked about the situation, sounding an optimistic note. Mussolini emphasized his desire to grant the Albanians a more and more liberal and autonomous local regime. This is the only policy possible— one that bears good fruit. Otherwise, Albania, too, would be a breeding place for revolt and intrigues like the other occupied countries. Revel, as might be expected, told me that he received Armenise and put an end to the cruel rivalry with a long embrace. Oh, women, women!

February 18, 1942

With Gailani to see Mussolini. Gailani insisted on immediately having a treaty and a declaration of independence for the Arab states. The Duce kept him guessing, because for some time the Germans have indicated their opposition to gestures of this sort. Mussolini said that he will make this declaration when it can have an immediate effect, that is, when our military forces are close enough to the Arab countries for the words to be immediately followed by deeds. What once appeared fantastic now seems possible. The Japanese victories are shattering British resistance hour by hour and may perhaps prepare a more rapid and successful conclusion which so far we could not foresee. In fact, the Anglo-Saxon situation has never appeared to me so desperate as it does now. But I believe they will hold on. Yesterday I announced at a luncheon for Kruia and in the presence of all the ministers a formula which was well received. We are not born young; we become young.

February 19, 1942

An address by Senator Kruia in the city hall of Rome. He spoke of the Italo-Albanian union, but it was more of a theoretical and academic than a political speech. The party should have organized things better. The hall was half empty.

Muti told me that Farnesi, Vidussoni's chief of cabinet, honestly declared to him that his boss is "an imbecile," and he is very worried when Vidussoni has to do anything without the help of his collaborators.

February 20, 1942

Alfieri sends a strange telegram, according to which Ribbentrop prophesies that England will ask for an armistice to save what can still be saved. Can it be that the Germans are actually beginning to realize the fearful tragedy which this war represents for the white race? It would be a good thing, but I can't believe it.

This morning Mussolini showed some concern about coal and steel. We lack these things, and the Germans only partially carry out their commitments to us. "Among the cemeteries," says Mussolini, "I shall someday build the most important of all, one in which to bury German promises. They have delivered nothing, or almost nothing, of what they promised. For this reason it is better not to insist. I persuaded Cavallero not to ask for the anti-tank guns and the anti-aircraft guns for our divisions going to Russia. I prefer to take the risk of taking twelve batteries from the Rome defenses." Naturally, he took it out on the Italian bourgeoisie, "which never troubled itself to develop the resources of the country," and which "he is sorry not to have physically exterminated in 1911."

Horthy's son was appointed Vice-Regent of Hungary. Anfuso telegraphs that the enthusiasm of the assemblies was moderate. The man is not at all up to the job. He is a gentleman, modest and courteous, but nothing more. Through this gesture Hungary tries to take out an insurance policy of an anti-German sort. I don't know if they have guessed right. In Berlin there is much coolness, and I am told they will not send congratulations to the Vice-Regent.

February 21, 1942

No news.

February 22, 1942

From Prague our Consul General reports that the deputy of the Reich Protector is treating our nationals if not worse than the Czechoslovaks certainly not much better. I showed the report to Mussolini, who is indignant and wants Alfieri to protest with some moderation, to von Ribbentrop. "And after this the Germans have the effrontery to protest against Japanese exclusivism. I much prefer the yellow people, even if the Japanese were to arrive as far as the Persian Gulf."

The coal situation is very bad. This month will be exceptionally good if we reach five hundred and forty thousand tons, that is one third of our needs. If we go on in this way, by April we shall have consumed all the available supplies for the railroads.

Rome is full of rumors about the Duce's violent anti-Vatican statements. In fact, he has said some things, but more theoretical than political, more historical than contemporary—such as the Duce has uttered many times. Vidussoni, who is a perfect imbecile, has interpreted them literally and repeated them in various quarters. He even told d'Aieta that an attack on the Vatican was being prepared. Hence the scandal. This is the result of letting children play with matters of importance.

February 23, 1942

I hadn't seen the King for some time. I found him in bad health, hardly able to stand up.

He said nothing of any particular importance, but reaffirmed his old thesis that the fall of Russia will put England and America out of the war. I again indicated my doubts.

The Duce is worried about the rumors which are circulating regarding his statements on ecclesiastical matters, and has asked me to have Guariglia deny them. Evidently Vidussoni, who has few ideas, and very confused ones at that, has a bee in his bonnet about the Vatican. When Guariglia presented himself to Vidussoni a few days ago at the city hall, as soon as he heard him say "Ambassador to the Holy See," he ostentatiously turned his back on him. He had confused him with the Nuncio.

I accompanied Clodius to the Palazzo Venezia. He offered some explanations on the non-delivery of coal. He said the winter was exceptionally cold, there was a shortage of labor and railroad transportation; the Russian front alone absorbed five thousand more locomotives than had been foreseen. But in the future things will go better. This, at any rate, he was good enough to promise us in the name of the Führer.

February 24, 1942

Mussolini expounds one of his new theories on war. Wars are necessary in order to see and appraise the true internal composition of a people, because during a war the various classes are revealed: the heroes, the profiteers, the indolent. I objected that in any case war is a selection in reverse, because the best die.

A speech by Roosevelt. A calm, measured, but nonetheless determined speech. It doesn't sound like the speech of a man who is thinking of suing for peace soon. Still, this strange belief is spreading. Even in Italy a good many honest people believe it.

The Papal Nuncio wants to know if it is true that the Padua University is preparing to offer Goebbels and Rosenberg honorary degrees. Honoring the two most bitter opponents of Catholicism in the city of Saint Anthony would be extremely obnoxious to the Church. However, the rumor had no foundation.

Bismarck talked to d'Aieta in a very pessimistic tone. In Germany they all believe that another winter of war would be unbearable. Everybody is convinced of this, from the supreme heads of the Army to the men close to Hitler. But no one dares tell Hitler. They ought, therefore, to find some way of coming to an understanding with the Anglo-Saxons, especially as the Nipponese advance is a disaster for the white race. The Germans can do nothing along this line. They are too much hated. They are "black sheep." Thus the Italians should assume the role of world peacemakers. According to Bismarck there isn't one intelligent German who doesn't believe this.

February 25, 1942

There are some signs of friction between the Germans and Japanese. For example, the latter frowned on some proposals made by von Ribbentrop, who, as usual, arrogates to himself the role of Grand Master of the Tripartite Alliance.

Mussolini, who is pro-Japanese, especially because of his anti-Germanism, expresses his satisfaction. "The Japanese are not a people," he said, "with whom the Germans can take liberties such as calling the Emperor or the Prime Minister out of bed at two o'clock in the morning in order to announce to them decisions that have already been made and carried out."

A strange attempt at murder at Ankara: von Papen, who was passing by, was knocked down but is unhurt. We shall see what De Peppo thinks of it. But from here, offhand, I should not be surprised to learn that the Germans have a hand in it and that they are beginning to pave the way for a crisis with Turkey. On the timeliness of this crisis I do not conceal my many doubts.

February 26, 1942

It is perhaps a stroke of fate, but every time the Germans issue a communiqué that everything is going well on the eastern front, they get a thrashing. Today has been the turn of Wiasma, which has fallen, and, judging from the Russo-English radio, the Russian thrust is continuing rapidly.

The Duce has issued a decree for the mobilization of civilians. For the time being it will include men between eighteen and fifty-five; later it will be the women's turn. However, there is a certain uneasiness because people do not understand what it is all about. In fact, they are afraid that it will be an imitation of the forced-labor decree imposed upon the Germans. Lombrassa will be in charge of the service as undersecretary. His name is a guarantee of moderation and competence.

The son of Oriani has become the mouthpiece of dissatisfaction existing in many Fascist circles over the line taken by the regime, especially in its social policy. "Let us turn back to the beginnings," is the motto of the old members of the party. The beginnings were anti-Bolshevik, traditionalistic, in defense of the family, of private property, and marked by respect for the Church. Now, on the other hand, we are slipping more and more to the left, and I fear that this Vidussoni, who does not understand anything, will attempt to drive the party too recklessly. Vito Mussolini, who had a conversation with him yesterday, and who is a prudent young man, told me that he was surprised by the idiocy, the ignorance, and the malice of the secretary of the party.

February 27, 1942

Nothing new.

February 28, 1942

Nothing new.

March 1, 1942

The English accede to our demands after the torpedoing of the *Lucania*. They again give the most ample guarantees, and to replace the *Lucania* they will release one of our confiscated oil tankers. Our Navy, which would like to boycott the enterprise at all costs, raises objections. It wants the tanker to be an English tanker. Unless this is done they say we shall have one tanker less when peace comes. Mussolini, although he is not enthusiastic about repatriation of the Italians, has reacted against this foolish objection. "Either we shall win the war," he commented, "and we shall have tankers to throw away, or we shall lose it and they will not even leave us eyes to weep with."

Notwithstanding the report by Alfieri, which assures us that the situation has become stabilized on the eastern front, we receive news of continual offensive thrusts by the Russians, which at some points are quite deep. Even Mussolini is now worried. "It's all right that the Germans have said that we had three hundred divisions. But even admitting that this is so, of what human material are these divisions composed? What is their real morale? Everything depends on the answers to these questions." Very bad news on the state of health of the Duke of Aosta. He has miliary tuberculosis, and hence his end is certain. Mussolini is not interested, and even the royal house does not seem to be greatly moved by it.

March 2, 1942

Jacomoni reports on the situation in Albania. In general it is good, considering the times. But there is one matter that has attracted my attention: the insufficiency of our military forces. We have scarcely four divisions, each composed of two regiments and the regiments composed of two battalions; a small number of carabinièri, not one tank. These are the forces that are garrisoning Albania. Now it is clear that if a blow were struck from the outside and if enemy propaganda succeeded in arousing large parts of the interior, we could not hold worth a damn. We must not forget that all the Balkans are in flames, that Albania has been under Italian rule for only three years, that we are at war with America and England, who have great resources, and with Russia, a master of guile. I shall speak very seriously of all this to the Duce. It is evident that before undertaking to send new forces to Russia we must assure ourselves of holding what we have.

Pareschi considers the present food situation better and he makes these prophecies for the future: the coming crop will be good because the earth is still well supplied with the fertilizers that were used in great profusion for the Battle of Wheat; bad crops in the future because of lack of fertilizer.

New and strong Russian attacks on all sectors of the front. The German communiqué is subdued in tone and our divisions, too, are having difficulties.

March 3, 1942

The Duke of Aosta is dead. With him disappears a noble figure of
a prince and an Italian, simple in his ways, broad in his outlook, human in his spirit. He did not want this war. He was convinced that
the empire could hold out for only a few months, and, besides, he
hated the Germans. In this conflict, which drenches the world with
blood, he feared a German more than an English victory. When he
left for Ethiopia in May 1940, he had a premonition of his fate. He
was determined to face it, but was filled with sadness. I communicated
the information to the Duce, who expressed his regret laconically.

In the afternoon Bismarck telephoned to say that his government
was preparing to launch a campaign against the English Secret Service because of the death of the Duke. He added that he personally
thought that the plan was in "bad taste." He is right. There is nothing
to support this accusation; on the contrary, it's quite absurd. I brought
this to the attention of the Duce, who expressed himself adversely. The
only value of the plan is its indication of the intelligence and morals
of the one who advanced it. Mussolini is more and more pro-Japanese
the less the Germans appear to be so. He would like to write an article
praising the Japanese people who, after centuries of misery and with
their faces turned to the future, have, in a few months, reversed their
situation, passing *"dall'ago al miliardo."* ["From a needle to a billion"—the title of an Italian light opera.] The Duce considers what is
happening in the Orient and in the Pacific as final.

March 4, 1942

I took Jacomoni to the Duce, so that he might speak clearly to him.
The internal situation is fundamentally good, but outside our frontiers are a thousand dangers which can quickly change the state of
mind of the population. The indispensable condition for calm is power
—to have power. Now we lack it. Probably more because of the duty
of his office than from conviction, the Duce said that he does not share
our apprehensions. In any case, he will send a third regiment and some
companies of light tanks which serve quite well in the city. Jacomoni,
who hadn't seen the Duce for many months, found him heavier and
with signs of exhaustion in his face. As a matter of fact it seemed to me
that the Duce was less somber than usual today.

Buffarini is very much concerned about the food situation. From every district in Italy come signs of alarm and cries of grief, and he believes that the situation is rapidly getting worse. To the scarcity of food must be added the steady rise in prices, which makes life really unbearable for all classes of people who live on fixed incomes.

The death of the Duke of Aosta made a great impression on the country. There was sincere sorrow shared by all. A young boy, whose brother is a prisoner, said to me, "Today my mother cried. All the mothers of prisoners are weeping today."

March 5, 1942

Nothing new.

March 6, 1942

A friend of one of Gambara's secretaries said that when he, Gambara, was replaced in his Libyan command, his aides in Rome were arrested and his office searched by General Maravigna and by the carabinièri. This was a blow delivered by Cavallero, who hates Gambara. I telephoned Cavallero to learn about this, but, as is his custom, he sidestepped everything, saying that he knew nothing about it and that it was the Ministry of War which had acted without his knowledge. He ends by admitting that they are on the trail of illicit business activity by Gambara's aides, but Gambara has nothing to do with it and he will go to Bolzano to command the army corps. He must not stay in Rome. He must not confer with anyone. We shall see where it will end, but there is no doubt that Cavallero has sought help from the Germans to strike this valorous general who was careless enough to talk too much. It appears that at an officers' mess in Libya he said, "I hope to live long enough to command an Italian Army marching on Berlin."

Vidussoni pays me a long visit to bring me up to date on his plans for the party. I maintain a careful reserve; it can't last long.

A heavy British bombardment of industrial Paris and, consequently, an attempt by the Germans to arouse French resentment. But Buti informs us that the French are not aroused, or aroused in a different way.

March 7, 1942

The Duce, who is dissatisfied with the way things are going, said, "This war is not for the Italian people. The Italian people do not have the maturity or the consistency for a test so grave and decisive. This war is for the Germans and the Japanese, not for us."

Luigi Cortese, Consul General in Geneva, informs us that fear of invasion is over in Switzerland because no one any longer believes in a complete German victory. In fact, forecasts are of an entirely different nature. It is believed that, having once more banged her head against Russia in the coming offensive without definite success, Germany will have to give up before winter. Feeling toward Italy has improved very much. In fact, it is quite favorable for certain future possibilities which are hopefully fostered in Switzerland.

Mussolini received Revel's report following the investigation of Graziani. It appears to be very hard on Graziani. The Duce will give me a copy of it. Mussolini does not know whether to have him court-martialed or liquidate him in an administrative way by retirement. I would be in favor of the latter solution in time of war. The Duce accuses Graziani of having been responsible for three serious losses to the country: a blow to its military prestige, the coming of the Germans into Italy, and the loss of the empire. The Duce now feels that we must attack Tobruk, else another blow will be dealt us by the British.

The Japanese admirals have informed us that they intend to proceed toward India. The Axis must move toward them in the Persian Gulf.

March 8, 1942

Nothing new.

[*No entry for March 9*]

March 10, 1942

Casero has me read a report from our air information office. It is deeply pessimistic. According to it Germany must bring its war with Russia to an end within a few months, for it is certain that the population will not stand for another winter of war. How much truth is there in it?

Meanwhile, there has been a strange development. Prince Urach, of von Ribbentrop's press bureau,-has come to Rome and asked to see d'Aieta. His conversation about Japan was strange, with an ambiguous tinge and bittersweet flavor. It is all very well for the Japanese to win because they are our allies, but after all they belong to the yellow race and their successes are gained at the expense of the white race. It is a leitmotiv which frequently appears in the conversation of the Germans. D'Aieta even had the impression that in a roundabout way Urach was trying to sound out our feelings about a separate peace between the Axis and England. Urach also said that the liquidation of Russia still appears to be a very hard task. D'Aieta restricted himself to generalities and did well.

I telephoned Bova-Scoppa to postpone my trip to Rumania until later. I see from the telegrams intercepted from the Rumanians that they are creating difficulties, and that they would like to attribute an anti-Magyar character to my trip. Hence there is nothing to be done.

March 11, 1942

The Duce reacted sharply to Urach's declarations. He affirmed, on the contrary, his extreme pro-Japanese attitude. "After all, what is the importance of enrichment of the Japanese at the cost of the European standard of life? Such materialistic reflections betray the traces of Marxism in the German soul, even though it is National Socialist."

This morning, at the Sudario, there was a requiem mass for the Duke of Aosta. Only the members of the Court were invited, and, of course, also the wearers of the Annunziata. The royal family was seated in a pew which was hidden from our view. The ceremony had just begun when the door opened and a woman in mourning entered, bent and aged. She was Donna Rachele. She took the first seat she could find, and wept throughout the whole ceremony. At the close of the service I called for her car, but it wasn't there. I offered her mine, but she refused. She came on foot, and she left on foot. I told the Duce, who was very much surprised. He didn't know that his wife would go to an intimate ceremony of the royal house. "This is the first time such a thing has happened," he said. But that old woman who was weeping in the Church of the Sudario today was not the wife of a great leader. She was simply the mother of a lieutenant of twenty killed in his airplane.

March 12 and 13, 1942

Nothing new.

March 14, 1942

Council of Ministers. There are no important measures except the regulation of registered bonds. [The title to these bonds can pass to any number of persons, but the state imposes a new tax on each successive owner.] This subject causes the Duce to make some extremist economic-financial declarations which end in a dark threat "to dig up another regulation, which has been ready for eight years, which, in just two clauses, modifies the entire situation of property in Italy, in case there is any attempt to oppose this law."

Further restrictive measures are adopted, due to the state of war, and in particular it is planned to limit the travel of private persons as much as possible. To go from one place to another will require a permit from the Prefect with a written justification for the trip.

March 15, 1942

In a conference with Indelli the Japanese have defined their plans. No attack on India, which would disperse their forces in a field that is too vast and unknown; no attack upon Russia; an extension of the conflict toward Australia, where it is evident that the Americans and the English are preparing a counterattack.

Before his departure I saw Ando, the Japanese Counselor, who is returning to Tokyo. I gave him a very friendly message for his government, especially as the Nipponese are sensitive and suspicious about the German attitude. Here, too, the pro-Japanese note is stressed by some just to spite Germany. I do not approve of this. No one can accuse me of being strongly pro-German, but I still prefer the white to the yellow race . . . and then Japan is far away and Germany is close, very close. . . .

Bastianini paints an ultra-pessimistic picture of the Croatian-Dalmatian situation. Except for the militia our armed forces are deplorable. They show no energy and no spirit. Anti-Fascism is general and widespread among them. Bastianini foresees many dark hours in the spring and summer. He is always rather pessimistic.

March 16, 1942

New and violent Russian attacks make the situation on the eastern front from Kharkov down rather uncertain. Mussolini does not hide his concern.

The Swedish Minister makes a report on Greece on behalf of his government. The English are disposed to open their blockade and to give the Greeks fifteen thousand tons of wheat per month. They naturally ask for some guarantees. I do not know whether the Duce and the Germans are disposed to accept the terms proposed. I shall work in their favor because only thus can some millions of innocent and unfortunate human beings escape certain death.

A long conversation with Pareschi on the food situation. It is not good. The recent 25 per cent cut in the bread ration was greeted with despair, even though there have not been many signs of protest. Pareschi, who has all the enthusiasm of a convert, looks to the future hopefully and believes that some measures he is going to take will at least accomplish a great deal to better the situation, if not change it completely. Nevertheless, all the most favorable hypotheses are based on the help of fate and depend on a number of ifs and buts. The facts are that fertilizers are reduced to one third, manual labor is lacking, agricultural implements are wearing out, and fuel is short.

March 17, 1942

Nothing new.

March 18, 1942

Nothing new.

March 19, 1942

Pavolini, on his return from a conversation with Goebbels, paints a pretty dark picture of the situation in Germany. Even his German colleague, who in the past has maintained a haughty tone, has had to pipe down this time. He spoke of a crisis in the regime, and about "walking on the razor's edge," and even when he passed to a consideration of the future beyond this dark period he could be only cautiously optimistic. They are no longer talking about destroying Bolshevism; they will be content if they get to the Caucasus.

The words "resistance" and "tenacity" have replaced assertions about "overwhelming victories," "dictated peace," and "New Orders." Pavolini also told a funny and significant story, significant for the Nazis as well as for their menials. When Goebbels sent Farinacci a bust of Hitler the bust was brought by Gauleiter Esser, who vaunts himself on his Italian. In handing over the gift, this is what he said: "Your Excellency Farinacci, Minister Goebbels has entrusted me to bring you this envelope." [*Busta,* an envelope, instead of *busto,* a bust. To the Italians this meant that Hitler was an envelope, having no original ideas but only those put into his head by others.] The story is making the rounds in Germany, and the first to tell it and laugh is Goebbels himself. Farinacci would laugh less.

This morning Mussolini discussed the Italian internal situation, and had to admit that the Italian people are not in the least for the war. He explains it by saying that immediate incentives are lacking, such as can be easily understood by the common people. He believes, therefore, that our line of propaganda should simply be to flaunt the banner of defeat as a threat. No generosity would be shown by our enemies, and we should be reduced to slavery for a century. But the people aren't even convinced of this. In Milan they are saying, "To end the war let's even win it."

March 20, 1942

Nothing new.

March 21, 1942

Nothing new.

March 22, 1942

A few days ago a young man called me by telephone, under the assumed name of the secretary of the party, asking to see me, as he had some "important disclosures to make about a plot." I received him. He is a boy from Trieste, Armando Stefani, twenty years old, enrolled in GUF [Gruppo Universitario Fascisto—Fascist University Group], lean, intelligent, nervous. He said that he had been approached by a journalist, Felice Chilanti, who suggested that he join a super-Fascist insurrectional movement, the purpose of which would be to eliminate all rightist or conservative elements in the party, and to impose upon the Duce a violent socialistic policy. Everything was thought out—attacks, seizure of the ministries, death of Ciano. The young man was very much worried about it, and so he hurried to tell me. I wouldn't attach too much importance to it but for the fact that the police believed there might be something to it. We must get to the bottom of this affair, and with a bit of concentration camp, or even jail, the hotheadedness of these young men will be cooled off. But this gives rise to a question: Why does all this happen? Might not these be obviously anti-Fascist beginnings, which dare not display the flag of revolution openly, but try to hide under the emblems of the party itself? Are not these elements which the party itself is lovingly nursing within its ranks, and which, in the opinion of some, are being kept under control by flattery and adulation, in reality being encouraged to follow a path which ought instead to be deplored and condemned?

March 23, 1942

Nothing new.

March 24, 1942

I brought the Duce a report on Germany by Luciolli. Even Mussolini said that he "had not read anything so significant and far-reaching for a long time." He is right. After mentioning the miserable internal situation of the country, Luciolli explains how there could be no political support for the military side of the war. They talked a lot about a New Order, but did nothing to bring it about. The whole of Europe today languishes under German occupation. The enemies of Germany have multiplied infinitely, even though they can do no more at the moment than to hate and hold their peace.

Luciolli says that in Germany they are now thinking of a possible defeat. For this reason they want all the countries of the continent exhausted, so that even in case of defeat the Germans will be relatively strong. The Duce was struck by this idea, and said that by the end of

1943 he intends to have fifteen perfect divisions ready in the valley of
the Po. Very good. I replied that this is now a war of attrition, the
progress of which is not easy to predict. Anything is possible. Therefore, it is necessary to prepare our forces, and to keep them *at home*.
Some day, maybe not too far away, a small but solid army at one's
disposal might decide the fate of Europe.

Cavallero came to see me, and I had a slight argument with him on
the Gambara question. The argument was solved by an embrace; but
is he sincere?

March 25, 1942

Some interesting telegrams from Turkey. De Peppo has spoken to
various personalities, and although there is some difference of opinion
on the military situation, they are in agreement in believing that the
German-Russian conflict will end by forcing Turkey to face the alternative it would like to avoid. But De Peppo is not in a position to
give the answer to the question whether with us or against us. However, it appears from numerous sources that the ties between Turkey
and the Anglo-Saxon world are growing stronger and stronger.

March 26, 1942

Colonel Amè speaks with great concern of the German situation.
He bases his conviction not only upon the information that had come
to him from our military intelligence service stationed in Germany,
but also upon what he personally has been told by his German colleague, Admiral Canaris; the internal situation is serious both from
the material and moral viewpoint. The Army is bitter and in disagreement with the political element. There is little confidence in the
spring offensive and at least a feeling that no definitive success can be
attained. The German people are tired of "victories" and no longer
believe in "victory."

On commenting on the steps taken by Hitler to detach the S.S.
[Schutzstaffel] from the regular army, in order to make a single large
unit out of it, the Duce sees the symptoms of a deep and perhaps incurable uneasiness.

An address by Churchill to the Conservatives. As usual he was
quick to recognize the disasters that have occurred, but he reaffirmed

his determination to carry on to the end and his certainty of ultimate victory. We must honestly recognize in Churchill an orator of singular power, capable of moving people deeply.

March 27, 1942

A long conversation with Squero on the Gambara affair. In spite of Cavallero's thousand insinuations Gambara is a perfect gentleman with a clear record. He came out of the investigation as clean as a whistle. Everything was exaggerated by Cavallero, for the purpose of wreaking vengeance on an overcourageous critic, and to eliminate an audacious young general who might have overshadowed him. In any case, Squero will act in defense of Gambara.

Squero is certainly a fine person. He may not be a genius, but he is sincere and honest. Mussolini also trusts him 100 per cent, and he does well to do so.

March 28, 1942

Distribution of gold medals awarded posthumously to fallen aviators. Balbo's son, who without looking like him yet reminds one of his father, received his father's decoration without batting an eye, pale and proud. Then it was the turn of Bruno's widow. She carried little Marina, who extended her arms toward her grandfather. There was sincere emotion in the air. Mussolini's expression was stonelike and did not change. He decorated Bruno's wife, the wife of his Bruno, as though she were just another of those who have been bereaved. Somebody asked whether the Duce was superhuman or inhuman. He is neither one nor the other. He was simply conscious of the fact that at that moment any weakness would have an echo in a thousand hearts. Later, for only a moment, when Marina was going away, I saw a light in his eyes—a light that fully betrayed everything that his iron will had sought to hide. I felt myself very close to his heart and to his sorrow.

In Venice we have had the first popular demonstrations caused by the bread shortage. Many people who had used all their ration stamps before they became due are protesting because the bakers refuse to sell. The Duce was resentful and sad; he gave orders that the crowds be scattered by *piattonate* [method used by the Austrian police to disperse crowds by beating them with their leather scabbards]. But this is an ugly occurrence which proves that many calculations in the matter of food were wrong and the coming weeks may hold some ugly surprises in store.

March 29, 1942

Today there have been bread riots at Matera [in the province of Potenza], where groups of women broke into the Littorio Club [Fascist party headquarters] and were dispersed by the carabinièri, who were forced to fire in the air. These are serious symptoms, especially as the harvest is far away and the available food supply scarcer and scarcer. Buffarini is expecting similar riots throughout the country and has sent his prefects a telegram of instruction which begins with the words "Keep calm." He wants to avoid bloodshed, and he is right.

Gastaldi, the former Federal Secretary of Turin, whom I hardly know, comes to me with the story of his dissensions with a partner, and up to this point there is nothing bad. But, as usual, the Petacci family is mixed up in the affair which he speaks about freely. It meddles and grants political protection, threatens from above, intrigues from below, and steals at all points of the compass. The chief of the carabinièri, Cerrica, had told me about this confidentially a few minutes before. Without doubt this scandal will spread and involve the person of the Duce. But what can one do to warn him, especially as two of his most intimate collaborators, De Cesare and Buffarini, are making loads of money in their underworld setting? Nevertheless, as far as I am concerned, I want to keep out of this, and out of respect for the Duce I cut short brusquely anyone who speaks to me about it.

At a meeting of the directors of the party yesterday Mussolini was violently critical of the youth and an apologist for the older members of the party. Is he beginning to realize the deep and engrossing crisis within the party?

March 30, 1942

Agostini violently attacked Cavallero. According to him, Cavallero has already chosen the new commander of the carabinièri, which he would like to control for ulterior purposes. There is a great deal of exaggeration, but a substratum of truth, in Agostini's words.

Vidussoni goes to Venice to discuss with Axmann the foundation of a European Youth Association, which would be under the honorary presidency of Schirach. Vidussoni would like to ask for an Italian presidency side by side with the German. I am certain that Schirach will not be favorably disposed, since this is his baby. I do not conceal from Vidussoni my doubts on the matter, but the young man, who is as ignorant as he is presumptuous, insisted on his point of view. Let him break his neck if he wants to.

March 31, 1942

Nothing new.

April 1, 1942

The Duce has learned from an industrialist of the Alto Adige that the following joke is circulating in Germany: "In two months we shall win the war against Russia, in four months against England, and in four days against Italy." He has asked me to obtain confirmation from Alfieri while "on his part he is beginning to prepare new divisions, because it is not known what surprises are in store for 1943." Mussolini is also very much concerned by a report from Anfuso regarding the behavior at Budapest of two groups of Italians who have gone to Hungary for the agricultural exposition. Drunken brawls in night clubs and raids on provisions on sale in the shops. This incident gave rise to a violent Mussolinian tirade against the middle class.

Pareschi is rather optimistic about our present harvest. On the other hand, he makes increasingly dark prophecies for the future.

April 2, 1942

The Prefect of Naples, Albini, reports that the Neapolitan situation is bad, but the Neapolitans are people who are accustomed to tightening their belts and suffering; hence, there is nothing to be feared, at least until some new and serious incident develops.

Hason, chief of the carabinièri, reports that the general situation is better, but the country has lost faith in the party, which is no longer an important element in national life. The Army still maintains unchanged its hostility toward Cavallero, although it recognizes that there is no general who enjoys a real and indisputable prestige and who, therefore, deserves to replace him. The appointment of Gariboldi as commander of the troops in Russia has created a good impression. It was known that he was a personal enemy of Cavallero and his appointment was not expected.

Farnesi expressed concern about the food situation and criticism of the attitude of the young men. The centers of infection are the classes on political leadership in the universities where one finds some ambitious, crooked, and untrustworthy individuals. From now on they will be scattered at various jobs in distant cities, and the press of the universities will be placed under the supervision of serious and responsible persons.

Borri, Prefect of Genoa, reports that the city is in good shape, but the lack of food supplies is beginning to be worrying.

Geloso, commander of the troops in Greece, reports that public order is good, public health in danger, the food outlook a little better for the future.

April 3, 1942

Nothing new.

April 4, 1942

A move by the Japanese Ambassador to get us to intervene at the Holy See. At the time it established diplomatic relations with Japan it did the same with Chiang Kai-shek. The Japanese prefer that the Chinese Minister should not come at all or that his arrival be postponed for some time at least. I do not know how much we can really do, but I have promised the Ambassador to act on his request.

April 5, 1942

Mussolini does not want to take from Hungary the thirteen thousand tons of wheat which Pareschi got Hungary to promise him. He considers this a pittance and believes that we can produce enough food without a further reduction in the ration.

Del Drago returns from Paris. In Berlin there is nothing new on the surface, while, on the other hand, Paris is really in a sad state. In some German circles he was told that after the offensive on the eastern front, which will practically liquidate Russia, they are hoping to obtain a compromise peace with the Anglo-Saxon countries.

Today I went to mass at the Santa Maria degli Angeli. The church was filled by a devout crowd. I do not at all believe, as some would like to have it, that Italy is not a fundamentally Catholic country.

April 6, 1942

When Goering was in Rome we spoke of the possibility of having returned to Italy certain Italian paintings now in France, particularly those which belonged to Jews and were seized by the Germans. Among the names that were mentioned in the conversation was that of Rothschild, who owned many Boldinis. Today Goering sent me a Boldini as a gift, and his letter began as follows: "Unfortunately, there was nothing left in the Rothschild house. . . ." If, someday, this letter is found, it will appear that it was I who instigated him to sack the homes of Jews and that he was sorry that he had arrived too late. This is an example of the political sharpness of the Germans.

The Vichy Government is attempting blackmail in the typical French manner regarding the repatriation of the Italians in East Africa. Whereas it had previously sanctioned the embarkation of our nationals at Jibuti, it now raises many objections unless we repatriate at the same time one hundred and fifty French civilians and six hundred and fifty military men. While it is possible to agree about the civilians, it is not possible for the military. Meanwhile, I believe that it would be worth while to turn them down hard. We shall see about it later.

We have received news of a Japanese air attack on Colombo. Does this represent a first move toward India? I believe, rather, that its object is to impress the Indians during the Cripps negotiations [Sir Stafford Cripps was on a mission to India to negotiate an agreement on eventual Indian independence], which just now seem to be moving in the general direction of a partially favorable conclusion.

April 7, 1942

Nothing new.

April 8, 1942

Somebody was talking about illiteracy in certain Italian regions, when Mussolini said: "Even if this were true, what is the difference? In the fourteenth century Italy was populated by nothing but illiterates, and this did not prevent the flowering of Dante Alighieri. Today, when everybody knows how to read and write, we have instead the poet Govoni, who, while not exactly insignificant, is certainly less than Dante."

The Prefect of Rome informs me that the Duce is indignant because he sees too many young men walking in the streets of the capital. He has given orders that they be inducted into the Army. But what will be done with them? How will they distinguish between the unemployed and those who are forced to walk the streets on account of their occupations? I recall that in Peking, when old Chang Tso-Lin was in need of soldiers, he would block off a few streets and his soldiers would then seize all male citizens who were passing by, shave their heads and immediately put them into uniform. No protest was of avail. The problem of conscription was reduced to a problem of street traffic. Are they thinking of adopting in Rome the ways of this old Pekinese despot?

I see Gambara, who is indignant but not saddened by Cavallero's hostility. It seems that they are going to send him to Russia. If this happens, I am sure that his name will once again become a synonym for success.

April 9, 1942

Alfieri has come to Rome on leave. He does not report anything particularly important, but is less optimistic than usual and thinks that the summer offensive can have only a limited success.

On the other hand, the statements made by Bismarck to Blasco d'Aieta in the greatest confidence are more interesting. I summarize them briefly. By October, no matter how things go, Germany must make peace. The Army cannot and will not take the initiative at that time, in the first place because it is not according to its tradition, and also because it has had its back broken by the removal of its best military leaders. There are many disturbances within the party. Himmler himself, who was an extremist in the past, but who now holds the real pulse of the country, wants a compromise peace. By October England will be ripe for negotiations, especially if the Germans would consider the possibility of an anti-Japanese collaboration for the reconquest of Asia by the whites. Italy should assume the initiative within the Axis to bring the war on to a diplomatic plane. Are these the imaginings of our Bismarck, or are they manifestations of real trends in German public opinion? I lack the information for an opinion, but it is noteworthy that Otto spoke after Admiral Canaris' visit to Rome and the many conversations he has had with him. Personally, I believe that the force of German resistance is far greater.

April 10, 1942

Conversation between the Duce and Alfieri. Mussolini talked less to seek information than to reaffirm his complete optimism on the progress of the war as well as its conclusion. He gave as much evidence of anti-German sentiment as of pro-Japanese feelings. He was in a happy mood, and talkative. Speaking of Charlemagne, he said that he admired his virility above all, since he agrees with the French philosopher who says, "Genius is a matter of guts."

Host Venturi told me about the origin and explanation of the abolition of railroad sleeping cars, restaurant cars, and first-class cars. It is Mussolini who wanted this step to put everybody on the same level, and against the opinion of the technicians. Mussolini said that he now feels the old revolutionary spirit more than ever. Meanwhile, the trains are filled with disorders of every sort, since the crowd is enormous and the accommodations limited. In Trieste last evening the Undersecretary of the Postal Service had to be put into his train through the window, as all the corridors were filled to the point where no one could get through. Naturally the government hasn't gained prestige by this incident.

April 11, 1942

Mussolini visits the Society of the Friends of Japan. He likes more and more to declare himself "the first pro-Japanese in the world," but he gives to his affirmation a distinct anti-German character. He uttered a few words of warm sympathy, and concluded: "The Italian soldiers and the Japanese soldiers and the *other armies* of the Tripartite Alliance will wage war until victory."

De Peppo from Ankara summarizes the situation thus: "The Turks will not fight against us and they may, perhaps, be on our side if the fate of the war brings a definitive success for the armies of the Axis. Enemy Number 1 is Russia, fear Number 2 is Germany. The Turkish ideal is that the last German soldier should fall upon the last Russian corpse. We are still very much under suspicion. In order to remove this suspicion it will be necessary to withdraw from the island of Castellorizzo, which is considered our offensive point in Turkish territory. But we cannot do that now. This gesture, at such an inopportune moment, would be interpreted as a sign of weakness and would lead to results that would have an effect contrary to what we are seeking.

April 12, 1942

Nothing new.

April 13, 1942

The Hungarian Chief of Staff comes to visit me, followed step by step by Cavallero. He says nothing of any importance.

I had a long conversation with Donna Edvige [Mussolini's eldest sister]. She asked to see me about a little favor, but this was obviously just a pretext. In reality she wanted to give me her impressions on the situation, listen to my own, and especially unburden her heart about a matter which has now become a national question: the Petacci family. She tells me, with much intelligence and great affection for her brother, what everybody is saying. She adds that she has proof in her hands concerning the shady business transactions of the Petacci clan, and the scandal resulting from them. She has made up her mind to confront the Duce with it and talk over the situation. I was very reserved, and told her what she already understands very well—my delicate position in the matter. Edvige told me that she had already talked about it last year, when it was said that Mussolini was going to the Cammilluccia [residence of the Petacci family] to play tennis. He had admitted going there, but definitely denied the tennis business.

Revel unburdened himself about the situation and expressed concern over the Duce's state of health, affirming that he saw him at times in such obvious pain as to be alarming. He wanted me to do something about it. But what? In the first place I am convinced that he is very well, and then, who has the courage to speak to him about a personal matter?

April 14, 1942

The Japanese have proposed a tripartite declaration on the independence of India and Arabia. First reactions in Berlin are unfavorable. The Japanese initiative is not welcome in regions close to Europe. Mussolini, on the other hand, wanted to adhere to the proposal immediately.

April 15, 1942

Laval is at the head of the government in France. Here are the results of long German labor, concerning which we have always been kept in the dark. Only after it was over did the German representative in Paris inform our Ambassador of what had happened, yet the matter concerns us directly. What promises have been made to the French in order to reach this conclusion? At whose expense? We shall see. For the moment it is hard to predict anything. But one thing is certain: Laval does not represent France, and if the Germans think they can conquer French hearts through him, they are mistaken, very much mistaken again.

April 16, 1942

Nothing new.

April 17, 1942

Nothing new.

April 18, 1942

The Laval government is formed. It is a government of undersecretaries and of unknowns. It remains practically a Pétain-Darlan government. Thus France prepares for all three eventualities: a British victory, de Gaulle; a German victory, Laval; a compromise, Pétain. If only all this does not end to our disadvantage.

The Americans have bombed Tokyo and other Japanese cities. This is their first offensive action since the beginning of the war. I do not think that, for the moment, they can do great things, their preparation being far behind; but as time passes they will make their weight felt more and more—especially in the air.

April 19, 1942

Mussolini was very much surprised at an order of the Führer which postpones to the second of May the national German holiday because it fell on a Friday. He is right. These Germans, he says, who bark against Catholicism, show themselves to be slaves of a prejudice which is distinctly Christian in origin. But, above all, they show that they lack nerve, and are not sure of what they are doing.

April 20, 1942

A strange speech by Goebbels on the occasion of Hitler's birthday. He talked in rather gloomy terms to reaffirm his faith in final victory. But why did he have to make this speech, if, as is repeated in many quarters, the coming of spring permits the Germans to look to the eastern front with greater confidence? Even Mussolini, who ordinarily inclines toward optimistic interpretations, commented bitterly on Goebbels' speech.

Anfuso, on his return from Budapest, also talks in a minor tone. The Hungarians affirm that German preparation for the offensive is not what is claimed, and on the southern front supplies are low.

April 21, 1942

The Germans intend to procrastinate for a few days on their reply to the Japanese about the declaration of independence for India and Arabia.

Bismarck tells d'Aieta that the German Consul General in Milan receives many offensive letters. The last one ran like this: "We hear that you are looking for a new residence. We offer you one which is very beautiful, and worthy of you and of your people and of your leader. The address is so and so." The Consul General went solemnly to the address indicated, and found himself at the doors of the jail.

Jacomoni makes a rather good report on the Albanian situation. The only difficulty is the shortage of materials, which makes it impossible for us to continue our public works.

April 22, 1942

The Duce informs me that Marshal Kesselring, on his return from Germany, brought Hitler's approval for the landing operation on Malta. It appears that the island has really been damaged by aerial bombardments. This does not, however, alter the fact that the coastal defenses are still intact. Therefore, in the opinion of some naval experts, the undertaking is still dangerous and in any case would be expensive.

April 23, 1942

I accompany Jacomoni to the Duce to discuss the question of the Albanian flag. The flag as it is now, the eagle framed in the fasces and topped by the crown of Savoy, is offensive to the Albanian Nationalists, who protest their respect for their own national symbols. We now revive the old flag, which will bear on the standard the Fascio Littorio and the blue band of Savoy. Naturally, before making the Duce's decision public I shall confer with the King.

Ambassador Boscarelli has died in Buenos Aires. As a diplomat he was my first friend in Rio de Janeiro, and had always kept alive his affection and devotion for me. He wasn't gifted with exceptional talent, but he was honest, a good worker, and courteous—all things which made him a very useful diplomatic agent. His death makes me very sad.

April 24, 1942

The Japanese military attaché, in talking to Prunas, vented his violent criticism of the German attitude and the German way of conducting political warfare—which is all wrong, according to the Japanese. If the Germans continue at this pace, they will meet with some painful surprises. I showed the Duce my notes on the subject and his comments were favorable to the Japanese.

During the evening Mackensen brings to the Duce a proposal that he meet the Führer at Salzburg by the end of the month. Mussolini would like to delay until the first of May. Hitler sends word by telephone that the delay is not possible "for reasons independent of his will." The meeting is thus set for the twenty-ninth and thirtieth.

Riccardi gave vent to his feelings about Petacci's brother and his band. He says that he talked openly to the Duce about it. I limited myself to listening. This is a buzz saw I don't want to put my finger into.

April 25, 1942

Nothing new.

April 26, 1942

Nothing new.

April 27, 1942

A long speech by Hitler. It is difficult to comment upon it because by now all his speeches are more or less alike. The tone is not very optimistic. More than anything else he looks to the past, how and why the Russian winter was so severe and they were yet able to overcome it. But there is not a hint of what all are waiting for—the ending of the war. On the contrary, he declared that he is making every preparation to face the eventuality of another winter on the Russian front with more adequate forces. Then he asked for full power over the German people. He already exercises complete power, but by appealing for it in this way he has aroused the feeling that the internal situation in Germany needs a still more rigid control. In general, the speech has had a depressing effect in Italy, while Mussolini has judged it to be "an excellent and strong speech."

Marcello Vaccari, the Prefect of Venice, speaks to me of the extravagances of young Petacci, how he has caused a big scandal in Venice, and how Buffarini had suppressed the reports of the carabinièri which Vaccari himself had given him. According to what Petrognano has said, Buffarini is financing Clara Petacci with two hundred thousand lire a month, and in this way Buffarini secures his complete impunity. However, now there is really too much talk about the affair.

April 28, 1942

We leave for Salzburg. This is a meeting that was desired by the Germans, and for which, as usual, they have given us no indication of an agenda. During the trip Cavallero talks to me about the Malta operation. He realizes that it is a tough nut. The preparations under way are being made with a maximum of attention and care, and with the conviction that the attack must be made. This is to give the maximum incentive to those concerned. But whether the operation will take place, and when, is another matter, and in regard to this Cavallero makes no commitment. As is his nature, he digs himself in behind a great quantity of ifs and buts. He talks about the future progress of the war. We must win during this year or, at least, place ourselves in a position to win. Otherwise, dangers will increase.

April 29, 1942

Arrival at Salzburg (the Puhl station). The usual scene: Hitler, Ribbentrop, the usual people, the usual ceremony. We are housed at the Klessheim Castle. This is a grandiose building, once owned by the prince-bishops of Salzburg, which has now become a guesthouse for the Führer. It is very luxurious and well arranged: furniture, hangings, carpets, all coming from France. Probably they did not pay too much for it.

There is much cordiality, which puts me on my guard. The courtesy of the Germans is always in inverse ratio to their good fortune. Hitler looks tired; he is strong, determined, and talkative. But he is tired. The winter months in Russia have borne heavily upon him. I see for the first time that he has many gray hairs.

Hitler talks with the Duce, I talk with Ribbentrop, but in two separate rooms, and the same record is played in both. Ribbentrop, above all, plays his usual record. I have recorded the conversation elsewhere. Napoleon, the Beresina, the drama of 1812, all this is brought to life in what he says. But the ice of Russia has been conquered by the genius of Hitler. This is the strong dish that is served up to me. But what of tomorrow? What does the future hold? On this matter Ribbentrop is less explicit. An offensive against the Russians in the south with the oil wells as a politico-military objective.

April 30, 1942 [*continuation of April 29*]

When Russia's sources of oil are exhausted she will be brought to her knees. Then the British Conservatives, and even Churchill himself, who, after all, is a sensible man, will bow in order to save what remains of their mauled empire. Thus spoke Ribbentrop. But what if all this doesn't happen? What if the English, who are stubborn, decide to continue? What course must be followed to change their minds? Airplanes and submarines, says Ribbentrop. We turn back to the 1940 formula. But this formula failed then and was put up in the attic. Now they pull it out again, and, after having dusted it thoroughly, they want to offer it to us again. I am little convinced by it, and I say this to Ribbentrop, much to Alfieri's dismay. Alfieri understands very little of what he hears but always says yes.

America is a big bluff. This slogan is repeated by everyone, big and little, in the conference rooms and in the antechambers. In my opinion, the thought of what the Americans can and will do disturbs them all, and the Germans shut their eyes in order not to see. But this does not keep the more intelligent and the more honest from thinking about what America can do, and they feel shivers running down their spines.

In regard to France they feel more doubt than friendship. Laval, too, is hardly convincing. The true spirit of the French is more clearly expressed by the gesture of the typesetter who risked his life to have the paper come out with the name of Pétain changed to Putain, than by all the words of the collaborationists in the pay of Vichy. In Germany they have no illusions, and are always ready to slug anybody who moves.

Hitler talks, talks, talks, talks. Mussolini suffers—he, who is in the habit of talking himself, and who, instead, practically has to keep quiet. On the second day, after lunch, when everything had been said, Hitler talked uninterruptedly for an hour and forty minutes. He omitted absolutely no argument: war and peace, religion and philosophy, art and history. Mussolini automatically looked at his wrist watch, I had my mind on my own business, and only Cavallero, who is a phenomenon of servility, pretended he was listening in ecstasy, continually nodding his head in approval. Those, however, who dreaded the ordeal less than we did were the Germans. Poor people. They have to take it every day, and I am certain there isn't a gesture, a word, or a pause which they don't know by heart. General Jodl, after an epic struggle, finally went to sleep on the divan. Keitel was reeling, but he succeeded in keeping his head up.

May 1, 1942 [continuation of April 30]

He was too close to Hitler to let himself go as he would have liked to do.

One does not see any physically fit men on the streets in the cities and towns of Germany. Women, children, and old men only. Also foreign laborers, slaves of the earth. Edda, who visited a camp of our Italian workers, found one who had been wounded on his arm by a brutal guard with a scythe. She told Hitler, who put on a fit of anger and ordered all sorts of arrests and investigations. Which, however, will not change the course of things.

Losses in Russia are heavy. Ribbentrop says two hundred and seventy thousand dead. Our General Marras raises it to seven hundred thousand. And between amputations, frostbite, and the seriously ill who will not recover by the end of the war, the figure rises to three million.

British aviation is striking hard. Rostock and Lübeck have been literally razed to the ground. Cologne has been heavily hit. The Germans react and strike back at the English cities but with less violence. Which only partly consoles the German population, accustomed as it has always been to dish it out but never to take it.

May 2, 1942 [continuation of May 1]

Which leads many of them, who have devastated half of Europe, to weep about the "brutality of the English, who make many innocent Prussian families homeless." The worst of it is that they really feel this way.

Mussolini is satisfied with the trip, and with his conversations with Hitler. This always happens. But, although he doesn't say it openly, this time he is led to reflect deeply about many things which are not yet apparent, but which one can feel in the air. This is the way he summarized the situation: "The German machine is still formidably powerful, but has suffered great wear. Now it will make a new and imposing effort. It must attain its goal."

The trip didn't arouse very much interest in Italy, and the war goes on. Real interest would come if people could begin to see peace in the offing. But peace has already been brushed aside by Hitler's speech, which could not have produced a worse impression. Everybody expected the announcement of the offensive against the Russians. Instead, he announced an offensive against the German people.

May 3, 1942

Yesterday a meeting of the Council of Ministers. The Duce summarized the results of his trip in a brief address. Grandi has found it "discomforting."

In agreement with Berlin, we reply to Tokyo that the moment has not yet come to make a declaration about Arab and Indian independence. It would be a platonic gesture with no practical results, and perhaps might have negative consequences. Only if and when the armies of the Axis have reached a point where they can impose the declaration of independence with armed force can they indulge in such a gesture.

I have given the Duce the stenographic report of my conferences with von Ribbentrop. I had given it a somewhat controversial flavor and thought that this would displease him. Instead, he found it satisfactory and has kept it because tomorrow he wants to show it personally to the King.

D'Aroma has come to tell me, with a tragic and mysterious air, all those commonplaces that everybody knows about the situation of the regime and the Duce. Nonsense. Naturally, the moment we are passing through is not one for elation, nor for many reasons could it be, but the approval of the people for the person of the Duce is unanimous. In order to sense this one had only to be at his train window during his trip from Tarvisio to Rome. There was not a person who, on recognizing the Duce, did not give signs of happy exaltation. Exactly as before. But, then, must we take a few professional gossipers seriously?

May 4, 1942

I report on the trip to the King and tell him that the Duce will give him personally the memorandum dictated by me. As usual, I speak quite frankly, and the King shows that he appreciates it. But today he looked more tired than usual. He makes some anti-German remarks. "If they did not need us they would cast us aside like old rags. I always tell the Duce that we must not trust those ugly Germans, and I know that he does not like my comments." However, in general he expresses himself calmly about the development of the conflict and is convinced that in England the situation is graver than it is thought to be.

I also speak to the King on the question of the Albanian flag. We talk about modifying it by removing the fasces and crown of Savoy, and putting these symbols on the standard. He accepts because needs must.

I receive Bose, head of the Hindu Nationalists. He feels badly when he learns that the declaration in favor of independence for India has been postponed *sine die*. He believes that in this way we are playing the game of Japan, which will act on its own account without considering the interests of the Axis. He now thinks that British domination in India is coming to an end. British forces are small and the Indian forces have no desire to fight. Naturally, we must take these declarations of Bose for what they are, because he is trying to turn the water to his mill.

May 5, 1942

The English have occupied Madagascar. It was to be expected, especially since Laval had announced to the four winds that he desired Nipponese occupation in order to forestall that of the Anglo-Saxons. Mussolini even thinks that Laval acted in this way in order to press the English to act and that he established an alibi in advance. He wanted Berlin informed of his suspicion.

I go with Bose to the Duce. A long conference without any new developments, except the fact that Mussolini allowed himself to be persuaded by the arguments adduced by Bose to obtain a tripartite declaration in favor of Indian independence. He has telegraphed the Germans proposing—contrary to the Salzburg decisions—proceeding at once with the declaration. I feel that Hitler will not agree to it very willingly.

Conference with Monsignor Bernardini, Papal Nuncio at Berne. He entertains considerable hope for a compromise peace in the fall, after the offensive in Russia. I disillusioned him. Germany is, and for a long time will be, extremely intransigent. Not even from a distance do I see what could be a good basis for discussion by the two parties in conflict. I advised the Holy See not to embark on a course that is surely bound to fail.

May 6, 1942

Nothing new.

May 7, 1942

Nothing new.

May 8, 1942

A great naval battle has taken place in the Coral Sea. Both sides claim great successes, but as yet we have no details as to how things have really gone.

An item which is important in the orientation of Italian political and social life: Vidussoni wanted to close the golf courses. I questioned him, and he, who is very simple-minded and is never able to find a way out, answered candidly that he intended to do this because "golf is an aristocratic sport." That's a fine reason! It is almost like those people we cudgeled in 1920 and 1921. The affair has, in itself, relatively little importance, but it has a great deal of importance as an indication of what will be done in the future. However, they must not exaggerate, because there are many people who are beginning to be annoyed. Let us not ask for greater rights than others merely because we wear a collar and wash our feet. But neither let us be disposed to accept this privation just for the reasons given. The Italian middle class is the one that endures the greatest sacrifices, that wages the war, and that constitutes the backbone of the country. Must we really strike at it every day and harass it to the point of making it an implacable enemy of the regime? I consider it a great mistake because nothing is gained and one does not even earn the gratitude of the masses, which are inconsistent and changeable as the sands.

May 9, 1942

It is not yet clear how things have gone in the Coral Sea. The Anglo-American communiqués, although they admit some unspecified losses, make loud claims of victory. On the other hand, the Japanese do the same. It is to be noted that the declaration of the Japanese General Staff placed the honor of the Emperor himself at stake. Therefore, they should not lie, although war lies are more or less like those that do not compromise the honor of a woman—permissible lies.

I accompanied Dindina [Ciano's daughter] to the altar for her first communion. She was as pretty as a dream and was very much touched. I, too, was somewhat touched.

May 10, 1942

Mussolini has left for Sardinia on a trip of military inspection. He will be absent one week.

Senise makes his usual attack on Buffarini, who, according to him, is at the bottom of all the filthy doings in Italy. Now he hopes he has finally caught him by the throat, through the scandal over the aryanization of the Jews. The band, which apparently was headed by Prefect Lepara, in reality was directed by Buffarini, who gorged himself with the profits. Buffarini has a bad conscience, and he trembles.

Senise has also sent me the reports of the questioning of the four bad boys who wanted to make a *coup d'état,* starting it in a manner of which I disapprove greatly, that is, with my assassination. More than their perversity, it is their idiocy which impresses one. They talked about these projects in the presence of people they had met for the first time and who were obviously spies of the police. I think that, except for one, all the rest should be given their liberty with a kick in the behind. They deserve no more. The Duce, talking about the matter, said to Senise: "I do not know whether the appointment of Vidussoni was a good or a bad thing." Well, it was a bad thing. But it is interesting that the question is raised so soon.

May 11, 1942

A violent speech by Churchill. He threatens to use gas against German cities in case Hitler uses gas on the Russian front. I hope that neither one nor the other will carry out such a sinister plan.

Hungarian uneasiness is expressed by this little story which is going the rounds at Budapest. The Minister of Hungary declares war on the United States, but the official who receives the communication is not very well informed on European matters and hence asks several questions.

He asks, "Is Hungary a republic?"

"No, it is a kingdom."

"Then you have a king?"

"No, we have an admiral."

"Then you have a fleet?"

"No, we do not have any sea."

"Do you have any claims, then?"

"Yes."

"Against America?"

"No."

"Against England?"

"No."

"Against Russia?"

"No."

"But against whom do you have these claims?"

"Against Rumania."

"Then will you declare war on Rumania?"

"No, sir. We are allies."

There is a great deal of truth in this series of paradoxes.

May 12, 1942

Cavallero outlines our program for carrying on the war in the Mediterranean. At the end of the month Rommel will attack in Libya with the aim of defeating the English forces. If he can, he will take Tobruk and will go as far as the old boundaries; if not, he will limit himself to forestalling an attack by the enemy by striking first. Then all the forces will be concentrated for an attack on Malta. The Germans are sending a parachute division commanded by General Student and are furnishing us with technical material for the assault. It will take place in July or August at the latest. Afterward it will no longer be possible because of the sea. Cavallero declares, "I know that it is a difficult undertaking and that it will cost us many casualties, and I know, too, that I am staking my head on this undertaking. But I am the one who wants it because I consider it absolutely essential for the future development of the war. If we take Malta, Libya will be safe. If not, the situation of the colony will always be precarious. I shall personally assume command of the operation. The Prince of Piedmont was considered, but for many reasons it was decided to leave him out." Cavallero does not conceal the fact that he hopes to derive a great deal of personal glory from this operation. But I believe he will never acquire it.

I saw the King at the exposition of the German Academy. The works are few and rather second-rate.

May 13, 1942

Colonel Casero does not share Cavallero's easy enthusiasms for the attack on Malta. Malta's anti-aircraft defense is still very efficient, and their naval defense is entirely intact. The interior of the island is one solid nest of machine guns. The landing of paratroops would be very difficult; a great part of the planes are bound to be shot down before they can deposit their human cargo. The same must be said for landings by sea. On the other hand, it must be remembered that only two days of minor aerial bombardment by us was enough to make their defense more stubborn. In these last attacks we, as well as the Germans, have lost many feathers. Even Fougier considers an eventual landing operation with much anxiety, and the German General Lörzer did not conceal his open disagreement. The supporters of the undertaking are Kesselring and Cavallero, the latter going through his usual tricks to put the responsibility on the shoulders of others.

Arpinati asks for a small favor. He is, as always, calm and dignified, and not at all anxious for his own personal position. He does not consider the internal situation of the country very good, and condemns two things: the too intimate union with the Germans, whom he does not like, and any demonstration of leftist tendencies.

May 14, 1942

Nothing new.

May 15, 1942

In Rome there is a good deal of gossip about the fact that there was a dance last Saturday in the Senni home, which was attended by a young secretary of the American Embassy. No one of those present had the courage to react against it, which is extremely deplorable. It seems that several of the attachés of our Ministry for Foreign Affairs were present, and for this reason I have asked the chief of police to make a careful investigation. Naturally, this gesture by a few inconsiderate irresponsibles is causing a great rumpus and casts discredit on an entire class of people, which, as a matter of fact, is giving its share of blood and faith to the conflict.

May 16, 1942

Mussolini returns. He is very happy about his trip and what he has seen. He doesn't seem at all tired; in fact, he is sunburned and thinner. He talks with enthusiasm about the people of Sardinia, from whom he didn't hear one protest about the scarcity of bread, or one plea for peace, "which would not have been lacking in the Valle Padana [the Po Valley], where there have been too many political experiments." Even with regard to the defense of the island, his visit has given him reasons for assurance: good troops, efficient armaments, and, in the zones of a possible invasion, a malaria such as to decimate the British troops in a few days, just as those of Frederick Barbarossa were decimated, when they stopped between Portonaccio and Ponte Galera.

Fougier inveighs against Cavallero, whom he accuses of being a dangerous clown, ready to follow every German whim without dignity, and a liar. He wanted to give vent to his feelings with the Duce, but I dissuaded him, at least for the time being. Things are not yet ripe for Cavallero's dismissal, which, however, will be necessary at the proper time. Fougier also mentions Rommel's plans to attack on the twenty-eighth, and to drive forward as far as the valley of the Nile. Cavallero, who in Rome says that he does not want such a risky offensive, sings a different song in Derna, encouraging Rommel to "make the maximum effort."

May 17, 1942

Starace. A brief visit to recommend two persons to me. He is calmer than before, which makes me think that he has found some satisfaction —if nothing else of a material variety.

Gariboldi. He will leave shortly for Russia to assume command of the expeditionary army. I have known him for many years, from the time of the capture of Addis Ababa. I have never had a very favorable opinion of him. Just now he seems even more tired and aged, notwithstanding the bleached-blondness of his heavy mustaches, trimmed *à la fin de siècle*. Cavallero has insisted on appointing him in order to get rid of Messe, who was beginning to acquire too much importance in the eyes of the Duce and of the country. Cavallero is a faithful follower of the theory which calls for the decapitation of poppies that grow too high. Gariboldi has been in Germany and has returned generally satisfied, but without clear ideas as to what is boiling in the kettle. However, he does not consider that the total liquidation of Russia will be possible before the coming of winter, which raises some very serious problems for us since we shall soon have three hundred thousand men on the eastern front.

May 18, 1942

The Duce telephones me to tell Edda "to talk to no one, absolutely no one, about what she saw and observed in Germany." The explanation is that the King told him, "All Rome knows that in a German hospital there is an Italian laborer with fingers cut off, and that your daughter energetically protested to Hitler." The Duce is concerned about this remark of the King, and realizes that it is a maneuver to feed the anti-German resentment of the Italian people, using the specific case of an important name. "The King, who always plays the part of the anti-German," said Mussolini, "has given a daughter to a German, his son to a Belgian woman of German race, and in his House marriages with Germans can be counted by the dozens."

In Slovenia things are not going so well. The High Commissioner asks us to send twenty-four thousand men. It appears that the streets of Lubiana are now unsafe for our troops; every doorway and every window hide potential danger.

All the youngsters who attended the dance in the Senni home, together with the American secretary, are now the object of Mussolini's just anger. Some of them, including the lady of the house, have been handcuffed. "The first to thank me," said the Duce, "should be her husband, because while he was fighting this flibbertigibbet was receiving the enemy in her home and dancing with them."

May 19, 1942

The English would like to send some hospital ships to Malta. Our Navy is favorable in principle, but the Germans are against it. The Duce decides against it, "especially because his experience has taught him the many things it is possible to hide in hospital ships when the blockade would otherwise prevent their passage. Last winter we were able to deliver some timely supplies of gasoline to Bengasi by making use of white ships" [ships of the Italian Red Cross].

Captain Dolmann, the S.S. man in Rome, has told d'Aieta that Himmler would like to come to Rome in October to talk things over with me, after the offensive in Russia that will certainly be brilliant but not decisive, making it necessary to prepare ourselves for a winter which will be hard, both materially and psychologically. Interesting declarations, especially because Himmler is the only man who really knows the pulse of the German people.

May 20, 1942

The Duce attached no importance to Dolmann's move. "Very well," he said. "We shall talk about it later. We know already that absolutely nothing will happen in Italy."

General Amè has secretly sent me two reports from General Marras on the morale of the German Army. According to the reports, it is bad from every point of view, discouragement has taken hold of everyone, and the idea of an unavoidable winter on the Russian front brings veritable despair to the military. Suicides are numerous among those who prefer death to returning to the front. Marras doesn't reach any conclusion, but these are his premises.

The British radio gives us to understand that Rommel's preparations for his coming offensive in Libya have not escaped them.

May 21, 1942

Mussolini has influenza. For the first time in many years I am told that he will not come to his office. I speak to him briefly over the telephone. His voice is hoarse and he has a bad cough. He must be in a very bad humor.

I speak with Colonna and some attachés who have returned from the United States. They say nothing sensational. They all agree in affirming, first, that the United States is not now in a position to do a great deal along military lines; second, that her industrial preparation is formidable and that within a few months we shall see a production of incalculable proportions; third, that the war is not popular, but that everyone is determined to fight even for twenty years, provided they get things settled; fourth, that feelings toward Italy are not at all hostile.

May 22, 1942

Nothing new.

May 23, 1942

The Duce telephoned indignantly, charging that the Japanese Ambassador, Shiratori, made certain statements which are not acceptable: the dominion of the world belongs to Japan, the Mikado is the only god on earth, and that both Hitler and Mussolini must become resigned to this reality. I remember Shiratori during his short stay in Rome. He was a fanatical extremist, but, above all, he was very ill-bred.

Bismarck has confirmed to d'Aieta that Himmler is playing a personal game by inciting people to grumble. Is this true? For the time being I think that the rumor must be accepted with a great deal of reserve.

May 24, 1942

Nothing new.

May 25, 1942

Nothing new.

May 26, 1942

Mussolini now interests himself only in the coming offensive in Libya, and he is definitely optimistic. He maintains that Rommel "will arrive at the Delta" unless he is stopped, "not by the British, but by our own generals." Even for the taking of Malta he makes good "forecasts." "A surprise has been prepared which will give formidable results." But he didn't say what the surprise is.

Serrano wants to come to Italy and Mussolini is favorable to the trip. I suggest that the meeting take place at Leghorn toward the middle of June. I don't think we shall have important things to say, but it is well not to lose this Spanish card which has cost blood and gold.

The situation between Hungary and Rumania is more and more tense. Mariassy sent a note today which is something of an alarm signal. I confess one suspicion, and that is that the Hungarians may be showing such concern in order to avoid any deep commitments in the offensive against Russia.

May 27, 1942

Sorrentino, on his return from Russia, gives his impressions and makes forecasts for the future. The first are not pleasant and the second not comforting. The brutality of the Germans, which has now reached the proportions of a continuing crime, stands out from his words so vividly and so movingly as to make one skeptical of its truthfulness. Massacres of entire populations, raping, killing of children— all this is a matter of daily occurrence. Against this there is the cold Bolshevik decision to resist and fight to the end, certain of victory. On the other hand, the morale of the Germans is lower than might be imagined. "The coming four months may mark the beginning of a catastrophe, the like of which has never been seen."

Fougier sends the first news of Rommel's attack in Libya. There is action of the air force and advance of armored columns, but it is too early to give even a partial account of what is happening. It appears that Rommel has somewhat reduced his original program, which was very comprehensive. Now he wants to reach the Nile Valley.

Bismarck told d'Aieta that food rations in Germany will soon be cut 25 per cent. Anna Maria Bismarck told me candidly yesterday evening, "I am pro-German because I married Otto, but I am anti-Nazi."

May 28, 1942

I understood that the Duce asked to see the declarations that I was going to make in the Senate on Saturday, so I sent him a copy of my speech. I hate to make speeches these days. One runs the risk of being called a liar or of being banal.

Pittalis, returning from Munich on his appointment as Ambassador to Buenos Aires, paints the German situation in dark colors. In 1942 it is necessary that careful decisions be made because the people have made every extreme sacrifice, and no more sacrifices can be expected of them. I must say that Pittalis, up to now, had, if anything, been guilty of optimism.

Venturi, Minister of Communications, says that sleeping cars and first-class cars will shortly be put back into operation on the Italian railroads. The experiment of abolishing them—one demagogically flavored—did not have good results but just the opposite.

Pavolini tells me that the Duce will have a slacker, who is a condemned assassin, shot in broad daylight at the Coliseum. I ask myself whether this lugubrious publicity will be of any help to the morale of the Italian people, whose psychology is a great deal more complex than is generally believed.

May 29, 1942

My speech to the Senate is approved by the Duce, without a word changed, which is something unusual for him, especially as he is in a very bad humor because of the drought which threatens to reduce the harvest by a million or so quintals of grain.

May 30, 1942

I spoke to the Senate. It appears that the speech was very much liked, as the senators, who are usually critical and reserved, were rather enthusiastic. They applauded very much and stood throughout the last part of my speech. Mussolini wanted a detailed report of the meeting and didn't hide his satisfaction.

In the afternoon I leave for Leghorn.

May 31, 1942

In Leghorn. A day of rest and fishing. But this does not save me from complaints about food, which is very short. Wine is lacking, and so is everything else. Renato, my fisherman, lost thirty pounds in a few months, and he tells me that the members of his family are losing weight at the same rate. In spite of this there is good humor and faith in the future.

I had a long and interesting conversation with Carboni. At the moment he is commanding one of the assault divisions which is to participate in the Malta operation. He is decidedly against it. He is convinced that we shall have heavy losses and nothing will come of it. He takes it out on Cavallero, whom he considers to be an intriguer and a man of bad faith. He is very pessimistic also about the Russian front. He doesn't think that during the summer the Germans can undertake any operations of far-reaching proportions. It is a war of position rather than anything else. From this he draws the most sinister conclusions for the German future. Carboni is a general of great ability. One must not forget, however, that he was dismissed by the SIM [Secret Military Intelligence] for his anti-German attitude, and that he is the son of an American mother.

June 1, 1942

The King praised my speech, of which I had sent him the complete text through Acquarone. As usual he takes it out on the Germans, whom he considers capable of all sorts of deceit and treachery. He shows interest in France and in the restoration of the Spanish monarchy, which he naturally approves, though at the same time he judges the future King with considerable reserve. He praises the future Queen, "who has a big nose, but a lot of good sense and clear judgment." He has modified his ideas about the future outlook. At first he believed in a British collapse, but now he does not talk about it any more and believes "that we must come to a compromise peace because no one will win, and the nations will add to their war sufferings the dissatisfaction of much inevitable disillusionment."

Mussolini repeats his praise of my speech and speaks with restraint about our offensive in Libya. According to him the main clash has not yet taken place because of the scarcity of supplies for the mechanized units. At the German Embassy, on the other hand, they are not satisfied with the course of things. It now seems that Tobruk has become an impossible objective and yet Cavallero was speaking of Cairo! True enough, on the day the attack began he went to bed with a very prudent attack of influenza.

June 2, 1942

The offensive in Libya has not yet taken a definite turn. On the whole, the Duce is optimistic, but at the High Command they are a little less so. Mussolini also thought of going to the front, but "he wouldn't like a repetition of what happened in Albania, when they made him a witness to an unfortunate battle."

Riccardi talks to me very critically about the Petacci family and about the business deals of Dr. Marcello Petacci. It appears that he had an open quarrel with them, and a violent exchange of words over the telephone. He showed me an interesting document. A non-commissioned officer of the carabinièri wrote in a report to his superiors that "a certain individual (whose name I do not remember) is a crook, but also the lover of a certain Petacci, sister of the Duce's mistress; therefore I can't touch him." This is incredible but true. I saw it with my own eyes.

Gambara writes that he has been retired. This is Cavallero's victory. Gambara asks for neither favor nor pity, but speaks sincerely. Was it necessary to harm the man who covered our flag with glory in Spain?

June 3, 1942

Optimism prevails at the Palazzo Venezia on the progress of operations in Libya. The Duce talks today about the imminent siege of Tobruk and about the possibility of carrying the action as far as Marsa Matruk. If these are roses . . . they will bloom. The Duce was very hostile to the Vatican because of an article appearing in the Osservatore Romano over the signature of Falchetto. The article spoke about

Greek philosophy, but the real purpose was evident. Guariglia will take the matter up with the Secretariat of State of the Vatican. "I hate priests in their cassocks," said Mussolini, "but I hate even more and loathe those without cassocks [Italians who follow the Vatican line], who are vile Guelfs, a breed to be wiped out."

I had lunch with Bottai. He said more or less the usual things, adding that as a matter of personal experience he found the Duce "spiritually and intellectually very low" in the last few months. I don't know on what he bases his impressions.

The Germans have prevented Alfieri going to Cologne, and barred his way at the station of Düsseldorf. Evidently the ruins of the city are such that they prefer our Ambassador not to see them. Also, Essen was bombed last night, and, it would seem, quite as heavily as Cologne.

According to Colonel Casero, the battle of Libya has become stationary, resolving itself into a battle of attrition.

June 4, 1942

Cavallero describes the results of the Libyan battle as "considerable," which, for anybody who knows the mysterious language of this mountebank general, means that things have gone very badly. He summarizes the situation as follows: it was a good thing we attacked, because the enemy was preparing to attack. But who says so? He goes on to say that we used up their matériel and thus won a tactical success. In reply to a question he says he doesn't believe that we can reach Tobruk or any more distant objective, but this does not prevent us from entertaining hopes. (Sic!) It is a little early to judge. We shall know later if this offensive of ours was good or bad.

I saw Messe on his return from Russia. He sees red because Cavallero made the old and stupid Gariboldi commander of the Army over his head, in spite of Messe's excellent record. Like everybody else who has had anything to do with the Germans, he detests them, and says that the only way of dealing with them would be to punch them in the stomach. He thinks the Russian Army is still strong and well armed, and that any idea of a complete collapse of the Soviets is an absolute Utopia. The Germans will still have some successes, perhaps some big successes, but they will solve nothing, and the winter will find them still in the field with further shortage of materials. Messe draws no conclusions, but does not conceal his doubts, which are very serious.

June 5, 1942

Grandi tells me that the Council of Ministers tomorrow, in connection with the doubling of the income tax, will introduce the oath as a way of ascertaining income, with all the consequences that this implies. This means that for the first time in the history of our tax system they are thinking of jailing tax evaders. This might do in countries educated in fiscal matters, but not with us, where everyone would be forced to take false oaths. If we closed our eyes to this, we would become ridiculous, or, wishing to apply the law, we would have to enlarge our jails to the point where half of the budget would go for the maintenance of prisoners. Thus Revel, after having taken everything from the Italians, wants also to take their honor. . . .

June 6, 1942

Meeting of the Council of Ministers. Mussolini inveighs violently against the merchants, of whom one hundred and thirty-two thousand have already been denounced. He accuses them of constituting another army which stabs the state in the back while it is engaged in a very hard war. Thus there will be new and tougher penalties added to those already set down. On the other hand, the tax oath, invented by Revel, was stillborn. The provision has been withdrawn. Naturally, it will be pulled out again, because the "Red Count," as they call this new Philippe Egalité Minister of Finance of ours, loses no opportunity to impose his demagogic policies.

Cavallero judges the situation in Libya as "logical." This is an adjective which he has now pulled out and dusted off and which he hasn't used since the time he was getting beaten in Albania. In the meantime, he stays in bed with his strange and rather suspicious illness.

June 7, 1942

Nothing new.

June 8, 1942

Nothing new.

June 9, 1942

Our military intelligence has uncovered a center of espionage in the German Embassy. Dr. Sauer, a cultural attaché, has already been arrested and has confessed. He made it clear that he did not act for money but out of hatred for Nazism and Fascism. He turned over to the Swiss military attaché information of a military nature. It also seems that a German colonel, an aide of von Rintelen, is also mixed up in the affair. The Duce commented bitterly on the matter and is afraid that it may damage the position of von Mackensen, the Ambassador. Bismarck, who has spoken on the subject with d'Aieta, did not attribute much importance to what has happened. He says that Sauer is a pederast and that he has been induced by his vice to commit this serious offense.

On the order of Mussolini the newspapers have for some days tried to show that during World War I the food situation in the country was worse than it is today. It is a sort of propaganda that produces an effect contrary to what was intended. We were all living then, and our memories are too fresh to accept these statements. Pavolini has, in fact, told me that the Duce complains that the newspapermen do not know how to carry on this campaign efficiently. The facts are that all those to whom Pavolini has gone have refused to write what was asked of them.

June 10, 1942

A ceremony at the monument to the unknown soldier in honor of naval heroes. As usual, the sailors and the cadets of Leghorn made a superb showing. However, the public showed little enthusiasm. No applause all along the line of march.

In Dalmatia the situation is very tense. The rebels, after having overwhelmed one of our brigades at Knin, are advancing toward Zara. Bastianini, who hurried to Rome, asserts that there isn't a minimum of forces to engage the rebels, thus their occupation of Dalmatia is to be feared. In the region of Fiume, also, there is a great deal of ferment. I talked with Testa, who is an energetic man who knows how to assume responsibility. Now Mussolini is furious with him, because without even a semblance of a trial he hanged five rebels whom he found wearing the shoes of our dead soldiers. Aside from the hangings, which

really are not in our tradition, recalling as they do the Austrian mentality of bygone days, Testa succeeds in keeping order, and the rebels
tremble at the very mention of his name.

Argentina protests strongly against the sinking of the *Victoria* by
Axis submarines. Ambassador Malbran, who is pro-Italian and who
has always been an optimist, now begins to see difficulties in the future
relations between our two countries.

June 11, 1942

Bir Akim has been taken. The garrison resisted strongly, because
there were many Frenchmen, Italians, Germans, and Jews convinced
that there would be no pity for them. Now we shall see if the action
can be followed up or will stop with this local success. This morning
the Duce expressed the opinion that it will be difficult to occupy
Tobruk. The action to date has cost us great losses.

I talked to Mussolini about Gambara. It appears that Cavallero
wishes to make an investigation even into the Spanish war period. This
is a shame, because in Spain Gambara was the only general who
brought glory to our colors. The Duce agreed and will put a stop to
this indecency. Every day Cavallero is becoming more and more harmful to the Army and to the country.

Pareschi is optimistic about the food situation, even though the heat
of the last few days has greatly damaged the grain harvest. At any
rate, he is convinced that the coming winter will be less hard than the
last.

Bismarck telephoned Blasco [d'Aieta] about an eventual alliance
between America, England, and Russia, and about an American commitment for the opening of a second front against the Germans. This
is like an injection to keep the Russians on their feet. Further news
must be awaited before forming an opinion on the subject.

June 12, 1942

Mussolini is more and more irritated against the *Osservatore Romano* because of certain articles signed by Falchetto in which there
really is a subtle vein of poison against the regime. He has decided to
have its director, Conte della Torre, arrested. I insisted that this act,
bound to produce a great crisis with the Vatican, be avoided, especially

now that we have no need of crises. He wasn't persuaded, but I hope that he will reconsider his decision.

Lequio's reports connect Serrano's visit with the question of the monarchy. Serrano has his visa for Switzerland, where the King of Spain is at this time. Mussolini is very much against the restoration of the monarchy and spoke along this line for a long time today. But nothing can be done about it. The monarchy will not solve anything, but all Spaniards want it. Therefore, if such a thing should happen, it is better that it take place with us rather than without us or against us. From Leghorn I shall take Serrano to luncheon with the King of Italy at San Rossore.

I saw Serena. He is just back from Croatia. He speaks despondently about the morale of the Army. He says, however, that a formula to improve it exists: kick out Cavallero. Every day he is less respected and more hated. General Guzzoni told me the same thing, but he is too much involved in the matter to be objective.

I learned from Bigliardi that the destroyer *Usodimare* has been sunk by mistake by one of our own submarines.

June 13, 1942

Nothing new. Off to Leghorn. Bad weather.

June 14, 1942

Nothing new.

June 15, 1942

Serrano arrives. The city greets him with an open heart and a formidable southwest wind.

June 16, 1942

At lunch with His Majesty. Conversation is conventional, but the King makes a very shrewd statement which I must set down. Serrano states that England, through Samuel Hoare, spends ten million pesetas a month for British propaganda in Spain. The King commented, "This is a lot of money, but fortunately experience teaches that a great part of these funds sticks to the fingers of the propagandists, and those who are to be propagandized get only the crumbs. This is a good thing, otherwise God only knows how many revolutions there would be."

June 17, 1942

Nothing new.

June 18, 1942

Nothing new.

June 19, 1942

I return to Rome. I made some notes on my conversations with Serrano. The Duce is still at Riccione.

June 20, 1942

I thought that after what had taken place in Libya and on the sea I would find the Duce in a boastful mood. Instead, he is reserved in his judgment and outlook. Nor does he give way to easy optimism. He is preparing to go to Africa if Tobruk is taken.

General Carboni has come to Rome to talk over the Malta enterprise, which is set for the time of the next new moon. He is convinced, technically convinced, that we are heading for an unheard-of disaster. Preparations have been childish, equipment is lacking and inadequate. The landing troops will never succeed in landing, or, if they land, they are doomed to total destruction. All the commanders are convinced of this, but no one dares to speak for fear of reprisals by Cavallero. But I am more than ever of the opinion that the undertaking will not take place.

The Duce receives Serrano, who repeats more or less what he said at Leghorn. Mussolini expresses hostility to monarchies which are potentially the natural enemies of totalitarian revolutions. He believes that in Spain the King will soon want to stifle Falangism. He cites some Italian precedents that tend to prove his point of view. As to the war, he makes predictions of absolute certainty on the success of the Axis, but foresees a very long war. He speaks of four or five years. He will see Serrano again before his departure. In today's conversation the Duce was particularly incisive and vivacious.

June 21, 1942

Tobruk has fallen and the British have left twenty-five thousand prisoners in our hands. This is a great success for us and opens new developments. On the other hand, I learned from a conversation with Bigliardi that the results of our aerial-naval battle were a great deal more modest than had been announced. The merchant ships were, in fact, hit, and many were sunk, but the British losses were limited to a cruiser probably sunk and a destroyer sunk.

Riccardi renews his broadsides against Clara Petacci. He also denounces an illegal traffic in gold, involving Buffarini, who lends his name to it. Riccardi, who is very violent and stubborn, is capable of starting a scandal. We shall see what develops.

Amè is pessimistic in judging the internal Anglo-American situation, but more so in judging the German situation. He, too, repeats the formula for the coming decisive four months. I think three months will be enough to see into the future.

June 22, 1942

The Duce is in very good humor and is preparing to go to Africa. In reality he was the man behind the decisive attack, even against the opinion of the High Command. Now he fears that they may not realize the magnitude of the success and therefore fail to take full advantage of it. He trusts only Rommel. From Rome a restraining telegram has already been sent, advising that they should not venture beyond the line of Fort Capuzzo-Sollum.

There is, on the other hand, some hesitation about the Malta undertaking. Mussolini wrote to Hitler, saying that if we did not have at our disposal forty thousand tons of oil, we should have to postpone it indefinitely.

This morning Petacci's sister was married in Rome, and the event was talked about throughout the city. There was talk of rich and fantastic gifts, forests of flowers, and Lucullan banquets. Much of it is probably fantasy, but there is a great deal of talk and this is what counts. The Duce said to Pavolini: "While we are talking, a marriage

is going on at Santa Maria degli Angeli. It is good from an economic
point of view, but bad for the girl, who had prospects of a successful
career in the movies. I hope, at any rate, that the newspapers will have
the sense not to talk about it. Only the *Messaggero,* to which her
father is a contributor, can make the announcement." It is interesting
that Mussolini broached the question openly with a minister.

June 23, 1942

A second conference between Serrano and the Duce. Nothing very
important except the affirmation by Serrano that if Portugal should be
attacked by the Anglo-Saxons Spain would not hesitate to come into
the war. In this connection there already exists an agreement between
Franco and Salazar. From the Duce comes the striking statement that
he, "like all Italians, is an Apostolic Roman Catholic, and that he does
not believe that Rosenberg's theory will be successful after the war."

From some intercepted telegrams from the American observer at
Cairo, Fellers, we learn that the English have been beaten and that if
Rommel continues his action he has a good chance of getting as far as
the Canal Zone. Naturally, Mussolini is pressing for prosecution of the
attack.

The promotion of Rommel to marshal raises some problems of
organization—in other words, the promotion of Bastico and Cavallero
to the same rank. I have told the Duce what I think. "Bastico's promotion will make people laugh; Cavallero's will make them indignant."
An authentic shake-up has taken place over the clandestine traffic in
gold with Spain through the diplomatic pouch. I have confiscated eighteen kilos and given them to the police. The information came from
Riccardi. The persons mixed up in it all belong to the Petacci gang.
Buffarini also has a part in it. I make no further comment.

June 24, 1942

The question of the gold and the Petaccis is becoming more acute.
Riccardi talked about it to the Duce, with whom Buffarini had already
tried to speak in self-defense. According to Riccardi, Mussolini is very
indignant at what has happened and has given orders that the guilty
be punished according to law, without respect for persons and without
pity. According to Buffarini, on the other hand, the Duce was angry

with Riccardi for having made a scene on the question which should
have been treated differently and with reserve. To complicate matters,
the name of the notorious Dr. Petacci has been added. Dr. Petacci has
come out of the shadow to address a violent letter to Buffarini, Riccardi,
and the Duce, in which he lays claim to special merit—"Fascist and
national merit"—for having gone in for such an operation, and insults
all those who are trying to put obstacles to the operation. The whole
affair cannot end too easily. It will be interesting to see who will foot
the bill.

In Libya, Rommel's action is progressing at full speed. The rosiest
forecasts can now be made.

June 25, 1942

After having made a tour of aviation camps for the distribution of
decorations, the Duce returned to Rome.

Victory has encouraged our forces in Libya and they are now
preparing to besiege Marsa Matruk.

Serrano has left, after an eleven-day visit. A too lengthy trip is never
useful; it creates boredom. Perhaps reciprocal, certainly unilateral.

June 26, 1942

Mussolini is happy over the progress of operations in Libya but unhappy over the fact that the battle is identified with Rommel, thus
appearing more and more as a German rather than an Italian victory.
Also Rommel's promotion to field marshal, "which Hitler evidently
made to accentuate the German character of the battle," causes the
Duce much pain. Naturally, he takes it out on Graziani, "who has
always been seventy feet underground in a Roman tomb at Cyrene
while Rommel knows how to lead his troops with the personal example
of the general who lives in his tank." For the moment Mussolini does
not make forecasts but hopes that "before fifteen days are over we can
establish our commissariat in Alexandria." He paints the Russian situation in darker colors: Russia, "where the Bolshevists have put into
execution the tactics of Lenin, who instructed the proletariat to fight
house by house against the armies of the bourgeois, thus obliging them
to abandon their artillery and aviation, to use only guns and bombs."
Our officers have prepared declarations of independence for Egypt,

changes in government, et cetera. We shall talk about it after Marsa Matruk has been taken.

I go to Leghorn on the anniversary of my father's death.

June 27, 1942

At Leghorn for the ceremonies in memory of my father; my memory of him is increasingly keen and sacred.

June 28, 1942

At Leghorn. Seashore and fishing. Operations in Libya are moving very fast. Marsa Matruk has fallen. The way to the Delta is now open.

June 29, 1942

Mussolini has left for Libya. I see Riccardi, who gives me a long account of his conversation with the Duce on the Petacci gold affair. It seems that the Chief is very indignant and has ordered Dr. Petacci to abstain from any such dealings in the future. We shall see. I do not know whether Riccardi has, perhaps, exposed himself too much. He said something that impressed me, "While I was speaking with the Duce I had before me a humiliated man. We were no longer on the same plane. I was two steps higher up." With Mussolini, it is very dangerous to believe that one is two steps above him.

June 30, 1942

I have had considerable difficulty in preventing Riccardi, for economic reasons, from creating a real political crisis with Switzerland, which I definitely want to avoid at this moment. I succeeded, but it was a burdensome and annoying discussion.

In Libya we are doing well, and our information gives the impression that the English are going through a grave crisis.

July 1, 1942

I leave for Leghorn, where I intend to spend a few days of rest at the seashore. News from Africa is still excellent.

July 2, 1942

Mussolini telegraphs, giving instructions to contact the Germans on the question of the future political government of Egypt. Rommel is to be the military commander, and an Italian is to be civilian delegate. I am asked to suggest a name. I suggest Mazzolini, who was our last Minister at Cairo. Blasco d'Aieta speaks with von Mackensen. If I had seen the Duce I would have dissuaded him from making a move which sounds too much like putting the cart before the horse.

July 3, 1942

Hitler answers that he agrees so far as Rommel is concerned, but he is postponing his answer as regards the Italian delegate, also in relation to the question of German representation. At any rate, he does not consider the question "urgent." He is not wrong, because a sudden and not unforeseen English reaction compels us to mark time before El Alamein. At the High Command in Rome they are very optimistic, and convinced that the lull is altogether temporary.

July 4, 1942

Cavallero has been made a marshal, evidently to offset the impression produced by the promotion of Rommel. The effect is negligible. The move is received with unanimous disfavor, especially in military circles.

July 5, 1942

Nothing new. We are still marking time in Libya. In Russia, on the other hand, the German offensive is moving slowly and with great difficulty. Either resistance has increased considerably or the force of penetration of the German Army is no longer what it was.

July 6, 1942

I have returned to Rome. There is in the air a vague concern on account of the lull before El Alamein. It is feared that after the impact of the initial attack is spent Rommel cannot advance farther, and whoever stops in the desert is truly lost. It is enough to think that every drop of water must come from Marsa Matruk, almost two hundred kilometers of road under bombardment of enemy aviation. It is reported to me that in military circles there is violent indignation against the Germans because of their behavior in Libya. They have grabbed all the booty. They thrust their claws everywhere, place German guards over the booty, and woe to anyone who comes near. The only one who has succeeded in getting plenty for himself, naturally, is Cavallero, and he has sent the goods to Italy by plane. This information is correct. It was given to me by Colonel Casero, the head of the air bureau. There is no question about it, Cavallero may not be a great strategist, but when it is a question of grabbing, he can cheat even the Germans.

July 7, 1942

Francesco Coppola, who, despite his advanced age, faced the long journey to East Africa in order to find his daughter, has returned disconsolate and alone. His daughter has been detained in Somaliland and may come home by the next Red Cross ship if there is to be one. Coppola has given a very unbiased account of his trip. The Italians, after the English occupation, for the most part maintained a very praiseworthy attitude. They do not complain of the treatment they receive. In general, the English have been fair, as well as the Abyssinians, especially in the large centers. It seems that the Negus has taken strong measures to protect the life and property of Italians, perhaps in the hope of establishing a future *modus vivendi* with us. The English, with whom Coppola had to deal during his trip, likewise behaved well. In general, they are not very enthusiastic about the war, and their morale is moderate.

Cavallero, who has left Libya for a brief visit, is 100 per cent optimistic on the approaching resumption of operations. He is certain that the superiority of the Axis forces will bring us immediately to Alexandria and in a short time to Cairo and the Canal. Meanwhile, the Germans have agreed that the Civil Commissioner of Egypt should be an Italian, a question on which they had previously raised some objections.

July 8, 1942

I see Sebastiani, Mussolini's ex-secretary, whom I have not seen for some time. He is upset because a request for an audience was not granted by the Duce. He attributes his misfortune to the sinister influence of the Petaccis. Sebastiani is a reserved man, and for the first time he spoke to me about this matter. He believes that the Duce will find it difficult to deal with the situation that has arisen. ("The girl is not bad, but the other members of the family are a bunch of blackmailers!") For some time he has been convinced of the necessity of breaking away. Once he said to Sebastiani, "This affair, too, will soon end." Pavolini thinks otherwise. He states that Mussolini took more interest in the marriage of the Petacci woman's sister than in the marriages of his own children. He even telephoned at midnight to learn the contents of the article in the society column of the *Messaggero.*

July 9, 1942

Again at Leghorn for ten days. I have not had any political contacts except a visit from Admiral Riccardi, who outlined a project to block the Sicilian passage, and one from Buffarini, who makes rather gloomy forecasts about the wheat harvest.

[*No entries for July 10 to 19, 1942, inclusive.*]

July 20, 1942

At Rome. Mussolini, too, will return during the evening. His return, together with news from Libya, convinces the public that many rosy dreams about Egypt have faded, at least for the time being. We shall now see if our deployment before El Alamein is wise or not. Some people on the General Staff are considering the advisability of a retreat.

Tamaro sends news from Switzerland about Anglo-German conversations that are supposed to be taking place at Lugano. He supplies a wealth of particulars. On behalf of the Germans, those present are said to be Seyss-Inquart, Rintelen, et al.; representing the English, personages of more or less equal rank. Tamaro enclosed some snapshots, but I honestly did not recognize anyone. How much truth is there in it? It is difficult to say. Nevertheless, it all has a strong flavor of a dime novel. But it is best to keep our eyes open. One never knows.

July 21, 1942

The Duce is in good humor, especially as he is satisfied that in the space of two or three weeks we can resume our forward march in Egypt and reach the great goals of the Delta and the Canal. He is so certain of it that he has left his personal baggage in Libya as guarantee of a quick return. (Bismarck, on the other hand, in view of information from General Rintelen, considers that our offensive is postponed for a long time, because the exhaustion of our troops has been very considerable, and because the reinforcements that have reached the English are greater than could have been foreseen.)

Naturally, Mussolini has been absorbing the anti-Rommel spirit of the Italian commander in Libya, and he takes it out on the German marshal who, by the way, did not pay him a visit during the three weeks and more Mussolini spent there. The attitude of the soldiers is also insolent. German motor vehicles do not yield the right of way to anyone, even to our generals, and at the least opportunity of acquiring a little booty they take everything. The Arabs behave very badly. "The policy of Balbo failed completely, and the only good thing done by him is Balbia [a town constructed by and named for Balbo]." He told me that he had found strong nuclei of New Zealand prisoners with "hangman faces and so far from reassuring that he always kept his gun close at hand." He said little about Russia, but he is convinced that for the time being operations are far from having a decisive character.

July 22, 1942

Mussolini has written a letter to Hitler: an account of his stay in Libya and his visit to Athens. In reality, the main purpose of the letter was to straighten things out on the matter of our Sabratha division, because Rommel had sent a telegram to Germany speaking ill of it— a telegram which "Mussolini will never forgive him." The tone of Mussolini's letter did not please my office colleagues. There were too many bureaucratic expressions, such as "I have the honor of transmit-

ting to you," "I permit myself to call your attention to," which gave
to the writing, according to them, the character of a report by a subordinate to his superior. Mussolini is now irritated at the Germans. He
deprecates their systematic impoverishment of Greece, and when I
called them "Lanzi" [a disparaging term generally used by Italians
from the thirteenth to the nineteenth century to describe brutish armed
forces of German origin] he, who usually does not like my phraseology,
agreed with enthusiasm, adding, "Perhaps many Germans deplore the
fact that they did not invade Italy, in order to take everything away
with them. But had they done this, they would have lost the war."

Mackensen pays me a visit on some pretext or other. He eulogizes
Cavallero, "who, in addition to technical competence, has also a great
political instinct and is a real friend of Germany." Friend? No, a
servant. Mackensen doesn't believe that the offensive can be resumed
before October, and makes many reservations. Di Cesare also said the
same thing. This concerns me more because Di Cesare has the evil
eye. During a trip to Libya his spell worked well: four dead in a plane
accident among the Duce's followers.

July 23, 1942

I recounted to the Duce the forecasts of the German Ambassador.
After two days of pretended assurance Mussolini has thrown off his
mask and has spoken clearly. He is furious with the military, who "for
the second time have made a fool of him by making him visit the front
at unfavorable moments." (Of course he is alluding to his trip to Albania.) This time he had given orders to Cavallero to send, by telegram, in clear [not in cipher] the word *"Tevere"* when Cavallero was
certain about the advance of our troops up to the Canal. The password
"Tevere" arrived Friday, the twenty-seventh of June. The Duce had
to delay his departure two days because of a cyclone. Only when he
was on the spot did he realize that things were not going well, and
that even "Rommel's strategy had its ups and downs." The promotion
of Cavallero to field marshal could not be avoided because he found
himself "between Rommel and Kesselring like Christ between the
thieves." In any case, Bastico will also be nominated field marshal, and
after him other generals, and "he doesn't exclude even Navarra, his
doorkeeper." Forecasts are now very reserved; in the opinion of Mussolini we must avoid any retreat because otherwise we would not
know where we would end.

July 24, 1942

The tone of the Duce's speeches is increasingly anti-German. Today he gave vent to his feelings on two points: a statement by General Marras on the meager esteem in which our military contribution is held by the German General Staff, and the lack of understanding of our needs and of our industrial aspirations. "The people," Mussolini said, "are now wondering which of the two masters is to be preferred, the English or the Germans." I reminded him what François-Poncet said upon leaving my room on the day of the declaration of war: *"Ne creusez pas des fosses trop profonds; n'oubliez pas que les allemands sont des maîtres durs."* [Beware of chasms that are too deep; don't forget that the Germans are hard masters.] I agree with him.

The Germans have occupied Rostov. From many sources the opening of a second front in France by the Anglo-Americans is reported to be certain. At Berlin, from what Alfieri telegraphs, the matter is not causing concern, but annoyance.

July 25, 1942

Nothing new. The Duce is leaving for Riccione.

July 26, 1942

The Mufti makes hard accusations against Gailani. As was to be foreseen, the two quarreled, and the one who added fuel to the fire was Minister Grobba, the German head of the Arab Service of the *Auswaertiges Amt* [German Foreign Office]. The incident has special importance if operations in Egypt are to be resumed favorably.

July 27, 28, 29, 30, 31, 1942

In Leghorn.

August 1, 1942

Buffarini was called to Riccione by Mussolini because the situation in Sicily gives much concern; the peasants are refusing to hand over their grain, and in many cases they fired on those charged with collecting it. On the basis of reports from the Health Service Buffarini called Mussolini's attention to the fact that in the working class edema caused by malnutrition is appearing. Even at Piombino, according to Aiello, similar cases are occurring.

Bottai pays me a visit. He has nothing to tell me, but he is more anti-Mussolini than ever. If he talks this way to me, imagine what he must say among his own friends!

August 2, 1942

We are warned from Lisbon that before long the Royal Air Force will bomb Milan in grand style. I don't know whether this will happen, but it is likely, and, in a certain sense, quite logical. I inform Buffarini.

Edda attacked me violently, accusing me of hating the Germans, saying that my hatred for the Germans is known everywhere, especially among the Germans themselves, who are saying that "they are physically repulsive to me." I cannot understand why Edda should be so excited about it, nor who talked about it to her. Generally when she does this she has been influenced by somebody. I said little or nothing in reply. After all, she knows very well how I feel on the matter. And I am not the only one. . . .

August 3, 1942

Nothing new.

August 4, 1942

Ambrosio, chief of the General Staff, tells me: (1) in Libya we shall not be able to resume our movements until the end of October; however, the prospects are good because English reinforcements are slower than had been foreseen while our reinforcements, especially the Germans (and this concerns the General Staff for evident reasons), are arriving regularly; (2) operations in Russia are developing well, and it is foreseen that German operations against the Caucasus will continue even during the winter; (3) personally, he does not believe in a victory that will liquidate our enemies. However, he thinks that Russia will probably be detached from the Allied camp, after which Great

Britain and America will be obliged to come to terms. This, in summary, is today the military-political thought of our General Staff.

Lombrassa foresees a strong accentuation of the labor shortage, and this is why, within a short time, the mobilization of civilians will begin on a large scale. I have advised him to remove from forced civilian service that odious flavor of punishment which has so far been attached to it. The citizen should know that civilian service is on the same moral plane as military service. Hence, we must do away with contemptible gossip, referring to such citizens as being pederasts, cardsharpers, dandies, and such people as we are in the habit of despatching to Carbonia [lignite mines in Sardinia]. It is not becoming and proves nothing.

August 5, 1942

A letter arrives from Hitler for the Duce. I send it unopened to Riccione.

August 6, 1942

There is great optimism on the possibilities in Libya according to General Marchesi, commander of the air squadron. Rommel is preparing to attack, and without a doubt he should settle matters within the space of ten days. Objectives: Cairo, Alexandria, Suez. The action to begin between the twentieth and twenty-sixth of this month.

A less rosy picture is painted for me by Renato Ricci. He talks about the industrial and food situations as they will be during the coming winter. He predicts that we shall have to pull in our belts; nothing compared to last winter.

Arpinati asks a favor for some of his friends. He describes the situation in Romagna as dull and dubious, attributing this in large measure to the fact that too many women of the Mussolini family are poking their noses into the local situation. To these is now added the Petacci woman, who, in Rimini, where she is staying for the baths, hands down judgments, orders people about, and is given to intrigues. Her spokesman and agent is a certain Spisani, a third-rate dancing teacher. Comic anecdotes are told. It appears that the Petacci recently went to Budapest, and it is likely, because she is trying to get a divorce. [As there is no divorce law in Italy some Italians apply to the courts in Hungary and Czechoslovakia.] To someone who asked her news of her trip, she replied, "I had neither receptions nor parties. I went there absolutely incognito."

August 7, 1942

At Forlì to attend the placing of Bruno's remains in a vault. On the train I spoke with Vidussoni. Besides being rather unintelligent, he shows a brazen ignorance. He spoke "of the history of Fascism by Oriani," but meant Orano. But for him it is all the same. He said that he did not know who "De Chirico was, because for two years he had been too occupied to read modern writers." What is pitiful is that he no longer holds his tongue; he talks too much and insists on having his say.

Mussolini desired that the ceremony in the cemetery of San Cassiano be altogether a family affair. There were eight of us in the crypt—his closest relatives and the widow. There was a good deal of sadness, a sort of catacomb air, and three tombs of gray stone—for the two parents of Mussolini and his son. On Bruno's tomb sadness is accentuated by a painting of him, gay and smiling. The mass was brief, and performed by a priest who drew out the Latin *s*'s like those of his Romagnolo dialect. The Duce was apparently impassive but inwardly tormented. After the ceremony he kissed Bruno's tomb, and, indicating the empty space between Bruno and the altar, said a number of times that that was to be his place. We then went to Rocca and to Carpena. Mussolini wanted to visit the scenes of Bruno's childhood. He was angry because the members of his family had accepted a basket of foodstuffs from the peasants. "I do not intend to return from the tomb of my son with chickens and pears," he commented. He was right.

August 8, 1942

Mussolini is back in Rome. I had a long conversation with him to discuss certain matters which had been waiting during his absence. Generally speaking, Hitler's letter was of no great importance, and with regard to Greece he avoids any and all commitments. It is the food situation which concerns the Duce. Not at this moment, since vegetables and fruit afford a temporary well-being, but for the morrow, for the winter, everything will be scarce and perhaps it will not be possible to increase the bread ration. There are cases of malnutrition in some provinces. It isn't too pervasive a phenomenon, but it is ugly. Mussolini thinks about it more than he talks about it, and more than he would have others believe. His stomach cramps have returned; the old ulcer has come to life again. This means that he is worrying.

Pareschi, who is usually optimistic, is far from being encouraging at present. He would like to find foodstuffs abroad. But it is useless. I believe that this year we shall receive very little, perhaps nothing. There will be suffering also on account of the cold. There is no coal, and wood will be rationed.

Alfieri made a useless trip to the Russian front, where he saw Hitler. He learned nothing concrete, and for this reason he chatters a lot. Mussolini, too, thinks that Alfieri has come to the end of his usefulness; maybe not today, but in any case I must have his successor ready.

August 9, 1942

Nothing new.

August 10, 1942

News of the day: The taking of Maikop by the Germans and agitation in India. Mussolini attributes to both facts a great deal of importance. The first will have the effect of relieving the Axis, but not immediately, and not altogether, of the pressing oil problem. The second could, in the judgment of the Duce, precipitate an Asiatic crisis. If Japan should decide to march on India, great and surprising developments might be expected. But will Japan do it? From here it is not possible to prophesy, considering the fact that China, according to what Ambassador Taliani telegraphs today, is more than ever of one mind in being anti-Japanese; and even Wang Ching-Wei, the Laval of Nanking, has given up trying to bring about a *rapprochement* between the two peoples. In my opinion, the struggle between China and Japan will be eternal. There will be lulls, it will have vicissitudes favoring first one side and then the other, but it will never quiet down. More than a political fact, it is a biological fact, and biologically China is very strong.

August 11, 1942

Meeting of the Council of Ministers. The measures considered had to do with ordinary administration, but they nonetheless gave Mussolini a cue to make certain interesting statements on his trip to Libya, on the fall of the empire, and on the progress of the war. He was more optimistic than ever in his forecast for the future: the war has already been won because the Anglo-Saxons, having divided their forces on so many fronts, cannot seriously engage in any offensive action.

Grandi commented with pessimism on the Duce's statements. Grandi is very much disturbed about the internal situation and said that for the first time in twenty years he has asked for carabinière protection at his villa. He exaggerates. He detests Cavallero. "That rascal," he said, "is preparing himself to become the Italian Pétain and would like to kill us all. But we shall bump him off first."

A great English convoy, well escorted, is directed from Gibraltar to the East. Our aero-naval forces have already taken position. Tomorrow will be a hard-fought day.

August 12, 1942

The aero-naval battle is in progress. For the time being details are lacking. Fougier and Casero are not too well pleased. The Germans have announced the sinking of the English airplane carrier *Eagle,* but there are many reasons to doubt this. By tomorrow at dawn a naval engagement is expected. However, we are in a position of inferiority. The big ships cannot move from port because of gasoline shortage and lack of light escort craft.

August 13, 1942

All attention is concentrated on the battle in the Mediterranean. It would seem that things are developing rather well for us, but we have paid with the loss of the *Bolzano,* and damage suffered by the *Attendolo* was a high price. At the moment only four ships of the convoy have reached Malta. Mussolini is moderately satisfied with the results, "because the guns of the Navy were not engaged in the battle."

August 14, 1942

No news.

August 15, 1942

The Roman midsummer holiday; the city is empty as usual. It seems that this morning at the railroad stations, as the trains were leaving, there was conduct worthy of barbarians. The people do not wish to change their habits, if they can get away with it, and everybody wants to have a good time. The war? They want to forget it.

A long conversation with Buti, who, according to his nature, delivers what he has to say in mouthfuls and morsels, saying nothing that commits him too much, and full of reticence. This is more or less what he thinks: French hatred is growing by leaps and bounds against the Germans, not against us. But nothing will happen; in any event, they will not go beyond their present demonstrations: shootings, sabotage, nothing more. The government believes in a victory of the Axis; the people believe in a victory of the Allies. De Gaulle, as a person, is despised by everybody, but at heart the country is de Gaullist. The blow has been heavy for the French, and this is more evident in things generally than it is in individuals. The French have remained what they were before: same habits, same ideas, same prejudices. They cannot say why, but they are convinced that in the future they will still have a great deal to say. Naturally they look more toward Moscow and Washington than toward London. "The feeling of the French with regard to the British is identical with that of the Italians with regard to the Germans." For once he couldn't have been more explicit.

August 16, 1942

Resistance on the Russian front seems to stiffen. In any event, there are no indications of a collapse either possible or imminent. From a Turkish telegram, intercepted by our services, it would seem that the standard of life in Russia is quite good and the spirit of the people hopeful. "Emaciated faces," telegraphs Ambassador Zobune, "I have seen only in Vienna and Munich. In Kuibyshev everybody lives well and eats very abundantly." He relates that the real enemy of the diplomatic set is boredom, and that in order to defeat it everybody has resorted to drink with great determination. I must say that I have seen many of my colleagues get drunk even without this excuse.

A discussion between Giannini and Clodius for the maintenance of food supplies to our Expeditionary Corps in Russia. The Germans want to put it entirely on our shoulders, contrary to the agreements made. Giannini insisted strongly, but the German Embassy in Rome has brought the matter up and we shall see what Mussolini will decide.

Bulgarian frontier break-through into Albania. It appears that the Germans are behind this; they have their eyes on the mines of Jezerina.

I am dissatisfied, and now believe that I shall recall Tamaro, Minister in Switzerland. He has got mixed up in a policy of resentments and I believe that it is to our interests, present and future, to be friendly with Switzerland.

August 17, 1942

In Leghorn.

[*Entries of August 18 to 24, 1942, inclusive, missing. Ciano at Leghorn.*]

August 25, 1942

I leave Leghorn for Budapest, for the funeral of Stephen Horthy, who was killed in an airplane accident.

August 26, 1942

I arrive in Budapest. The city is in mourning and very sad. From the windows and from the archways long black streamers are hanging, which contrast with the enamel blue of the sky. The Regent is the first person I see. Our meeting at the gateway is casual. He is very much touched, and leaves at once. Later he receives me in his study. He speaks with relative calm, and would like to discuss general politics. But he is still upset by his sorrow for the loss of his son, and is thinking of the succession. The death of Stephen today seems to indicate the collapse of what he has accomplished so far. He has no clear ideas, but from various hints I take it that he is thinking of having the designation go to his son's son, who is a baby one year old. Nonsense. Everybody in Hungary, even those who were favorable to the vice-regency of Stephen Horthy, is very much opposed to a solution that would tie the hands of the Magyar people for a period of twenty or thirty years. Kallay himself tells me this, and in Hungarian politics he is a strong follower of the Regent.

I have drawn up a statement on the conference with Kanya. It has been suggested that a solution would be to have Victor Emmanuel III become the nominal sovereign of both countries. I have noted in another place my remarks and objections. I believe the idea is impossible, or at least very premature.

August 27, 1942

Hungarian ceremonial funerals have a certain oriental and imposing quality. Much commotion and many tears, but more for the grief of the mother than for the loss of Stephen Horthy.

Long conversations with Ribbentrop. His courtesy is really unusual. He comes to see me first, invites me to lunch, steps back at every doorway, even though with the Hungarians he wants to make it clear that he occupies first place, contrary to every right and tradition. (The Hungarians, who hate the Germans but who tremble in their presence, try to please him by suggesting that precedence be determined according to the French alphabetical order of nations: Allemagne, Italie, et cetera. Much ado about nothing!)

Ribbentrop's tone is moderate, even though he continues to be optimistic. The German "Krieg ist schon gewonnen" [the war is already won] of the old days has now become [in English] "We cannot lose this war." He is obviously coming off his high horse. He gave no particulars, but he judges Russia to be a hard nut, very hard, and thinks that not even if Japan should attack her would she be entirely knocked out. He makes no forecasts on the length of the war; it might have a rapid conclusion, "but one must not count too much on that."

He repeated his invitation for the usual hunting party at Schönhof toward the end of October.

August 28, 1942

In Venice. A visit to the biennial exposition. Paintings and sculpture are very interesting. In general, the Spanish pavilion is the best. We had two painters who are important: De Chirico and Sciltian.

August 29, 1942

I report to Mussolini on my trip to Budapest and give him my notes on the meeting with Kanya. One hundred per cent indifference. The

principal reason for this is concern over the Germans. He is certain—
and he is right—that Hitler, even if he were to accept such a thing,
would bill us for it, and would make us pay dearly as soon as possible.
The second element has to do with the growing hostility of Mussolini
toward the monarchies and toward our own monarchy. [Mussolini
said:] "I entertained a similar proposition in regard to the Duke of
Aosta, but with him dead nothing else will be done."

With the approval of the Duce, Grandi had arranged for a trip to
Spain. Now I have received instructions to tell him to forget about it.
Grandi grasped the idea and has postponed the trip without objection.

August 30, 1942

Ghigi sends an S O S from Greece. The Germans are insisting on
astronomical indemnities, the government threatens to resign, trouble
may begin any minute. In any case, I advise Mussolini not to take any
initiative. He had promised the Greeks to plead for them with Hitler,
and wrote him a letter, but Hitler refused. One cannot fail twice without losing too much prestige. This argument of mine led Mussolini to
expatiate on an article which appeared in a German review. The New
Order is here described in detail, also what will be the role of all peoples, including the allies of Germany. No liberty, no rights, except that
of serving the nation "who will be at the head." I telegraphed Alfieri to
learn whether the ideas in the article reflected those of the leading
classes in Germany. I think that even if the answer is no it means yes.

August 31, 1942

Yesterday evening at eight o'clock Rommel attacked in Libya. He
has chosen the day and the hour well, at a time when no one was expecting the attack and whisky had begun to appear on the English
tables. Mussolini expresses no opinion, but is substantially optimistic.
Cavallero, who had shown no signs of life for a long time, telephones to
give me news of the operation. As usual he wavers between "yes" and
"no." He does not wish to compromise himself, but intends to remain
sufficiently near to gather the fruits of victory, if there are any. Churchill, according to what the Turkish Ambassador has telegraphed to his
government, has said that if Rommel had not attacked in two weeks he
would have taken the initiative in the operations. He believes that the

English forces are sufficient for any eventuality, but wishes to adopt a phrase used by Stalin: "Anything is possible, since war is war."

September 1, 1942

There is no great news. In Egypt the English are withdrawing toward the sea, offering a minimum of resistance. Mussolini believes that they want to resist on the coast, where they can have the support of the naval forces.

Jacomoni makes a rather reassuring report on the Albanian situation. It suffices to be assured of a minimum of foodstuffs to maintain order in the country, notwithstanding the fact that enemy propaganda is now aiming at Albania, which represents the only oasis of peace in all the Balkans. From documents that have come into possession of the government it seems that the English are attempting to start uprisings and disorders in order to be able, at the moment of peace, to compromise those who have been in favor of union with Italy, and to destroy any legal basis in the relations between the Albanians and us.

September 2, 1942

Rommel is halted in Egypt on account of lack of fuel. Three of our oil tankers have been sunk in two days. Cavallero maintains that this will not change the course of operations, and that other means will be found to forward the gasoline. Instead of the oil tankers, which are too easily identified, ordinary boats and hospital ships can be used. (This is an old system that goes well as long as it goes well.) Nevertheless, Cavallero repeats that Rommel's push is this time destined to reach the Canal.

September 3, 1942

Rommel's pause continues, and, what is worse, the sinking of our ships continues. Tonight there have been two. Cavallero repeats his optimistic declarations, and says that within a week the march will be resumed. Rintelen, who has just arrived from Libya today, is less sure. Everything, not only fuel, is lacking. Hence, action this time is, according to him, a little risky, and may turn out well or badly. Mussolini is in a black mood. He does not express himself; in fact, he has been silent on the subject of Egypt for three days. Once more he suffers from stomach pains. Yesterday he had himself examined by a radiologist. There was nothing serious the matter with him, except gastritis, but it is painful and debilitating. Today, while he was conferring with Jacomoni and me on the Albanian situation, he was unable to hide his suffering. Yesterday the Duce sent a telegram to the industrial workers. He praised them and violently threatened other greedy, odious, and egotistical groups. Everybody thought that he was aiming at the middle class, as usual, but, on the contrary, he was striking at the farmers, who, "after the regime has followed a policy in their favor for twenty years, take everything and are greedy for money to the point of deserving the worst punishment, the infliction of which would, after all, result in benefiting only the state. Nevertheless, this year no one will die of hunger, and if many Italians have to grow lean, it will do them good."

September 4, 1942

What is happening in Libya is not clear. Rommel is drawing back his left flank under the attack of British aviation even before the enemy tanks come into action. Tonight two other ships were sunk. Our supply problem is difficult. Rintelen maintains that the offensive should be postponed indefinitely. Casero is of the same opinion.

A governmental crisis in Spain. It had grown to be inevitable. I was convinced of this in Leghorn when I heard how Serrano was talking about Franco. He talked of him as one speaks of a moronic servant. And he said this without caution, in the presence of everybody. It is too early to say what the consequences of this development will be. The only indication might be the choice of Jordana, and this is not favorable. Jordana has always been a man not wholeheartedly with the Axis and a sympathizer with France and Great Britain. On the other hand, in these latter times, many events prove that the Iberian Peninsula is beginning to entertain doubts as to the future, and wishes to remain on friendly terms with everybody. Maybe Serrano will come to Rome. I am not enthusiastic about the idea, because Serrano is an intriguer and a gossip, and may be the cause of great embarrassment. We must be extremely careful about him.

September 5, 1942

Three days with influenza.

September 6, 1942

Nothing.

[*Entries of September 7 and 8, 1942, missing.*]

September 9, 1942

I call the attention of Mussolini to the Albanian situation. More of the inevitable undercurrent of discontent. I am concerned about our lack of troops. There are four divisions, but in name only; in reality, eleven thousand men. Under the circumstances, any surprise is possible. Cavallero, to whom I communicated the alarm, could do nothing more than give me fifty tanks; not enough. The Duce lets off one of his periodic attacks on the Army, with which everything is going badly and nothing is improving. He talks also of operations in Libya. The idea of an offensive is now given up, at least for some time. Let us hope that the enemy will not take too much advantage of it. Then, too, he is angry at Rommel, who, according to English sources, has telegraphed accusing several of our officers of having revealed some of his future plans to the enemy. As always, victory finds a hundred fathers, but defeat is an orphan. Now in Libya they are quarreling, and Kesselring ran to Berlin to complain about Rommel. They are talking about a possible recall of Rommel.

Gambara came out intact from the investigation directed against him. He will have another command. I am happy about it, because he is a patriotic Italian and a soldier, and for these very reasons they were trying to stab him in the back.

Churchill has spoken after a long silence. It is an unruffled speech, and substantially optimistic.

September 10, 1942

I accompany the secretary of the Albanian National party to see the Duce.

Casero summarizes the question of airplane production as regards ourselves, the Germans, and the Allies. The proportions are changing every day to our disadvantage and on a large scale.

September 11, 1942

I leave for Leghorn, where I will stay until the twenty-third of September.

September 12 to 21, 1942, inclusive, no entries in diary.]

September 22, 1942

This is what happened during my stay in Leghorn.

Fougier describes our airplane production in dark colors. Between us and Germany we produce less than one fifth or one sixth of what the Allies produce. The enlistment of pilots is also short and falling off. During the summer of 1943 the Allies will definitely have control of the skies.

D'Aieta reports to me a very confidential conversation with Bismarck, who now is sure that Germany will be defeated but will go on to the "bitter end." Italy will find a way out; and to this end may contribute the measured policy that I have always maintained toward England and America. It is because of this policy that Ribbentrop especially, and the Germans in general, hate me. If "they should win the war, my head would be the first one they would want." There are also many Italians who denounce me to the German Embassy as pro-English. Mackensen reports on everything, but he comments on me in a friendly way.

Bottai stayed with me two days. He also is hopeful for the future. According to his nature, he indulges in useless details. He says that the war is illegal, because the Grand Council was not consulted. He is, as always, hostile to Mussolini. He calls him "a self-taught man who had a bad teacher, and who was a worse student."

September 23, 1942

I find nothing new in Rome. On this first day I have no conversations of any importance. I talk with Mackensen about organizing certain celebrations for the Tripartite Pact. Ribbentrop misses no occasion to exalt this beloved child of his.

Guariglia says nothing new on Myron Taylor's trip. It is clear, at any rate, that at the Vatican they keep us informed only on what they want us to know. The only interesting thing is that the Germans have asked the Pope to intervene to stop the bombardments on German open cities. The word "Coventrize" was coined in Germany, as I recall.

September 24, 1942

The lull on the two fronts has undoubtedly made a bad impression on public opinion. For the first time people are no longer asking themselves about the length of the war, but about its progress. That is how people with whom I have had occasion to talk express themselves.

A brief conversation with Arpinati, who recommends to me an employee of the Office of Corporations. Arpinati makes little mention of the general situation, and what he says is not interesting. The few conversations I have had with him give me the impression that this man has a very modest mind. They say that he is an honest man. This may be true, but that is all there is to him.

Albini is skeptical on the Neapolitan situation. There is much misery, a great deal of hunger, and concern that bombings on a large scale will begin again.

Ricci wants me to concern myself a little more with the internal situation, which, according to him, is at its lowest. But on what authority could I mix up in it?

September 25, 1942

I had a few more conversations, and all those with whom I spoke were depressed. Morgagni, who is anything but a friend of mine, was more explicit than the others. Things are not going well at the front, and very badly inside the country. What, then, will the future bring? I limited myself to replying that while I was always prudent when others are optimistic, I am calm and serene when others are in despair. I don't know how, nor can I say why, but I am certain that things cannot go completely wrong with us. Bastianini also sees black. But this is habitual with him, and I don't remember ever having had a conversation with him in which he didn't make dark forecasts. He isn't a great intellect and doesn't see very far ahead; what he sees is always damnably dark.

The most pessimistic report which has lately come to us from Germany is from young Consul Farinacci. What would his father think?

From Berlin through Alfieri, who approves of it, comes the proposal that we give Myron Taylor a "solemn booing." How foolish! I can't say whether it is more ridiculous or disgusting. It would appear that the inventor of this idea was that cripple Goebbels. It doesn't even deserve an answer.

September 26, 1942

I receive a letter from Edda, which disturbs me a great deal. I attach it to this page. Tomorrow I shall see Donna Rachele and will see what can possibly be done. Under the circumstances, an illness of the Duce would be really disastrous.

Alfieri telegraphs that the German Chief of Staff, Halder, has been liquidated. Halder is a big figure in the German military world. An ugly sign.

(Letter from Edda Ciano to her husband, attached to diary.)

"DEAR GALLO: I arrived last evening at eleven, after a terrible trip. I was told, with that idiotic inconsistency which makes mine the most impossible of families, that they were all leaving today, but that if I wanted to remain I could. . . . My mother has no sense of humor. She says and does the most fantastic things. . . . Anyway, this is not why I am writing you. My father is not well. Stomach pains, irritability, depression, et cetera. My mother draws a rather dark picture. In my opinion it's the old ulcer again. (His private life of the last few years gives us much to think about, its effects, et cetera. . . . Well, let's not talk about it.) They made X-ray pictures of every kind—all negative—but a doctor was never called. When, having called for Frugoni, they learned that he would not be in Rome until the fourth, they gave it up and . . . let it all slide! I have known few such scatterbrain people. Please get on the job yourself. If it isn't Frugoni, then let it be Pontano; if not him, then somebody else, anything so that my father is seen and examined and examined properly. Communicate with my mother and help her. So far the only measures taken have been blasphemy and curses. In an illness, a clinic is to be preferred, though, naturally, with a certain secrecy. Though it was a beautiful day, I had a sense of suffocation and fear. Maybe because I am so tired that I feel as if I were poisoned. Tonight I haven't slept a wink, because, as the song says, 'All through the night in vain, with candle in hand, I hunted the ugly beast.' On my unprotected bed hundreds of mosquitoes charged forth. That's Capri for you. Some time today I shall leave for Castrocaro, where I hope to sleep. The children, as you will see, are well. The governess has been given her instructions. Hurray for Colonel Oliva! Dear Gallo, let's take it as it comes, chins up! I urge you to get to work about the doctors, et cetera. I embrace you affectionately,

"EDDA."

September 27, 1942

I see the Duce again, after a long absence. I find him thinner but solid, and his appearance seems in no way to confirm Edda's troubled impression. He is, as always, calm, but he realizes that military events have cut deeply into the morale of the population, especially the Stalingrad resistance, which makes clear to the minds of the masses the great attachment of the Russian people to the regime—a thing proved by the exceptional resistance and the spirit of sacrifice. I have had a visit from Rommel, who said that he is leaving on a six weeks' furlough. Mussolini is convinced that Rommel will not come back. He finds Rommel physically and morally shaken. I didn't conceal from the Duce my estimate of the situation, synthesizing it in the following formula: "We are starting the winter with a state of mind in which, at the worst, we should be at the end of the winter."

A dinner for the Tripartite group. A rather heavy atmosphere. The only thing of note was Cavallero's boner when, to endear himself to the Japanese Ambassador, he gave him news of successes at Stalingrad. When Cavallero's English and that of Horichiri got together, it came out that Stalingrad had fallen. The rumor spread through the hall, until the Germans, to the great shame of Cavallero, took measures to deny it. Bottai heard the Japanese general offer the German assistant military attaché his congratulations for the victory. The German, in his hard Italian, said dryly and in a military style, "Nonsense."

September 28, 1942

Nothing new.

September 29, 1942

Host Venturi is concerned about the many sinkings in our merchant fleet. Replacements are slow and completely inadequate. In all, we have little more than a million tons left. At this rate the African problem will automatically end in six months, since we shall have no more ships to supply Libya. Venturi will give me a documented report in a few days.

September 30, 1942

From Berlin and Vienna come very pessimistic reports. Even Alfieri, as is his nature, with many perhapses and buts, says that things are not going well, and that the summer offensive has failed to accomplish its purpose. Air bombings are terrorizing the German populations, frequently paralyzing all life.

D'Agostino, Director of the Bank of Labor, will go to Switzerland soon. I charge him with many good-will messages to his banker friends. I believe in the future function and possibilities of Switzerland, and am convinced that we must cultivate Swiss friendship.

October 1, 1942

Hitler has spoken. *Quantum mutatus ab illo.* [How much he's changed.] Last year, too, at about this time, he made an address that was a paean of victory. Now, at best, it may be said that he has made a defensive address. As usual on such an occasion, Alfieri is silent.

A very realistic note on the food question was brought me today by Pareschi. Winter will be harder than expected, and if the Germans do not really give us a hand we do not know where to go to obtain an adequate food supply.

October 2, 1942

No new event of importance, but both from within and without pessimistic reports continue to reach us. From without, it is especially our consuls in Germany and our Balkan legations that give us discouraging news. From within, almost everybody does so. Today, for example, I have seen Federzoni and Del Croix. Both have just arrived here after their vacation. Well, they spoke as if they had had some previous understanding, the same observations, the same forecast, and identical regrets.

October 3, 1942

Nothing new.

October 4, 1942

Castellani sends me the results of the diagnosis that he made of the Duce. Naturally in this case, too, Castellani has discovered his usual amoeba. As for myself, I believe he invented it. Nevertheless, Mussolini, although he feels some slight pain, looks well, and his capacity for work has not at all diminished.

Otherwise there is nothing new.

October 5, 1942

Nothing new.

October 6, 1942

Clodius is in Rome to discuss the Greek financial question which is becoming more and more thorny. If it continues at this rate sensational and unavoidable inflation will result, with all its consequences. Ghigi foresees that the situation will be very bad. The amount of Greek money in circulation is one hundred and sixty billions.

Before the war it was nine billions. The Greeks are required to supply fifty-three billions a month. All this is absurd, but the German Army does not intend to reduce its interest rate. Clodius agrees with us, but cannot do anything about it. He will return to Berlin to confer with his superiors. He makes no comment on the general situation, but says only that by the end of October the cycle of summer operations may be considered at an end, and that this year the Russian front will cause "much less anxiety than last winter."

October 7, 1942

Dr. Kesterer, the man whom Himmler calls the magic Buddha, and who cures everything by means of massage, told me today that Himmler and von Ribbentrop are at swords' points, but that the first is powerful and the second will be liquidated because he is "insane and ill." Hitler hardly ever receives him. This must be true in part, because von Ribbentrop energetically opposed the coming of Himmler to Italy, and even now is maintaining that the program of the visit be reduced to its essentials.

Mussolini is disturbed over the gossip about the arrival of Myron Taylor in Rome. All this gossip is without importance and without foundation, because we know nothing as to what he has said and done. But all this talk is provoking and I am certain that in future it will make more difficult any further visits to the Vatican by Anglo-Saxon personages.

October 8, 1942

Mussolini is very much disturbed by the attitude of the Germans in the occupied countries, especially in Greece. The claims that have been advanced are simply absurd. This means that the Germans are trying to create disorders and complications at all costs. The Duce said, "I have no qualms about the military course of the war. There will be neither surprises nor second fronts, but if we lose the war it will be because of the political stupidity of the Germans, who have not even tried to use good sense and restraint, and who have made Europe as hot and treacherous as a volcano." He is thinking of speaking to Himmler about this next Sunday, but he will not get the spider out of the hole.

I receive Count Capodistria, the Mayor of Corfu. He is a serious, restrained, and distinguished old man, and expresses himself in excellent Italian. He declares that the Ionian populations would like to have some administrative freedom, but that they do not at all want to return to the odious Hellenic government, and prefer to link their destinies to those of Italy. A plebiscite on this matter today would give almost unanimous results. The work of Parini has been highly praised and he really deserves it.

October 9, 1942

A long conference with General Amè, head of the Military Secret Service, who was distinctly pessimistic. All the information and the conversation lead one to conclude that the Anglo-Saxons are preparing to land in force in North Africa, whence, later on, they intend to launch their blows against the Axis. Italy is geographically and logically the first objective. How long shall we have the strength to resist a determined, strong, and methodical aerial and naval offensive? On the Russian front there will be no important news, and if there were it would probably not be in our favor.

The situation in the interior of Germany is heavy and oppressive. Prospects cannot be good and, according to him, that is what the majority of the officers think who are not drawing any conclusions. They observe but do not talk, and do not offer any forecasts. Amè reported these and other things to Cavallero who, however, pretends to be too deaf to understand.

Clodius informs me that Germany is ready to cut down its claims to eighteen or perhaps fifteen billions a month, but a certain Gotzamanis rejects these proposals. I shall have a meeting in my office tomorrow. Mussolini is convinced of the harmful uselessness of the Ministry of Exchange and Foreign Moneys and has promised me that he will abolish it soon. It will be an excellent move.

October 10, 1942

Council of Ministers. Routine matters. But this did not prevent the Duce from repeating his optimistic statements about the future. His opinion, too, of the morale of the Italian people is full of assurance. "We cannot expect enthusiasm from a people who know that they must still face long sacrifices before victory, and must show discipline, obedience, tenacity—virtues which they have beyond all measure."

In the afternoon a meeting to discuss Greece. Clodius withdraws the proposals which he had made through official channels. On the other hand, Gotzamanis explains that Greece can no longer yield anything for the simple but definite reason that it has nothing to offer. If we continue on the present basis the most complete bankruptcy will result within two months. Today the middle class is already obliged to give up its jewels, its beds, at times its daughters, in order to live. Hence, we are facing uprisings and disorders, the proportions of which it is impossible to estimate accurately at this time. But nothing can make the Germans change their absurd and idiotic attitude, and the worst of it is that we Italians must stand for 80 per cent of the consequences.

Mussolini's health is unchanged. We do not notice anything special and he says nothing, but he suffers severe stomach pains. Castellani now thinks he has had a recurrence of his ulcer condition.

October 11, 1942

I receive Himmler at the station. He has just returned from the front. He does not hide his joy at being in a beautiful city again and under a blue sky. The memory of the front is a nightmare to him, nor does he hide it. At Castel Fusano I see the Prince of Piedmont. He reproaches me because I have not been to see him for a long time. He says little about the situation and speaks as he must in public, somewhat optimistically, but when I speak frankly about today and tomorrow he becomes expansive and recalls that I had the honest courage to say the same thing two or three years ago. He tells me that he has seen Mussolini, who said that 1943 will be a hard year for the Axis but that 1944 will be more favorable and that 1945 will bring us victory, but in repeating this the Prince did not hide his skepticism.

A long conversation with Himmler. He says nothing very important, but what counts is the extremely reserved tone of his conversation. He is no longer the Himmler who in Munich in 1938 was in despair because an agreement had been reached and war seemed to be averted. Now he speaks of the difficulties, of the sacrifices, of what has been done, and, above all, what remains to be done. He wanted to find out a good deal about Italy. In particular he wanted to know about the monarchy and about the Vatican. He praised the loyalty of the first and the discretion of the second.

October 12, 1942

Nothing new in politics. The Duce was about to leave for Rocca, but had to postpone his trip because of a bad attack of gastritis, which forced him to stay in bed.

October 13, 1942

I received Castellani, who talked to me about the Duce's health. His diagnosis, and that of Frugoni, would seem to indicate that the old ulcer has reappeared, and is now complicated by an acute attack of dysentery. Castellani maintains that the Duce must have a long rest, but denies that there is anything to worry about. I am happy about it, because now, more than ever, the Duce's health is indispensable.

[*Entries of October 14 and 15, 1942, missing.*]

October 16, 1942

The Spaniards ask that we accept Fernandez-Cuesta as Ambassador. I met him immediately after the fall of Madrid and had a good impression of him. It appears that in Brazil he did very well. In any event, he is to be preferred to Serrano Suñer, who evidently didn't know his place and had turned the Spanish Embassy into a dangerous center of gossip.

The Germans inform us that Sapuppo talks defeatism in Copenhagen, and that therefore it is desirable that he be recalled. I have taken measures for his recall, without attempting to defend him. And this because Sapuppo is essentially a fool, and to defend fools is always hopeless.

From the Duce's entourage we learn that he may not be in a condition to receive Goering on Monday. In any event, he will have to receive him at home, and the Duce is somewhat embarrassed on account of the modesty of his living quarters. Yesterday, however, I was told that he was almost well, and his voice over the telephone seemed sure and strong.

October 17, 1942

After a conference with Ghigi, Giannini, and Baldoni, I telephoned the Duce about the real situation in the Greek negotiations. Tough going! The Germans, with utter obtuseness, insist on demanding a crazy sum which in the space of a few months would cause the total collapse of the drachma. Even before this we shall have a political crisis, because the Greek Government will resign, and then we can hold the country only by force of arms. The Duce agrees with me, and expresses himself in harsh terms against the Germans. He goes so far as to say that "the only way to explain such a bestial attitude on the part of the Germans is that they are convinced that they are lost, and since they have to die, they want to create general confusion."

But a little later Ribbentrop called by telephone to tell me that he has sent new proposals to Rome by Neubacher. He added that things were going very well on the Stalingrad front, where yesterday they had made great progress. He was ostentatiously cordial and repeated many times that we ought to get together.

October 18, 1942

Nothing new.

October 19, 1942

Mussolini was getting ready to go to the Palazzo Venezia to receive Goering when Mackensen informed us that the field marshal had been stricken tonight by a violent dysentery which did not "permit him to leave his throne, even for ten minutes." The expression isn't very respectful, but it was used textually in the message. It was also repeated by Bismarck, in a more ludicrous tone. It must be recognized that such an ailment is not particularly becoming to the glamorous vanity of the Reichsmarshal.

Neubacher, nominated by Ribbentrop as Commissioner Extraordinary for Greek economic and financial affairs, has come to Rome. We shall appoint one of our own with the same powers. I suggested D'Agostino, who has the necessary qualifications, and he was accepted. The Duce was favorable to a solution that "probably will help us find the end of the thread in the skein."

Jacomoni makes a rather favorable report on the Albanian situation. He believes that the critical period is now over, and that, with some gesture of force against the rebels, it may be possible to bring order and quiet back to the country.

October 20, 1942

Nothing new.

October 21, 1942

A meeting on the economic affairs of Greece, at which are present Mackensen, Neubacher, D'Agostino, Ghigi, and Gotzamanis. Neubacher is the only one who is convinced that big things can be accomplished. The others are quite skeptical, especially Gotzamanis, who undoubtedly is the one who best knows the conditions and the possibilities of his country. I more or less share his skepticism, but naturally guard myself against saying so.

October 22, 1942

To Leghorn for the anniversary of the death of my poor dear Maria.

October 23, 1942

Genoa has been heavily bombed by the English air force, though the number of planes was no more than twenty. Anyway, we should realize that, as time passes, aerial bombardments will become our daily fare.

I see Farinacci and Bottai. They are both exasperated by the internal situation, which is aggravated by the absolute inadequacy of the party, in connection with which there is much talk about a report by the Federali [provincial secretaries of the Fascist party] of a meeting presided over by Farnesi at Lucca, during which the "Petacci affair" was officially discussed—whether it was a good thing or whether it was an evil, what was being said about it, et cetera. I wouldn't believe it, except that it was confirmed to me by Aiello himself, who is serious, and who, with some others, spoke up to end this ugly spectacle.

October 24, 1942

The British have attacked in Libya. For the moment news is favorable to us. No progress was made on land. But von Stumm is dead, the over-all commander who had taken the place of Rommel. Genoa and Milan were again the targets of heavy bombings.

October 25, 1942

Bismarck tells me that in German military quarters they look on the situation in Libya with a certain optimism, provided the British offensive isn't too long. Our supply problem is very difficult, and reserves are entirely inadequate. This is confirmed by Colonel Casero, who says that we have no fuel stocks in Libya, even to the point where we are sending fuel by air from Italy.

Politically, nothing new, except a short letter from Alfieri, who speaks of "the lead weight which now physically and psychologically weighs on the capital of the Reich."

The Duce, who intended to speak before a great gathering of party leaders on the twenty-ninth, has given orders to cancel everything. What's the reason? There are three current interpretations: (1) that his doctors have forbidden the strain of a long speech; (2) that he does not wish to say anything until the Libyan offensive is decided; (3) that he intends to make big changes in the party, and, as would be logical, he wants to speak to the new leaders. Personally, I incline toward the second interpretation.

October 26, 1942

Today I saw the Duce for the first time in two weeks. He has lost a great deal of weight, but his eyes are clear, his voice firm, and he looks bold. I would say that the ailment, in drying up his face and body, has made him more youthful. There wasn't anything of great importance to say, and that is clear, because there is silence in the field of foreign policy. The Duce was irritated with Myron Taylor and with the Vatican. He attributes to the reports of the American envoy the heavy bombardments of our northern Italian cities. "This buffoon," he said, "went back to America to report that the Italians are on their last legs, and that with one or two hard blows they can easily be beaten." Anyway, "he learned these things from the Holy See, where information comes by way of the parish priests. But," says the Duce, "there they don't see that the people who follow the priests are the least courageous, and the worst, always ready to weep and to beg." In any case, he wanted me to let the Vatican know that "Concordat or no Concordat, if Myron Taylor tries to return to Italy he will be put in handcuffs."

I do not share the Duce's diagnosis of the causes which have led the Anglo-Saxons to aim these hard blows at Italy. Maybe Myron Taylor is involved in it, but very little. It is rather that the whole offensive plan of the Americans and the British is being applied.

In Libya it seems that they are holding well, but with heavy losses, and with the hope that pressure will not be maintained too long.

October 27, 1942

Ley has come here to head the National Socialist Mission of the Twentieth Anniversary of the March on Rome. Vidussoni brings him to me. Ley is vulgar, both in appearance and in the way he thinks. In fact, such a bum that I ask myself how he was ever able to attain a position of leadership. He says nothing new, but adds a new lie to the propaganda line: the whole Stalingrad action has cost the Germans only three thousand dead. I wouldn't believe it, even if he multiplied it by ten.

Pavolini informs me that the Duce talked to him about the incident which occurred during the report of the Federali at Lucca, when they discussed the "Petacci affair." He faced the argument squarely and said that no one has the right to "investigate and judge the emotional life of anybody else," and then he went into the history of the Renaissance to show that all men had their love affairs. He was annoyed at the party. He has every reason.

October 28, 1942

The Twentieth Anniversary celebration. It was a single ceremony, the inauguration of the new quarters for the Exhibit of the Revolution. Mussolini appeared in public for the first time since his illness. In the open, in uniform, surrounded by many people, he seemed thin and more tired than two days ago at the Palazzo Venezia. He was welcomed in a way that I would call affectionate. But the organization of the ceremony was far from coming up to par, lacking even the least sense of camaraderie among its members. The fact is that the present secretariat of the party is made up of unknown men, to whom we are, in turn, unknown. This explains the coolness of the ceremony. It explains also a good many of the serious difficulties of the internal situation. On this very day of the recurrence of the Fascist celebration, the inefficiency of the party is felt more strongly than ever, because the party is headed by incapable, discredited, and questionable men.

The fight in Libya continues to be tough. We are holding on tenaciously. To hear the High Command talk, the only danger is our deficiencies in stocks and transportation. Tactical situation good, logistic situation dangerous. I am no technician, but I believe that in a battle of this kind logistics will play the decisive role.

October 29, 1942

Another oil tanker was sunk this evening. This is a black mark on the situation in Libya. Bismarck has learned from Rintelen that Rommel is optimistic about the military quality of the troops, but that he is literally terrified by the supply situation. Just now not only is fuel lacking but also munitions and food.

The humor of the Chief is good. We have spoken of a certain Roseo, who has gone to intrigue at Court for a separate peace. He will be handcuffed. The Duce gave me a letter from Hitler on the twentieth anniversary of the founding of the Fascist party, which is extremely laudatory and sugar-coated. Mussolini expressed himself in harsh terms against the Genoese people, who are "certainly the most hostile to the war and who have given proof of moral weakness." On the other hand, he praised the Neapolitans, who have been made fatalistic by centuries of difficulties and misery to the point of composing ironical songs on the English during bombing from the air.

A long visit from Donna Edvige Mussolini. She judges the internal situation with much good sense and is concerned about the future. She serves as a mouthpiece of what is said in various circles and would like me to take the Ministry of the Interior. She believes—and she is right —that we must give our policy a more humane character, but for nothing in the world would I want to go to the Ministry of the Interior.

October 30, 1942

Nothing of any particular importance.

October 31, 1942

General Ambrosio, who in the past was very optimistic, is now notably less so. With regard to Libya, he maintains that if the British continue to develop a battle of attrition it will be difficult for us to avoid a retreat; and with regard to Russia, he fears that during the winter there will be a Soviet counteroffensive and that it will start against our armies. Although everything has been done to assure our troops decent living conditions, yet we must expect difficulties greater than last year, because now they have no native houses to live in, nor have they the coal that was available in the Donetz basin. All this leads General Ambrosio to modify his rosy predictions of the past.

I received the Swiss banker, Vieli, to whom I offered many olive branches. I strongly believe in the present and future European function of Switzerland. Furthermore, we have great need of her now.

Alessi informs me that Petacci's brother wrote a letter to Prefect

Tamburini, saying that Castellani had made a wrong diagnosis and cure for the Duce. He wanted Tamburini to put pressure on Donna Rachele, with whom he has cordial relations, to persuade her to call in a new doctor.

November 1, 1942

Sorrentino, who is an intelligent journalist, even if odd and a little bit sectarian, returns from a long stay in Russia with marked pessimism. To listen to him, even the sanctum sanctorum of the German spirit— the Army—is weakened by its worst enemy: the doubting mind. "This year they were fighting to avoid defeat. It hasn't gone very well. Now the Germans themselves believe in defeat, and perhaps many among them even hope for it."

I spoke to our Minister in Lisbon, Fransoni, who is not exactly an ace, but an honest man. The attitude toward the Axis has changed very much in Portugal, and all the Anglo-Saxon preparations lead one to believe that in a short while a powerful blow will be delivered in the Mediterranean to strike at Italy, which is judged to be the Achilles' heel of the Axis. Mussolini has written a letter to Hitler in answer to his. He concludes by setting the date of a meeting in Salzburg by the end of November.

At golf I meet Senator Castellani, who expresses himself favorably on the health of the Duce. The crisis is over, convalescence may still require some time, but it will only be convalescence.

November 2, 1942

The Duce is in very good humor. Maybe because the progress of operations in Libya is quite satisfactory. He vents his displeasure on the *Osservatore Romano,* which is hurling anti-dictatorial darts, and this leads him to observe that Catholicism and Christianity are on the decline "because they wish to make people believe a number of things which do not agree with our modern concept of life. For example, at a certain point I decided that even in the matter of miracles it was necessary to adopt autarchy, and I referred this to the Vatican. As a result, they launched the Madonna of Loreto in competition with that of Lourdes, and one has to agree that they did a swell business."

Farnesi has come to see me. He feels the earth giving way beneath him, and would like to build some bridges. I did not conceal from him that on many questions I disagree with the present directors of the party, for reasons of substance and form, but I haven't slammed the door on them. They will be, I think, short-lived, and for my part I am not going to help them keep their jobs. But I don't think it is sensible to start internal contention in the party at a moment like this.

November 3, 1942

A new and more violent English attack renders our Libyan situation very dangerous. Our forces are wearing out and supplies are arriving as if delivered through an eyedropper. We really seem to be condemned to fight wars overseas. That crook of a Cavallero continues to give the watchword of optimism at headquarters, but on the side lines they see the future very black, and are already thinking of withdrawing to defend Tripolitania. Rommel judges the situation to be "very serious." This, at any rate, is what Bismarck reports. Bismarck is in deadly fear of betraying himself, and urges that his confidential information be given to no one.

November 4, 1942

After a long interval I see Cavallero in the Duce's antechamber. He tells me how things are going in Libya. Two days ago Rommel supposedly wanted to begin his withdrawal, but Hitler nailed him to the spot with the order to "show the troops the way of victory or death." Mussolini did the same with our forces. Now the battle is in full swing, and Cavallero, who is usually unduly optimistic, maintains an attitude of reserve, though he adds quickly that "his faith is intact." I believe little in any of the virtues of this faker, and especially his type of faith convinces me least of all. From Gibraltar we learn that a great convoy is being prepared, in which are included even monitors with three hundred-and-eighty-one-caliber guns. This suggests the possibility of a landing in Morocco.

The Duce is resentful against the Vatican because of the attitude of the *Osservatore Romano,* and he wishes to "break a few wooden heads." He has had this in mind for a long time, especially as the party encourages him along this line. I disagree with this, and, up to the moment, have succeeded in avoiding any crisis with the Vatican. But now he wants to give personal instructions to Guariglia, who will come with me to the Palazzo Venezia tomorrow. I do not think this is really the time to create a new problem, and such a serious one, especially now that without a doubt the prestige of the Church is very high.

November 5, 1942

The Libyan front collapses. Mussolini telephones early in the morning to have me postpone Kallay's trip to Rome. In fact, this is not the moment to welcome any guests. Later I see the Duce at the Palazzo Venezia. He is pale. His face is drawn; he is tired. But he still keeps his balance. He judges the situation to be serious, but he still has some hope that the English can be held on the line of Fukra-El-Qattara. (Even Cavallero, who is really the one responsible for all our troubles, affirms, on the other hand, that no attempt at resistance can be concentrated except on the Sollum-Halfaia line.) The Duce also speaks with Guariglia about relations with the Vatican, and has calmed down a great deal since yesterday, giving instructions for a completely moderate step. I see Grandi and some others. The news from Libya makes them unhappy, but does not surprise them. For some time past a sense of irrepressible pessimism has taken possession of the Italians.

November 6, 1942

The Libyan retreat is assuming more and more the character of a rout. We know nothing of our 10th Army Corps, cut off by the English forces, and even the detachments which are withdrawing are massacred by bombing from the air. Even the Duce thinks that as matters stand Libya will probably be lost, and he quickly adds "that from some points of view this represents an advantage because this region has cost us our merchant fleet and we can better concentrate on the defense of Italy itself." Nevertheless, we cannot say today on what line resistance will be attempted, even if we do not take into account possible attacks from the west, whence a convoy of exceptionally large proportions is advancing.

Mussolini asked me if I was keeping my diary up to date. When I answered affirmatively, he said that it will serve to prove how the Germans, both in military and political fields, have always acted without his knowledge. But what does his strange question really hide?

I have seen Gambara, Fougier, Pirelli, and Admiral Mancini. They are all staggered by the news from Libya, and today even the most optimistic temperaments see the morrow in dark colors. The rank and file, on the other hand, believe that this time it is a question of one of the usual seesaw races across the desert.

November 7, 1942

Today the Duce sees the situation favorably. A certain amount of resistance which Rommel has offered the English at Marsa Matruk, as well as the arrival of reinforcements in Libya, lead him to believe that some change may take place in the course of events.

But what will he do, or, rather, what will the various convoys do that have left Gibraltar and are eastward bound? There are various conjectures. According to the Germans, the provisioning of Malta or an attempt at landing in Tripolitania in order to fall upon Rommel's rear. According to our General Staff, the occupation of French bases in North Africa. The Duce, too, is of this opinion; in fact, he believes that the landing will be accomplished by the Americans, who will meet almost no resistance from the French. I share the Duce's opinion; in fact, I believe that North Africa is ready to hoist the de Gaullist flag. All this is exceedingly serious for us.

November 8, 1942

At five-thirty in the morning von Ribbentrop telephoned to inform me of American landings in Algerian and Moroccan ports. He was rather nervous, and wanted to know what we intended to do. I must confess that, having been caught unawares, I was too sleepy to give a very satisfactory answer.

The reaction of the Duce was lively as usual. He speaks at once of a landing in Corsica and of the occupation of France. But what forces are there for such undertakings? In the opinion of the most responsible people of our General Staff this is not at all feasible, but the Germans are certainly ready. Officially, I have not learned anything from the Germans. I know from Anna Maria Bismarck that at the Embassy they are literally terrified by the blow, which is very severe and above all absolutely unexpected.

During the evening I see General Amè, who brings me up to date.

There is still resistance in the cities, but pressure from the de Gaullists and the Americans will soon overcome the small amount of French resistance. Amè believes that within the next week the Allies will have extended their dominion over all the colonies, including Tunisia, and that within two weeks they will be able to attack Libya from the west. The situation that will result from this is extremely serious. Italy will become the center of attack by the Allies in the offensive against the Axis. Amè says that the morale of the Army is sensationally low.

November 9, 1942

During the night von Ribbentrop telephoned. Either the Duce or I must go to Munich as soon as possible. Laval will also be there. It is time to consider our line of conduct toward France. I wake up the Duce. He is not very anxious to leave, especially since he is not yet feeling at all well. I shall go, and these are the instructions: If France is ready to collaborate loyally it will receive all possible aid from us; if, on the other hand, it plays hot and cold, we are going to adopt preventive measures: occupation of the free zone and landing in Corsica.

In Munich I find von Ribbentrop at the station. He is tired out, thin, and courteous. Laval, who is making a long trip by automobile, will arrive during the night.

I have my first conversation with Hitler this evening. He has not built up any illusions on the French desire to fight, and now among the rebels is General Giraud, who has brains and courage. Hence, we must make our supreme decisions before it is too late. He, Hitler, will listen to Laval. But whatever he says will not modify his already definite point of view: the total occupation of France, landing in Corsica, a bridgehead in Tunisia. Hitler is neither nervous nor restless, but he does not underrate the American initiative and he wants to meet it with all resources at his disposal. Goering does not hesitate to declare that the occupation of North Africa represents the first point scored by the Allies since the beginning of the war.

November 10, 1942

Hitler, Goering, von Ribbentrop, and myself at the Führerbahn. Decisions have been made to move, especially because the position of Admiral Darlan at Algiers is quite ambiguous and leads one to suspect some understanding with the rebels. A conference with Laval is almost superfluous, because he will be told nothing, or almost nothing, of what has been decided.

Laval, with his white tie and middle-class French peasant attire, is very much out of place in the great salon among so many uniforms. He tries to speak in a familiar tone about his trip and his long sleep in the car, but his words are unheeded. Hitler treats him with frigid courtesy. The conversation is brief. The Führer is the first to speak and asks pointedly if France is in a position to assure us landing points in Tunisia. Laval, like a good Frenchman, would like to discuss it and take advantage of the occasion to obtain concessions from Italy. I do not have time to interrupt because Hitler, with the firmest decision, declares that he does not intend to take up at this time a discussion of Italian claims, which are more than modest. Laval cannot take upon himself the responsibility of yielding Tunis and Bizerte to the Axis, and he himself advises that he be faced with a *fait accompli;* that is that we draw up a note for Vichy in which it is stated what the Axis has decided to do.

November 11, 1942 [continuation of November 10]

The poor man could not even imagine the *fait accompli* that the Germans were to place before him. Not a word was said to Laval about the impending action—that the orders to occupy France were being given while he was smoking his cigarette and conversing with various people in the next room. Von Ribbentrop told me that Laval would be informed only the next morning at eight o'clock, that on account of information received during the night Hitler had been obliged to proceed to the total occupation of the country. Laval owes it to me that a communiqué was not published in which, even though it was not stated in so many words, the impression was left that Laval had given his approval to all the measures decided by the Axis. And yet the words loyalty and honor are always on the lips of our dear Germans!

I come back to Rome. I find Mussolini nervous because our military operations are not going as they should. Those in Corsica are carried out with a flotilla of cutters, which is crazy, and Vercellino has requested a five-hour delay before moving. In Libya, too, Rommel's withdrawal continues at an accelerated pace. Now Mussolini thinks that we shall have God to thank if he can succeed in stopping at the old Agedabia line. I see a few people, and gather the impression that the events of the last few days have been a sad blow for the country, which, for the first time, is asking many questions without finding answers.

November 12, 1942

The march of the Italo-German troops is proceeding in France, and also in Corsica, without encountering the least opposition. The French people are certainly unrecognizable. I thought there would be some gesture of opposition, at least for the honor of the flag. But nothing of the kind. Only the French Navy made it known to us that the fleet would remain loyal to Vichy, and that it does not want the occupation of Toulon by the Axis. The Germans agreed and also, willy-nilly, the Duce, who, however, does not trust their word of honor and thinks that someday we shall wake up to find the port of Toulon empty.

We shall see what will happen in Tunisia, where the first German contingents are supposed to arrive tonight.

Rommel continues to withdraw from Libya at breakneck speed. There is a great deal of friction between Italian and German troops. At Halfaia they even fired on one another, because the Germans took all our trucks in order to withdraw more rapidly, leaving our divisions in the middle of the desert, where masses of men are literally dying of hunger and thirst.

Churchill has made a great speech in the House. It is clear from what he said that all the British and American forces will hurl themselves on Italy for the purpose of putting us out of the fight.

November 13, 1942

Nothing new.

November 14, 1942

This evening conversations are taking place with the Germans. Von Mackensen is the bearer of a message to be sent to the French troops and to the population in Tunisia, as well as a plan for an answer to the Spanish Government on the entire problem of the American landings. With this kind of stuff he might have allowed me to sleep in peace. In fact, I advised von Mackensen "to find some good sleeping pills for von Ribbentrop, who has insomnia and pesters too many people."

I see Messe, who has returned from Russia. His opinion on the eastern front is that the Bolsheviks do not have the strength to attempt action on a large scale, but have enough to hold almost all the German Army on the steppes. His diagnosis regarding Africa is worse. He does not believe that it is possible to maintain a new line, and hence considers the loss of Tripolitania inevitable. Neither does he believe that the attempt to establish a bridgehead in Tunisia can have any lasting success.

Buti reports that Weygand has been arrested by the Germans. The Duce enthusiastically approves of this.

November 15, 1942

The Japanese Chargé d'Affaires asks for news on the situation, and in such a way as to make it clear that his government is very anxious to know the whole truth on the European-African situation. I reassure him, of course, within the limits of possibility.

Today the Duce views the situation with greater optimism, and is irritated with Cavallero, who, having been sent by him to Libya, came back quickly without having seen anything. His return, as the Duce himself asserts, is due to worry about his personal safety.

Otherwise, nothing new.

November 16, 1942

Nothing new.

November 17, 1942

The Duce is convinced that in the next few days, for better or worse, the crisis in Africa will come. An American column is at Sfax, or in the vicinity; other columns are advancing on Bizerte and Tunis. The French attitude is very ambiguous, and we must expect hostility rather than indifference. Will the forces of the Axis be able to resist the blow? It will all depend on what can be transferred to Tunisia in the next few days. At present not much has been done, and German support is very much inferior to what was hoped and promised. If Tunisia should fall, we would lose our last defensive bastion, and the Italian situation would become extremely difficult in a short time. The Duce seems thoughtful, and today his face showed fatigue.

Galbiati tells me about what he is doing so that the militia can face any internal crisis decisively and successfully. I am not entirely convinced of what he says. I believe that police and carabinièri represent all that is left to guarantee our institutions.

Spain is beginning to mobilize. What for? I think that above all she wishes to warn both sides that she is ready to defend her territories against anyone who wants to violate them.

November 18, 1942

The Consul General at Tunis, Silimbani, has left Tunis with the attachés of the consulate. Admiral Salza, the commander of the armistice commission in North Africa, has also returned to Italy. Silimbani declares over the telephone that the situation in Tunis is untenable, that the Americans are advancing unopposed, and that the city is already practically in the hands of the de Gaullists, who will stage an uprising on the first appearance of the Stars and Stripes. The Duce was not informed of this, then he later telephones me, asking whether Silimbani has had orders to leave from the Ministry for Foreign Affairs. He added that Salza had returned temporarily and for other reasons. He says that the military situation is "becoming clarified." Has Silimbani gone crazy or is Cavallero lying, as usual?

The Nuncio protests about some stupid article by Farinacci, according to which the Holy See and Myron Taylor are to blame for the bombings. The Vatican is not going to stand for such an accusation and is ready to start a lot of trouble. Mussolini instructs me to ask Farinacci for a retraction. Farinacci reacts, saying that he had the information from the Duce himself. We shall see about it tomorrow.

November 19, 1942

I see the King, after not having seen him for a long time. I find him physically well and spiritually serene. He keeps me for a long conversation—an hour and twenty minutes. He wants to be informed on everything that was done in Munich, and explores the situation fully. He asks particularly for news on Spain, Switzerland, and Turkey. He says very little about what has happened and is happening in the

Mediterranean, but is particularly concerned about the scarcity of troops in Italy, and especially in Rome, where even the Grenadiers have been taken away. He asks me to insist to the Duce that some troops be returned to Italy, begging me at the same time not to tell him that the King asked this, "because otherwise he might suspect secret dealings." He defends the armed forces passionately, pronounces no judgment on Cavallero, but "if they are thinking of a new head of the armed forces, they should consider the oldest who are the best," and he cites "Ago, Amantea, and Geloso." He talks in a friendly way about Guzzoni. As always, there is not lacking in his words a certain element of Germanophobia. On the progress of the war he repeats a rather generic statement of faith, but he asks me many questions about Washington and London, advising me to cling to any thread which may yet be reknotted, "even if it is as thin as a spider's web."

I saw Del Croix. He is unhappy, but not surprised about the situation. He, too, condemns the absence from Italy of our best divisions. He inveighs against dictatorship of the type of the Roman, Marius, "because, with us, all plebeian dictatorships have degenerated into tyrannies," and he adds that the single great merit of Marius was that of having beaten the Teutons.

November 20, 1942

Nothing new.

November 21, 1942

Council of Ministers dealing with routine matters. At the end the Duce spoke to summarize and to throw light on the present situation. In brief, he said: (a) that the food situation is a great deal better than forecasts, which had been very gloomy; (b) that the military situation in Cyrenaica is such as to lead to stopping the enemy at Agheila Marada, and perhaps to get the upper hand, while the trend of operations in Tunisia is favorable to the Axis; (c) that the internal situation is excellent, except for the alarmists; (d) that Hitler, acting on a suggestion made by him, has agreed to send one hundred anti-aircraft batteries for the protection of our cities, which are suffering severe punishment every night from the R.A.F.

Tonight, in fact, it has been Turin's turn, and the city was the object of a bombing that was heavier than any other attacks, including those on Genoa. This now raises serious problems: the evacuation of the cities, the question of supplies, and the reduction of the industrial potential in Italy. It is useless to build up illusions. All this has a considerable bearing on morale, and the spirit of resistance is less than one might expect. We must not confuse endurance with resistance; they are two very different things.

November 22, 1942

The Duce remarks that His Majesty talked to him about replacing Cavallero, mentioning the same names as he did to me, but Mussolini, who in these days is again optimistic, says that we should not make changes in our command while we are engaged on two fronts.

A Russian offensive on the Don has achieved notable success, and deserves the most prudent attention.

November 23, 1942

Bismarck says that General von Pohl, returning from Libya, was pessimistic, notwithstanding the fact that "Rommel is in good humor." From the confidential talks that Colonel Montezemolo of our General Staff has had with our foreign office liaison officer, it appears that the Germans intend to make another try at saving Tripolitania, while we believe that it would be more useful to concentrate everything on the defense of Tunisia. This causes a certain uneasiness in our High Command, except, naturally, Cavallero, who, having become the servant of the Germans, puts his personal interests before the interests of his country.

In the country, pessimism and concern are growing beyond all measure. One cannot speak with any person of any class or station in life without hearing the same thing.

November 24, 1942

All West Africa has joined the Darlan movement. The fact is of great importance. A large reserve of men passes over to the Allies as well as the base of Dakar, and a considerable part of the Navy. Reactions are just beginning to come in, but the event is important.

Alfieri from Berlin. He still harps upon the official optimism in German circles. Personally, he appears to be concerned because he believes that the Italian people may consider him one of those mainly responsible for our entry into the war. He does not even suspect that the Italian people merely consider him a fool.

New and more accurate X rays of the Duce, which tend to prove that his trouble is caused by a rheumatic localization in the spinal column. If this is true, as I hope it is, within a short time he can completely recover his health.

November 25, 1942

Nothing new.

November 26, 1942

Information from Africa is, in general, worse. Both in Tunisia and in Tripolitania the position of our forces becomes more critical; at the same time pressure from the enemy increases. Last night forty American tanks arrived at the gates of Tunis. Fougier, who is a realist and an honest man, thinks that within a few days we shall be driven from Tunis, and within a month from all of Africa. Mussolini, too, must more or less have this same idea, since he said in telephoning to me about the commercial agreement with Rumania, "We should not insist too much on increasing our quota of gasoline. I believe that next year our needs will be distinctly less."

Von Mackensen communicates to me the details of a letter from Laval to Hitler. He offers full French collaboration to the Axis, but what does a Laval from Auvergne represent in reality? How can he speak for France? The German answer was prudent indeed. Not Hitler, but von Ribbentrop thanked Laval in vague terms, and another conference has been deferred without setting a date.

The Russian attack on the Volga-Don basin continues, and it appears that the results are really very important. But on this matter we know nothing very specific. We must accept what the Germans tell us.

November 27, 1942

The important event of the day is the occupation of the port of Toulon by German troops. During the night a communication reached the Duce from Hitler regarding the decision taken. Communication took place through the military, and I was kept in the dark about everything until noon, when Cavallero telephoned me. No one knows yet how things have gone. Two things are certain: that there was a certain resistance, and that the French Navy is completely scuttled. I do not yet know the French reaction to what has happened, but in any event it would not seem such as to increase sympathy for Laval and for the Germans. For us Italians there is one advantage—that in any eventuality a naval power in the Mediterranean has been canceled for many years. The necessity for carefully preserving our own Navy becomes more and more evident.

November 28, 1942

Nothing new.

November 29, 1942

I go to Leghorn.

November 30, 1942

Goering comes to Rome without advance notice. From what is said by members of the General Staff, the trip was prompted by the fact that Rommel has left Libya secretly to see the Führer. We reacted and the assistant German military attaché has been told that if an Italian general had behaved in this way he would have been brought before a court-martial. Now Goering comes to settle the trouble, but this discord is not merely a matter of form. Rommel does not consider it possible to hold Tripolitania and would like to withdraw into Tunisia at once. Bastico is of the contrary opinion, and among the members of the Italian General Staff many share the ideas of Bastico. We shall see what decisions come out of the conference that is to be held today at the Palazzo Venezia.

Amè is very pessimistic about our resistance in Tunisia. Taking everything into consideration, he thinks that we shall be dislodged in about ten days. By Christmas we shall be out of Libya. This raises very serious problems for us.

Churchill makes a speech which relates particularly to Italy. Unfortunately, I do not see what means are at our disposal today to frustrate his program of a scientific and demolishing offensive against our country. In these last few days Turin has suffered more hard ordeals.

December 1, 1942

I have seen the Duce again after an interval of ten days, during which he had stayed at Villa Torlonia for reasons of health. Physically he is thinner, but energetic and vivacious. Tomorrow he will address the Chamber. The occasion for this is Churchill's attack, and in it he intends "to debate with him without, however, resorting to insults as he has done. Besides," he added, "Churchill's address honors me because it proves that I am the real antagonist of Great Britain." Later he sent me a report of his conversation with Goering. The Germans will send three armored divisions to Africa, the Adolf Hitler, the Hermann Goering, and the Deutschland—"three names that mean much to German honor." In Libya the situation is confused. Everything is in the hands of the English, who, by quickly taking the initiative, can easily dislodge us from our present line of defense. We are planning to make Buerat the line to which we shall retreat, and it has the advantage of placing the Sirte desert in front of us rather than at our backs. In general, I found the Duce optimistic both as regards the war and the internal situation. The officers in Goering's party speak with assurance. They declare they are certain that within three months the German armored forces will reach Morocco. With respect to the conflict in Russia they also make rosy prophecies.

From Bucharest telegrams arrive from Bova-Scoppa which give evidence of the nervousness caused by the information from the Don River front. They accuse Antonescu of having involved Rumania too much in a struggle in which it has no direct interest.

December 2, 1942

After a long silence Mussolini has spoken to the Chamber. The reception of the speech by the National Council was very warm, even if in the hall it was easy to recognize people who disagree in private. Physically the Duce appeared quite thin, but nonetheless vigorous and at times as fiery as ever. The speech? It is too early to say what effect it will have. But it is clear that it does not introduce new facts or opinions, nor indeed could it have done so. It will not be difficult for English propaganda to refute it effectively, even if it does not avail itself of

Mussolini's glaring slip about the "dinner jackets worn by the English while drinking their five o'clock tea." (Edda was aghast at this boner. She knows the English and knows how they will laugh at it, and she immediately wrote me a letter to have the newspaper version corrected.)

Bismarck spoke confidentially to d'Aieta on the coming of Goering. He says that the Germans are the first to be convinced that there is nothing more to be done in Africa, and that all the promises of Goering are bound to be left up in the clouds. But it is a matter of saving the reputation of Rommel, who has a big name in Germany and is one of the military men most loyal to the Nazis. Hence the principal aim of Goering is to create confusion and give documentary proof that the blame for everything rests upon our poor organization of transports, ships, railroads, et cetera. For this reason he has begun to snub everyone, including Admiral Riccardi. Bismarck added that the military technicians of the Embassy are surprised at the amount of nonsense which the Reichsmarshal has been capable of putting together.

December 3, 1942

Scannavacca confirms our opinion that Goering has made an extremely bad impression, even on our officers of the High Command. Colonel Montezemolo, secretary of the meeting of the four marshals (Goering, Kesselring, Rommel, and Cavallero), said that he was surprised by the "proud ignorance" of the Reichsmarshal. Now, Goering has gone to Naples, declaring that he intends to appoint "as Superintendent of Transportation the secretary of the party in Naples, who is a young and active man, and who thinks as he does." For the sake of history, Secretary Milone, an excellent boy, is a doctor. Can it be that Goering is really thinking of appointing himself the Reichsprotektor of Italy?

December 4, 1942

Nothing new.

December 5, 1942

Guariglia has spoken with Maglione on the question of the bombing of Rome. The Holy See is doing its best to avoid it, and the Anglo-

Americans have been informed that the Pope, the Bishop of Rome, could not witness with apathy the destruction of the Eternal City. The English Minister, Osborne, answered that Rome is not only the city of the Catholics, but also the headquarters of the High Command, a large German command, many airports, as well as a very important railway dispersal point. The Allies, therefore, assume full freedom of action, at least against military objectives. Cardinal Maglione therefore pointed out that the removal of the commands from Rome would strengthen the Holy Father in his task. I informed the Duce of this, but as yet do not know his reaction. On the other hand, I have learned that the King is favorable to this and he himself had thought of such an action.

Goering continues to preside over meetings to which he invites people in civil life, Buffarini, technical ministers, et al. Buffarini reports that the meetings are banal and useless, and he is quite displeased at the servile attitude of Cavallero toward the Reichsmarshal. Yesterday, when Goering arrived at the High Command, he was received in the courtyard by our military chiefs. This made the young officers present indignant, and they have reported it to me.

December 6, 1942

The Duce has dictated to me a brief summary of his conferences with Goering, which I have preserved elsewhere. No conclusion has been reached in the political field, but in the military sector the Reichsmarshal has observed that our efforts will have to be redoubled if we wish to avoid further grief in Africa. We, too, had come to this conclusion without the need of his precious insight.

In principle Mussolini is not against the transfer elsewhere of the High Command, "in order that it may not be said that he has remained under the big umbrella of Catholicism to protect himself from English bombs."

Von Mackensen officially invites the Duce to go to Germany between the fifteenth and twentieth of the month. Laval will attend the second part of the conference. Tomorrow the Duce will give his answer.

D'Aieta has had a long conversation with the Prince of Piedmont. In general, it was satisfactory even though he is inclined to see the situation everywhere in dark colors.

December 7, 1942

Conference with the King. We went into details about the situation. We spoke of the advisability of transferring the High Command elsewhere in order to avoid the bombing of Rome and, accepting my suggestion, he told me that he will propose Fiuggi to the Duce as the most suitable site.

Then he mentioned a bit of advice once given by his grandfather, King Victor Emmanuel II. In speaking with people, one must say two things in order to be assured of a good reception, "How beautiful your city is!" and "How young you look!" The King maintains that in his long experience they never fail. But some minutes later, when he began to speak well to me about Leghorn, I took the liberty of interrupting, and this amused him.

The Duce agrees to the trip to Germany at the time proposed, but without enthusiasm.

December 8, 1942

The Duce has said that he will go to Germany only on one condition: namely, that he be allowed to take his meals alone in his apartment, "because he does not want a lot of ravenous Germans to notice that he is compelled to live only on rice and milk." But, I may add, his health has considerably improved during the last few days, so that it seems almost normal.

He is optimistic about the African military situation, especially because he has decided not to defend the Agheila-Marada line in Tripolitania, but to fall back to Buerat so as to leave before the English the four hundred kilometers of the Sirte desert.

December 9, 1942

New and effective bombing of Turin by the R.A.F.

I see Amè on his return from Nice, where he met Admiral Canaris. He repeats his usual pessimism, which he bases above all on news coming from Russia regarding Soviet attacks and German exhaustion. For Africa, also, he makes dark forecasts, though for the distant future.

Amè, for his part, sees the situation with a little more optimism than he did ten days or so ago. This, naturally, only for the immediate aspect; for the future his ideas have not changed.

But the proofs of bad strategy given by the Anglo-Americans in Tunisia lead him to believe that the fight will still be a long one. The Duce, to whom Amè reported Canaris' concern, showed no interest in it. In fact, he asserted his confidence in quick victory.

Franco spoke in very friendly terms about the Axis. Mussolini sent him congratulations through our Ambassador, but "he does not intend to move a finger to accelerate the intervention of Spain in the war, because it would be more of a hindrance than a help."

December 10, 1942

No news.

December 11, 1942

Nothing new.

December 12, 1942

The removal of our commands [from Rome] has been decided and I shall pass the news on to Guariglia so that he may bring it to the knowledge of the Holy See. Bombing of Rome must be avoided absolutely; the population is very much disturbed, and the two alarms of yesterday were enough to create profound uneasiness.

December 13, 1942

The British have attacked Libya. For the moment we are resisting well, but this disturbs the withdrawal from the Buerat line.

Mussolini is calm. This morning he was going through the reports from the censorship and came to very pessimistic conclusions on humanity. Two things, he believes, have really eternal value, "bread and guts." The rest are pipe dreams, ideals, sacrifices—nothing.

Notwithstanding the fact that we let the Germans know that we did not consider Cavallero's presence advisable at the coming meeting at Klessheim, they have still insisted that he come. It becomes more and more evident that they consider him their man.

Guariglia talked to the Vatican about the removal of the command. It appears that Osborne insists especially on the removal of the Germans. When Guariglia said to Monsignor Montini that even the Duce would leave the capital, the Monsignor replied, "I think he will have to make another march on Rome to come back."

Jacomoni is quite optimistic on the Albanian situation, in spite of the many incidents which are taking place. He believes, and with good reason, that it depends solely on international events. He would change Kruia, but he doesn't regret the experiment. "He is a man," he said, "who, in our own interest, we should have destroyed gradually."

December 14, 1942

Ribbentrop informs us that "because of operations in the East" it is advisable to postpone the meeting at Klessheim for a few days. He is not precise on when the meeting will take place, but hopes that it will still be possible before Christmas.

In Libya the British attack is rather heavy, but our greatest difficulty is the scarcity of fuel. In these days our Navy has also suffered severe losses.

December 15, 1942

Nothing new.

Late in the evening Mackensen asks to see me. New proposals are made for the meeting. Hitler cannot leave the High Command, nor can he postpone the meeting. And since he does not want the Duce to face such a long trip, almost to the old borders of Lithuania, he invites me to go as soon as possible with Cavallero. He tells us beforehand that the conversations will be important and will last a day or so. I will answer him tomorrow.

December 16, 1942

As I had anticipated, the Duce does not feel inclined to face such a long trip, nor does he care to interrupt his electrotherapeutic cure, which seems to be doing him a great deal of good. I shall have to go, and this time provided with exact instructions. Mussolini is especially anxious to have Hitler know (and he has already spoken of it to Goering) that he considers it extremely advisable to come to an agreement with Russia, or at least to fix upon a defensive line that can be held by small forces. Nineteen forty-three will be the year of the Anglo-Saxon effort. Mussolini considers that the Axis must have on hand the greatest possible number of divisions in order to defend itself in Africa, in the Balkans, and perhaps even in the West. I shall note elsewhere the instructions received and shall have stenographic notes made of the conference. Just now it is interesting to note that Bismarck has told d'Aieta that the Führer has tried to avoid the meeting with the Duce, because he does not want to enter into general political discussions. It seems that we shall speak only of France if Laval is present.

Things are going badly in Cyrenaica, where the English have succeeded in making our retreat somewhat disorderly, while obliging us to fight under the worst tactical and logistic conditions.

The Duce confirms the removal of the German commands from Rome, and I give instructions that Cardinal Maglione be informed immediately. Perhaps it will be worth while to put in writing the negotiations that have taken place. We shall never have an English assurance that they will not bomb, but I continue to be optimistic.

December 17, 1942

On my way to Hitler's headquarters.

December 18, 1942

I recorded my conversations in the forest of Görlitz and made notes of my general impressions. Now, as usual, a few particulars.

The atmosphere is heavy. To the bad news there should perhaps be added the sadness of that humid forest and the boredom of collective living in the barracks of the command. There isn't a spot of color, not one vivid note. Waiting rooms filled with people smoking, eating, chatting. Kitchen odor, smell of uniforms, of boots. All this is in great measure needless, at least for a mass of people who have no need to be here. First among them is Ribbentrop, who compels the greater number of his employees to live a troglodyte life to no purpose and which, in fact, impedes the normal working of the Foreign Ministry.

When I arrive no one tried to conceal from me or from my collaborators the unhappiness over the news of the break-through on the Russian front. There were open attempts to put the blame on us.

Hewel, who is very close to Hitler, had the following conversation (in English) with Pansa. Pansa: "Had our Army many losses?" Hewel: "No losses at all; they are running." Pansa: "As you did in Moscow last year?" Hewel: "Exactly."

December 19, 1942

Laval made a trip that he could have spared himself. After two days on the train they first sat him at a tea table, then at a dinner table, and did not let him open his mouth. The moment he tried to speak the Führer would interrupt him and deliver a long dissertation. (I believe that at heart Hitler is happy at being Hitler, since this permits him to talk all the time.) Altogether, Laval is a filthy Frenchman —the filthiest of all Frenchmen. To get into the good graces of the German bosses he doesn't hesitate to betray his own compatriots and to defame his own unhappy country. He said one clever thing, that for him it is difficult to govern France, since everywhere he turns he hears people call out, *"Laval au poteau* [Laval to the scaffold]."

Still, how the Germans feel the charm of the French! Even of this Frenchman. Except for Hitler, all the others were milling around trying to talk to him, or to get close to him; it looked like the entrance of the great fallen lord in a circle of new-rich bastards.

Ribbentrop also did his best, but he ended with a *faux pas*. He reminded Laval that his "eminent compatriot" Napoleon had once been in that same forest.

December 20, 1942 [continuation of December 19]

If I am not mistaken, Napoleon was there under entirely different conditions.

A fact that should be remembered: In 1939 Cavallero went to Germany bearing a letter from Mussolini. Now Keitel, recalling that meeting, said that they had already then decided on the war against Poland, even to the setting of the date. And all this, naturally, while they were committed with us to a period of at least three years of peace.

December 21, 1942

Return trip.

December 22, 1942

I return to Rome. I find considerable panic over the news from the Russian front, especially since the Duce, in speaking to people of a possible peace with Russia, had kindled many hopes.

Mussolini is in a rather bad humor. I turned over to him the report on my trip, in which I clearly stated what I think. In my verbal comments, also, I do not conceal my unfavorable impressions. I speak to him of Cavallero and of the servility he shows in his relations with the Germans. The Duce says: "The usefulness of Cavallero is over. A few years ago he had a keen brain, but that is no longer true." However, he does not allude to the person who is to replace him. He invites me to send His Majesty a copy of my report.

Colonel Stephens has made a radio comment on my trip to Germany which is quite amusing. He recalls my speech before the Chamber on December 16, 1939, and maintains that I am the person best fitted to speak clearly to the English because I have done so since that time.

December 23, 1942

Nothing new.

December 24, 1942

The King has words of approval for my report on my return from Germany. He is indignant about the fact that Ribbentrop has asked for part of our light fleet. The tone of the King's conversation is, as always, anti-German, but he says nothing in particular and concludes with the usual formal and unconvincing affirmation of victory.

We are at loggerheads again on the question of the bombing of Rome. From an intercepted British telegram we learn that in addition to the departure of the Duce and the commands from Rome, Eden also wants that of the King and of the whole government, with Swiss officials controlling the evacuation. Naturally Mussolini reacted vigorously and is preparing to refuse. Yesterday I was in his room while he was listening to the speech of the Pope on the radio. He commented on it with sarcasm, "The Vicar of God, that is the representative of the Ruler of the Universe on Earth, should never speak; he should remain in the clouds. This is a speech of platitudes which might better be made by the parish priest of Predappio [Mussolini's native village]."

News from Russia still bad, but at the High Command they believe that this time the Russians will not succeed in taking strategic advantage of the initial successes.

December 25, 1942

At Algiers Darlan has been assassinated—three revolver shots. Are the de Gaullists, the English, or the Germans to be blamed? He was shot by a young man, twenty years of age, and hence either a fanatic or an agent. Perhaps we shall come to know the truth. However, it is interesting to note the cold indifference with which the English press has commented on the news.

Fougier is very deeply pessimistic. As far as he is concerned the war is already lost; in fact, it was lost some time ago, and now the only thing that remains is to find the way to end it as soon as possible and with the least harm to us. In his opinion the scarcity of equipment has become so acute as to render any kind of serious military operation inconceivable—at least for the air force.

December 26, 1942

Horia Sima, head of the Rumanian legion, has arrived in Italy. Since he got out of Germany with a false passport, Himmler demands his extradition. For my part, I advised the Duce to grant his extradition forthwith, especially since his presence here would create friction with Antonescu. And then, all things considered, there will be one less crook.

Today Princess di Gangi, who had a cordial friendship with the Duce, opened her heart to me on the Petacci affair, without any suggestion from me, talking, as she said in her Sicilian accent, "like in the confessional." According to her, Mussolini has had enough of Claretta, her brother, her sister, and all of them, but he can't get rid of them because they are bad people, ready to blackmail and create a scandal. Speaking with the Princess di Gangi, the Duce is supposed to have said that he once loved this girl [Claretta Petacci], but that now she is "revolting" to him. How much truth is there in this and how much of it is dormant feminine jealousy? Anyway, the Gangi woman blames the Petaccis for everything that is going badly in Italy, including the Duce's ailments, which seem to me, frankly, a bit exaggerated.

December 27, 1942

I go to Leghorn to say good-by to Emilia, my dear old faithful Tata, who is slowly dying. To the weight of her eighty-two years is added that of many ailments. I have loved her very tenderly. Yesterday afternoon was one of the unhappiest days of my life.

December 28, 1942

No news of any importance in Rome. I don't see the Duce because he is in bed with a kind of influenza. His health is not what I should like it to be.

Mackensen sends me in the name of the German Government the telegram in answer to Laval, regarding what he asked for in the forest of Görlitz. It has to do with very modest concessions, entirely matters of form. Not hard to agree with so far as we are concerned.

December 29, 1942

Buffarini shows me the written reports of the Rimini police which the Duce asked for today. It is nothing more than a mediocre and banal piece of gossip spread in Tirana by people I don't know and who gossiped about me, saying that I was seeking to become the Duce's successor and other such absurdities. I told Buffarini to show the reports immediately to Mussolini, who will easily judge them for what they are worth. I am only sorry that there are people who bring such silly reports to the Duce, and that he, after knowing me for so many years, can listen to them even without taking them seriously.

Buti is here in transit. He says nothing substantially new. The whole of France is now convinced that Germany will lose the war, and everybody awaits the day. Laval is despised, but he is supported because they fear the worst; that is, they fear Doriot, who is considered a gangster. Buti found a picturesque simile in talking about Franco-German relations: a wagon driver who whips his mule crying "collaboration, collaboration!"

December 30, 1942

Donegani rushed to the Palazzo Chigi to advise against the proposed customs union with Germany. In reality somebody had mentioned it, though I can't remember who, but the idea had been bluntly rejected because the enormous loss which would result for our country is too evident. It would be like opening the doors of our house while the doors of others remained locked. The Germans have had enough from us. Are they still dissatisfied?

A good point on the question of the bombing of Rome: from an intercepted telegram we learn that the Americans have said no to Eden's Draconian request, declaring that they do not intend to bomb the city of St. Peter because there would be more disadvantages than advantages for the Allies. Thus it seems to me that the matter can be tabled. At least for the time being.

December 31, 1942

Emilia died tonight. With her dies another part of my youth. Perhaps no one in the world has lavished upon me such a sweet and constant tenderness. In her opinion I have never grown up; man, youth, adolescent, it was all the same. She surrounded me with the same concern that she had for me as a child. She was generous, honest, and extremely faithful. Today I have suffered the deepest sorrow of my life, after the death of Father and that of Maria.

I received Colonel Montezemolo, sent to me by Cavallero with the approval of the Duce, to explain what is to be done in Tripolitania; namely, to evacuate it. It is impossible to send sufficient supplies and reinforcements. Everything that goes to Libya is used up in Tunisia and supplies are already very scarce. Now Cavallero's order of the day is: optimism regarding Tunisia, pessimism regarding Tripolitania. Only a few days ago he was an optimist with respect to all sectors. We shall see. Montezemolo, whom I asked about his personal opinion on our prospects in Tunisia, answered: "I believe that we shall be able to resist for a long time." He did not wish to compromise himself.

An interesting conference with Colonel Lucca who has just come from Constantinople. As is well known, he is a very good friend of Saragioglu. The latter told him two or, rather, three things: that what is happening to the Axis is no longer looked upon with optimism in Turkey; that Russia would not be adverse to making a separate peace; that Turkey would behave just like the Bulgarians with respect to Germany if England violated her neutrality. I have asked Lucca for a written report.

CROCE ROSSA ITALIANA
COMITATO CENTRALE · ROMA

A G E N D A 1 9 4 3
ANNO XXI-XXII · E. F.

EDIZIONE DELLA CROCE ROSSA ITALIANA

January 1, 1943

Nothing particularly new except a great flowering of telegrams from the German Nazi chiefs which are very courteously worded. It is a sign of the times.

Hitler's message to the German people and the one that he sent to the armed forces I did not like very much. They reveal a great deal of concern, which is logical, but it is not wise to announce it to a public which is already perplexed.

January 2, 1943

Pietromarchi has had a long conference with the Pope. Without assuming any obligation, the Holy Father said that he now believes that the danger of the bombing of Rome has been averted. He also informed whom it may concern that his reaction would be energetic and immediate. He has found better comprehension in Washington than in London, and this is understandable. He did not give any opinion on the situation but shows that he is informed as to what the Ministry for Foreign Affairs is doing to prevent massacre and ruin in the occupied territories. He ended by sending me his greetings and his blessing.

I took Colonel Lucca to the Duce. The former is now convinced that we cannot make a separate peace with Russia. Two months ago he considered it feasible, but now that the Cossacks are advancing toward the Donetz basin and Veliki Lukki has fallen, Stalin wants to impose impossible terms. However, he feels that before long the situation may offer better prospects. That the situation on the Russian front is very depressing is confirmed by Antonescu, who considers the German mistakes as "strategic and hence susceptible of serious consequences."

I have prepared a memorandum for the Duce on the real situation in Croatia, Dalmatia, and Montenegro as it is developing after our understanding with the Chetniks. It is very precarious and dangerous.

January 3, 1943

Nothing new.

January 4, 1943

The Duce asked me to give von Mackensen a copy of a telegram the Turkish Ambassador Zorlu sent to his government from Kuibyshev. It is a description of the Soviet situation. It seems impartial and quite informative. According to him, the war weighs heavily on the Russians, but Russia is still strong and, in the judgment of the diplomatic corps in Kuibyshev, Axis stock is falling.

I am thinking about gifts for Goering on his fiftieth birthday. The Duce is giving him a gold sword carved by Messina (which was originally meant to go to Franco, but times have changed). I will give him a star of San Maurizio studded with diamonds (originally meant for Zog and kept in the safe all this time). The personal indifference of the Duce to personal possessions is moving. At home he owns only one good piece: a self-portrait by Mancini, which was a gift from the painter. Well, when he heard that a gift had to be made to Goering and that the Belle Arti [Ministry of Fine Arts] had difficulty in locating something worth while, he immediately thought of giving his Mancini. I had to argue a great deal to change his mind.

January 5, 1943

I see the Duce after two days. I find him tired. Edda says that the pains in his stomach have increased though he takes only liquid food. He is depressed about the situation in Libya. He realizes that the loss of Tripoli will cut deeply into the morale of the people. He would like a desperate house-to-house defense like that in Stalingrad. He knows that this will not happen. Furthermore, it is impossible. The city can be broken into from all sides, and can be shelled from the sea. He has harsh words for Cavallero and for "that madman Rommel, who thinks of nothing but retreating in Tunisia."

January 6, 1943

I talked with Roatta and Geloso. With the first we discussed the Chetnik problem. He also realizes the danger that the Chetniks represent now and will represent in the future. He declares that in order to carry out the German plan of extermination we need a great many more troops than both we and Germany can afford. I believe that, as things stand, he is not wrong. But how about tomorrow? The fact is that military forces are scarce. In Africa, Russia, and the Balkans, the occupied countries, everywhere new and greater forces are needed. At times I have the impression that the Axis is like a man who is trying to cover himself with a bedspread that is too small. His head is cold if he warms his feet, and his feet freeze if he wants to keep his head warm.

Geloso, too, draws a rather modest picture of the situation in Greece. He thinks, however, that the forces at his disposal are sufficient to repel a British attack, at least in the initial phase. Both of these generals see a gloomy future, and, without confessing it openly, make unhappy forecasts.

Alfieri sends a long report on the German situation. For the first time he comes to pessimistic conclusions without even bothering to suggest palliatives. This must be hard for him, since he has been the zealous representative of unconditional optimism.

January 7, 1943

Japan wants to sign economic agreements with Germany and us, in which the living spaces of the three countries would be defined and specific preferential tariffs agreed upon. Since our position of inferiority is obvious I put a spoke in the wheel.

Pirelli talks to me with all his cards on the table. He describes his conversation with a Swiss banker just arrived from London, and frankly admits that he now believes that the war has been won by the Allies. He gives no news; confirms the fact that it is easier for us to find understanding in Washington than in London.

General Dalmasso views the Albanian situation with remarkable tranquillity so long as there is no attack from the outside. This would bring many painful surprises.

January 8, 1943

I have seen the Duce again after three days and find him looking worse. It seems that Frugoni, too, in these last few days has expressed his concern. But in my humble opinion, what is hurting his health more than anything else is his uneasiness about the situation. He has rage in his heart over the abandonment of Tripoli and suffers from it. As usual, he hurled bitter words at the military men who do not make war with the "fury of the fanatic, but rather with the indifference of the professional."

I have lunch with Bottai and Farinacci. Both are furious. In speaking of the loss of Libya, Bottai says: "After all it is another goal that has been reached. In 1911 Mussolini uttered his 'away from Libya.' After thirty-two years he has kept his word."

The brazen-faced Dr. Petacci has sent me through De Giacomo a letter which in peremptory terms advances the candidacy of his partner, Vezzari, to the Spanish Embassy. Vezzari is an old jailbird, an ignorant man, a swindler, and obscene. I have rejected the letter. If it were not that Mussolini is unwell and I do not want to worry him I would speak of it to him. But there will be time to do so.

January 9, 1943

Vittorio [eldest son of Mussolini] speaks to me about the health of the Duce. In the last few days he has had very severe gastric pains, which is serious, because they drastically reduce his consumption of food. All the doctors agree in saying that there is no organic trouble. Vittorio, as well as I, is convinced that the source of the disturbance is nervousness.

Wang Ching-Wei declares war on the Allies. The event is of no practical importance, even though we play it up with large headlines for home consumption. I speak frankly to the Duce about it. As far as Italy is concerned, we are giving up our concession at Tientsin which is not very important, but it was, nevertheless, a heritage of the past and is personally very dear to me.

January 10, 1943

I think the Germans would do well to watch the Rumanians. I see an about-face in the attitude and words of Mihael and Antonescu. The sudden will for conciliation with Hungary is suspicious to me. If the Russian offensive had not been so successful I doubt that all this would have taken place. There is something peculiar going on in Finland also; watch it.

Goering, to whom Martin Franklin today handed the first Gold Star of the Roman Eagle, expressed his thanks so vociferously that his childish joy was obvious.

January 11, 1943

Von Mackensen telephoned during the night on Ribbentrop's orders to inform us that Pétain was preparing to leave Vichy, bound for his villa near Marseilles. The move is suspicious: preparations for an escape to Algeria? In any case, orders have been given to the troops to watch the movements of the old marshal closely, and the French Government was told that it would be best for Pétain not to move. Mussolini telephoned me early, wishing further particulars, which I didn't have. Then, suddenly, he left for Forlì. His leaving can be explained by his bad health; and as the meeting of the Council of Ministers, planned for the sixteenth, has been indefinitely postponed, this will cause inevitable gossip.

Marshal Antonescu, talking with Bova-Scoppa, mentioned something about the German secret weapon, which is supposed to do wonders: a multiple-barreled electric gun; no armor could withstand its blow. Any truth in it? Is this the arm that Hitler alluded to in his speech? Or is it the usual hot air?

January 12, 1943

The Prince of Piedmont has sent for d'Aieta to tell him that in military circles the action carried out by me to avert the bombing of Rome has been favorably received, but adds that all now desire the actual removal of the German commands, who are shilly-shallying about it. Blasco d'Aieta showed the Prince the transcript of my report on my recent trip to the German High Command.

A long conference in the Colonna residence with Monsignor Montini, who, from what is said, is a really close collaborator of the Holy Father. He acted prudently, reservedly, and like an Italian. He did not express any opinion on the military situation but said only that in the Vatican they think that the struggle will still be hard and long. He added that in so far as he is able to do anything in favor of our country he is completely at our disposal. I spoke to him of the importance that we must attach to the internal order of our country at all times, and he agreed. The Church will always work in this direction. Though he is anti-Bolshevistic, he nevertheless expresses admiration and surprise at what Stalin has been able to do. He said: "One thing is important: whatever the future may bring our people have given singular proof of strength, faith, and discipline. These are qualities that will bring about a complete revival."

January 13, 1943

Senator Kruia has submitted his resignation. The governor is planning to replace him with Ekrem Libohova, who was Minister for Foreign Affairs at the time of Zog, or with Kensal Vrioni. In fact, it is planned to return to the government of the beys, who still have a considerable influence in the country and are in a position strongly to influence public opinion.

Suardo tells me that he once asked Senator Borea d'Olmo, who was the secretary of Cavour, his own personal reminiscences of the great statesman. "He used to eat a great deal," was the only answer that he got. Certain ideas come to mind spontaneously.

January 14, 1943

Nothing new.

January 15, 1943

Mussolini telephones, wishing to know if it is true that I went to a luncheon at Farinacci's home with Bottai, Scorza, and Turaboni. It is very true. But also nothing was more insignificant. Farinacci had invited me to see his new country home; a bad luncheon, a banal conversation. Evidently somebody is trying to sow distrust and suspicion in the mind of the Chief, and I am sorry that he could fall for it even for a moment.

January 16, 1943

Among our interceptions there is a telegram in which are summarized the terms of a conversation between the German General von Thoma and Montgomery. If it is true it is serious. Von Thoma said that the Germans are convinced they have lost the war, and that the Army is anti-Nazi because it holds Hitler completely responsible. By order of the Duce I gave a copy of it to von Mackensen. There must be some truth in it because Thoma, passing through Rome, said more or less the same thing to Bismarck.

Edda spoke with Frugoni about the health of the Duce. A consultation with Cesabianchi will take place tomorrow at the Castle of Rocca. Although the ailment is of such long standing, Frugoni said there is every reason to believe that the Duce will be all right. This is good news.

January 17, 1943

Nothing new.

January 18, 1943

During the night a telegram from Tirana, in which the police inspector sounds an alarm: they can't form a government, the rebellion is growing, and we must hand over the government to the military. From Jacomoni no news. Now one thing is clear: either somebody is too cool or too nervous. I call him on the telephone, and in a veiled way he says things are quite bad, especially because Marka Gioni, the Catholic leader of Scutari, wants everything or nothing: either the whole government or no collaboration on his part. Jacomoni will not be blackmailed and solves the crisis with Ekrem Libohova. This is a return to the government of the beys, that is, the aristocratic local families. I inform the Duce, who was rather disturbed, and advised Jacomoni in any case to take precautionary measures with the military authorities. We shall see what will come of this situation, but it is clear that even in Albania we are getting the reflection of events on the larger checkerboard. And these events are not good. They are bad in Russia, with the German retreat assuming greater and greater proportions, and they are bad in Libya, where the threat against Tripoli appears more and more imminent.

I receive from Frugoni a rather reassuring letter about the Duce's health.

January 19, 1943

It has been a very oppressive day. News from all sectors is bad. The retreat in Russia continues and seems to have become a rout in some sections. In Libya, the infantry divisions are abandoning Tripoli and are marching westward, while the rear guards are trying to delay the prudent but inexorable advance of Montgomery. I speak with Mussolini over the telephone. He seems discouraged. Since the Germans have informed us that they can no longer send the armored forces promised us in Tunisia, he is thinking of finding a corrective in an eventual declaration of war on the Anglo-Saxon powers by the Bey. I tried to explain that this is impossible, useless, and ineffective. But he insists, and wants me to call Silimbani to Rome for a conference.

Bova-Scoppa has made a report on his long conference with young Antonescu, who has returned from German headquarters. The latter was very explicit about the tragic condition of Germany and foresees the need for Rumania and Italy to contact the Allies in order to establish a defense against the bolshevization of Europe. I shall take the report to the Duce and shall make it the subject of a conversation which I have been planning for some time. Let us not bandage our heads before they are broken, but let us look at the situation realistically and remember that charity begins at home.

January 20, 1943

A long and interesting conversation with Ambrosio and Vercellino. These two generals, both worthy and honest men, and of patriotic integrity, are very anxious about what is happening. Convinced as they are that Germany will lose the war, and that there is nothing left for us but destruction, death, and disorder, they ask how far we intend to go. Naturally they attack Cavallero violently—Cavallero who lies, consorts with the Germans, and steals all he can. I promise that I will talk frankly to the Duce, concealing nothing from him; this is what I can and must do in order to have peace with my own conscience.

In fact, taking my cue from Bova's report, I told the Duce what I thought. The Duce began by replying that "he was sure that the Germans would hold tenaciously." Then he listened to me attentively. He naturally refused Antonescu's offer, saying that "the Danube is not the way we must follow." But he did not react when at a certain point I said openly that we, too, should try to make some direct contact.

Physically he is the same as three weeks ago. He seemed a little thinner but looks well. Mentally he is depressed.

We have chosen De Peppo for Madrid and Rosso for Ankara. They are both good.

January 21, 1943

As I anticipated, Mussolini wanted to reread the Bova report. He described Antonescu's language as oversubtle and he reaffirmed in terms much stronger than those of yesterday his decision to march with Germany to the end. In addition he hopes "that five hundred Tiger tanks, five hundred thousand men in reserve, and the new German gun may yet change the situation." Even as far as Africa is concerned, he expresses himself in the most optimistic fashion: "Our Libyan forces are entering Tunisia and we still have many trump cards to play." I do not know what they can be. I speak frankly about Albania: what we are doing is merely to apply hot compresses. We must send troops and more troops. It is now clear that we have lost the Albanians' approval as well as their trust. Only force will win—not to be used in the beginning, but at least we should show that it is there.

General Amè is in a very black humor. He is convinced that 1943 will witness the collapse of Germany. He believes that we must begin to think of our own affairs, perhaps not at once, but certainly within a short time. As to Cavallero's successor, whom Mussolini intends to appoint very soon, he believes that Ago is the best candidate.

January 22, 1943

The Duce thinks that today's German communiqué is the worst since the beginning of the war. And it certainly is. Rout at Stalingrad, retreat everywhere on the front, and Tripoli about to fall. It appears that Rommel has again maneuvered in such a way as to save his forces, leaving the Italian troops in the lurch. Mussolini is very much irritated, and plans to have it out with the Germans. He is very unhappy over the fall of Tripoli, but isn't at all convinced that we can't counterattack from Tunisia and retake it. Thus he continues to lull himself with many dangerous illusions, which distort his clear vision of reality —a reality which is now apparent to everybody. Naturally, Cavallero and his following are the ones really responsible for the creation of this fool's paradise.

January 23, 1943

Meeting of the Council of Ministers. After the administrative agenda Mussolini talks of the military situation. The negative side is the allied initiative on all land fronts, a positive side is the success of the submarine campaign. He puts a great deal of emphasis on this. (But really I can't understand why the Axis, where the element of power is represented by the German Army, should find its reasons for hope on the seas!) The Duce makes no predictions. He says, instead, incisively that this war will last "another three or four years."

Today the communiqué announced the fall of Tripoli. On many faces, the most humble and the most sincere, I saw deep lines of pain. Many hopes are now concentrated on Tunisia by our propaganda. I fear that these are all false hopes.

January 24, 1943

General Messe informs me of a conference he had yesterday with the Duce in the presence of Cavallero. He has been made commander of the Italian forces that are flowing into Tunisia. "Commander of the dispersed forces," so Messe defines his job. He considers it a left-handed blow struck at him by Cavallero to get rid of him, since he, too, must be convinced that there are no prospects for us in Tunisia and he wants Messe to lose his reputation in a desperate gamble or even to end up in a prison camp. What surprised Messe was the language of Mussolini, who spoke of certain successes, offensive possibilities, African recoveries, et cetera, et cetera. All this is due to the fact that Cavallero pictures a situation which is far from the truth and is deliberately deceiving the Duce.

January 25, 1943

The Royal Signature. His Majesty had a serious cold, his voice was raucous, and he coughed. He spoke in rather general terms, avoiding any reference to the situation. As a matter of fact, he indulged in some perfunctory optimism, without missing the occasion for a dig at the Germans. He talked at length about Giolitti, exalting his callousness and ignorance. Giolitti managed Parliament like no one in the world. He had a notebook, each page of which was dedicated to some deputy, on which he wrote the "life, death, and miracles" of each man. Not one deputy ever escaped Giolitti's blackmail. The King himself read the page having to do with Eugenio Chiesa, who was particularly susceptible to threats on account of an old bankruptcy. To show Giolitti's ignorance, His Majesty related that when he proposed that Michetti be made a senator, Giolitti asked who he was, and then telegraphed the Prefect of Naples to secure information about "a certain Michetti." [Michetti was one of the most famous artists in Italy at the time.]

Today's German communiqué is depressing, and announces the evacuation of Voronez.

January 26, 1943

Nothing new.

January 27, 1943

Favagrossa confers with me on our supply situation. There are no changes, either good or bad, but now that a major effort must be made in the field of production, he thinks that there will be a notable diminution in the stocks available. However, our contribution to the production of arms is very modest: more than half and less than three quarters of one per cent of world production.

Bismarck was received by the Duce, to whom he brought a horse offered him by the city of Bremen. Mussolini expounded a theory which he had once told me about, according to which German bulletins are purposely pessimistic in order to prepare more pleasant surprises for the German people. Bismarck does not share this theory, and was very much surprised by it.

We receive news of the Casablanca meeting [between Roosevelt and Churchill when the "unconditional surrender" formula was announced]. It is too early to judge, but it seems to be a serious thing, very serious indeed. I neither share nor approve the easy ironies of our press.

January 28, 1943

The Duce continues to interpret the Russian situation rather optimistically. He believes that the Germans have men, resources, and energy to dominate the situation, and perhaps to turn it in their favor. Even for Africa he doesn't see things in gloomy colors. But he speaks more and more unfavorably about Cavallero.

One cannot say that the Duce's ideas are different from those of Colonel Battaglini, Chief of Staff of the Third Celere Division, just back from Russia. He painted the darkest picture possible, and though it was the first time he talked to me he said that the only way left to save Italy, the Army, and the regime itself is a separate peace. This is an idea that is taking root. It was mentioned to me with some approval, even by Mussolini's sister.

January 29, 1943

I go to the Duce with our Consul General at Tunis, Silimbani. He reports with some objectivity on the situation, which he considers serious. He does not see how, without the aid of very considerable armored forces, it is possible to hold the thin strip of land to which we are now clinging when the double Anglo-American pressure begins. The conference will continue tomorrow.

Anfuso has written from Budapest a keen and interesting letter which Mussolini praised very much. There are no actual facts as yet, but many indications lead one to believe that Hungary has already had some contacts with the Anglo-Saxons. Besides, Mariassy asked d'Aieta with a good deal of anxiety today if it were true that the Rumanians had been negotiating with the English and that conversations were under way in Lisbon. D'Aieta denied this but, in reality, what do we know about it?

Grandi is insisting that I send the foreign service functionary, Casardi, as First Secretary to Madrid. It may be a coincidence, but Casardi is half English, has an American wife, and was with Grandi when Samuel Hoare, who is today Ambassador to Spain, was Secretary for Foreign Affairs.

January 30, 1943

Ambrosio takes the place of Cavallero as Chief of Staff. This is a good change, imposed by honesty, by events, and by the resentment of all Italians against a man who has always lied for his own self-interest and for the sake of his career. Ambrosio is respected in the Army. He isn't considered a thunderbolt, but anyway, under present conditions, I don't think that even a Napoleon Bonaparte could work miracles. What is important is that at the head of our armed forces there is an Italian, a patriot who sees with honest eyes the reality of things, and who intends to put the interest of the country above everything else. Ambrosio, to judge from the conversations I have had with him, is of this sort.

January 31, 1943

The replacing of Cavallero has produced joy among Italians and delusion among the Germans. Bismarck has become the mouthpiece of the latter, and praises the excellent collaboration which the marshal had given to the German armed forces. Naturally, I said that the event did not have any political significance: reasons of an internal and military nature had determined it. Besides, the Germans had changed their chief of staff three times and the removal of Admiral Raeder took place only yesterday.

In a conference with me Ambrosio confirms what we had to say the last time we met. He is an honest man who will act in the interests of the country rather than in his own interest.

The event of the day: the meeting of Churchill and members of the Turkish Government. De Peppo and Alfieri do not attach too much weight to the meeting. Mussolini, when informed by telephone, said that this proves the weakness of the English "if Churchill must go to the trouble of begging for Turkish help." I cannot share this much too optimistic interpretation. It is the Casablanca plan that is finding its application, and Turkey is a base of too much importance not to be exploited. I do not yet feel sure that the Turks have been neutralized as Berlin believes or says.

February 1, 1943

Mussolini delivered a very proud speech for the Twentieth Anniversary of the Fascist militia. It wasn't an optimistic speech; he talked not of victory, but of fighting.

News from Albania is disturbing; the government of Libohova is also up to tricks. The men who were most faithful to us are trying to abandon ship. Even Vrioni. Even Verlaçi. These are signs of the times.

I think that before long it will be necessary to put all power in the hands of the military.

February 2, 1943

Nothing new.

February 3, 1943

I talked to the Duce on three problems:

Albania. The situation is such that I think it is necessary to replace Jacomoni. For a certain period he did very well, but now his policies are turning sour. We need a man who can talk about force, and who can also employ it. I propose Guzzoni or Pariani, two generals who know the country and are well regarded. Mussolini said he would think about it and decide.

Cavallero. His replacement has alarmed the Germans. He was their servant. Now they fear that with his going the whole system will be changed. I reassure Bismarck, but I think it would be well if the Duce wrote to Hitler on the matter.

Tunis. Silimbani is pretending that he is sick, and does not want to return. No use pushing him; he has made enough of a fool of himself. I will send, instead, Bombieri, who was for many years consul general.

A meeting with Missiroli. He informs me in detail of the opinions on the situation, expressed by eminent men of the past.

February 4, 1943

A long visit with Thaon de Revel. He has been one of the most ardent interventionists, who believed 100 per cent in a German victory. Now he is facing a crisis, a real crisis. He opened his heart to me with a sincerity that is unusual in politics. He expects the country to be saved by the monarchy. He is even ready to invoke the help of his uncle, the Grand Admiral, who seems to have a great deal of influence with the King.

In the afternoon I go to the royal palace for the registration of the birth of Princess Beatrice. His Majesty had a bad cold and a tired air. The Prince of Piedmont was very cordial, and we had a brief conversation. He sees things very clearly, and no wonder he is disturbed.

February 5, 1943

At four-thirty in the afternoon the Duce calls me. The moment I enter the room I perceive that he is very much embarrassed. I grasp what he is prepared to tell me. "What are you going to do now?" he begins, and then adds in a low voice that he is changing his entire cabinet. I understand the reasons. I share them, and I do not intend to raise the least objection. Among the various solutions of a personal nature that he offers me I decisively reject the governorship of Albania, where I would be going as the executioner and hangman of those people to whom I promised brotherhood and equality. I choose to be Ambassador to the Holy See. It is a place of rest that may, moreover, open up many possibilities for the future. And the future, never so much as today, is in the hands of God. To leave the Ministry for Foreign Affairs, where for seven years—and what years—I have given my best, is certainly a hard and sad blow. I have lived too much, in the full sense of the word, between those walls not to feel the anguish of my removal. But that does not matter. I know how to be strong and to look to the morrow, which may require an even greater liberty of action. The ways which Providence chooses are at times mysterious.

February 6, 1943

The Duce telephones quite early in the morning, to hold up my nomination to the Holy See. "They will say that you have been kicked upstairs, and you are too young to be kicked upstairs." But I, who had foreseen Mussolini's vacillations, had already sent Ambassador Guariglia to ask the Secretariat of State for my acceptance. *Cosa fatta capo ha* [A thing done is done]. The Duce accepted the accomplished fact with indifference.

Acquarone informs me that the King knew nothing about my leaving the government when he saw me on Thursday. The King is happy about my appointment to the Vatican. Acquarone is personally enthusiastic about it.

February 7, 1943

Nothing new except the official announcement of my appointment to the Holy See.

February 8, 1943

I hand over my office at the Ministry for Foreign Affairs. Then I go to the Palazzo Venezia to see the Duce and take leave of him. He tells me: "Now you must consider that you are going to have a period of rest. Then your turn will come again. Your future is in my hands, and therefore you need not worry." He thanks me for what I have done and rapidly enumerates my most important services. "If they had given us three years' time we might have been able to wage war under different conditions or perhaps it would not have been at all necessary to wage it." He then asked me if I had all my documents in order. "Yes," I answered. "I have them all in order, and remember, when hard times come—because it is now certain that hard times will come —I can document all the treacheries perpetrated against us by the Germans, one after another, from the preparation for the conflict to the war on Russia, communicated to us when their troops had already crossed the frontier. If you have need of them I shall furnish the details, or, better still, I shall, within the space of twenty-four hours, prepare that speech which I have had in my mind for three years, because I shall burst if I do not deliver it." He listened to me in silence and almost agreed with me. Today he was concerned about the situation because the retreat on the eastern front continues to be almost a rout. He has invited me to see him frequently, "even every day." Our leave-taking was cordial, for which I am very glad, because I like Mussolini, like him very much, and what I shall miss most will be my contact with him.

[No entries February 9 to December 22, inclusive.]

[Final entry—December 23, 1943]

If these notes of mine one day see the light, it will be because I took precautions to put them in safety before the Germans, through base trickery, made me a prisoner. It was not my intention, while I was writing these hasty notes, to release them to the press just as they are; rather it was my desire to fix events, particulars, facts which would have been useful to me in the future. If Providence had granted me a quiet old age, what excellent material for my autobiography! They do not, therefore, form part of a book, but rather the raw material with which the book could have been prepared later.

But perhaps in this skeleton form and in the absolute lack of the superfluous are to be found the real merit of these diaries. Events are photographed without retouching, and the impressions reported are the first, the most genuine, uninfluenced by the criticism or wisdom of later years. I was accustomed to jot down the salient happenings day by day, hour by hour, and perhaps at times repetitions or contradictions can be found, in the same way in which, very often, life repeats and contradicts itself.

Certainly if the opportunity to expand these notes had not suddenly been taken away from me, I should have wished on the basis of other documents, or my personal recollections, to amplify the chronicle of certain days which have had peculiar and dramatic influence on the history of the world.

I should have liked to fix responsibility both of men and governments with a greater wealth of detail, but unfortunately this was impossible, even though there might come to my mind, in these last hours, so many details that I should like to have known to those who tomorrow will analyze and judge events.

The Italian tragedy, in my opinion, had its beginnings in August 1939, when, having gone to Salzburg on my own initiative, I suddenly found myself face to face with the cynical German determination to provoke the conflict. The alliance had been signed in May. I had always been opposed to it, and for a long time I had so contrived that the persistent German offers were allowed to drift. There was no reason whatever, in my opinion, for us to be bound in life and death to the destiny of Nazi Germany. Instead, I was in favor of a policy of collaboration, for in our geographical situation we are bound to detest the eighty million Germans, brutally set in the heart of Europe, but we cannot ignore them. The decision to conclude the alliance was taken by Mussolini, suddenly, while I was in Milan with von Ribbentrop. Some American newspapers had reported that the Lombard metropolis had received the German Minister with hostility, and that this fact was proof of the diminished personal prestige of Mussolini.

Hence his wrath. I received by telephone the most peremptory orders to accede to the German demands for an alliance, which for more than a year I had left in a state of suspense and had thought of leaving there for a much longer time. So "The Pact of Steel" was born. A decision that has had such a sinister influence upon the entire life and future of the Italian people is due entirely to the spiteful reaction of a dictator to the irresponsible and valueless utterances of foreign journalists.

However, the alliance had a clause; namely, that for a period of three or four years neither Italy nor Germany would create controversies capable of disturbing the peace of Europe.

Instead, in the summer of 1939 Germany advanced its anti-Polish claims, naturally without our knowledge. Moreover, von Ribbentrop repeatedly denied to our Ambassador Germany's intention to push the polemic to its final conclusion. In spite of these denials I was somewhat incredulous and wanted to be sure, and on the eleventh of August I went to Salzburg. It was at his residence at Fuschl that von Ribbentrop, while we were waiting to be seated at the dinner table, told me of the German decision to set a match to the European powder keg. This he told me in much the same tone that he would have used about an inconsequential administrative detail.

"Well, Ribbentrop," I asked, as we were walking together in the garden, "what do you want? The Corridor or Danzig?"

"Not that any more," he said, gazing at me with his cold metallic eyes. "We want war!"

I felt that the decision was irrevocable, and in a flash I saw the tragedy that threatened humanity. The conversations, not always cordial, which I had with my German colleague lasted for ten hours that day. Those that I had with Hitler lasted for as many hours on the two successive days. My arguments made absolutely no impression on either of them. They were like water on a duck's back. Nothing could have prevented the execution of this criminal project long meditated and fondly discussed in those somber meetings the Führer had every evening with his intimates. The madness of the Chief had become the religion of his followers. Every objection was ruled out even if it was not ridiculed.

Their calculation was fundamentally wrong. They were sure that both France and England would remain passive during the slaughter of Poland. Convinced of this, Ribbentrop insisted on making a bet with me during one of those gloomy meals at the Oesterreichischerhof in Salzburg. If England and France remained neutral I would give him an Italian painting. If those Powers intervened he would give me a collection of old armor. There were many witnesses to this bet. Not long ago Ambassador Mackensen and I were talking about the incident. But von Ribbentrop has preferred to forget the bet and has never paid up—unless he believes that he is discharging his debt by having me shot in his name by a platoon of wretches in the pay of the enemy.

(At last Hitler reached the point of telling me that I, a southerner, could not understand how much he, a German, needed to get his hands on the timber of the Polish forests. . . .)

From Salzburg on, during the period of Italian neutrality and during the war, the policy of Berlin toward Italy was nothing but a network of lies, intrigue, and deceit. We were treated, never like partners, but always as slaves. Every move took place without our knowledge; even the most fundamental decisions were communicated to us after they had been put into execution. Only the base cowardice of Mussolini could, without reaction, tolerate this and pretend not to see it.

The attack on Russia was brought to our knowledge half an hour after the German troops had passed the eastern border. Yet this was an event of no secondary importance in the course of the conflict, even if our appraisal of the matter differed from that of the Germans.

The preceding Sunday, on the sixteenth of June, I was with von Ribbentrop in Venice to discuss the inclusion of Croatia in the Tripartite Pact. The world was filled with rumors about an impending act of aggression against the Soviets, despite the fact that the ink was not yet dry on the friendship pact signed between the Germans and the Soviets. I asked my Axis colleague about it in a gondola while we were going from the Hotel Danieli to a dinner given by Count Volpi in his palace.

"Dear Ciano," said von Ribbentrop with studied deliberation. "Dear Ciano, I cannot tell you anything as yet because every decision is locked in the impenetrable bosom of the Führer. However, one thing is certain: *if we attack them, the Russia of Stalin will be erased from the map within eight weeks.*"

Thus, in addition to a notable case of bad faith against Italy, there is a conspicuous misunderstanding of realities, sufficient at least to help lose a war. . . .

I am aware of the fact that in this explanatory note which was meant to be no more than that I have allowed myself to drift into the narration of some facts which are not altogether negligible nor deserving of oblivion.

Within a few days a sham tribunal will make public a sentence which has already been decided by Mussolini under the influence of that circle of prostitutes and white slavers which for some years have plagued Italian political life and brought our country to the brink of the abyss. I accept calmly what is to be my infamous destiny. I take some comfort in the thought that I may be considered a soldier who has fallen in battle for a cause in which he truly believed. The treatment inflicted upon me during these months of imprisonment has been shameful and inhuman. I am not allowed to communicate with anyone. All contacts with persons dear to me have been forbidden. And yet I feel that in this cell, this gloomy Veronese cell where I am confined during my last days of this earthly life, I am surrounded by all those whom I have loved and who love me. Neither walls nor men can prevent it. It is hard to think that I shall not be able to gaze into the eyes of my three children or to press my mother to my heart, or my wife, who in my hours of sorrow has revealed herself a strong, sure, and faithful companion. But I must bow to the will of God, and a great calm is descending upon my soul. I am preparing myself for the Supreme Judgment.

In this state of mind which excludes any falsehood I declare that not a single word of what I have written in my diaries is false or exaggerated or dictated by selfish resentment. It is all just what I have seen and heard. And if, when making ready to take leave of life, I consider allowing the publication of my hurried notes, it is not because I expect posthumous revaluation or vindication, but because I believe that an honest testimonial of the truth in this sad world may still be useful in bringing relief to the innocent and striking at those who are responsible.

Galeazzo Ciano

December 23, 1943, Cell 27 of the Verona Jail.

CPSIA information can be obtained at www.ICGtesting.com
Printed in the USA
LVOW042156261111

256569LV00001B/275/A